Stated Choice Methods

Understanding and predicting the behaviour of decision makers when choosing among discrete goods has been one of the most fruitful areas of applied research over the last thirty years. An understanding of individual consumer behaviour can lead to significant changes in product or service design, pricing strategy, distribution-channel and communication-strategy selection, as well as public-welfare analysis.

This book is a reference work dealing with the study and prediction of consumer choice behaviour, concentrating on stated preference (SP) methods rather than revealed preferences (RP) – placing decision makers in controlled experiments that yield hypothetical choices rather than actual choices in the market. It shows how SP methods can be implemented, from experimental design to econometric modelling, and suggests how to combine RP and SP data to get the best from each type. The book also presents an update of econometric approaches to choice modelling.

JORDAN J. LOUVIERE is Foundation Chair and Professor of Marketing in the Faculty of Economics and Business at the University of Sydney.

DAVID A. HENSHER is Founding Director of the Institute of Transport Studies and Professor of Management in the Faculty of Economics and Business at the University of Sydney.

JOFFRE D. SWAIT is a Vice-President of Advanis Inc. (previously Intelligent Marketing Systems), based in Florida, and an adjunct Professor of Marketing at the University of Florida (Gainesville).

Stated Choice Methods

Analysis and Applications

Jordan J. Louviere
University of Sydney

David A. Hensher
University of Sydney

Joffre D. Swait
University of Florida

(with a contribution by Wiktor Adamowicz)

CAMBRIDGE
UNIVERSITY PRESS

PUBLISHED BY THE PRESS SYNDICATE OF THE UNIVERSITY OF CAMBRIDGE
The Pitt Building, Trumpington Street, Cambridge, United Kingdom

CAMBRIDGE UNIVERSITY PRESS
The Edinburgh Building, Cambridge CB2 2RU, UK   www.cup.cam.ac.uk
40 West 20th Street, New York, NY 10011-4211, USA   www.cup.org
10 Stamford Road, Oakleigh, Melbourne 3166, Australia
Ruiz de Alarcón 13, 28014 Madrid, Spain

First published 2000

Printed in the United Kingdom at the University Press, Cambridge

Typeface *Times*   System *3B2*

A catalogue record for this book is available from the British Library

Library of Congress Cataloguing in Publication data

Louviere, Jordan J.
    Stated choice methods / Jordan J. Louviere, David A. Hensher, Joffre Swait, Jr.
      p. cm.
    Includes bibliographical references and index.
    ISBN 0 521 78275 9
      1. Consumer behavior–Mathematical models. 2. Decision-making–Mathematical
models. I. Hensher, David A., 1947– II. Swait, Joffre Dan.

HF5415.32.L687 2000
658.8'342–dc21   00-023024

ISBN 0 521 78275 9 hardback
ISBN 0 521 78830 7 paperback

Contents

Figures

Tables

Acknowledgements

Many individuals have contributed intellectually to this book. The literature on discrete choice analysis, combining sources of preference data and experimental design, is vast, with a history spanning at least sixty years. This book is a contribution to that literature, inspired by a need at the end of the twentieth century for a single source accessible to both practitioners and researchers who need some assistance in 'travelling' through the essential components of the extant literature in order to undertake an appropriate systematic study of consumer choice behaviour.

To Daniel McFadden, Norman Anderson and Moshe Ben-Akiva we owe a special debt for their contribution to the literature and for their inspiration to all authors. Wiktor Adamowicz and graduate students and staff in the Faculty of Economics and Business at the University of Sydney read earlier versions of the book and guided us in revisions. The influence of a number of other colleagues has been substantial in our appreciation of the topic. We especially thank Bill Greene, Don Anderson, Axel Boersch-Supan, Bob Meyer, Frank Koppelman, Deborah Street and Chandra Bhat. We would like to express our gratitude to Advanis Inc., and particularly to Michael Williams, its President, for his support.

We dedicate this book to Cathy Louviere, Johanna Hensher and Carolyn Swait for their support and patience and understanding during all the long hours needed to bring this work to fruition.

1   Choosing as a way of life

1.1   Introduction

Understanding the behavioural responses of individuals to the actions of business and government will always be of interest to a wide spectrum of society. Whether a simple application such as gauging the effect of an increase in the price of a specific good or service, or a more complex one such as evaluating the introduction of a new product with private and public impacts, understanding and predicting the nature of individual and aggregate responses is vital to the evaluation of the resulting costs and benefits. Choosing to do or not to do something is a ubiquitous state of activity in all societies. Choosing manifests itself in many ways such as supporting one outcome and rejecting others, expressed through active responses (e.g., choosing to use products or services through purchases), or through passive responses, such as supporting particular views (e.g., choosing to support a conservation rather than a logging position in a dispute over wood chipping). Individuals' choices are influenced by habit, inertia, experience, advertising, peer pressures, environmental constraints, accumulated opinion, household and family constraints, etc. This set of influences reflects the temporal nature of choice outcomes and segments within the constraint set (e.g., income classes of households).

Our objective in writing a book on stated choice methods, analysis and applications, is to demonstrate the benefits of developing a formal structure within which to investigate the responsiveness of potential and actual participants in markets for particular goods, services and positions. Our challenge will be to describe, in simple terms, the practical benefits of using the tools of data specification, modelling and application that have evolved through research activity over the last thirty years. Many disciplines have contributed to the advances made in these areas, most notably econometrics, transportation, marketing, decision science and biostatistics. The one common thread in these diverse and often non-overlapping literatures is a search for better theory and methods to explain individual and aggregate choice behaviour, and predict behavioural responses to changing opportunities. An important corollary is the desire to develop practical analytical tools, so that the benefits of research can be transferred to practitioners in a timely manner, allowing for incremental updates as knowledge of individual choice behaviour improves.

Great progress has been made in developing frameworks within which to explore, understand, analyse and predict individual choice behaviour. The objective of this book is to fill a gap in reference sources for those who seek to understand, gain expertise in and apply stated choice methods and models. Like any reference work, there are limits to what can be covered in a single source; hence, from the outset we impose bounds on our topic, largely determined by our own personal biases and views as to the interesting and important advances in theory, analytical tools and applications. The topics included are:

- random utility theory,
- the associated family of discrete-choice models such as multinomial logit, nested logit, heteroscedastic extreme value logit, random parameter or mixed logit, and multinomial probit,
- families of controlled experimental designs consistent with various members of the discrete-choice modelling family, and
- data enrichment and comparison of preference data sources via integration of revealed preference and stated choice data, as well as the combination and comparison of various sources of stated choice and preference data.

1.2   Decision making and choice behaviour

> The traditional economic model of consumer behaviour has disappointingly few implications for empirical research. (Muth 1966: 699)

The theoretical underpinnings of discrete-choice models contain elements of the traditional microeconomic theory of consumer behaviour, such as the formal definition of rational choice and other assumptions of traditional preference theory. However, the essential point of departure from the traditional theory, germane to the subject matter of this book, is the postulate that utility is derived from the *properties* of things, or as in the now classical work of Lancaster (1966, 1971), from the characteristics (in an objective dimension) which goods possess, rather than the goods *per se*. Goods are used either singly or in combination to *produce* the characteristics that are the source of a consumer's utility.

This section takes Lancaster's contribution as a point of departure and modifies it to make clear the connection between the spirit of Lancaster's precise approach and the approach in this book. The connection with the traditional characteristics approach remains strong, although Lancaster and others (e.g., Rosen 1974) concentrated mainly on developing a detailed subset of the elements of what we will term the paradigm of choice.

To appreciate the connection between the 'standard Lancaster approach' (SLA) and our modifications, let us briefly outline the SLA for the case in which goods are divisible (Lancaster 1966, 1971) and indivisible (Rosen 1974). Furthermore, so that one can interpret (and assess) the arguments in terms of their relationship to discrete-choice models, it is appropriate to formally state the paradigm of choice now and discuss its elements later. Formally the paradigm of choice underlying discrete-choice models can be expressed as a set of three interconnected equations:

$$s_k = f_{kr}(t_r) \tag{1.1a}$$

$$u_j = g(s_{kj}) \tag{1.1b}$$

$$P_j = h(u_j) \tag{1.1c}$$

and

$$P_j = h\{g[f_{kr}(t_r)]\}, \tag{1.1d}$$

where s_k is the perceived (marginal) utility of consumption service k,
t_r is the observable value of objective characteristic r,
u_j is the overall utility (preference) associated with the jth alternative,
s_{kj} is the level of attribute k (representing consumption service k) associated with alternative j,
P_j is the likelihood of choices allocated to alternative j, and
f, g, h are linear or non-linear functions, yet to be determined.

The standard Lancaster approach postulates that goods (X) are transformed into objective characteristics, t, through the relation

$$t = \mathbf{B}X, \tag{1.2}$$

where B is an R by J matrix which transforms the J goods (i.e., alternatives in a choice set) into R objective characteristics (i.e., attributes of alternatives). Hence, **B** defines the consumption technology, assumed to be objective since it is invariant for all consumers (e.g., the number of cylinders in the engine of a particular make and model of car is the same for everyone). A range of mappings can exist, such that several goods can produce one characteristic, and several characteristics can be produced by one good. Lancaster asserts that the relevant characteristics should be defined not in terms of an individual's reaction to the good (which we will refer to as consumption service), but rather in terms of objective measures; that is, in terms of the properties of the good itself. Lancaster did not say that there could not be differences between consumers in the way in which they perceive an objective characteristic. However, if such differences exist, they relate to the formation of a preference function for t that is outside the domain of his theory.

The rationale given for the emphasis on t is that economists are primarily interested in how people will react to changes in prices or objective characteristics embodied in the goods that produce t, and not in how the function $U(t)$ is formed. This further implies that the functions h, g and f_{kr} in equations (1.1a) to (1.1c) can be reduced to a composite function $B(.)$ with no loss of information and a one-to-one correspondence in content and form between s_k and t_r, u_j and s_{kj}. The latter implies that utility is a function of commodity characteristics:

$$u = U(t_1, t_2, \ldots, t_R) \tag{1.3}$$

where t_r is the amount of the rth characteristic that a consumer obtains from consumption of commodities, $r = 1, \ldots, R$.

The particular formulation outlined above assumes that goods are infinitely divisible, frequently purchased and of low unit value. Yet many goods are not perfectly divisible, especially goods relevant to discrete-choice applications, which often deal with goods that are infrequently purchased or evaluated. Rosen (1974) developed a goods characteristics model for indivisible (or discrete) goods in which he assumed that alternatives were available for a continuous range of objective characteristics. This latter assumption enabled him to eliminate Lancaster's transformation from goods to characteristics, and to state a model directly in terms of prices and quantities of characteristics (still defined objectively by Rosen). If Hicks' (1946) composite good theorem holds, we can hold the prices of all other goods constant except those under study. That is, we can assume one intrinsic group of goods (e.g., modes of transport, brands of cereals, an endangered wildlife species, residential accommodation) yields objective characteristics $(t_1, t_2, \ldots, t_R)$ and define all other (composite) goods consumed as d. Then Rosen's model can be stated as

$$\text{maximise} \quad U(t_1, t_2, \ldots, t_R) \tag{1.4}$$

$$\text{subject to} \quad p(t_1, t_2, \ldots, t_R) + d = M, \tag{1.5}$$

where the price of d is arbitrarily set equal to one dollar, M is the consumer's income, and $p(t_1, t_2, \ldots, t_R)$ represents the price of one good yielding objective characteristics $t_1, t_2, \ldots, t_R$ which are actually acquired. The budget constraint, defined in terms of the objective characteristics, is non-linear. If goods are not divisible, $p(t_1, t_2, \ldots, t_R)$ need not be linear, and hence it is not appropriate to define objective characteristics in terms of characteristics per dollar (or any other unit price), but rather in terms of their absolute levels. Thus, price must be represented as a separate dimension, as seen in the discrete-choice models discussed in later chapters.

Rosen's model is more appropriate to a discrete-choice theoretic framework, although it continues to link utility directly to the objective characteristics of goods. The paradigm of choice links utility to goods and thence to objective characteristics via a complex function of function(s), as suggested in equation (1.1d). The latter is our point of departure from the Lancaster–Rosen contribution, but we retain the spirit of their approach and use it as the starting point for developing the full set of relationships outlined in the paradigm of choice. In particular, random utility theory based discrete-choice models focus primarily on equations (1.1b) and (1.1c), and accept the need to map attributes or consumption services into objective characteristics and, vice versa, to develop predictive capability. In practice, analysts commonly assume a one-to-one correspondence between s_k and t_r, such that s_k is a perfect representation of t_r.

The relationship between utility and the sources of utility is clearly central to the decision on selection of commodities. We now conceptually outline alternative ways to represent the sources of utility, given that we accept the limitations of using the Lancaster–Rosen standard approach. We present three modifications, subsequent ones building directly on the preceding, and use the final modified formalisation as the link with the basic choice model developed in chapter 3. The discrete-choice model is essentially an analytical representation of equations (1.1b) and (1.1c), with alternative assumptions on g and h.

The objective properties of commodities may not be an appropriate measure of services if we assume that individuals act as if they maximise utility based on their perceptions of characteristics. Thus, a 'modified Lancaster–Rosen approach' can be derived by assuming that individuals consume commodities by consuming the services provided by the commodities; that is, utility is a function of services rendered by commodities:

$$u = U(s_1, s_2, \ldots, s_K) \tag{1.6}$$

where s_k is the amount of kth consumption service that a consumer obtains from consumption of commodities, $k = 1, \ldots, K$. Furthermore, given the uncertainty of the level of service offered by commodities, a 'further modified Lancaster–Rosen approach' can be derived by assuming that individuals consume commodities by consuming the *expected services* provided by the characteristics associated with commodities; that is, utility (assuming deterministic utility maximisation) is a function of the expectation of consuming a required level of service provided by characteristics which group to define a commodity:

$$u = U(se_1, se_2, \ldots, se_K) \tag{1.7}$$

where se_k is the expected amount of kth consumption service that a consumer obtains from consumption of commodity characteristics, $k = 1, \ldots, K$.

Equation (1.7) represents an individual's decision calculus and the expected levels of service, the latter assumed to be known by the individual agent with the degree of 'certainty' that an individual attaches to the expectation. The analyst, in contrast, does not have access to the same level of information used by the consumer in processing a decision leading to a choice. The analyst is unable to 'peep into an individual decision maker's head' and accurately observe the set of attributes which define the expected level of service on offer. We can make this restriction explicit by defining the utility function observed by the analyst as given in equation (1.8):

$$u = U((se_o + se_{uo})_1, \ldots, (se_o + se_{uo})_K), \tag{1.8}$$

where subscripts o and uo indicate the division of consumption services that an individual associates with the consumption of commodity characteristics that are, respectively, observed and unobserved by analysts. In practice, the unobserved component (denoted as ε in the discrete-choice literature – see chapter 3), is assumed to be distributed across the population in some defined way, and a specific sampled individual is randomly allocated a value on the pre-specified distribution (e.g., a normal or extreme value distribution – see section 3.4).

Equations (1.3), (1.6), (1.7) and (1.8) are not independent, and can be combined to define components of a paradigm of choice. Let us call the objective characteristics 'features', and the quantitative dimension in which consumption services are defined 'attributes'. Many attributes may map exactly into a feature; but an attribute may be functionally related to more than one feature and vice versa. For example, a feature on a mobile phone might be 'call holding while attending another call'; two attributes related to this feature would be 'making an inquiry call to another extension while holding an outside call' and 'holding an existing call while dealing with an incoming outside call'.

Throughout this book the separation of supply 'price' into a vector of features and demand 'price' into a vector of attributes is used to account for the important distinction between the value of a commodity to an individual and the objective nature of the commodity. The latter provides a useful way to identify the possible source of bias in using supply 'prices' as determinants of choice because such prices have an indirect influence via their role in the definition of demand price. An important element of choice models is the translation of features into attributes, allowing one to assess the impact of a change in the objective properties of commodities; and the translation of an attribute-level change into a feature-level change to determine the appropriate supply change. In some circumstances, attributes and features only differ in terms of magnitude (e.g., actual and perceived travel time), whereas in other cases they may differ in dimension (i.e., two different characteristics). Thus the term 'characteristics' is usefully defined on both feature and attribute dimensions, and the mapping of features into attributes and/or attributes into features may involve one or more characteristics. The paradigm of choice is summarised below:

$$u = U[(se_o + se_{uo})_1, (se_o + se_{uo})_2, \ldots, (se_o + se_{uo})_K], \tag{1.9}$$

$$(se_o + se_{uo})_k = f_k(t_1, t_2, \ldots, t_R), k = 1, \ldots, K, \tag{1.10}$$

or

$$s_k = f(t_{11}, t_{21}, \ldots, t_{R1}, t_{12}, t_{22}, \ldots, t_{RJ}), \tag{1.11}$$

or

$$(se_o + se_{uo})_k = f_k(t_{11}, t_{21}, \ldots, t_{R1}, t_{12}, t_{22}, \ldots, t_{RJ}), r = 1, \ldots, R, j = 1, \ldots, J. \tag{1.12}$$

In equation (1.10), t_r is the rth feature, assumed independent of the jth commodity, and is an appropriate formulation when explicit commodities cannot be formally defined in a choice framework (i.e., if each mix of features is a (potentially) unique commodity).

Alternatively, because a particular consumption service (defined in terms of attributes) can be obtained from various bundles of features and varying levels of features, service can be defined across a range of R features in a framework of J commodities, as shown in equation (1.10). Equation (1.9) is a commodity-independent relationship between attributes and features. Equation (1.11) is a commodity-specific relationship. To complete the paradigm, two additional expressions are required. The first, equation (1.13), indicates the dependence of t_{rj} on the unit offering by the jth commodity of the total quantity of feature r:

$$t_{rj} = g_{rj}(y_{rj}), \ldots, r = 1, \ldots, R, j = 1, \ldots, J, \tag{1.13}$$

where y_{rj} is the quantity of feature r available in one unit of commodity j. The final equation (1.14) relates the total amount of the rth feature obtained from the jth commodity to the quantity of the commodity consumed (i.e., G_j):

$$tr_j = g_{rj}(G_1, G_2, \ldots, G_J), j = 1, \ldots, J. \tag{1.14}$$

The approach assumes that a particular consumption service (defined on one or more attributes) can be met by one or more objective characteristics (defined on one or more features and translated into a perceived set of attributes), and that a particular objective characteristic can exist in one or more commodities.

The paradigm of choice, together with alternative specifications of the relationship between u_j, s_{kj} and t_r, is consistent with the general approach to consumer behaviour in economics, although the analysis of the relationship between consumption of commodities and sources of utility begins earlier in the individual's decision process than is normally considered within the traditional economic paradigm. We accept that a consumer does not directly acquire objective characteristics or consumption services, but rather purchases commodities. Commodities are acquired in those amounts that provide the quantities of t_{rj}s that provide the amount of desired s_ks (or $(se_o + se_{uo})_k$) that maximises utility. This is equivalent to saying that

('price' j)($\partial u/\partial$ expenditure on j)

$$= \sum_j \sum_k (\partial u/\partial((se_o + se_{uo})_k) . (\partial(se_o + se_{uo})_k/\partial t_r)(\partial(se_o + se_{uo})_k/\partial t_{rj})$$

$$. (\partial t_{rj}/\partial G_j), \quad G_j > 0.$$

In words, given a positive level of consumption of the jth commodity, the value of a commodity j, equal to the product of the price of j and the marginal utility derived from the expenditure on j, is equal to the product of the marginal utility of the kth attribute, the marginal rate of substitution between the kth attribute and the rth objective characteristic, the marginal rate of substitution between the kth attribute and the rth objective characteristic contained in commodity j, and the marginal rate of substitution between the rth objective characteristic contained in the jth commodity and the quantity of the jth commodity consumed, all other things being equal.

We are now in a position to take the paradigm of choice as central to the formulation of a conceptual framework for studying choice behaviour, adding assumptions as needed to qualify the particular analytical form of the model's specification of the relationship between P_j, u_j and s_{kj}. The next section expands on this conceptual framework, integrating ideas drawn from a diverse set of literatures with an interest in decision making. The paradigm is broader in practice than the contributions from economics, with very strong contributions from psychology, decision science, marketing and engineering.

1.3 Conceptual framework

A general order or stages in a consumer's decision process are summarised in figure 1.1. The consumer first becomes aware of needs and/or problems to be solved, which is followed by a period of information search in which he or she learns about products that can satisfy these needs or solve the problems. During search and learning, consumers form beliefs about which products are available to attain their objectives, product attributes germane to a choice and attribute values offered by products, as well as any associated uncertainties. Eventually consumers become sufficiently informed about the product category to form a utility function (or decision rule) which involves valuing and trading off product attributes that matter in the decision. Given a set of beliefs or priors about attributes possessed by product alternatives, consumers develop a preference ordering for products, and depending upon budget and/or other constraints/considerations make decisions about whether to purchase. If they decide to purchase, consumers finally must choose one or more alternatives, in certain quantities and with particular purchase timings.

Figure 1.2 concentrates on the last decision stage, during which consumers form utilities or values and begin to compare products to form overall (holistic) preferences for an available set of alternatives. Figure 1.3 formalises this process as a series of interrelated processes, links each process to a formal stage in the decision-making process and describes the general area of research connected to that topic in marketing, psychology and/or economics/econometrics. The conceptual framework outlined

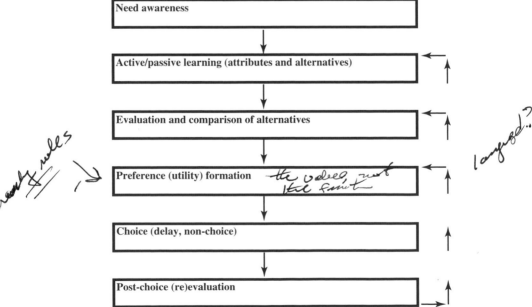

Figure 1.1 Overview of the consumer's choice process

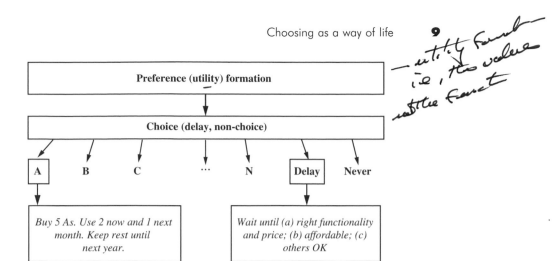

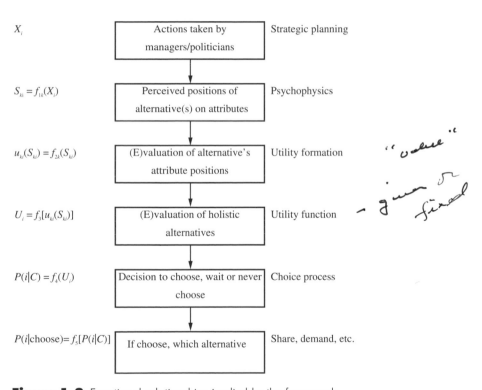

Figure 1.2 Complex decision making and the choice process

Figure 1.3 Functional relationships implied by the framework

in figures 1.1 to 1.3 is consistent with economic theory, accommodates random utility type choice and decision processes; and most importantly, allows one to 'mix and match' measures from various levels in the process, assuming such measures are logically or theoretically consistent with the framework and each other. The advantage of the latter integration is that it allows explanation of the choice behaviour in terms of:

1. physically observable and measurable (engineering) characteristics,
2. psychophysical variables (beliefs/product positions),
3. part-worth utility measures, or
4. holistic measures of each alternative's utility.

Depending on one's research and/or analytical objectives, explanatory variables at one level can serve as instruments or 'proxy' variables for measures at other levels. Such instruments can be used to reduce specification errors and/or improve estimation efficiency. Equally important, the conceptual framework suggests the potential contribution of many types of data to understanding choice; this catholic view of preference data is a focal point of this book. In particular, stated choice methods and measures used to model intermediate stages in the decision-making process can be integrated with parallel revealed preference or market methods and models. For example, the framework permits choices to be explained by direct observation and measurement of physical product characteristics and attributes and/or managerial actions such as advertising expenditures. Direct estimation alone, however, may obscure important intermediate processes, and overlook the potential role of intermediate models and measures in an overall behavioural framework that explains consumer choices.

1.4   The world of choice is complex: the challenge ahead

A major objective in writing this book is to bring together, in one volume, tools developed over the last thirty years that allow one to elicit and model consumer preferences, estimate discrete-choice models of various degrees of complexity (and behavioural realism), apply the models to predict choices, and place monetary (and non-monetary) values on specific attributes (or, better said, levels of attributes) that explain choices.

1.4.1   Structure of the book

The sequence of chapters has been guided by the authors' beliefs about the most natural steps in the acquisition of knowledge on the design, collection and analysis of stated choice data for problems involving agents making choices among mutually exclusive discrete alternatives. Subsequently we shall discuss the contents of each chapter in some detail, but first it is useful to present an overview of the book's structure. Figure 1.4 contains a flowchart depicting the overall structure of the book, which is broadly divided into (1) methodological background (chapters 2–7), (2) SP data use and study implementation (chapters 8 and 9), (3) applications (chapters 10–12) and (4) external validity of SP methods (chapter 13).

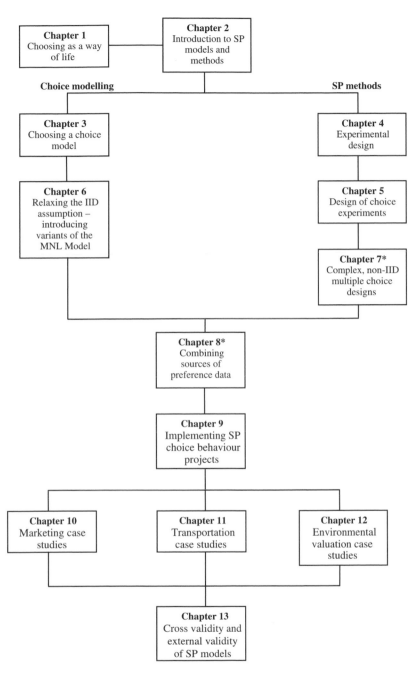

Figure 1.4 Overview of book structure (* denotes advanced material)

The chapters constituting the methodological component of the book are further subdivided (see figure 1.4) into (1) an introduction (chapter 2), (2) topics in choice modelling (chapters 3 and 6) and (3) experimental design for SP choice studies (chapters 4, 5 and 7). Appendix B to chapter 6 provides a catalogue of advanced choice modelling techniques, and should serve as a reference for the more advanced reader. The same can be said for chapter 7, which deals with complex designs to support estimation of the more complex choice models. Note that the advanced status of chapter 7 is denoted by an asterisk; all chapters so denoted are to be considered advanced material.

Chapter 8 is a useful how-to for students, researchers and practitioners interested in the combining of multiple data sources. Since this topic may not be of interest to everyone, it is designed as stand-alone material that can be accessed as need arises. Chapter 9, on the other hand, is intended as a primer on how to design and implement SP choice studies; after some overview considerations, a case study is followed through from conception to model estimation. Most readers should find this material useful.

Depending upon one's profession, one of the three application chapters should be of greater relevance (chapter 10 for marketing, 11 for transportation and 12 for environmental valuation). However, we strongly urge readers to study all three chapters because each deals with different aspects of preference elicitation and policy analysis that every choice modeller should be acquainted with.

The question of how good SP methods are at capturing 'real' preferences often arises in both academic and commercial applications. Some disciplines and individuals, in fact, have a strong bias against SP methods due to the perception that preferences elicited in hypothetical settings must be reflecting artificial preferences generated by the respondent 'on the spot', so to speak; these disciplines rely strongly on revealed preference, or RP, choices to infer preferences. In chapter 9 we discuss many of the things the SP practitioner should do to safeguard against real biases that can affect an SP choice study, but in chapter 13 we address directly the issue of the external validity of SP methods. We show how SP and RP preference elicitations can be compared using the methods of chapter 8 and other, less formal, methods. Practically speaking, we show through a significant number of examples that SP and RP preferences seem to match up surprisingly well in different choice contexts, cultures and time periods.

We now take a more detailed look at the book's contents.

1.4.2 Detailed description of chapters

Chapter 2 provides an introduction to alternative types of data available for studying choices. The particular emphasis is on the distinction between data representing choices in observed markets and data created through design to study new responses in real and potential markets. Another important distinction is the nature of the response metric (i.e., ratio, interval, ordinal and nominal) and the meaning of such responses as guided by the theoretical antecedents from axiomatic utility theory (Keeney and Raiffa 1976), order-level axiomatic theory (Luce and Suppes 1965), information integration theory (Anderson 1981) and random utility theory (RUT). This book adopts RUT as the theoretical framework for studying human behaviour and explaining choice behaviour. In contrast, some of the antecedents, such as axiomatic utility theory, are heavily focused on a theory about numbers and measurement.

One important and often not realised strength of the random utility theoretic approach is that it can study choice behaviour with choice responses obtained from any of the available response metrics. To be consistent with random utility theory, one data metric (e.g., an interval scaled rating) must be able to be transformed to a weaker ordering (e.g., an ordinal scale where the highest ranked = chosen (1) vs the rest = non-chosen (0)), and when re-analysed, produce statistically equivalent results up to a scale transformation (see chapter 9). This is known as the principle of invariance over any arbitrary monotonic transformation of the data. Only if this principle is satisfied can we accept the behavioural validity of stronger ordered response data such as ranking and ratings.

Chapter 3 develops the behavioural framework within which revealed and stated choices are modelled. Specifically, the idea of random utility maximisation is introduced, and used as the theoretical context in which to derive a family of estimable discrete-choice models. We devote time to a formal derivation of one of the most basic discrete-choice models, the multinomial logit (MNL) model, the 'workhorse' of choice models. Having grasped the behavioural and econometric properties of the MNL model, including possible ranges of policy outputs such as direct and cross share elasticities, probability predictions, marginal rates of substitution between pairs of attributes, we are ready in later chapters (especially chapter 6) to relax some of the strong assumptions supporting the relatively simple (and often robust) MNL model, in order to obtain gains in empirical validity. The majority of the enhancements to the MNL specification discussed in this book are associated with properties of the variances and covariances of the unobserved influences on choice, and the distribution of taste weights or parameters associated with the observed attributes defining sources of indirect utility.

Chapter 4 is the kernel of our presentation of experimental designs, the construct used to develop an empirical data framework within which to study choices. Agents consider combinations of attributes and associated levels across a set of alternatives in a fixed or varying choice set, and make choices. The analytical toolkit used to design experiments is presented in chapter 4 in some detail. Factorial designs, fractional factorials, design coding, main effects plans and orthogonality are some of the essential concepts that have to be understood in order to progress to the design of choice experiments with appropriate statistical properties. Without them, the analyst may be unable to study the full complexity of agent choice, unravelling the many sources of variability in behaviour.

Researchers studying choice processes soon come to realise how complicated the design of choice experiments is and how tempting it becomes to simplify experiments at the high risk of limiting the power of the choice instrument in explaining sources of behavioural variability. Confoundment of influences on choice behaviour is an often occurring theme in stated choice modelling, in large part attributable to poor experimental design. Some of the candidates of poor design include limited selection of attributes and levels, and selection of a fraction from a full factorial, which prevents uncorrelated testing of non-linear effects such as quadratic and two-way interactions amongst attributes potentially influencing choice. The accumulated experience of the authors is imparted in the book through many practical suggestions on the balance between parsimony and complexity necessary to provide behavioural realism in choice modelling. This starts with the quality of the data input into the modelling process. Choice experiments are discussed in detail in chapter 5. They provide the richest form of behavioural data for studying the phenomenon of choice, in almost any application context. An example of a choice experiment is given in figure 1.5. A more complex choice experiment is shown in appendix A1.

Chapters 1–5 provide sufficient material to enable the reader to design a choice experiment, collect the data and estimate a basic choice model. All of the major

Say a local travel agency has contacted you and told you about the three vacation packages below. Assuming that both you and your spouse would have time available to take a vacation together in the near future, please indicate your most preferred vacation option or whether you'd rather stay home.

PACKAGE	Package A	Package B	Package C	Stay
Type of Vacation				
Location	Large urban area	Mountain resort	Ocean side resort	
Duration	Weekend	One week	Two weeks	
Distance From Home	1500 miles	1000 miles	300 miles	
Amenities and Activities	Sightseeing	Hiking	Beach activities	
	Theater	Horse riding	Diving lessons	
	Restaurants	Lake swimming	Parasailing	
Distance to nearest urban area of 300,000 people or more		10 miles	100 miles	
Travel Arrangements				
Air travel cost (per person, round trip)	$400	$350	$300	
Accommodations				
Hotel (per night, double occupancy)	$120	$150	$75	
Quality of hotel restaurant or nearest other restaurant	**	***	*	
Which package would you and your spouse choose for your next vacation together, or would both of you rather stay at home if these were the only options available? (✓ only one)	A ☐1	B ☐2	C ☐3	Stay home ☐4

Figure 1.5 Example of a choice experiment

behavioural response outputs are deliverable from this model, such as choice elasticities, marginal rates of substitution between attributes as empirical measures of valuation of attributes in utility or dollar units (the latter possible if one of the attributes is measured in dollars), and aggregate predictions of choosing each alternative in a choice set.

The multinomial logit model remains the most popular choice modelling framework for the great majority of practitioners, for some very convincing reasons. Amongst these are:

- its simplicity in estimation – the solution set of estimated parameters is unique (there is only one set of globally optimal parameters),
- the model's closed-form specification, which enables easy implementation of predictive tests of changing market shares in response to scenarios of changing levels of attributes without complex evaluation of integrals,
- the speed of delivering 'good' or 'acceptable' models on the accepted tests of model performance (i.e., overall goodness of fit, t-statistics for the parameters of each attribute, and correct signs of parameters),
- accessible and easy to use packaged estimation software, and,
- where one has very rich and highly disaggregate data on attributes of alternatives and agents, the model is often very robust (in terms of prediction accuracy) to violation of the very strong behavioural assumptions imposed on the profile of the unobserved effects, namely that they are independently and identically distributed (IID) amongst the alternatives in the choice set.

These appealing features of the multinomial logit model are impressive and are not lightly given up.

However, the many years of modelling of discrete choices has produced many examples of applied choice problems in which the violation of the IID condition is sufficiently serious to over or under predict choice shares, elasticities and marginal rates of substitution between attributes. Chapter 6 introduces the set of models that have been proposed in the literature as offering behaviourally richer interpretations of the choice process. At the centre of these alternative choice models are degrees of relaxation of the IID assumption.

IID implies that the variances associated with the component of a random utility expression describing each alternative (capturing all of the *unobserved* influences on choice) are identical, and that these unobserved effects are not correlated between all pairs of alternatives. If we have three alternatives, this can be shown as a 3 by 3 variance–covariance matrix (usually just referred to as a covariance matrix) with 3 variances (the diagonal elements) and $J^2 - J$ covariances (the off-diagonal elements):

$$\begin{bmatrix} \sigma^2 & 0 & 0 \\ 0 & \sigma^2 & 0 \\ 0 & 0 & \sigma^2 \end{bmatrix}.$$

The most general variance–covariance matrix allows all elements to be unique (or free) as presented by the following matrix for three alternatives:

$$\begin{bmatrix} \sigma_{11}^2 & \sigma_{12}^2 & \sigma_{13}^2 \\ \sigma_{21}^2 & \sigma_{22}^2 & \sigma_{23}^2 \\ \sigma_{31}^2 & \sigma_{32}^2 & \sigma_{33}^2 \end{bmatrix}.$$

There are $J*(J-1)/2$ unique covariance elements in the above matrix. For example, the second element in row 1 equals the second element in column 1. The multinomial probit model (MNP) and the mixed logit (or random parameter logit) (ML, RPL) models are examples of discrete-choice models that can test for the possibility that pairs of alternatives in the choice set are correlated to varying degrees. For example, a bus and a train may have a common unobserved attribute (e.g., comfort) which makes them more similar (i.e., more correlated) than either is to the car. These choice models can also allow for differences in variances of the un-observed effects. For example, the influence of reliability (assumed to be important but not measured) in the choice of transport mode is such that it varies much more across the sample with respect to the utility of bus than train and car. For identi-fication requirements, some covariance and variance elements are set equal to zero or one.

When we relax only the MNL's assumption of equal or constant variance, then we have a model called the heteroscedastic logit model (HL), discussed in detail in chapter 6 (appendix B). It is also referred to as the heteroscedastic extreme value (HEV) model. The covariance matrix has zero valued off-diagonal elements and uniquely subscripted diagonal elements:

$$\begin{bmatrix} \sigma_{11}^2 & 0 & 0 \\ 0 & \sigma_{22}^2 & 0 \\ 0 & 0 & \sigma_{33}^2 \end{bmatrix}.$$

The degree of estimation complexity increases rapidly as one moves away from MNL and increasingly relaxes assumptions on the main and off-diagonals of the variance–covariance matrix. The most popular non-IID model is called the nested logit (NL) model. It relaxes the severity of the MNL condition between subsets of alternatives, but preserves the IID condition across alternatives within each nested subset, which we henceforth refer to as IID within a partition. The popularity of the NL model stems from its inherent similarity to the MNL model. It is essentially a set of hierarchical MNL models, linked by a set of conditional relationships. For example, we might have six alternatives, three of them being public transport modes (train, bus, ferry – called the a-set) and three being car modes (drive alone, ride share and taxi – called the b-set). The NL model is structured such that the model predicts the probability of choosing each of the public transport modes conditional on choosing public transport. It also predicts the probability of choosing each car mode condi-tional on choosing car. Then the model predicts the probability of choosing car and public transport (called the c-set):

$$\begin{bmatrix} \sigma_a^2 & 0 & 0 \\ 0 & \sigma_a^2 & 0 \\ 0 & 0 & \sigma_a^2 \end{bmatrix} \begin{bmatrix} \sigma_b^2 & 0 & 0 \\ 0 & \sigma_b^2 & 0 \\ 0 & 0 & \sigma_b^2 \end{bmatrix} \begin{bmatrix} \sigma_c^2 & 0 \\ 0 & \sigma_c^2 \end{bmatrix}.$$

Since each of the 'partitions' in the NL model are of the MNL form, they each display the IID condition between the alternatives within a partition (e.g., the three public transport modes). However the variances are different between the partitions. Furthermore, and often not appreciated, some correlation exists between alternatives within a nest owing to the common linkage with an upper-level alternative. For example, there are some attributes of buses and trains that might be common owing to both being forms of public transport. Thus the combination of the conditional choice of a public transport mode and the marginal choice of public transport invokes a correlation between the alternatives within a partition. Chapter 6 shows how this occurs, despite the fact that all the covariances at the conditional level (i.e., the a-set above) are zero.

The possibility of violation of the IID condition translates into requirements for the design of choice experiments. Chapter 5 assumes that the model form is consonant with the IID assumption, and hence that certain relationships between alternatives in the design can be simplified. If behavioural reality is such that the possibility of correlation between alternatives and differential variances may exist, then the design of the choice experiment must be sufficiently rich to capture these extra relationships. IID designs run the risk of being unable to separate the effect of such influences. Chapter 7 addresses this issue by introducing non-IID choice designs.

One of the most important developments in stated choice methods is the combining of multiple preference data drawn from either the same or different samples. The opportunity to draw on the richness of multiple data sources while hopefully minimising the impact of the less-appealing aspects of particular types of data has spawned a growing interest in how data can be combined within the framework of random utility theory and discrete-choice models. Given the importance of this topic, chapter 8 is devoted entirely to showing how data can be combined while satisfying the behavioural and econometric properties of the set of discrete-choice models. The breakthrough is the recognition that preference data sources may differ primarily in the variance (and possibly covariance) content of the information captured by the random component of utility. If we can identify the differences in variability and rescale one data set relative to another to satisfy the covariance condition, then we can (non-naively) pool or combine data sets and enrich the behavioural choice analysis.

The popular enrichment strategy centres on combining revealed preference (RP) and stated preference (SP) data, although some studies combine multiple stated preference data sets. The appeal of combining RP and SP data is based on the premise that SP data are particularly good at improving the behavioural value of the parameters representing the relative importance of attributes in influencing choice, and hence increasing the usefulness of resulting marginal rates of substitution between pairs of attributes associated with an alternative. RP data, however, are more useful in predicting behavioural response in real markets in which new alternatives are introduced or existing alternatives are evaluated at different attribute levels. Combined models can rely on parameters imported from the SP component for the observed attributes, except the alternative-specific constants (ASCs) of existing alternatives. These ASCs should be aligned to actual market shares in the existing (or base) market; hence, the SP model stated choice shares are of no value and actually misleading (since they reflect the average of conditions imposed by the experiment, not those of the real market). This nullifies the predictive value of a stand-alone, uncalibrated SP model. It is extremely unlikely that the stated choice shares will match the market shares for a sampled individual (especially when new alternatives are introduced) and very unlikely for the sample as a whole. Thus the appeal of joint RP–SP models to service a number of application objectives.

Chapters 1–8 provide the reader with a large number of tools to design a choice experiment and estimate a discrete-choice model. The translation of this body of theory into action, however, often remains a challenge. Chapter 9 is positioned in the book to bring together the many elements of a complete empirical study in a way that reveals some of the 'hidden' features of studies that are essential to their efficient and effective implementation. In many ways this chapter is the most important in bringing all the pieces together, and provides a very useful prelude to chapters 10–12, which present examples of applications in transportation, marketing and environmental sciences.

We expect that this book will provide a useful framework for the study of discrete-choice modelling as well as choice behaviour. We are hopeful that it will be a valuable reference source for many in the public sector, private industry, private consultancies and academia who have discovered the great richness offered by stated choice methods in understanding agent behaviour and in predicting responses to future new opportunities. We know that the methods are popular. What we sincerely hope is that this book will assist in improving the practitioner's knowledge of the methods so that they are used in a scientific and rigorous way.

Appendix A1   Choosing a residential telecommunications bundle

In the future there will be competition for all types of telecommunications services. In this section, we would like you to consider some hypothetical market situations where such competition exists. Assume for each situation that the competitors and features shown are the only choices available to you. For each situation, compare the possible range of services offered by each company and choose which type of services you would select from each company.

Please note, if you choose two or more services from the same company, you may qualify for a bundle discount. This bundle discount is a percentage off your total bill from that company.

*We have enclosed a **glossary** to explain the features that are included in the packages offered. Please take a few minutes to read the glossary before completing this section. The following example will show you how to complete this task.*

EXAMPLE:

FEATURES	Bell South	Sprint	AT&T	NYNEX	GTE
LOCAL SERVICE					
Flat Rate	$12.00	$14.00			$12.00
LONG DISTANCE SERVICE					
Fee		$0.15 peak - $0.12 off peak	$0.20 peak - $0.16 off peak	$0.15 peak - $0.12 off peak	
CELLULAR SERVICE					
Monthly Service Charge	$20.00	$40.00	$40.00	$20.00	$40.00
Free Minutes	30 minutes	60 minutes	30 minutes	30 minutes	30 minutes
Home Air Time Charges	$0.45	$0.45	$0.65	$0.45	$0.65
Roaming Charges	$0.45	$0.45	$1.00	$0.45	$1.00
"Rounding" of Charged Air Time	Nearest minute	No rounding (exact)	No rounding (exact)	Nearest minute	No rounding (exact)
Free Off Peak Minutes	Weekends free	Weekends not free	Weekends free	Weekends free	Weekends free
DISCOUNTS AND BILLING					
Multiple Service Discounts if 2 or More Services	10% off total bill	5% off total bill	10% off total bill	5% off total bill	5% off total bill
Billing	Separate bills per service	Separate bills per service	Separate bills per service	Combined, single bill	Combined bill

Step 1: Compare the features offered by each of the five companies.

Step 2: Indicate which company you would choose for each service by checking one box in each row.

Which provider would you choose or remain with for your residential services?
(check one box in each row)

	Bell South	Sprint	AT&T	NYNEX	GTE	None
a. Local Service (✓ *one only*)	☑	☐	N/A	N/A	☐	
b. Long Distance Service (✓ *one only*)	N/A	☑	☐	☐	N/A	None ☐
c. Cellular Service (✓ *one only*)	☐	☐	☐	☑	☐	☐

Figure A1.1 Choosing a residential telecommunications bundle

2 Introduction to stated preference models and methods

2.1 Introduction

This chapter provides the basic framework for stated preference (SP) and stated choice (SC) methods. We first provide a brief rationale for developing and applying SP theory and methods. Then we briefly overview the history of the field. The bulk of attention in this chapter is devoted to an introduction to experimental design, with special reference to SP theory and methods. The next and subsequent chapters deal specifically with the design of (stated) choice experiments, which are briefly introduced in this chapter.

Let us begin by discussing the rationale for the design and analysis of stated preference and choice surveys. By 'survey' we mean any form of data collection involving the elicitation of preferences and/or choices from samples of respondents. These could be familiar 'paper and pencil' type surveys or much more elaborate multimedia events with full motion video, graphics, audio, etc., administered to groups of respondents in central locations or single respondents using advanced computerised interviewing technology. The type of 'survey' is dictated by the particular application: relatively simple products which are well known to virtually all respondents usually can be studied with familiar survey methods, whereas complex, new technologies with which most respondents are unfamiliar may require complex, multimedia approaches.

2.2 Preference data come in many forms

Economists typically display a healthy scepticism about relying on what consumers say they will do compared with observing what they *actually* do; however, there are many situations in which one has little alternative but to take consumers at their word or do nothing. Moreover, the historical basis for many economists' reliance on market data (hereafter termed *revealed preference*, or RP data) is a classical paper in which Samuelson (1948) demonstrates that if market observations have thus-and-such properties, then systems of demand equations consistent with market behaviour can be estimated. Frequently overlooked, however, is the fact that Samuelson's paper and subsequent work in economics in no way exclude the design, analysis and modelling of SP data, although many economists incorrectly believe that they do. The premise of this chapter, and indeed of the entire book, is that SP surveys can produce data consistent with economic theory, from which econometric models can be estimated which are indistinguishable from their RP data counterparts. Thus, the issue is not if one can or should obtain SP data, but whether models estimated from SP data yield valid and reliable inferences about and predictions of real market behaviour. Later chapters review the empirical record, which we note here is at least as (if not more) impressive compared with RP data models.

Thus, despite well-developed economic theory (e.g., Lancaster 1966, McFadden 1981) for dealing with real market choices, there are a number of compelling reasons why economists and other social scientists should be interested in *stated preference* (SP) data, which involve choice responses from the same economic agents, but evoked in hypothetical (or virtual) markets:

- *Organisations need to estimate demand for new products with new attributes or features.* By definition, such applications have no RP data on which to rely; hence, managers face the choice of guessing (or a close substitute, hiring an 'expert') or relying on well-designed and executed SP research. Despite economists' opinions about the lack of reliability and validity of SP data, real organisations need the best information about market response to new products that they can afford. Since the late 1960s, many organisations worldwide have relied on some form of SP data to address this need, and it should be obvious to even the most obdurate economists that such a practice would not have persisted this long, much less increased many-fold, if organisations did not see value in it. (This is, as it were, revealed preference for SP data!)
- *Explanatory variables have little variability in the marketplace.* Even if products have been in the market for many years, it is not uncommon for there to be little or no variability in key explanatory variables (see, for example, section 8.2 of chapter 8). As a case in point, in many industries competitors match each other's prices; in other cases prices or levels of service may remain unchanged for long periods of time, as was the case for airfares to/from Australia and Europe in the 1970s. In still other cases, all competitors may provide a core set of specifications, obviating the use of these variables as a way to differentiate choices. Thus, RP data exist, but are of limited or no use for developing reliable and valid models of how behaviour will change in response to changes in the variables.
- *Explanatory variables are highly collinear in the marketplace.* This is probably the most common limitation of RP data, and one might well wonder why many economists would argue that severely ill-conditioned RP data are superior to SP data just because they reflect 'true' market choices. As most statisticians know all too well, seriously ill-conditioned data are problematic regardless of their source. More interesting, perhaps, are the reasons why we expect this to occur in almost all

real markets. That is, as markets mature and more closely satisfy the assumptions of free competition, the attributes of products should become more negatively correlated, becoming perfectly correlated in the limit. Thus, the very concept of a Pareto (or 'efficient') frontier requires negative correlations, which in turn all but preclude even the cleverest econometrician from drawing reliable and valid inferences from RP data. Additionally, technology drives other correlations between product attributes, so as to place physical, economic or other constraints on product design. For example, one cannot design a car that is both fuel efficient and powerful because the laws of physics intervene. Thus, reliance on RP data alone can (and often does) impose very significant constraints on a researcher's ability to model behaviour reliably and validly.

- *New variables are introduced that now explain choices.* As product categories grow and mature, new product features are introduced and/or new designs supplant obsolete ones. Sometimes such changes are radical, as when 3.5″ floppy disks began to replace 5.25″ disks for PCs. It is hard to imagine how one could reliably use RP data to model the value of the 3.5″ disk innovation prior to its introduction. Similarly, virtually all PCs now come equipped with drives for 3.5″ disks, so this feature cannot explain current choices, nor can it provide insight into the demand for CD, DVD or external storage drives. Thus, it is often essential to design SP projects to provide insight into the likely market response to such new features.

- *Observational data cannot satisfy model assumptions and/or contain statistical 'nasties' which lurk in real data.* All models are only as good as their maintained assumptions. RP data may be of little value when used to estimate the parameters of incorrect models. Further, all empirical data contain chance relationships which may mitigate against development of reliable and valid inferences and predictions. A major advantage of SP data is that they can be designed to eliminate, or at least significantly reduce, such problems.

- *Observational data are time consuming and expensive to collect.* Very often RP data are expensive to obtain and may take considerable time to collect. For example, panel data involve observations of behaviour at multiple points in time for the same or independent samples of individuals. Thus, for new product introductions very long observation periods may be required to model accurately changes in trial and repeat rates. It frequently is the case that SP data are much less expensive to obtain and usually can be collected much faster, although SP panels may involve the same lengthy observation periods as RP panels.

- *The product is not traded in the real market.* Many goods are not traded in real economic markets; for example, environmental goods, public goods such as freeways or stadia. Yet, society and its organisations often require that they be valued, their costs and benefits calculated, etc. (Hanemann and Kanninen 1999 provide an excellent recent review of the valuation of environmental goods). In some cases consumers expend such resources as time or travel effort to consume these types of goods, and RP data can be used to proxy the true underlying dimension of interest (Englin and Cameron (1996) discuss such 'travel cost' methods). But in many other

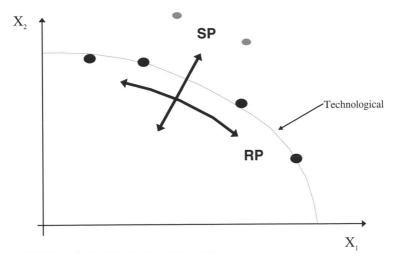

Figure 2.1 The technological frontier and the roles of RP and SP data

cases, such as environmental damage due to an oil spill or the existence value of a wild caribou herd in a remote forest, no RP data exist to model the behaviour of interest. Consequently, some resource economists have come to rely on SP theory and methods to address such problems.

The preceding comments can be understood with reference to figure 2.1. By definition, RP data are generally limited to helping us understand preferences within an existing market and technology structure. In contrast, although also possibly useful in this realm, SP data provide insights into problems involving shifts in technological frontiers.

Shifts in technological frontiers are at the heart of much academic and applied research in marketing, particularly issues related to demand for new product introductions, line extensions, etc., and are common concerns for many organisations. Forecasts of likely demand, cannibalisation, appropriate target markets, segments and the like are often needed to develop appropriate corporate and marketing strategies. Both business and government need reliable and valid models to reduce uncertainties associated with such decisions, which in turn has encouraged the development of various SP methods and models which we later discuss. Although the positive features of SP data were emphasised in the preceding, it is important to note that the two data sources generally are complementary, so that the weaknesses of one can be compensated by the strengths of the other. Indeed, recognition of this complementarity underlies the growing interest in combining RP and SP choice (and more generally, preference) data in transportation, marketing and environmental and resource economics during the past decade. Combination of preference data sources is discussed in chapter 8.

It seems apropos at this point to briefly summarise the features of each source of preference data, which can be described as below.

RP data typically

- depict the world as it is now (current market equilibrium),
- possess inherent relationships between attributes (technological constraints are fixed),
- have only existing alternatives as observables,
- embody market and personal constraints on the decision maker,
- have high reliability and face validity,
- yield one observation per respondent at each observation point.

SP data typically

- describe hypothetical or virtual decision contexts (flexibility),
- control relationships between attributes, which permits mapping of utility functions with technologies different from existing ones,
- can include existing and/or proposed and/or generic (i.e., unbranded or unlabelled) choice alternatives,
- cannot easily (in some cases, cannot at all) represent changes in market and personal constraints effectively,
- seem to be reliable when respondents understand, are committed to and can respond to tasks,
- (usually) yield multiple observations per respondent at each observation point.

RP data contain information about current market equilibria for the behaviour of interest, and can be used to forecast short-term departures from current equilibria. In contrast, SP data are especially rich in attribute tradeoff information, but may be affected by the degree of 'contextual realism' one establishes for respondents. So, SP data are more useful for forecasting *changes* in behaviour. Given the relative strengths of both data types, there can be significant value in combining them (see chapter 8). This value lies primarily in an enhanced ability (a) to map trade-offs over a (potentially much) wider range of attribute levels than currently exists (adding robustness to valuation and prediction), and (b) to introduce new choice alternatives by accommodating technological changes in expanded attribute spaces. Figure 2.2 illustrates how alternatives in a stated choice experiment imply specific consumption technological constraints of their own. That is, the nine specific combinations of travel time and travel cost, constrained by the time and money budgets of a sampled individual, are only part of the possible set of time–cost combinations. Stated choice experiments focus on combinations which can be generalised in application to evaluate any combinations in the square bounded by combinations 1–9.

A key role for SP data in combined SP–RP analyses lies in *data enrichment*; that is, providing more robust parameter estimates for particular RP-based choice models, which should increase confidence in predictions as analysts *stretch* attribute spaces and choice sets of policy interest. However, if one's primary interest is valuation, SP data alone often may be sufficient. In particular, each replication of a choice experiment provides a rich individual observation, so as few as three SP replications plus one RP observation per respondent generate four observations per respondent. In such cases

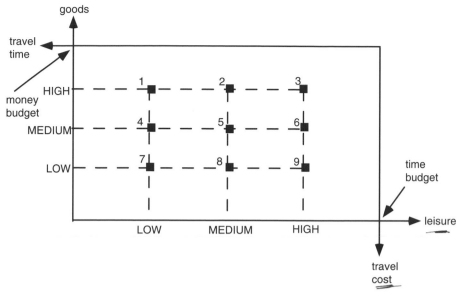

Figure 2.2 Travel alternatives in a stated choice experiment

small samples (100–300 respondents) are often sufficient to obtain consistent and efficient parameter estimates. An SP–RP model can be estimated either jointly or sequentially to obtain all the parameters for such samples, as we demonstrate in later chapters.

At this point many other issues germane to the use of SP theory and methods could be raised. Rather than attempt encyclopedic coverage, the preceding represent some of the major reasons why SP theory and methods have attracted growing research attention in many social science disciplines over the past decade. Having established a need and justification for the use of SP theory and methods, let us now turn our attention to laying the foundations needed to understand SP theory and methods.

2.3   Preference data consistent with RUT

Generally speaking there can be no valid measurement without an underlying theory of the behaviour of the numbers which result from measurement. Thus, it is a premise of this chapter, and indeed of this book, that measurement in the absence of theory is at best uninterpretable, and at worst meaningless. For example, it is difficult to know how to interpret the category rating scale measures that many marketing and survey researchers routinely collect to 'measure' attitudes, beliefs, values and preferences for subjective quantities such as 'customer satisfaction'. Specifically, if a survey enquires 'How satisfactory was the wait in the queue to be served at the counter?', and consumers can respond on a scale from 0 (= extremely unsatisfactory) to (say) 10 (= extremely satisfactory), what does a '6' mean?

A '6' response might mean that a consumer found the experience 'not altogether satisfactory' (whatever those words mean), 'slightly better than average waits previously experienced', 'about what was expected', etc. Now, should organisations who commission such surveys improve waits in line from '6' to (say) '7' or '8'? Is a '6' really bad? Perhaps compared with other organisations, a '6' is very good, but the consumer thinks it could be better. Who's to say? Thus, answers to such questions require a theory of the process which leads consumers to respond with a '6'. Specifically, an organisation needs to know how consumers value waits in line compared with service efficiency once at the counter, or charges for service, etc. A model of the process allows one to anticipate (predict) how consumers are likely to respond to changes in service within and between organisations.

That brings us to the issue of measurement and its role in modelling preferences and choices. Several types of measures are germane to our discussion: (1) measures of preferences and choice, (2) measures of attributes, (3) measures of consumers or decision-making units, and (4) measures of decision environments. For the time being we restrict our discussion to measures of preference and choice, but later in the book (chapter 9) we will return to the issue of reliable and valid measurement of these other crucial dimensions.

Preference and choice measures fall into the general domain of measures called dominance measures. Simply put, 'dominance' measures are any form of numerical assignment that allows the analyst to determine that one or more objects being measured are indistinguishable in degree of preference from one another (i.e., equal) or are more/less preferred to one another (i.e., not equal, with information about direction and order of inequalities). Many types of dominance measures can be identified which are, or can be transformed to be, consistent with Random Utility Theory (Luce and Suppes 1965). For example, consider the following brief list of possibilities:

- Discrete choice of one option from a set of competing ones. This response measures the most preferred option relative to the remaining, but provides no information about relative preferences among the non-chosen. That is, it is a true nominal scale.
- 'Yes, I like this option' and 'No, I do not like this option'. This response clearly separates alternatives (options) into liked and not liked, and provides information about preferences in the sense that all 'liked' options should be preferred to all 'disliked' options. Hence, assuming the consumer can and will choose an option, the choice will be one of the 'liked' options.
- A complete ranking of options from most to least preferred. This response orders all options on a preference continuum, but provides no information about degree of preference, only order. Variations are possible, such as allowing options to be tied, ranking only options that respondents actually would choose, etc. That is, it is a true ordinal scale.
- Expressing degrees of preference for each option by rating them on a scale or responding via other psychometric methods such as magnitude estimation, 'just

noticeable differences' (JNDs), bisection measures, etc. If consumers can supply reliable and valid estimates of their degrees of preference this response contains information about equality, order and degrees of differences or magnitudes. That is, their responses are consistent with interval or ratio measurement properties.

• Allocation of some fixed set of resources, such as money, trips, chips, etc. If consumers can reliably and validly allocate resources to indicate degrees of preference, this type of response provides information about equality, order, differences, ratios, etc. (i.e., ratio scale information).

• And, potentially many more ...

Mathematical psychologists, psychometricians and utility theorists have studied properties of measurement systems (behavioural models, associated measurement methods and tests of consistency) for many decades. Thus, we will not try to review this impossibly large body of work. Instead, we provide a very brief conceptual overview of the properties of the above types of preference (dominance) response measures, and their correspondence with random utility theory, and hence, discrete-choice models. Our purpose is to explain (1) that there are many sources of data from which preference and choice models can be estimated, and (2) that random utility theory allows us to compare and combine these various sources of preference data to make inferences about behavioural processes with greater statistical efficiency.

2.3.1 Discrete choice of one option from a set of competing ones

Listed in table 2.1 are five transport modes that consumers might use to commute to work. We observe a consumer to drive her own auto to work today, and by implication reject the four other modes, which provides one discrete piece of information about behaviour. Note that we also could design a survey in which a consumer was offered the five mode choices for her work trip, and observe which one she would choose for tomorrow's trip. We also might vary attributes of modes or trips, and ask which one she would have chosen for her last trip or would choose for her next trip given the changes. The key point is that the response is a report of which one option is chosen from a set of competing options.

Consider a survey question which asks a consumer to report which one of the five modes she would be most likely to use for her work trip tomorrow. As shown in

Table 2.1. *Discrete choice of commuting option*

'Brands' for journey to work	Consumer chooses
Take bus	
Take train	
Take ferry	
Drive own auto	✓
Carpool	

table 2.1, a tick (check) mark in the table tells us only that this consumer prefers driving her own auto to the other four options.
That is, we know:

- auto > bus, train, ferry, carpool, and   *i.e. No more info*
- bus = train = ferry = carpool.

Thus, we can say that these data are very 'weakly ordered', and a complete preference ordering cannot be determined for this consumer from this one response. To anticipate future discussions, if we want to know the complete ordering as well as how it is likely to change in response to changes in the attributes of the modes, the transport system, characteristics of individuals or the general environment, we need either (a) more discrete responses from one individual and/or (b) responses from more individuals under a wider range of attributes.

2.3.2 'Yes, I like this option' and 'No, I do not like this option'

pairwise

More generally, any binary discrete response that categorises a set of options into two groups (like, dislike; consider, not consider; etc.) can yield preference information. Continuing our commuter mode choice example, the data below can be viewed as coming from the following two sources:

- Observing a commuter's choices over one work week (five days).
- Asking a commuter which modes she would seriously consider for the journey to work, such that she should say 'no' to any she knows she would not use except in unusual circumstances (e.g., auto in repair shop).

As an example, consider the following hypothetical consumer 'would seriously consider/would not seriously consider' responses to questions about using each of the five transport modes for the journey to work listed in table 2.2. The responses above yield the following information about the consumer's preferences:

- auto > bus, train, ferry
- carpool > bus, train, ferry
- auto = carpool; bus = train = ferry.

Table 2.2. *Acceptance or rejection of commuting options*

'Brands' for journey to work	Consumer will consider (y/n)
Take bus	no
Take train	no
Take ferry	no
Drive own auto	yes
Carpool	yes

Thus, these data also are 'weakly ordered'; and to obtain a complete preference order we need either (a) more yes/no responses from this consumer and/or (b) responses from more consumers. Having said that, it should be noted that we have more information about preferences from this data source than was the case in our previous single discrete-choice example.

2.3.3 A complete ranking of options from most to least preferred

Table 2.3 contains a consumer's complete preference ranking, or at least a complete ranking by 'likelihood of use', which we take to imply preference. In this case, we could obtain the ranking by either (a) asking a consumer to rank the modes directly and/or (b) observing her choices over a long time period and then ranking by frequency of use. There are a variety of issues associated with complete ranking responses, which should be carefully considered before attempting to obtain such data:

- Task difficulty increases substantially with the number of options to be ranked.
- Response reliability is likely to be affected by the number of options ranked and the degree of preference for each. That is, reliability should decrease with more options. Reliability should be higher for the most liked and disliked options, and should be lower for options in the middle.
- The reliability and validity of information about the ranking of options that would never be chosen in any foreseeable circumstances is not clear.
- The reliability and validity of information about the ranking of options that either are not known, or are not well known to the consumer, is not clear.

Many choice modelling problems require information about non-choice; that is, the option to choose none of the options offered. A complete ranking may provide ambiguous information in this regard, and although one could restrict the complete ranking only to those options that the consumer actually would choose, there is little agreement about reliable and valid ways to do that. As there are other ways to obtain dominance data, we suggest that researchers look elsewhere for sources of data to model and understand preference until there is more empirical evidence and/or a consensus among researchers. Thus, one probably would be best advised to avoid the use of complete rankings for the present, especially in light of other options.

Having said that, suppose that consumers can provide reliable and valid complete preference rankings for a set of options. Table 2.3 provides an example of such a complete ranking.

The responses imply the following about the consumer's preferences:

- auto > bus, train, ferry, carpool
- carpool > bus, train, ferry
- ferry > bus, train
- train > bus.

Thus, we can say that the above data are 'strongly ordered', and provide a complete preference order, albeit with no information about preference degree or differences.

Table 2.3. *Complete preference ranking of commuting options*

'Brands' for journey to work	Ranking by likelihood of use
Take bus	5
Take train	4
Take ferry	3
Drive own auto	1
Carpool	2

2.3.4   Expressing degrees of preference by rating options on a scale

There are many ways to obtain direct measures of degrees of preference, but for the sake of example we restrict ourselves to rating each option on a category rating scale, which is undoubtedly the most popular in applications. In this case, we must assume that consumers can provide a reliable and valid measure of their degree of preference for each option. Different response methods may be used depending on one's beliefs about consumers' abilities to report degrees of preference differences in options, option preference ratios, etc. It is important to note that the latter constitute *very strong* assumptions about human cognitive abilities. Generally speaking, the stronger the assumptions one makes about such measures, the less likely they will be satisfied; hence, the more likely measures will be biased and invalid (even if reliable).

The preceding response measures make much less demanding assumptions about human cognitive abilities; hence, they are much more likely to be satisfied, and therefore the models that result from same are more likely to be valid. In any case, for the sake of completeness, table 2.4 illustrates how one consumer might rate the commuting options of previous examples.

As before, we ask what these responses imply about preferences. In this case we claim that it is not obvious because there is no theory available to allow us to interpret the meaning of a difference between a rating of '4' and a rating of '7'. What we can say, however, is that there is ordinal information in the data which allows us to transform the ratings into implied rankings, and interpret them. Note that if we use the ratings to infer rankings, we make a much less demanding assumption about the measurement

Table 2.4. *Scale rating of commuting options*

'Brands' for journey to work	Consumer likelihood to use (0–10)
Take bus	4
Take train	4
Take ferry	6
Drive own auto	10
Carpool	7

properties of the responses, namely that ratings reflect an underlying ranking. We suggest that researchers consider transforming ratings data in this way rather than blindly assuming that ratings produced by human subjects satisfy demanding measurement properties. Thus, if we transform the ratings to infer a preference ranking we would have the following:

- auto > bus, train, ferry, carpool
- carpool > bus, train, ferry
- ferry > bus, train
- train = bus.

Thus, these data are more weakly ordered than a complete ranking, but less 'weakly ordered' than the discrete and yes/no response data.

We eschew further discussion of response modes such as resource allocations in the interest of brevity, but note in passing that it is important to understand the kinds of measurement property assumptions implied by various response modes, and their implications for understanding and modelling preferences and choices. Generally speaking, one is better off making as few demanding assumptions as possible; hence, serious consideration should be given to discrete and binary responses in lieu of more common, but more assumption-challenged alternatives.

2.3.5 Implied choice data provided by each response

In order to estimate a choice model, one generally needs data that indicate chosen and rejected alternatives, as well as the set of alternatives (i.e., choice set) from which the consumer chose (see chapter 1). For each choice set faced by each consumer, one must identify the chosen and rejected option(s). The (single) chosen option is coded one (1), and the rejected option(s) is(are) coded zero (0). Table 2.5 illustrates how choice sets are created, and how chosen and rejected options are coded based on response information, consistent with the preceding discussion.

The types of preference data discussed above can be (and are) obtained in a wide variety of survey settings. As long as one also has available information about the attribute values associated with each alternative, consumer characteristics and the like, one can develop SP models from such data. It is worth noting at this point that such SP models are exact analogues to RP models. That is, one observes some preference or choice data from a sample of individuals, measures (observes) attributes associated with choice alternatives, measures characteristics of the individual choosers and develops a random utility based probabilistic discrete-choice model as discussed in chapters 1 and 3. Such SP data have all of the aforementioned disadvantages of RP models that lead us to seek complementary alternatives (e.g., no information on new products or features, limited ranges, collinearity, etc.).

Thus, we are motivated to seek alternative ways of dealing with these problems, although we must be mindful that such SP measures may yet prove to be useful for enriching estimation, cross-validating models and/or rescaling models from choice experiments to match choices in the real market. Chapter 4 provides an introduction

Table 2.5. *Creating choice sets and coding choices from response data*

Implied choice set	Alternative	Implied choice
Discrete choice		
1	Auto	1
1	Bus	0
1	Train	0
1	Ferry	0
1	Carpool	0
Yes/No		
1	Auto	1
1	Bus	0
1	Train	0
1	Ferry	0
1	Carpool	0
2	Auto	0
2	Bus	0
2	Train	0
2	Ferry	0
2	Carpool	1
Complete ranking		
1	Auto	1
1	Bus	0
1	Train	0
1	Ferry	0
1	Carpool	0
2	Bus	0
2	Train	0
2	Ferry	0
2	Carpool	1
3	Bus	0
3	Train	0
3	Ferry	1
4	Bus	0
4	Train	1
Rating		
1	Auto	1
1	Bus	0
1	Train	0
1	Ferry	0
1	Carpool	0
2	Bus	0
2	Train	0
2	Ferry	0
2	Carpool	1
3	Bus	0
3	Train	0
3	Ferry	1

to the notion of controlled experiments as a vehicle for designing options and collecting response data. In succeeding chapters we expand the basic ideas of this chapter and of chapter 4 to allow us to design and analyse discrete-choice experiments to obtain SP data that closely simulate possible analogue RP situations. We eventually return to the ideas of this chapter by demonstrating that all sources of preference data can be used to inform modelling, including those discussed in this chapter. The next chapter provides an introduction to choice models, the framework for taking SP and RP choice data and revealing the statistical contribution of each attribute to the explanation of a choice response.

3 Choosing a choice model

3.1 Introduction

Two elements of the paradigm of choice proposed in chapter 1 are central to the development of a basic choice model. These elements are the function that relates the probability of an outcome to the utility associated with each alternative, and the function that relates the utility of each alternative to a set of attributes that, together with suitable utility parameters, determine the level of utility of each alternative. In this chapter, we develop the basic choice model known as the multinomial logit (MNL) model. Beginning with this basic form, making a detailed examination and extending it to accommodate richer behavioural issues is an effective way to understand discrete-choice models in general, and provides a useful vehicle to introduce a wide range of relevant issues.

In section 3.3 the conventional microeconomic demand model with continuous commodities is outlined and used to demonstrate its inadequacy when commodities are discrete. A general theory of discrete-choice is developed around the notion of the existence of population choice behaviour defined by a set of individual behaviour rules, and an indirect utility function that contains a random component. The random component does not suggest that individuals make choices in some random fashion; rather, it implies that important but unobserved influences on choice exist and can be characterised by a distribution in the sampled population, though we do not know where any particular individual is located on the distribution. Hence we assign this information to that individual stochastically. The random utility model is then generalised to develop a formula for obtaining selection probabilities. Section 3.4 takes the (presently) analytically intractable general model, introduces a number of assumptions about the distribution and form of the relationship between utility and selection probability, and produces a computationally feasible basic choice model, the multinomial logit model.

Having derived the basic MNL choice model in sufficient detail, a procedure for estimating the parameters in the utility expression of the MNL model (known as maximum likelihood estimation) is introduced in Section 3.5. Various statistical measures of goodness-of-fit are outlined in Section 3.6, along with the main policy outputs, such as choice elasticities and probabilities. The chapter concludes with a commentary of important variants of the basic MNL choice model which ensure more realistic behavioural prospects in explaining choice. Chapter 3 provides a comprehensive introduction to the basic elements of a choice model, and is sufficiently detailed that the reader should be able to follow and appreciate more clearly how a final model is derived.

3.2 Setting out the underlying behavioural decision framework

> In conventional consumer analysis with a continuum of alternatives, one can often plausibly assume that all individuals in a population have a common behaviour rule, except for purely random 'optimisation' errors, and that systematic variations in aggregate choice reflect common variations in individual choice at the intensive margin. By contrast, systematic variations in aggregate choice among lumpy alternatives must reflect shifts in individual choice at the extensive margin, resulting from a distribution of decision rules in the population. (McFadden 1974: 106)

Many economic decisions are complex and involve choices that are non-marginal, such as choices of occupations, particular consumer durables, house types and residential locations, recreation sites, and commuting modes. Although economists are mainly interested in *market* demand, the fact that each individual makes individual consumption decisions based on individual needs and environmental factors, and that these individual decisions are complex, makes the relationship between market and individual demand even more complicated. For example, the framework of economic rationality and the associated assumption of utility maximisation allow the possibility that unobserved attributes of individuals (e.g., tastes, unmeasured attributes of alternatives) can vary over a population in such a way that they obscure the implications of the individual behaviour model.

Given such a state of affairs, one might question whether it is feasible to deduce from an individual choice model properties of population choice behaviour that have empirical content. In particular, one can observe the behaviour of a cross-section of consumers selected from a population with common observed (but differing levels of) socioeconomic characteristics, money budgets M_q and demands G_q associated with each individual ($q = 1, \ldots, Q$). A reasonable behavioural model, derived from the individual's utility function $u = U(G, \omega)$ and maximised subject to the budget constraint (M), is $G = h(M; \omega)$ (ω represents the tastes of an individual), can be used to test behavioural hypotheses such as those relating to the structural features of parametric demand functions, particularly price and income elasticities, and the revealed or stated preference hypothesis that the observed data are generated by utility-maximising individuals.

Because of measurement errors in G_q, consumer optimisation errors and unobserved variations in the population, the observed data will not fit the behavioural equation exactly. In fact, most empirical demand studies ignore the possibility of taste variations in the sample, and instead assume that the sample has randomly distributed observed demands about the exact values G for some *representative* utility $\bar{\omega}$, i.e., $G_q = h(M_q; \bar{\omega}) + \varepsilon_q$, where ε_q is an unobserved random term distributed independently of M_q. Hence, $\bar{\omega}$ has no distribution itself.

In a population of consumers who are homogeneous with respect to monetary budgets, this specification of aggregate demand will equal individual demand in the aggregate, and all systematic variations in market demand will be generated by a common variation at the *intensive margin* of the identical individual demands. If there are no unobserved variations in utilities or budgets, there is no *extensive margin* affecting aggregate demand (McFadden 1974). Conventional statistical techniques can be applied to $G_q = h(M_q; \bar{\omega}) + \varepsilon_q$ to test hypotheses about the structure of h. If quantities demanded vary continuously such that marginal optimisation and measurement errors are likely to be particularly important, and possibly dominate the effect of utility variations, the specification above is realistic.

If the set of alternative choices is finite, how can we interpret the traditional model, and what role can it play? In the case of discrete alternatives, the standard utility maximisation model with the corresponding demand equation $G_q = h(M_q; \bar{\omega})$ predicts a single chosen G (referred to as an alternative) if tastes and unobserved attributes of alternatives are assumed uniform across the population. The conventional statistical specification $G_q = h(M_q; \bar{\omega}) + \varepsilon_q$ would then imply that all observed variation G_q in demand over the finite set of alternatives is the result of behaviour described by some global disturbance term. That is, heavy demands are imposed on the random disturbance term.

Continuing this line of argument, McFadden states:

> Aggregate demand can usually be treated as a continuous variable, as the effect of the discreteness of individuals' alternatives is negligible. As a result, aggregate demand may superficially resemble the demand for a population of identical individuals for a divisible commodity. However, systematic variations in the aggregate demand for the lumpy commodity are all due to shifts at the extensive margin where individuals are switching from one alternative to another, and not at the intensive margin as in the divisible commodity, identical individual case. Thus it is incorrect to apply the latter model to obtain specifications of aggregate demand for discrete alternatives. (McFadden 1979: 309)

If commodities are not continuous there is no intensive margin at which changes in the magnitudes of attributes produce responses measured by a change in the criterion variable. That is, small marginal adjustments are not feasible consequences at the level of the individual. It is not possible with a single cross-section of preference data to accommodate discrete-choice in an atomistic individual choice framework in which the unit of analysis is the individual or household (current practice being limited to such data). Panel or repeated measures data with many waves would be required to facilitate estimation of a unique model for each individual. However, if we invoke a model of population choice behaviour defined on a set of individual behaviour(s), the marginal calculus can be maintained through a redefinition of the margin.

That is, the margin becomes the *extensive margin* for the population, and is relevant to each individual member of the population because an individual behaviour rule is contained within the set of individual behaviour rules. This is guaranteed because of the assumption that an element of utility is stochastic, individual specific and connected to the criterion variable (i.e., probability of selection) by a defined distribution. The latter distribution is the one that accommodates the way in which the individual behaviour rule is mapped into the set of individual behaviour rules. Individual specificity arises due to idiosyncrasies (conditioned on the representative utility), that produce a distribution of decision rules in the population. This permits the population margin to be used to assess the effect of a change in an observable attribute on each individual.

The foregoing will strike many as unsatisfactory because it suggests that the model needs to be reformulated so that the effects on the error structure due to individual difference in tastes and optimisation behaviour in the conventional specification are made explicit. Alternatively, a general procedure for formulating models of population choice behaviour from distributions of decision rules in the population when commodities are discrete is needed. We develop the latter in the next section.

3.3　Random utility maximisation

A general model of individual choice behaviour requires that three key factors be taken into account:

1.　objects of choice and sets of alternatives available to decision makers, known as choice set generation;
2.　the observed attributes of decision makers and a rule for combining them; and
3.　a model of individual choice and behaviour, and the distribution of behaviour patterns in the population.

To develop this more general model, we need to introduce some notation. Let G represent the set of alternatives in a (global) choice set, and S the set of vectors of measured attributes of the decision makers. Then a randomly drawn individual from the population (e.g., in a simple random sample), will have some attribute vector $s \in S$, and face some set of available alternatives $A \subseteq G$. (Hereafter G and S are not needed.) Hence, the actual choice for an individual, described by particular levels of a common set of attributes s and alternatives A across the sampled population, can be defined as a draw from a multinomial distribution with selection probabilities (multinomial refers to the existence of two or more possible outcomes)

$$P(x|s, A) \quad \forall x \in A \text{ (the probabilities of each alternative)}. \tag{3.1}$$

In words, equation (3.1) states the probability of selecting alternative x, given the individual's socioeconomic background and set of alternatives A, for each and every alternative contained in the set A. The vector x denotes consumption services or attributes, and is used to emphasise that the alternative is defined in terms of a set of attributes.

To operationalise the preceding condition, we need to establish an individual behaviour rule (defined as a function IBR), which maps each vector of observed attributes s and a possible alternative set A into a selected alternative of A. Our interest centres on a model of individual behaviour, which is an analytical device to represent the set of individual behaviour rules (SIBR) relevant to all individuals who define the sampled population. For example, IBR may be a particular choice function that results from maximising a specific utility function, whereas SIBR may be a set of choice functions resulting from the maximisation of a particular utility function. If unmeasured attributes vary across the sampled population, many possible IBRs can exist in a model SIBR. If there are multiple IBRs in the population, a model SIBR that describes a population must have a probability defined on the measurable subsets of SIBR that specify the distribution of the SIBRs in the population.

The selection probability that an individual drawn at random from the population will choose alternative x, given the observed attributes s and the alternative set A, is given by:

$$P(x|s, A) = P\{\text{IBR} \in \text{SIBR}|\text{IBR}(s, A) = x\}. \tag{3.2}$$

In words, the right-hand side states that the probability of choosing a particular individual behaviour rule, given that the particular individual behaviour rule, defined on s and A, is to choose x. Hence the right-hand side defines the probability of occurrence of a behavioural rule producing this choice. It is not the probability that the IBR is contained in the set (known as choice set generation), but the probability of choosing that IBR within the SIBR, given that the IBR maps the attributes into the choice x. This relationship is an initial condition for a model of choice behaviour. If P is assumed to be a member of a parametric family of probability distributions (e.g., normal, extreme value, lognormal, see section 3.4), and the observed choices are distributed multinomial with probabilities as given in equation (3.2), estimates of the parameters may be identified.

Having postulated the SIBR model, we need to relate the selection probabilities to the utility maximisation assumption that is central to the classical rational economic consumer. This requires us to represent the sources of utility in the choice model, and initially, we can assume that each individual defines utility in terms of attributes via a common functional form.

Let U_{iq} be the utility of the ith alternative for the qth individual. Further assume each utility value can be partitioned into two components: a systematic component or 'representative utility', V_{iq}, and a random component, ε_{iq}, the latter reflecting unobserved individual idiosyncrasies of tastes. Then,

$$U_{iq} = V_{iq} + \varepsilon_{iq}. \tag{3.3}$$

V_{iq} is subscripted q, even though we define V as representative, because the levels of attributes contained in the expansion of $V_{iq}(= \sum_{k=1}^{K} \beta_{ik} s_{ikq})$ can and often do vary across individuals. The βs are utility parameters, initially assumed to be constant across individuals. That is, only utility parameters are independent of q (not attribute levels). Utility parameters can be allowed to vary across the sampled observations (as random parameters) or be expressed as a function of contextual influences such as the socioeconomic characteristics of an individual or the nature of data being analysed (e.g., RP vs. SP). The latter adds further complexity, as outlined in chapter 6.

The partitioning of the utility function is used for operational reasons when populations of individuals are modelled. That is, one assumes that one part of utility is common to all individuals while the other is individual specific. This is a crucial assumption, implying that the existence of a significant element of the full attribute set is associated with homogeneous utility across the population under study. That is, one element, V_{iq}, is assumed homogeneous across the population in terms of the relative importance of those attributes contained in V_{iq} (hence β_i, not β_{iq}). Clearly, the particular definition of the dimensions of V_{iq} will depend largely on the population studied, the ability to segment the sampled population in such a way that each segment satisfies homogeneity of utility (see chapter 10), and the extent to which one can measure known or assumed attributes yielding representative utility.

The systematic component is assumed to be that part of utility contributed by attributes that can be observed by the analyst, while the random component is the utility contributed by attributes unobserved by the analyst. This does not mean that individuals maximise utility in a random manner; to the contrary, individuals can be deterministic utility maximisers. Randomness arises because the analyst cannot 'peep into the head' of each individual and fully observe the set of influencing factors and the complete decision calculus; which in turn, implies that the analyst can only explain choice up to a probability of event selection. The systematic utility maximisation function can be thought of as a 'perceived maximisation' function, because imperfect markets should encourage individuals to try to maximise utility to levels they perceive as maxima. This raises the interesting question of how one introduces actual levels of attribute changes in application and adjusts them for perceptual differences (equation (1.1a) in chapter 1), given that a behavioural model is estimated on the perceived levels of attributes describing alternatives.

The above discussion provides most of the basic concepts necessary for us to formulate a model. In particular, we assume that individuals will try to choose an alternative that yields them the highest utility. Hence, the empirical structure of the utility function is critical to modelling individual choice, and represents the process by which the attributes of alternatives and individuals' socioeconomic environments combine to influence choice probabilities, and in turn, the predictive capability of the choice model. We will return to this topic in more detail later when we discuss alternative specifications of the relationship between V_{iq} and the attributes. For the present, however, we concentrate on developing the general structure of an individual choice model.

The key assumption is that individual q will choose alternative i if and only if (iff)

$$U_{iq} > U_{jq} \qquad \text{all } j \neq i \in A. \tag{3.4}$$

From equations (3.3) and (3.4), alternative i is chosen iff

$$(V_{iq} + \varepsilon_{iq}) > (V_{jq} + \varepsilon_{jq}). \tag{3.5}$$

Rearranging to place the observables and unobservables together yields:

$$(V_{iq} - V_{jq}) > (\varepsilon_{jq} - \varepsilon_{iq}). \tag{3.6}$$

The analyst does not observe $(\varepsilon_{jq} - \varepsilon_{iq})$, hence cannot determine exactly if $(V_{iq} - V_{jq}) > (\varepsilon_{jq} - \varepsilon_{iq})$. One can only make statements about choice outcomes up to a probability of occurrence. Thus, the analyst has to calculate the probability that $(\varepsilon_{jq} - \varepsilon_{iq})$ will be less than $(V_{iq} - V_{jq})$. This leads to the following equations:

$$P_{iq} \equiv P(x_i|s, A) = P[\text{IBR}_\varepsilon \in \text{SIBR}|\text{IBR}_\varepsilon(s, A) = x_i], \tag{3.7}$$

$$P(x_{iq}|s_q, A) = P_{iq} = P[\{\varepsilon(s, x_j) - \varepsilon(s, x_i)\} < \{V(s, x_i) - V(s, x_j)\}],$$
$$\text{for all } j \neq i. \quad (3.8)$$

Equation (3.8) can be interpreted as a translation of equation (3.7) into an expression in terms of V and ε. The translation of (3.7) to (3.8) is not a straight substitution as such, but instead takes the conceptual notion of an IBR given in (3.2) and gives it an operational flavour. That is, given the assumptions that utility can be decomposed into systematic and random components, and that individuals will choose i over j if $U_i > U_j$, then IBR implies equation (3.8).

In other words, the probability that a randomly drawn individual from the sampled population, who can be described by attributes s and choice set A, will choose x_i equals the probability that the difference between the random utility of alternatives j and i is less than the difference between the systematic utility levels of alternatives i and j for all alternatives in the choice set. The analyst does not know the actual distribution of $\varepsilon(s, x_j) - \varepsilon(s, x_i)$ across the population, but assumes that it is related to the choice probability according to a distribution yet to be defined.

The model of equation (3.8) is called a random utility model (RUM). Unlike the traditional economic model of consumer demand, we introduced a more complex but realistic assumption about individual behaviour to account for the analyst's inability to fully represent all variables that explain preferences in the utility function.

Thus far we have specified the theoretical relationship between the selection of an alternative and the sources of utility that influence that selection, but have made no assumptions about the distribution of the elements of utility across the population. In order to begin relating the random utility model represented by equation (3.8) to a useful statistical specification for empirical applications, two fundamental probability concepts must be understood: the distribution function, particularly the cumulative form, and the joint density function. We discuss these concepts next, which will allow us to specify the structure of a random utility model that can be used in empirical applications. Intuitively, there is a utility space and an IBR, which implies that we must formulate the model in an n-dimensional space.

3.3.1 A brief introduction to the properties of statistical distributions

Consider a continuous random variable Z, and define the function $F(Z)$ to be such that $F(a)$ is the probability that Z takes on a value $\leq a$ (i.e., $F(a) = P(Z \leq a)$). We call $F(Z)$ a *cumulative* distribution function (CDF), because it cumulates the probability of Z up to the value a. It is monotonically increasing over all values of Z. If we limit ourselves to cases where the CDF is continuous, the derivative of $F(Z)$ is given by $F'(Z)$ (or $\partial F/\partial Z) = f(Z)$, which is called the probability density function (PDF) of the random variable Z. An example of a CDF and its associated PDF is given in figure 3.1.

The probability that Z falls between any two points, say a and b, is simply the area under f between the points a and b. This can be calculated by the formula

$$P(a \leq Z \leq b) = \int_a^b f(z)\,\mathrm{d}z,$$

where z is a dummy variable of integration. From this, the probability that $Z \leq a$ (our definition of the CDF $F(a)$) is given by:

$$F(a) = \int_{-\infty}^a f(z)\,\mathrm{d}z.$$

Extending these ideas to the case of n random variables $Z_1, Z_2, \ldots Z_n$, the probability that $Z_1 \leq a_1, Z_2 \leq a_2, \ldots, Z_n \leq a_n$ *simultaneously* (i.e., jointly) is equal to:

$$F(a_1, a_2, \ldots, a_n) = \int_{-\infty}^{a_1} \int_{-\infty}^{a_2} \cdots \int_{-\infty}^{a_n} f(z_1, z_2, \ldots, z_n)\,\mathrm{d}z_1, \mathrm{d}z_2, \ldots, \mathrm{d}z_n.$$

$F(a_1, a_2, \ldots, a_n)$ is the *joint CDF* and $f(z_1, z_2, \ldots, z_n)$ is the joint PDF for the random variables $z_1, z_2, \ldots, z_n$.

Finally, given the joint PDF of n random variables, we can calculate the *joint marginal* PDF of any subset of k of these random variables by integrating out

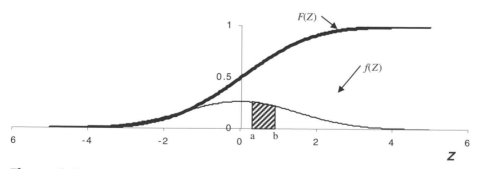

Figure 3.1 An example of a CDF and its PDF

(from $-\infty$ to $-\infty$) the other $n - k$ variables. For example, the joint marginal PDF of Z_1 and Z_2 is given by

$$\int_{-\infty}^{\infty} \cdots \int_{-\infty}^{\infty} f(z_1, z_2, \ldots, z_n) \, dz_3, dz_4, \ldots, dz_n,$$

which leaves the joint marginal density (PDF) of Z_1 and Z_2 because all other variables were integrated out. Furthermore, the *joint marginal CDF* of Z_1 and Z_2 is given by:

$$\int_{-\infty}^{a_1} \int_{-\infty}^{a_2} \int_{-\infty}^{\infty} \cdots \int_{-\infty}^{\infty} f(z_1, z_2, z_n) \, dz_1, dz_2, \ldots, dz_n.$$

This result obtains because we integrated the joint marginal PDF of Z_1, and Z_2 over Z_1 and Z_2 from $-\infty$ to a_1 and a_2 respectively. In other words, the joint marginal CDF of Z_1 and Z_2 can be interpreted as $F(a_1, a_2, \infty, \infty, \ldots, \infty)$. A more detailed discussion of this can be found in standard textbooks on mathematical statistics or econometrics (e.g., Greene 1999).

3.3.2 Specifying the choice problem as a distribution of behavioural responses

We can specify the structure of the choice model in more detail, but first we briefly recap the goal of choice modelling to make the distributional and density assumptions more meaningful and apparent. Specifically, the goal of a choice model is to estimate the significance of the determinants of $V(s, x)$ in equation (3.8). For each individual q, the analyst observes an ordering (see next paragraph) of the alternatives, and from them infers the influence of various attributes in the utility expression $V(s, x)$, which is represented more compactly as V_{jq}. Specification of the functional form of V_{jq} in terms of attributes (i.e., the relationship between decision attributes and observed choices) must be determined insofar as this will influence the significance of attributes. However, there is little loss of generality in assuming a linear, additive form. A linear, additive form represents the composition rule that maps the multi-dimensional attribute vector into a unidimensional overall utility of the form $V_{jq} = \beta_{1j} f_1(s_{1jq}) + \cdots + \beta_{kj} f_k(s_{kjq})$.

The attributes can enter in strictly linear form, as logarithms, as various powers, as well as a variety of other forms. The term 'linear' means linear in the parameters. The linear additive assumption is testable and can be replaced with more complex non-linear functional forms. For consistency and expositional clarity, however, we continue to use V_{jq} rather than the expression in terms of attributes.

The procedure developed for the basic choice model requires the analyst to observe only the individual's choice and the defined choice set, not the rank order of all alternatives. Alternatively, one could observe a complete or partial ranking of alternatives, but the reliability of such information is questionable if alternatives are not frequently used (as discussed in chapter 2). This ranking procedure yields more information from a given individual (by 'exploding' the data), resulting in multiple observations per individual, but this comes at the expense of (possible) violation of the underlying properties of the basic choice model (see chapter 6).

The next step is to specify a probability model for the observed data as a function of the parameters associated with each attribute, and apply probabilistic assumptions that permit adequate statistical tests. A statistical estimation technique is required to obtain estimates of the parameters associated with attributes. The approach we use to estimate the parameters of the basic choice model is called 'maximum likelihood estimation' (MLE). MLE is outlined in section 3.5 and in appendix A to this chapter, but briefly, the maximum likelihood estimates are obtained by maximising a probabilistic function with respect to the parameters or utility parameters.

In summary, therefore, choice model development proceeds in a series of logical steps:

1. First we assume that an individual q will select alternative i iff U_{iq} is greater than the level of utility associated with any other alternative in the choice set (equation (3.4)).
2. Second, we (or rather, computers) calculate the probability that the individual would rank alternative i higher than any other alternative j in the choice set, conditional on knowing V_{jq} for all j alternatives in the individual's choice set. Assuming that the known value of V_{jq} is v_j, then equation (3.8) can be expressed as

$$P_{iq} = P(U_{iq} > U_{jq}|V_{jq} = v_j, j \in A_q) \quad \forall j \neq i. \tag{3.9}$$

Equation (3.9) is a statement about the probability that the unobserved random elements, the ε_{iq}s, take on a specific relationship with respect to the quantities of interest, the V_{jq}s. Once an assumption is made about the joint distribution of the ε_{jq}s, and the V_{jq}s are specified in terms of their utility parameters and attributes, we can apply the method of maximum likelihood estimation to estimate the empirical magnitude of the utility parameters.

Let us rearrange equation (3.8) to express the right-hand side in terms of the relationship between ε_{jq} and the other elements:

$$P_{iq} = P[\varepsilon_{jq} < V_{iq} - V_{jq} + \varepsilon_{iq}, \; \forall j \in A_q, \; j \neq i].$$

For a particular alternative, i, we need to identify the level of ε_i. Because ε_i has a distribution of values in the sampled population, we denote all possible values of ε_{iq} by b_ℓ ($\ell = 1, \ldots, r$), and initially assume some discrete distribution (i.e., a limited number of levels of ε_{iq}). Then

$$P_{iq} = P[\varepsilon_{iq} = b_\ell, \varepsilon_{jq} < V_{iq} - V_{jq} + b_\ell, \quad \forall j \in A_q, j \neq i](b_\ell = b_1, b_2, \ldots, b_r). \tag{3.10}$$

Equation (3.10) can be expanded:

$$\begin{aligned} P_{iq} = \; & P[\varepsilon_{iq} = b_1, \text{ and } \; \varepsilon_{jq} < V_{iq} - V_{jq} + b_1, \; \forall j \in A_q, j \neq i] \\ & + P[\varepsilon_{iq} = b_2 \text{ and } \; \varepsilon_{jq} < V_{iq} - V_{jq} + b_2, \; \forall j \in A_q, j \neq i] + \cdots \\ & + P[\varepsilon_{iq} = b_r \text{ and } \; \varepsilon_{jq} < V_{iq} - V_{jq} + b_r, \; \forall j \in A_q, j \neq i]. \end{aligned}$$

Alternatively,

$$P_{iq} = P[\varepsilon_{iq} = b_1][P(\varepsilon_{iq} < V_{iq} - V_{jq} + b_1, \; \forall j \in A_q, \; j \neq i)] + \cdots$$
$$+ P[\varepsilon_{iq} = b_r][P(\varepsilon_{jq} < V_{iq} - V_{jq} + b_r, \; \forall j \in A_q, \; j \neq i)],$$

or

$$P_{iq} = \sum_{\ell=1}^{r} [\varepsilon_{iq} = b_\ell][P(\varepsilon_{jq} < V_{iq} - V_{jq} + b_\ell), \; \forall j \in A_q, \; j \neq i]. \tag{3.11}$$

Equation (3.11) can be modified further by assuming a continuous distribution of b_ℓs (with a range of $-\infty$ to $+\infty$), giving equation (3.12):

$$P_{iq} = \sum_{g=1}^{\infty} P[\varepsilon_{iq} = b_g] \Delta b_g [P(\varepsilon_{jq} < V_{iq} - V_{jq} + b_g), \; \forall j \in A_q, j \neq i]. \tag{3.12}$$

Thus, in the limit, as $\Delta b_g \to 0$,

$$\lim_{\Delta b \to 0} P_{iq} = \int_{-\infty}^{\infty} P[\varepsilon_{iq} = b_g][P(\varepsilon_{jq} < V_{iq} - V_{jq} + b_g), \; \forall j \in A_q, j \neq i]. \tag{3.13}$$

Equation (3.13) is a general expression for the relationship between a selection probability and the attributes of the alternatives in the choice set for a utility maximising consumer under the assumed condition of random utility (i.e., randomness due to the information gap between utility maximisers and analysts). This equation constitutes a general expression for a choice model. Several additional assumptions are required to convert equation (3.13) to an operational model. The remainder of this chapter introduces assumptions that permit a very simple (or basic) operational model. Later chapters introduce further assumptions that result in more complex, albeit more behaviourally appealing, models.

3.4   The basic choice model — a particular model formulation

To make the individual choice model operationally tractable, a number of axioms have been developed to condition the interpretation placed on the empirically identifiable selection probabilities. That is, in practice one specifies formulae for the selection probabilities, and then determines whether these formulae could be obtained via equation (3.13) from some distribution of utility-maximising consumers. Thus, a defined parametric specification associated with a particular operational model used to obtain selection probabilities does not have a *strict* choice theoretic foundation.

The main selection probability axiom used to develop a simple operational model is known as the Independence-from-Irrelevant Alternatives (IIA) axiom. This states that *the ratio of the probabilities of choosing one alternative over another (given that both alternatives have a non-zero probability of choice) is unaffected by the presence or absence of any additional alternatives in the choice set.*

This condition is both a strength and weakness of a choice model: its strength is that it provides a computationally convenient choice model, and permits introduction and/or elimination of alternatives in choice sets *without re-estimation*. Its weakness is that the observed and unobserved attributes of utility may not be independent of one another, and/or if the unobserved components of utility are correlated among alternatives, this leads to biased utility parameters and added errors in forecasts. Satisfaction of the IIA condition, however, should not be of general concern because the independence assumption is a priori neither desirable nor undesirable, but should be accepted or rejected on empirical grounds depending on the circumstances. A series of tests to identify potential violation of IIA are presented in Chapter 6.

McFadden (1974) introduced two additional assumptions for completeness:

1. *Positivity*: Given the chooser's socioeconomic characteristics and the alternatives in the choice set, the probability that a particular alternative is chosen must be greater than zero for all possible alternative sets A, vectors of measured attributes s, and $x \in A$.
2. *Irrelevance of alternative set effect*: This holds that without replications on each individual it is not possible to identify an 'alternative choice set effect' (z). Thus, another restriction must be introduced to isolate the 'choice alternative effect'.

In particular, we assume that $V(s, x, z) = V(s, x) - V(s, z)$. That is, the function $V(s, x, z)$ used to determine selection probabilities has an additive separable form. The latter assumption should be innocuous if the model is limited to situations in which the alternatives can plausibly be assumed to be distinct and weighed independently by each decision maker, and there is one set of alternatives across replications (i.e., the present choice alternatives). If these conditions obtain, the selection probabilities can be calculated with some degree of confidence, but this does not guarantee that any particular selection probability structure conforms precisely to the choice theory.

The IIA property implies that the random elements in utility (i.e., ε_j s) are independent across alternatives and are identically distributed. There are many statistical distributions available, but the one used extensively in discrete-choice modelling is the extreme value type 1 (EV1) distribution. Historically this distribution has been referred to by a number of names, including Weibull, Gumbel and double-exponential. The mean and variance of this distribution are derived in chapter 6 as a natural prelude to a range of models that relax some of the strict assumptions of the basic MNL model. The task we now face is to use the selected distribution as the mechanism for translating the unobserved random index associated with each alternative into an operational component of the probability expression. This component can then be integrated out of the model to arrive at a choice model in which the only unknowns are utility parameters associated with each attribute in the observed component of the random utility expression.

The structural solution for the basic choice model can be derived by starting with a definition of the EV1 distribution in terms of ε_j s, given in equation (3.14):

$$P(\varepsilon_j \leq \varepsilon) = \exp(- \exp -\varepsilon) = e^{-e^{-\varepsilon}}. \tag{3.14}$$

Recall that equation (3.8) indicated that

$$P_{iq} = P((\varepsilon_{jq} - \varepsilon_{iq}) < (V_{iq} - V_{jq})) \quad \text{for all } j \neq i, \, j = 1, \ldots, J, q = 1, \ldots, Q.$$
(3.15)

Rearranging equation (3.15) to reflect the condition in equation (3.14), and dropping the subscript q to clarify the exposition with no loss of information, yields equation (3.16). This is a respecification of the left-hand side of equation (3.14):

$$P_i = P(\varepsilon_j < (\varepsilon_i + V_i - V_j)), \text{ assuming that } U_j \neq U_i \text{ (hence } < \text{ not } \leq).$$
(3.16)

Because each ε_j is assumed to be independently distributed, the probability of choosing alternative i, P_i, may be written as the product of $J - 1$ terms specified using (3.14) as follows for some given value of ε_i (say b):

$$P_i = P(\varepsilon_j < (b + V_i - V_j) \text{ for all } j \neq i) = \prod_{j=1}^{J} \exp(-\exp -[b + V_i - V_j]).$$
(3.17)

This simplifies to

$$\exp(-b) \exp\left[-\sum_{j=1}^{J} \exp -(b + V_i - V_j)\right].$$
(3.18)

Thus, analogous to equation (3.13), the probability of choosing a particular alternative i, can be calculated by integrating the probability density function (3.18) over all possible values of ε:

$$P_i = \int_{b=-\infty}^{b=\infty} \exp(-b) \exp\left[-\sum_{j=1}^{J} \exp -(b + V_i - V_j)\right] db.$$
(3.19)

To obtain the final result, we rearrange equation (3.19) to separate out elements containing b, as follows:

$$P_i = \int_{b=-\infty}^{b=\infty} \exp(-b) \exp\left\{-\exp(-b)\left[\sum_{j=1}^{J} \exp(V_j - V_i)\right]\right\} db.$$
(3.20)

We integrate equation (3.20) which has a definite integral from $-\infty$ to $+\infty$, which is not straightforward to do in this form. Thus, we apply a transformation of variables by replacing $\exp(-b)$ with z, noting that z does not replace b but the exponential of the negative of b. Thus $b = -\ln z$. The expression to be integrated then becomes:

$$z \exp[-za],$$

where

$$a = \sum_{j=1}^{J} \exp(V_j - V_i),$$

which is a constant containing only Vs. However, because the integration in equation (3.20) is over the random utility space with respect to db, not $d(\exp(-b))$, then a transformation has to occur to replace db with dz. Because $\exp(-b) = z$ implies that $b = -\ln z$, we can replace db by $-(1/z) \, dz$ in (3.20). This requires a change to the limits of integration because db is now $-(1/z) \, dz$. Note that $z = \infty$ when $b = -\infty$ (from $z = \exp(-(-\infty))$) and $z = 0$ when $b = \infty$. Hence, equation (3.20) now can be rewritten in terms of z as:

$$P_i = \int_\infty^0 z \exp[-za](-1/z) \, dz. \tag{3.21}$$

Simplifying and reversing the order of integration (the latter simply changes the sign), yields:

$$P_i = \int_0^\infty \exp(-za)] \, dz. \tag{3.22}$$

This is a more conventional form of a definite integral, so now we can integrate

$$P_i = -\exp(-za)/a|_0^\infty.$$

Note that $\int \exp(-az) = -\exp(-az)/a$, and that when $z = \infty$, $\exp(-\infty) = 0$; when $z = 0$, $\exp(0) = 1$. Thus,

$$P_i = -\left[\frac{1}{a}(0-1)\right] = \frac{1}{a} \qquad \text{where} \qquad a = \sum_{j=1}^J \exp(V_j - V_i). \tag{3.23}$$

Equation (3.23) can be rearranged to obtain:

$$P_i = \frac{1}{\displaystyle\sum_{j=1}^J \exp -(V_i - V_j)}. \tag{3.24}$$

Equation (3.24) is the basic choice model consistent with the assumptions outlined above, and is called the conditional logit choice or multinomial logit (MNL) model. In the remaining sections of this chapter the procedure for estimating the MNL model is outlined, important estimation outputs are identified and a simple empirical example is used to illustrate a complete framework for a basic choice model. The remaining chapters in the book use the basic model as the starting position for more detailed discussions of a wide range of issues, including alternative assumptions on the co-variance structure of the matrix of unobserved influences across the choice set.

3.5 Statistical estimation procedure

We now discuss estimation of the utility parameters of the utility expressions in equation (3.24). There are several alternative statistical approaches to estimating the parameters of choice models. Our objective in this chapter is to discuss *maximum likelihood estimation* (MLE), which is the most commonly used estimation method. To accomplish our purpose, we develop the general concept of MLE and then apply it to the specific case of the MNL model.

3.5.1   Maximum likelihood estimation

The method of maximum likelihood is based on the idea that a given sample could be generated by different populations, and is more likely to come from one population than another. Thus, the maximum likelihood estimates are that set of population parameters that generate the observed sample most often. To illustrate this principle, suppose that we have a random sample of n observations of some random variable Z denoted by $(z_1, \ldots, z_n)$ drawn from a population characterised by an unknown parameter θ (which may be a mean, a variance, etc.).

Z is a random variable, hence it has an associated probability density function (PDF) which can be written $f(Z|\theta)$. This implies that the probability distribution of Z depends upon the value of θ ($f(Z|\theta)$). This is read as 'a function of Z *given* some value for θ'. If all the n values of Z in the sample are independent, the joint (conditional) probability density function (PDF) of the sample can be written as follows:

$$f(z_1, z_2, \ldots, z_n|\theta) = f(z_1|\theta)f(z_2|\theta), \ldots, f(z_n|\theta). \tag{3.25}$$

The Zs are considered variable for a fixed value of θ in the usual interpretation of this joint PDF. However, if the Zs are fixed and θ is variable, equation (3.25) can be interpreted as a likelihood function instead of a joint PDF. In the present case, there is a single sample of Zs; hence, treating the Zs as fixed seems reasonable. Maximising equation (3.25) with respect to θ (allowing θ to vary) yields an estimate of θ that maximises equation (3.25). This latter estimate is called the maximum likelihood estimate of θ. In other words, it is that value of θ (i.e., characteristic of the population) which is most likely to have generated the sample of observed Zs.

The concept of maximum likelihood can be extended easily to situations in which a population is characterised by more than a single parameter θ. For example, if the Zs above follow a normal probability distribution, without additional knowledge we know that the population is characterised by a mean (μ) and a variance (σ^2). If θ is defined as a 2-dimensional vector of elements (μ, σ^2) instead of a single parameter, the likelihood function of the sample may be written in the same form of equation (3.25), and maximised with respect to the vector θ. The parameter values that maximise equation (3.25) are the MLEs of the elements of the vector θ.

A likelihood function is maximised in exactly the same way as any function is maximised. That is, the MLE estimates of θ are those values at which $\partial L/\partial \theta_i = 0$ (i indexes the elements of θ and L denotes the likelihood function). Often, it is mathematically simpler to work with the (natural) logarithm of the likelihood function because the MLEs of θ are invariant to monotonically increasing transformations of L. Hence, we seek those values of θ which maximise $\ln L = L^*$ (i.e., those values of θ_i for which $\partial L^*/\partial \theta_i = 0$). For completeness one should check the second-order conditions for a maximum; but to avoid complication at this point we will assume that L (or L^*) is such that the maximum exists and is unique. McFadden (1976) proved that a unique maximum exists for the basic MNL model except under special conditions unlikely to be encountered in practice. Further details of MLE are given in appendix A to this chapter.

3.5.2 Maximum likelihood estimation of the MNL choice model

We are now ready to discuss estimation of the parameters of the basic MNL choice model developed in the last section. Recall that the probability of individual q choosing alternative i can be written as the following closed-form MNL model (equation 3.24):

$$P_{iq} = \exp(V_{iq}) \left/ \sum_{j=1}^{J} \exp(V_{jq}) \right.$$

Recall that the V_{jq} are assumed to be linear, additive functions in the attributes (Xs) which determine the utility of the jth alternative. That is, let V_{jq} be written as:

$$V_{jq} = \sum_{k=1}^{K} \beta_{jk} X_{jkq}. \tag{3.26}$$

It is possible, for a given j, to set one of the Xs (say X_{j1q}) equal to 1 for all q. In this case, the utility parameter β_{j1} is interpreted as an *alternative-specific constant* for alternative j. However, we cannot specify such constants for all V_j because this would result in a perfectly collinear set of measures, such that no estimator can be obtained for any βs. Thus, we may specify *at most* $(J-1)$ alternative-specific constants in any particular MNL model. As for the other Xs in equation (3.26), if an element of X_{jk} appears in the utility expression (V_{jq}) for all J alternatives, such a variable is termed *generic*, and β_{jk} may be replaced by β_k (i.e., the utility parameter of X_{jk} is the same for all j). On the other hand, if an element of X_{jk} appears only in the utility expression for one alternative, say V_{jq}, it is called alternative-specific. For the moment we will continue to use the notation of equation (3.26), which implies alternative-specific variables because a generic variable basically is a restriction on this more general form (i.e., we impose equality of utility parameters). We will have more to say on this matter later.

Suppose we obtain a random sample of Q individuals, and for each individual we observe the choice actually made and the values of X_{jkq} for all alternatives. Given that individual q was observed to choose alternative i, the PDF for that observed data point is $f(\text{Data}_q|\beta)$, where Data_q is the observed data for individual q and β is the vector of utility parameters contained in the functions V_{jq}. This PDF can be represented simply by P_{iq} in equation (3.24). Thus, if all observations are independent, we can write the likelihood function for the sample by replacing $f(\text{Data}_q|\beta)$ by the expression for the probability of the alternative actually chosen by individual q. It therefore follows that if we order our observations such that the first n_1 individuals were observed to choose alternative 1, the next n_2 to choose alternative 2, etc., the likelihood function of our sample may be written as follows:

$$L = \prod_{q=1}^{n_1} P_{1q} \cdot \prod_{q=n_1+1}^{n_1+n_2} P_{2q}, \ldots, \prod_{q=Q-n_J+1}^{Q} P_{Jq}. \tag{3.27}$$

The expression for L can be simplified somewhat by defining a dummy variable f_{jq}, such that $f_{jq} = 1$ if alternative j is chosen and $f_{jq} = 0$ otherwise. The latter simplification allows us to rewrite equation (3.27) as follows:

$$L = \prod_{q=1}^{Q} \prod_{j=1}^{J} P_{jq}^{f_{jq}}. \tag{3.28}$$

We can confirm that equation (3.28) is the same as (3.27) by examining a few observations. First, consider one of the n_1 observations in which the individual chose alternative 1. P_{iq} should appear in L for that value of q. For that q in equation (3.28) we multiply the terms $P_{jq}^{f_{jq}}$ over j. The first term will be P_{1q}^1 because alternative 1 was chosen, hence $f_{1p} = 1$. The next (and all subsequent terms) will be $P_{2q}^0 = 1 (P_{jq}^0 = 1)$ because $f_{2q}, \ldots, f_{J_q}$ will be zero since alternative 1 was not chosen. For one of the n_2 individuals who chose alternative 2, $f_{2q} = 1$ and all other $f_{jq} = 0$; hence, only P_{2q} enters equation (3.28) for that observation. Thus, equation (3.28) is exactly the same as equation (3.27).

Now, given L in equation (3.28), the log likelihood function L^* can be written as

$$L^* = \sum_{q=1}^{Q} \sum_{j=1}^{J} f_{jq} \ln P_{jq}. \tag{3.29}$$

Replacing P_{jq} in equation (3.29) by the expression (3.24) yields an equation that is a function only of the unknown βs contained in the expression V_{jq} because all other quantities in equation (3.28) are known (the Xs and f_{jq}s). L^* can then be maximised with respect to the βs in the usual manner (see appendix A to this chapter). The estimates that result are the MLEs for the model's utility parameters. The set of first-order conditions necessary to maximise L^* can be derived (see appendix A), but are not particularly useful at this point because our objective is to understand the basic estimation methodology.

We conclude our discussion of maximum likelihood estimation of the parameters of the MNL model by noting that equation (3.29) should be maximised with respect to the utility parameters (βs) using some non-linear maximisation algorithm. Such algorithms are usually iterative, and typically require the analyst to provide an initial guess for the values of β. These 'guessed' values are used in equation (3.26) to calculate the V_{jq}s, which are inserted in equation (3.24) to calculate the P_{iq}s. Then they are used in equation (3.29) to calculate a starting value of L^*.

The standard procedure is to use some search criterion to find 'better' values of the βs to use in equation (3.26), such that the value of L^* in equation (3.29) increases. Such iterative procedures continue until some (predetermined) level of tolerance is reached; for example, either L^* increases by an amount less than a given tolerance and/or the βs change by less than some predetermined amount (see appendix A for more details). Several methods are used to search for the optimal value of each β; Goldfeld and Quandt (1972) and Greene (1999) provide an excellent survey of many of the methods.

3.6   Model outputs

Having covered the basics of maximum likelihood estimation of the utility parameters of the MNL choice model in the previous section, we now discuss the various results which can be obtained as a consequence of the application of such a procedure. These include the following: (1) estimated βs and their asymptotic t-values, (2) measures of goodness of fit for the model as a whole and (3) estimated elasticities of choice with respect to the various attributes (Xs) for both individuals and aggregates of individuals.

3.6.1   Estimation of utility parameters

An estimate of β_{jk} (say $\hat{\beta}_{jk}$) can be interpreted as an estimate of the weight of attribute k in the utility expression V_j of alternative j. Given estimates of the βs, an estimate of V_{iq} (say $\hat{V}_{iq}$) can be calculated by taking the βs and the Xs for individual q and alternative i and using equation (3.26). The resulting $\hat{V}_{iq}$ can be interpreted as an estimate of the (relative) utility U_{iq} of alternative i to individual q. Analysts can evaluate generic and alternative-specific specifications for an attribute that exists in more than one utility expression across the choice set.

3.6.2   Statistical significance of utility parameters

Most empirical applications require the ability to statistically test whether a particular $\hat{\beta}_{jk}$ is significantly different from zero or some other hypothesised value. That is, we require a choice model analogue to the types of statistical tests performed on ordinary least squares regression weights (e.g., t-tests). Fortunately, the MLE method provides such capability if the asymptotic property of the method is satisfied; that is, strictly speaking, the tests are valid only in *very* large samples. The tests require the matrix of second partial derivatives of L (or L^*) with respect to the βs. The negative of the inverse of this matrix evaluated at the estimated values is the estimated asymptotic variance–covariance matrix for the MLEs. The square roots of the diagonal elements can be treated as estimates of the asymptotic standard errors.

If you are unfamiliar with matrix algebra, it is important that you at least understand that the maximum likelihood procedure permits you to calculate asymptotic standard errors for the $\hat{\beta}s$ in the MNL model and use these to test the statistical significance of individual βs using asymptotic t-tests. The appropriate standard errors and t-statistics normally are produced as part of the output of any MNL computer program. Typically, analysts will seek out mean utility parameters which have sufficiently small standard errors (think of this as the variation around the mean) so that the mean estimate is a good representation of the influence of the particular attribute in explaining the level of relative utility associated with each alternative.

The ratio of the mean parameter to its standard error is the *t*-value (desirably 1.96 or higher so that one can have 95 per cent or greater confidence that the mean is statistically significantly different from zero). Practitioners often accept *t*-values as low as 1.6, although this is stretching the usefulness of a mean estimate. It suggests a number of specification improvements, such as segmentation, to enable an attribute to have a different mean and smaller standard error within each segment compared to the whole sample or more aggregate segments.

There are many other possible reasons why an attribute may not be statistically significant. These include presence of outliers on some observations (i.e., very large or small values of an attribute which lie outside the range of most of the observations), missing or erroneous data (often set to zero, blank, 999 or −999), non-normality in the attributes distribution which limits the usefulness of *t*-statistics in establishing levels of statistical significance, and of course the fact that the attribute simply is not an important influence of the choice under study.

3.6.3   Overall goodness-of-fit tests

At this point, it is useful to consider the following statement by Frisch about statistical tests, made almost forty years ago.

> Mathematical tests of significance, confidence intervals etc. are highly useful concepts ... All these concepts are, however, of relative merit only. They have a clearly defined meaning only within the narrow confines of the model in question ... As we dig into the foundation of any economic ... model we will always find a line of demarcation which we cannot transgress unless we introduce another type of test of Significance (this time written with a capital *S*), a test of the applicability of the model itself ... Something of relevance for this question can, of course, be deduced from mathematical tests properly interpreted, but no such test can ever do anything more than just push the final question one step further back. The final, the highest level of test can never be formulated in mathematical terms. (Frisch 1951: 9–10)

Frish's quote reminds us of the relative role of statistical tests of model significance. That is, all too often statistical measures are used as the dominant criteria for acceptance or rejection of a particular model. Analyst judgement about overall model validity should have the ultimate decision power during model development, as a function of the analyst's experience. Nevertheless, there are a number of statistical measures of model validity that can assist assessment of an empirically estimated individual-choice model. This section describes some of the key measures.

To determine how well the basic MNL model fits a given set of data, we would like to compare the predicted dependent (or endogenous) variable with the observed dependent variable relative to some useful criterion. Horowitz and Louviere (1993)

(HL) provide a test that allows one to evaluate predicted probabilities against a vector of observed discrete-choices. It can be used to evaluate the out-of-sample fit of any MNL model by taking repeated samples of the data.

The HL test is a test of process equivalence in that it takes an estimated model and associated variance–covariance matrix of the estimated parameters and uses the model to forecast the expected probabilities. The forecast probabilities are then regressed against the 1, 0 observed choices using a modified regression based on the variance–covariance matrix, which takes the sampling and estimation errors into account. The null is that the predicted probabilities are proportional to the observed 1, 0 choice data. This test loses no power from aggregation and can be used to compare models across full data sets and holdout samples (and a second data source).

3.6.3.1 The likelihood ratio test

The log likelihood function evaluated at the mean of the estimated utility parameters is a useful criterion for assessing overall goodness-of-fit when the maximum likelihood estimation method is used to estimate the utility parameters of the MNL model. This function is used to test the contribution of particular (sub)sets of variables. The procedure is known as *the likelihood ratio test* (LR). To test the significance of the MNL model in large samples, a generalised likelihood ratio test is used. The null hypothesis is that the probability P_i of an individual choosing alternative i is independent of the value of the parameters in the MNL function (equation 3.24). If this hypothesis is retained, we infer that the utility parameters are zero; that is, analogous to an overall F-test in OLS regression, the null is that all βs in equation (3.26) are zero (except alternative-specific constants). Similar to the case of testing the significance of R^2 in OLS regression, the hypothesis of independence is almost always rejected for a specific model. Thus, the usefulness of the likelihood ratio test is its ability to test if subsets of the βs are significant. The generalised likelihood ratio criterion has the following form:

$$L^* = \max L(\omega) / \max L(\Omega), \qquad (3.30)$$

where L^* is the likelihood ratio, $\max L(\omega)$ is the maximum of the likelihood function in which M elements of the parameter space are constrained by the null hypothesis. For example, in testing the significance of a set of βs in the MNL model, $L(\omega)$ is the maximum with these βs set equal to zero (constrained) and $\max L(\omega)$ is the unconstrained maximum of the likelihood function. Wilks (1962) shows that $-2 \ln L^*$ is approximately chi-square distributed with M degrees of freedom for large samples if the null hypothesis is true. Therefore, one maximises L for the full MNL model, and subsequently for the model with M βs set to zero (i.e., some Xs are removed). The next step is to calculate L^* and see if the quantity $-2 \ln L^*$ is greater than the critical value of χ_M^2 from some preselected significance level (e.g., $\alpha = 0.05$). ($\ln L^*$ is the difference between two log likelihoods.) If the calculated value of chi-square exceeds the critical value for the specified level of confidence, one rejects the null hypothesis that the particular subset of βs being tested are equal to zero.

The likelihood ratio test can be used to compare a set of nested models. A common comparison is between a model in which an attribute has a generic taste weight across all alternatives and a model in which alternative-specific utility parameters are imposed. For example, if there are four alternatives then we compare the overall influence of one generic taste weight versus four alternative-specific utility parameters. Thus, after estimating two models with the same data, we can compare the log likelihood (at convergence) for each model and calculate the likelihood ratio as $-2 \ln L^*$. This can be compared to the critical value for three degrees of freedom (i.e., three extra d.f.s for the alternative specific variable model compared to the generic model) using a chi-squared test at, say, 5 per cent significance. If the calculated value is greater than the critical value we can reject the null hypothesis of no statistically significant difference at 5 per cent significance. If the calculated value is less than the critical value then we cannot reject the null hypothesis.

The likelihood function L for the basic MNL choice model takes on values between zero and one because L is the product of Q probabilities, and therefore, the log likelihood function L^* will always be negative. Let us define $L^*(\hat{\beta})$ as the maximised value of the log likelihood and $L^*(0)$ as the value of the log likelihood evaluated such that the probability of choosing the ith alternative is exactly equal to the observed aggregate share in the sample of the ith alternative (call this S_i). In other words, let

$$L^*(0) = \sum_{q=1}^{Q} \sum_{j=1}^{J} f_{jq} \ln S_i. \tag{3.31}$$

Clearly, L^* will be larger if evaluated at $\hat{\beta}$ than if the explanatory variables (Xs) are ignored, as in equation (3.31). Intuitively, the higher the explanatory power of the Xs, the larger $L^*(\hat{\beta})$ will be in comparison to $L^*(0)$. We use this notion to calculate a *likelihood-ratio index* that can be used to measure the goodness-of-fit of the MNL model, analogous to R^2 in ordinary regression. To do this we calculate the statistic

$$\rho^2 = 1 - (L^*(\hat{\beta})/L^*(0)). \tag{3.32}$$

We noted that $L^*(\hat{\beta})$ will be larger than $L^*(0)$, but in the case of the MNL model this implies a smaller negative number, such that $L^*(\hat{\beta})/L^*(0)$ must lie between zero and one. The smaller this ratio, the better the statistical fit of the model (i.e., the greater the explanatory power of the Xs relative to an aggregate, constant-share prediction); and hence, the larger is the quantity 1 minus this ratio. Thus, we use ρ^2 (rho-squared) as a type of pseudo-R^2 to measure the goodness-of-fit of the MNL model. Values of ρ^2 between 0.2 and 0.4 are considered to be indicative of extremely good model fits. Simulations by Domencich and McFadden (1975) equivalenced this range to 0.7 to 0.9 for a linear function. Analysts should not expect to obtain ρ^2 values as high as the R^2s commonly obtained in many stated choice ordinary least squares regression applications.

Some MNL computer programs compute ρ^2 not on the basis of $L^*(0)$ assuming that P_i is equal to S_i, the sample aggregate share, but rather under the assumption of equal aggregate shares for all alternatives (e.g., if $J = 3$, $S_i = 1/3$ in equation (3.31)). Our definition of ρ^2 is preferable to the latter because the Q observations allow us to calculate the share of each alternative in the sample, which is the best estimate of P_i in the absence of a choice model that can improve the predictions.

We can improve on ρ^2 in equation (3.32) by adjusting it for degrees of freedom, an adjustment that is useful if we want to compare different models. The corrected ρ^2, given by $\bar{\rho}^2$ (rho-bar squared) is[1]

$$\bar{\rho}^2 = 1 - \frac{L^*(\hat{\beta}) \Big/ \sum_{q=1}^{Q} (J_q - 1) - K}{L^*(0) \Big/ \sum_{q=1}^{Q} (J_q - 1)} \tag{3.33}$$

where J_q refers to the number of alternatives faced by individual q, and K is the total number of variables (Xs) in the model. As an aside, note that prior to (3.33) J has been assumed to be the same for all Q individuals, which need not be the case.

The likelihood ratio (LR) test is an appropriate test for an exogenous sample. If we had selected a choice-based sample (Ben-Akiva and Lerman 1985, Cosslett 1981) in order to increase the number of observations of relatively less frequently chosen alternatives and decrease the incidence of more frequently chosen alternatives, then the LR test is not valid since the LR test statistic does not have a chi-square distribution under non-random sampling schemes. Rather it is distributed as a weighted average of chi-square variates with one degree of freedom. In this case a *Lagrange multiplier* (LM) test would be preferred since it handles both choice-based and exogenous samples. The LM test statistic is part of the output of most estimation packages, just as the LR test is. A choice-based sample test is given in chapter 6.

3.6.3.2 Prediction success

Tests of prediction success have been developed which involve a comparison of the summed probabilities from the models (i.e., *expected* number choosing a particular alternative) with the observed behaviour for the sample. However, it is possible that a model might predict well with respect to the estimation sample, but poorly predict the outcome of policy changes defined in terms of movements in one or more of the model variables. The best test of predictive strength is a before-and-after (i.e., external validity) assessment procedure.

McFadden (1979) synthesised prediction tests into a prediction success table. Each entry (N_{ij}) in the central matrix of the table gives the expected number of individuals who are *observed* to choose i and *predicted* to choose j. Alternatively, it is the probability of individual q selecting alternative j summed over all individuals who actually

---

[1] An alternative definition for $\bar{\rho}^2$, due to Ben-Akiva and Swait (1986), is given in chapter 9. That definition is useful for testing non-nested specifications.

select alternative i. Thus

$$N_{ij} = \sum_{q=1}^{Q} f_{iq} P_{jq} = \sum_{q=1}^{Q} P_q(j|A_q), \qquad (3.34)$$

where f_{iq} equals one if i is chosen, zero otherwise. (Note that the last term in (3.34) only applies if choice responses are of the 1, 0 form. For aggregate choice frequencies such as proportions and total sample frequencies, the methods in appendix B to this chapter should be used.) A_q is the set of alternatives out of which individual q chooses, and Q_i is the set of individuals in the sample who actually choose alternative i. Column sums (predicted count) are equal to

$$\sum_{i \in A_q} \left[\sum_{q \in Q_i} P_q(j|A_q) \right] = \sum_{q=1}^{Q} P_q(j|A_q) = N.j \qquad (3.35)$$

and are used to calculate predicted shares. Row sums (observed counts) are equal to

$$\sum_{q \in Q_i} \left[\sum_{j \in A_q} P_q(j|A_q) \right] = \sum_{q \in Q_i} 1 = N._i \qquad (3.36)$$

and are used to calculate observed shares. $N_{ii}/N._i$ indicates the proportion of the predicted count (i.e., individuals expected to choose an alternative) who actually choose that alternative. $(N_{11} + \cdots + N_{JJ})/N..$ gives the overall proportion successfully predicted.

To interpret the percentage correctly predicted, it is useful to compare it to the percentage correct that should be obtained by chance. Any model which assigns the same probability of choosing an alternative to all individuals in the sample would obtain a percentage correct for each alternative equal to the actual share for that alternative. The prediction success index is an appropriate goodness-of-fit measure to account for the fact that the proportion successfully predicted for an alternative varies with the aggregate share of that alternative. This index may be written as

$$\sigma_i = \frac{N_{ii}}{N._i} - \frac{N._i}{N..}, \qquad (3.37)$$

where $N_{ii}/N._i$ is the proportion of individuals expected to choose an alternative who actually choose that alternative, and $N._i/N..$ is the proportion who would be successfully predicted if the choice probabilities for each sampled individual were assumed to equal the predicted aggregate share. Hence, if σ_i is equal to zero, a model does not predict alternative i better than the market-share hypothesis.

An overall prediction success index can be calculated by summing the σ_is over the J alternatives, weighting each σ_i by $N._i/N..$. This may be written as

$$\sigma = \sum_{i=1}^{J} (N._i/N..)\sigma_i. \qquad (3.38)$$

Table 3.1. *An example of a prediction success table*

Actual alternatives	Predicted alternatives			Row total (N_i)	Observed share % ($N_i/N_{..}$)* 100
	(1)	(2)	(3)		
(1) Fully detached house	100	20	30	150	45.5
(2) Town house	30	50	20	100	30.3
(3) Flat 20	10	20	50	80	24.2
Column total ($N_{.i}$)	140	90	100	330	100.0
Predicted share (%) ($N_{.i}/N_{..}$)* 100	42.4	27.3	30.3	100	
Proportion successfully predicted ($N_{ii}/N_{.i}$)* 100	71.4	55.6	50.0		
Success index (eq. (3.37))	29.0	28.3	19.7		
Percent error in predicted share − 100* ($N_{.i} - N_i$)/$N_{..}$	−3.03	3.03	6.06		
Overall prediction success index (eq. (3.38))* (predicted share* success index)		0.2599			

Note: *[(42.4*29.0) + (27.3*28.3) + (30.3*19.70)/100²] = 0.

We can expand equation (3.38) as follows:

$$\sigma = \sum_{i=1}^{J} (N_{.i}/N_{..}) \left(\frac{N_{ii}}{N_{.i}} - \frac{N_{.i}}{N_{..}} \right), \tag{3.39}$$

$$\sigma = \sum_{i=1}^{J} \left(\frac{N_{ii}}{N_{..}} - \frac{N_{.i}}{N_{..}} \right)^2. \tag{3.40}$$

This index will generally be non-negative with a maximum value occurring when $\sum_{i=1}^{J} N_{ii} = N_{..}$ (the model perfectly predicts), or

$$1 - \sum_{i=1}^{J} (N_{.i}/N_{..})^2. \tag{3.41}$$

Hence, we can normalise σ to have a maximum value of one. The higher the value, the greater the predictive capability of the model. An example of a prediction success test is given in table 3.1 for choice of establishment type.

3.7 Behavioural outputs of choice models

The random utility model represented by the MNL function provides a very powerful way to assess the effects of a wide range of policies. Policies impact individuals to varying degrees, hence, it is important to be able to determine individual-specific effects prior to determination of market-share effects. If an estimated model was carefully developed so that the systematic utility is well-specified empirically (i.e., the choice set and structural representation of the decision process is reasonable), the model should be a very flexible, policy-sensitive tool. At this point it seems apropos to outline the key policy-related outputs of individual-choice models, and comment on the types of policy issues which ideally can be investigated with this framework.

It should be noted that errors associated with any modelling approach are not necessarily due to the approach *per se*, but often are due to errors in data exogenously supplied (e.g., exogenous forecasts of future levels of population, transport, retail services and recreation facilities). Individual models require smaller samples than aggregate models (the latter use grouped data based on information from many individual interviews/questionnaires); hence, additional costs to obtain such detail are offset by cost savings and increased accuracy of predictive performance and policy indicators.

The types of policy outputs arising from choice models are similar to most statistical models. The models can be used to estimate the responsiveness of a population group to changes in levels of particular attributes (i.e., elasticities of particular choices with respect to certain attributes), to marginal rates of substitution between attributes (i.e., valuation), and to obtain individual and group estimates of the likelihood of choosing a particular activity, given the levels of the attributes offered as the significant choice discriminators.

3.7.1   Elasticities of choice

The appropriateness of various policies can be evaluated with the measures of responsiveness of market shares to changes in each attribute. Direct and cross elasticities can be estimated. A direct elasticity measures the percentage change in the probability of choosing a particular alternative in the choice set with respect to a given percentage change in an attribute of that *same* alternative. A cross elasticity measures the percentage changes in the probability of choosing a particular alternative in the choice set with respect to a given percentage change in an attribute of a *competing* alternative. A full matrix of direct and cross elasticities can be derived for the complete choice set. The size of the change in the level of an attribute has an important bearing on whether the elasticity measure should be point or arc (see below).[2] Software packages can automatically generate point elasticities, which is useful for interpreting small changes in the level of an attribute.

To derive a general formula for the calculation of elasticities in the basic MNL model, consider the equation for P_{iq} (equation (3.24)) and recall the definition of V_{jq} (equation (3.26)). The elasticity of any variable Y with respect to another variable Z is $(\Delta Y/Y)/(\Delta Z/Z)$, which reduces to $(\partial Y/\partial Z)(Z/Y)$ as ΔZ becomes very small. Therefore, direct point elasticities in the MNL model can be written as follows:

$$E_{X_{ikq}}^{P_{iq}} = \frac{\partial P_{iq}}{\partial X_{ikq}} \cdot \frac{X_{ikq}}{P_{iq}}. \tag{3.42}$$

Equation (3.42) can be interpreted as the elasticity of the probability of choosing alternative i for individual q with respect to a marginal (or 'small') change in the kth variable which describes the utility of the ith alternative for individual q.

---

[2] If the terms arc and point elasticities are unfamiliar, see figure 9.7 and its associated discussion.

An operational formula for this elasticity requires an evaluation of the partial derivative in equation (3.42), which can be obtained by using the quotient rule for derivatives (i.e., $\partial e^{az}/\partial Z = ae^{az}$):

$$\frac{\partial P_{iq}}{\partial X_{ikq}} = \frac{\left(\sum_j e^{V_{jq}}\right)\frac{\partial(e^{V_{iq}})}{\partial X_{ikq}} - (e^{V_{iq}})\frac{\partial\left(\sum_j e^{V_{jq}}\right)}{\partial X_{ikq}}}{\left(\sum_j e^{V_{jq}}\right)^2}. \tag{3.43}$$

Simplifying equation (3.43), noting that the partial derivatives are the utility parameters, we get equation (3.44):

$$\frac{\partial P_{iq}}{\partial X_{ikq}} = P_{iq}\beta_{ik} - P_{ik}^2\beta_{ik}. \tag{3.44}$$

The direct point elasticity in equation (3.42) for the MNL model is, therefore, given by equation (3.45):

$$E_{X_{ikq}}^{P_{iq}} = P_{iq}\beta_{iq}(1 - P_{iq})X_{ikq}/P_{iq} = \beta_{ik}X_{ikq}(1 - P_{iq}) \tag{3.45}$$

Cross point elasticities are obtained similarly, evaluating $\partial P_{iq}/\partial X_{jkq}$ as follows:

$$\frac{\partial P_{iq}}{\partial X_{jkq}} = \frac{\left(\sum_j e^{V_{jq}}\right)(0) - (e^{V_{iq}})(e^{V_{jq}})\beta_{jk}}{\left(\sum_j e^{V_{jq}}\right)^2} = -P_{iq}P_{jq}\beta_{jk}. \tag{3.46}$$

The cross elasticity can be evaluated as follows:

$$E_{X_{jkq}}^{P_{iq}} = \frac{\partial P_{iq}}{\partial X_{jkq}} \cdot \frac{X_{jkq}}{P_{iq}} = -P_{iq}P_{jq}\beta_{jk}X_{jkq}/P_{iq} = -\beta_{jk}X_{jkq}P_{jq}. \tag{3.47}$$

The cross-elasticity formula in equation (3.47) depends on variables associated with alternative j, and is independent of alternative i. Thus, MNL cross elasticities with respect to a variable associated with alternative j are the same for all $i \neq j$. This property of *uniform cross elasticities* is a consequence of the assumption that the actual utilities are distributed about their means with independent and identical distributions (IID). When we relax the IID condition (see chapter 6), the elasticity formulae will be different, although the behavioural interpretation is the same.

Equations (3.45) and (3.47) can be combined to yield a single point elasticity formula for the basic MNL model in a simple way:

$$E_{X_{jkq}}^{P_{iq}} = \beta_{jk}X_{jkq}(\delta_{ij} - P_{jq}) \tag{3.48}$$

$$\text{where } \delta_{ij} = \begin{cases} 1 & \text{if } i = j \text{ (a direct point elasticity)} \\ 0 & \text{if } i \neq j \text{ (a cross point elasticity)} \end{cases}.$$

The direct elasticity approaches zero as P_{jq} approaches unity, and approaches $\beta_{jk}X_{jkq}$ as P_{jq} approaches zero. The converse applies for the cross elasticity.

Equation (3.48) yields elasticities for each individual. For aggregate elasticities, one might be tempted to evaluate equation (3.48) at the sample average X_{jk} and $\hat{P}_j$ (average estimated P_j). However, this is not generally correct because the MNL model is non-linear, hence, the estimated logit function need not pass through the point defined by these sample averages. Indeed, this mistake commonly produces errors as large as 20 percent (usually over-estimates) in estimating the responsiveness of choice probabilities with respect to some variable X_{jk}. A better approach is to evaluate equation (3.48) for each individual q and then aggregate, weighting each individual elasticity by the individual's estimated probability of choice. This technique is known as the 'method of sample enumeration', the formula for which is given in equation (3.49):

$$E^{\bar{P}_i}_{X_{jkq}} = \left(\sum_{q=1}^{Q} \hat{P}_{iq} E^{P_{iq}}_{X_{jkq}} \right) \bigg/ \sum_{q=1}^{Q} \hat{P}_{iq}. \tag{3.49}$$

$\hat{P}_{iq}$ is an estimated choice probability. $\bar{P}_i$ refers to the aggregate probability of choice of alternative i. It should be noted that the *weighted aggregate cross elasticities* calculated from an MNL model are likely to differ across alternatives, which may seem odd given the limiting condition of constant cross elasticities in a model derived from the IIA property. This occurs because the IIA condition guarantees identical cross elasticities at the *individual level*, before probability weighting is undertaken. Some software packages give the user the option to select an unweighted aggregation based on a summation across the sample and a division by sample size. This naive aggregation will produce identical cross elasticities, but it is not correct since it fails to recognise the contribution of each observation to the choice outcome of each alternative.

The elasticity formulation in (3.48) and (3.49) is derived from partial differentiation of the choice function, assuming any changes in X are marginal. If changes are non-marginal, as frequently happens in practice, an *arc elasticity* formula is appropriate, provided that the change in the level of the attribute does not result in a level of X outside of the distribution of values used in estimation. This elasticity is calculated using differences rather than differentials:

$$E^{P_{iq}}_{X_{ikq}} = [(P^1_{iq} - P_{iq})/(X^1_{ikq} - X_{ikq})]/[(P^1_{iq} + P_{iq})/(X^1_{ikq} + X_{ikq})], \tag{3.50}$$

$$E^{P_{iq}}_{X_{jkq}} = [(P^1_{iq} - P_{iq})/(X^1_{jkq} - X_{jkq})]/[(P^1_{iq} + P_{iq})/(X^1_{ikq} + X_{ikq})]. \tag{3.51}$$

The elasticities can be combined in many ways, which can be very convenient and useful if one wants to know the average level of responsiveness across a number of market segments. McFadden (1979) summarised some aggregation rules which we list for reference below:

1. Aggregate elasticity over *market segments*, which is the sum of segment elasticities weighted by segment market shares. This rule assumes that the percentage change in the policy variables is the same in each segment.

2. Aggregate elasticities over *alternatives*, which is the sum of component alternative elasticities weighted by the component share of the compared alternative (e.g., all public transport). This rule assumes an equal percentage change in each component alternative as the result of a policy.
3. Elasticity with respect to a *component of an attribute*, which is the elasticity with respect to the variable multiplied by the component's share in the variable (e.g., the elasticity with respect to bus fare when we only have the estimated elasticity with respect to total trip cost).
4. Elasticity with respect to a policy that causes an equal percentage change in several variables equals the sum of elasticities with respect to each variable.

In the same reference, McFadden discusses further how these rules may be combined to arrive at the elasticity needed for policy analysis.

3.7.2 Valuation of attributes

Increasingly, discrete-choice models are being used to derive estimates of the amount of money an individual is willing to pay (or willing to accept) to obtain some benefit (or avoid some cost) from a specific action. In a simple linear model where each attribute in a utility expression is associated with a single taste weight, the ratio of two utility parameters is an estimate of the willingness to pay (WTP) or willingness to accept (WTA), holding all other potential influences constant. If one of the attributes is measured in monetary units, then the marginal rates of substitution arising from the ratio of two utility parameters is a financial indicator of WTP or WTA.

The literature on the use of discrete-choice models to derive empirical values of the WTP or WTA is extensive. Throughout the book we cross-reference to this literature and devote considerable space to valuation. Chapters 11 and 12 present a number of empirical studies to illustrate how choice models are used in practice to obtain valuations of attributes such as travel time savings, convenience of a shopping store and the preservation of an endangered species. The possibility of allowing the valuation of an attribute to be a function of the level of the attribute enriches the point estimates into a distribution of values, referred to as a valuation function (see chapter 11 for more details).

Valuation implies the measurement of the welfare implications of a specific policy. Choice models can be used to identify changes in consumer surplus as an indicator of changes in benefits. As will be shown in chapter 6, the difference in the natural logarithm of the denominator of the MNL model before and after a change in the level of an attribute is a measure of the change in expected maximum utility, or change in consumer surplus (assuming a zero income effect), in utility units. This can be expressed in monetary units by scaling it by the inverse of the utility parameter of an attribute in the model that is expressed in monetary units.

3.8   A simple illustration of the basic model

We conclude the chapter by providing a simulated empirical example of the use of the MNL model that enables us to assess its major inputs and outputs. The example focuses on the choice of mode of transport for the journey to work. The data consist of $Q = 1000$ observations, in which the choice set ($J = 4$) available to each commuter includes drive alone car driver (da), ride share (rs), train (tn) and bus (bs). Five alternative-specific attributes (Xs) were used to specify the utility of each mode. Personal income (persinc) is included in the utility expression for car drive alone, to test whether individuals with higher incomes are more likely to choose to drive to work by themselves. In-vehicle cost was defined to be generic, i.e., the utility parameter of X_{invc} is the same in each utility expression (i.e., $\beta_{jk} = \beta_k$ for all $j = 1, 2$). The other attributes are defined as alternative-specific. These attributes of the four modes are:

1. wlk = total walk time (minutes)
2. wt = total wait time (minutes)
3. invt = total in-vehicle time (minutes)
4. invc = total in-vehicle cost (cents)
5. pkc = parking cost (cents).

In addition, an alternative (or mode) specific constant is included for $J - 1$ alternatives. It is arbitrary which alternative the constant is excluded from. The utility expressions are:

$$U_{\text{da}} = \text{MSC}_{\text{da}} + \beta_{\text{da1}}\text{invt}_{\text{da}} + \beta_2\text{invc}_{\text{da}} + \beta_{\text{da3}}\text{pkc}_{\text{da}} + \text{pinc}_{\text{da}}\text{persinc}_{\text{da}},$$

$$U_{\text{rs}} = \text{MSC}_{\text{rs}} + \beta_{\text{rs1}}\text{invt}_{\text{rs}} + \beta_2\text{invc}_{\text{rs}} + \beta_{\text{rs3}}\text{pkc}_{\text{rs}},$$

$$U_{\text{tn}} = \text{MSC}_{\text{tn}} + \beta_{\text{tn1}}\text{invt}_{\text{tn}} + \beta_2\text{invc}_{\text{tn}} + \beta_3\text{wlk}_{\text{tn}} + \beta_4\text{wt}_{\text{tn}},$$

$$U_{\text{bs}} = \beta_{\text{bs1}}\text{invt}_{\text{bs}} + \beta_2\text{invc}_{\text{bs}} + \beta_3\text{wlk}_{\text{bs}} + \beta_4\text{wt}_{\text{bs}}.$$

The results of maximum likelihood estimation of the model (which required ten iterations to reach a solution, such that L^* changed by less than 0.01) are summarised in table 3.2.

All attributes have t-statistics greater than 1.96 (95 per cent confidence) except for the parking cost associated with ride share and two mode-specific constants. Overall the model has a pseudo-R^2 of 0.346 when comparing the log likelihood at zero and log likelihood at convergence. The constants alone contribute 0.13 of the 0.346, suggesting the attributes in the utility expressions do have an important role to play in explaining mode choice. A simple MNL model with a full set of ($J - 1$) alternative-specific constants will always exactly reproduce the aggregate market shares, even though the predicted choice for an individual (as a probability) is unlikely to equal the actual choice. This is not a major concern since the model has external validity at the sample level and not for a specific individual, unless the analyst has sufficiently rich data to be able to estimate a model for each individual. This is sometimes possible with stated choice data with many replications (the number required will be a function of the

Table 3.2. *Parameter estimates for the illustrative example*

Attribute	Alternative	Taste weight	t-statistic
Drive alone constant	drive alone	0.58790	2.32
Ride share constant	ride share	0.32490	1.23
Train constant	train	0.29870	1.86
In-vehicle cost	all modes	−0.00255	−2.58
In-vehicle time	drive alone	−0.05251	−4.32
In-vehicle time	ride share	−0.04389	−3.21
In-vehicle time	train	−0.03427	−2.67
In-vehicle time	bus	−0.03523	−2.75
Walk time	train	−0.07386	−3.57
Walk time	bus	−0.06392	−3.25
Wait time	train	−0.11451	−2.18
Wait time	bus	−0.15473	−4.37
Parking cost	drive alone	−0.07245	−2.59
Parking cost	ride share	−0.00235	−1.24
Personal income	drive alone	0.03487	5.87
Log likelihood at zero	−2345.8		
Log likelihood at constants	−2023.7		
Log likelihood at convergence	−1534.8		
Likelihood ratio (pseudo R^2)	0.346		

number of attributes and levels of each) or a large and long panel of repeated observations on the same individuals.

The signs of all utility parameters are correct and unambiguous in the example – we would expect that a negative sign would be associated with time and cost since an individual's relative utility will increase when time or cost decreases (and vice versa). The sign on personal income might be positive or negative, although we would reasonably expect it to be positive in the utility expression for drive alone. That is, all other things being equal, we would expect an individual to have a higher probability of choosing to drive alone as their income increases. In contrast, if we had placed the income variable in the public transport alternative's utility expression we might have expected a negative sign.

A characteristic of an individual, or any other variable that is not an attribute of an alternative in a choice set, cannot be included as a separate variable in *all* utility expressions since it does not vary across the alternatives. That is, a person's income does not vary by mode unless it is defined as net of modal costs. To enable a non-modal attribute to be included in all utility expressions, it must be interacted with an alternative-specific attribute. For example, we could include income in all utility expressions by dividing cost by income; or we could interact travel time with income by multiplication. There are many ways of doing this, but a sensible behavioural hypothesis is required to justify this additional complexity.

The in-vehicle time utility parameters for bus and train are almost identical, suggesting that we could save one degree of freedom by imposing an equality restriction on these two utility parameters, treating them as generic to these two modes. The parking cost attribute could be eliminated from the ride share alternative given its statistical non-significance, saving an additional degree of freedom. All the other variables should be retained for the derivation of elasticities and for policy analysis.

Weighted aggregate point elasticities for all variables and choices were calculated by applying the method of sample-enumeration discussed in the last section. Direct elasticities only are calculated, since the identical cross elasticities in a simple MNL model have little behavioural value (owing to the IID condition). Alternative specifications of discrete-choice models (such as nested logit and heteroscedastic extreme value, presented in chapter 6) allow us to obtain behaviourally plausible cross elasticities. The direct elasticities for in-vehicle time for each of drive alone, ride share, train and bus are, respectively, -0.362, -0.324, -0.298 and -0.260. All are negative, since we expect an increase in a travel time component or cost to, *ceteris paribus*, reduce the probability of choosing a particular mode and hence result in a reduced market share.

Interpreting the estimated elasticities is straightforward. For example, the value of -0.362 for in-vehicle time associated with drive alone implies that a 1 per cent increase in the time travelling by car as a sole driver will, all else equal, cause a 0.362 per cent decrease in the overall probability of drive alone choice of commuter mode. Other elasticities may be interpreted similarly. The empirical evidence in this example suggests that commuters are more sensitive to travel time changes than to cost changes, and are most sensitive to changes in time waiting for a public transport mode.

The more dispersed the distribution of attribute values, the lower the weighted aggregate elasticity relative to the aggregate elasticity, the latter calculated at the sample average (X_{jk} and $\hat{P}_j$). This happens because, as the differential in the relative levels of an attribute increases, the response of aggregate demand to changes in that variable decreases (Westin 1974). Gillen (1977) illustrates this effect by calculating weighted and unweighted aggregate elasticities for four variables, and obtains $(-0.29, -0.34)$, $(-0.59, -0.68)$, $(-0.31, -0.38)$ and $(-0.19, -0.25)$.

The estimated utility expressions can be processed in a spreadsheet to identify the impact of a change in one or more attributes on market shares. This gives the MNL model a very strong policy role by assisting analysts in evaluating the impact of many policies (as defined by specific mixes of attributes modelled in the utility expressions). The marginal rate of substitution between in-vehicle travel time and in-vehicle cost can be calculated as the ratio of the travel time utility parameter and the in-vehicle cost utility parameter. For example, the value of in-vehicle travel time savings for drive alone would be $(-0.05251$ utiles per minute$)/(-0.00255$ utiles per cent$)$ or 20.60 cents per minute. This converts to \$12.36 per person hour. It tells us that a sampled individual is willing to pay, on average, \$12.36 to save 1 hour of time spent in a car (driving alone) on the journey to work. By contrast, the equivalent value of in-vehicle time savings for train users is \$8.06 per person hour. A comparison of the utility parameters for the components of travel time illustrates the differences in value attached to different attributes. For example, a unit of walk time has a disutility that is 2.155 times higher than in-vehicle time (-0.07386 compared to -0.05251). Thus, a sampled individual is willing to pay, on average, 2.155 times more to save a unit of walk time to the train than to save a unit of time in the train.

3.9 Linking to the later chapters

The basic logit model presented in this chapter is likely to be the workhorse for most discrete-choice modelling for many years. Its robustness in many applications to violation of its underlying behavioural assumptions is impressive in the aggregate. Despite this praise, practitioners and researchers have recognised the limitations of the simple model for many applications, and have sought out more complex, albeit more behaviourally appropriate, choice models which relax one or more of the strong assumptions imposed on the variance–covariance matrix of the MNL model.

The extensions to the MNL model are mainly associated with varying degrees of additional freedoms in the treatment of the variances and covariances associated with the unobserved influences on utility. The most popular variant is the nested logit model, often referred to as tree logit or hierarchical logit. Chapter 6 introduces the nested logit (NL) model as a way of accommodating violation of the IIA property through relaxing the identically distributed component of IID for subsets of alternatives where violation is a problem for applications. Once the nested logit model is appreciated, we can go a further step and introduce a number of more general models. These include the heteroscedastic extreme value (HEV) model in its random and fixed effects form, which frees up all of the variances associated with the unobserved influences on each alternative in the choice set. A random parameter logit (RPL) or mixed logit (ML) model is also introduced which adds further flexibility in the treatment of the variances and covariances of the random component. Another very general model – multinomial probit (MNP) – is also considered in chapter 6. A case study compares the approaches – MNL, NL, random HEV, fixed HEV, RPL (ML) and MNP.

Before addressing these additional modelling complexities, however, chapters 4 and 5 will focus on the important topic of experimental design for stated choice applications. These chapters will address how to design choice experiments so that the simple MNL and its more complex cousins can be estimated from SC data. Since choice data is often analysed as aggregate choice frequencies, in contrast to the disaggregated 1,0 response developed in this chapter, appendix B summarises the essential statistical features of aggregate choice models.

Appendix A3   Maximum likelihood estimation technique

A3.1   Theoretical background

A3.1.1 Introduction to maximum likelihood

The underlying rationale for the method of maximum likelihood may be indicated briefly as follows. Suppose that the function expressing the probability of the particular outcome x of an experiment, X, having a discrete set of possible outcomes is represented by $P_X(x|\theta)$, where this nomenclature indicates that the function has parameter(s) $\theta = \theta_1, \theta_2, \ldots, \theta_r$. If the parameter(s) θ is (are) known, then the joint probability function of a random sample of experiments, $X_1, X_2, \ldots, X_T$, can be written as:

$$P_{X_1,X_2,\ldots,X_T}(x_1, x_2, \ldots, x_T|\theta) = P_{X_1}(x_1|\theta).P_{X_2}(x_2|\theta)\ldots P_{X_T}(x_T|\theta)$$

$$= \prod_{t=1}^{T} P_{X_t}(x_t|\theta). \tag{A3.1}$$

Next, consider the situation in which the parameter vector θ is unknown, but a specific sample set of experiments, $X_1, X_2, \ldots, X_T$, has been observed to have outcomes $X_1, X_2, \ldots, X_T$. Then the view can be taken that the right-hand side of (A3.1) expresses the probability of having observed this particular sample, *as a function of θ*. To emphasise this, it is written as:

$$L(\theta|x_1, x_2, \ldots, x_T) = \prod_{t=1}^{T} P_{X_t}(x_t|\theta). \tag{A3.2}$$

A3.2 is called the *likelihood function* of the sample. The likelihood function can be evaluated for different θ and, intuitively, the larger the value obtained for a particular θ, the more likely it should be considered that θ represents an appropriate estimate of the parameters for the probability function for the population from which the sample was drawn.

Such considerations lead to the following rule for maximum-likelihood estimation: *The maximum-likelihood estimator of θ is the value $\hat{\theta}$ which causes the likelihood function $L(\theta)$ to be a maximum.*

In many cases, the form of the probability function $P_X(x|\theta)$ is such that it is easier to maximise the logarithm of the likelihood function, rather than the likelihood function itself. (Owing to the monotonic, one-to-one relationship between the likelihood function and its logarithm, they have a maximum at the same value, $\hat{\theta}$.) In such cases the criterion is:

$$\text{Maximise } L^*(\theta) = \ln(L(\theta)) = \ln\left(\prod_{t=1}^{T} P_{X_t}(x_t|\theta)\right)$$

$$= \sum_{t=1}^{T} \ln(P_{X_t}(x_t|\theta)). \tag{A3.3}$$

If the necessary computations are mathematically tractable, the maximum of $L^*(\theta)$ can be found by identification of its stationary points, through solution of the set of simultaneous equations:

$$\sum_{t=1}^{T} \frac{\partial}{\partial \theta_k} \ln(P_{X_t}(x_t|\theta)) = 0, \qquad k = 1, 2, \ldots, r. \tag{A3.4}$$

In many situations, however, it is necessary to use an iterative gradient search technique such as the Newton–Raphson method that is discussed below.

A3.1.2 Gradient search and the Newton–Raphson method

The general concept of a gradient search technique for maximisation of a function $L^*(\theta)$ is to start from an initial solution $\theta^0 = (\theta_1^0, \theta_2^0, \ldots, \theta_r^0)$ and, in a series of iterations, move to other solutions, $\theta^1, \theta^2, \ldots$, in such a way as to always improve (increase) the value of $L^*(\theta)$. The change at iteration $(p+1)$ is given by:

$$\theta^{p+1} = \theta^p + d^p t, \tag{A3.5}$$

where $d^p = (d_1^p, d_2^p, \ldots, d_r^p)$ is a direction vector chosen such that the value of $L^*(\theta)$ increases as the solution θ moves in that direction from θ^p, and t is a (scalar) step-size defining the magnitude of the movement in the direction d^p.

The choice of the step-size t is important because even though d^p defines a direction of improving value of $L^*(\theta)$ at θ^p, any non-linearity of $L^*(\theta)$ means that its value may eventually start to worsen (decrease) as t is made larger. The optimal step-size can be found by solution of the following equation in the single variable t:

$$\frac{\partial}{\partial t} L^*(\theta^p + d^p t) = 0. \tag{A3.6}$$

The choice of the direction vector d^p can be achieved by a number of methods, one of the most common being the method of steepest ascent in which:

$$d_k^p = \frac{\partial L^*(\theta)}{\partial \theta_k} \quad \begin{array}{l} \text{evaluated at } \theta^p \\ \text{for } k = 1, 2, \ldots, r. \end{array} \tag{A3.7}$$

Faster convergence is often found by use of the Newton–Raphson method in which d^p is determined by solution of the matrix-vector equation

$$\left[\frac{\partial^2 L^*(\theta)}{\partial \theta_\ell \, \partial \theta_k} \right] [d_k^p] = \left[-\frac{\partial L^*(\theta)}{\partial \theta_\ell} \right], \tag{A3.8}$$

where $k = 1, 2, \ldots$, $\ell = 1, 2, \ldots, r$, and the first and second derivatives of $L^*(\theta)$ are evaluated at θ^p. In the case of $L^*(\theta)$ having a quadratic form, for example, the Newton–Raphson method converges in a single iteration with a step-size of one.

A3.2 Application to the multinomial logit model

The multinomial logit model states that in a choice situation t, the probability that alternative i is chosen from the set of available alternatives A_t is given by:

$$P(i: A_t) = \frac{U_{it}}{\sum\limits_{j \in A_t} U_{jt}} = \frac{e^{V_{it}}}{\sum\limits_{j \in A_t} e^{V_{jt}}}, \qquad (A3.9)$$

where V_{jt} = the utility of alternative j in choice situation t. The value of any V_{jt} is assumed to depend on the values of a number of variables x_{kjt} which are considered to affect the choice, and often the functional relationship is assumed to take the linear-in-parameters form:

$$V_{jt} = \sum\limits_{k=1}^{r} \theta_k x_{kjt}. \qquad (A3.10)$$

Assume now that a sample set of choice situations $1, 2, \ldots, T$ has been observed, together with the corresponding values of x_{kjt}, and let i designate the alternative chosen in situation t. Then the likelihood function for this sample is

$$L(\theta) = \prod\limits_{t=1}^{T} P(i : A_t) \qquad (A3.11)$$

and the log likelihood function of the sample is

$$L^*(\theta) = \ln(L(\theta)) = \sum\limits_{t=1}^{T} \ln(P(i : A_t)); \qquad (A3.12)$$

i.e., $$L^*(\theta) = \sum\limits_{t=1}^{T} \ln\left(\frac{e^{V_{it}}}{\sum\limits_{j \in A_t} e^{V_{jt}}}\right). \qquad (A3.13)$$

We can express (A3.13) as (A3.14) to identify the chosen alternative:

$$L^*(\theta) = \sum\limits_{t=1}^{T} \left[V_{it} - \ln\left(\sum\limits_{j \in A_t} e^{V_{jt}}\right) \right]. \qquad (A3.14)$$

For any t, i represents the alternative observed to have been chosen from the set of available alternatives A_t.

First Derivatives of $L^*(\theta)$

From (A3.14),

$$\frac{\partial L^*(\theta)}{\partial \theta_k} = \sum\limits_{t=1}^{T} \left[\frac{\partial V_{it}}{\partial \theta_k} - \frac{\sum\limits_{j \in A_t} e^{V_{jt}} \frac{\partial V_{it}}{\partial \theta_k}}{\sum\limits_{j \in A_t} e^{V_{jt}}} \right], \qquad (A3.15)$$

or

$$\frac{\partial L^*(\theta)}{\partial \theta_k} = \sum_{t=1}^{T} \left[\frac{\partial V_{it}}{\partial \theta_k} - \sum_{j \in A_t} P(j : A_t) \frac{\partial V_{jt}}{\partial \theta_k} \right]. \tag{A3.16}$$

Now, if all V_{jt} are linear functions of the x_{kjt} as in equation (A3.10), then:

$$\frac{\partial V_{jt}}{\partial \theta_k} = x_{kjt} \tag{A3.17}$$

and equation (A3.15) becomes:

$$\frac{\partial L^*(\theta)}{\partial \theta_k} = \sum_{t=1}^{T} \left[x_{kit} - \frac{\sum_{j \in A_t} U_{jt} x_{kjt}}{\sum_{j \in A_t} U_{jt}} \right], \tag{A3.18}$$

using the nomenclature $U_{jt} = e^{V_{jt}}$ introduced in equation (A3.9).

Equation (A3.16) is similarly modified to:

$$\frac{\partial L^*(\theta)}{\partial \theta_k} = \sum_{t=1}^{T} \left[x_{kit} - \sum_{j \in A_t} P(j : A_t) x_{kjt} \right]. \tag{A3.19}$$

Second derivatives of $L^*(\theta)$

Extending from equation (A3.16), it is found that:

$$\frac{\partial^2 L^*(\theta)}{\partial \theta_k \, \partial \theta_\ell} = \sum_{t=1}^{T} \left[\frac{\partial^2 V_{it}}{\partial \theta_k \, \partial \theta_\ell} - \sum_{j \in A_t} P(j : A_t) \frac{\partial^2 V_{jt}}{\partial \theta_k \, \partial \theta_\ell} - \sum_{j \in A_t} \frac{\partial P(j : A_t)}{\partial \theta_\ell} \frac{\partial V_{jt}}{\partial \theta_k} \right]. \tag{A3.20}$$

For all V_{jt} linear in the x_{kjt} as in equation (A3.10), equation (A3.17) holds and

$$\frac{\partial^2 V_{jt}}{\partial \theta_k \, \partial \theta_\ell} = 0, \tag{A3.21}$$

so that equation (A3.20) simplifies to

$$\frac{\partial^2 L^*(\theta)}{\partial \theta_k \, \partial \theta_\ell} = - \sum_{t=1}^{T} \sum_{j \in A_t} \frac{\partial P(j : A_t)}{\partial \theta_\ell} x_{kjt}. \tag{A3.22}$$

Further evaluation of the derivative in equation (A3.22) for the linear utility function case leads to

$$\frac{\partial^2 L^*(\theta)}{\partial \theta_k \, \partial \theta_\ell} = - \sum_{t=1}^{T} \sum_{j \in A_t} P(j : A_t) x_{kjt} \left[x_{\ell jt} - \sum_{h \in A_t} P(h : A_t) x_{\ell ht} \right]. \tag{A3.23}$$

It can be shown that equation (A3.23) can be expressed in the form

$$
\frac{\partial^2 L^*(\theta)}{\partial \theta_k \, \partial \theta_\ell} = - \sum_{t=1}^{T} \left[\frac{\left(\sum_{j \in A_t} U_{jt} x_{kjt} x_{\ell jt} \right) \left(\sum_{j \in A_t} U_{jt} \right) - \left(\sum_{j \in A_t} U_{jt} x_{kjt} \right) \left(\sum_{j \in A_t} U_{jt} x_{\ell jt} \right)}{\left(\sum_{j \in A_t} U_{jt} \right)^2} \right],
$$

(A3.24)

which is a more suitable form for computer programming purposes.

A3.3   Description of the estimation process

Maximum likelihood estimation of the multinomial logit model using the Newton–Raphson iterative technique involves three major loops in the process (see figure A3.1). The inner loop iterates over all available alternatives $j \in A_t$ for each observation t, accumulating the quantities

$$
SU = \sum_{j \in A_t} U_{jt},
$$

(A3.25)

$$
SU1_k = \sum_{j \in A_t} U_{jt} x_{kjt}, \text{ all } k,
$$

(A3.26)

$$
SU2_{k\ell} = \sum_{j \in A_t} U_{jt} x_{kjt} x_{\ell jt}, \text{ all } k, \ell.
$$

(A3.27)

The middle loop iterates over all observations during each Newton–Raphson iteration and makes use of the quantities computed in the inner loop, plus the values of U_{it} for the alternative i chosen in each observation t, to accumulate

$L =$ the value of the log likelihood function for the iteration, computed according to equation (A3.13),

$[DL] =$ the vector of first derivatives of the log likelihood function, computed according to equation (A3.18), and

$[DDL] =$ the matrix of second derivatives of the log likelihood function, computed according to equation (A3.24).

The outer loop corresponds to the Newton–Raphson iterations. At the end of each of these, the changes in the parameters θ are computed using equation (A3.8) and a step-size of 1. That is, $[\Delta \theta]$ corresponds to $[d_k^p]$ in equation (A3.8). The parameter values are updated and convergence of the process is ascertained by examining the magnitude of the change in the log likelihood function from the previous iteration, the magnitude of the first derivatives of the log likelihood function and/or the magnitude of the computed changes in θ. The result of this investigation determines whether the process continues to a further iteration or terminates.

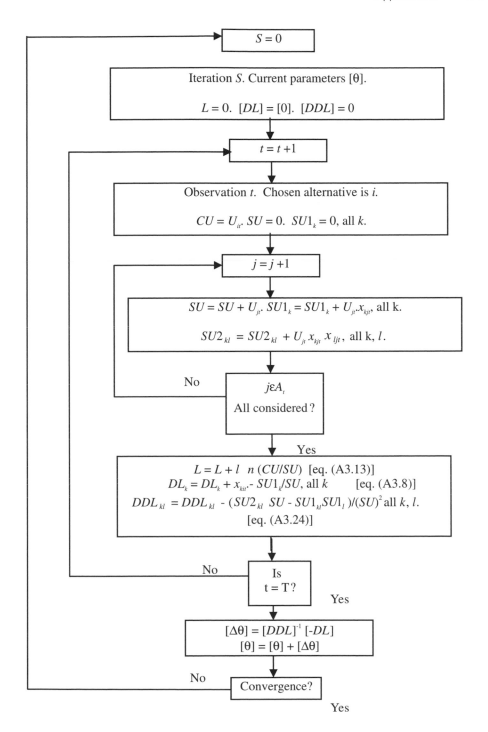

Figure A3.1 MLE of the MNL model using the Newton–Raphson technique

Appendix B3 Linear probability and generalised least squares models

B3.1 Introduction

Chapter 3 discussed the basic choice model and extensions on the assumption that the estimation technique is maximum-likelihood and that the model is a member of the non-linear logit family. In this appendix we examine two alternative estimation procedures and model forms which are popular in the applied modelling literature – the linear probability model, which requires the least squares regression technique for estimation, and the linear logit model, which requires generalised least squares.

B3.2 Linear probability model and least squares regression

Consider a situation where there are only two possible choices (e.g., choose a small or large car, vote yes or no). Furthermore, instead of specifying the basic MNL choice model assume that this choice is a linear function of a set of explanatory variables. This simple choice model may then be written (in its stochastic form) as equation (B3.1):

$$f_q = \beta_0 + \beta_1 x_{1q} + \cdots + \beta_K x_{Kq} + \varepsilon_q, \qquad q = 1, \ldots, Q, \tag{B3.1}$$

where $f_q = \begin{cases} 0 & \text{if the first option is chosen} \\ 1 & \text{if the second option is chosen,} \end{cases}$

X_{kq} = the kth explanatory variable,

ε_q = a stochastic error term assumed to be normally distributed with zero mean and constant variance.

This model is known as the linear probability model (LPM), since the estimating equation is linear and can be interpreted as describing the probability of the second option given values of the K explanatory variables. The reason for this interpretation can be seen by examining the expected value of each f_q. Because f_q can take on only two values, the probability distribution of f_q can be denoted as prob $(f_q = 1) = P_q$ and prob $(f_q = 0) = 1 - P_q$. Hence $E(f_q) = 1(P_q) + 0(1 - P_q) = P_q$. Therefore, the expected value of f_q is the probability that $f_q = 1$ and thus the interpretation of equation (B3.1) as a probability model.

Given observations for Q individuals on the K explanatory variables and the f_qs (i.e., the choices actually made), ordinary least squares estimates of the coefficients (βs) in equation (B3.1) may be obtained using standard regression techniques. Let us denote this estimated equation by

$$\hat{f}_q = \hat{\beta}_0 + \hat{\beta}_1 X_{1q} + \cdots + \hat{\beta}_K X_{Kq} \quad q = 1, \ldots, Q, \tag{B3.2}$$

where a 'hat' denotes an estimated value. Then $\hat{\beta}_K$ is an estimate of the change in the probability of choosing the second alternative given a unit change in X_K. From this we can estimate the elasticity of choice with respect to variable X_K at the sample mean by multiplying $\hat{\beta}_K$ by $(\bar{X}_K/\bar{f})$, where $\bar{X}_K$ and $\bar{f}$ are the sample averages of X_K and f respectively. This elasticity is an estimate of the percentage change in the probability of choosing the second alternative given a one per cent change in X_K.

The major advantage of the linear probability model is its simplicity, in both estimation and interpretation. However, there are major disadvantages that, when weighed against the advantage of simplicity, make the LPM much less satisfactory than other models which are available, such as the basic MNL model and the linear logit model (see section B3.3).

In a binary choice situation, there are several difficulties with the LPM. A specific problem stems from the fact that the statistical properties of the ordinary least squares (OLS) regression estimates of the parameters given in equation (B3.2) depend upon certain assumptions about the error term ε_q. One of these assumptions is that the variance of the error terms is constant for each observation. However, the error term in the LPM does not have a constant variance, and so the OLS estimates of the regression coefficients will not be efficient (i.e., have smallest variance), although they will still be unbiased and consistent (as long as other necessary assumptions still hold). We can see this by noting that

$$\varepsilon_q = f_q - \beta_0 - \beta_1 X_{1q} - \cdots - \beta_K X_{Kq} = f_q - \beta_0 - \sum_{K=1}^{K} \beta_K X_{Kq},$$

so that the only two values that ε_q can take are

$$\varepsilon_q = 1 - \beta_0 - \sum_{K=1}^{K} \beta_K X_{Kq} \quad \text{if } f_q = 1,$$

$$\varepsilon_q = -\beta_0 - \sum_{K=1}^{K} \beta_K X_{Kq} \quad \text{if } f_q = 0.$$

Now, since prob $(f_q = 1) = P_q$ and prob $(f_q = 0) = 1 - P_q$, and since one of the assumptions made about the error term is that it has an expected value of zero (i.e., $E(\varepsilon_q) = 0$), we know that:

$$E(\varepsilon_q) = \left(1 - \beta_0 - \sum_{k=1}^{K} \beta_k X_{kq}\right)(1 - P_q) = 0.$$

Solving for P_q gives

$$P_q = \beta_0 + \sum_{k=1}^{K} \beta_k X_{kq}, \tag{B3.3}$$

and so $1 - P_q = 1 - \beta_0 - \sum_{k=1}^{K} \beta_k X_{kq}$. We may now calculate the variance of ε_q as follows:

$$\text{var}(\varepsilon_q) = E(\varepsilon_q^2) = \left(1 - \beta_0 - \sum_{k=1}^{K} \beta_k X_{kq}\right)^2 P_q$$

$$+ \left(-\beta_0 - \sum_{k=1}^{K} \beta_k X_{kq}\right)^2 (1 - P_q)$$

which, using B3.3,

$$= \left(1 - \beta_0 - \sum_{k=1}^{K} \beta_k X_{kq}\right)^2 \left(\beta_0 + \sum_{k=1}^{K} \beta_k X_{kq}\right)$$

$$+ \left(-\beta_0 - \sum_{k=1}^{K} \beta_k X_{kq}\right)^2 \left(1 - \beta_0 - \sum_{k=1}^{K} \beta_k X_{kq}\right)$$

and factoring

$$= \left(1 - \beta_0 - \sum_{k=1}^{K} \beta_k X_{kq}\right) \left(\beta_0 + \sum_{k=1}^{K} \beta_k X_{kq}\right)$$

$$\times \left(1 - \beta_0 - \sum_{k=1}^{K} \beta_k X_{kq} + \beta_0 + \sum_{k=1}^{K} \beta_k X_{kq}\right)$$

so,

$$\text{var}(\varepsilon_q) = \left(1 - \beta_0 - \sum_{k=1}^{K} \beta_k X_{kq}\right) \left(\beta_0 + \sum_{k=1}^{K} \beta_k X_{kq}\right)$$

$$= (1 - P_q)P_q. \tag{B3.4}$$

The variance of ε_q is *not constant* (a condition known as heteroscedasticity), but depends upon the individual observations. One can easily note that the variance will be larger the closer P_q is to a half. One possible solution to this problem of heteroscedasticity is known as *weighted least squares* (WLS). WLS in the present case requires one to divide each of the variables in equation (B3.1), including the constant term, by the standard deviation of $\varepsilon_q(\sigma_q)$. This would result in a transformed model given by

$$\frac{f_q}{\sigma_q} = \beta_0 \frac{1}{\sigma_q} + \beta_1 \frac{X_{1q}}{\sigma_q} + \cdots + \beta_K \frac{X_{Kq}}{\sigma_q} + \frac{\varepsilon_q}{\sigma_q}. \tag{B3.5}$$

Since the error term in equation (B3.5) has constant variance

$$\left(\text{var}\left(\frac{\varepsilon_q}{\sigma_q}\right) = \frac{1}{\sigma^2} \text{Var}(\varepsilon_q) = \frac{\sigma_q^2}{\sigma_q^2} = 1\right),$$

OLS estimation of the parameters of equation (B3.5) will now be efficient (see, e.g., Theil 1971). In the above, it would be preferable to use the actual standard deviation of ε_q, but as can be seen from equation (B3.4), we would need to know each P_q, whereas we only know which alternative the qth individual has chosen, not his probability of choice. Therefore, we must first estimate the standard deviation (or variance) of each ε_q, and then use these estimates as weights instead of the actual standard deviations, as in equation (B3.5). To do this, we apply OLS to the original specification (B3.1) and then, using the estimated regression coefficient to calculate f_q as in equation (B3.2), find a consistent estimate of the variance of ε_q by

$$\hat{\sigma}_q^2 = \hat{f}_q (1 - \hat{f}_q),$$ (B3.6)

which uses the result (B3.4) for the actual variance of ε_q and the fact that $\hat{f}_q$ is an estimate of P_q.

On the surface, then, it seems that the above WLS procedure solves one of the problems associated with the LPM, and that efficient estimates of the model's coefficients may be found. However, there is a serious problem associated with the estimation of variances using equation (B3.6) that is not as easy to solve, and as we shall presently see, seriously weakens the LPM as a vehicle for estimation. The problem is that with the LPM there is no guarantee that the estimated value $\hat{f}_q$ will be between 0 and 1! Any $\hat{f}_q$ outside this interval will result in a negative estimated $\hat{\sigma}_q^2$ which is, of course, nonsense. Arbitrarily setting any $\hat{\sigma}_q^2$ to 0.99 or 0.01 (say) for any observation with $\hat{f}_q$ outside the unit interval is one solution to this problem, but not a particularly satisfactory one, since WLS may not be efficient in that case. WLS is actually only efficient asymptotically (i.e., as the sample size gets arbitrarily large), so that for relatively small samples it may be preferable to use OLS anyway.

The possibility of obtaining predicted $\hat{f}_q$s outside the unit interval is disturbing for another reason; simply put, given the interpretation of $\hat{f}_q$ as a probability, it makes no sense to arrive at a predicted $\hat{f}_q$ of 1.3 or -0.4, for example. It has been suggested that a solution to this problem would be to estimate the model (B3.1) subject to a restriction that $\hat{f}_q$ lie in the unit interval. This becomes a problem in non-linear programming which we will not discuss here because, although the resulting estimated coefficients have smaller variances, they are not necessarily unbiased.

If we overlook all of the above-mentioned problems with the LPM and use OLS or WLS to estimate the *coefficients* (βs) of the model, it would be useful to be able to test hypotheses about these coefficients. The problem here is that the usual testing procedures (e.g., t-tests) rely on the assumption that the ε_q in equation (B3.1) are normally distributed, which is equivalent to assuming that the $\hat{f}_q$ are normally distributed. This is not the case since $\hat{f}_q$ takes on only the values 0 or 1, and so the usual tests are not valid. Warner (1963, 1967) has developed tests which are valid asymptotically, but again, unless sample sizes are quite large, the results of such tests may be suspect. We will not pursue the issue further here. From the above discussion, one may get the idea that the linear probability model is not to be recommended in a binary choice situation. Clearly, the problems with the model seem to far outweigh its advantage of simplicity. However, since it is *quite* simple to estimate the LPM using OLS, it may be used as a preliminary screening device to get a feel for the data before using one of the alternative models which have been developed. Another use frequently made of the LPM (e.g., Struyk 1976) is as a mechanism for comparing alternative specifications of the attribute set defined in the utility expressions, where prediction is not an issue.

We began this section by assuming a binary choice situation for the linear probability model. However, Domencich and McFadden (1975: 75–80) have shown that if one takes the basic choice model derived in chapter 3 and makes some specific assumptions about the nature of V_j in that model, the result will be a model of the form given by the LPM. The assumptions on V_j are specifically that

$$V_{jq} = \ln\left[\sum_{k=1}^{K} \beta_k X_{jkq}\right], \tag{B3.7}$$

$$0 \le \sum_{k=1}^{K} \beta_k X_{jkq} \le 1 \quad (j = 1,\ldots,J), \tag{B3.8}$$

$$\sum_{j=1}^{J}\sum_{k=1}^{K} \beta_k X_{jkq} = 1. \tag{B3.9}$$

Given these assumptions, insertion of equations (B3.7 to B3.9) in equation (3.24) yields:

$$P_{iq} = \frac{\exp\left(\ln\left[\sum_{k=1}^{K}\beta_k X_{ikq}\right]\right)}{\sum_{j=1}^{J}\exp\left(\ln\left[\sum_{k=1}^{K}\beta_k X_{jkq}\right]\right)} = \frac{\sum_{k=1}^{K}\beta_k X_{ikq}}{\sum_{j=1}^{J}\sum_{k=1}^{K}\beta_k X_{jkq}} = \sum_{k=1}^{K}\beta_k X_{ikq}. \tag{B3.10}$$

Formulation (B3.10) is the LPM (B3.1) with P_{iq} replacing f_q, and is exactly (B3.1) when we add an error term ε_q. Notice that equation (B3.10) is not limited to a binary choice situation but holds for any $j = 1,\ldots,J$. However, it is difficult to use equation (B3.10) (i.e., the LPM) in the multinomial case since the sum of estimated probabilities over alternatives for each individual must sum to one (equation (B3.9)), but this implies that the representative utility of one alternative (V_{jq}) depends upon the attributes of all other alternatives, contrary to the usual assumption of independence of tastes. Furthermore, the imposition of the inequality constraints (equation (B3.8)) provides a computational non-linearity, which means that linear least squares is no longer applicable. It is also difficult to see how we would specify the dependent variable, f, in the case of more than two alternatives.

Given these problems with the LPM in general, other estimation procedures are seen as preferable, in particular the basic MNL model (3.24) with V_{jq} *not* defined as in equation (B3.7).

B3.3   Linear logit model and weighted/generalised least squares regression

We have seen in chapter 3 that the basic MNL model may be estimated with Q individual observations using maximum-likelihood techniques. An alternative method of estimating a choice model involves variants of least squares regression, to which we now turn. Although one can use maximum likelihood methods for estimating choice models where the choice variable is a binary index 1, 0, a frequency, proportions or even ranks, many practitioners who estimate models using stated choice data which is aggregated into frequencies or proportions use the method of generalised least squares, as described in this section. The method is often referred to as linear logit.

Consider the binary choice case where the probability of choosing the first of two alternatives (P_1) is given by the (binary) logit model

$$P_{1q} = \exp V_{1q} / (\exp V_{1q} + \exp V_{2q}), \tag{B3.11}$$

where V_{1q} and V_{2q} are again linear functions of the characteristics associated with alternatives 1 and 2, respectively. Equation (B3.11) may be rewritten as

$$P_{1q} = 1 / (1 + \exp -(V_{1q} - V_{2q})) = 1. \tag{B3.12}$$

Hence

$$P_{1q}(1 + \exp -(V_{1q} - V_{2q})) = 1,$$

so,

$$\exp -(V_{1q} - V_{2q}) = \frac{1 - P_{1q}}{P_{1q}}$$

and

$$\exp(V_{1q} - V_{2q}) = \frac{P_{1q}}{1 - P_{1q}}.$$

Taking the natural logarithm of both sides, we get

$$V_{1q} - V_{2q} = \ln(P_{1q}/(1 - P_{1q}))$$

or, upon substituting for Vs using equation (3.26) and assuming that a total of K variables, including alternative-specific constants, appear in the model, we obtain

$$\ln\left(\frac{P_{1q}}{1 - P_{1q}}\right) = \sum_{k=1}^{K} \beta_k X_{kq}. \tag{B3.13}$$

The left-hand side of equation (B3.13) is known as the *logit* of the probability of choice, and it represents the logarithm of the odds that individual q will choose alternative 1. An appeal of the logistic transformation of the dependent variable is that it transforms the problem of predicting probabilities within a (0, 1) interval to the problem of predicting the odds of an alternative being chosen within the range of the entire real line $(-\infty, +\infty)$.

Direct estimation of equation (B3.13) is not possible. If P_{1q} (actually, f_{q1} is what we observe) is equal to either 0 or 1, then $P_{1q}/(1 - P_{1q})$ will equal zero or infinity and the logarithm of the odds is undefined. Thus the application of ordinary least squares (OLS) estimation to equation (B3.13) when $P_{1q} = 1$ or 0 is inappropriate. We do, however, have two situations in which this equation is useful.

B3.3.1 Group data

What we are about to describe is only possible if observations are repeated for each value of an explanatory variable. If this condition is met, OLS or weighted least squares (WLS) can be used to estimate (B3.13).

Define $\hat{P}_1 = r_1/n_1 r_1$ as the number of replications (observations) choosing alternative 1 that are contained in the cell representing the particular value of the explanatory variable, and n_1 is the number of observations relevant to that particular cell. Then,

$$\ln\left(\frac{r_1/n_1}{1 - r_1/n_1}\right) = \ln\left(\frac{r_1}{n_1 - r_1}\right) = \sum_{k=1}^{K} \beta_k X_k, \tag{B3.14}$$

where X_k is the value of the explanatory variable for that cell. This equation, referred to as linear logit, can be estimated using OLS and will yield consistent parameter estimates when the number of repetitions for each of the levels of the Xs grows arbitrarily large. A large sample size is required to ensure approximation to a normal distribution when the dependent variable is of the form in equation (B3.14). To accommodate error variance heteroscedasticity, particularly if the sample is not large, we can apply WLS and weight each cell by $n_1/(r_1(n_1 - r_1))$ since $\ln[r_1/(n_1 - r_1)]$ is approximately normally distributed with mean 0 and variance $\sigma_1 = n_1/[(r_1(n_1 - r_1))]$.

This weight will assist when a small sample is used. However, regardless of sample size, this approach is suitable only when sufficient repetitions occur. With extreme values or outliers the OLS and WLS approaches perform poorly. As r_1/n_1 approaches 0 or 1, σ_1 could be adjusted to accommodate this as in equation (B3.15):

$$\sigma_1 = \frac{(n_1 + 1)(n_1 + 2)}{n_1(r_1 + 1)(n_1 - r_1 + 1)} \tag{B3.15}$$

However, for successful application of the approach, given that heteroscedasticity and required repetition can be accommodated, continuous explanatory variables would have to be categorised. This can introduce bias because of the potentially serious errors-in-variables problem. Fortunately an appealing alternative is available, namely, the maximum likelihood estimation of the basic MNL model outlined in chapter 3 and appendix A3.

B3.3.2 Disaggregate data

In the majority of consumer research applications, where there exists more than one determinant of the choice of an alternative from a choice set, only one choice is associated with each set of explanatory variables. The maximum likelihood estimation procedure is ideally suited to this task, and has the added advantage of data economy (relatively small sample sizes). For example, 300 observations, with 10 explanatory variables and a choice split of 30 per cent to 70 per cent is sufficient to estimate a choice model. The data economy is due, amongst other reasons, to the maintenance of the decision-making unit as the unit of analysis, rather than an aggregate unit as in the grouped case, hence increasing the amount of variance to be explained and maintaining maximum relevant information. The aggregation error need not, however, be serious with grouped data. It is very much dependent on the nature of the policies being investigated – in particular the extent of the homogeneous effect across the members of the aggregated unit of analysis. Because a unique maximum always exists for a logit model (McFadden 1974), maximum likelihood estimation is appealing. The additional cost in computer time is more than compensated for by the practical advantages of not having to group observations. This also greatly increases the flexibility of data manipulation.

The above discussion notwithstanding, we can extend the linear logit model to the case of more than two alternatives quite easily. Assuming J alternatives, we can express the logarithm of the odds of choosing any alternative compared to any base alternative (arbitrarily, alternative l) by

$$\ln\left(\frac{P_{iq}}{P_{lq}}\right) = \sum_{k=1}^{K} \beta_{kil} X_{kq}. \tag{B3.16}$$

There are $J - 1$ equations of the form (B3.16) with alternative l as a base, the parameters of which (i.e. β_{kil}) reflect the effect of the kth explanatory variable on the choice of alternative i versus alternative l. To examine other binary pairs, for example i versus j, we need only look at binary pairs (i, l) and (j, l) and combine them as follows.

$$\ln\left(\frac{P_{iq}}{P_{lq}}\right) + \ln\left(\frac{P_{lq}}{P_{jq}}\right) = \sum_{k=1}^{K} \beta_{klj} X_{kq}$$

$$\ln\left(\frac{P_{iq}}{P_{lq}} \times \frac{P_{lq}}{P_{jq}}\right) = \ln\left(\frac{P_{iq}}{P_{jq}}\right) = \sum_{k=1}^{K} (\beta_{kil} + \beta_{klj}) X_{kq}. \tag{B3.17}$$

Now, using the general format (B3.16), we can also write this as

$$\ln\left(\frac{P_{iq}}{P_{jq}}\right) = \sum_{k=1}^{K} \beta_{kil} X_{kq}, \tag{B3.18}$$

and hence, $\beta_{kij} = \beta_{kil} + \beta_{klj}$, so that $\beta_{kil} = \beta_{kij} - \beta_{klj}$. Theil (1971: 119) has noted that β_{kil} above may be written $\beta_{kil} = \beta_{ki} - \beta_{kl}$ so that equation (B3.16) may be written

$$\ln\left(\frac{P_{iq}}{P_{lq}}\right) = \sum_{k=1}^{K} (\beta_{ki} - \beta_{kl}) X_{kq}. \tag{B3.19}$$

As the above analysis shows, the linear logit model depends on analysis of the difference in response from some base alternative (in our case alternative l).

Furthermore, we may impose initialisation constraints on β_{kl} such that $\beta_{kl} = 0$ for all k, without loss of information. Therefore, the basic model becomes

$$\ln\left(\frac{P_{iq}}{P_{lq}}\right) = \sum_{k=1}^{K} \beta_{ki} X_{kq}. \tag{B3.20}$$

Let us define $\ln(P_{iq}/P_{lq})$ as $L_{i1/q}$. In order to estimate the parameters of equation (B3.20), we must first categorise the explanatory variables (Xs), assuming that the variables are continuously measured. For example, if there are two Xs, X_1 and X_2, we might group X_1 into ten sets and X_2 into five sets so that there are fifty possible combinations of X_1 and X_2. We may then find the frequency of occurrence of any alternative for each cell in a 10×5 contingency table and use these as estimates of P_{iq}s in $L_{il/g}$. Hence, from this point on we refer to group g instead of individual q.

Denoting these frequencies as $fr_{i|g}$, the estimable version of equation (B3.20) becomes

$$\tilde{L}_{i1|g} = \ln\left(\frac{fr_{i|g}}{fr_{1|g}}\right) = \sum_{k=1}^{K} \beta_{ki} X_{kg} + (\tilde{L}_{i1|g} - L_{i1|g}), \tag{B3.21}$$

where the model is specified in terms of group g instead of individual q and where the last term is an error term reflecting the fact that the observed relative frequencies only approximate the relative probabilities in equation (B3.20). $J - 1$ equations are implied by equation (B3.21).

To illustrate the estimation procedure, suppose there is a 5-alternative choice scenario (alternatives numbered 0–4). For the 5-choice situation, we can write the following equations (ignoring the distinction between P and fr at present and dropping the subscript g):

$$\begin{aligned}
\ln(P_0/P_1) &= \beta_0 + \beta_{10}X_1 + \cdots + \beta_{K0}X_K \\
\ln(P_2/P_1) &= \beta_2 + \beta_{12}X_1 + \cdots + \beta_{K2}X_K \\
\ln(P_3/P_1) &= \beta_3 + \beta_{13}X_1 + \cdots + \beta_{K3}X_K \\
\ln(P_4/P_1) &= \beta_4 + \beta_{14}Z_1 + \cdots + \beta_{K4}X_K.
\end{aligned} \tag{B3.22}$$

Although one could continue with other pairs such as P_0/P_2, P_0/P_3, P_0/P_4, P_2/P_3, P_2/P_4, P_3/P_4, a 'circulatory' condition guarantees sufficiency by considering only the number of equations where all response categories are different from a selected base or denominator category, arbitrarily selected in our case as alternative l. The system of equations is constrained so that the sum of the probabilities is equal to 1 for any given group.

Some adjustments to the estimable model are required to allow for the error introduced by grouping observations. We have already mentioned the adjustment $\tilde{L}_g - L_g$ to account for the use of relative frequencies as estimates of probabilities. However, the error variances between cells are not constant (a requirement for ordinary least squares regression); hence an adjustment is required to remove heteroscedasticity.

Theil (1970: 317) has demonstrated that these error variances take the asymptotic form $1/(n_g P_g(1 - P_g))$.

Thus, in estimation, given the knowledge of heteroscedasticity, the ordinary least squares estimators of $\beta_0, \beta_1, \ldots, \beta_K$ are replaced by another set of weighted least squares estimators using weights of the form:

$$w_g = n_g F_g(1 - F_g) \qquad (B3.23)$$

where F_g = relative frequency for group g (n_g/Q).

These weights imply that as the number of observations n_g in a cell increases, more weight is allocated to that cell in the estimation procedure. Given n_g, however, as F_g approaches 0 or 1, less weight is allocated because $\tilde{L}_g$ takes large negative or positive values and is thus highly sensitive to small changes in F_g. This system of weights thus effectively excludes a cell g in which the observed relative frequency is 0 or 1. Berkson (1953) proposed alternative working values in order to reduce information loss:

$$1/rn_g \text{ to replace 0 when } F_g = 0$$
$$1 - 1/rn_g \text{ to replace 1 when } F_g = 1,$$

where r is the number of response categories. So far, the model is as follows:

$$\tilde{L}_{01g} = \ln\left(\frac{F_0}{F_1}\right)_g = w_g\beta_0 + w_g X_{1g0}\beta_{10} + \cdots + w_g X_{Kg0}\beta_{K0} + (\tilde{L}_{01g} - L_{01g})$$

(with the 0 subscript dropped for X if the X-variable is generic),

$$\tilde{L}_{21g} = \ln\left(\frac{F_2}{F_1}\right)_g = w_g\beta_2 + w_g X_{1g2}\beta_{12} + \cdots + w_g X_{Kg2}\beta_{K2} + (\tilde{L}_{21g} - L_{21g})$$

(with the 2 subscript dropped for X if X is generic),

$$\tilde{L}_{31g} = \ln\left(\frac{F_3}{F_1}\right)_g = w_g\beta_3 + w_g X_{1g3} + \cdots + w_g X_{Kg3}\beta_{K3} + (\tilde{L}_{31g} - L_{31g})$$

(with the 3 subscript dropped for X if X is generic),

$$\tilde{L}_{41g} = \ln\left(\frac{F_4}{F_1}\right)_g = w_g\beta_4 + w_g X_{1g4}\beta_{14} + \cdots + w_g X_{Kg4}\beta_{K4} + (\tilde{L}_{41g} - L_{41g})$$

(with the 4 subscript dropped for X if X is generic), and the W_g matrix is

$$n_g \begin{bmatrix} f_{0j}(1-f_{0j}) & -f_{0j}f_{2j} & -f_{0j}f_{3j} & -f_{0j}f_{4j} \\ -f_{2j}f_{0j} & f_{2j}(1-f_{2j}) & -f_{2j}f_{3j} & -f_{2j}f_{4j} \\ -f_{3j}f_{0j} & -f_{3j}f_{2j} & f_{3j}(1-f_{3j}) & -f_{3j}f_{4j} \\ -f_{4j}f_{0j} & -f_{4j}f_{2j} & -f_{4j}f_{3j} & f_{4j}(1-f_{4j}) \end{bmatrix}$$

and f_{2g}, for example, is the relative frequency of the choice of response category 2 in cell g. The estimates of βs are obtained (in matrix form) by generalised least squares (see Theil (1971) for a more detailed explanation):

$$\underline{\hat{\beta}} = (X'w^{-1}\underline{x})^{-1}\underline{x}'w^{-1}\underline{\tilde{L}}. \tag{B3.24}$$

The estimated probabilities are then given by

$$\hat{P}_{0g} = \exp \hat{L}_{0g} / (1 + \exp \hat{L}_{0g} + \exp \hat{L}_{2g} + \exp \hat{L}_{3g} + \exp \hat{L}_{4g})$$

$$\hat{P}_{1g} = 1 \left/ \left(1 + \exp \hat{L}_{0g} + \sum_{i=2}^{4} \exp \hat{L}_{ig} \right) \right.$$

$$\hat{P}_{2g} = \exp \hat{L}_{2g} \left/ \left(1 + \exp \hat{L}_{0g} + \sum_{i=2}^{4} \exp \hat{L}_{ig} \right) \right.$$

$$\hat{P}_{3g} = \exp \hat{L}_{3g} \left/ \left(1 + \exp \hat{L}_{0g} + \sum_{i=2}^{4} \exp \hat{L}_{ig} \right) \right. \tag{B3.25}$$

$$\hat{P}_{4g} = \exp \hat{L}_{4g} \left/ \left(1 + \exp \hat{L}_{0g} + \sum_{i=2}^{4} \exp \hat{L}_{ig} \right), \right.$$

where $\hat{L}_g = \hat{\beta} + \hat{\beta}_1 x_{g1} + \hat{\beta}_2 x_{g2} + \cdots$ (note that the $\hat{\beta}$s are obtained from a generalised least squares regression with weights as defined above). Since the model is estimated using relative frequencies as estimates of probabilities, then the output should be interpreted as 'estimates of estimates of probability'. A comparison between $\tilde{L}_g$, the observed logit based on relative frequencies, and $\hat{L}_g$, the predicted logit, appropriately weighted, provides a basis for testing the predictive capability of the model. That is,

$$\sum_g (\tilde{L}_g - \hat{L}_g)^2 w_g \tag{B3.26}$$

is a goodness-of-fit statistic asymptotically distributed as χ^2 with $(J - K)$ degrees of freedom.

We re-emphasise the point that the linear logit method is inferior to non-linear maximum-likelihood logit, especially in situations when some or all of the explanatory variables are quantitative (i.e., measured on a continuous scale). This occurs due to a loss of information from intracell variation occurring from the grouping process. However, linear logit is quite useful in experimental situations where the Xs can be controlled by the investigator, as in the case of stated choice experiments. An extended discussion of linear logit (or log-linear models) using contingency tables is given in Payne (1977) and Goodman (1970, 1972).

4 Experimental design

4.1 Introduction

Revealed preference (RP) or market data are commonly used by economic, marketing and transport analysts to estimate models that explain discrete choice behaviour, as discussed in chapter 2. Such data may have substantial amounts of *noise* that are the result of many influences, e.g., measurement error. In contrast, stated preference (SP) or choice (SC) data are generated by some systematic and planned design process in which the attributes and their levels are pre-defined without measurement error and varied to create preference or choice alternatives. Similarly, RP choices can be measured with relatively little (if any) error when direct observation is possible (e.g., one can record brands chosen by consumers in supermarkets, or modes chosen by travellers in the act of making trips). However, an individual's self-report of a choice 'actually' made is likely to be uncertain, and the uncertainty or noise probably increases as the time between the actual choice and the report of that choice increases. Additionally, SP and SC responses are 'stated' and not actual, and hence are uncertain because individuals may not actually choose the alternatives that they say they will/would.

In later chapters we will discuss the benefits of combining RP and SC data to take advantage of their strengths and (we hope) minimise their individual weaknesses. Before doing so, we have to introduce a set of analytical tools that provide the building blocks for the design of choice experiments. Chapter 5 uses these tools to design families of choice experiments.

The concept of designed experiments, while unfamiliar to many economists and econometricians, is widespread in the physical, biological and behavioural sciences, engineering, statistics, marketing and many other fields. An experiment, in its simplest form, involves the manipulation of a variable with one or more observations, taken in response to each manipulated value of the variable. In the experimental design literature the manipulated variable is called a 'factor', and the values manipulated are called 'factor levels'. Such variables are also referred to in various disciplines as independent or explanatory variables, or *attributes* when they are features or characteristics of products and services (as described in chapter 1).

Each unique factor level is also termed a 'treatment', or if more than one factor is manipulated, each combination of factor levels is called a 'treatment combination'. Marketers tend to call the latter 'profiles'; hence different disciplines have evolved different terms for the same concepts, which only compounds the confusing jargon for newcomers to this area. We will use the terms 'attribute' and 'attribute levels' instead of 'factors' and 'factor levels' in this book, and where other terms are used we will be careful to define them using the least possible amount of jargon.

A designed experiment is therefore a way of manipulating attributes and their levels to permit rigorous testing of certain hypotheses of interest. In the general case of SP and SC models, the hypotheses of interest typically concern terms in utility and choice models. More generally, the term 'design' refers to the science of planning in advance exactly which observations to take and how to take them to permit the best possible inferences to be made from the data regarding the hypotheses of research interest. Designed experiments can be very simple, involving as little as one attribute level (e.g., a particular price discount) and an associated control condition in which there is no discount. The design aspect deals with planning the experiment in such a way that as many other influences as possible can be ruled out. So, our price discount example, whilst simple, is not well designed because it does little to control for many other possible influences on the behaviour of interest (e.g., purchase volumes, trends, etc.).

The field of experimental design is now quite mature, especially in the case of testing hypotheses based on general linear models, such as the ANOVA and multiple regression models. However, experimental design for non-linear models, such as designs for the families of choice models discussed in this book, is still in its infancy, though advances we later discuss are being made. Not only is the general experimental design field mature, it is also remarkably diverse and varied. Hence, we restrict our discussion to the class of designs known as factorial designs, both complete (when all treatment combinations are used) and fractional (when a subset of all the treatments are used). It is important to note, however, that this restriction is merely for pedagogical convenience, and a serious student of stated choice theory and methods must be prepared to master a much wider design literature to solve real problems with any degree of complexity (e.g., Street and Street 1987, Winer 1995).

4.2   Factorial designs

Factorial designs are designs in which each level of each attribute is combined with every level of all other attributes. Consider a simple problem involving three attributes, each of which has exactly two levels. For example, suppose the attributes are associated with canned soups, and they are type of meat (beef or chicken), noodles (present or absent) and vegetables (present or absent). Each combination of the levels of the three attributes describes a unique soup (e.g., chicken noodle with vegetables), and all possible soups that can be created from this particular set of attributes and levels are given by the factorial combination of attribute levels. That is, there are $2 \times 2 \times 2$, or eight total soups, as can be seen in table 4.1.

Table 4.1. *Example factorial design*

Soup combination	Meat	Noodles	Vegetables
1	chicken	present	present
2	chicken	present	absent
3	chicken	absent	present
4	chicken	absent	absent
5	beef	present	present
6	beef	present	absent
7	beef	absent	present
8	beef	absent	absent

Table 4.2. *The 2 × 2 (or 2^2) and 2 × 2 × 2 (or 2^3) factorial designs*

Treatment combination	Attributes of the ×2		Attributes of the 2 × 2 × 2		
	A (2 levels)	B (2 levels)	A (2 levels)	B (2 levels)	C (2 levels)
1	1	1	1	1	1
2	1	2	1	1	2
3	2	1	1	2	1
4	2	2	1	2	2
5			2	1	1
6			2	1	2
7			2	2	1
8			2	2	2

More generally, a factorial design consists of two or more attributes, each of which has two or more levels. For example, table 4.2 illustrates a 2 × 2 (or 2^2) factorial and a 2 × 2 × 2 (or 2^3) factorial. Note that the attribute levels are coded 1 or 2, but any other coding scheme that is unique could have been used. Generally speaking, in the experimental design literature it is common to code L levels of attributes as $0, 1, 2, \ldots, L - 1$. For the present, we use $1, 2, \ldots, L$, but eventually we will use the $0, 1, \ldots, L - 1$ convention as we move away from simple concepts.

In general, therefore, a factorial design is simply the factorial enumeration of all possible combinations of attribute levels. Such a complete enumeration is often called a 'complete factorial' or a 'full factorial'. Factorial designs have very attractive statistical properties from the standpoint of estimating the parameters of general linear models and/or testing hypotheses based on such models. In particular, complete factorial designs guarantee that all attribute effects of interest are truly independent. In fact one might say that the attributes are independent 'by design'. Thus, the statistical effects or parameters of interest in such models can be estimated independently of one another. Additionally, all possible effects associated with analysis of variance

(ANOVA) or multiple linear regression models can be estimated from a complete factorial.

The effects of interest in the case of ANOVA and multiple regression models are, respectively, means, variances and regression parameters or slopes. In the case of the general polynomial regression model, the regression parameters are the exact counterparts of the ANOVA means, and constitute the basis for 'tests on trends' widely used in the ANOVA paradigm. We will frequently use the term 'effect' (or, more generally, 'effects') with reference to model results. An effect is a difference in treatment means relative to a comparison, such as the grand (or overall) mean. In the design literature in mathematical statistics, an effect is a comparison of the means of the factor levels by means of orthogonal constraints.

A 'main effect' is the difference in the means of each level of a particular attribute and the overall or 'grand mean,' such that the differences sum to zero. Because of this constraint, one of the differences is exactly defined once the remaining $L - 1$ are calculated for an L level attribute. The latter constraint gives rise to the concept of degrees of freedom, and leads naturally to the conclusion that there are $L - 1$ degrees of freedom in each main effect because one difference is exactly determined. In general, if an attribute has no statistical effect on the dependent variable (more generally, the 'response'), then the mean of each of its levels (called the 'marginal mean') will be the same and equal to the grand mean in theory, or statistically equivalent in practice.

In the regression paradigm the main effect of a quantitative (and continuous) attribute can be defined by a polynomial of degree $L - 1$, where $j = 1, 2, \ldots, L$ indexes the levels of the attribute, and L is again the total number of such levels. If an attribute has no statistical effect, all regression parameters will be exactly zero in theory and non-significant in practice. In the case of a qualitative attribute, the main effect can be defined by $L - 1$ dummy or effects-coded variables, each of which represents one of the attributes' $L - 1$ levels. That is, if an attribute has L levels, we can represent any arbitrary subset of $L - 1$ of them as follows:

- Create a dummy variable, D_1, such that if the treatment contains the first level selected, $D_1 = 1$, otherwise $D_1 = 0$.
- Create a second dummy variable, D_2, such that if the treatment contains the second level selected, $D_2 = 1$, otherwise $D_2 = 0$.
- Continue in this fashion until $L - 1$ dummies are created, i.e., $D_1, D_2, \ldots D_{L-1}$.

Thus, the main effect of a factor represented by $L - 1$ dummy variables can be expressed as follows:

$$Y_{ij} = \beta_0 + \beta_1 D_{i1} + \beta_2 D_{i2} + \cdots + \beta_{L-1} D_{iL-1},$$

where Y_{ij} represents the ith response to treatment (level) j of the factor. In this coding scheme, it should be obvious that the Lth (or arbitrarily omitted) level is exactly equal to β_0, and $\beta_1, \beta_2, \ldots, \beta_{L-1}$ are the means of each level of the factor. Thus, the Lth effect is perfectly correlated with the intercept or grand mean.

Effects codes constitute a useful alternative to dummy codes. As with dummy codes, the main effect of a qualitative attribute can be defined by $L - 1$ effects-coded variables that represent an arbitrary $L - 1$ of its levels. That is, if an attribute has L levels, we can represent any arbitrarily chosen $L - 1$ of them as follows:

- Create a dummy variable, D_1, such that if the treatment contains the first level selected, $D_1 = 1$, if the treatment contains the Lth level, $D_1 = -1$, otherwise $D_1 = 0$.
- Create a second dummy variable, D_2, such that if the treatment contains the second level selected, $D_2 = 1$, if the treatment contains the Lth level, $D_2 = -1$, otherwise $D_2 = 0$.
- Continue in this fashion until $L - 1$ effects codes are created, i.e., $D_1, D_2, \ldots D_{L-1}$.

As before, the main effect of a factor represented by $L - 1$ effects coded variables can be expressed as follows:

$$Y_{ij} = \beta_0 + \beta_1 D_{i1} + \beta_2 D_{i2} + \cdots + \beta_{L-1} D_{iL-1},$$

where Y_{ij} represents the ith response to treatment j of the factor. In this coding scheme, the Lth (or arbitrarily omitted) level is exactly equal to $\sum_{j \neq L-1} [-1 \cdot (\beta_{j \neq L-1})]$ and $\beta_1, \beta_2, \ldots, \beta_{L-1}$ are the means of the remaining $L - 1$ attribute levels. In contrast to dummy codes, effects codes are uncorrelated with the grand mean or intercept in the model (β_0), and their column sum is 0. However, effects-coded variables are not orthogonal with one another, but are instead constantly correlated. Thus, each represents a non-orthogonal contrast between the Lth level and the jth level (i.e., a comparison of treatment means).

Although 'main effects' are of primary interest in practical applications of SP theory and methods, they are not the only effects that may be of interest. In particular, 'interaction effects' frequently are of theoretical interest, and despite the fact that they are ignored in the overwhelming majority of practical applications, it is important to understand their role in any application. In fact, even though interactions frequently are ignored by practitioners (and many academics!) this does not mean that they do not matter. Indeed, including interactions suggested by theory or previous empirical evidence often provides insights otherwise not possible, and ignoring (i.e., omitting) or assuming non-significance of interactions in applications can be dangerous.

This raises the issue of the meaning of interactions and how to interpret them. Simply put, an interaction between two attributes will occur if consumer preferences for levels of one attribute depend on the levels of a second. For example, if preferences for levels of product quality depend on levels of price, there will be an interaction. That is, if consumers are less sensitive to prices of higher than lower quality products, price slopes will differ by level of quality, and therefore preferences for combinations of price and quality will require this interaction to correctly represent preferences in statistical models.

Early research in stated preference consumer transport mode choice decisions frequently revealed interactions among such attributes as travel time, fare, walking distance to/from stops and frequency of service (e.g., Norman and Louviere 1974). These interactions were large and meaningful, and typically displayed the same pattern in different studies: the utilities followed a multiplicative-like rule in which all the attributes behaved like complements. Thus, the response to a change in any one attribute, such as fare, depends on the values of these other attributes, such that the lower the fare and the better the values of the other attributes the larger the impact of fare, all else equal. Similar interpretations hold for the other attributes. Recently, Ohler et al. (2000) demonstrated that this same interaction pattern obtained in mode choice data, so it is unlikely to be context-dependent or study-specific.

Continuing the mode choice example, a strictly additive model would under- and over-predict at the extremes of the utility space. Hence, additive models should over-predict the responses to changes when attribute levels are relatively worse from a utility standpoint, and under-predict responses when attribute levels are relatively better. In the middle of the space, additive models will predict relatively well even when the true specification contains interactions, as in the case of the fully multi-plicative model. It is worth noting that the multiplicative models to which we referred are *not* additive under a logarithmic transform of both sides because the utility scale is not a ratio scale, and hence does not contain a natural zero that would allow a log-log transformation. Another example of an important interaction term is the very large commuting distance by city-size interaction found by Lerman and Louviere (1978) in their study of SP and RP residential choice decisions. The key takeaway from the foregoing discussion should be that there is ample evidence that interactions exist in many decision rules. Hence, assuming strictly additive utility functions is likely to be very naive and quite ill-advised in many applications from a prediction and policy inference viewpoint. The latter is true despite the fact that we later demonstrate that additive models often will predict well in practical situations in which the middle region of the utility space is of primary interest.

Ideally, one would like some theoretical and/or empirical guidance in deciding which (if any) interactions to include and estimate. Unfortunately, economic theory, including axiomatic utility theory and its counterpart in psychology, behavioural decision theory, generally are silent about the issue of interactions, with some notable exceptions in information integration theory and risky decision-making (e.g., Anderson 1981, 1996; Keeney and Raiffa 1976). Thus, it is important to note that the assumptions that must be satisfied for utility functions to be strictly additive (i.e., preferential independence of all attributes) are unlikely to be satisfied in many real markets; hence, additivity of utility should be regarded from the outset as very naive and simplistic. On the other hand, the more complex an applied problem, the more one has to make assumptions about additivity of marginal utilities, and we later note that in some applications it may not be practical (or even possible) to use designs that provide relatively efficient estimates of all main effects and two-way interactions.

Hence, in many cases, one must use main effects designs or do nothing. This state of affairs may not be altogether unfortunate because, as previously noted, models derived from such designs often predict well in attribute regions of greatest interest even if their parameters are biased. It is important, therefore, to recognise two different and often conflicting objectives in empirical research on consumer decision making and choice behaviour:

1. Understanding decision and choice processes depends on having the greatest possible amount of information, which typically means complete factorials, or at least designs that permit one to estimate some or all two-way (or possibly higher-order) interactions in addition to main effects. Science typically is best served by designs that permit as wide an array of utility specifications as possible to be estimated and tested.

2. Practical prediction of consumer response to changes in one or more attributes often can be achieved without real understanding. In fact, we later show that many, if not most, decision experiments satisfy certain conditions that ensure reasonable predictive accuracy even when utility functions are quite misspecified. Practical prediction often can be achieved by highly fractionated designs, including designs that permit one to estimate only main effects. The latter are so-called 'main effects only' designs, and require assumptions/knowledge that *all* interactions are zero or not statistically significant.

Academics typically are interested in the first objective, and practitioners in the second. It is worth noting, however, that understanding generally leads to better prediction, but better prediction does not necessarily lead to understanding. In either case, however, there are limits to the size of experiments. Complete factorials grow exponentially in size and complexity as we increase the number of attributes, the number of attribute levels or both. Also, the more attributes to be studied, the more likely it is that a high proportion of higher-order interactions will be of little to no interest. Indeed, in the absence of theory, it is difficult to know how to interpret three-, four- or higher-way interactions, even if they prove to be significant. (In fact, one might even go so far as to say that the interpretation of such high-order interactions is risky in the absence of highly controlled laboratory conditions.) Finally, we later discuss the fact that even if such high-order interactions are significant, they rarely produce much bias in main and two-way interaction estimates.

So, the key takeaway from the preceding discussion is that one needs seriously to consider the fact that at least some interactions will exist and be meaningful and significant, which brings us to the topic of fractional factorial designs. Fractional designs are ways to systematically select subsets of treatment combinations from the complete factorial such that the effects of primary interest can be estimated under the assumption that (often, many) interactions are not significant.

4.3   Fractional factorial designs

Notwithstanding the statistical advantages possessed by complete factorials, such designs are practical only for small problems involving either small numbers of

Table 4.3. *Standard design notation*

Factor A	Factor B	Factor C	Notation	Simple effects
0	0	0	(1)	
1	0	0	A	A − (1)
0	1	0	B	
1	1	0	AB	AB − B
0	0	1	C	
1	0	1	AC	AC − C
0	1	1	BC	
1	1	1	ABC	ABC − BC

attributes or levels or both. In our experience the vast majority of SP problems are too large to allow one to use complete factorials. For example, consider a relatively small problem involving five attributes denoted by capital letters, with levels indicated in parentheses: $A(2) \times B(4) \times C(4) \times D(5) \times E(8)$, or $2 \times 4 \times 4 \times 5 \times 8$, or more simply yet, $2 \times 4^2 \times 5 \times 8$. The complete factorial involves 1280 total combinations, each of which requires a minimum of one observation in order to estimate all the possible effects. It may also be the case (and usually is) that many fewer than all possible effects are of real interest, which suggests that complete factorials rarely will be of interest except for fairly small problems.

As the number of possible combinations in complete factorial designs increase one is motivated to reduce the size of such problems to undertake practical work in the field. Such problems can be reduced to practical sizes by using fractional factorial designs. Fractional factorial designs involve the selection of a particular subset or sample (i.e., fraction) of complete factorials, so that particular effects of interest can be estimated as efficiently as possible. Instead of sampling randomly from the complete factorial, statistical design theorists have developed a large range of sampling methods that lead to practical designs with particular statistical properties. In general, all fractional designs involve some loss of statistical information, and the information loss can be large. That is, all fractions require assumptions about non-significance of higher-order effects, i.e., interactions between two or more attributes. We will discuss the types of assumptions one has to make, and their consequences later in this chapter, but for the present it is sufficient to note that failure to satisfy such assumptions may result in biased and misleading model estimates. Econometricians will recognise this as an omitted-variables problem.

We begin our discussion by presenting a formal system for representing factorials and fractional factorials.[1] Consider a complete factorial design, consisting of three factors A, B and C, each of which varies over two levels. The notation we will use for this design and the effects therein is provided in table 4.3.

---

[1] This discussion benefited considerably from discussions with and presentations in the University of Sydney SP interest group seminars by Dr Deborah Street, University of Technology, Sydney.

Table 4.4. *Defining relations for 2^3 designs*

(1)	A	B	AB	C	AC	BC	ABC	Effect
−1	+1	−1	+1	−1	+1	−1	+1	ME(A)
−1	−1	+1	+1	−1	−1	+1	+1	ME(B)
+1	−1	−1	+1	+1	−1	−1	+1	INT(AB)
−1	−1	−1	−1	+1	+1	+1	+1	ME(C)
+1	−1	+1	−1	−1	+1	−1	+1	INT(AC)
+1	+1	−1	−1	−1	−1	+1	+1	INT(BC)
−1	+1	+1	−1	+1	−1	−1	+1	INT(ABC)

Notes: ME = main effect; INT = Interaction.

Now we can define the various effects as given next:

1. The main effect of $A = 1/4(A - (1) + AB - B + AC - C - ABC - BC) = 1/4(A - 1)(B + 1)(C + 1)$.
2. The main effect of $B = 1/4(A + 1)(B - 1)(C + 1)$.
3. The main effect of $C = 1/4(A + 1)(B + 1)(C - 1)$.
4. The AB interaction $= (AB - B + ABC - BC) - (A - (1)) + (AC - C) = (A - 1)(B - 1)(C + 1)$.
5. The AC interaction $= (A - 1)(B + 1)(C - 1)$.
6. The BC interaction $= (A + 1)(B - 1)(C - 1)$.
7. The ABC interaction $= (A - 1)(B - 1)(C - 1)$.

We can rearrange the above into table 4.4 such that if we multiply the codes in each row by the corresponding columns we can obtain the exact effects defined above.

Now, suppose that we cannot deal with the complete factorial, and instead want only a subset (e.g., we may not be able to observe all eight treatment combinations, or think that asking subjects to evaluate all eight may be too burdensome). In particular, let us decide to choose 1 in 2 of the eight treatment combinations (i.e., a 1/2 fraction).

For pedagogical reasons we ignore all fractions that are not regular fractions, but generally speaking unless one is familiar with advanced design theory, it probably is wise to avoid irregular fractions (regularity is defined below). To understand fractions, one needs to understand aliasing. The 'alias' of an effect in a regular fraction consists of one or more omitted effects. For example, in the case of an experiment with three attributes at two levels, the main effect of attribute A may be aliased with the BC interaction. In larger experiments, the main effect of attribute A may be aliased with several interactions of different orders.

Thus, in regular fractions the aliasing (sometimes also called 'confounding') structure of the design consists of known and exact subsets of effects in the design. By way of contrast, in irregular fractions the aliasing structure consists of a linear combination of effects in the design. That is, the main effect of attribute A is a perfect linear combination of one or more omitted effects, but is not a perfect correlate of any one of them. In the case of regular fractions, therefore, it is easy to determine exactly which effects are aliased (or confounded) with what other effects, but in the latter case, this structure is neither obvious nor necessarily easy to determine. Readers with econometric backgrounds should view this as a case of exact collinearity of omitted and included effects. To emphasise, in the case of regular fractions, one or more omitted effects are exactly correlated ($r \equiv \pm 1.0$) with included effects; in the case of irregular fractions, included effects are either exact linear combinations of omitted effects or are highly correlated with them.

Recall that we decided to sample only half the treatment combinations; hence we are free to select any four columns in table 4.4 to define our fraction. It is relatively easy to determine if one has selected a regular fraction because all regular fractions contain one row in which all the entries equal one. The effect represented by this row is called a 'defining relation'. For example, let us choose columns A, B, C and ABC to represent the four treatments in our one-half fraction that we wish to construct (cols 2, 3, 5 and 8 of table 4.4).

Note that, for these four treatments, the row INT(ABC) entries are all $+1s$, hence this now is the 'defining relation'. We define each alias structure in the design by multiplying each effect by the defining relation as follows:

- $A = A \times ABC = A^2BC = BC$
- $B = B \times ABC = AB^2C = AC$
- $C = C \times ABC = ABC^2 = AB$
- $AB = AB \times ABC = A^2B^2C = C$
- $AC = AC \times ABC = A^2BC^2 = B$
- $BC = BC \times ABC = AB^2C^2 = A$
- $ABC = ABC \times ABC = A^2B^2C^2 = 1$.

Each squared effect above equals one, and hence can be ignored. Thus, if we choose this particular subset of effects to make our one-half fraction, each main effect (A, B, C) is perfectly aliased with a two-way interaction, and the three-way interaction is exactly equal to one, or the grand mean (or intercept). That is, if we use the four treatment combinations implied by this choice of columns, and we estimate the main effect of factor A from SP response data, we actually estimate the main effect of A *if and only if* the two-way interaction BC is not significant (equals zero). Otherwise, we cannot know if our estimate is in fact the main effect of A, the BC interaction or some combination of both A and BC. All regular fractions have properties similar to this, and all effects that one estimates from regular fractions will be perfectly aliased with one or more omitted effects.

Another way of considering the foregoing problem of the selection of a 1/2 fraction of the $2 \times 2 \times 2$ (or 2^3) factorial is shown in table 4.5a. The table contains both halves of the 2^3, and each contains exactly four treatment combinations. It is easy to see that the first two columns in both halves are identical (factors A and B), but the third column differs. In fact, the third column is exactly equal to the AB interaction. The latter can be seen easily if we modify the coding of the attribute levels by replacing 1,2 with their corresponding orthogonal codes. Orthogonal codes are a transformation of

Table 4.5a. *Two 1/2 fractions of the 2^3 factorial*

Combination	A (2 levels)	B (2 levels)	C (2 levels)
Fraction 1			
1	1	1	1
2	1	2	2
3	2	1	2
4	2	2	1
Fraction 2			
1	1	1	2
2	1	2	1
3	2	1	1
4	2	2	2

Table 4.5b. *Orthogonally coded 1/2 fraction of the 2^3 factorial*

Combination	A (2 levels)	B (2 levels)	C (2 levels)
Fraction 1			
1	−1	−1	−1
2	−1	+1	+1
3	+1	−1	+1
4	+1	+1	−1
Fraction 2			
1	−1	−1	+1
2	−1	+1	−1
3	+1	−1	−1
4	+1	+1	+1

the original codes such that each column sums to zero and the inner product of each pair of columns is zero. In the present case, replacing 1 and 2 with −1 and +1 satisfies the transformation. However, in the case of two levels, subtracting the mean also satisfies the transformation because of the constraint on the effects of the L (=2 in this case) levels to sum to zero.

We replace codes 1,2 with −1,+1 in table 4.5b to demonstrate that the cross-product of columns A and B reproduce the values in column C in both fractions. Thus, column C is the interaction (cross-product) of columns A and B in both fractions. This illustrates our earlier point about assumptions required to use fractions: column C represents the main effect of attribute C, the AB interaction or some combination of both. Note also that four interactions are possible with three attributes: AB, AC, BC and ABC. These interactions are orthogonal cross-products in the complete factorial, but are perfectly confounded (correlated) with one of the columns in each fraction. For example, BC = A in both fractions, whereas ABC identically equals

−1 in fraction 1 and +1 in fraction 2; hence, ABC exactly equals the intercept (grand mean). Thus, design columns represent not only main effects assigned to them (i.e., A, B and C), but also unobserved (and unobservable) interaction effects.

The latter point is particularly important. If the omitted interaction effects are not zero (i.e., at least one is significantly different from zero), the effects estimated by such a fraction will be biased, and the nature and extent of the bias cannot be known in advance because it depends on the unobserved effects. This important aspect of fractional designs seems to have escaped the attention of large numbers of academics and practitioners who undertake SP research. More problematic is the widespread use of designs such as table 4.5a, which allow identification *only* of main effects, and require assumptions about *all* unobserved interactions.

The fractions in table 4.5b involve four unobserved interactions, but consider a modest extension involving five attributes, each with four levels (or 4^5). Once again, suppose that the complete factorial contains too many treatment combinations (1024) for an experiment involving individual consumers. Hence, we want a much smaller number of treatment combinations. Let us assume that 16 combinations is the most we can tolerate, which is 1/64 of the total design, or 4^{5-3}. Also assume that we are willing to ignore all two-way and higher-order interactions, either because we have no other choice or because we have reason to believe that they are not significant.

The foregoing problem translates into a design that allows estimation of only the main effects of the five attributes. Efficient estimation of the parameters of a linear model that represents the utility function of interest (i.e., 'main effects only') can be accomplished if we select the treatments such that the resulting main effects columns in our design are orthogonal. The five-attribute main effects contain fifteen degrees of freedom because each attribute has four levels (i.e., three degrees of freedom each). Bear in mind, however, that we explicitly ignored all interactions and/or assumed them away (i.e., $1024 - 15 = 1009$ other effects). Frankly, it would be miraculous if all remaining 1009 interaction terms (degrees of freedom) were not significant, especially as there is no theory to suggest otherwise.

4.4   Practical considerations in fractional designs

At this point, one may well ask why one would want to use fractional factorial designs to study and model decision processes given the large number of potentially unobserved interaction effects in most designs. Indeed, researchers interested in understanding decision process, as opposed to practical prediction, should think seriously about using fractions. In the case of practical prediction, however, bias may be less of an issue, although problems of incorrect inference remain. In any case, aliasing interaction effects with main effects to create regular fractions can be somewhat justified by the following well-known results for linear models (e.g., Dawes and Corrigan 1974):

- main effects typically account for 70 to 90 per cent of explained variance,
- two-way interactions typically account for 5 to 15 per cent of explained variance, and
- higher-order interactions account for the remaining explained variance.

Thus, even if interactions are significant and large, they rarely account for a great deal of explained variance. This suggests that a wise approach to design strategy should be to use designs that allow estimation of (at least) all two-way interactions whenever possible because main effects and two-way interactions account for virtually all the reliable explained variance. Thus, little variance is accounted for by omitted effects, and bias in the estimates of interest should be minimised (although not eliminated).

Additionally, if attribute preference directionality is known a priori, this also should ensure high levels of explained variance (e.g., Dawes and Corrigan 1974; Anderson and Shanteau 1977). Specifically, regardless of true (but unknown) forms of utility or decision rules, if attribute levels are monotonically related to responses, or can be transformed to be so related, any additive model will fit the data from which it is estimated very well, and also will cross-validate well to hold-out (test-retest) samples. Thus, as long as a consumer's decision rule is of the general form that more good attribute levels result in more positive responses, additive models will fit and predict well within the domain of attribute levels encompassed by the experiment.

A corollary to the preceding discussion of conditional attribute monotonicity is that interaction effects also will have properties that benefit practical prediction. That is, most of the variance explained by interactions should be captured by their linear-by-linear (or bilinear) components. A bilinear component is a simple cross-product of two linear components in a polynomial expansion. That is, if two attributes X and Z each have L levels, their means (or marginals in the case of discrete-choice experiments) can be fitted exactly with a polynomial of degree $L - 1$. As well, their two-way interaction can be exactly fitted by expanding the cross-products to include all $(L - 1) \times (L - 1)$ polynomial components: $XZ, X^2Z, \ldots, X^{L-1}Z, XZ^2, XZ^3, \ldots, XZ^{L-1}, X^2Z^2, \ldots, X^{L-1}Z^{L-1}$. The bilinear component is the XZ term in this expansion, and if both X and Z are monotonically related to the response, almost all the reliable variance explained by the two-way interaction of X and Z should be in XZ.

This property of conditionally monotone attributes suggests a useful design strategy that is consistent with the objective of minimising the variance attributable to unobserved but significant effects (i.e., omitted effects). *The majority of variance explained by two-way interactions should be in the bilinear component, which can be captured by generating an 'endpoint design' based on the extreme levels of each attribute.* The 'extreme levels' are the highest and lowest levels of each attribute in terms of its relation to the response. For example, if price and travel time are two attributes, then the 'extreme levels' would be the highest and lowest fares and times, respectively, that one wants to vary in the experiment.

One way to make such an 'endpoint' design is to use a regular fraction of a 2^J factorial (J = the total number of attributes) in which all main and two-way interaction effects are independent of one another. This endpoint design can be combined with another regular fraction of the L^J factorial in which all main effects are independent of one another (L = all original attribute levels of interest) to estimate (a) non-linear main effects and (b) all linear × linear two-way interaction effects. The combined design may not be orthogonal, but typically is well-conditioned, and can estimate all effects with reasonable statistical efficiency.

For example, the complete factorial design for six attributes at four levels has 4096 total combinations (4^6). The smallest regular fraction in which the main effects are independent contains a subset of 32; hence, thousands of potentially significant effects are unobserved if one uses only the main effects design. If all levels are restricted to their two extremes (end points), there will be six main and fifteen two-way interactions, or twenty-one total degrees of freedom (i.e., $6 \times 5/2$ or $J \times (J-1)/2$). We can estimate all main and two-way interaction effects independently of one another by constructing (1) a thirty-two-treatment 2^{6-1} orthogonal fraction to estimate all linear main and bilinear two-way interactions, combining it with (2) a thirty-two-treatment main effects design to estimate the four-level main effects. The combined design has sixty-four treatment combinations, but there may be duplicates in each design, which can be reduced by eliminating them at the expense of a small degree of design non-orthogonality. Alternatively, one may wish to use duplicate profiles to estimate response reliability (test-retest reliability). Table 4.6a uses the 4^5 design as an example, and creates two sixteen-treatment designs. Duplicate profiles in the two designs are 1/17 and 12/21, which can be eliminated, slightly reducing orthogonality.

It also should be noted that technically 'extreme levels' must be identified for each respondent separately. That is, unless all attributes are quantitative and/or their preference directions known a priori for all respondents, extreme levels will not be obvious. However, it is normally straightforward to identify the extremes for each respondent based on initial interviews, computerised interviewing techniques and the like. Hence, identifying extremes is at worst a minor problem with current technology.

Treatment (hereafter 'profile') duplication usually can be eliminated or minimised by reversing the order of attribute levels in some columns. For example, if the codes in column A1 for profiles 17 to 32 are 0, 1, 2, 3, codes in every other column can be reversed beginning with column A1 or A2 (i.e., $0 = 3, 1 = 2, 2 = 1, 3 = 0$). Table 4.6b illustrates this process for both endpoint and main effects designs: reverse columns A2 and A4 in the endpoint design, and columns A1, A3 and A5 in the main effects design to eliminate duplicates.

4.5 Design strategies for simple SP experiments

Table 4.7 contains nine possible attributes of airline flights between Boston and Los Angeles. Two of the attributes have four levels and seven have two levels. Thus, the complete factorial is a $4^2 \times 2^7$. The effects and degrees of freedom in this factorial can be decomposed as follows:

- Main effects (13 d.f.)
- Two-way interactions (72 d.f.)
- Other interactions ($2048 - 13 - 72 - 1 = 1952$ d.f.).

It would be difficult (if not impossible) to ask each consumer in a sample to evaluate and respond to 2048 ticket combinations. Even if one believes that responses can be

Table 4.6a. *Combining two designs to capture*
most sources of variance

Profile no.	A1	A2	A3	A4	A5
2^5 *orthogonal fraction to estimate main effects and*					
two-way interactions					
1	0	0	0	0	0
2	0	0	0	1	1
3	0	0	1	0	1
4	0	0	1	1	0
5	0	1	0	0	1
6	0	1	0	1	0
7	0	1	1	0	0
8	0	1	1	1	1
9	1	0	0	0	1
10	1	0	0	1	0
11	1	0	1	0	0
12	1	0	1	1	1
13	1	1	0	0	0
14	1	1	0	1	1
15	1	1	1	0	1
16	1	1	1	1	0
4^5 *orthogonal fraction to estimate main effects*					
17	0	0	0	0	0
18	0	1	1	2	3
19	0	2	2	3	1
20	0	3	3	1	2
21	1	0	1	1	1
22	1	1	0	3	2
23	1	2	3	2	0
24	1	3	2	0	3
25	2	0	2	2	2
26	2	1	3	0	1
27	2	2	0	1	3
28	2	3	1	3	0
29	3	0	3	3	3
30	3	1	2	1	0
31	3	2	1	0	2
32	3	3	0	2	1

aggregated over groups (segments) of individuals, the number of profiles is probably
too large for practical use. Thus, we are motivated to consider more parsimonious
statistical models of the potential response surface than one that involves all possible
effects. Such models can be derived from theory, hypotheses, empirical evidence,
curve-fitting, or other sources. In the present case, some statistical model possibilities

Table 4.6b. *Eliminating or reducing profile
duplication in two designs*

Profile no.	A1	A2	A3	A4	A5
2^5 *orthogonal fraction to estimate all main effects and two-way interactions*					
1	0	1	0	1	0
2	0	1	0	0	1
3	0	1	1	1	1
4	0	1	1	0	0
5	0	0	0	1	1
6	0	0	0	0	0
7	0	0	1	1	0
8	0	0	1	0	1
9	1	1	0	1	1
10	1	1	0	0	0
11	1	1	1	1	0
12	1	1	1	0	1
13	1	0	0	1	0
14	1	0	0	0	1
15	1	0	1	1	1
16	1	0	1	0	0
4^5 *regular fraction to estimate main effects*					
17	3	0	3	0	3
18	3	1	2	2	0
19	3	2	1	3	2
20	3	3	0	1	1
21	2	0	2	1	2
22	2	1	3	3	1
23	2	2	0	2	3
24	2	3	1	0	0
25	1	0	1	2	1
26	1	1	0	0	2
27	1	2	3	1	0
28	1	3	2	3	3
29	0	0	0	3	0
30	0	1	1	1	3
31	0	2	2	0	1
32	0	3	3	2	2

include the following (in increasing order of complexity):

- only main effects
- main effects plus some two-way interaction effects
- main effects plus all two-way interaction effects
- Polynomial and dummy variable approximations.

Table 4.7. *Example attributes for airline flights*

Attributes of flights from Boston to LA	Levels of features
Return fare	$300, $400, $500, $600
Departure time	8am, 9am, noon, 2pm
Total time to LA	5, 7 hours
Non-stop service	Non-stop, 1 stop
Music/audio entertainment	Yes, no
TV video clips, news	Yes, no
Movie(s)	Yes, no
Hot meal	Yes, no
Airline	United, Delta

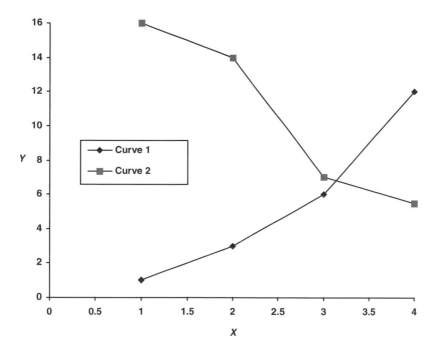

Figure 4.1 Possible functional forms for main effects

In the case of the latter, consider two possible representations of the main effects of a four-level attribute shown in figure 4.1.

Curve 1 can be approximated by a second-degree polynomial and curve 2 by a third-degree polynomial as shown below:

$$Y = \beta_0 + \beta_1 X + \beta_2 X^2 \tag{4.1}$$

$$Y = \alpha_0 - \alpha_1 X - \alpha_2 X^2 + \alpha_3 X^3. \tag{4.2}$$

Table 4.8. *Effects codes for as many as five attribute levels*

No. of levels	Levels	Effects code 1	Effects code 2	Effects code 3	Effects code 4
2	1	+1			
	2	−1			
3	1	+1	0		
	2	0	+1		
	3	−1	−1		
4	1	+1	0	0	
	2	0	+1	0	
	3	0	0	+1	
	4	−1	−1	−1	
5	1	+1	0	0	0
	2	0	+1	0	0
	3	0	0	+1	0
	4	0	0	0	+1
	5	−1	−1	−1	−1

As previously discussed, dummy variables or effects codes (EC) can be used to represent the effects of $L - 1$ of the levels of qualitative attributes (L = total levels). Effects codes for five or fewer levels are illustrated in table 4.8, and the statistical model commonly used to specify the effect of a single qualitative attribute is

$$Y = \beta_0 + \beta_1 EC_1 + \beta_2 EC_2 + \cdots + \beta_{L-1} EC_{L-1}. \tag{4.3}$$

β_1, β_2 and β_{L-1} estimate the utilities of levels assigned to columns labelled, respectively, 'effects code 1', 'effects code 2', ..., 'effects code $L - 1$'. The utility of the 'missing' or omitted level is exactly $\beta_1(-1) + \beta_2(-1) + \cdots + \beta_{L-1}(-1)$.

Before leaving the topic of attributes, attribute levels and approximating conditional and joint response surfaces, for completeness we need to discuss nesting of attributes. Briefly, attribute levels are nested if at least some levels of two or more attributes cannot logically occur together, or levels of one attribute necessarily differ due to levels of a second, or levels of one attribute are associated with levels of a second. For example, the length of a flight (short vs. long) and associated fares; the makes/models of auto and associated prices; type of transport mode and travel times to destinations; package size and associated prices or installation fee and installation fee waiver. Nesting of attributes/levels often can be handled by combining levels:

- short trip ($2.75, $3.75); long trip ($4.00, $5.50), for a total of 4 levels;
- installation fee and fee waiver ($0 if 3 or more, $10, $20, $30 each if less than 3), or a total of 4 levels.

Nesting should be avoided if possible, but if nested levels/attributes are required, it is important to try to minimise the resulting number of levels because they can quickly escalate in the combined attribute. Thus, nesting generally complicates design, and may require large designs if 'combined' (new) attributes contain eight or more levels.

4.5.1   Experiments for binary responses

Recall that binary responses are of the form, 'I like this, I do not like that', or 'Yes, I'd consider that, No, I would not', etc. Thus, subjects provide a 0,1 binary indicator of preference in response to some stimulus profile. Our design objectives should be as follows:

- *Identification.* Identification refers to the form(s) of utility functions that can be estimated from a given experiment. For example, as previously discussed, some experiments allow strictly additive, main-effects only specifications, whereas others allow estimation of more general forms involving various types of non-additivities (or interactions).
- *Precision.* Precision refers to confidence intervals of parameter estimates, given particular specifications and sample sizes. More precise estimates have smaller confidence intervals, hence, greater statistical efficiency.
- *Cognitive complexity.* This refers to the degree of task complexity and difficulty arising from the experiment. There is little consensus, and even less empirical data regarding optimum levels of complexity. Suffice it to say that proper pilot tests usually inform this decision.
- *Market realism.* This refers to the degree to which the experiment and associated task match the actual decision environment faced by subjects. At one extreme, one could design experiments to manipulate key aspects of real markets; at the other extreme, the experiment could be completely unrelated to real market behaviour. Logically, the closer the experiment resembles the actual market, the higher the face validity. Thus, the objective should be to simulate the real market as closely as possible, within the constraints posed by the other objectives.

As discussed in previous chapters on discrete-choice models, designs must satisfy properties of the probabilistic discrete-choice models hypothesised to underlie the response data, and whose parameters one therefore wishes to estimate. This necessarily dictates that we consider these properties and their relevance to design strategies, as well as other aspects of the research that may bear on design, such as sampling methods and sample sizes.

Our design discussion concentrates on the simple binary logit model (BLM) because software for estimating this model is widely available, and it is practically indistinguishable from its major competitor, the binary probit model. Recall that the BLM can be expressed as:

$$P(\text{yes}|\text{yes}, \text{no}) = \exp(V_{\text{yes}})/[\exp(V_{\text{yes}}) + \exp(V_{\text{no}})], \tag{4.4}$$

where the Vs are the systematic utility components. Recall that the value of V_{no} can be set to zero with no loss of generality, satisfying the identification restriction in the

BLM. Thus,

$$P(\text{yes}|\text{yes}, \text{no}) = \exp(V_{\text{yes}})/[\exp(V_{\text{yes}}) + 1]. \tag{4.5}$$

Furthermore, if we consider the odds of responding 'yes' relative to 'no', we see that

$$\frac{P(\text{yes}|\text{yes}, \text{no})}{P(\text{no}|\text{yes}, \text{no})} = \frac{\dfrac{\exp(V_{\text{yes}})}{\exp(V_{\text{yes}}) + 1}}{\dfrac{\exp(V_{\text{no}})}{\exp(V_{\text{yes}}) + 1}} = \frac{\exp(V_{\text{yes}})}{\exp(V_{\text{no}})}. \tag{4.6}$$

But $\exp(V_{\text{no}}) = 1$; hence, the odds of responding 'yes' relative to 'no' involve only influences on 'yes'. If we take natural logarithms of both sides, we see that:

$$\log_e\left[\frac{P(\text{yes}|\text{yes}, \text{no})}{P(\text{no}|\text{yes}, \text{no})}\right] = V_{\text{yes}}, \tag{4.7}$$

where all terms were previously defined. Now, recall that V_{yes} can be specified as a linear-in-the-parameters expression, such that:

$$V_{\text{yes}} = \sum_k \beta_k X_k + \sum_m \alpha_m Z_m, \tag{4.8}$$

where β_k is a vector of taste weights associated with K attribute vectors, X_k; and α_m is a vector of effects associated with M individual characteristics interacted with either the 'yes' intercept or elements of the X vector, Z_m.

Equation (4.8) involves attributes of alternatives and characteristics of individuals. We have control over the X_k, in the sense that we can design them to satisfy the properties of interest; but generally we have far less control over the Z_m. Specifically, the X_k can be designed such that the K columns of the design are orthogonal, ensuring relatively efficient estimates β_k. Efficient estimates of the α_m can be obtained only by similar design of individual characteristics. That is, the sampling plan itself must be based on orthogonal columns of characteristics, a daunting proposition in most applied settings. The latter is accomplished by sampling from the complete factorial implied by the array of individual characteristics of interest (e.g., income, age, education, etc.), which grows exponentially as numbers of characteristics, levels of characteristics or both increase. As discussed earlier in this chapter, fractional design principles are used to sample from the complete factorial by sacrificing information about some interactions.

The preceding discussion suggests that we can use design strategies not only to design alternatives to achieve experimental objectives, but also to design the sampling plan. However, in the interests of exposition, we confine our attention in the remainder of this chapter to the design of experiments involving attributes of alternatives, and we therefore assume that the sample from which responses are to be obtained is appropriate to the research purpose.

Equation (4.8) suggests that the key property that designs need to satisfy is that the effects of the X_k be independently estimable. At a minimum, X_k consists of the attribute main effects, but may also include various attribute interactions. Hence, model forms that can be identified (estimated) depend upon the design of the X_k columns. We restrict our attention to main effects and two-way interactions, following the logic of our earlier discussion of design for general linear models.

4.5.2 Random assignment (sampling) strategies

Theoretically, one should be able to satisfy the 'independence-of-effects' property by designing profiles based on random sampling from the complete factorial. As discussed in chapter 3, the statistical properties of probabilistic discrete-choice models hold only for large samples. There are therefore two sampling problems that must be addressed in this approach: (1) sampling profiles from the complete factorial that spans the space defined by X_k, and (2) sampling individuals from the target population(s).

Random sampling theory guarantees that if we take large enough samples from the complete factorial, we should closely approximate the statistical properties of the factorial itself. The property we wish to obtain is the orthogonality of columns representing the main and interaction effects of interest. If our research objective is to present all subjects with the same set of profiles and observe their responses, there is no consensus regarding how many profiles respondents will complete before reliability, bias or response rates are compromised. Based on our experience with hundreds of such experiments, the following rules of thumb seem apropos:

- Many experiments have employed at least thirty-two profiles successfully.
- As the number of attributes increase, task complexity increases because of the number of things to which respondents must attend.
- As the complexity of levels increases, task complexity increases because of cognitive effort involved in comprehending and attending to information.
- Thus, if there are more than ten attributes, and/or the attribute levels are complex in the sense that extra cognitive effort must be expended to comprehend them, one probably should consider reducing the number of profiles to which individuals are asked to respond (Carson et al. 1994).

4.5.3 Design strategies for binary responses

The foregoing implies that in the case of large factorials, a randomly chosen sample of thirty-two or fewer is unlikely to closely approximate the statistical properties of the complete factorial. Hence, design columns are unlikely to be orthogonal, and many columns may be quite highly correlated, which suggests that this strategy is not advisable, despite its simplistic appeal. As a corollary, this suggests that a random sampling approach to the design of experimental profiles might be feasible if one is willing to select relatively large samples from the complete factorial, divide the profiles into subsets (blocks) and randomly assign respondents to the blocks. This procedure requires assumptions about respondents, primarily homogeneity of preferences; or, alternatively, a way to account for preference heterogeneity. We return to this

Table 4.9. *Attributes and levels for flights from Boston to Los Angeles*

Attributes describing Boston to LA flights	Levels of features
Return fare	$300, $400, $500, $600
Departure time	8am, 9am, noon, 2pm
Total time to LA	4,5,6,7 hours
Non-stop service	Non-stop, 1 stop
Music/audio entertainment	Yes, no
TV video clips, news	Yes, no
Hot meal	Yes, no
Airline	United, Delta

topic in later chapters, but note in passing that Bunch and Batsell (1989) show that a minimum of six respondents per profile are required to satisfy large sample statistical properties. Hence, sampling and design are interrelated, and both must be considered in concert. Good design will not compensate for inadequate sampling, and vice versa.

Although easy to implement, random samples of profiles leave much to chance, motivating us to ensure that effects of interest can be identified and estimated relatively efficiently for a given sample size. Because profiles need to be designed only for 'yes' responses, the problem is isomorphic to linear model designs. That is, one develops a fractional factorial to permit identification of all effects of interest, possibly in this sequence of increasing design complexity:

- main effects only independent of one another (but not independent of two-way interactions),
- main effects independent of some (or all) unobserved two-way interactions (but not independent of other omitted effects),
- main effects plus some two-way interactions independent of one another (but not omitted effects),
- main effects plus some or all 'bilinear' two-way interactions independent of one another (but not omitted other two-way and higher-order effects),
- main effects plus all two-way interactions independent of one another (but not omitted higher-order effects),
- designs that permit estimation of main effects plus two-way interactions plus some or all three-way interactions independently of one another (but not of omitted effects).

Consider the example in table 4.9, which involves attributes of airline flights. The complete factorial implied by table 4.9 contains 2048 profiles. A single random sample of thirty-two profiles represents 1.5625 per cent of the total, which is unlikely to represent the statistical properties of the full factorial closely. Thus, we seek a designed solution, rather than rely on chance. For example, a 'main effects only' design can be used to illustrate the basic idea. Such a design is shown in table 4.10.

Table 4.10. *'Main effects only' design codes for the flight example*

Flight	Fare	Depart	Time	Stops	Audio	Video	Meals	Airline
				Design codes for regular orthogonal main effects				
1	0	0	0	0	0	0	0	0
2	0	1	1	1	0	1	1	0
3	0	2	2	1	1	0	1	1
4	0	3	3	0	1	1	0	1
5	1	0	1	0	1	0	1	1
6	1	1	0	1	1	1	0	1
7	1	2	3	1	0	0	0	0
8	1	3	2	0	0	1	1	0
9	2	0	2	1	0	1	0	1
10	2	1	3	0	0	0	1	1
11	2	2	0	0	1	1	1	0
12	2	3	1	1	1	0	0	0
13	3	0	3	1	1	1	1	0
14	3	1	2	0	1	0	0	0
15	3	2	1	0	0	1	0	1
16	3	3	0	1	0	0	1	1

The design codes in table 4.10 can be translated into profiles by replacing each code with a unique, corresponding level in table 4.9 to produce the profiles in table 4.11. This process is analogous to a 'find and replace' process in a word processor, such that each design code is replaced by the corresponding string of verbal, quantitative, graphical or other information that represents the description of the attribute level.

Once profiles are designed, they are placed into an appropriate survey format (often called a 'card sort') and administered. Table 4.12 adds hypothetical 'yes/no' responses from 100 respondents who evaluated each flight profile for their next flight from Boston to Los Angeles.

Once response data are obtained from the survey, they can be analysed with binary logistic (shown in table 4.13) or probit regression. The results in table 4.13 should be qualified because successive responses of each respondent may not be independent, as assumed in chapter 2. That is, the IID assumption may not hold within or between individuals. Within individuals, responses to successive profiles may depend in some way on previous responses. Between individuals, differences in preferences lead to violation of the IID assumption because the joint distribution of taste (β) parameters (marginal utilities) is not the convolution of independent random variables. Thus, the model results in table 4.13 would be correct if, instead of 100 individuals evaluating all sixteen profiles, each of the 16 profiles was randomly assigned to 100 respondents (i.e., 1600 total respondents). Even in this ideal situation, however, differences in individuals could give rise to response dependence. Having said that, the parameter

Table 4.11. *Matching design codes with levels to construct profiles*

Flight	Translating design codes into profiles using 'find and replace'							
	Fare	Depart	Time	Stops	Audio	Video	Meals	Airline
1	$300	8 am	4 hrs	0	No	No	No	Delta
2	$300	9 am	5 hrs	1	No	Yes	Yes	Delta
3	$300	Noon	6 hrs	1	Yes	No	Yes	United
4	$300	2 pm	7 hrs	0	Yes	Yes	No	United
5	$400	8 am	5 hrs	0	Yes	No	Yes	United
6	$400	9 am	4 hrs	1	Yes	Yes	No	United
7	$400	Noon	7 hrs	1	No	No	No	Delta
8	$400	2 pm	6 hrs	0	No	Yes	Yes	Delta
9	$500	8 am	6 hrs	1	No	Yes	No	United
10	$500	9 am	7 hrs	0	No	No	Yes	United
11	$500	Noon	4 hrs	0	Yes	Yes	Yes	Delta
12	$500	2 pm	5 hrs	1	Yes	No	No	Delta
13	$600	8 am	7 hrs	1	Yes	Yes	Yes	Delta
14	$600	9 am	6 hrs	0	Yes	No	No	Delta
15	$600	Noon	5 hrs	0	No	Yes	No	United
16	$600	2 pm	4 hrs	1	No	No	Yes	United

Table 4.12. *Hypothetical 'yes/no' responses to flight profiles*

Profile	Responses		Attributes of flights in experiment ($n = 100$)							
	Yes	No	Fare	Depart	Time	Stops	Audio	Video	Meals	Airline
1	80	20	$300	8 am	4 hrs	0	No	No	No	Delta
2	60	40	$300	9 am	5 hrs	1	No	Yes	Yes	Delta
3	50	50	$300	Noon	6 hrs	1	Yes	No	Yes	United
4	30	70	$300	2 pm	7 hrs	0	Yes	Yes	No	United
5	60	40	$400	8 am	5 hrs	0	Yes	No	Yes	United
6	50	50	$400	9 am	4 hrs	1	Yes	Yes	No	United
7	20	80	$400	Noon	7 hrs	1	No	No	No	Delta
8	35	65	$400	2 pm	6 hrs	0	No	Yes	Yes	Delta
9	10	90	$500	8 am	6 hrs	1	No	Yes	No	United
10	15	85	$500	9 am	7 hrs	0	No	No	Yes	United
11	40	60	$500	Noon	4 hrs	0	Yes	Yes	Yes	Delta
12	20	80	$500	2 pm	5 hrs	1	Yes	No	No	Delta
13	30	70	$600	8 am	7 hrs	1	Yes	Yes	Yes	Delta
14	5	95	$600	9 am	6 hrs	0	Yes	No	No	Delta
15	10	90	$600	Noon	5 hrs	0	No	Yes	No	United
16	15	85	$600	2 pm	4 hrs	1	No	No	Yes	United

Table 4.13. *Results of binary logistic regression of flight responses*

Effect	Coefficient	Std error	t-Value
Return fare	−0.007	0.001	−12.649
Depart 8 am	0.604	0.103	5.873
Depart 9 am	−0.098	0.112	−0.876
Depart Noon	−0.215	0.107	−2.011
Total time	−0.361	0.054	−6.642
No. of stops	−0.003	0.123	−0.026
Audio entertain (no = −1)	0.340	0.125	2.728
Video entertain (no = −1)	0.058	0.123	0.476
Meals (no = −1)	0.523	0.122	4.285
Airline (Delta = +1)	−0.181	0.062	−2.912
Intercept	3.927	0.398	9.860

Statistics: $-2[L(0) - L(\beta)] = 501.86$, d.f. $= 11$, $\rho^2 = 0.839$

estimates are the mean effects of each attribute in the sample, which are consistent but inefficient.

The parameter estimates in table 4.13 are of two types: (1) in the case of quantitative attributes, they reflect the rate of change in the odds of a yes relative to a no response for a unit change in the attribute level, and (2) in the case of a qualitative attribute, they are an estimate of the odds ratio for each level coded as +1. Thus, fare and flight time are both negative and significant, as expected, with the following interpretation: for each one dollar increase in fare, the log odds of a 'yes' decrease by 0.007; and for each one hour increase in travel time, the log odds decrease by 0.361. In the case of departure times, the most preferred is 8am (highest log odds), and the least preferred is 2pm. Other effects are interpreted similarly. Strictly speaking, the effects in the table are defined in terms of the log odds of the response, but the log odds ratios are linearly related to the true, but unobserved, utility, and in that sense are our best estimates of the utility of each attribute level. The latter can be seen more clearly by conducting the analysis in terms of log odds ratios, and using ordinary least squares methods to calculate the effects by hand, as we shall now exemplify.

Table 4.14 is the same as table 4.13, with 'yes' and 'no' responses replaced by their respective odds and log odds. Because equation (4.8) is the linear form of the binary logit model expressed in terms of the log odds, we can treat the log odds as being the outcome of a process described by a general linear model. This allows us to explain the analysis by calculating the marginal means associated with each level of each attribute, which are the best OLS estimates of the main effects. That is, the effect of the kth attribute, X_k, say $\tau_k = \mu_k - \mu$, which reveals that the main effect of the kth attribute is simply a difference in treatment means for the levels of that attribute. Logically, if none of the levels affects the outcome or response, then $\mu_1 = \mu_2 = \cdots = \mu$, or $\tau_k = \mu_1 - \mu = 0$.

Earlier, we showed how marginal effects (means) of attributes can be captured statistically by using polynomials of degree $L - 1$, or $L - 1$ dummies or effects

Table 4.14. *Odds and log odds responses to 'yes/no' flight profiles*

	Responses		Attributes of flights in experiment (n = 100)							
Profile	Odds	Log odds	Fare	Depart	Time	Stops	Audio	Video	Meals	Airline
1	80/20	1.386	$300	8 am	4 hrs	0	No	No	No	Delta
2	60/40	0.405	$300	9 am	5 hrs	1	No	Yes	Yes	Delta
3	50/50	0.000	$300	Noon	6 hrs	1	Yes	No	Yes	United
4	30/70	−0.847	$300	2 pm	7 hrs	0	Yes	Yes	No	United
5	60/40	0.405	$400	8 am	5 hrs	0	Yes	No	Yes	United
6	50/50	0.000	$400	9 am	4 hrs	1	Yes	Yes	No	United
7	20/80	−1.386	$400	Noon	7 hrs	1	No	No	No	Delta
8	35/65	−0.619	$400	2 pm	6 hrs	0	No	Yes	Yes	Delta
9	10/90	−2.197	$500	8 am	6 hrs	1	No	Yes	No	United
10	15/85	−1.734	$500	9 am	7 hrs	0	No	No	Yes	United
11	40/60	−0.405	$500	Noon	4 hrs	0	Yes	Yes	Yes	Delta
12	20/80	−1.386	$500	2 pm	5 hrs	1	Yes	No	No	Delta
13	30/70	−0.847	$600	8 am	7 hrs	1	Yes	Yes	Yes	Delta
14	5/95	−2.944	$600	9 am	6 hrs	0	Yes	No	No	Delta
15	10/90	−2.197	$600	Noon	5 hrs	0	No	Yes	No	United
16	15/85	−1.735	$600	2 pm	4 hrs	1	No	No	Yes	United

coded variables. The latter are equivalent to calculating the marginal means of the levels of each attribute. In fact, the marginal means of the log odds ratios are linearly related to the unknown utilities for each attribute level (Louviere 1988a), and we can estimate the parameters from the marginal means with OLS (i.e., estimate attribute slopes or level contrasts from the marginal means). Because the attributes are orthogonal, simple regression estimates must equal multiple regression estimates. More generally, one should use the method of maximum likelihood (chapter 3) to estimate the parameters because the OLS estimates won't satisfy the constant variance assumption of OLS.

The marginal means of the kth attribute in X_k can be calculated from the log odds in table 4.14. Definition (and calculation) of marginal means can be illustrated with reference to the fare attribute. Marginal means of the log odds of fare levels are calculated as shown below, and are contained in table 4.15.

- Marginal mean for 300 = $(1.386 + 0.405 + 0.000 − 0.847)/4 = 0.236$.
- Marginal mean for 400 = $(0.405 + 0.000 − 1.386 − 0.619)/4 = −0.400$.
- Marginal mean for 500 = $(−2.197 − 1.734 − 0.405 − 1.386)/4 = −1.431$.
- Marginal mean for 600 = $(−0.847 − 2.944 − 2.197 − 1.735)/4 = −1.931$.

The relationship between the marginal means and their corresponding fare levels can be visualised by graphing each mean against its corresponding fare level as shown in figure 4.2.

Table 4.15. *Marginal means calculated from table 4.14*

Attributes and levels	Marginal means (utilities) of levels			
Fare ($300, $400, $500, $600)	0.236	−0.400	−1.431	−1.931
Departure time (8, 9, 12, 2)	−0.313	−1.068	−0.304	−1.147
Total time to LA (4, 5, 6, 7 hrs)	−0.189	−0.693	−1.440	−1.204
Non-stop service (0, 1 stops)	−0.869	−0.893		
Music/audio entertain. (No, Yes)	−0.924	−0.836		
TV-video clips, news (No, Yes)	−1.196	−0.564		
Hot meal (No, Yes)	−0.631	−1.129		
Airline (Delta, United)	−0.631	−1.129		

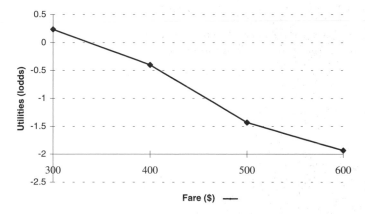

Figure 4.2 Marginal means vs. fare levels

As can be seen in figure 4.2, the relationship between fare levels and the (log odds) marginal means is approximately linear. Hence, we can estimate the slope of the relationship using simple regression. The slope obtained from ordinary least squares regression is −0.008, which is very close to the maximum likelihood result in table 4.13. The other marginal means in table 4.15 also can be analysed with simple regression, and compared. We invite the reader to perform these analyses and do a similar comparison: some ordinary regression estimates will not match corresponding maximum likelihood estimates well. Thus, estimation methods that do not account for non-constant error variances should be treated with suspicion.

The preceding discussion focused on a linearisation of the binary logit model (Theil 1971), which involves aggregate choice frequencies. More generally, however, choice data involve disaggregated, binary observations (i.e., 0,1), and therefore maximum likelihood estimation must be used to ensure satisfaction of asymptotic statistical properties. More importantly, equation (4.8) reveals that, in order to estimate individual difference effects, data must be disaggregated. That is, differences within individuals are constant across choice sets, hence cannot affect an individual's responses. Instead, socio-demographic and/or psychographic measures at best account for differences between individuals. That is, individual characteristics in binary logit models can be hypothesised to account for differences in propensity to respond 'yes' vs. 'no' (i.e., the odds of saying 'yes'), or differences in responses to changes in attribute levels. Additionally, large sample sizes may be needed to achieve sufficient power to reject the null for individual characteristics. The latter situation also may be exacerbated if individual characteristics are highly collinear (McClelland and Judd 1993).

Now that we have covered the fundamentals of experimental design, including an extension to the case of simple binary response problems, we have the basic conceptual framework to introduce the topic of multiple choice experiments. We now turn our attention to that topic in the next chapter.

5 Design of choice experiments

5.1 Introduction

Choice experiments consist of a sample of choice sets selected from the universal set of all possible choice sets that satisfy certain statistical properties. The key statistical properties relevant to the design of choice experiments are identification and precision, which must be considered together with non-statistical properties such as realism and complexity.

Chapter 3 introduced two types of choice alternatives: generic and alternative-specific. The former type have no specific name or label, but rather are members of a class of alternatives. The latter are alternatives to which a name or label naturally applies, such as brands of detergent, names of retail chains, names of holiday destinations, etc., and it is the label itself which is the object of choice. Thus, generic alternatives are members of a general class of options, whereas alternative-specific alternatives are specific members of a general class.

Not surprisingly, the preceding discussion implies that there are two general types of choice experiments: (1) *labelled* (alternative-specific), and (2) *unlabelled* (generic). There are two general ways to design choice experiments for both types: (a) sequentially design alternatives and then design the choice sets into which they are placed, and/or (b) simultaneously design alternatives and assign them to choice sets. The types of effects that can be estimated from the two main types of choice experiments differ by type.

As discussed in chapter 3, if parameters representing the effects of attributes and/or individual characteristics are constant across alternatives, we say that such effects are generic for those alternatives. In contrast, if such effects differ for at least one alternative, we say that they are alternative-specific for the one or more alternatives for which they differ. It should be noted that both main and interaction effects (as defined in chapter 4) can be generic or alternative-specific. Two other types of effects can be estimated from choice experiments, and bear on whether IID error assumptions in the utility specification are violated. An *own effect* refers to the main and/or interaction effects of an alternative on its own utility or choices. A *cross effect* refers to main and/or interaction effects of other alternatives on a particular alternative's utility or choices. If the IID error assumption holds, only own attribute effects will be statistically significant; but if the assumption is violated more cross effects than would be expected by chance should be statistically significant.

This chapter takes the principles of experimental design of chapter 4 and applies them in the context of experiments where an individual makes a choice from a mutually exclusive set of alternatives. Choice designs can be labelled or unlabelled and can accommodate the availability and non-availability of subsets of alternatives. The latter implies that alternatives may be fixed or varying across choice sets, enabling a study of the influence on choice of the composition of the choice set and the attributes (and associated levels) defining each alternative in a choice set. An appendix provides an overview of a number of popular choice designs.

5.2 Multiple choice experiments

The objective of multiple choice experiments is to design alternatives and the choice sets in which they appear such that the aforementioned types of effects can be estimated with reasonable levels of statistical precision. That is, estimation of these effects implies particular utility specifications; hence a sine qua non from a design standpoint is that if one wants to estimate or test particular effects, by definition, the design must support their estimation. The art and science of design rests on the analyst's ability to estimate different utility specifications conditional on a maintained hypothesis about the form of the choice process.

The following briefly summarises the distinguishing features of multiple choice experiments:

1. there are more than two alternatives (e.g., two brands and non-choice; eight brands, etc.), and
2. choice set sizes may vary (i.e., some sets with two brands, some with four, some with eight, etc.).

The overarching design issues involve the types of alternatives and the types of effects mentioned in the introduction: (a) labelled vs. unlabelled, (b) generic vs. alternative-specific, and (c) own vs. cross effects.

5.2.1 Designs for MNL models

Let us first consider design strategies for IID models in general, and the multinomial logit (MNL) model in particular. To motivate the development we begin by linearising the MNL model in order to use intuition from the design of statistical experiments for linear models. The probability of choosing alternative a from a set of J total alternatives can be written as equations (5.1) or (5.2), equivalent to equation (3.24) in chapter 3, if the MNL model is a good approximation to the true, but unknown choice process:

$$P(a \mid a, b, \ldots, j) = \frac{\exp(V_a)}{[\exp(V_a) + \exp(V_b) + \cdots + \exp(V_j)]} \tag{5.1}$$

or,

$$P(a \mid a, b, \ldots, j) = \frac{\exp(V_a)}{\sum_j \exp(V_j)}. \tag{5.2}$$

Now, consider the result of forming the odds of choosing a over r (a reference alternative) and taking the logarithmic odds:

$$\frac{P(a \mid a, b, \ldots, j)}{P(r \mid a, b, \ldots j)} = \frac{\exp(V_a)}{\exp(V_r)} = \exp(V_a - V_r); \tag{5.3}$$

$$\log_e \left[\frac{P(a \mid a, b, \ldots, j)}{P(r \mid a, b, \ldots, j)} \right] = V_a - V_r. \tag{5.4}$$

The log of the odds of choosing a over r is an estimate of the utility difference of the two alternatives a and r. The word 'logit' is a contraction of the **log**arithmic **t**ransformation of an odds ratio. The utility value of one alternative must be set to some constant, typically zero, because only $J - 1$ of the utilities are identified. Thus, alternative r can be conveniently set to a utility of zero, which implies that the log odds of choosing a over r is a direct estimate of the utility of alternative a. Because r is the reference for all alternatives, the log odds of choosing any of the $J - 1$ alternatives relative to r is an estimate of the utility of each.

More generally, r is not a constant, but rather possesses attributes which vary over choice sets. In this case, if utility effects are generic, specifications (5.5a) and (5.5b) would define the utility expressions

$$V_a = \sum_k \beta_k X_{ka}, \tag{5.5a}$$

$$V_r = \sum_k \beta_k X_{kr}; \tag{5.5b}$$

and,

$$V_a - V_r = \sum_k \beta_k X_{ka} - \sum_k \beta_k X_{kr} = \sum_k \beta_k (X_{ka} - X_{kr}). \tag{5.6}$$

Thus, MNL models are *difference-in-attributes* models, characterised by a vector of generic parameters β_k. In turn, this implies that if the choice process of interest is well approximated by MNL and at least some attributes of all alternatives vary across choice sets, choice experiments will involve the manipulation of attribute differences, *not* absolute values of attributes.

Logically, however, if the reference alternative does not have attributes that vary, designs can involve absolute attribute levels rather than differences in levels. That is, if the reference alternative's utility is fixed (e.g., zero), $(V_{a\neq r} - V_r)$ is a constant, which is a linear transformation of the absolute levels. Linear transformations of variables affect only intercepts and not slopes in models such as MNL. Hence, if the reference alternative is constant, one can use standard design theory developed for linear models to design choice experiments based on the MNL model.

If the reference itself varies from consumer to consumer, but is constant in all sets faced by any particular individual, the same results hold. That is, if each consumer faces an orthogonal design matrix (or subset of that matrix) of attribute levels, and the reference for each consumer differs across consumers, but is constant within consumers, $(V_{a\neq r} - V_r)$ is a constant for each consumer. Thus, orthogonality within consumers is preserved.

To test the *generic* nature of the β_k for each attribute, a design must permit one to estimate alternative-specific effects, or β_{ka}, independently of one another and of the attributes of competing alternatives. That is, the test for generic parameters is the rejection of parameter *alternative-specificness*. This is accomplished by using the likelihood ratio test (equation (3.30) in chapter 3), testing if the log likelihood of the generic form, which constitutes a restriction on the parameters, is significantly worse than the log likelihood of the less-restricted, alternative-specific form. Ideally we would like such a test to be based on truly independent attribute effects to minimise the impact of shared covariances between attribute columns. This can be accomplished by designing choice experiments so that attribute levels (or differences) are orthogonal to one another both within and between alternatives.

If one is certain that MNL is appropriate and utility functions are generic, design economies are available. In particular, one need only design an initial set of P total alternatives (profiles) to create choice sets containing one or more additional alternatives, say *M* total, in any of the following ways:

1. Make $M - 1$ copies of the initial set of *P* total profiles, and place the *M* sets of profiles in *M* separate urns. Randomly select one of the *P* profiles from each of the *M* urns without replacement to construct a choice set of exactly *M* alternatives, ensuring that none of the *M* profiles in the set are the same. Continue this process until all *P* profiles in each urn have been assigned to *P* total choice sets of *M* alternatives.
2. Improve the statistical efficiency of the first design procedure, as well as enhancing the identification properties of the design, by creating *M* different, statistically equivalent designs. In this case, each urn contains a different design, which means that across the *M* urns the designs span *M* times the design space of the first option. As well, when one randomly draws profiles from the *M* urns to make the *P* total choice sets, one does not have to eliminate duplicate profiles from sets because all profiles are different.
3. Further improve design efficiency by first constructing the *P* total profiles and then constructing the *P* total choice sets by a method known as *shifting* (Bunch, Louviere and Anderson 1996; Huber and Zwerina 1996), in which

modular arithmetic is used to shift each combination of initial attribute levels by adding a constant that depends on the number of levels.

4. Make P initial profiles and construct all possible pairs of each. There will be exactly $P(P-1)/2$ pairs. The total number of pairs will increase geometrically with P. Thus, although consistent with MNL and generic utility functions, this approach becomes less feasible and desirable as P increases.

Each of the above design methods depends on satisfaction of the IID error assumption. If IID is violated, these design methods at best will yield biased estimates of an incorrect model, and at worst will yield results which are unreliable and invalid, inferences from which may be seriously misleading. For example, if the preferences of consumers are heterogeneous and the differences are not completely explained by the observed attributes of alternatives and/or the measured characteristics of consumers, the IID assumption may not be satisfied. The greater the heterogeneity in terms of any one or a combination of attributes (or alternatives), the more likely are model estimates to be incorrect and misleading.

The foregoing suggests that unless one is certain that the IID error assumption will be satisfied, it is probably unwise to use the simplistic design strategies described above. Many commercial experimental design software products implement these or similarly simplistic design strategies, hence, it is probably wise to learn as much about the properties of designs produced by such software as possible before blindly using them. Indeed, *it may be wise to consider design strategies that allow rigorous tests of the IID error assumption.* The latter always can be accomplished by designing experiments such that the attributes (or attribute level differences) of all alternatives are orthogonal to one another within and between alternatives. We will return to this topic in greater detail later in this chapter, but before doing so we need to introduce other experimental issues and details.

5.2.2 Designs for availability problems

Many problems involve sets of alternatives that vary in nature and composition. For example, in marketing, channels of distribution are used to transfer products and services from producers to consumers. Frequently, producers cannot choose all channels; hence, not all products are ubiquitously available. So, too, in transport: it is rare for commuters to have all transport modes available for their commute. Such problems naturally fall within the purview of *availability designs*.

Despite the logical appeal of availability designs, they grow in complexity rapidly as numbers of alternatives and/or attributes and levels increase. Consider the simplest case in which only brand names (labels) appear as choice alternatives, and no attributes are varied. If IID is satisfied, label-specific intercepts (i.e., overall label utilities) for $J-1$ alternatives can be estimated by designing experiments such that the presence and absence of each alternative is independent of the presence and absence of all other alternatives, and the probability of choosing an alternative is independent of the probability that it is available to be chosen.

Table 5.1a. *An example of a simple presence/absence design*

Set	United	Delta	Northwest	US Airways	Southwest
1	P	P	P	P	P
2	P	P	A	P	A
3	P	A	P	A	A
4	P	A	A	A	P
5	A	P	P	A	P
6	A	P	A	A	A
7	A	A	P	P	A
8	A	A	A	P	P

Note: P = present; A = absent.

There are several ways to design such experiments, but one of the simplest and easiest to understand is to treat each of the J labels as a two-level variable (present and absent). Louviere and Hensher (1983) and Louviere and Woodworth (1983) showed that if there are J total present/absent alternatives and MNL holds, a nearly optimally efficient strategy is to design the choice sets using a 2^J fractional factorial design. If one is sure that IID will be satisfied, one only need select the smallest orthogonal main effects fraction from the 2^J factorial, and use it to assign the labels to sets (i.e., 'present'). If IID may be violated, Anderson and Wiley (1992) show that a minimum strategy is to design the smallest orthogonal 2^J main effects design plus its *foldover* (a foldover is a mirror image of the original design; i.e., replace each 0 by 1, and each 1 by 0). More generally, rigorous tests of the IID assumption can be made by designing the experiment such that all main and two-way interactions between labels (the presence/absence columns in the design) can be estimated independently.

The latter strategy is based on the fact that the portion of the design subtended by each label's presence constitutes an orthogonal main effects design for the other $J - 1$ alternatives. Thus, given that a particular label is 'present' (say, label 'a'), the presence and absence of all other labels will be orthogonal and balanced, which allows the IID assumption to be tested by estimating the most general MNL model possible, known as the *mother logit* model (McFadden, Train and Tye 1978).

For example, consider the simple airline choice experiment in table 5.1a which involves only *labels* or airline names. One easily can verify that each airline appears equally often, and the presence/absence of each airline is independent of the presence/absence of other airlines. The former is verified by counting the number of 'Ps' in each column, which totals four for all airlines; the latter can be verified by tabulating the co-occurrence of presence/absence for each pair of airlines. Each airline pair has the pattern shown in table 5.1b. Table 5.1b is as a 2×2 contingency table, which reveals that the presence/absence of each pair of airlines is independent, in the classical sense of probabilistic independence. That is, if two events are probabilistically independent their joint probabilities should equal the product of their *marginals* (i.e., column totals and row totals), or in the present case the expected frequency = $(4 \times 4)/8 = 2$, which

Table 5.1b. *Presence/absence design details*

	Airline A	
Airline B	Present	Absent
Present	2	2
Absent	2	2

exactly obtains in table 5.1b. Similarly, the correlation of the co-occurrences is exactly zero. Thus, any pair of columns in the design is orthogonal. The properties of such a design are as follows:

- The marginals for each airline can be estimated independently of the marginals of every other airline.
- The marginal of each airline is the best estimate of the alternative-specific intercept or constant in the MNL model.

At this point we have sufficient background to understand the basics of an availability design and simple choice experiments. That is, it should now be obvious that there is a one-to-one correspondence between marginal and joint probabilities that are observed in choice experiments and terms in choice models. In fact, choice experiments are actually incomplete contingency tables, often very incomplete or sparse tables as we will see in later discussions of design issues. Those familiar with log-linear and logistic regression models applied to analyse contingency tables would be aware of this correspondence (e.g., Bishop, Feinberg and Holland 1975), and choice models have much in common with this literature. This naturally leads us to discuss different levels of aggregation of choice experiment data; that is, as we proceed from sample aggregate frequency to totally disaggregate discrete choices different types of effects can be estimated. However, it should be obvious that the basic effects discussed above will be the same at the mean at every aggregation level. Let us now consider the levels of aggregation and their interpretation.

5.2.3 Choice frequency aggregation

The simple airline presence/absence design above gives us an opportunity to discuss the effects of choice frequency aggregation.

Alternative-specific intercepts can be estimated from several data aggregation levels, and each will yield the same coefficients up to multiplication by a positive constant. That is, each set of estimates is exactly proportional to every other; hence, they differ only in scale. Each level of aggregation can best be appreciated by introducing notation for the choices. Let Y_{ijc} be the binary choice indicator ($=1$ if consumer i is observed choosing alternative j in choice set c, otherwise $= 0$). Then

- $\sum_{ic} Y_{ijc} = T_j$, or the total number of times the jth airline was chosen in all choice sets by subjects in the experiment;
- $\sum_i Y_{ijc} = T_{jc}$, or the total number of times the jth alternative was chosen in each choice set, summed over all subjects in the cth choice set;
- $\sum_c Y_{ijc} = T_{ic}$, or the total number of times the jth alternative was chosen by the ith subject, summed over all choice sets in which that subject participated;
- Y_{ijc}, or the choice observed for alternative j by the ith subject in choice set c.

Each of the above choice totals, or more generally, choice frequencies, will provide statistically identical estimates of the alternative-specific intercepts, insofar as all are exactly proportional to one another. The constants of proportionality are exactly equal to the ratio of the scale constants, and each scale constant is inversely related to the proportion of unexplained variation in choice (i.e., size of the random components). The more one aggregates data, the more one hides individual and choice set variation; hence, this will leave less unexplained variation. Thus, model estimates will increase with increasing levels of aggregation simply because one averages out lower-level sources of variation with aggregation. For a given model specification, model estimates from different levels of choice data aggregation will be equivalent once scale differences are taken into account.

Thus, data aggregation is a matter of (a) convenience and (b) the level and detail of explanation one wishes to achieve. In the case of the former, if one merely wishes to describe sample average trends in the data, a model estimated from sample aggregate choice frequencies may serve that purpose. In the case of the latter, to the degree that one wishes to introduce attributes to account for differences in choice behaviour at different levels of aggregation, one must disaggregate to that level which is most appropriate for explaining the data.

There is a final, but important, set of issues to do with aggregation of choice data. The higher one aggregates data, the more one runs the risk of missing or ignoring violations of the IID error assumption. Thus, it is particularly dangerous to aggregate data over subjects because consumers typically exhibit heterogeneous preferences, which in turn can lead to serious violations of the IID assumption. Similarly, it is naive and dangerous to assume that one can adequately model disaggregate choice data by simply including individual consumer characteristics in models. As discussed in chapter 6, the state-of-the-art recognises that the random components of different alternatives may exhibit non-constant variances, and alternatives may share common unobserved attributes, leading to non-zero off-diagonal covariances. Such IID violations must be considered in any application of choice models, and at a minimum, tests should be conducted to determine the nature and extent of the violations and the implied modelling steps needed to deal with them appropriately. We discuss the latter throughout chapters 6–9.

Aggregation is particularly problematic for choice experiment data because it may give the impression that one or at most a few *segment-level* models can be applied to predict choice behaviour. It is now well known that the method of sample enumeration

Table 5.2. *An example of a generic choice experiment*

	Option A			Option B		
Set	Fare	Service	Time	Fare	Service	Time
1	$1.20	5	10	$2.00	15	15
2	$1.20	5	20	$2.00	30	30
3	$1.20	15	10	$3.00	30	30
4	$1.20	15	20	$3.00	15	15
5	$2.20	5	10	$3.00	30	15
6	$2.20	5	20	$3.00	15	30
7	$2.20	15	10	$2.00	15	30
8	$2.20	15	20	$2.00	30	15

should be used to forecast choices from choice models because it avoids aggregation bias (see chapter 3). Failure to include attributes which operate at lower levels of disaggregation can lead to biased and misleading models, and in turn, possibly seriously flawed choice predictions.

5.3 General design principles for choice experiments

Having completed the preliminary discussion of concepts, we are now ready to attend to more general issues in the design of choice experiments. We are strongly influenced by many years of practical experience in designing and analysing choice experiments, which experience suggests that the simple, conditional MNL models are rarely appropriate for real choice problems. In particular, most real choice problems involve violations of the IID error assumption that leads to the simple MNL model. Thus, we focus on design strategies that allow one to estimate and test more general probabilistic discrete-choice models than the MNL model. Less risk-averse researchers may wish to consult other sources for advice on designs suitable for MNL models (e.g., Huber and Zwerina 1996; Kuhfeld, Tobias and Garrat 1994; Bunch, Louviere and Anderson 1996). Designs suitable only for MNL models usually are unable to detect IID violations, potentially resulting in large prediction errors and biased policy inferences in practice.

5.3.1 Unlabelled, generic alternatives

This type of experiment is the easiest to understand and conceptualise. The choice outcomes are purely generic in the sense that the *labels* attached to each option convey no information beyond that provided by their attributes. For example, in table 5.2 options are simply labelled 'A' and 'B'. Each option is described by three transport mode-related attributes, namely fare, service frequency and travel time.

As noted in chapter 4, all-pairs and random assignment of (a priori) designed profiles generally are inferior to statistically designed experiments. For the sake of example, let there be M total generic choice outcomes and A total attributes, each of which has exactly L levels. A general way to design choice experiments for this case is to combine all the attributes of all the choice outcomes into a collective factorial, and select the smallest main effects design from that factorial. That is, the collective design is an L^{MA} factorial, from which one selects the smallest, orthogonal main effects plan.

For example, if there are four choice outcomes, and each is described by nine four-level attributes, the collective factorial is a $4^{9\times4}$, or 4^{36}. The smallest possible main effects plan is determined by the total degrees of freedom required to estimate all implied main effects. That is, the total degrees of freedom are determined by summing the separate degrees of freedom in each main effect. Each main effect has exactly $L-1$ degrees of freedom ($=3$ in the present example). There are exactly thirty-six main effects (4×9 attributes); hence there is a total of 36×3, or 108 degrees of freedom.

Therefore, the smallest orthogonal main effects plan for this example requires 128 choice sets. Numbers of choice sets required for problems of various sizes are presented in table 5.3, which displays the smallest, orthogonal main effects plans. If one is willing to sacrifice some design orthogonality, the total number of choice sets usually can be reduced (e.g., Kuhfeld, Tobias and Garratt 1994), but any reduction is subject to the restriction that the minimum number of sets by number of choice alternatives must equal or exceed the total degrees of freedom to be estimated. In general, it is poor practice to use design minima because the smaller the quantity *number of sets × alternatives* relative to parameters to be estimated, the less statistical power. Unbalanced designs should also be avoided where possible because statistical power differs within attribute levels and/or between attributes, and artificial correlations with grand means or model intercepts are introduced. Unbalanced designs are those for which (a) attributes have unequal numbers of levels, and (b) the numbers of levels are not multiples of one another. For example, if three attributes have levels, respectively of 2, 3 and 4, the design properties will be unbalanced. If the three-level attribute can be reduced to two or increased to four levels, design properties will be improved. Consequently, designs in table 5.3 are balanced and based on powers of 2, which should suffice for many applications.

5.3.2 Specification issues for labelled alternatives

The design principles for unlabelled alternatives also apply to designs for labelled alternatives. The key difference so far as the outcomes are concerned is that the *label* or name of the alternative itself conveys information to decision makers. This matters in choice and other decision tasks because (a) subjects may use labels to infer missing (omitted) information, and (b) these inferences may be (and usually are) correlated with the random component. In the main, both these issues have been ignored by academics and practitioners, particularly in the large conjoint analysis literature, but they may have a very significant impact on model estimates and interpretation of results.

Table 5.3. *Details of multiple choice designs based on factorials*

No. of options	No. of attributes	No. of levels	Full factorial	Smallest design
2	4	2	2^8	16 sets
2	4	4	4^8	32 sets
2	8	2	2^{16}	32 sets
2	8	4	4^{16}	64 sets
2	16	2	2^{32}	64 sets
2	16	4	4^{32}	128 sets
4	4	2	2^{16}	32 sets
4	4	4	4^{16}	64 sets
4	8	2	2^{32}	64 sets
4	8	4	4^{32}	128 sets
4	16	2	2^{64}	128 sets
4	16	4	4^{64}	256 sets
8	4	2	2^{32}	64 sets
8	4	4	4^{32}	128 sets
8	8	2	2^{64}	128 sets
8	8	4	4^{64}	256 sets
8	16	2	2^{128}	256 sets
8	16	4	4^{128}	512 sets
16	4	2	2^{64}	128 sets
16	4	4	4^{64}	256 sets
16	8	2	2^{128}	256 sets
16	8	4	4^{128}	512 sets
16	16	2	2^{256}	512 sets
16	16	4	4^{256}	1024 sets

For example, it is common practice to use brand names or similar labels as levels of the attribute 'brand name' in unlabelled choice (and conjoint analysis) tasks in marketing. Unfortunately, however, consumers can (and often do) use these monikers to infer omitted information about choice alternatives, and the omitted information may be correlated with the random component. Likely manifestations of this form of omitted variables bias are (a) significantly different alternative-specific attribute effects for some alternatives and/or (b) violations of the IIA property of simple MNL models. The latter two effects arise owing to differences in (i) random component variances among the choice alternatives, (ii) random component covariances among the choice alternatives and/or (iii) preferences among consumers. The former may be a consequence of the latter, but in general does not have to be.

This form of omitted variables bias can be quite serious, and is frequently misinterpreted by naive analysts to imply that there are significant differences in the sensitivity of consumers to various attributes, price often being a prime contender. For example, seemingly significant differences in price effects will occur to the extent that consumers associate good or bad omitted variables with brands. That is, *good* inferences lead to apparently lower price sensitivity, whereas *bad* inferences lead to seemingly higher price sensitivity. Unfortunately, such apparent effects are driven by failure to include in the task all the relevant information on which consumers base their choices. Hence, models estimated from such tasks will be of limited value for future forecasting if the covariance structure of the omitted variables changes. Such changes should be slower in established, mature product markets, but may be rapid in new and emerging markets.

The latter phenomenon is a form of the so-called *Lucas effect* in economics, but also noted by Rushton (1969) and Louviere (1988b) in geography and transport. That is, models which fail to capture how consumer preferences or choice processes change in response to changes in producer actions are merely descriptions of the behaviour of the recent past, devoid of theoretical or empirical insights about future dynamics. In other words, models derived from observations of consumer responses to a particular sample of past producer actions are incorrect by definition, and if one uses them to formulate and implement policy, successful policies will change the empirical covariance structure of the choices that consumers face. In turn, the latter manifests itself as a change in one or more model parameters, rendering a previously estimated model unsuitable for further prediction.

In the case of choice experiments, such effects can be minimised by spending as much time as possible in advance of the design of experiments and field work to understand the choice problem faced by consumers as thoroughly as possible. The latter include not only identifying the attributes and appropriate levels, but also gaining insights into how consumers make choices, the role of experiences and expectations and individual differences. Such insights rarely can be gained by sitting in one's office speculating about the behaviour of real consumers. Nor can they be gained by waiting for data from scanner panels or other sources to be supplied, and formulating models based on data collected by others for purposes other than that explicitly intended by the researcher. Statistical and econometric ability is no substitute for theory, thinking, observation and just plain hard, empirical detective work. Complex models that 'demonstrate' one's statistical and/or mathematical superiority are not 'better' models. Rather, better models come from real understanding of the behaviour of interest and its antecedent links, which leads to significant insights into behaviour *before* parameter estimation. In turn, this leads to informed and well-designed experiments or data-collection efforts that produce accurate and valid empirical insights about choice processes.

5.3.3 Statistical properties of labelled choice experiments

As previously mentioned, two statistical properties are of interest in labelled and unlabelled choice experiments, namely identification and precision. Recall that the former refers to the type(s) of utility and choice process specifications that can be estimated, and the latter refers to the statistical efficiency of parameters estimated from the experiment conditional on a maintained specification. Unfortunately, these two properties are not independent, and precision also depends on sample size, whatever the maintained specification.

Specification is entirely under the researcher's control. That is, whatever form of choice process and associated utility function, in principle there is a way to design a choice experiment to estimate all implied free parameters. In practice, an experiment may be too large for practical application, but for now we assume that an experiment can be designed and implemented that is consistent with a particular maintained specification. Thus, the real issue is precision, which bears on the ability of an experiment to reject the null hypothesis for a given parameter vector. For a fixed sample size, precision will be a function of the number of non-zero attribute level differences (continuous attributes) or contrasts (qualitative attributes). In general, the fewer non-zero differences or contrasts, the more precise confidence intervals will be.

Because MNL model parameters are associated with differences or contrasts between attribute levels, zero differences or contrasts in attribute levels provide no statistical information about choice because consumers do not have to compare or trade-off information about that attribute to make a choice. Thus, all else equal, the more zero attribute level differences in a choice set, the fewer attributes that can influence choice. Thus, from a design perspective, we seek to develop designs that minimise the number of zero attribute differences.

In practice, however, this is a very difficult objective to achieve when there are more than two choice alternatives. One approach is to develop what are termed *difference designs* (Louviere and Woodworth 1983). Difference designs require one to begin with an initial set of profiles, designed or otherwise. Let A total attributes describe this original set of profiles. An additional M choice alternatives can be designed by using an orthogonal difference design based on the L^{MA} factorial, where L is the number of levels, assumed constant for all attributes. Thus, if an original set of profiles is created from an orthogonal fraction of a 4^A factorial, an additional $M \times A$ difference columns are required to generate the other competing alternatives.

For example, let all attributes be quantitative and let $L = 4$. Let the levels of each attribute in the difference design be $-3, -1, +1$ and $+3$; and let the levels of a certain attribute in the original profiles, say price, be measured in appropriate units (e.g., dollars). Then price levels in the original design are operated on by a price difference column in the difference design associated with a second such that its price attribute takes on levels $\pm 1, 3$ dollars relative to the price levels in the original profiles. Thus, if the original price levels are $5, $7, $9 and $11, the price levels of the second alternative would be $5 \pm 1, 3; 7 \pm 1, 3; 9 \pm 1, 3$ and $11 \pm 1, 3$ (i.e., $2, $4, $6, $8, $10, $12, $14). Although the original profiles have four levels, the designed competing profiles all will have seven levels. The resulting design will be orthogonal in its attribute level differences, but will not be orthogonal in the absolute attribute levels.

All effects will be defined as attribute level differences relative to the original profile base. Thus, to estimate non-linear attribute difference main effects and/or interaction effects, a difference design must accommodate them. One advantage of difference designs relative to the designs previously proposed for unlabelled alternatives is that the design matrix requires A fewer columns because all differences are relative to the original profile columns. A second potential advantage of difference designs is that the attribute columns in the original profile design need not be orthogonal; instead, only the differences must be orthogonal. Thus, one can design the original (base) profiles to reflect whatever correlations apply to the real market of interest if this is a desirable feature of an experiment.

A second design strategy is one previously discussed with reference to unlabelled experiments (section 5.3.1): all attribute columns of all alternatives are treated as a collective factorial, and a constant, reference alternative is added to each choice set. That is, given M options, each described by A attributes with exactly L levels, the collective factorial is an L^{MA}. One selects the smallest orthogonal design from this factorial that satisfies the desired identification properties. Each choice set is a row in this fractional factorial design matrix to which a constant is added. The 'constant' can be a fixed attribute profile or an option such as 'no choice'. As previously noted, this involves subtraction of a constant from each attribute column, which leaves design orthogonality unaffected.

The preceding design strategy is generally straightforward to implement and based on well-known design principles for linear models. It also makes sense in many experimental contexts to use a constant option such as 'no choice', which adds realism and value to experiments because it allows estimation of true demand models, rather than conditional demand (i.e., share) models. This strategy does have limitations: (a) a significant number of between-alternative attribute differences will be zero, (b) some choice sets will contain dominant alternatives, and (c) a relatively large number of choice sets will be required. Regarding the first and second limitations, Huber and Zwerina (1996) suggest ways to interchange columns and/or swap attribute levels to reduce these problems, a procedure that we have long used in practice. That is, one can rotate the order of columns in a design and/or reorder the levels in one or more columns to eliminate or at least reduce dominance and zero attribute level differences. The second limitation also may be less serious if a constant alternative such as 'no choice' is used. Finally, choice set numbers often can be reduced by computerised optimal design methods that produce some (usually, small) inter-attribute correlations (Kuhfeld, Tobias and Garratt 1994), subject to the earlier caveat that design minima rarely can be considered wise empirical practice.

Table 5.4 illustrates a design for two labelled alternatives, each described by three, two-level attributes based on an orthogonal main effects 2^{6-3} fraction of the 2^6 factorial. As explained above, the three attributes of commuter train and city bus are treated as a collective 2^6 factorial, and the smallest orthogonal main effects design is used to create the choice alternatives and the choice sets. Each row in the design is a choice set. Inspection of attribute differences (train minus bus) reveals two zero differences for the frequency of service attribute. Thus, this design is not optimally efficient. Also, the attribute differences are not orthogonal because the correlation between service frequency and travel time = 0.474. The other correlations are zero.

Table 5.5a is of the same design as table 5.4, to which the constant alternative 'I'd choose some other mode of travel to work' has been added. Table 5.5b is of the same design as table 5.5a, but with a constant difference subtracted from each column. The constant alternative used in this example differs for each respondent, hence, it

Table 5.4. *Example of a labelled design and resulting attribute differences*

	Commuter train			City bus			Attribute differences		
Set	1-way	Freq.	Time	1-way	Freq.	Time	1-way	Freq.	Time
1	$1.20	5	10	$2.00	15	15	−0.80	−10	−5
2	$1.20	5	20	$2.00	30	30	−0.80	−25	−10
3	$1.20	15	10	$3.00	30	30	−1.80	−15	−20
4	$1.20	15	20	$3.00	15	15	−1.80	0	+5
5	$2.20	5	10	$3.00	30	15	−0.80	−25	−5
6	$2.20	5	20	$3.00	15	30	−0.80	−10	+5
7	$2.20	15	10	$2.00	15	30	+0.20	0	−5
8	$2.20	15	20	$2.00	30	15	+0.20	−15	−10

Table 5.5a. *A labelled experiment with constant third option*

Commuter train			City bus			
1-way	Freq.	Time	1-way	Freq.	Time	Option
$1.20	5	10	$2.00	15	15	Choose another mode
$1.20	5	20	$2.00	30	30	of travel to work
$1.20	15	10	$3.00	30	30	
$1.20	15	20	$3.00	15	15	
$2.20	5	10	$3.00	30	15	
$2.20	5	20	$3.00	15	30	
$2.20	15	10	$2.00	15	30	
$2.20	15	20	$2.00	30	15	

Table 5.5b. *Treatment of constant option in table 5.5a*

Commuter train			City bus			
1-way	Freq.	Time	1-way	Freq.	Time	Attribute differences
$2.20	5	20	$2.00	30	15	All columns have a
$1.20	5	20	$3.00	15	15	constant difference
$2.20	15	10	$3.00	30	15	subtracted (e.g., k).
$2.20	15	20	$2.00	15	15	Thus, difference =
$1.20	15	20	$3.00	15	30	column − k.
$2.20	5	10	$2.00	15	30	
$1.20	5	10	$2.00	30	30	
$1.20	15	10	$3.00	30	30	

Table 5.6. *Attribute level differences resulting from random design*

	Commuter train			City bus			Attribute differences		
Set	1-way	Freq.	Time	1-way	Freq.	Time	1-way	Freq.	Time
1	$1.20	5	10	$3.00	15	30	−1.80	−10	−20
2	$1.20	5	20	$2.00	15	30	−0.80	−10	−10
3	$1.20	15	10	$3.00	30	15	−1.80	−15	−5
4	$1.20	15	20	$2.00	30	15	−0.80	−15	−55
5	$2.20	5	10	$2.00	15	15	+0.20	−10	−5
6	$2.20	5	20	$3.00	15	15	−0.80	−10	+5
7	$2.20	15	10	$2.00	30	30	+0.20	−15	−20
8	$2.20	15	20	$3.00	30	30	−0.80	−15	−10

represents a distribution instead of a single, fixed alternative. In real applications, one must observe (i.e., measure) the attributes of the travel options faced by each respondent, and include these in the estimation data set. This also illustrates why many real applications will require one to include additional, non-experimental choice information in model estimation. The present example requires one to disaggregate the choice data to the level of (subjects × alternative × choice set) and each respondent's constant options must be included in the model estimation as a choice option. Predictions must be based on the method of sample enumeration.

Consider using random assignment to construct a design as discussed earlier in this chapter. That is, use separate designs to make profiles for train and bus, put the bus and train profiles in different urns and generate pairs by randomly selecting a profile from each urn without replacement, as illustrated in table 5.6. Interestingly, this design is statistically more efficient than the design in table 5.5a. That is, the correlation between the service frequency and travel time differences is 0.16, about a third of that in the table 5.5a design. As before, correlations between the other attribute difference columns are zero. Thus, *a randomly generated design can be more efficient than an orthogonal design, but this result need not hold in general, and in our experience, is not common.*

5.4 Availability designs for labelled alternatives

Thus far our discussion has dealt with designs that generate choice sets of fixed size; i.e., sets in which the number of competing alternatives is constant. However, there are many applications that involve labelled alternatives for which variable set size designs are appropriate. The design problem in this section differs from the previous introduction to availability designs due to the additional complication that the alternatives also can differ in 'their attributes' when 'present' (or available). These design problems arise when choice options are characterised by differential 'availability' of options, the simplest class of which were previously introduced. Some problems to which such designs apply include:

- *Out of stock.* How do supply interruptions or difficulties affect choices?
- *Closures or service interruptions.* How do choices change if a bridge collapses or a road to a ski area is closed owing to an avalanche or a rock slide?
- *New product introductions.* How do choices change in response to new entrants that may or may not be introduced?
- *Retention/switching.* How do choices change in response to systematic changes in availability?

There are a number of ways to create availability designs. We will limit our discussion to a few basic approaches; a more detailed discussion of these and other design methods can be found in Lazari and Anderson (1994) and Anderson and Wiley (1992). There are two general types of problem: (a) all alternatives vary in availability, and (b) some alternatives are fixed (i.e., always available), while the availability of others varies. There are also two levels of design complexity: (i) availability is the only aspect of alternatives that varies, or (ii) when some alternatives are available, their attributes also vary.

5.4.1   More complex availability designs

Recall the simple case in which presence/absence of options varies, but no attributes vary. In this case designs can be created by treating alternatives as two-level factors (i.e., present/absent), and selecting orthogonal fractions from the 2^J factorial. It was mentioned previously that if the IID error assumption does not hold, different design strategies are needed, such as combining an orthogonal main effects design with its exact foldover; or designs in which all main and two-way interaction effects are orthogonal. A disadvantage of basing availability designs on 2^J fractions is that average choice set size $= J/2$, so choice set size increases rapidly with J. Now consider table 5.7a, which contains an orthogonal main effects design plus its foldover (Rhagavrao and Wiley 1994). Choice options are numbered (1 to 6) and presence/absence represented by P/A.

Alternatives which are *present* are marked P in table 5.7a. The subdesign that applies when alternative 1 is 'present' is in table 5.7b. Such orthogonal subdesigns are nested under the 'presence' and 'absence' of each other option. For example, the subdesign spanned by alternatives 2 to 6 is orthogonal and balanced, which allows us to independently estimate the cross-effects of these options $(2, 3, \ldots, 6)$ on choice 1, which will capture violations of the IID assumption that are related to attribute variations.

We did not previously mention, but it is worth noting that such availability experiments are excellent vehicles to study and model switching behaviour. Indeed, availability designs offer significant advantages for modelling switching behaviour over scanner and other sources of panel choice data: option presence/absence is orthogonal

Table 5.7a. *Availability design plus foldover*

Set	Option 1	Option 2	Option 3	Option 4	Option 5	Option 6
Original 2^{6-3} orthogonal main effects design						
1	P	A	P	A	P	A
2	P	A	A	A	A	P
3	P	P	P	P	A	P
4	P	P	A	P	P	A
5	A	A	P	P	P	P
6	A	A	A	P	A	A
7	A	P	P	A	A	A
8	A	P	A	A	P	P
Foldover of original 2^{6-3} orthogonal main effects design						
9	A	P	A	P	A	P
10	A	P	P	P	P	A
11	A	A	A	A	P	A
12	A	A	P	A	A	P
13	P	P	A	A	A	A
14	P	P	P	A	P	P
15	P	A	A	P	P	P
16	P	A	P	P	A	A

Table 5.7b. *Subdesign for alternative 1 'present'*

Set	Option 1	Option 2	Option 3	Option 4	Option 5	Option 6
Subdesign of original 2^{6-3} orthogonal main effects design						
1	P	A	P	A	P	A
2	P	A	A	A	A	P
3	P	P	P	P	A	P
4	P	P	A	P	P	A
5	P	P	A	A	A	A
6	P	P	P	A	P	P
7	P	A	A	P	P	P
8	P	A	P	P	A	A

and balanced; hence, all options occur equally often. Thus, switching is independent of co-occurrence and switching probabilities are independent of the probability that options are available.

5.4.2 Alternatives vary in availability and attributes

The next level of complexity involves nesting a design to vary the attributes of the alternatives under the level 'present' in the availability design. We consider two design approaches for this problem: (a) an orthogonal fraction of a 2^J design is used to design presence/absence conditions, and designed attribute profiles are randomly assigned without replacement to make choice sets in each condition; (b) a fraction of a 2^J design is used to design presence/absence conditions, and a second orthogonal fraction of the collective factorial of the attributes of the alternatives 'present' is used to make the choice sets in each presence/absence condition.

These two design strategies are illustrated in table 5.8 for alternatives A to E, each described by three two-level attributes. Hence, profiles for each alternative can be designed as the entire 2^3 or $1/2$ of the 2^3 (i.e., 2^{3-1}). We use the latter to illustrate the process to save space, and instead of using random assignment, a Latin square is used to rotate profiles across alternatives within and between sets because there are as many alternatives as profiles. The latter ensures that each alternative receives the same profiles an equal number of times and no profile is combined with itself. In the interest of space, we omit the foldover conditions, which add another thirty-two choice sets.

Table 5.9 illustrates an attribute nested availability design based on a fraction of the 2^J factorial to design availability conditions, and a second fraction of the $2^{3 \times J}$ to design attribute profiles and choice sets in each condition (J_c is the number of alternatives in the cth condition). To save space, the design involves three alternatives (A, B, C), each with three two-level attributes. The availability conditions are based on the 2^{3-1}, which yields four conditions, coded as follows for options A, B, C: 000, 011, 101, 110 (0 = absent, 1 = present); hence one condition can be eliminated (= all options absent). Although the availability conditions design involves all pairs, this is coincidental and due solely to the use of this particular fractional design.

A large number of variations on this design theme are possible, but it should be noted that such designs may be very large. The key properties of these designs of interest in choice modelling are as follows:

- Presence/absence of alternatives is orthogonal and balanced.
- Attributes of alternatives are nested within 'presence' levels.
- Non-IID error models require an orthogonal availability and/or nested attribute availability sub-design that spans the space of the 'presence' levels of each alternative.
- Certain non-IID models require attribute orthogonality within and between alternatives as well as within and between availability conditions.

The latter properties generally lead to very large designs as the number of alternatives and/or the number of attributes (levels) increases.

Chapter 7 deals with designs for complex non-IID models. Generally, such designs require explicit assumptions to be made about the nature of the random error components, although one can relax the assumptions by constructing ever more general designs. The appendix to this chapter contains several example designs for common multiple choice problems which allow IID violations to be treated in what are now routine ways, by relaxing assumptions about the variance or covariance structures of the random components.

Table 5.8. *Orthogonal fraction of 2^J design used for nesting conditions*

Set no.	A	B	C	D	E
Condition 1					
1	000	A	011	A	101
2	011	A	101	A	110
3	101	A	110	A	000
4	110	A	000	A	011
Condition 2					
5	110	A	A	A	A
6	000	A	A	A	A
7	011	A	A	A	A
8	101	A	A	A	A
Condition 3					
9	011	101	110	000	A
10	101	110	000	011	A
11	110	000	011	101	A
12	000	011	101	110	A
Condition 4					
13	101	110	A	000	011
14	110	000	A	011	101
15	000	011	A	101	110
16	011	101	A	110	000
Condition 5					
17	A	A	110	000	011
18	A	A	000	011	101
19	A	A	011	101	110
20	A	A	101	110	000
Condition 6					
21	A	A	A	000	A
22	A	A	A	011	A
23	A	A	A	101	A
24	A	A	A	110	A
Condition 7					
25	A	000	011	A	A
26	A	011	101	A	A
27	A	101	110	A	A
28	A	110	000	A	A
Condition 8					
29	A	011	A	A	101
30	A	101	A	A	110
31	A	110	A	A	000
32	A	000	A	A	011

Table 5.9. *Attribute availability*
nesting based on fractional design

Set no.	A	B	C
Condition 1 (011): based on the			
smallest fraction of the 2^6			
1	A	000	000
2	A	001	011
3	A	010	111
4	A	011	100
5	A	100	101
6	A	101	110
7	A	110	010
8	A	111	001
Condition 2 (101): based on the			
smallest fraction of the 2^6			
9	000	A	000
10	001	A	011
11	010	A	111
12	011	A	100
13	100	A	101
14	101	A	110
15	110	A	010
16	111	A	001
Condition 3 (110): based on the			
smallest fraction of the 2^6			
17	000	000	A
18	001	011	A
19	010	111	A
20	011	100	A
21	100	101	A
22	101	110	A
23	110	010	A
24	111	001	A

Note: A in table body = absent.

Appendix A5   Some popular choice designs

In what follows we use capital letters to designate attributes (e.g., A, B, ...) and design codes to denote levels of those attributes (e.g., 0, 1, ...) to illustrate several different ways to design choice experiments. The end section of the appendix contains several concrete design examples using attributes and levels of light rail transit systems. For consistency, all examples use six two-level attributes to illustrate design options. We use an orthogonal fraction of the 2^6 to illustrate the options in which attributes are denoted by uppercase letters, and attribute levels by 0s and 1s.

			Attributes			
Profiles	A	B	C	D	E	F
1	0	0	0	0	0	0
2	0	0	1	0	1	1
3	0	1	0	1	1	1
4	0	1	1	1	0	0
5	1	0	0	1	1	0
6	1	0	1	1	0	1
7	1	1	0	0	0	1
8	1	1	1	0	1	0

The above design creates eight attribute profiles described by six two-level attributes. We now illustrate several ways to design choice experiments based on these profiles.

1. Randomly pair the 8 profiles without replacement or duplication to create eight pairs or choice sets:

Profile	Order 1	Profile	Order 2	Differences in levels
3	0 1 0 1 1 1	6	1 0 1 1 0 1	−1 1 −1 0 1 0
5	1 0 0 1 1 0	2	0 0 1 0 1 1	1 0 −1 1 0 −1
2	0 0 1 0 1 1	7	1 1 0 0 0 1	−1 −1 1 0 1 0
7	1 1 0 0 0 1	4	0 1 1 1 0 0	1 0 −1 −1 0 1
1	0 0 0 0 0 0	3	0 1 0 1 1 1	0 −1 0 −1 −1 −1
6	1 0 1 1 0 1	1	0 0 0 0 0 0	1 0 1 1 0 −1
8	1 1 1 0 1 0	5	1 0 0 1 1 0	0 1 1 −1 0 0
4	0 1 1 1 0 0	8	1 1 1 0 1 0	−1 0 0 1 1 0

2. Randomly pair the eight profiles and a foldover or a statistically equivalent design without replacement to create eight choice sets:

Set no.	Random original profiles	Random foldover profiles	Differences in attribute levels
1	0 1 0 1 1 1	6 1 0 1 0 0 0	−1 1 −1 1 1 1
2	1 0 0 1 1 0	2 0 0 1 1 1 0	1 0 −1 0 0 0
3	0 0 1 0 1 1	7 1 1 0 1 0 0	−1 −1 1 −1 1 1
4	1 1 0 0 0 1	4 0 1 1 0 0 1	1 0 −1 0 0 0
5	0 0 0 0 0 0	3 0 1 0 0 1 0	0 −1 0 0 −1 0
6	1 0 1 1 0 1	1 0 0 0 1 0 1	1 0 1 0 0 0
7	1 1 1 0 1 0	5 1 0 0 0 1 1	0 1 1 0 0 −1
8	0 1 1 1 0 0	8 1 1 1 1 1 1	−1 0 0 0 −1 −1

3. Pair each of the eight profiles with their exact foldover to create eight choice sets:

Set no.	Original profiles	Foldover profiles	Differences in attribute levels
1	0 0 0 0 0 0	1 1 1 1 1 1	−1 −1 −1 −1 −1 −1
2	0 0 1 0 1 1	1 1 0 1 0 0	−1 −1　1 −1　1　1
3	0 1 0 1 1 1	1 0 1 0 0 0	−1　1 −1　1　1　1
4	0 1 1 1 0 0	1 0 0 0 1 1	−1　1　1　1 −1 −1
5	1 0 0 1 1 0	0 1 1 0 0 1	1 −1 −1　1　1 −1
6	1 0 1 1 0 1	0 1 0 0 1 0	1 −1　1　1 −1　1
7	1 1 0 0 0 1	0 0 1 1 1 0	1　1 −1 −1 −1　1
8	1 1 1 0 1 0	0 0 0 1 0 1	1　1　1 −1　1 −1

4. Treat both left- and right-hand attributes as 12 total, and construct the smallest orthogonal main effects design of the 2^{12-8} factorial to make the choice sets:

Choice set no.	1st 6 Atts A B C D E F	2nd 6 Atts A B C D E F	Attribute diffs A B C D E F
1	0 0 0 0 0 0	0 0 0 0 0 0	0　0　0　0　0　0
2	0 0 0 1 0 1	0 1 1 1 0 1	0 −1 −1　0　0　0
3	0 0 1 0 0 1	1 0 1 1 1 0	−1　0　0 −1 −1　1
4	0 0 1 1 0 0	1 1 0 0 1 1	−1 −1　1　1 −1 −1
5	0 1 0 0 1 0	0 1 1 0 1 1	0　0 −1　0　0 −1
6	0 1 0 1 1 1	0 0 0 1 1 0	0　1　0　0　0　1
7	0 1 1 0 1 1	1 1 0 1 0 1	−1　0　1 −1　1　0
8	0 1 1 1 1 0	1 0 1 0 0 0	−1　1　0　1　1　0
9	1 0 0 0 1 0	1 0 1 1 0 1	0　0 −1 −1　1 −1
10	1 0 0 1 1 1	1 1 0 0 0 0	0 −1　0　1　1　1
11	1 0 1 0 1 1	0 0 0 0 1 1	1　0　1　0　0　0
12	1 0 1 1 1 0	0 1 1 1 1 0	1 −1　0　0　0　0
13	1 1 0 0 0 0	1 1 0 1 1 0	0　0　0 −1 −1　0
14	1 1 0 1 0 1	1 0 1 0 1 1	0　1 −1　1 −1　0
15	1 1 1 0 0 1	0 1 1 0 0 0	1　0　0　0　0　1
16	1 1 1 1 0 0	0 0 0 1 0 1	1　1 −1　0　0 −1

We use LRT (light rail transit) systems to illustrate design options for profiles (alternatives). The attributes and levels in the table below are pedagogically convenient but do not necessarily represent realistic values. Once profiles are generated, the above design strategies can be used to make choice designs based on sequential or simultaneous design methods.

Cleanliness (Clean)	Yes/no
Service frequency (Serv. frq)	Every 15/30 mins
Nearest home stop (Stop H)	3, 16 blocks
Nearest work stop (Stop W)	3, 16 blocks
Seat available (Seat)	Yes/no
Air conditioned (A/C)	Yes/no
Safety patrols (Patrols)	Yes/no
Fare × trip length	Short trips ($1.29/$1.59); long trips ($1.79/$2.09)

Factorial combination of these attributes and levels results in $4 \times 2^7 (= 512)$ profiles (i.e., LRT 'systems'), involving ten main effects and forty-two two-way interactions. Generally one wants designs with high ratios of observations to parameters. In the present case the smallest orthogonal design that can estimate all main and two-way interaction effects requires sixty-four profiles. The latter is a large number of profiles for consumers to evaluate, but may be feasible if sufficient incentives are offered to respondents.

For example, recent research (Brazell and Louviere 1997; Johnson and Orme 1996) suggests that at least twenty and perhaps more than forty choice sets may be feasible in some choice experiments. As well, Brazell and Louviere found that increasing the number of choice sets affects reliability instead of validity. Swait and Adamowicz (1996) studied the impact of choice task complexity and cumulative cognitive burden on respondent taste parameters in choice tasks of the type being discussed. Their results also support the contention that the number of choice sets affects reliability; however, on a cautionary note, their results also indicate that there may exist an optimal level of complexity and an optimal number of repeated choices that may be elicited from respondents. Thus, although the optimum number of sets still remains unknown, it is likely that it may be greater than some now believe. Note also that other than the cited papers, there is virtually no research on this subject. So, if one believes that sixty-four profiles are too many for consumers to evaluate, one may wish to consider these options instead:

1. The smallest orthogonal main effects fraction for the LRT example produces sixteen profiles, from which ten main effects and an intercept are estimated, a high ratio of estimates to data points. If significant interactions are omitted, the estimates of the main effects will be biased, and the nature and magnitude of this bias cannot be determined.

2. The smallest orthogonal main effects design can be folded over to make another sixteen profiles, or a total of thirty-two, from which ten main effects and an intercept can be estimated. This design protects main effects from unobserved and significant linear × linear 2-way interactions. We noted earlier that most model variance is explained by main effects, the next largest proportion by two-way interactions, the next by three-way interactions, etc. Thus, orthogonalising the linear × linear two-way interactions protects them against the most likely

source of bias, although it leaves them open to bias from other omitted significant higher-order interactions.

3. If the likely two-way interactions involve a key attribute such as fare × trip-length (FTL), these interactions can be estimated by combining each FTL level (4) with a main effects design for the other seven attributes, such as 2^{7-4}, which creates eight profiles or a total of thirty-two profiles across all FTL levels. This design strategy permits one to estimate all FTL interactions with other attributes (ten main effects + twenty-one interactions) independently, but the model is saturated. Other main effects are not protected from unobserved and significant two-way and higher order interactions, hence will be biased if other omitted two-way or higher-order interactions are significant.

Let us now illustrate two of the foregoing possibilities. The table below contains sixteen LRT profiles. These profiles can be copied and placed in two or more 'urns' and pairs, triples, M-tuples, etc., can be drawn at random without replacement to make sixteen choice sets of pairs, triples, M-tuples etc. Statistically equivalent sets of sixteen profiles can be made by simply reversing the labels on the codes (e.g., 0 = yes and 1 = no or vice versa) systematically to create different sets of sixteen profiles. One also can rotate the two-level attribute columns to create different profiles. Finally, more statistically equivalent profiles can be generated by creating the foldover because the foldover of each statistically equivalent design is also statistically equivalent. Thus, systematic rotation of columns or swapping/reversing levels can be used to create statistically equivalent designs, which in turn, can be folded over to make yet more equivalent designs that can be used to make choice alternatives. We can use an orthogonal main effects design to construct sixteen profiles as shown in the following table.

Profile	Fare × trip length	Clean	Serv. frq.	Stop H	Stop W	Seat	A/C	Patrols
1	0 = sht @$1.29	0 = No	0 = 15	0 = 16 b	0 = 16 b	0 = Yes	0 = Yes	0 = Yes
2	0 = sht @$1.29	0 = No	1 = 30	0 = 16 b	1 = 3 b	1 = No	0 = Yes	1 = No
3	0 = sht @$1.29	1 = Yes	0 = 15	1 = 3 b	0 = 16 b	1 = No	1 = No	0 = Yes
4	0 = sht @$1.29	1 = Yes	1 = 30	1 = 3 b	1 = 3 b	0 = Yes	1 = No	1 = No
5	1 = sht @$1.59	0 = No	0 = 15	0 = 16 b	1 = 3 b	0 = Yes	1 = No	0 = Yes
6	1 = sht @$1.59	0 = No	1 = 30	0 = 16 b	0 = 16 b	1 = No	1 = No	1 = No
7	1 = sht @$1.59	1 = Yes	0 = 15	1 = 3 b	1 = 3 b	1 = No	0 = Yes	0 = Yes
8	1 = sht @$1.59	1 = Yes	1 = 30	1 = 3 b	0 = 16 b	0 = Yes	0 = Yes	1 = No
9	2 = lon @$1.79	0 = No	0 = 15	1 = 3 b	0 = 16 b	1 = No	0 = Yes	1 = No
10	2 = lon @$1.79	0 = No	1 = 30	1 = 3 b	1 = 3 b	0 = Yes	0 = Yes	0 = Yes
11	2 = lon @$1.79	1 = Yes	0 = 15	0 = 16 b	0 = 16 b	0 = Yes	1 = No	1 = No
12	2 = lon @$1.79	1 = Yes	1 = 30	0 = 16 b	1 = 3 b	1 = No	1 = No	0 = Yes
13	3 = lon @$2.09	0 = No	0 = 15	1 = 3 b	1 = 3 b	1 = No	1 = No	1 = No
14	3 = lon @$2.09	0 = No	1 = 30	1 = 3 b	0 = 16 b	0 = Yes	1 = No	0 = Yes
15	3 = lon @$2.09	1 = Yes	0 = 15	0 = 16 b	1 = 3 b	0 = Yes	0 = Yes	1 = No
16	3 = lon @$2.09	1 = Yes	1 = 30	0 = 16 b	0 = 16 b	1 = No	0 = Yes	0 = Yes

The final example illustrates one way to create a design that can estimate all two-way interactions with one of the attributes. In the example below we use the four-level fare × trip length (FTL) attribute as the one with which two-way interactions with all other attributes are of interest. A design can be constructed in the following way: (a) use the smallest orthogonal main effects design (i.e., the 2^{7-4}) to make eight descriptions of the other seven attributes, and then (b) combine the profiles with each of the four levels of FTL to make thirty-two total profiles. This construction method insures that each of the FTL levels contains an orthogonal array representing the main effects of the other seven attributes. Hence, each level of FTL is completely crossed with the same main effects design for the other attributes, ensuring that each two-way interaction with FTL can be estimated. The final design is shown below.

Profile	Fare × trip length	Clean	Serv. frq.	Stop H	Stop W	Seat	A/C	Patrols
1	0 = sht @$1.29	0 = 3 b	0 = No	0 = 15	0 = Yes	0 = 16 b	0 = Yes	0 = Yes
2	0 = sht @$1.29	0 = 3 b	0 = No	1 = 30	0 = Yes	1 = 3 b	1 = No	1 = No
3	0 = sht @$1.29	0 = 3 b	1 = Yes	0 = 15	1 = No	0 = 16 b	1 = No	1 = No
4	0 = sht @$1.29	0 = 3 b	1 = Yes	1 = 30	1 = No	1 = 3 b	0 = Yes	0 = Yes
5	0 = sht @$1.29	1 = 16 b	0 = No	0 = 15	1 = No	1 = 3 b	0 = Yes	1 = No
6	0 = sht @$1.29	1 = 16 b	0 = No	1 = 30	1 = No	0 = 16 b	1 = No	0 = Yes
7	0 = sht @$1.29	1 = 16 b	1 = Yes	0 = 15	0 = Yes	1 = 3 b	1 = No	0 = Yes
8	0 = sht @$1.29	1 = 16 b	1 = Yes	1 = 30	0 = Yes	0 = 16 b	0 = Yes	1 = No
9	1 = sht @$1.59	0 = 3 b	0 = No	0 = 15	0 = Yes	0 = 16 b	0 = Yes	0 = Yes
10	1 = sht @$1.59	0 = 3 b	0 = No	1 = 30	0 = Yes	1 = 3 b	1 = No	1 = No
11	1 = sht @$1.59	0 = 3 b	1 = Yes	0 = 15	1 = No	0 = 16 b	1 = No	1 = No
12	1 = sht @$1.59	0 = 3 b	1 = Yes	1 = 30	1 = No	1 = 3 b	0 = Yes	0 = Yes
13	1 = sht @$1.59	1 = 16 b	0 = No	0 = 15	1 = No	1 = 3 b	0 = Yes	1 = No
14	1 = sht @$1.59	1 = 16 b	0 = No	1 = 30	1 = No	0 = 16 b	1 = No	0 = Yes
15	1 = sht @$1.59	1 = 16 b	1 = Yes	0 = 15	0 = Yes	1 = 3 b	1 = No	0 = Yes
16	1 = sht @$1.59	1 = 16 b	1 = Yes	1 = 30	0 = Yes	0 = 16 b	0 = Yes	1 = No
17	2 = lon @$1.79	0 = 3 b	0 = No	0 = 15	0 = Yes	0 = 16 b	0 = Yes	0 = Yes
18	2 = lon @$1.79	0 = 3 b	0 = No	1 = 30	0 = Yes	1 = 3 b	1 = No	1 = No
19	2 = lon @$1.79	0 = 3 b	1 = Yes	0 = 15	1 = No	0 = 16 b	1 = No	1 = No
20	2 = lon @$1.79	0 = 3 b	1 = Yes	1 = 30	1 = No	1 = 3 b	0 = Yes	0 = Yes
21	2 = lon @$1.79	1 = 16 b	0 = No	0 = 15	1 = No	1 = 3 b	0 = Yes	1 = No
22	2 = lon @$1.79	1 = 16 b	0 = No	1 = 30	1 = No	0 = 16 b	1 = No	0 = Yes
23	2 = lon @$1.79	1 = 16 b	1 = Yes	0 = 15	0 = Yes	1 = 3 b	1 = No	0 = Yes
24	2 = lon @$1.79	1 = 16 b	1 = Yes	1 = 30	0 = Yes	0 = 16 b	0 = Yes	1 = No
25	3 = lon @$2.09	0 = 3 b	0 = No	0 = 15	0 = Yes	0 = 16 b	0 = Yes	0 = Yes
26	3 = lon @$2.09	0 = 3 b	0 = No	1 = 30	0 = Yes	1 = 3 b	1 = No	1 = No
27	3 = lon @$2.09	0 = 3 b	1 = Yes	0 = 15	1 = No	0 = 16 b	1 = No	1 = No
28	3 = lon @$2.09	0 = 3 b	1 = Yes	1 = 30	1 = No	1 = 3 b	0 = Yes	0 = Yes
29	3 = lon @$2.09	1 = 16 b	0 = No	0 = 15	1 = No	1 = 3 b	0 = Yes	1 = No
30	3 = lon @$2.09	1 = 16 b	0 = No	1 = 30	1 = No	0 = 16 b	1 = No	0 = Yes
31	3 = lon @$2.09	1 = 16 b	1 = Yes	0 = 15	0 = Yes	1 = 3 b	1 = No	0 = Yes
32	3 = lon @$2.09	1 = 16 b	1 = Yes	1 = 30	0 = Yes	0 = 16 b	0 = Yes	1 = No

The above design strategies are only two of many ways to reduce profile numbers. For example, a foldover can be made from the first example by replacing each attribute level by its mirror image ($0 = 3, 1 = 2, 2 = 1, 3 = 0$ for four levels; $0 = 1$ and $1 = 0$ for two). Many other designs can be constructed from these basic building blocks. For example, instead of combining each FTL level with a main effects design for the remaining seven attributes, one can use a design that allows all main and two-way interactions to be estimated. Such a design can be constructed in thirty-two profiles, and if combined with each of the four FTL levels, results in 128 total profiles. All main effects and two-way interactions and all three-way interactions of each attribute with FTL can be estimated from this design. More designs can be constructed by combining other designs in this way.

6 Relaxing the IID assumption — introducing variants of the MNL model

6.1 Setting the context for behaviourally more plausible models

Many applications in marketing, transport, and the environment use the simple multi-nomial (MNL) logit model presented in chapter 3. This approach is common to studies using stand-alone stated preference (SP) or revealed preference (RP) data, as well as cases with multiple data sets, such as combined SP and RP data (see chapter 8). A great majority of empirical studies go no further than this. Some studies progress to accommodating some amount of difference in the structure of the random component of utility, through a nested logit (NL) model. The NL model partitions the choice set to allow alternatives to share common unobserved components among one another compared with a non-nested alternative.

Despite the practitioner's support for the MNL model and occasionally for the NL model (the latter being the main focus of this chapter), much research effort is being devoted to increasing the behavioural realism of discrete-choice models. This effort is concentrated on relaxing the strong assumptions associated with IID (independent and identically distributed) error terms in ways that are behaviourally enriching, computationally tractable and practical. Choice models are now available in which the identically distributed structure of the random components is relaxed (e.g., Bhat 1995, 1997b, Hensher 1997b). Extensions that permit non-independence between alternatives, such as mixed logit (ML) and multinomial probit (MNP) models, have also been developed, adding further behavioural realism but at the expense of additional computational complexity (see Greene 1997; Geweke, Keane and Runkle 1994; Bolduc 1992; Daganzo 1980, McFadden and Train 1996; Brownstone, Bunch and Train 1998).

To gain an appreciation of the progress made in relaxing some of the very strict assumptions of the multinomial logit model, the essential generality of interest can be presented through the specification of the indirect utility expression U_{it} associated with the ith mutually exclusive alternative in a choice set at time period t, and the structure of the random component(s) (equation (6.1) below). Time period t can be interpreted in an SP context as an SP profile or treatment. The reader may not fully appreciate the behavioural implications of all elements of equation (6.1) until working through the entire chapter (including appendices). However, this equation does usefully synthesise the range of behavioural improvements that might be made as we move beyond the MNL model.

$$U_{it} = \alpha_{it} + \psi_{i,t-1} \frac{\lambda_{it}}{\lambda_{i,t-1}} \text{Choice}_{i,t-1} + \lambda_{it}\beta_{ikt}X_{ikt} + \lambda_{it}\gamma_{qt} + \varepsilon_{it}, \quad (6.1)$$

where

$\alpha_{it} =$ alternative-specific constant (ASC) representing the mean of the distribution of the unobserved effects in the random component ε_{it} associated with alternative i at time period t (or alternative i in choice set t). This is also referred to as the location parameter.

$\psi_{i,t-1} =$ the utility parameter associated with the lagged choice response from period $t-1$, which takes the value 1 if the chosen alternative in period t is the same as the chosen in period $t-1$ (i.e., $it = i, t-1$) (see Hensher et al. 1992).

$\lambda_{it} =$ the scale (or precision) parameter, which in the family of extreme-value random utility models is an inverse function of the standard deviation of the unobserved effects for alternative i at time period t. This parameter can be set to 1 across all alternatives when the standard deviations are identically distributed. λ_{it} may vary between data sets (e.g., stated choice and revealed preference data drawn from the same or different samples of individuals in a closed population) and between alternatives, and/or time periods/decision contexts for the same individual.

$\beta_{ikt} =$ the utility parameters which represent the relative level of satisfaction or saliency associated with the kth attribute associated with alternative i in time period t (or choice set t in repeated SP tasks).

$X_{ikt} =$ the kth (exogenous) attribute associated with alternative i and time period t.

$\gamma_{qt} =$ individual-specific effect or unobserved heterogeneity across the sampled population, for each individual q in time period (or choice set) t. This parameter may be a fixed effect (i.e., a unique estimate per individual) or a random effect (i.e., a set of values randomly assigned to each individual drawn from an assumed distribution). As a random effect, this unobserved term is part of an error component's structure, assumed to be independent of other unobserved effects but permissible to be correlated across alternatives. Identification of γ_{qt} requires multiple observations per individual from a panel of RP data and/or repeated SP tasks – see Appendix B6.

$\varepsilon_{it} =$ the unobserved random component comprising a variance and a set of covariances linking itself to the other alternatives. The full variance–covariance matrix across the choice set permits J variances and $J * (J - 1)/2$ covariances; at least one variance must be normalised to 1.0 and at least one row of covariances set to zero for identification (Bunch 1991) (note that the model is estimated as a series of differences between the chosen and each non-chosen alternative). By separating the unobserved heterogeneity (γ_{qt}) across the sample, from ε_{it} we have a components form of the random sources of indirect utility. Any suppression of other sources of unobserved influences not included in equation (6.1), such as errors-in-variables (i.e., measurement error of the observed attributes), is confounded with the residual sources of random utility.

The utility parameters and the scale parameters may themselves be a function of a set of exogenous characteristics that may or may not define the attributes of alternatives. This can include socioeconomic characteristics of the sample and contextual effects such as task complexity, fatigue, data collection method and interviewer identifier. The functional form can be of any estimable specification, for example:

$$\lambda_{it} = \delta_{0i} + \delta_{1it}\text{Income}_{it} + \delta_{2it}\text{TaskComplexity}_{it}, \qquad (6.2a)$$

$$\beta_{ikt} = \varphi_{0i} + \varphi_{1it}\text{Age}_{it} + \varphi_{2it}\text{HouseholdSize}_{it}. \qquad (6.2b)$$

A comparison of equation (6.1) and equation (3.24) in chapter 3 will show that the MNL model assumes:

- a single cross-section and thus no lagged structure,
- non-separation of taste and other component 'weights' defining the role of attributes in each indirect utility expression (due to a confoundment with scale),
- scale parameters that are constant across the alternatives (i.e., constant variance assumption), arbitrarily normalised to one in (3.24),
- random components that are not serially correlated,
- fixed utility parameters, and
- no unobserved heterogeneity.

As one permits complex structures for the unobserved effects through introducing variation and covariation attributable to contemporaneous patterns among alternatives, and temporal patterns among alternatives (e.g., autoregressive structures), there exist complex and often 'deep' parameters associated with the covariance matrix which necessitate some simplification to achieve any measure of estimability of a model with application capability. The set of models presented in this chapter have the potential to be practically useful and to enrich our understanding of behaviour and behavioural response.

To illustrate why paying attention to the behavioural source of the error terms in a choice model leads to new insights into how a choice model should be estimated, interpreted and applied, consider a simple random utility model, in which there are heterogeneous preferences for observed and unobserved labelled attributes:

$$U_{qjt} = \alpha_{qj} + \gamma_q P_{qjt} + \beta_{qj} X_{qjt} + \varepsilon_{qjt}. \qquad (6.2c)$$

U_{qjt} is the utility that individual q receives given a choice of alternative j on occasion t. In a stated choice experiment, t can index choice tasks. P_{qjt} denotes price, and X_{qjt} defines an observed attribute of j. α_{qj} is the individual-specific intercept for alternative j arising from q's preferences for unobserved attributes j. γ_q and β_q are individual-specific utility parameters intrinsic to the individual and hence invariant over choice occasions. ε_{qjt} are occasion-specific shocks to q's tastes, assumed to be independent over choice occasions, alternatives and individuals.

Suppose we estimate an MNL model for process (6.2), invalidly assuming that all parameters are homogeneous in the population. The random component in this model will be:

$$w_{qjt} = \hat{\alpha}_q + \hat{\gamma}_i P_{qjt} + \hat{\beta}_{qj} X_{qjt} + \varepsilon_{qjt}, \tag{6.3a}$$

where $\hat{\ }$ denotes the individual-specific deviation from the population mean. From the analyst's perspective, the variance of this error term for individual q on choice occasion t is (Keane 1997)

$$\text{var}\,(w_{qjt}) = \sigma_\alpha^2 + P_{qjt}^2 \sigma_\gamma^2 + X_{qjt}^2 \sigma_\beta^2 + \sigma_\varepsilon^2, \tag{6.3b}$$

and the covariance between choice occasions t and $t-1$ is

$$\text{cov}\,(w_{qjt}, w_{qjt,t-1}) = \sigma_\alpha^2 + P_{qjt} P_{qj,t-1} \sigma_\gamma^2 + X_{qjt} X_{qj,t-1} \sigma_\beta^2. \tag{6.3c}$$

Equations (6.3b) and (6.3c) reveal two interesting consequences of ignoring heterogeneity in preferences (Keane 1997). First, the error variance will differ across choice occasions as price P and attribute X are varied. If one estimates an MNL model with a constant error variance, this will show up as variation in the intercept and slope parameters across choice occasions. In a stated choice experiment context, this could lead to a false conclusion that there are order effects in the process generating responses.

Second, equation (6.3c) shows how preference heterogeneity leads to serially correlated errors. (That heterogeneity is a special type of serial correlation is apparently not well understood.) To obtain efficient estimates of choice model parameters one should include a specification of the heterogeneity structure in the model. But more importantly, if preference heterogeneity is present it is not merely a statistical nuisance requiring correction. Rather, one must model the heterogeneity in order to obtain accurate choice model predictions, because the presence of heterogeneity will alter cross-price effects and lead to IIA violations.

The chapter is organised as follows. Understanding the role of the unobserved influences on choice is central to choice modelling, so we begin with a formal derivation of the mean and variance of the random component, assumed to be distributed extreme value type 1 (EV1); the distribution imposed on the majority of discrete-choice models. These parameters summarise important behavioural information (as shown in equations (6.1)–(6.3)). The chapter then introduces the nested logit model in which IID errors hold within subsets of alternatives but not between blocks of alternatives (including single or degenerate alternatives). Much of the chapter is devoted to the NL model since it offers noticeable gains in behavioural realism for the practitioner without adding substantial complexity in estimation. It remains the most advanced *practical* tool for modelling choices involving many decisions, as well as choices in which a single decision involves consideration of many alternatives. The

NL model provides the springboard for further relaxation of the structure of the random errors.

Given the significant increase in technical complexity of models beyond MNL and NL, they are assigned to appendix B of the chapter. All such models no longer maintain a closed-form expression associated with MNL and NL models, such that the analyst has to undertake complex analytical computations to identify changes in choice probabilities through varying the levels of attributes. We present the following models in the appendix: heteroscedastic extreme value (HEV), covariance hetero-geneity logit (CovHet), random parameter logit (RPL) or mixed logit (ML), latent class heteroscedastic MNL, multinomial probit (MNP) and multiperiod multinomial probit (MPMNP).

We use a single data set throughout the chapter and appendix B (except for MPMNP) to illustrate the differences between various choice models, as well as to undertake tests of the violation of the independence of irrelevant alternatives property linked to IID. We conclude the chapter with some practical hints on modelling with more complex procedures.

6.2   Deriving the mean and variance of the extreme value type 1 distribution

It is relatively straightforward to derive the first two moments of the EV1 distribution. The EV1 distribution is defined by the density function

$$f(x) = \lambda e^{-\lambda x} e^{-e^{-\lambda x}} \quad -\infty < x < \infty.$$

$$\left(\text{NB: } \int_{-\infty}^{\infty} f(x)\, dx = \int_{-\infty}^{\infty} \lambda e^{-\lambda x} e^{-e^{-\lambda x}}\, dx = [e^{-e^{-\lambda x}}]_{-\infty}^{\infty} = 1 \right).$$

The *mean* is given by the mode of the distribution $(\eta) + J$, where

$$J = \int_{-\infty}^{\infty} x f(x)\, dx = \int_{-\infty}^{\infty} \lambda x e^{-\lambda x} e^{-e^{-\lambda x}}\, dx = 1/\lambda \int_{-\infty}^{\infty} y e^{-y} e^{-e^{-y}}\, dy.$$

Write $e^{-y} = z \therefore J = \dfrac{1}{\lambda} \int_{0}^{\infty} e^{-z} \log z\, dz = \dfrac{\gamma}{\lambda}$, where γ is Euler's constant $(= 0.577)$.

The *variance* is given by $\kappa = \int_{-\infty}^{\infty} x^2 f(x)\,dx - \mu^2$, where μ is the mean.

Write $\kappa^1 = \int_{-\infty}^{\infty} x^2 f(x)\, dx = \int_{-\infty}^{\infty} \lambda x^2 e^{-\lambda x} e^{-e^{-\lambda x}}\, dx = \dfrac{1}{\lambda^2} \int_{-\infty}^{\infty} y^2 e^{-y} e^{-e^{-y}}\, dy$

Write $e^{-y} = z \therefore \kappa^1 = \dfrac{1}{\lambda^2} \int_{0}^{\infty} e^{-z} (\log z)^2\, dz = \dfrac{1}{\lambda^2} \left(\dfrac{\pi^2}{6} + \gamma^2 \right) \therefore \kappa = \dfrac{\pi^2}{6\lambda^2}.$

This derivation of the mean and variance of the extreme value type 1 distribution provides important behavioural information on the nature of unobserved sources of influence on overall relative utility, and hence choice outcomes. For the MNL model the variances of the unobserved effects are the same (equivalently, $\lambda_1 = \lambda_2 = \lambda_i = \cdots = \lambda_J$). The means can differ but could be the same by coincidence. λ is the only unknown element of the variance formula ($\pi = 3.14159$). The variance of the unobserved effects is inversely proportional to λ^2. *Alternatively, λ is inversely proportional to the standard deviation of the unobserved effects.* λ is known as the scale parameter, set by assumption to 1.0 for MNL models, hence not explicitly modelled in the MNL model (equation (3.24)). If the constant variance assumption is relaxed, then λ_i becomes an additional (constant) multiplicand of each of the attributes influencing choice:

$$V_{iq} = \lambda_i \alpha_i + \lambda_i \beta_{il} X_{ilq} + \cdots + \lambda_i \beta_{ik} X_{ikq} + \cdots + \lambda_i \beta_{iK} X_{iKq}, k = 1, \ldots K, \quad (6.4a)$$

where β_{ik} is the utility parameter associated with the kth attribute and ith alternative. It is common practice to specify equation (6.4a) in the form of (6.4b), which in the MNL form would be:

$$(V_{iq}/\lambda_i) = \alpha_i + \beta_{il} X_{ilq} + \cdots + \beta_{ik} X_{ikq} + \cdots + \beta_{iK} X_{iKq}, \quad (6.4b)$$

$$P_{iq} = \frac{\exp(V_{iq}/\lambda_i)}{\sum_{j=1}^{J} \exp(V_{jq}/\lambda_j)}, \quad (6.4c)$$

noting that, from McFadden's generalised extreme value model, the utility function for alternative i is defined as $\gamma_i^{1/\lambda_i} = \exp(V_i)^{1/\lambda_i} = \exp(V_i/\lambda_i)$.

The scale parameter, λ, is a critical parameter in the estimation of choice models when data sets are combined (e.g., market data and stated choice data on the same choice such as choice of shopping destination). Differences in λ in an EV1 model specification determine if the information in the utility expressions associated with alternatives from one data set need to be rescaled to make it comparable with the underlying distributional properties associated with the other data set. See chapter 8 for more details.

λ is also the source of information to identify the extent to which the standard deviations of the unobserved components differ across alternatives in a single data set. When the latter occurs, it suggests a need to partition a choice set so that sets of alternatives with the same (or similar) standard deviations are studied differently from other sets of alternatives with their own similar standard deviation profiles, to preserve as far as possible the practical appeal of the MNL form. The nested logit (NL) model can be thought of as a way to estimate a choice model recognising that, within a choice set, there can be sets of alternatives that can be partitioned, such that some alternatives have similar or identical standard deviations that differ from other alternatives whose standard deviations are similar to each other but different from the first group.

However the overall variance of unobserved random components of all alternatives in a nested logit model is constant. This is the only way the NL model can be derived from utility maximisation. In addition, the NL model permits covariances to be different in certain restrictive ways (see below) in order to deliver a closed-form structure for the choice probabilities.

6.3 Introduction to the nested logit model

The MNL model is subject to potential violations of the *identically distributed* assumption associated with the random components of each alternative. This implies that cross-substitutions between pairs of alternatives are equal and unaffected by the presence/absence of other alternatives. Although one could move to a more general model such as multinomial probit (MNP) which can totally relax IID (see appendix B6), it does so at the expense of substantially greater computational complexity as the number of alternatives increases (Maddala 1983; McFadden 1981; Geweke, Keane and Runkle 1994). Estimation techniques for these models involve simulated maximum likelihood, or more recently, advanced Bayesian methods, and require very sophisticated knowledge and expertise. Currently even modest problems require relatively high performance computing platforms and substantial elapsed time, neither of which is commonly available to many practitioners.

The IID limitation of MNL has long been recognised. McFadden (1979, 1981) proposed a more general random utility theory model that can accommodate various degrees of cross-alternative substitution and is consistent with utility maximisation. This generalised extreme value (GEV) model generalises the multinomial logit model, with NL a special case. GEV models partially relax IID such that the random components are correlated within a partition of a choice set but not across partitions. The latter naturally leads to a consideration of partitioning choice sets so that richer substitution patterns can be accommodated to reflect differential degrees of similarity or dissimilarity.

The NL model provides a way not only to link different but interdependent decisions, but also to decompose a single decision to minimise the restriction of equal cross-alternative substitution. NL includes additional parameters for each choice set partition, equal to the inverse of λ (see below) attached to an index variable commonly referred to as the inclusive value (IV) or alternatively as the *logsum* or *expected maximum utility*, defined by a set of utility expressions associated with a partitioned set of alternatives. NL provides a way to identify the behavioural relationship between choices at each level of the nest and to test the consistency of the partitioned structure with random utility maximisation. It is important to note that partitioning occurs not (necessarily) for behavioural reasons but to comply with the underlying conditions imposed on the unobserved effects for each indirect utility expression. However, behavioural intuition can often assist in specifying nested structures because differences in variances of unobserved effects (and associated correlations among alternatives) are often linked to unobserved attributes common to subsets of alternatives.

6.3.1 Specifying a hierarchical choice context

Consider a two-level choice decision involving a generic choice set (G) of private and public transport, and an elemental choice set (M) of car driver, car passenger, train and bus. The indirect utility function associated with an elemental mode m contained

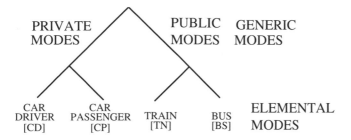

PRIVATE MODES

PUBLIC MODES

GENERIC MODES

CAR DRIVER [CD]

CAR PASSENGER [CP]

TRAIN [TN]

BUS [BS]

ELEMENTAL MODES

Figure 6.1 An hierarchical model structure

within the generic category g is given in equation (6.5):

$$U_{gm} = U_g + U_{m|g}, m \in M_g, g \in G. \tag{6.5}$$

The hierarchical structure is given in figure 6.1.

Let us write the U_{gm} expression in terms of component vectors for the observed (V) and unobserved (μ, ε) influences on choice:

$$U_{gm} = V_g + V_{m|g} + \mu_g + \varepsilon_{m|g}, m = 1, \ldots, M_g, g = 1, \ldots, G \tag{6.6}$$

and define the variance–covariance matrix in terms of the associated elements

$$\sum_{gm,g'm'} = E[(\mu_g + \varepsilon_{m|g}) * (\mu_{g'} + \varepsilon_{m'|g'})]. \tag{6.7}$$

Invoking the independence assumption of the distributions in the two choice dimensions and random utility maximisation, numerous authors (e.g., McFadden 1981; Williams 1977, 1981; Daly and Zachary 1978) show that the joint probability of choosing alternative gm is defined by equation (6.8), or a nested logit model.

$$P_{gm} = \frac{\exp(\lambda_g(V_g + V_{g*}))}{\sum_{g' \in G} \exp(\lambda_g(V_{g'} + V_{g'*}))} \cdot \frac{\exp((\lambda_m V_{m|g})}{\sum_{m' \in M_g} \exp(\lambda_{m'} V_{m'|g}}, \tag{6.8}$$

where

$$V_{g*} = I_{g*} = (1/\lambda_m) \log \sum_{m' \in M_g} \exp(\lambda_m V_{m'|g}) + \text{Euler's constant}. \tag{6.9a}$$

By substitution of (6.9a) into (6.8), we get:

$$P_{gm} = \frac{\exp\left(\lambda_g V_g + \frac{\lambda_g}{\lambda_m} \log \sum_{m' \in Mg} \exp(\lambda_m V_{m'|g})\right)}{\sum_{g' \in G} \exp\left(\lambda_{g'} V_{g'} + \frac{\lambda_{g'}}{\lambda_{m'}} \log \sum_{m' \in Mg} \exp(\lambda_{m'} V_{m'|g})\right)} \cdot \frac{\exp(\lambda_m V_{m|g})}{\sum_{m' \in Mg} \exp(\lambda_{m'} V_{m'|g})}$$

$$\tag{6.9b}$$

I_{g*} is the inclusive value (IV) index with parameter λ_g/λ_m. The scale parameter λ_g in equation (6.8) associated with the upper level of the tree is often set equal to 1.0

(i.e., normalised). The scale parameter(s) for the conditional choice (λ_m) between the elemental modes in each partition are left free to be estimated. Alternatively, one could set $\lambda_m = 1$ and allow λ_g to be estimated. It should be noted, however, that the alternative normalisations only produce identical results (e.g., overall goodness-of-fit and elasticity) when the inclusive value parameters are the same across all branches at a level. This point is not often appreciated (Koppelman and Wen 1998, Hensher and Greene 1999). Allowing IVs to be different within a level will produce different results. In addition, when one selects a normalisation scale parameter, the non-normalised scale has to be the same across all branches in a level of the nest to be consistent with utility maximisation. If, as is often the situation, one wishes to have different scale parameters, one way to comply with utility maximisation involves using a dummy node and link 'trick' (see section 6.5 for more detail). The 'trick' involves adding another level to the tree below the elemental alternatives and constraining the scale parameters at the dummy nodes to equal the scale parameter of the other branches in the tree (Koppelman and Wen 1998, Hensher and Greene 1999).

A *global* sufficiency condition for the nested choice model in equation (6.8) to be consistent with random utility maximisation is that the parameter of inclusive value be in the 0–1 range and not increase as we go to higher levels of the tree (McFadden 1981). This is due to the presence of greater variance in the upper-level error components which include the variance components from both the lower-level choices and upper-level choices. Thus the scale parameters, inversely related to the standard deviations, must satisfy the weak inequalities $\lambda_g \leq \lambda_m$, or $\lambda_g/\lambda_m \leq 1$. The MNL model, which sets $\lambda_g = \lambda_m$, produces $\lambda_g/\lambda_m = 1$. Furthermore, since each scale parameter is inversely related to the standard deviation, each will be positive, and hence their ratio is positive. Thus the IV parameters will lie in the open unit interval $0 \leqslant (\lambda_g/\lambda_m) \leqslant 1$.

In any two-level nested structure there will be at least two scale parameters (with one arbitrarily normalised to 1.0). The ratio of any two scale parameters (e.g., λ_g/λ_m) can be interpreted as the correlation between any two indirect utility expressions for alternatives below the node of the branch where I_{g*} is defined.

The proof of this is based on Ben-Akiva and Lerman, 1985: 289:

$$\frac{\lambda_g}{\lambda_m} = \frac{\pi/(\sqrt{6}\sigma(\varepsilon_g + \varepsilon_{g*}))}{\pi/(\sqrt{6}\sigma(\varepsilon_{m|g}))}$$

$$= \sigma(\varepsilon_{m/g})/\sigma(\varepsilon_g + \varepsilon_{m|g})$$

$$= \sigma(\varepsilon_{m/g})/\sigma(\varepsilon_g + \varepsilon_{m|g}) \tag{6.10a}$$

(noting the common variance of ε_{g*} and $\varepsilon_{m|g}$)

$$= [\text{var}\,(\varepsilon_{m|g})/\text{var}\,(\varepsilon_g + \varepsilon_{m|g})]^{0.5}.$$

By further rearrangement of (6.10a), we get (6.10b):

$$\frac{\lambda_g}{\lambda_m} = \{1 - [\text{var}(\varepsilon_{g*})/\text{var}(\varepsilon_{g*} + \varepsilon_{m|g})]\}^{0.5} \tag{6.10b}$$

noting that the covariance of the utilities of two alternatives within a partition is equal to var (ε_{g*}), we get

$$= \{1 - [\text{cov}(V_{m_1|g}, V_{m_2|g})/\text{var}(\varepsilon_{g*} + \varepsilon_{m|g})]\}^{0.5}.$$

By noting that the variance of two unobservable components (from upper and lower levels) of the utility of alternative $m|g$, equals the variance of $V_{m|g}$, we get

$$= \{1 - [\text{cov}(V_{m_1|g}, V_{m_2|g})/\text{var}(V_{m_1|g})]\}^{0.5}$$

$$= \{1 - [\text{cov}(V_{m_1|g}, V_{m_2|g})/[[\text{var}(V_{m_1|g})\text{var}(V_{m_2|g})]]^{0.5}]\}^{0.5}$$

$$= [1 - \text{corr}(V_{m_1|g}, V_{m_2|g})]^{0.5}.$$

Thus $1 - (\lambda_g/\lambda_m)^2$ equals the correlation of the indirect utilities for any pair of alternatives sharing a common branch in a nest (e.g., for train and bus in figure 6.1). The closer the correlation is to unity, the closer the IV parameter is to zero. Conversely, if the correlation is zero, the IV parameter is 1.0, which is the special case of the MNL model in which alternatives share no common utility elements.

This discussion signals a statistical test to determine if the correlation structure of NL differs from MNL. That test is as follows: a t-test suggests that if the IV parameter $1/\lambda_m$ for a branch (setting $\lambda_g = 1$) does not differ statistically from 1.0, then an NL specification (or a part representing a particular partition) can be collapsed to MNL. In practice, if λ_m approaches zero, a very large negative number results, that can be interpreted as a degenerate case. Values between zero and one imply degrees of similarity, but values significantly different from one justify NL structures.

A primary role for NL is to allow the variances of the random components to vary across subsets of alternatives (subject to the overall variance of unobserved random components of all alternatives being constant). This implies, for example, that there will be a different λ_m for the private and public transport nests in figure 6.1. However, as stated above, NL models allow *covariance* in the random components among subsets of alternatives (assuming an alternative is assigned to only one partition) because random utility components at lower levels (e.g., train and bus) are partitioned into a common *public transport* error component and an independent component with the variances of bus and train summing to 1.0. The common *public transport* random component generates a covariance in the utilities of bus and train. Thus one tries to assign alternatives in a partition of the nested structure so that they display an identical degree of increased sensitivity relative to alternatives not in that partition. The IV parameter often is interpreted as a measure of *dissimilarity*, capturing correlations among unobserved components of alternatives in the partition. This correlation supports the claim that NL provides relaxation of *independence* (for alternatives sharing a partition) as well as the identical distribution assumption between alternatives in *different* partitions.

It is important to note that even if the λs for each branch are significantly different from 1.0, this does not necessarily mean that the tree structure is the best in a statistical (and/or behavioural) sense. A number of tree structures may produce variations in λs within the 0–1 bound. Therefore, analysts have to evaluate a number of trees, and if the λs differ from 1.0, compare the log likelihood of each tree at convergence using a likelihood ratio test (see chapter 3). The tree with the lowest log likelihood at convergence that improves on a null hypothesis of no gain in goodness-of-fit is the preferred structure (in a statistical sense).

There are 2^M possible combinations of elemental alternatives (Cameron 1982: 90); hence, a priori criteria are required in the initial partitioning of the alternatives. The main a priori criterion that should be employed is the anticipated correlation between the random components among elements of each subset. This should not be used to necessarily imply a truly sequential decision process.

The 0–1 bound to ensure consistency with global random utility maximisation is a strong test. A local sufficiency condition was proven by Boersch-Supan (1990) and corrected by Herriges and Kling (1996), in which IV can exceed unity (practice suggests a limited amount, such as 1.3). Boersch-Supan (1990) suggested that the sufficient conditions for consistency (known as the Daly–Zachary–McFadden conditions in Boersch-Supan 1990), that require the IV parameters to lie within the unit interval are too stringent. Hence, the nested logit specification should be viewed as an approximation (as are many functional forms in demand systems), which suggests that random utility maximisation should not be expected to hold globally, but only within the region of data points sensible for a specific application of the choice model. A relaxed set of conditions to test for consistency developed by Boersch-Supan (1990) and Herriges and Kling (1996) are (for a two-level nest):

$$(1/\lambda)_b = 1/(1 - Q_b), b = 1, \ldots, B \tag{6.11}$$

and

$$(1/\lambda)_b = 4/[3(1 - Q_b) + (1 + 7Q_b)(1 - Q_b)]^{0.5} \nabla b \in G_3 \equiv \{h | I(h) \geq 3\}, \tag{6.12}$$

where Q_b is the marginal probability that an alternative from within branch b is selected, $I(h)$ is the number of alternatives in the hth branch, and G_3 is a choice set of at least three alternatives in each branch.

6.3.2 Elasticities in NL models

The IV parameter(s) provide a basis for assessing differences in cross-substitution elasticities. The elasticity formula for NL models differs according to whether alternatives (direct elasticities) or pairs of alternatives (cross elasticities) are associated with the same or different branches of a nested partition. Direct elasticities are identical to MNL elasticities (see chapter 3) for alternative m not in a partitioned branch (e.g., in a non-nested partition). If alternative m is in a partitioned part of the tree, the formula must be modified to accommodate the correlation between alternatives in the branch. The NL direct elasticity for a partitioned alternative (using notation from equation (6.9)) is:

$$\left[(1 - P_m) + \left\{\frac{1}{\lambda_m - 1}\right\}(1 - P_{m|G})\right]\beta_k X_{mk}, \tag{6.13a}$$

where P_m is the marginal probability of choosing alternative m and $P_{m|G}$ is the probability of choosing alternative m conditional on choice set G. The NL cross elasticity for alternatives m and m' in a partition of the nest is:

$$-\left[P_m + \left\{\frac{1}{\lambda_m} - 1\right\}P_{m|G}\right]\beta_k X_{mk}. \tag{6.13b}$$

Estimation of NL models can be sequential or simultaneous. Software is readily accessible for the preferred simultaneous estimation; however, it is informative to include a brief discussion of sequential estimation. Analysts studying integrated choices or nested partitions that involve more than four levels often analyse the entire choice process as a mixture of simultaneous and sequential estimations.

6.3.3 Sequential estimation

Sequential estimation involves separate estimation of each choice situation as the lowest level in the hierarchy (e.g. CD vs. CP and TN vs. BS in figure 6.1), followed by calculation of inclusive values I_{g*}, then estimation at the upper level(s) using the estimated IVs as explanatory variables. Because separate models are estimated for each branch at the lower level, there is potential for a considerable loss of information, which affects both sample size and distribution of the levels of attributes. In the lower level estimation, the sequential approach includes only those observations that have a chosen alternative and at least one other alternative in that branch. Hence, sequential estimation is statistically inefficient because parameter estimates at all levels above the lowest level do not have minimum variance parameter estimates (Hensher 1986). This is a result of using *estimates of estimates* to calculate the contribution of aggregate utility or IV indices of the subsets of alternatives below the relevant node. It also is inefficient from a practical point of view, because the task of calculating IVs and relating them to an upper level is quite demanding.

Procedures are available to correct the standard errors estimated from a sequential procedure at all levels above the lowest level, but are complicated even for relatively simple two-level S-NL models (Amemiya 1978, Cameron 1982, Small and Brownstone 1982, Boersch-Supan 1984), although some modern estimation software does the correction automatically. A sequential approach is commonly implemented for large multi-level nested models. If the tree has two to four levels, it is more common to estimate model systems jointly using full information maximum likelihood (FIML).[1]

[1] FIML estimation is available in LIMDEP/W (Econometric Software 1998) for up to four levels and in ALOGIT (Daly 1997) for any number of levels, although the author of the latter program has advised that it is common to go to sequential estimation for the levels above four (personal communication with Andrew Daly June 22, 1997). HIELOW by Brielare (since 1995) and HLOGIT by Boersch-Supan (since 1987) are other programs specialising in MNL and NL estimation.

The literature tends to give the misleading impression that sequential nested logit modelling requires less data than simultaneous NL. For example, with six travel destinations and four travel modes there are twenty-four mode by destination combinations of data required to estimate an MNL model. A nested logit model of (conditional) mode given destination choice requires four data points for each individual and the marginal destination choice requires up to six data points. However, calculation of the IV requires data points for all modes to all destinations current in each individual's choice set, regardless of which destination is chosen. Thus, the ultimate data saving is nil. Another potential disadvantage of sequential estimation is linked to economic theory. If theory argues for certain restrictions on the utility parameters of particular attributes (e.g., equality of cost parameters throughout the structure, see Truong and Hensher 1985, Jara-Diaz 1998), this cannot be accommodated globally, but can be handled locally within a level by stacking, such that each branch is treated as a separate observation. Restricting upper level utility parameters to the levels estimated at the bottom level of a tree will not guarantee the same utility parameters as those obtained from FIML estimation.

6.3.4   Simultaneous estimation

Most applications typically have fewer than four nested levels; hence, a better alternative is to use FIML techniques to obtain fully efficient parameter estimates. In practice, analysts use nested choice models with varying and fixed choice sets. Yet to satisfy the equal cross-substitution property globally it is necessary to include all (physically available) alternatives in the choice set (McFadden 1979). Subsets of observations may, however, have different choice sets as a consequence of the availability of particular alternatives, and thus statistical sampling of alternatives is not permitted. The simple MNL model has the attractive feature of IIA which allows analysts to estimate models with differentially *sampled* choice sets for each respondent while satisfying global conditions for equal cross substitution amongst subsets of alternatives.

FIML introduces some new issues:

1. Structurally, the NL model corresponds to a set of independently estimated MNL models, each with a unique optimal solution when considered individually. However, while FIML–NL does have a unique global optimal solution (unless there is a lack of identification), it may have suboptimal local maxima; hence great care must be exercised in the selection of starting values for all parameter estimates.

2. Optimisation procedures will accept analytical first and analytical second derivatives, but the latter are not available in simple form. Thus the practice has been to accept either approximate analytical second derivatives (e.g., Small and Brownstone 1981, Hensher 1986, Daly 1985) or numerical second derivatives (e.g., Matzoros 1982, Borsch-Supan 1984). Given the highly non-linear behaviour

of the IV parameters, use of first derivatives only is not recommended. Simulated maximum likelihood methods can also be used, as discussed in appendix B6.

The full log-likelihood expression for a FIML nested model extended to three levels is of the form:

$$\log L = \sum_{q=1}^{Q} \sum_{m \subseteq (1,...,M)} \delta_{mq} \log[P(m|x_m, \beta, \theta, \lambda)], \tag{6.14}$$

where $q = 1, \ldots, Q$ are observations, $m = 1, \ldots, M$ are alternatives in a universal finite choice set, θ and λ are the parameter estimates of inclusive value for the top and middle levels, x_m are the set of other exogenous attributes, and β their utility parameters. $\delta_{mq} = 1$ if alternative m is chosen by observation q and zero otherwise. For a three-level logit model of the form:

$$P_{agm} = P(a)^*P(g|a)^*P(m|a,g), \tag{6.15}$$

the joint cumulative distribution function of the unobserved random components is (McFadden 1979, 1981):

$$F(\varepsilon_1, \varepsilon_2, \ldots, \varepsilon_z) = \exp\{-G[\exp(-\varepsilon_1), \ldots, \exp(-\varepsilon_z)]\} \tag{6.16}$$

with

$$G(y_1, \ldots, y_z) = \sum_a \left[\sum_{g' \in a'} \left(\sum_{m \in g'} y'^{(1/\lambda_m)} \right)^{\lambda_m/\theta} \right]^{\theta} \tag{6.17}$$

where the sum is over the highest level containing alternative a', the subsets of alternative g' contained in each branch of the top level, and then over the elemental alternative m' in each of the middle level branches.

To facilitate understanding of the precise form of the utility and probability expressions, we will write out the expressions for six alternatives in a three-level nested model of the structure given in figure 6.2. Three attributes (cost, time, income) and alternative-specific constants (ASC$_i$) are included together with the IV index. These expressions can be used to undertake policy analysis of a 'what-if' nature, changing the levels of one or more attributes, feeding the expressions through the data sets to obtain sample and expanded population market shares.

Lower level:
$V_{1L} = \lambda_1 \text{ASC}_{1L} + \lambda_1 \beta_1 \text{Cost} + \lambda_1 \beta_{1L} \text{Time}$
$V_{2L} = \lambda_2 \text{ASC}_{2L} + \lambda_2 \beta_1 \text{Cost} + \lambda_2 \beta_{2L} \text{Time}$
$V_{3L} = \lambda_3 \text{ASC}_{3L} + \lambda_3 \beta_1 \text{Cost} + \lambda_3 \beta_{3L} \text{ Time}$
$V_{4L} = \lambda_4 \text{ASC}_{4L} + \lambda_4 \beta_1 \text{Cost} + \lambda_4 \beta_{4L} \text{ Time}$
$V_{5L} = \lambda_5 \text{ASC}_{5L} + \lambda_5 \beta_1 \text{Cost} + \lambda_5 \beta_{5L} \text{ Time}$
$V_{6L} = \qquad\qquad \lambda_6 \beta_1 \text{Cost} + \lambda_6 \beta_{6L} \text{ Time}$
$\lambda_1 = \lambda_2; \lambda_4 = \lambda_5$

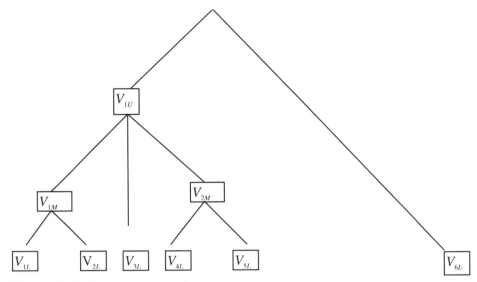

Figure 6.2 A three-level nested structure

Middle level (note: no IV_{3M}):
$V_{1M} = \lambda_{1M}[(\text{ASC}_{1M} + \beta_2\text{Income}) + (1/\lambda_{12L})\text{IV}_{1M}]$
$\text{IV}_{1M} = \ln(\exp\lambda_{1L}V_{1L} + \exp\lambda_{2L}V_{2L})$, noting $\lambda_{1L} = \lambda_{2L} = \lambda_{12L}$
$V_{2M} = \lambda_{2M}[(\beta_3\text{Income} + \beta_4\text{Caravail}) + (1/\lambda_{45L})\text{IV}_{2M}]$
$\text{IV}_{2M} = \ln(\exp\lambda_{4L}V_{4L} + \exp\lambda_{5L}V_{5L})$, noting $\lambda_{4L} = \lambda_{5L} = \lambda_{45L}$

Upper level:
$V_{1U} = \lambda_{1U}[(\text{ASC}_{1U} + \beta_5\text{Partysize}) + (1/\lambda_{123M})\text{IV}_{1U}]$
$\text{IV}_{1U} = \ln(\exp\lambda_{1M}V_{1M} + \exp\lambda_{2M}V_{2M} + \exp\lambda_{3L}V_{3L})$,
noting $\lambda_{1M} = \lambda_{2M} = \lambda_{3L} = \lambda_{123M}$

Probability calculations:
$P_{1L} = P_{1L|1M,1U}{}^*P_{1M|1U}{}^*P_{1U}$
$P_{2L} = P_{2L|1M,1U}{}^*P_{1M|1U}{}^*P_{1U}$
$P_{3L} = P_{3L|1U}{}^*P_{1U}$
$P_{4L} = P_{4L|1M,1U}{}^*P_{2M|1U}{}^*P_{1U}$
$P_{5L} = P_{5L|2M,1U}{}^*P_{2M|1U}{}^*P_{1U}$
$P_{6L} = P_{6L}$
$P_{1L|1M,1U} = \exp V_{1L}/(\exp V_{1L} + \exp V_{2L})$
$P_{1M|1U} = \exp V_{1M}/(\exp V_{1M} + \exp V_{3L} + \exp V_{2M})$
$P_{1U} = \exp V_{1U}/(\exp V_{1U} + \exp V_{6L})$
$P_{2L|1M,1U} = \exp V_{2L}/(\exp V_{1L} + \exp V_{2L})$
$P_{3L|1U} = \exp V_{3L}/(\exp V_{1L} + \exp V_{2L} + \exp V_{3L})$
$P_{4L|2M,1U} = \exp V_{4L}/(\exp V_{4L} + \exp V_{5L})$
$P_{2M|1U} = \exp V_{2M}/(\exp V_{1M} + \exp V_{3L} + \exp V_{2M})$
$P_{5L|2M,1U} = \exp V_{5L}/(\exp V_{4L} + \exp V_{5L})$
$P_{6L} = \exp V_{6L}/(\exp V_{6L} + \exp V_{1U})$.

6.3.5 Handling degenerate branches in a nested logit model

It is common for NL models to have branches with only one alternative. When this occurs, the role of the inclusive value needs special treatment. An NL model with M partitions of the elemental choice alternatives is partially degenerate when the number of degenerate partitions of M, D_M, satisfies the inequality $0 < D_M < M$. If $D_M = M$, then there is complete degeneracy, and each of the basic choices forms its own 'cluster'. This is the MNL model. If $D_M = 0$, then we have an NL model with all clusters containing more than one basic alternative (Hunt 1998).

In the partially degenerate choice structure, the non-degenerate partitions have marginal and conditional probability equations given in (6.8) and inclusive values as given in (6.9). With a degenerate partition the formulation is different. Let us define a degenerate partition m and set the scale as $\lambda_m = 1$. The conditional choice probability for the degenerate partition is:

$$
\begin{aligned}
P(j|m) &= \exp[\lambda_m V_{mj}] / \sum \exp[\lambda_m V_{mk}] \forall k \in B_m \\
&= \exp[\lambda_m V_{mj}] / \exp[\lambda_m V_{mj}] \\
&= 1.
\end{aligned}
\tag{6.18}
$$

Because alternative j is the only alternative in the degenerate partition m, by definition the probability of choosing the single available alternative in the cluster, conditional on the choice of the cluster, will always be unity. The inclusive value for the degenerate partition is:

$$
\begin{aligned}
\mathrm{IV}_m &= \ln \sum \exp[\lambda_m V_{mj}] j \in B_m \\
&= \lambda_m V_{mj}
\end{aligned}
\tag{6.19}
$$

which follows because the partition B_m is degenerate and therefore contains only the alternative j. The marginal choice probability for the degenerate partition is:

$$
\begin{aligned}
P(m) &= \exp[V_m + (1/\lambda_m)\mathrm{IV}_m] / \sum \exp[V_n + (1/\lambda_m)\mathrm{IV}_n] \forall n \in B \\
&= \exp[V_m + (1/\lambda_m)\lambda_m V_{mj}] / \sum \exp[V_n + (1/\lambda_m)\mathrm{IV}_n] \forall n \in B \\
&= \exp[V_m + V_{mj}] / \{\exp[V_m + V_{mj}] + \sum \exp[V_n + (1/\lambda_m)\mathrm{IV}_n]\} \\
&\quad \forall n \in B, n \neq m \\
&= 1 + \exp[V_m + V_{mj}] / \sum \exp[V_n + (1/\lambda_m)\mathrm{IV}_n].
\end{aligned}
\tag{6.20}
$$

The IV parameter for the degenerate partition cancels out of the numerator and denominator, showing that there is no IV parameter, $(1/\lambda_m)$, associated with a degenerate partition.

The absence of an inclusive value (and, therefore, a similarity) parameter for degenerate partitions is quite intuitive. In a degenerate partition, there is only one basic alternative represented. Since the concept of similarity is a comparative one, it therefore requires more than one alternative to be meaningful. This intuition extends to the special case of MNL in which all partitions are degenerate. In this case, all inclusive value parameters factor out.

In a partially degenerate NL model, the utility parameters are identified (accounting for the fact that the normalised scaling, $\lambda = 1$, is absorbed in them), and all the non-degenerate partitions' inclusive value parameters are identified, along with each non-degenerate partition's lower-level scale parameter, λ_n. The degenerate partition has no corresponding IV parameter, and therefore the issue of identification does not arise with respect to such a parameter. In estimating a model with a degenerate branch, we essentially ignore the lower level(s) and simply include all attributes of the degenerate alternative (e.g., travel time) and any observation-specific effects (e.g., income) in a utility expression for the top level. Another way of saying this is that the IV index is empty and hence does not exist, as shown in (6.20). All that exists from lower levels would be the attributes and their parameter estimates, which can be obtained readily at the uppermost level of the tree, or carried forward as V_{mj}.

6.4   Empirical illustration

We use a single data set with sufficient richness to provide a context within which to compare the family of choice models. The data, collected as part of a 1987 intercity mode choice study, are a subsample of 210 non-business travellers travelling between Sydney, Canberra and Melbourne who could choose from four alternatives (plane, car, bus and train). The sample is choice-based (Cosslett 1981), with oversampling of the less-popular modes (plane, train and bus) and undersampling of the more popular mode, car. The data set also enables us to evaluate the implications of failing to correct for choice-based sampling.[2]

The level of service data was derived from highway and transport networks in Sydney, Melbourne, non-metropolitan NSW and Victoria, including the Australian Capital Territory. The data file contains the following information:

MODE	Equal 1 for the mode chosen and 0 otherwise
TTME	Terminal waiting time for plane, train and bus (minutes)
INVC	Invehicle cost for all stages (dollars)
INVT	Invehicle time for all stages (minutes)
GC	Generalised cost = Invc + (Invc*value of travel time savings) (dollars)
CHAIR	Dummy for chosen mode is Air (1,0)
HINC	Household income ($'000s)
PSIZE	Travelling group size (number)

---

[2] All model estimation was performed with the 1999 Windows version of LIMDEP (Econometric Software 1999). The 1999 version gives the user the option to specify the McFadden nested logit structure which is consistent with random utility maximisation, and to normalise on either the upper or lower scale parameters in a two-level model.

Table 6.1. *Two observations from the intercity mode data set*

MODE	TTME	INVC	INVT	GC	CHAIR	HINC	PSIZE	Choice specific effects				
Observation 1												
0.0	69.0	59.0	100.0	70.0	0.0	35.0	1.0	1.0	0.0	0.0	0.0	Air
0.0	34.0	31.0	372.0	71.0	0.0	35.0	1.0	0.0	1.0	0.0	0.0	Train
0.0	35.0	25.0	417.0	70.0	0.0	35.0	1.0	0.0	0.0	1.0	0.0	Bus
1.0	0.0	10.0	80.0	30.0	0.0	35.0	1.0	0.0	0.0	0.0	1.0	Car
Observation 2												
0.0	64.0	58.0	68.0	68.0	0.0	30.0	2.0	1.0	0.0	0.0	0.0	Air
0.0	44.0	31.0	354.0	84.0	0.0	30.0	2.0	0.0	1.0	0.0	0.0	Train
0.0	53.0	25.0	399.0	85.0	0.0	30.0	2.0	0.0	0.0	1.0	0.0	Bus
1.0	0.0	11.0	255.0	50.0	0.0	30.0	2.0	0.0	0.0	0.0	1.0	Car

The 210 observations expand to 840 lines of data (or cases) for a fixed choice set of four alternatives, as illustrated in table 6.1 with car as the chosen mode in observations 1 and 2. A set of choice-specific effects are included in the last four columns of data to represent alternative-specific constants (ASCs), although in most software packages these ASCs can be identified in the model specification without having to include them in the base data set. We show in table 6.1 two observations from the data set so that the structure becomes clearer.

The models estimated in this chapter and in the appendix are not all nested. That is, one cannot use a simple likelihood ratio test to evaluate pairs of models such as an HEV model and an NL model. Our preferred basis for comparison is behavioural responses revealed through the calculation of marginal effects and elasticities. To demonstrate the value of marginal effects, let us begin with the MNL model with only the characteristics of each sampled individual in the utility expression, and generic utility parameters. The notation P_j is used for prob $(y = j)$. By differentiation and ignoring the scale parameter(s), we find that:

$$\partial \operatorname{prob}(y_q = j)/\partial \beta_k = P_k(1 - P_k)\mathbf{x} \quad \text{if } j = k,$$
$$= -P_0 P_k \mathbf{x} \quad \text{if } j \neq k. \tag{6.21}$$

That is, every utility parameter vector affects every probability. The utility parameters in the model are not the marginal effects. Indeed these marginal effects need not even have the same sign as the utility parameters. Hence the statistical significance of a utility parameter does not imply the same significance for the marginal effect:

$$\partial \operatorname{prob}(y_q = j)/\partial \mathbf{x} = P_j(\beta_j - \overline{\beta}), \overline{\beta} = \Sigma_j P_j \beta_j \text{ (defined below as } \delta_j). \tag{6.22}$$

Neither the sign nor the magnitude of δ_j need bear any relationship to those of β_j. The asymptotic covariance matrix for an estimator of δ_j would be computed using

$$\operatorname{asy.var.}[\hat{\delta}_j] = \mathbf{G}_j \operatorname{asy.var}[\hat{\beta}]\mathbf{G}_j', \tag{6.23}$$

where $\hat{\beta}$ is the full parameter vector, and

$$\text{asy.var}(\hat{\delta}_j) = \sum_l \sum_m \mathbf{V}_{jl}\text{asy.cov}\,(\hat{\beta}_l, \hat{\beta}'_m)\mathbf{V}'_{jm},\ j = 0,\dots,J, \tag{6.24}$$

where

$$\mathbf{V}_{jl} = [\mathbf{1}(j = l) - P_l]\{P_j\mathbf{I} - \delta_j\mathbf{x}'\} - P_j\delta_l\mathbf{x}'$$

and

$$\mathbf{1}(j = l) = 1 \text{ if } j = l, \text{ and } 0 \text{ otherwise.}$$

β_j, equal to $\partial \log(P_j/P_0)/\partial \mathbf{x}$, has been suggested as an interpretation of the utility parameters. 'Logit' is not a natural unit of measurement, and is definitely not an elasticity. Utility parameters in MNL are less informative than marginal effects. Marginal rates of substitution (e.g., value of travel-time savings), marginal effects and elasticities are the most useful behavioural outputs. For an MNL model in which attributes of alternatives are included as well as characteristics of sampled individuals, the marginal effects defined as derivatives of the probabilities are given as:

$$\delta_{jm} = \partial P_j/\partial \mathbf{x}_m = [\mathbf{1}(j = m) - P_jP_m]\beta. \tag{6.25}$$

The presence of the IIA property produces identical cross effects. The derivative above is one input into the more general elasticity formula:

$$\eta_{jm} = \partial \log P_j / \log \mathbf{x}_m = (\mathbf{x}_m/P_j)[\mathbf{1}(j = m) - P_jP_m]\beta. \tag{6.26}$$

For the sample as a whole one can derive unweighted or weighted elasticities (as discussed in chapter 3). To obtain an unweighted elasticity for the sample, the derivatives and elasticities are computed by averaging sample values. The empirical estimate of the elasticity is:

$$\hat{\eta}_{jm} = \left(\frac{1}{Q}\sum_{q=1}^{Q}\frac{1}{\hat{P}_j(q)}[\mathbf{1}(j = m) - \hat{P}_j(q)\hat{P}_m(q)]\right) = \left(\sum_{q=1}^{Q}w(q)\hat{\theta}_{jm}(q)\right), \tag{6.27}$$

where $\hat{P}_j(q)$ indicates the probability estimate for the qth observation and $w(q) = 1/Q$. A problem can arise if any single observation has a very small estimated probability, as it will inordinately increase the estimated elasticity. There is no corresponding effect to offset this. Thus, a single outlying estimate of a probability can produce unreasonable estimates of elasticities. This could, however, be the result of mis-specification, in which case the weighting may be a palliative. To deal with this, one should compute 'probability weighted' elasticities, as proposed in chapter 3, by replacing the common weight $w(q) = 1/Q$ with

$$w_j(q) = \frac{\hat{P}_j(q)}{\sum_{q=1}^{Q}\hat{P}_j(q)}. \tag{6.28}$$

With this construction, the observation that would cause the outlying value of the elasticity automatically receives a correspondingly small weight in the average.

For a nested logit form, the generalised definition of the elasticity of choice in (6.27) with respect to the kth attribute g^* obtained from a nested logit model, $P_s.P_{b|s}. P_{m|sb}$, is:

$$\partial \log P_{aht} \partial \log g^*_{aht} = \partial P_{aht}/\partial g^*_{aht} \cdot g^*_{aht}/P_{aht} \tag{6.29}$$

$$= g^*_{sbm,k} x_k [\delta - P_{sbm}], \tag{6.30}$$

where

$$\delta = \Delta_{sv} \cdot \Delta_{bw} \cdot \Delta_{mx} \cdot 1/\lambda_{sb} + \Delta_{bw} \cdot \Delta_{mx} \cdot [1/\lambda_{sb} - 1/\tau_s] \cdot P_{m|sb}$$

$$+ \Delta_{mx} \cdot [\tau_s - 1] \cdot \tau_s \cdot P_{b|s} \cdot P_{m|sb} \tag{6.31}$$

and $\Delta_{sv} = 1$ if $s = 1$, otherwise $= 0$. s, b and m define the three levels of a nested logit tree.

6.4.1   Setting the scene with a base multinomial logit model

A simple multinomial logit model is given in table 6.2. It is useful to spend some time interpreting the base output because it will be the basis for comparisons with other models.

Table 6.2. *Summary results for a simple multinomial logit model*

Variables	Utility parameters	t-values
GC	−0.0235	−4.62
TTME	−0.1002	−9.51
HINC (Air)	0.0238	2.13
PSIZE (Air)	−1.1738	−4.55
A_AIR	7.3348	7.75
A_TRAIN	4.3719	9.14
A_BUS	3.5917	7.55
Log likelihood	−185.91	
Log likelihood (constants only)	−283.76	
Log likelihood at zero	−291.12	
Pseudo-R^2	0.35	

Note: A_i are alternative-specific constants.

Typical output includes an indication of the sample shares and, where a choice-based sample is used with choice-based weights, an indication of the weights defined as the ratio of the population size to the number in the sample choosing an alternative. In the data, the sample shares for air, train, bus and car are respectively 27.6, 30, 14.3 and 28.1 per cent. The actual population shares are respectively 14, 13, 9 and 28 per cent. The base model in table 6.2 assumes no choice-based weights. The overall

goodness-of-fit is defined by the log likelihood function at convergence, equal to
-185.91. This is compared to the log likelihood with no alternative-specific constants
and utility parameters of -291.12, producing a likelihood ratio index (or a pseudo-R^2)
of 0.361 without adjustment for degrees of freedom, and 0.354 after adjusting for
degrees of freedom (see chapter 3 for more details). A comparison with the log likelihood function when only the constants are included in the model (i.e., when the only
information we have is sample shares), given by -283.75, suggests that the attributes
influencing choice (i.e., GC, TTME, HINCA and PSIZEA) are the major contributors
to the reduction in the log likelihood. The constants contribute very little to the overall
goodness-of-fit, equivalent to 0.0167 in the overall pseudo-R^2 of 0.354.

The utility parameters for each of the attributes are all of the expected sign and
statistically well above the 95 per cent confidence limit of 1.96. As might be expected,
ceteris paribus, as household income increases, the probability of selecting to fly
increases; as the size of the travelling party increases, the probability of flying
decreases. Household income and party size are observation-specific characteristics
that do not vary across the alternatives for each sampled observation. In order to
establish some variation, they can only enter in utility expressions for up to $J - 1$
alternatives. Without any variation, there is nothing to contribute to sources of
explanatory variance across the choice set. If the analyst wished to incorporate an
observation-specific effect in all utility expressions, it must be interacted with an
alternative-specific effect; for example, dividing GC by HINCA. The alternative-
specific constants are all statistically significant, which tells us that these 'utility parameters', which represent the mean of the distribution of the unobserved effects, are a
statistically important measure of the influence of all values in the distribution of
random components across the sample (i.e., the variances are particularly small
around the mean). This model has captured the major sources of variability in choice
behaviour by the set of attributes in the observed component of the utility expression.

The matrix of direct and cross elasticities for generalised cost is presented in table
6.3. We will limit our comparison of elasticities to this one important attribute. As
expected, the direct elasticities are negative; thus a 1 per cent increase in the generalised cost of flying decreases the probability of flying by 1.702 per cent on average,
ceteris paribus. The sensitivity is similar for car but is much greater for bus and·train.
The results in table 6.3 assume an unweighted aggregate elasticity in column 2 and a
probability weighted sample average in column 3. The cross elasticities should all be
the same for a specific alternative, owing to the presence of the IIA effect. In the
presentation of aggregate elasticities, the constant cross effect for an alternative will
be identical only when the aggregation uses the unweighted indicator '1/sample size'.
Even though the identical cross effects exist at the individual level before aggregation,
the preferred weighted aggregate elasticity will produce different cross elasticities for
an alternative, simply because of the weighting by choice probabilities. This is potentially misleading to analysts who might think that they have established variation in
the cross elasticities (and cross effects) for a simple MNL model subject to the IIA
property. We strongly advise analysts to ignore the cross elasticities for the simple
MNL model.

Table 6.3. *Estimated GC elasticities for basic logit model*

	Unweighted average	Probability weighted
Alternative = Air		
Choice = Air	−1.702	−1.069
Choice = Train	0.711	0.300
Choice = Bus	0.711	0.416
Choice = Car	0.711	0.519
Alternative = Train		
Choice = Air	0.735	0.392
Choice = Train	−2.326	−1.197
Choice = Bus	0.735	0.542
Choice = Car	0.735	0.617
Alternative = Bus		
Choice = Air	0.363	0.223
Choice = Train	0.363	0.226
Choice = Bus	−2.346	−1.495
Choice = Car	0.363	0.299
Alternative = Car		
Choice = Air	0.631	0.500
Choice = Train	0.631	0.416
Choice = Bus	0.631	0.507
Choice = Car	−1.612	−1.193

6.4.2 Introducing choice-based weights into the base multinomial logit model

If an MNL model is estimated with $J - 1$ alternative-specific constants, the model will reproduce the sample shares. By weighting the sample by the ratio of the population to sample shares, we reproduce the population shares. The estimated MNL model with choice-based weights is summarised in table 6.4. The main interest in the revised model is the improvement in the overall goodness-of-fit and the comparison of the marginal effects (table 6.5). Compared to the unweighted MNL model, the choice-based weighted model has improved the log likelihood from −185.91 to −138.36, which on the likelihood ratio test is a major improvement at any accepted level of statistical significance. The pseudo-R^2 is now 0.519 (compared to 0.354) after correcting for degrees of freedom. Note that a comparison of the utility parameters for the unweighted and choice-based weighted models as shown in table 6.4 reveals that only the alternative-specific constants change substantially. The mean estimates of the other utility parameters differ only by sampling error. Given this knowledge, we could have corrected the alternative-specific constants (ASCs) analytically by taking each estimated ASC and deducting from it the natural logarithm of the ratio of the true population share to the choice-based sample share.

Table 6.4. *Basic MNL model with choice-based weights*

Variables	Utility parameters	t-values
Choice-based weighted:		
A_AIR	8.2193	6.03
A_TRAIN	3.9216	7.99
A_BUS	3.4956	6.10
GC	−0.0236	−3.91
TTME	−0.1323	−7.38
HINC (Air)	0.0185	1.46
PSIZE (Air)	−1.274	−2.90
Unweighted:		
A_AIR	7.3348	7.75
A_TRAIN	4.3719	9.14
A_BUS	3.5917	7.55
GC	−0.0235	−4.62
TTME	−0.1002	−9.51
HINC (Air)	0.0238	2.13
PSIZE (Air)	−1.1738	−4.55
Log likelihood	−138.37	
Log likelihood at zero	−219.12	
Pseudo-R^2	0.519	

When one compares the marginal effects, it is clear that the influence of a one-unit change in the level of an attribute has a noticeably different impact in the presence and absence of correction of choice-based sampling (CBS). For example, for air travel, with naive averaging, the direct marginal effect of −0.269 in the absence of CBS correction is significantly greater than −0.161 in the presence of CBS correction. The same relativity applies when probability weights are used, yielding respectively −0.321 and −0.241. Thus the impact of a one-unit change in generalised cost varies from −0.161 to −0.321 (essentially double), depending on the assumption made about CBS correction and aggregation of marginal effects across the sample. This range is substantial.

6.4.3 Testing for violation of the independence of irrelevant alternatives property

The simplicity and empirical appeal of the MNL model is a consequence of the IIA property. For any MNL choice model, the presence or absence of an alternative preserves the ratio of the probabilities associated with other alternatives in the choice set (i.e., P_i/P_j is unaffected by changes in characteristics of alternative k). This restriction enables analysts to add a new alternative or delete an existing alternative without having to re-estimate the model. All other choice models require re-estimation. To decide if the IIA property is satisfied in an application, it is necessary to implement a

Table 6.5. *Comparison of GC marginal effects for unweighted and choice-based MNL models*

	Naive averaging		Probability weighted	
	Unweighted MNL	Choice-based weighted MNL	Unweighted MNL	Choice-based weighted MNL
Alternative = Air				
Choice = Air	−0.269	−0.161	−0.321	−0.241
Choice = Train	0.086	0.023	0.094	0.033
Choice = Bus	0.052	0.019	0.102	0.042
Choice = Car	0.131	0.119	0.185	0.132
Alternative = Train				
Choice = Air	0.086	0.023	0.096	0.028
Choice = Train	−0.299	−0.185	−0.351	−0.317
Choice = Bus	0.067	0.024	0.132	0.055
Choice = Car	0.146	0.138	0.198	0.143
Alternative = Bus				
Choice = Air	0.052	0.019	0.059	0.025
Choice = Train	0.067	0.024	0.078	0.035
Choice = Bus	−0.192	−0.133	−0.378	−0.344
Choice = Car	0.073	0.090	0.088	0.092
Alternative = Car				
Choice = Air	0.131	0.119	0.165	0.187
Choice = Train	0.146	0.138	0.179	0.248
Choice = Bus	0.073	0.090	0.144	0.247
Choice = Car	−0.350	−0.347	−0.471	−0.367

test to establish violation of the condition. One should always undertake such a test before proceeding to less restrictive models, since a major reason for moving to establish greater realism, but more complex estimation, is to avoid the IIA property. Where it is not being violated in a simple MNL model, one should stay with splendid simplicity.

Hausman and McFadden (1984) have proposed a specification test for the MNL model to test the assumption of the independence of irrelevant alternatives. First estimate the choice model with all alternatives. The specification under the alternative hypothesis of IIA violation is the model with a smaller set of choices, estimated with a restricted set of alternatives and the same attributes. The set of observations is reduced to those in which one of the smaller sets of choices was made. The test statistic is

$$q = [b_u - b_r]'[V_r - V_u]^{-1}[b_u - b_r], \tag{6.32}$$

where 'u' and 'r' indicate unrestricted and restricted (smaller choice set) models and V is an estimated variance matrix for the estimates.

Table 6.6. *Results of an IIA test for an MNL model*

Variables	Utility parameters	*t*-values
GC	−0.04012	−5.50
TTME	0.00239	0.042
Log likelihood	−132.88	
Log likelihood at zero	−210.72	
Pseudo-R^2	0.365	

Number of obs. = 210, *skipped 58 bad obs.* ← (chose air)
Hausman test for IIA. Excluded choices are AIR
Chi-sq [2] = 21.3402, prob (C > c) = 0.000023 ← (test result)

There is a possibility that restricting the choice set can lead to a singularity. When you drop one or more alternatives, some attribute may be constant among the remaining choices. For example, in the application above, HINCA is non-zero only for the AIR choice, so when AIR is dropped from the choice set, HINCA is always zero for the remaining choices. In this case, a singular Hessian will result. Hausman and McFadden suggest estimating the model with the smaller number of choice sets and a smaller number of attributes. There is no question of consistency, or omission of a relevant attribute, since if the attribute is always constant among the choices, its variation is obviously not affecting the choice. After estimation, the subvector of the larger parameter vector in the first model can be measured against the parameter vector from the second model using the Hausman–McFadden statistic (6.32). The test results for our example data are given in table 6.6. On the basis of the Hausman–McFadden test, the IIA restriction is rejected. That is, we have violated the constant variance assumption and need to consider a less restrictive specification of the choice model. We will now consider more complex models that do not impose the assumption, and incrementally evaluate the behavioural gains.

6.5 The nested logit model — empirical examples

Two two-level NL models are estimated: an NL model in which each branch has two elemental alternatives (also referred to as a non-degenerate NL model), and an NL model in which one branch has three elemental alternatives and the other branch has one elemental alternative (also referred to as a partially degenerate NL model). In the non-degenerate case, it is assumed that one partition of the choice set contains the air and car modes. The other partition contains the train and bus modes. In the model with partial degeneracy, the degenerate partition is assumed to contain the air mode with the non-degenerate partition containing the other three (ground) modes. For each elemental alternative, mode-specific constants are specified for air (A_AIR), train (A_TRAIN), and bus (A_BUS). All modes include generalised cost (GC), while terminal waiting time (TTME) is included in the non-car alternatives. Household income (HINC) is added into the utility expressions for the branch composite alternatives 'other' and 'fly', respectively, for the non-degenerate and partially degenerate NL specifications. The notation within parentheses indicates the descriptors used in the tables to denote the corresponding parameters. Section 6.5 draws heavily on joint research by Hensher and Greene (1999).

6.5.1 Setting out the notation for estimating NL models

We propose the following notation as a method of unifying the different forms of the NL model. Each observed (or representative) component of the utility expression for an alternative (usually denoted as V_k for the kth alternative) is defined in terms of four items – the parameters associated with each explanatory variable, an alternative-specific constant, a scale parameter and the explanatory variables. The utility of alternative k for individual t is

$$U_{tk} = g_k(\alpha_k, \mathbf{b}'\mathbf{x}_{tk}, \varepsilon_{tk}) \tag{6.33a}$$

$$= g_k(V_{tk}, \varepsilon_{tk}) \tag{6.33b}$$

$$= \alpha_k + \mathbf{b}'x_{tk} + \varepsilon_{tk}, \tag{6.33c}$$

$$\text{var}\,[\varepsilon_{tk}] = \sigma^2 = \kappa/\theta^2. \tag{6.34}$$

The scale parameter, θ, is proportional to the inverse of the standard deviation of the random component in the utility expression, σ, and is a critical input into the set up of the NL model (Ben-Akiva and Lerman 1985; Hensher, Louviere and Swait 1999). Under the assumptions now well established in the literature, utility maximisation in the presence of random components which have independent (across choices and individuals) extreme value distributions produces a simple closed form for the probability that choice k is made;

$$\text{prob}\,[U_{tk} > U_{tj} \forall j \neq k] = \frac{\exp\,(\alpha_k + \mathbf{b}'\mathbf{x}_{tk})}{\displaystyle\sum_{j=1}^{K} \exp\,(\alpha_j + \mathbf{b}'\mathbf{x}_{tj})}. \tag{6.35}$$

Under these assumptions, the common variance of the assumed IID random components is lost. The same observed set of choices emerges regardless of the (common) scaling of the utilities. Hence the latent variance is normalised at one, not as a restriction, but of necessity for identification.

One justification for moving from the MNL model to the NL model is to enable one to *partially relax* (and hence test) the independence assumption of the unobserved components of utility across alternatives. The standard deviations (or variances) of the random error components in the utility expressions can be different across groups of alternatives in the choice set (see equation (6.10)). This arises because the sources of utility associated with the alternatives are not fully accommodated in V_k. The missing sources of utility may differentially impact on the random components across the alternatives. To accommodate the possibility of partial differential covariances, we

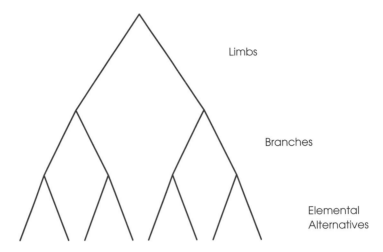

Figure 6.3 Descriptors for a three-level NL tree

must explicitly introduce the scale parameters into each of the utility expressions. (If all scale parameters are equal, then the NL model 'collapses' back to a simple MNL model.) Hunt (1998) discusses the underlying conditions that produce the nested logit model as a result of utility maximisation within a partitioned choice set.

The notation for a three-level nested logit model covers the majority of applications. The literature suggests that very few analysts estimate models with more than three levels, and two levels are the most common. However it will be shown below that a two-level model *may* require a third level (in which the lowest level is a set of dummy nodes and links) simply to ensure consistency with utility maximisation (which has nothing to do with a desire to test a three-level NL model).

It is useful to represent each level in an NL tree by a unique descriptor. For a three level tree (figure 6.3), the top level will be represented by limbs, the middle level by a number of *branches* and the bottom level by a set of *elemental alternatives*, or twigs. We have $k = 1, \ldots, K$ elemental alternatives, $j = 1, \ldots, J$ branch composite alternatives and $i = 1, \ldots, I$ limb composite alternatives. We use the notation $k|j,i$ to denote alternative k in branch j of limb i and $j|i$ to denote branch j in limb i.

Define parameter vectors in the utility functions at each level as follows: **b** for elemental alternatives, **a** for branch composite alternatives, and **c** for limb composite alternatives. The branch level composite alternative involves an aggregation of the lower level alternatives. As discussed below, a branch specific scale parameter $\mu(j|i)$ will be associated with the lowest level of the tree. Each elemental alternative in the jth branch will actually have scale parameter $\mu'(k|j,i)$. Since these will, of necessity, be equal for all alternatives in a branch, the distinction by k is meaningless. As such, we collapse these into $\mu(j|i)$. The parameters $\lambda(j|i)$ will be associated with the branch level. The inclusive value (IV) parameters at the branch level will involve the ratios $\lambda(j|i)/\mu(j|i)$. For identification, it will be necessary to normalise one of these parameters, either $\mu(j|i)$ or $\lambda(j|i)$ to one. The inclusive value (IV) parameters associated with the composite alternative at each level are thus defined either by scale parameters $\mu(j|i)$ or $\lambda(j|i)$ for branches, and $\gamma(i)$ for limbs. The IV parameters associated with the IV variable in a branch, calculated from the natural logarithm of the sum of the exponential of the V_k expressions at the elemental alternative level directly below a branch, implicitly have associated parameters defined as the $\lambda(j|i)/\mu(j|i)$, but, as noted, some normalisation is required. Some analysts do this without acknowledgement of which normalisation they have used, which makes the comparison of reported results between studies difficult. Normalisation is simply the process of setting one or more scale parameters equal to unity, while allowing the other scale parameters to be estimated.

The literature is vague on the implications of choosing the normalisation of $\lambda(j|i) = 1$ versus $\mu(j|i) = 1$. It is important to note that the notation $\mu'(m|j, i)$ used below refers to the scale parameter for each elemental alternative. However, since a nested logit structure is specified to test for the presence of identical scale within a subset of alternatives, it comes as no surprise that all alternatives partitioned under a common branch have the same scale parameter imposed on them. Thus $\mu'(k|j, i) = \mu(j||i)$ for every $k = 1, \dots, K|j, i$ alternatives in branch j in limb i.

We now set out the probability choice system (PCS) for the situation where we normalise on $\mu(j|i)$ – called random utility model 1 (RU1), and the situation where we normalise on $\lambda(j|i)$ – called random utility model 2 (RU2). We ignore the subscripts for an individual. For later purposes, we now define the three-level PCS,

$$P(k, j, i) = P(k|j, i) \times P(j|i) \times P(i). \tag{6.36}$$

Random utility model 1 (RU1)

The choice probabilities for the *elemental alternatives* are defined as:

$$P(k|j, i) = \frac{\exp\left[\mathbf{b}'\mathbf{x}(k|j, i)\right]}{\displaystyle\sum_{l=1}^{K|j,i} \exp\left[\mathbf{b}'\mathbf{x}(l|j, i)\right]} = \frac{\exp\left[\mathbf{b}'\mathbf{x}(k|j, i)\right]}{\exp\left[\text{IV}(j|i)\right]}, \tag{6.37}$$

where $k|j, i =$ elemental alternative k in branch j of limb i, $K|j, i =$ number of elemental alternatives in branch j of limb i, and the inclusive value for branch j in limb i is

$$\text{IV}(j|i) = \log \sum_{k=1}^{K|j,i} \exp\left[\mathbf{b}'\mathbf{x}(k|j, i)\right]. \tag{6.38}$$

The *branch level* probability is

$$p(j|i) = \frac{\exp\left\{\lambda(j|i)[\mathbf{a}'\mathbf{y}(j|i) + \text{IV}(j|i)]\right\}}{\displaystyle\sum_{m=1}^{J|i} \exp\left\{\lambda(m|i)[\mathbf{a}'\mathbf{y}(m|i) + \text{IV}(m|i)]\right\}}$$

$$= \frac{\exp\left\{\lambda(j|i)[\mathbf{a}'\mathbf{y}(j|i) + \text{IV}(j|i)]\right\}}{\exp\left[\text{IV}(i)\right]}, \tag{6.39}$$

where $j|i =$ branch j in limb i, $J|i =$ number of branches in limb i, and

$$\text{IV}(i) = \log \sum_{j=1}^{J|i} \exp\{\lambda(j|i)[\mathbf{a}'\mathbf{y}(j|i) + \text{IV}(j|i)]\}. \tag{6.40}$$

Finally, the *limb level* is defined by

$$p(i) = \frac{\exp\{\gamma(i)[\mathbf{c}'\mathbf{z}(i) + \text{IV}(i)]\}}{\displaystyle\sum_{n=1}^{I} \exp\{\gamma(n)[\mathbf{c}'\mathbf{z}(n) + \text{IV}(n)]\}} = \frac{\exp\{\gamma(i)[\mathbf{c}'\mathbf{z}(i) + \text{IV}(i)]\}}{\exp(\text{IV})}, \tag{6.41}$$

where $I =$ number of limbs in the three-level tree and

$$\text{IV} = \log \sum_{i=1}^{I} \exp\{\gamma(i)[\mathbf{c}'\mathbf{z}(i) + \text{IV}(i)]\}. \tag{6.42}$$

RU1 has been described (e.g., by Bates 1999) as corresponding to a non-normalised nested logit (NNNL) specification, since the parameters are scaled at the lowest level (i.e., for $\mu'(k|j, i) = \mu(j|i) = 1$).

Random utility model 2 (RU2)

Suppose, instead, we normalise the upper-level parameters and allow the lower-level scale parameters to be free. The *elemental alternatives* level probabilities will be:

$$P(k|j, i) = \frac{\exp[\mu'(k|j, i)\mathbf{b}'\mathbf{x}(k|j, i)]}{\displaystyle\sum_{l=1}^{K|j,i} \exp[\mu'(l|j, i)\mathbf{b}'\mathbf{x}(l|j, i)]} = \frac{\exp[\mu'(k|j, i)\mathbf{b}'\mathbf{x}(k|j, i)]}{\exp[\text{IV}(j|i)]} \tag{6.43}$$

$$= \frac{\exp[\mu(j|i)\mathbf{b}'\mathbf{x}(k|j, i)]}{\displaystyle\sum_{l=1}^{K|j,i} \exp[\mu(j|i)\mathbf{b}'\mathbf{x}(l|j, i)]} = \frac{\exp[\mu(j|i)\mathbf{b}'\mathbf{x}(k|j, i)]}{\exp[\text{IV}(j|i)]} \tag{6.44}$$

(with the latter equality resulting from the identification restriction $\mu'(k|j, i) = \mu'(m|j, i) = \mu'(j|i)$) and

$$\text{IV}(j|i) = \log \sum_{k=1}^{K|j,i} \exp[\mu(j|i)\mathbf{b}'\mathbf{x}(k|j, i)]. \tag{6.45}$$

The *branch level* is defined by:

$$p(j|i) = \frac{\exp\left\{\gamma(i)\left[\mathbf{a}'\mathbf{y}(j|i) + \frac{1}{\mu(j|i)}\,\mathrm{IV}(j|i)\right]\right\}}{\sum\limits_{m=1}^{J|i}\exp\left\{\gamma(i)\left[\mathbf{a}'\mathbf{y}(m|i) + \frac{1}{\mu(m|i)}\,\mathrm{IV}(m|i)\right]\right\}}$$

$$= \frac{\exp\left\{\gamma(i)\left[\mathbf{a}'\mathbf{y}(j|i) + \frac{1}{\mu(j|i)}\,\mathrm{IV}(j|i)\right]\right\}}{\exp\left[\mathrm{IV}(i)\right]} \qquad (6.46)$$

$$\mathrm{IV}(i) = \log \sum_{j=1}^{J|i}\left\{\gamma(i)\left[a'y(j|i) + \frac{1}{\mu(j|i)}\,\mathrm{IV}(j|i)\right]\right\}. \qquad (6.47)$$

The *limb level* is defined by:

$$p(i) = \frac{\exp\left[\mathbf{c}'\mathbf{z}(i) + \frac{1}{\gamma(i)}\,IV(i)\right]}{\sum\limits_{n=1}^{I}\exp\left[\mathbf{c}'\mathbf{z}(n) + \frac{1}{\gamma(n)}\,\mathrm{IV}(n)\right]} = \frac{\exp\left[\mathbf{c}'\mathbf{z}(i) + \frac{1}{\gamma(i)}\,IV(i)\right]}{\exp\left(\mathrm{IV}\right)} \qquad (6.48)$$

$$\mathrm{IV} = \log \sum_{i=1}^{I}\exp\left[c'z(i) + \frac{1}{\gamma(I)}\,\mathrm{IV}(i)\right]. \qquad (6.49)$$

It is typically assumed that it is arbitrary as to which scale parameter is normalised (see Hunt (1998) for a useful discussion). Most applications normalise the scale parameters associated with the branch level utility expressions [i.e., $\lambda(j|i)$] at 1 as in RU2 above, then allow the scale parameters associated with the elemental alternatives $((j|i))$ and hence the inclusive value parameters in the branch composite alternatives to be unrestricted. It is implicitly assumed that the empirical results are identical to those that would be obtained if RU1 were instead the specification (even though parameter estimates are numerically different). *But, within the context of a two-level partition of a nest estimated as a two-level model, unless all attribute parameters are alternative-specific, this assumption is only true if the non-normalised scale parameters are constrained to be the same across nodes within the same level of a tree (i.e., at the branch level for two levels, and at the branch level and the limb level for three levels).* This latter result actually appears explicitly in some studies of this model (e.g., Maddala 1983: 70; Quigley 1985), but is frequently ignored in recent applications. Note that in the common case of estimation of RU2 with two levels (which eliminates $(\gamma(i))$ the 'free' IV parameter estimated will typically be $1/\mu(j|i)$. Other interpretations of this result are discussed in Hunt (1998).

6.5.2 Conditions to ensure consistency with utility maximisation

The previous section set out a uniform notation for a three-level NL model, choosing a different level in the tree for normalisation (i.e., setting scale parameters to an arbitrary value, typically unity). We have chosen levels one and two respectively for the RU1 and RU2 models. We now are ready to present a range of alternative empirical specifications for the NL model, some of which satisfy utility maximisation either directly from estimation or by some simple transformation of the estimated parameters. Compliance with utility maximisation requires that the addition of a constant value to all elemental alternatives has no effect on the choice probabilities of the alternatives (McFadden 1981). We limit the discussion to a two-level NL model and initially assume that all branches have at least two elemental alternatives. The important case of a degenerate branch (i.e., only one elemental alternative) is treated separately later.

Table 6.7 presents full information maximum likelihood (FIML) estimates of a two-level non-degenerate NL model. The tree structure for table 6.7 has two branches, PUBLIC = (train, bus) and OTHER = (car, plane). In the PCS for this model, household income enters the probability of the branch choice directly in the utility for OTHER. Inclusive values from the lowest level enter both utility functions at the branch level. Table 6.8 presents FIML estimates of a two-level partially degenerate NL model. The tree structure for the models in table 6.8, save for model 7 which has an artificial third level, is FLY (plane) and GROUND (train, bus, car).

Estimates for both the non-normalised nested logit (NNNL) model and the utility maximising (GEV-NL) parameterisations are presented. In the case of the GEV model parameterisation, estimates under each of the two normalisations (RU1: $\mu = 1$ and RU2: $\lambda = 1$) are provided, as are estimates with the IV parameters restricted to equality within a level of the tree and unrestricted.

Eight models are summarised in table 6.7 and six models in table 6.8. Since there is only one limb, we drop the limb indicator from $\lambda(j|i)$ and denote it simply as $\lambda(j)$:

model 1: RU1 with scale parameters equal within a level ($\lambda(1) = \lambda(2)$);
model 2: RU1 with scale parameters unrestricted within a level ($\lambda(1) \neq \lambda(2)$);
model 3: RU2 with scale parameters equal within a level (not applicable for a degenerate branch) ($\mu(1) = \mu(2)$);
model 4: RU2 with scale parameters unrestricted within a level ($\mu(1) \neq \mu(2)$);
model 5: non-normalised NL model with dummy nodes and links to allow unrestricted scale parameters in the presence of generic attributes to recover parameter estimates that are consistent with utility maximisation. This is equivalent up to scale with RU2 (model 4);
model 6: non-normalised NL model with no dummy nodes/links and different scale parameters within a level. This is a typical NL model implemented by many practitioners (and is equivalent to RU1 (model 6.7));
model 7: RU2 with unrestricted scale parameters and dummy nodes and links to comply with utility maximisation (for partial degeneracy). Since model 7 is identical to model 8 in table 6.7, it is not presented; and, in table 6.8 only;
models 8 and 9: for the non-degenerate NL model (table 6.7), these are RU1 and RU2 in which all parameters are alternative-specific and scale parameters are unrestricted across branches.

Table 6.7. *Summary of alternative model specifications for a non-degenerate NL model tree*

	Alternative	Model 1: RU1	Model 2: RU1	Model 3: RU2	Model 4: RU2	Model 5: NNNL***	Model 6: NNNL***	Model 8: RU1*	Model 9: RU2
Variables									
Train constant	Train	4.542 (6.64)	3.757 (5.8)	5.873 (5.8)	6.159 (5.7)	3.6842 (2.34)	3.757 (5.8)	17.396 (2.2)	2.577 (3.8)
Bus constant	Bus	3.924 (5.83)	2.977 (4.4)	5.075 (6.0)	5.380 (5.8)	3.218 (2.18)	2.977 (4.4)	19.523 (2.4)	2.892 (3.73)
Plane constant	Plane	5.0307 (6.81)	4.980 (6.7)	6.507 (5.7)	6.154 (5.2)	3.681 (2.34)	4.980 (6.7)	4.165 (3.3)	4.165 (3.5)
Generalised cost ($)	All	−0.01088 (−2.6)	−0.0148 (−3.5)	−0.01407 (−2.6)	−0.01955 (−1.8)	−0.01169 (−1.8)	−0.0148 (−3.5)		
Transfer time (mins.)	All excl car	−0.0859 (−7.4)	−0.0861 (−7.3)	−0.1111 (−5.5)	−0.1064 (−5.2)	−0.0637 (−2.5)	−0.0861 (−7.3)		
Hhld income ($000s)	Other	0.03456 (3.2)	0.0172 (2.9)	0.0447 (4.0)	0.0426 (3.8)	0.0426 (3.8)	0.0416 (3.4)	0.04269 (4.24)	0.04269 (3.8)
Generalised cost ($)	Air							0.00492 (0.56)	0.00492 (0.60)
Generalised cost ($)	Train							−0.0943 (−3.0)	−0.0139 (−2.8)
Generalised cost ($)	Bus							−0.1065 (−2.9)	−0.0158 (−2.9)
Generalised cost ($)	Car							−0.0143 (−2.5)	−0.0143 (−3.0)
Transfer time (mins)	Air							−0.1048 (−6.2)	−0.1048 (−7.1)
Transfer time (mins)	Train							−0.0787 (−2.5)	−0.0116 (−1.9)
Transfer time (mins)	Bus							−0.1531 (−3.5)	−0.0227 (−1.9)
IV parameters									
IV Other	Other	1.293 (5.3)	2.42 (4.6)	0.773 (3.8)	0.579 (3.3)	0.969 (3.2)**	2.42 (4.6)	1.00 (fixed)	1.00 (fixed)
IV Public transport	Public transport	1.293 (5.3)	1.28 (5.1)	0.773 (3.8)	1.03 (3.2)	1.724 (3.3)**	1.28 (5.1)	0.148 (2.0)	6.75 (1.9)
Log-likelihood		−190.178	−184.31	−190.178	−188.43	−188.43	−184.31	−177.82	−177.82
Direct Elasticities									
	Plane	−0.544	−0.797	−0.544	−0.666	−0.666	−0.797	0.228	0.228
	Car	−0.651	−1.081	−0.651	−0.762	−0.762	−1.081	−0.799	−0.799
	Train	−0.629	−0.854	−0.629	−0.910	−0.910	−0.854	−0.188	−1.27
	Bus	−0.759	−1.014	−0.759	−1.174	−1.174	−1.014	−0.343	−2.32

Notes: Structure: other {plane, car} vs. public transport {train, bus} except for model 5 which is other {planem (plane), carm (car)} vs. public transport {trainm (train), busm (bus)}. There is no model 7 in order to keep equivalent model numbering in tables 6.7 and 6.8.

Generalised cost (in dollars) = out-of-pocket fuel cost for car or fare for plane, train and bus + time cost; where time cost = linehaul travel time and value of travel time savings in $/minute. Transfer time (in minutes) = the time spent waiting for and transferring to plane, train, bus.

* Model 8 with all alternative-specific attributes produces the exact parameter estimates, overall goodness of fit and elasticities as the NNNL model (and hence it is not reported). ** = IV parameters in model 5 based on imposing equality of IV for (other, trainm, busm) and for (public transport, planem, carm). *** = standard errors are uncorrected.

Table 6.8. *Summary of alternative model specifications for a partially degenerate NL model tree*

	Alternatives	Model 1: RU1	Model 2: RU1	Model 4: RU2	Model 5: NNNL**	Model 6: NNNL**	Model 7: RU2
Variables							
Train constant	Train	5.070 (7.6)	5.065 (7.7)	2.622 (5.9)	9.805 (3.4)	5.065 (7.7)	4.584 (2.7)
Bus constant	Bus	4.145 (6.7)	4.096 (6.7)	2.143 (5.5)	8.015 (3.3)	4.096 (6.7)	3.849 (2.7)
Plane constant	Plane	5.167 (4.3)	6.042 (5.04)	2.672 (3.0)	9.993 (3.8)	6.042 (5.04)	5.196 (2.7)
Generalised cost ($)	All	-0.0291 (-3.6)	-0.0316 (-3.9)	-0.0151 (4.32)	-0.0564 (2.8)	-0.0316 (-3.9)	-0.0187 (-2.4)
Transfer time (min.)	All excl car	-0.1156 (8.15)	-0.1127 (-7.9)	-0.0598 (-5.9)	-0.2236 (3.7)	-0.1127 (-7.9)	-0.0867 (-2.7)
Hhld income ($000s)	Fly	0.02837 (1.4)	0.0262 (1.5)	0.0143 (1.35)	0.01467 (1.4)	0.01533 (1.6)	0.02108 (1.4)
Party Size	Auto						0.4330 (2.0)
IV parameters							
IV	Fly	0.517 (4.1)	0.586 (4.2)	1.00 (0.67 + 15)*	1.00 (0.67 + 15)*	0.586 (4.2)	Not applicable
IV	Ground	0.517 (4.1)	0.389 (3.1)	1.934 (5.0)*	0.517 (5.0)	0.389 (3.1)	
IV	Auto						Not applicable
IV	Public Transport						1.26 (2.3)
IV	Other						0.844 (2.1)
IV	Land PT						Not applicable
Log-likelihood		-194.94	-193.66	-194.94	-194.94	-193.66	-194.27
Direct Elasticities							
	Plane	-0.864	-1.033	-0.864	-0.864	-1.033	-0.859
	Car	-1.332	-1.353	-1.332	-1.332	-1.353	-0.946
	Train	-1.317	-1.419	-1.317	-1.317	-1.419	-1.076
	Bus	-1.650	-1.878	-1.650	-1.650	-1.878	-1.378

Notes: Structure: fly {plane} vs ground {train, bus, car}. Model 3 is not defined for a degenerate branch model when the IV parameters are forced to equality. Forcing a constraint on model 4 (i.e., equal IV parameters) to obtain model 3 produced exactly the same results for all the parameters. This is exactly what should happen. Since the IV parameter is not identified, no linear constraint that is imposed that involves this parameter is binding. Model 7 tree is Other{fly (plane) vs auto (car)} vs land PT{public transport (train, bus)}.

* = IV parameters in Model 5 based on imposing equality of IV. ** = standard errors are uncorrected.

All results reported in tables 6.7 and 6.8 are obtained using LIMDEP Version 7 (Econometric Software 1998; revised December 1998). The IV parameters for RU1 and RU2 that LIMDEP reports are the μs and the λs that are shown in the equations above. These μs and λs are proportional to the reciprocal of the standard deviation of the random component. The t-values in parenthesis for the NNNL model require correction to compare with RU1 and RU2. Koppelman and Wen (1998) provide the procedure to adjust the t-values. For a two-level model, the corrected variance and hence standard error of estimate for the NNNL model is:

$$\text{var}\,(\beta_{RU}) = \beta_{NN}^2\,\text{var}\,(\mu_{NN}) + \mu_{NN}^2\,\text{var}\,(\beta_{NN}) + 2\mu_{NN}\beta_{NN}\,\text{cov}\,(\mu_{NN},\beta_{NN})$$

$$(6.50)$$

6.5.2.1 The case of generic attribute parameters

Beginning with the non-degenerate case, it can be seen in table 6.7 that the GEV parameterisation estimates with IV parameters unrestricted (models 2 and 4) are *not* invariant to the normalisation chosen. Not only is there no obvious relationship between the two sets of parameter estimates, the log likelihood function values at convergence are not equal (-184.31 vs. -188.43). When the GEV parameterisation is estimated subject to the restriction that the IV parameters be equal (models 1 and 3), invariance is achieved across normalisation after accounting for the difference in scaling. The log likelihood function values at convergence are equal (-190.178), and the IV parameter estimates are inverses of one another ($1/0.773 = 1.293$, within rounding error). Multiplying the utility function parameter estimates at the elemental alternatives level (i.e., $\alpha_{\text{Plane}}, \alpha_{\text{train}}, \alpha_{\text{bus}}$, GC, TTME) by the corresponding IV parameter estimate in one normalisation (e.g., model 1) yields the utility function parameter estimates in another normalisation (e.g., model 3). For example, in model 3, $(1/1.293)*5.873$ for train constant $= 4.542$ in model 1.

The points made above about invariance, or the lack of it, scaling, and the equivalence of GEV and NNNL under the appropriate set of parametric restrictions are also illustrated in table 6.8 for the case of a partially degenerate NL model structure. However, an additional and important result emerges for the partial degeneracy case. If the IV parameters are unrestricted, the GEV model 'estimate' of the parameter on the degenerate partition IV is unity under the $\lambda = 1$ normalisation. This will always be the case because of the cancellation of the IV parameter and the lower-level scaling parameter in the GEV model in the degenerate partition. The results will be invariant to whatever value this parameter is set to. To see this, consider the results for the unrestricted GEV model presented as model 4 in table 6.8. The IV parameter is 'estimated' to be 1.934, and if we were to report model 3, all of the other estimates would be the same as in model 4 and the log likelihood function values at convergence are identical (-194.94). In a degenerate branch, whatever the value of $(1/\mu)$, it will cancel with the lower-level scaling parameter, μ, in the degenerate partition marginal probability. If we select $\mu = 1$ for normalisation (in contrast to λ) in the presence of a degenerate branch, the results will produce restricted (model 1) or unrestricted (model 2) estimates of λ which, unlike μ, do not cancel out in the degenerate branch (Hunt (1998) pursues this issue at length).

To illustrate the equivalence of behavioural outputs for RU1 and RU2, tables 6.7 and 6.8 present the weighted aggregate direct elasticities for the relationship between the generalised cost of alternative kji and the probability of choosing alternative $k|ji$. As expected the results are identical for RU1 (model 1) and RU2 (model 3) when the IV parameters are equal across all branches at a level in the GEV model. The elasticities are significantly different from those obtained from models 2 and 4, although models 4 and 5 produce the same results (see below). Model 6 (equivalent to model 2) is a common model specification in which parameters of attributes are generic and scale parameters are unrestricted within a level of the NL model with no constraints imposed to recover the utility-maximisation estimates.

6.5.2.2 Allowing different scale parameters across nodes in a level in the presence of generic and/or alternative-specific attribute parameters between partitions

When we allow the IV parameters to be unrestricted in the RU1 and RU2 GEV models and in the NNNL model we fail to comply with normalisation invariance, and for models 2 and 6 we also fail to produce consistency with utility maximisation. RU1 (model 2) fails to comply with utility maximisation because of the absence of explicit scaling in the utility expressions for elemental alternatives. We obtain different results on overall goodness-of-fit and the range of behavioural outputs such as elasticities.

For a given nested structure and set of attributes there can be only one utility maximising solution. This presents a dilemma, since we often want the scale parameters to vary between branches and/or limbs or at least test for non-equivalence. This is, after all, the main reason why we seek out alternative nested structures. Fortunately there is a solution, depending on whether one opts for a specification in which either some or all of the parameters are generic, or all are alternative-specific. Models 5 to 9 are alternative specifications.

If all attributes between partitions are unrestricted (i.e., alternative-specific), unrestricted scale parameters are compliant with utility maximisation under all specifications (i.e., RU2 = 1, RU2 and NNNL). Intuitively, the fully alternative-specific specification avoids any artificial 'transfer' of information from the attribute parameters to the scale parameters that occurs when restrictions are imposed on parameter estimates. Models 8 and 9 in table 6.7 are totally alternative-specific. The scale parameters for models 8 and 9 are the inverse of each other. That is, for the unrestricted IV, 0.148 in model 8 equals (1/6.75) in model 9. The alternative-specific parameter estimates associated with attributes in the public transport branch for model 8 can be recovered from model 9 by a scale transformation. For example, 0.148*17.396 for the train constant equals 2.577 in model 9. The estimated parameters are identical in models 8 and 9 for the 'other' modes since their IV parameter is restricted to equal unity in both models.

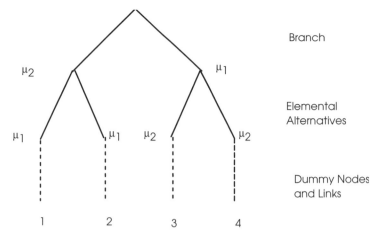

Figure 6.4 Estimating a two-level model to allow for unrestricted scale parameters within a level

This demonstrates the equivalence up to scale of RU1 and RU2 when all attribute parameters (including IV) are unrestricted.

When we impose the generic condition on an attribute associated with alternatives in different partitions of the nest, Koppelman and Wen (1998) (and Daly in advice to ALOGIT subscribers) have shown how one can recover compliance with utility maximisation in an NNNL model under the unrestricted scale condition (within a level of the NL model) by adding dummy nodes and links below the bottom level and imposing cross-branch equality constraints as illustrated in figure 6.4. Intuitively, what we are doing is allowing for differences in scale parameters at each branch but preserving the (constant) ratio of the IV parameters between two levels through the introduction of the scale parameters at the elemental level; the latter requiring the additional lower level in an NNNL specification. The NNNL specification does not allow unrestricted values of scale at the elemental level, unlike RU2, for example. Preserving a constant ratio through crossover equality constraints between levels in the nest satisfies the necessary condition of choice probability invariance to the addition of a constant in the utility expression of all elemental alternatives.

Adding an extra level is not designed to investigate the behavioural implications of a three-level model; rather it is a 'procedure' to reveal the scale parameters at upper levels where they have not been identified. This procedure is fairly straightforward for two branches (see model 5 in tables 6.7 and 6.8). With more than two branches, one has to specify additional levels for each branch. The number of levels grows quite dramatically. However, there is one way of simplifying this procedure: if we recognise that the ratio of the scale parameters between adjacent levels must be constant. Thus, for any number of branches, consistency with utility maximisation requires that the product of all the ratios of scale parameters between levels must be identical from the root to all elemental alternatives. To facilitate this, one can add a single link below each real alternative with the scale of that link set equal to the product of the scales of all scale parameters not included in the path to that alternative. For example, in the case of three branches with scales equal to λ_1, λ_2 and λ_3, the scale below the first branch would be $(\lambda_2 * \lambda_3)$, below the second branch it would be $(\lambda_1 * \lambda_3)$ and below the third branch it would be $(\lambda_1 * \lambda_2)$.

Model 5 is estimated as an NNNL model with the addition of a lower level of nodes and links with cross-branch equality constraints on the scale parameters. For example, in table 6.7, the tree structure is as follows: {Other [planem (plane), carm (car)], Public Transport [trainm (train), busm (bus)]}. The cross-over constraint for two branches sets the scale parameters to equality for {Other, trainm, busm} and {Public Transport, planem, carm}. Model 5 (table 6.7) produces results which are identical to RU2 (model 4) in respect of goodness-of-fit and elasticities, with all parameter estimates equivalent up to scale. Since we have two scale parameters in model 5, the ratio of each branch's IV parameters to their equivalent in model 4 provides the adjustment factor to translate model 5 parameters into model 4 parameters (or vice versa). For example, the ratio of $0.579/0.969 = 1.03/1.724 = 0.597$. If we multiply the train-specific constant in model 4 of 6.159 by 0.597, we obtain 3.6842, the train-specific constant in model 5. This is an important finding, because it indicates that *the application of the RU2 specification with unrestricted scale parameters in the presence of generic parameters across branches for the attributes is identical to the results obtained by estimating the NNNL model with an extra level of nodes and links.*

RU2 thus avoids the need to introduce the extra level.[3] The equivalent findings are shown in table 6.8 where the scale ratio is 3.74. Intuitively, one might expect such a result, given that RU2 allows the scale parameters to be freely estimated at the lower level (in contrast to RU1 where they are normalised to 1.0). One can implement this procedure under an exact RU2 model specification to facilitate situations where one wishes to allow scale parameters at a level in the nest to be different across branches in the presence or absence of a generic specification of attribute parameters. *The estimation results in model 4 are exactly correct and require no further adjustments.* The procedure can also be implemented under an NNNL specification (with an extra level of nodes and links) (model 5). The elasticities, marginal rates of substitution, goodness-of fit are identical in models 4 and 5. The parameter estimates are identical up to the ratio of scales.

6.5.5   Conclusions

The empirical applications and discussion has identified the model specification required to ensure compliance with the necessary conditions for utility maximisation.

This can be achieved for a *GEV-NL model* by either

- setting the IV parameters to be the same at a level in the nest in the presence of generic parameters, or

---

[3] From a practical perspective, this enables programs such as **LIMDEP** that limit the number of levels which can be jointly estimated to use all levels for real behavioural analysis.

- implementing the RU2 specification and allowing the IV parameters to be free in the presence of generic attribute parameters between partitions of a nest, or
- setting all attribute parameters to be alternative-specific between partitions, allowing IV parameters to be unrestricted.

This can be achieved for a *non-normalised NL model* by either

- setting the scale parameters to be the same at a level in the nest (for the non-normalised scale parameters) and rescaling all estimated parameters associated with elemental alternatives by the estimated IV parameter, or
- allowing the IV parameters to be free, and adding an additional level at the bottom of the tree through dummy nodes and links, and constraining the scale parameters at the elemental-alternatives level to equal those of the dummy nodes of all other branches in the total NL model, or
- setting all attribute parameters to be alternative-specific between partitions, allowing IV parameters to be unrestricted.

6.5.6   A three-level GEV-NL model

To identify other possible nested structures, we estimated a number of two- and three-level NL models. The 'best' of the set was a three-level model of the hierarchical structure shown in figure 6.5, with results in table 6.9. We have an upper-level choice between plane and slow modes; a middle-level choice of public vs. private (i.e., car) modes conditional of being slow modes; and at the bottom level, a choice between train and bus conditional on public mode, which is conditional on being a slow mode. We have replaced the generalised cost with its component attributes. Theta (θ) is the parameter of IV that links the train vs. bus choice to the public branch, and tau (τ) is the IV parameter linking the public vs. private choice to the slow branch. The air mode is degenerate at the lowest and middle levels, as is the car mode at the lowest level in the tree. Intuitively, individuals choose between the fast and slow modes, then within the slow modes they choose between public and private transport, and then within the

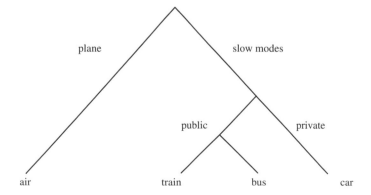

Figure 6.5 A three-level NL model

Table 6.9. *A three-level NL model estimated as FIML*

Exogenous variable	Mode(s)	MNL model		Nested model	
		Utility parameters	t-values	Utility parameters	t-values
Invehicle cost	All	−0.006017	−0.85	−0.013705	−0.98
Terminal time	All	−0.021389	−1.97	−0.011379	−0.66
Hhld income	Plane	0.00232	1.97	0.004142	2.97
Size of group	Plane	−0.495204	−2.10	−0.881091	−2.97
Travel time	All	−0.191950	−2.51	−0.116918	−0.81
A_AIR	Plane	−0.138229	−0.09	0.056551	0.030
A_TRAIN	Train	2.269314	2.88	1.907287	0.75
A_BUS	Bus	0.145447	0.25	0.972361	0.71
θ PUBLIC				0.097236	6.39
τ SLOW				0.296311	1.86
Log likelihood		−125.5502		−96.9558	
Log likelihood at zero		−163.5827		−163.5827	
Pseudo-R^2		0.23		0.41	

slow public modes they choose between train and bus. Each level has only one IV parameter, given the degenerate branches, and hence the single scale parameter at each level specifies a GEV-NL model (of the RU2 form) which complies with utility maximisation.

A comparison of the models suggests a substantial improvement in the overall goodness-of-fit of the model when a three-level FIML-NL model replaces the two-level FIML-NL model and the MNL model. Using the likelihood ratio test at any generally acceptable level of confidence, we can confidently reject the null hypothesis of no significant difference between the three-level and MNL models. We might have anticipated this in the intercity context (in contrast to an urban commuter context) given the greater variation in levels of service and possibly more binding financial constraint on the travelling family, and hence the benefit of a conditional structure. The pseudo-R^2 increases from 0.23 to 0.41. IV(public) and IV(slow) are much closer to zero than unity, suggesting that the tree structure is justified relative to the MNL specification.

6.6 Tests of overall model performance for nested models

6.6.1 The simplest test for nested models

The most common test undertaken to compare any two nested models (not to be confused with nested logit models) is the likelihood ratio test as detailed in chapter 3 and applied in the previous sections. When comparing two models estimated on the same data set, the analyst needs to know the log likelihood at convergence for each model and the difference in the degrees of freedom. The *calculated* likelihood ratio is derived as minus twice the absolute difference in log likelihood at convergence (equation 3.30). The resulting calculation is compared to the *critical value* from a chi-squared test table at an appropriate level of statistical significance (0.05 being the most used level in academic and other settings) for the number of degrees of freedom. If the calculated value is greater than the critical value, then we can conclude that the two models are statistically different, rejecting the null hypothesis of no difference.

The number of degrees of freedom is the difference in the number of free parameters (given a fixed sample size). For example, if model one has twelve parameters, one of which is generic across three alternatives, and we replace the single generic parameter with three alternative-specific parameters, then the number of degrees of freedom is two ($= 3 - 1$). Using a log likelihood of -125.55 (MNL) and -96.95 (NL, table 6.9), with two degrees of freedom, we get the calculated value of $-2(-28.59) = 57.19$. The critical χ^2 value at two degrees of freedom for 0.05 significance is 5.99; thus we can safely reject the null hypothesis of no difference between the nested logit model and the MNL model.

6.6.2   Other tests of model comparability for exogenous sampling

6.6.2.1 Small–Hsiao LM test

Small and Hsiao (1985) investigated the Lagrange multiplier (LM) test for the equality of cross-substitution of pairs of alternatives. Using an asymptotically unbiased likelihood ratio test, a sample of individuals is randomly separated into subsets S_1 and S_2 and weighted mean parameters obtained from separate models of the subsamples:

$$\hat{\alpha}_k^{S_1 S_2} = (1/2^{-1/2})\hat{\alpha}_k^{S_1} + (1 - 1/2^{-1/2})\hat{\alpha}_k^{S_2}. \tag{6.51}$$

Then a restricted (R) choice set is obtained as a subsample from the universal set and the subsample S_2 is reduced to include only individuals who have chosen alternatives in the restricted set. A constrained (i.e., parameter$= \hat{\alpha}_k^{S_1 S_2}$) and an unconstrained ($\hat{\alpha}_k^{S_2}$) model are estimated. A test of the null hypothesis of an MNL structure involves a chi-square statistic

$$\chi^2 = -2[L_R^{S_2}(\hat{\alpha}_k^{S_1 S_2}) + L_R^{S_2}(\hat{\alpha}_{k'}^{S_2})] \tag{6.52}$$

with degrees of freedom equal to the number of parameters in the vectors $\hat{\alpha}_k^{S_1 S_2}$ and $\hat{\alpha}_{k'}^{S_2}$. The procedure should be repeated with reversal of S_1 and S_2 subsamples.

6.6.2.2 McFadden's LM regression test

McFadden (1987) demonstrated that regression techniques can be used to conduct an LM test for deviations from MNL. An auxiliary regression is estimated over observations and alternatives. The dependent variable is (McFadden 1987: 65):

$$u_i = [\delta_i - P_C(i)]/(P_C(i))^{1/2}, \tag{6.53}$$

where $\delta_i = 1$ if an alternative in a partition $A(k)$ of the full set C is chosen and zero otherwise, and $P_C(i)$ is the MNL selection probability for alternative i contained in the full choice set C. The explanatory variables are x_{iC} and $w_{ii}, \ldots, w_{iK}$, where

$$x_{iC} = (x_i - x_C)/(P_C(i))^{1/2}, \tag{6.54}$$

$$X_C = \sum_{j \in C} x_j P_C(j), \tag{6.55}$$

and

$$w_{ik} = \left[v_{ik} - \sum_{j \in C} P_C(j) v_{jk} \right] (P_C(i))^{1/2} \tag{6.56}$$

with

$$v_{ik} = \begin{cases} -\ln P_{A(k)}(i) & \text{if } i \in A(k) \\ 0 & \text{if } i \notin A(k), \end{cases} \tag{6.57}$$

where $A = (A_1, \ldots, A_K)$ is a partition of C. The data are obtained from the MNL model. McFadden shows that $(N - T)R^2$ and LM are asymptotically equivalent with a limiting distribution which is χ^2 (K degrees of freedom). N is the number of observations in the auxiliary regression, or individuals by alternatives; the sample of T individuals used to estimate the MNL model is also used for the auxiliary regression. R^2 is the unadjusted multiple correlation coefficient from the auxiliary regression. Although the procedure suggested by McFadden is relatively straightforward, it requires some effort in data reformatting and programming to prepare the input variables.

6.6.3 A test for choice-based samples for nested and non-nested models[4]

Suppose we are interested in testing the probability that alternative $i(i = 1, \ldots, J)$ is chosen conditional on a vector of attributes z. Let the maintained hypothesis, H_0, be that this probability is $g(i|z, b)$ for some parameter vector b and a given conditional probability function g. H_0 is maintained in the sense that it is assumed satisfactory unless proven otherwise.

Let H_1 be the alternative hypothesis that the choice probability conditional on z is $f(i|z, a)$ for some probability function f and parameter vector a. Assume that f and g

---

[4] The reader is directed to section 9.2.6, chapter 9, for the description of a non-nested test procedure for random or exogenous samples. Here we treat only the choice-based case.

are non-nested, i.e., there are no values of a and b such that $f(i|z, a) = g(i|z, b)$ with probability equal to one. For example, f and g might correspond to nested logit models with different tree structures. The problem is to test H_0 against H_1, i.e., to test the hypothesis that $g(i|z, b)$ is correct for some b against the alternative that $f(i|z, a)$ is correct for some a.

Horowitz (1983) considered this problem but assumed random or exogenous stratified sampling of (i, z). Here, we assume that the estimation data form a choice-based sample and that parameter estimation is carried out by the weighted exogenous maximum likelihood (WESML) method of Manski and Lerman (1977). The test is more complex than for exogenous samples; however it is important to understand that choice-based samples, which are increasingly common in discrete-choice studies, require a different test. Accordingly, the *log likelihood* functions for models g and f are:

$$L_{Ng}(\beta) = \sum_{n=1}^{N} w(i_n) \log g(i_n|z_n, \beta) \tag{6.58}$$

$$L_{Nf}(\alpha) = \sum_{n=1}^{N} w(i_n) \log f(i_n|z_n, \alpha), \tag{6.59}$$

where the sum is over the choice-based sample $\{i_n, z_n\}(n = 1, \ldots, N)$ and

$$w(i) = Q(i)/H(i), \tag{6.60}$$

where $Q(i)$ = population share of alternative i and $H(i)$ = share of alternative i in the choice-based sample. We assume that $Q(i)(i = 1, \ldots, J)$ is known. To introduce the test, let us assume the following notation:

$\Delta L_N(b, a) = L_{Ng}(b) - L_{Nf}(a)$, the difference in the log likelihood under alternative models;

$\hat{b}_N, \hat{a}_N$ = WESML estimators of b and a if these quantities exist;

b^*, a^* = almost sure limits of $\hat{b}_N$ and $\hat{a}$ as $N \to \infty$. They are the true values of a and b;

$\Delta \hat{L}_N = \Delta L_N(\hat{b}_N, \hat{a}_N)$ and $\Delta L_N^* = \Delta L_N(\beta^*, \alpha^*)$.

It can be shown that if H_0 is true, $\Delta \hat{L}_N$ diverges in probability to $+\infty$ as $N \to \infty$ (a formal justification of this statement is given in Horowitz, Hensher and Zhu 1993). Under H_1, on the other hand, $\Delta \hat{L}_N$ diverges in probability to $-\infty$ as $N \to \infty$. Therefore, in large samples, occurrence of the event $\Delta \hat{L}_N < 0$ suggests that H_0 is false and that $f(i|z, a^*)$ is a better approximation to the true choice model than is $g(i|z, b^*)$. However, random sampling errors can cause the event $\Delta \hat{L}_N < 0$ to occur even if N is large and H_0 is true. So accepting or rejecting H_0 according to the sign of $\Delta \hat{L}_N$ can lead to erroneous inference. Under H_0, small negative values of $\Delta \hat{L}_N$ occur with higher probability than large negative values. Therefore, large negative values constitute stronger evidence against H_0 than do small ones.

The purpose of the test is to determine how large a negative number $\Delta \hat{L}_N$ must be to justify rejecting H_0. More precisely, the objective is to identify a critical number $\xi^* > 0$ such that under H_0 (and for sufficiently large N) the event $\Delta \hat{L}_N < -\xi^*$ has a probability not exceeding a specified small number $p > 0$. In other words, if $\Delta \hat{L}_N < -\xi^*$ then H_0 is rejected at a significance level not exceeding p. The inequality which forms the basis of the test is given in equation (6.61) for a sufficiently large N, given $\varepsilon > 0$.

$$\text{prob} \left(\Delta \hat{L}_N < -\xi^* \right) < \Phi \{ -[2\xi^*/w(i)^*]^{1/2} \} + \varepsilon. \tag{6.61}$$

Inequality (6.61) holds for any fixed alternative $f(i|z, \alpha^*)$ since, for a fixed alternative,

$$-(\xi^* + NE_L)/N^{1/2} V_L^{1/2} \rightarrow -\infty \quad \text{as} \quad N \rightarrow \infty, \tag{6.62}$$

where

$$E_L = E\{w(i) \log [g(i|z, \beta^*)/f(i|z, \alpha^*)]\} \tag{6.63}$$

$$V_L = \text{var} \{w(i) \log [g(i|z, \beta^*)/f(i|z, \alpha^*)]\}, \tag{6.64}$$

where E and var, respectively, are the expected value and variance relative to the sampling distribution $\lambda(i, z)$. Inequality (6.61) holds regardless of whether H_1 is a sequence of local alternatives. Given $\xi^* > 0, H_0$ is rejected at a significance level not exceeding $\Phi \{ -[2\xi^*/w(i^*)]^{1/2} \}$ if $\Delta \hat{L}_N < -\xi^*$. For example, if $\xi^*/w(i^*) = 1.35, H_0$ is rejected at a significance level not exceeding 0.05 if $\Delta \hat{L}_N < -1.35w(i^*)$.

This test is called the *bounded-size likelihood ratio* (BLR) test since its size is known only up to an upper bound. Hypothesis tests whose sizes are known only up to upper bounds are well known in statistics. For example, the uniformly most powerful test of the hypothesis that the mean of a normal distribution is less than or equal to a specified constant is given in terms of an upper bound. The BLR test is implemented next.

To illustrate the application of the BLR test for large samples, three comparisons of hierarchical models were undertaken (figures 6.6–6.9). The specification of figure 6.6 is taken as a base model for the comparison, i.e., g in hypothesis H_0, while figures 6.7, 6.8 and 6.9 are denoted as alternative models (tests 1, 2 and 3), i.e., denoted as f_1, f_2, and f_3 in H_1. The specification test draws on the utility parameter estimates together with other data required to calculate the various covariance matrices and other matrix inputs required.

The utility expression for the air mode was defined in terms of GC, TTME, HINCA, PSIZEA and the mode-specific constant (AASC). The exogenous effects in

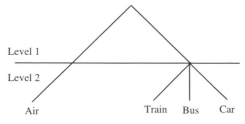

Figure 6.6 Air ↔ land logit model

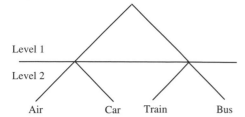

Level 1

Level 2

Air   Car   Train   Bus

Figure 6.7 Private ↔ public logit model

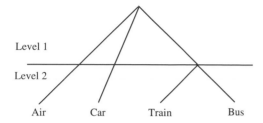

Level 1

Level 2

Air   Car   Train   Bus

Figure 6.8 Others ↔ public logit model

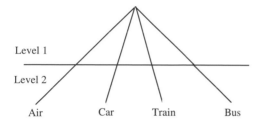

Level 1

Level 2

Air   Car   Train   Bus

Figure 6.9 MNL logit model

the utility expression for the other modes are GC, TTME (except for the car) and the respective mode-specific constants for train (TASC), bus (BASC) and car (CASC). An IV links the upper and lower choice processes.

Given the emphasis on the specification test, we do not detail the parameter estimates for each of the NL models. For each pair of tree structures, we undertook the large sample test. For all hypothesis tests, we set the significance level as 0.05, i.e., letting $\Phi(-[2\xi^*/w(i^*)]^{1/2}) = 0.05$ in inequality (6.61). Thus we have $-[2\xi^*/w(i^*)]^{1/2} = -1.64$. The population shares of alternatives car, plane, train and bus are 0.64, 0.14, 0.13 and 0.09 respectively. The sample shares of these alternatives are 0.281, 0.276, 0.3 and 0.143 in the sample. Thus, we have $\xi^* = 3.081$ for the test. The first example includes the same attributes in the base model and alternative model structures. By running the test, the values of L_{ng}, L_{nf1}, L_{nf2} and L_{nf3} are -191.44, $-208.32, -395.71$ and -476.19. The conclusions for the tests are summarised in table 6.10.

Table 6.10. *Parameter estimates for the tests: example 1*

Test	L_{ng}	L_{nf}	ΔL_{ngf}	$-\xi*$	Conclusion
1	−191.44	−208.32	16.88	−3.08	not reject
2	−191.44	−395.71	204.27	−3.08	not reject
3	−191.44	−476.19	284.75	−3.08	not reject

Table 6.11. *Parameter estimates for the tests: example 2*

Test	L_{ng}	L_{nf}	ΔL_{ngf}	$-\xi*$	Conclusion
1	−161.91	−208.32	46.41	−3.08	not reject
2	−161.91	−395.71	233.80	−3.08	not reject
3	−161.91	−476.19	314.28	−3.08	not reject

The maintained hypothesis cannot be rejected at a significance level of 0.5 for all comparisons. A second and more interesting example was evaluated in which we modified the set of attributes in the air alternative for the base nested structure (figure 6.5). GC, TTME and HINCA were removed, leaving PSIZEA, IV and AASC. The results given in table 6.11 again provide comparisons for each test which lead to non-rejection at the 0.5 significance level.

6.7 Conclusions and linkages between the MNL/NL models and more complex models

The MNL and NL models will remain useful analytical and behavioural tools for studying choice responses. In the first section of this chapter, we identified a number of potentially important sources of influence on choice behaviour (summarised in equation (6.1)). The great majority of practitioners will continue to estimate and implement models based on the MNL paradigm, and increasingly are expected to progress to the NL specification now that readily accessible software is available and interpretation of results is relatively straightforward. For these reasons alone, we have limited the main body of this chapter to a comprehensive presentation of the NL model, as well as a number of useful procedures for establishing the gains in moving beyond MNL to NL. Appendix A6 provides a quick reference guide to the properties of these two choice models.

A book on stated choice methods and analysis would be incomplete without consideration of more advanced discrete-choice models. The literature focusing on choice models 'beyond MNL and NL' is growing fast, aided by advances in numerical and simulation methods for estimation, and the increasing power of desktop computers. In appendix B6 we introduce a number of advanced discrete-choice models, each of which relaxes one or more of the behavioural assumptions dictating the structure of the MNL and NL models. The great challenge for researchers and practitioners is to explore these advances with at least one objective in mind – that of establishing grounds for rejecting the simpler choice models in the interests of increasing our understanding of the choice process, and hence improving the predictive capability of our set of behavioural response tools.

Appendix A6   Detailed characterisation of the nested logit model

This appendix summarises the major statistical and behavioural features of the NL model, to provide the reader with a quick reference guide. We use a two-level example in two dimensions M (model of travel) and D (destination), as shown in the figure A6.1.

The components $u(m, d)$ may be written as:

$$U(m, d) = u_d + u_{md}; \; m = 1, \ldots, M; \; d = 1, \ldots, D. \tag{A6.1}$$

We have the mth mode (e.g., car as driver) and dth destination (e.g., central city). We want to identify the existence of correlation between the utility distributions for different (m, d) pairs of alternatives. Write $u(m, d)$ in terms of a representative component v and the random component ε:

$$u(d, m) = v_d + v_{md} + \varepsilon_d + \varepsilon_{md}. \tag{A6.2}$$

The variance–covariance matrix $\sum$ is defined in terms of its elements (E = expectation value). Define the structure of the relation between alternatives as A6.3:

$$\sum_{dm,d'm'} = E[\varepsilon_d + \varepsilon_{md}, \varepsilon_{d'} + \varepsilon_{d'm'}]. \tag{A6.3}$$

If components u_d and u_{dm} are independently distributed, and we further impose the requirements that

$$E(\varepsilon_d \varepsilon_{d'}) = \sigma_D^2 \delta_{dd'} \tag{A6.4}$$

$$E(\varepsilon_{dm} \varepsilon_{d'm'}) = \sigma_{DM}^2 \delta_{dd'} \delta_{mm'} \tag{A6.5}$$

$$E(\varepsilon_m \varepsilon_{m'}) = \sigma_M^2 \delta_{mm'}, \tag{A6.6}$$

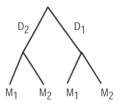

Figure A6.1

then there are *no* cross terms such as $E(\varepsilon_d + \varepsilon_m)$. Given the independence assumption, we then assume that the unobserved (random) effects are IID – independently and identically distributed – according to some density function (e.g., extreme value type I).

Example I (see figure A6.2) $E(\varepsilon_d + \varepsilon_m) = \sigma_D^2 \delta_{dd'}$ (equation (A6.4))

$$\delta_{dd'} \begin{cases} = 1 & \text{if } d = d' (\text{e.g.}, d = \text{city}, d' = \text{city}) \\ = 0 & \text{otherwise} = d \neq d' (\text{e.g.}, d = \text{city}, d' = \text{other}). \end{cases}$$

Example II (see figure A6.3) $E(\varepsilon_{dm}\varepsilon_{d'm'} = \sigma_{DM}^2 \delta_{dd'}\delta_{mm'}$ (equation (A6.5))

$$\sigma_D = 0, \quad \sigma_M = 0, \quad \sigma_{DM}^2 \neq 0$$

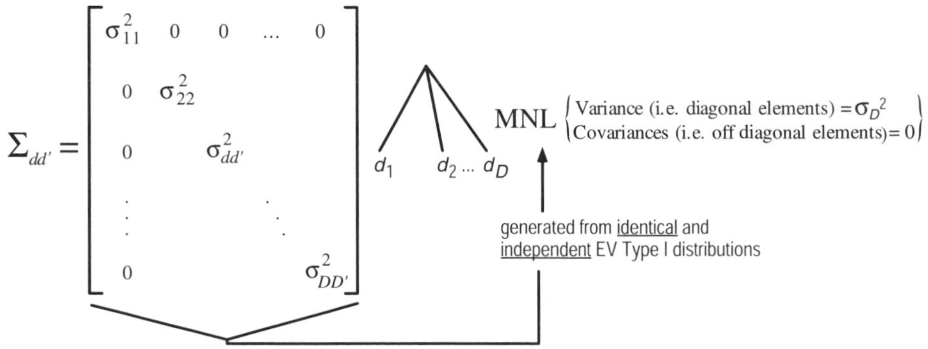

Figure A6.2

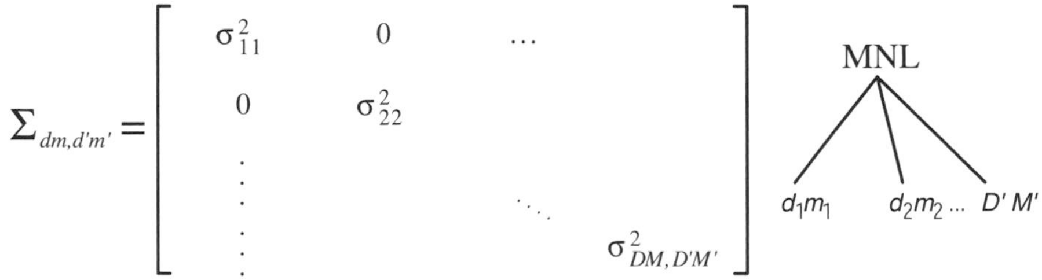

Figure A6.3

Example III (see figure A6.4.) $E(\varepsilon_{d'}\varepsilon_{d'} + E(\varepsilon_{dm}\varepsilon_{d'm'}) = \sigma_{DM}^2 \delta_{dd'} + \sigma_{DM}^2 \delta_{dd'}\delta_{mm'}$ (equations (A6.4), (A6.5)) We can then write matrix elements of $\sum$ as

$$\sum_{dm,d'm'} = \sigma_D^2 \delta_{dd'} + \sigma_{DM}^2 \delta_{dd'}\delta_{mm'}, \tag{A6.7}$$

where the first term on the right-hand side is the marginal choice and the second term is the conditional choice. Note: we could have made 'm' marginal and 'd' conditional, but that would make less empirical sense.

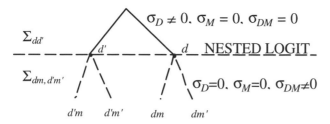

Figure A6.4

Independence of the e vectors means:

$$E(\varepsilon_d \varepsilon_m) = 0$$

$$E(\varepsilon_d \varepsilon_{d'm'}) = 0$$

$$E(\varepsilon_m \varepsilon_{d'm'}) = 0 \text{ for all } d, d' \in D, \text{ and, } m, m' \in M, \tag{A6.8}$$

$\varepsilon_d =$ unobservables which relate to d only
$\varepsilon_m =$ unobservables which relate to m only
$\varepsilon_{dm} =$ unobservables which relate to d and m.

Model structure appropriate to (A6.7)
The probability, P_{dm}, that alternative (d, m) will be selected is

$$P_{dm} = \text{prob}\,[u(d,m) > u(d',m') \forall d \in D, m \in M], \tag{A6.9}$$

characterised as

$$P_{dm} = F_{dm}[\underline{v}_D, \underline{v}_{DM}; \underline{\sigma}_D, \underline{\sigma}_{DM}], \tag{A6.10}$$

where vectors V_D, V_{DM} contain all mean values of indirect utility components in $\{D, M\}$ choice set (e.g., $v_D = \sum_k \alpha_{kj} X_{kjq}$) and σ_D, σ_{DM} are corresponding vectors of standard deviations (associated with random components of $u(d, m)$). For example:

$$\underline{V}_D = (\nu_1, \ldots, \nu_d, \ldots, \nu_D)$$

$$\underline{V}_{DM}(\nu_{11}, \ldots, \nu_{dm}, \ldots, \nu_{DM})$$

$$\underline{s}_D = (\sigma_1, \ldots, \sigma_d, \ldots \sigma_D)$$

$$\underline{s}_{DM} = (\sigma_{11}, \ldots \sigma_{dm}, \ldots \sigma_{DM}).$$

Given equations (A6.4) and (A6.5) – our decomposition of structure requirements – we can simplify the structure of the error matrix (A6.10), which currently is very general, to become:

$$P_{dm} = F_{dm}[\underline{v}_D, \underline{v}_{DM}; \sigma_D, \sigma_{DM}]. \tag{A6.11}$$

Note: the standard deviations are now scalars, i.e., constants across alternatives contained in $D(d \in D)$, and constants across alternatives contained in $DM(dm \in DM)$. They are not underlined as vectors. Alternatively, the inverse of the standard deviation,

λ, is constant within the marginal and within the conditional choice sets, but can vary in magnitude between the marginal and conditional choices:

$$\left\{ \begin{array}{l} (\lambda_d = \lambda_{d'} \ldots) \\ \lambda_{dm} = \lambda_{d'm'} \ldots) \end{array} \right\}.$$

Now we can conceptualise the choice process as follows:

- The additive separable utility function lends itself naturally to partitioning of alternatives in a hierarchy (like Strotz's utility tree; see figure A6.5).

$$\sum_{dm,d'm'} = \sigma_D^2 \delta_{dd'} + \sigma_{DM}^2 \delta_{dd'} \delta_{mm'}$$

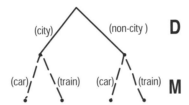

Figure A6.5

- For each alternative, D_d, an individual q will determine the maximum value

$$U_{d*}^q = \max_m u_{dm}^q \qquad (A6.12)$$

and select D_d if

$$U_d^q + U_{d*}^q = \max_{d'}[u_d^q + u_{d*}^q]. \qquad (A6.13)$$

Over the whole population of choice makers,

$$P_{dm} = \text{prob}\,[u_d + u_{d*} > u_{d'} + u_{d'*}, \forall d' \in D, \text{and } u_{dm} > u_{dm'} \forall m' \in M], \qquad (A6.14)$$

where u_{d*} is a random 'composite utility' variable drawn from a distribution of maximum utility

$$\underline{U}_{d*} = \max_d \{\underline{u}_{d1}, \ldots, \underline{u}_{dm}, \ldots, \underline{u}_{dM}\}. \qquad (A6.15)$$

Note: d is unchanged but m varies.

Because of the independence assumption of the distributions in the separate choice dimensions we can write

$$P_{dm} = \text{prob}\,[u_d + u_{d*} > u_{d'} + u_{d'*}, \forall d' \in D]\text{prob}\,[u_{dm} > u_{dm'} \forall m' \in M], \qquad (A6.16)$$

where $u_d + u_{d*}$ is distributed according to the sum of the independent random variables u_d and u_{d*}. The distribution has a mean:

$$v_d + \tilde{v}_{d*} \qquad (A6.17)$$

and a standard deviation

$$(\sigma_d^2 + \sigma_{d*}^2)^{1/2}. \tag{A6.18}$$

In product form, (A6.16) becomes

$$P_{dm} = P_d(.)P_{m|d}(.). \tag{A6.19}$$

To derive an estimable model structure we must assume a specific form for the utility distributions, i.e., the random components.

The MNL model assumes u_{dm} are EV type 1 distributed with standard deviation:

$$\sigma_{DM} = \frac{\pi}{\sqrt{6}\lambda}, \text{giving:}$$

$$P_{m|d} = \frac{\exp[\lambda v_{dm}]}{\sum_{m'\in M}\exp[\lambda v_{dm'}]}, m' = 1,\dots, M. \tag{A6.20}$$

The distribution of $\underline{u}_{d*}$ (A6.14) has a mean of

$$v_{d*} = \frac{1}{\lambda}\log\sum_{m'\in M}\exp(\lambda v_{dm'}) + \text{Euler's constant}. \tag{A6.21}$$

This is alternatively referred to as the inclusive value (IV), expected maximum utility (EMU), logsum, or composite utility, and

$$\sigma_{D*} = \frac{\pi}{\sqrt{6}}. \tag{A6.22}$$

To derive an expression for the marginal probability, P_d, we have to determine the distribution of the sum of $\underline{u}_d$ and $\underline{u}_{d*}$. Since we have assumed that $\underline{u}_d$ and $\underline{u}_{d*}$ are independent (so we can add them up), the mean of

$$\underline{u}_d + \underline{u}_{d*} \Rightarrow \underline{v}_d + \tilde{v}_{d*} \equiv \underline{v}_d^+ \text{ (this is an estimate of equation A6.21)}$$

$$\underline{v}_d^+ = \underline{v}_d + \frac{1}{\lambda}\log\sum_{m'\in M}\exp(\lambda\bar{v}_{dm'}) \tag{A6.23}$$

$$= \underline{v}_d + \frac{1}{\lambda}(\text{EMU}_{dm'}) \tag{A6.24}$$

and the variance is

$$(\sigma_d^+)^2 = \sigma_d^2 + \frac{\pi^2}{6\lambda^2}. \tag{A6.25}$$

If, again, we assume U_d^+ is EV1 distributed with standard deviation σ_d^+ and mean value given by equation (A6.23) we obtain equation (A6.26):

$$P_{dm} = \frac{\exp[\beta(\underline{v}_d + \underline{v}_{d*})]}{\sum_{d'\in D}\exp[\beta(\underline{v}_{d'} + \underline{v}_{d'*})]} \cdot \frac{\exp(\lambda\underline{v}_{dm})}{\sum_{m'\in M}\exp(\lambda\underline{v}_{dm'})} \tag{A6.26}$$

with

$$\underline{v}_{d*} = \frac{1}{\lambda} \log \sum_{m' \in M} \exp(\lambda \bar{v}_{dm'}) \tag{A6.27}$$

$$\beta = \frac{\pi}{\sqrt{6}\sigma_D}$$

$$= \frac{\pi}{\sqrt{6}} \left[\sigma_D^2 + \frac{\pi^2}{6\lambda^2} \right]^{-1/2}. \tag{A6.28}$$

A change in expected maximum utility (EMU) is also referred to in the economic literature as a change in consumer surplus, ΔCS, assuming no income effect. It can be defined, from equation (A6.26) as

$$\Delta\text{CS} = \frac{1}{\beta} \log \left\{ \sum_{d' \in D} \left[\sum_{m' \in M} \exp(\lambda(\underline{v}_d + \underline{v}_{dm'})) \right]^{\beta/\lambda} \right\}. \tag{A6.29}$$

A simple proof of the link between IV or EMU and consumer surplus (simplifying notation and ignoring β, λ) is given below.

$$E\left[\max_{m \in M_q} U_q \right] = \int_0^1 \frac{\exp \underline{V}_{dmq}}{\sum_{m' \in M} \exp \underline{V}_{dm'q}} \, d\underline{V}_{dmq} \tag{A6.30}$$

$$= \int \frac{\exp \underline{v}_{dmq}}{\exp \underline{v}_{dmq} \pm \sum_{m' \neq m \in M} \exp \underline{v}_{dm'q}} \, d\underline{v}_{dmq}. \tag{A6.31}$$

Let $x = \exp \underline{V}_{dmq}$ and define:

$$a = \sum_{m' \neq m \in M} \exp \underline{V}_{dm'q}.$$

Then $dx = \exp \underline{V}_{dmq} \, d\underline{V}_{dmq} = x \, d\underline{V}_{dmq}$. That is, $d\underline{V}_{dmq} = dx/x$; hence

$$E[\max U_q] = \int \frac{x}{x+a} \, dx/x$$

$$= \int \frac{dx}{x+a}$$

$$= \log(x+a) + \text{constant}$$

$$= \log \left[\sum_{m' \in M} \exp V_{dm'q} \right] + \text{constant} \tag{A6.32}$$

$$\equiv (A6.23) \text{ and } (A6.29).$$

From (A6.28), because $\sigma_D \leq 0$, the dispersion parameters must satisfy

$$\beta \leq \lambda \quad \text{and} \quad \beta/\lambda \leq 1 \tag{A6.33}$$

if the choice model (A6.26) is to be consistent with global utility maximisation. Clearly (A6.26) *as a whole* violates the IIA property. For example:

$$
\frac{P_{dm}}{P_{d'm'}} = \frac{\exp\left[\beta\underline{v}_d + \lambda\underline{v}_{dm}\right]}{\exp\left[\beta\underline{v}_{d'} + \lambda\underline{v}_{d'm'}\right]} \left[\frac{\sum_m \exp\left(\lambda\underline{v}_{dm}\right)}{\sum_{m'} \exp\left(\lambda\underline{v}_{dm'}\right)}\right]^{(\beta-\lambda)/\lambda}.
\tag{A6.34}
$$

The term $\sum_m \ldots / \sum_m \ldots$ is the part of the denominator of dm which does not cancel out since it contains different modes.

Equation (A6.34) depends on the utility values of alternatives other than (d, m) and (d', m'). Only if $\beta = 1$ will the independence property be satisfied, and $\sigma_D^2 = 0$ (in A6.28). That is, there must be a common dispersion parameter for all alternatives. The independence property will not hold in the presence of correlation between alternatives.

Appendix B6   Advanced discrete choice methods

B6.1   The heteroscedastic extreme value (HEV) model

Chapter 6 partially relaxed the constant variance assumption through NL partitioning. We can go one step further and completely relax the assumption of *identically distributed* random components. The heteroscedastic extreme value (HEV) model provides the vehicle for *free variance* (up to identification) for all alternatives in a choice set. Allenby and Ginter (1995), Bhat (1995) and Hensher (1997a, 1998a,b) amongst others, have implemented the HEV model. A nested logit model with a unique inclusive value parameter for each alternative (with one arbitrarily chosen variance equal to 1.0 for identification) is equivalent to an HEV specification.

The probability density function $f(.)$ and the cumulative distribution function $F(.)$ of the standard type 1 extreme value distribution (see Johnson, Kotz and Balakrishnan 1995 and chapter 3) associated with the random error term for the ith alternative with unrestricted variances and scale parameter λ_i are given as equations (B6.1a) and (B6.1b):

$$
f(\varepsilon_i) = \frac{1}{\lambda_i} e^{-(t_i/\lambda_i)} e^{-e^{-(\varepsilon_i/\lambda_i)}}
\tag{B6.1a}
$$

$$
F_i(z) = \int_{\varepsilon_i=-\infty}^{\varepsilon_i=z} f(\varepsilon_i)\, \mathrm{d}\varepsilon_i = e^{-e^{-(z/\lambda_i)}}
\tag{B6.1b}
$$

λ_i is the inverse of the standard deviation of the random component; hence its presence with the subscript i indicates that the variances can be different for each alternative in a choice set. If we imposed the constant variance assumption, then (B6.1) would be replaced by (B6.2):

$$f(t) = e^{-t}e^{-e^{-t}},$$ (B6.2a)

$$F(t) = e^{-e^{-t}}.$$ (B6.2b)

The probability that an individual will choose alternative i (P_i) from the set C of available alternatives, given the probability distribution for the random components in equation (B6.1) and non-independence among the random components, is summarised in equation (B6.3):

$$P_i = \text{prob}\,(U_i > U_j), \text{for all } j \neq i, j \in C$$
$$= \text{prob}\,(\varepsilon_j \leq V_i - V_j + \varepsilon_i), \text{for all } j \neq i, j \in C$$ (B6.3)
$$= \int_{\varepsilon_i=-\infty}^{\varepsilon_i=+\infty} \prod_{j \in C, j \neq i} F\left[\frac{V_i - V_j + \varepsilon_i}{\lambda_j}\right] \frac{1}{\lambda_i} f\left(\frac{\varepsilon_i}{\lambda_i}\right) \mathrm{d}\varepsilon_i,$$

Following Bhat (1995) and substituting $z = \varepsilon_i/\lambda_i$ in equation (A6.3), the probability of choosing alternative i can be rewritten, as equation (B6.4):

$$P_i = \int_{z=-\infty}^{z=+\infty} \prod_{j \in C, j \neq i} F\left[\frac{V_i - V_j + \lambda_i z}{\lambda_j}\right] f(z)\,\mathrm{d}z.$$ (B6.4)

The probabilities given by the expression is equation (B6.4) sum to one over all alternatives (see Bhat 1995; appendix A). If the scale parameters of the random components of all alternatives are equal, then the probability expression in equation (B6.4) collapses to the MNL (equation (3.24)).

The HEV model avoids the pitfalls of the IID property by allowing different scale parameters across alternatives. Intuitively, we can explain this by realising that the random term represents unobserved attributes of an alternative; that is, it represents uncertainty associated with the expected utility (or the observed part of utility) of an alternative. The scale parameter of the error term, therefore, represents the level of uncertainty (the lower the scale, the higher the uncertainty). It sets the relative weights of the observed and unobserved components in estimating the choice probability. When the observed utility of some alternative l changes, this affects the observed utility differential between another alternative i and alternative l. However, this change in the observed utility differential is tempered by the unobserved random component of alternative i. The larger the scale parameter (or equivalently, the smaller the variance) of the random error component for alternative i, the more tempered is the effect of the change in the observed utility differential (see the numerator of the cumulative distribution function term in equation (B6.4)) and the smaller is the elasticity effect on the probability of choosing alternative i.

The HEV model is flexible enough to allow differential cross elasticities among all pairs of alternatives. Two alternatives will have the same elasticity only if they have the same scale parameter on the unobserved components of the indirect utility expressions for each alternative. The effect of a marginal change in the indirect utility of an alternative m on the probability of choosing alternative i may be written as equation (B6.5) – see also Bhat (1995) and Hensher (1998a):

$$\frac{\partial P_i}{\partial V_m} = \int_{z=-\infty}^{z=+\infty} -\frac{1}{\lambda_m} \exp\left[\frac{-V_i + V_m - \lambda_i z}{\lambda_m}\right] \prod_{j \in C, j \neq i} F\left[\frac{V_i - V_j + \lambda_i z}{\lambda_j}\right] f(z) \ dz.$$

(B6.5)

The impact of a marginal change in the indirect utility of alternative i on the probability of choosing i is given in equation (B6.6):

$$\frac{\partial P_i}{\partial V_i} = -\sum_{l \in C, l \neq i} \frac{\partial P_i}{\partial V_l}.$$

(B6.6)

The cross elasticity for alternative i with respect to a change in the kth variable in the mth alternative's observed utility, x_{km}, can be obtained as equation (B6.7):

$$\eta_{x_{km}}^{P_i} = \left[\frac{\partial P_i}{\partial V_m}/P_i\right] * \beta_k * x_{km},$$

(B6.7)

where β_k is the estimated utility parameter on the kth variable (assumed to be generic in equation (B6.7)). The corresponding direct elasticity for alternative i with respect to a change in x_{ki} is given as equation (B6.8):

$$\eta_{x_{ki}}^{P_i} = \left[\frac{\partial P_i}{\partial V_i}/P_i\right] * \beta_k * x_{ki}.$$

(B6.8)

The equivalence of the HEV elasticities when all the scale parameters are identically equal to one and those of MNL is straightforward to establish. If, however, the scale parameters are unconstrained, the relative magnitudes of the cross elasticities of any two alternatives i and j with respect to a change in the level of an attribute of another alternative l are characterised by the scale parameter of the random components of alternatives i and j (Bhat 1995):

$$\eta_{x_{kl}}^{P_i} > \eta_{x_{kl}}^{P_j} \text{ if } \lambda_i < \lambda_j; \eta_{x_{kl}}^{P_i} = \eta_{x_{kl}}^{P_j} \text{ if } \lambda_i = \lambda_j; \eta_{x_{kl}}^{P_i} < \eta_{x_{kl}}^{P_j} \text{ if } \lambda_i > \lambda_j.$$

(B6.9)

This important property of the HEV model allows for a simple and intuitive interpretation of the model, unlike mixed logit (ML) or multinomial probit (MNP) – see sections B6.3 and B6.5, respectively – which have a more complex correspondence between the covariance matrix of the random components and the elasticity effects. For ML and MNP, one has to compute the elasticities numerically by evaluating multivariate normal integrals to identify the relative magnitudes of cross-elasticity effects.

To estimate the HEV model, the method of full information maximum likelihood is appropriate. The parameters to be estimated are the utility parameter vector β and the scale parameters of the random component of each of the alternatives (one of the scale parameters is normalised to one for identifiability). The log likelihood function to be maximised can be written as:

$$L = \sum_{q=1}^{q=Q} \sum_{i \in C_q} y_{qi} \log \left\{ \int_{z=-\infty}^{z=+\infty} \prod_{j \in C_q, j \neq i} F \left[\frac{V_{qi} - V_{qj} + \theta_i z}{\lambda_j} \right] f(z) \, dz \right\}, \quad (B6.10)$$

where C_q is the choice set of alternatives available to the qth individual and y_{qi} is defined as follows:

$$y_{qi} = \begin{cases} 1 & \text{if the } q\text{th individual chooses alternative } i \\ & (q = 1, 2, \dots Q, i = 1, 2 \dots I), \\ 0 & \text{otherwise,} \end{cases} \quad (B6.11)$$

One has to find a way of computing $\int f(x) \, dx$. Simpson's rule is a good startingpoint. For some improper integrals in both tails, $\int_{-\infty}^{+\infty} f(x) \exp(-x^2) \, dx$ and $\int_{-\infty}^{+\infty} g(x) \, dx$, the value can be approximated by Hermite quadrature $\int_{-\infty}^{+\infty} f(x) \exp(-x^2) \, dx \approx \sum(s = -1, +1) \sum(i = 1, k) \, w(i) * f[s * z(i)]$, where $w(i)$ is a weight and $z(i)$ is the abscissa of the Hermite polynomial. The number of points is set by the user.

The log likelihood function in (B6.10) has no closed-form expression. An improper integral needs to be computed for each alternative-individual combination at each iteration of the maximisation of the log likelihood function. For integrals which can be written $\int_0^{+\infty} f(x) \exp(-x) \, dx$ and $\int_0^{+\infty} g(x) \, dx$, the use of conventional numerical integration techniques (such as Simpson's method or Romberg integration) for the evaluation of such integrals is cumbersome, expensive and often leads to unstable estimates because they require the evaluation of the integrand at a large number of equally spaced intervals in the real line (Butler and Moffitt 1982).

On the other hand, Gaussian quadrature (Press et al. 1986) is a more sophisticated procedure. It can obtain highly accurate estimates of the integrals in the likelihood function by evaluating the integrand at a relatively small number of support points, thus achieving gains in computational efficiency of several orders of magnitude. However, to apply Gaussian quadrature methods, equation (B6.4) must be expressed in a form suitable for application of one of several standard Gaussian formulas (see Press *et al.* 1986 for a review of Gaussian formulas).

To do so, define a variable $u = e^{-w}$. Then, $\lambda(w) \, dw = -e^{-u} \, du$ and $w = -\ln u$. Also define a function G_{qi} as

$$G_{qi}(u) = \prod_{j \in C_q, j \neq i} F \left[\frac{V_{qi} - V_{qj} - \lambda_i \ln u}{\lambda_j} \right]. \quad (B6.12)$$

Then we can rewrite (B6.10) as

$$L = \sum_q \sum_{i \in C_q} y_{qi} \log \left\{ \int_{u=0}^{u=\infty} G_{qi}(u) e^{-u} \, du \right\}. \quad (B6.13)$$

Table B6.1. *Heteroscedastic extreme value model*

Variables	Utility parameters	*t*-values
Attributes in the utility functions		
AASC	6.025	2.58
TASC	4.214	3.10
BASC	3.942	2.90
GC	−0.0309	−2.47
TTME	−0.0917	−2.29
HINCA	0.0282	1.30
PSIZEA	−1.106	−2.18
Scale parameter of extreme value distributions		
s_AIR	0.585	2.00
s_TRAIN	0.742	1.61
s_BUS	1.682	1.51
s_CAR	1.00	
*Standard deviations – sigma*pi/sqr(6) for HEV distribution*		
s_AIR	0.750	2.00
s_TRAIN	0.951	1.61
s_BUS	2.157	1.51
s_CAR	1.282	
Log likelihood function	−185.97	
Log likelihood at zero	−291.12	
Pseudo-R^2	0.350	

The expression within braces in equation (B6.13) can thus be estimated using the Laguerre Gaussian quadrature formula, which replaces the integral by a summation of terms over a certain number (say K) of support points, each term comprising the evaluation of the function $G_{qi}(.)$ at the support point k multiplied by a mass or weight associated with the support point. The support points are the roots of the Laguerre polynomial of order K and the weights are computed based on a set of theorems provided by Press et al. (1986: 124). For this procedure, a 40 to 65 point quadrature is often used.

We have estimated an HEV model using the data in chapter 6 that can be directly compared to the MNL and NL models. The results are summarised in table B6.1. The elasticity matrix of probability weighted elasticities is given in table B6.2. The attributes influencing choice contribute most of the explanatory power, with the alternative-specific constants adding very little (0.350–0.334). The most important results for our purposes are the standard deviations associated with the unobserved random components, and the elasticities. The standard deviations are different across all four alternatives, suggesting a nested structure in which all alternatives are degenerate. If any grouping were to occur, the HEV model would have suggested grouping air and train. That is, the unobserved effects associated with air and train have a much more similar distribution structure in respect of variance, than does each with the other two

Table B6.2. *Probability weighted HEV GC elasticities compared with MNL elasticities*

	Random effects HEV	MNL
Alternative = Air		
Choice = Air	−1.162	−1.069
Choice = Train	0.334	0.300
Choice = Bus	0.571	0.416
Choice = Car	0.583	0.519
Alternative = Train		
Choice = Air	0.432	0.392
Choice = Train	−1.372	−1.197
Choice = Bus	0.818	0.542
Choice = Car	0.748	0.617
Alternative = Bus		
Choice = Air	0.278	0.223
Choice = Train	0.311	0.226
Choice = Bus	−2.191	−1.495
Choice = Car	0.470	0.299
Alternative = Car		
Choice = Air	0.497	0.500
Choice = Train	0.439	0.416
Choice = Bus	0.767	0.507
Choice = Car	−1.485	−1.193

alternatives. Indeed, the grouping of bus and train as having a priori behavioural appeal is not as good in achieving compliance with IIA within each partition in a nested logit structure.

The selected three-level structure reported in table 6.10, identified from our search of a number of partitions of the choice set, is not the preferred tree structure on a free variance test. These behavioural insights are indicative of the benefits of modelling heteroscedasticity in choice models, and are the basis for formulating potentially rewarding avenues of research to explain the behavioural foundations of the hetero-scedastic errors.

A comparison of the direct and cross choice elasticities for GC (table B6.2) suggests some similar and some quite different mean estimates. The bus estimates in particular are quite different, with the HEV direct and cross elasticities significantly greater than the MNL estimates. The direct elasticity of −2.191 is substantially higher than the MNL estimate of −1.495. The car direct elasticity and the cross elasticity of car use with respect to bus GC are also noticeably higher for the HEV model. On these six elasticities, one would conclude that the MNL model significantly underestimates the sensitivity of the model to changes in the generalised cost of travel.

B6.2   Covariance heterogeneity (CovHet) fixed effects HEV model

The HEV model in section B6.1 is often referred to as the random effects HEV model because of the way it treats the distribution of the unobserved random components. An alternative and more general model is the fixed effects HEV model, or what has been referred to as the *covariance heterogeneity* (CovHet) model. As a generalisation of the random effects-HEV model, it is equivalent to estimating a model in which a single scale parameter (across the alternatives) is a function of alternative-specific variables: attributes associated with an alternative and each sampled individual can be included as sources of scale decomposition, adding useful behavioural information of sample heterogeneity. This extension is the source of heterogeneity introduced through covariates. For example, given the relative similarity of the standard deviations of air and train (identified in the HEV model, table B6.1), we might assume that the variances of ε_a and ε_t are given by the same function of $\mathbf{z}$; and that ε_b and ε_c are a different function of the covariates $\mathbf{z}$. That is,

$$\text{var}\left[\varepsilon_a\right] = \text{var}\left[\varepsilon_t\right] = \sigma_1^2 \exp\left(\gamma' \mathbf{z}_1\right) \tag{B6.14a}$$

$$\text{var}\left[\varepsilon_b\right] = \text{var}\left[\varepsilon_c\right] = \sigma_1^2 \exp\left(\gamma' \mathbf{z}_1\right). \tag{B6.14b}$$

The analyst can specify a particular functional form for the covariate expression. This model has a lot of similarity to the nested logit model. It can be formulated as a nested logit model with IV parameters multiplied by the exponential functions. For choice k given branch j,

$$P(k|j) = \frac{\exp\left(\beta' \mathbf{x}_{k|j}\right)}{\displaystyle\sum_{s|j} \exp\left(\beta' \mathbf{x}_{s|j}\right)} \tag{B6.15}$$

$$\text{For branch } j, P(j) = \frac{\exp\left(\alpha' \mathbf{y}_j + \sigma_j I_j\right)}{\displaystyle\sum_j \exp\left(\alpha' \mathbf{y}_j + \sigma_j I_j\right)}, \tag{B6.16}$$

where

$$\sigma_j = \tau_j \exp\left(\gamma' \mathbf{z}_j\right). \tag{B6.17}$$

A two-level model generalises the nested logit model through specifying the IV utility parameter (i.e., σ_j) to be an exponential function of covariates. Analysts may be able to formulate a theory to explain the heteroscedasticity structure present in preference data of the type described by (B6.17). For example, depending upon its content, exposure to advertising might lead to more or less variability in the observed choice behaviour of a population. While this effect might be captured partially by a random effects specification of the scale parameters (i.e., the HEV model in section B6.1), the origin of the variability would not be explicit. The latter consequence was one motivation for the development of the CovHet model (Swait and Adamowicz 1996, Swait and Stacey 1996). Equation (B6.17) thus can be transformed in terms of the scale parameter as equation (B6.18):

$$\lambda_{iq} = \exp(\psi Z_{iq}), \qquad \qquad (B6.18)$$

where ψ is a parameter row-vector and Z_{iq} are covariates. CovHet choice probabilities are given by equation (B6.19):

$$P_{iq} = \frac{\exp(\lambda_{iq}\beta X_{iq})}{\displaystyle\sum_{j \in C_q} \exp(\lambda_{iq}\beta X_{jq})}. \qquad \qquad (B6.19)$$

As with the HEV model, CovHet allows complex cross-substitution patterns among the alternatives. The derivation of CovHet when the scale factor does not vary by alternative is different than when it does. If the scale factor is *not* alternative-specific, the model can be derived using a heteroscedasticity argument (see Swait and Adamowicz 1996); when the scale factor is alternative-specific, the model can be derived as a special case of the nested logit model (Daly 1985, McFadden 1981, Hensher 1994, Swait and Stacey 1996). In either case, the final expression for the choice probability is given by expression (B6.19).

Swait and Adamowicz (1996) hypothesise that task complexity (for SP data) and choice environment (e.g., market structure for RP data) influence levels of variability found in preference data. They propose a specific measure to characterise complexity and/or environment, and find evidence of its impact in a number of SP data sets, as well as in an RP data source. Their measure of complexity does not vary across alternatives; consequently, scale parameters in their model vary across individuals and SP replications, but not across alternatives. They also found that different degrees of complexity between preference data sources can impact the propriety of combining RP/SP data. Swait and Stacey (1996) apply CovHet to scanner panel choice data, allowing the variance (i.e., scale) to vary by person, alternative and time period as a function of brand, socio-demographic characteristics, interpurchase time, and state dependence. They show that accounting for non-stationarity of the variance in terms of the explanatory variables Z_{iq} enhances insight about panel behaviour and greatly improves model fit with respect to standard choice models such as the MNL, NL and even MNP models with fixed covariance matrices. We have implemented this model with our case study data set. The results are summarised in table B6.3.

The CovHet model is specified as the four elemental alternatives plus the 'composite' alternative FLY at the upper level. The covariates included in the exponential form of the fixed-effects function are size of the travelling party (PSIZE) and household income (HINC). We could have included alternative-specific constants, but did not in the example. We chose not to include a composite utility expression for GROUND, although the IVs for both upper level branches are generated and reported in table B6.3. The covariates have negative utility parameters although only HINC is statistically significant. What this suggests is that as household income increases, *ceteris paribus*, the scale parameter decreases in value. Another way of saying this is that the standard deviation of the random component increases

Table B6.3. *Covariance heterogeneity logit model*

Variables	Utility parameters	*t*-values
Attributes in the utility functions		
A_TRAIN	4.470	6.44
A_BUS	3.121	5.26
BC	−0.0638	−6.86
BT	−0.0699	−5.88
A_AIR	6.072	1.44
AF	−1.379	−0.71
Attributes of branch choice equation		
A_FLY	−6.309	−3.06
Inclusive value parameters		
FLY	3.988	0.38
GROUND	4.870	0.46
Lmb[1|1]	1.00	
Trunk{1}		1.00
Covariates in inclusive value parameters		
s_PSIZE	−0.914	−1.02
s_HINC	−0.173	−2.71
Log likelihood function	−204.89	
Log likelihood at zero	−312.55	
Pseudo-R^2	0.332	

with increasing household income. Thus we might conclude that the variance of the unobserved effects is larger for the higher household income segment, and consequently the attributes associated with the utility expressions at the lower level (noting that we only have a constant at the upper level for FLY) are indeed representing the heterogeneity in choice for individuals from lower income households (after controlling for HINC) better than for higher income households.

A comparison of the elasticities (table B6.4) suggests noticeable differences in behavioural responses to a one-unit change in generalised cost. Selecting the preferred model structure is not straightforward, although the CovHet model is the most general and could be preferred on these grounds alone. We cannot guarantee, however, that we have identified the 'best' CovHet model. The direct elasticities for the ground modes are extremely high and worrisome, given the extant evidence that estimates in the −0.3 to −1.2 range are most likely. None the less, this example has demonstrated the opportunity to explore decomposition of the variance of the random components, adding important behavioural information in understanding the differences in the distributions of the unobserved effects. By comparison, the random-effects HEV model is limited in that we are unable to reveal attribute-specific influences on variation.

Table B6.4. *Comparison of GC elasticities of covariance heterogeneity, NL and MNL models*

	Covariance heterogeneity			Nested logit			Unweighted MNL
	Upper level	Lower level	Total effect	Upper level	Lower level	Total effect	
Alternative = Air							
Branch = FLY							
Choice = Air	−0.444	0.000	−0.444				−0.161
Branch = GROUND							
Choice = Train	0.072	0.000	0.072				0.023
Choice = Bus	0.072	0.000	0.072				0.019
Choice = Car	0.072	0.000	0.072				0.119
Alternative = Train							
Branch = FLY							
Choice = Air	0.331	0.000	0.331	−0.458	0.414	−0.045	0.023
Branch = GROUND							
Choice = Train	−0.050	−5.955	−6.005	−0.458	−0.627	−1.086	−0.185
Choice = Bus	−0.050	2.353	2.303	0.735	0.0	0.735	0.024
Choice = Car	−0.050	2.353	2.303	0.735	0.0	0.735	0.138
Alternative = Bus							
Branch = FLY							
Choice = Air	0.100	0.000	0.100	0.314	0.0	0.314	0.019
Branch = GROUND							
Choice = Train	−0.018	1.524	1.506	0.314	0.0	0.314	0.024
Choice = Bus	−0.018	5.830	−5.848	−0.307	−0.738	−1.045	−0.133
Choice = Car	−0.018	1.524	1.506	−0.307	0.303	−0.004	0.090
Alternative = Car							
Branch = FLY							
Choice = Air	0.071	0.000	0.071	0.420	0.000	0.420	0.119
Branch = GROUND							
Choice = Train	−0.020	2.571	2.552	0.420	0.0	0.420	0.138
Choice = Bus	−0.020	2.571	2.552	−0.674	0.534	−0.140	0.090
Choice = Car	−0.020	−3.517	−3.537	−0.674	−0.229	−0.903	−0.347

B6.3 The random parameters (or mixed) logit model

Accommodating differences in covariance of the random components and unobserved heterogeneity (also referred to as random effects or individual-specific effects) is the next extension to the HEV and CovHet models. Although the latter model begins to decompose the variances to identify sources of differences across the sampled population, there are other ways to allow for individual-specific segment differences. Two approaches have been developed: the random parameters logit (RPL) model and the mixed logit (ML) model. Both approaches differ only in interpretation, being derivatives of a similar approach. There are a small but growing number of empirical studies implementing the RPL or ML method. The earliest studies include Ben-Akiva and Bolduc (1996), Revelt and Train (1998), Bhat (1997a), McFadden and Train (1996), and Brownstone, Bunch and Train (1998).

The model is a generalisation of the MNL model, summarised in equation (B6.20):

$$P(j|\mu_i) = \frac{\exp\left(\alpha_{ji} + \theta_j \mathbf{z}_i + \varphi_j \mathbf{f}_{ji} + \beta_{ji} \mathbf{x}_{ji}\right)}{\sum_{j=1}^{J} \exp\left(\alpha_{ji} + \theta_j \mathbf{z}_i + \varphi_j \mathbf{f}_{ji} + \beta_{ji} \mathbf{x}_{ji}\right)} \tag{B6.20}$$

where

α_{ji} is a fixed or random alternative-specific constant associated with $j = 1,\ldots,J$ alternatives and $i = 1,\ldots,I$ individuals; and $\alpha_J = 0$,

φ_j is a vector of non-random parameters,

β_{ji} is a parameter vector that is randomly distributed across individuals; μ_i is a component of the β_{ji} vector (see below),

$\mathbf{z}_i$ is a vector of individual-specific characteristics (e.g., personal income),

$\mathbf{f}_{ji}$ is a vector of individual-specific and alternative-specific attributes,

$\mathbf{x}_{ji}$ is a vector of individual-specific and alternative-specific attributes,

μ_i is the individual-specific random disturbance of unobserved heterogeneity.

A subset or all of α_{ji} alternative-specific constants and the parameters in the β_{ji} vector can be randomly distributed across individuals, such that for each random parameter, a new parameter, call it ρ_{ki}, can be defined as a function of characteristics of individuals and other attributes which are choice invariant. Examples of the latter are the method of data collection (if it varies across the sample), interviewer quality, length of SP experiment (if it varies across the sample) and data type (e.g. RP or SP). The layering of selected random parameters can take a number of pre-defined functional forms, typically assumed to be normally or lognormally distributed, as presented respectively in equations (B6.21) and (B6.22):

$$\rho_{ki} = \gamma_k + \delta_k \mathbf{w}_i + \sigma_k \mu_{ki} \tag{B6.21}$$

$$\rho_{ki} = \exp\left(\gamma_k + \delta_k \mathbf{w}_i + \sigma_k \mu_{ki}\right), \tag{B6.22}$$

where

$\mathbf{w}_i$ is a vector set (excluding a constant) of choice invariant characteristics that produce individual heterogeneity in the averages of the randomly distributed parameters,

γ_k is the constant,

δ_k is a vector of *deep* parameters that identify an individual-specific mean,

μ_{ki} is a random term assumed to be normally distributed with mean zero and unit standard deviation, and hence σ_k is the standard deviation of the marginal distribution of ρ_{ki}.

The lognormal (or exponential) form is often used if the response parameter needs to be a specific sign.

The μ_{ki}s are individual and choice-specific, unobserved random disturbances, which are the source of the *unobserved heterogeneity*. The RPL or ML model is equivalent in form to the MNP model (set out below), even though the variances of the random component take on a different distribution (i.e., EV1 compared to normal), if we assume (a) that the alternative-specific constants are random, (b) $\delta_k \mathbf{w}_I$ is excluded, and (c) that the full (i.e., including the variances) lower triangular (Cholesky) matrix of covariance is unrestricted. This equivalence is very important, since this special case of the RPL or ML model provides an alternative method of estimation to MNP. Estimation of the RPL/ML model is usually undertaken using simulation methods, in contrast to direct integration. This method is increasingly the approach adopted for all complex choice models (see McFadden and Ruud 1994). The unconditional probabilities are obtained by integrating the μ_{ki}s out of the conditional probabilities $P_j = E\mu_i(P(j|\mu_i))$.

In the most general case we need to evaluate $E = (C-1){*}T$ dimensional integral for each agent and each iteration in the maximisation of the (log) likelihood function. C is the choice set size and T is the number of time periods (or choice sets if an SP data set). This multiple integral does not exist in closed form. What makes this particularly complex is the inter-alternative correlation on one or more of the error components. Numerical integration is not computationally feasible since the number of operations increases with the power of E, which dimensions the covariance matrix. Simulation of the choice probabilities is now the preferred method of estimating all parameters, by drawing pseudo-random realisations from the underlying error process (Boersch-Supan and Hajivassiliou 1990). The popular method is one initially introduced by Geweke (and improved by Keane, McFadden, Boersch-Supan and Hajivassiliou – see Geweke, Keane and Runkle 1994; McFadden and Ruud 1994) of computing random variates from a multivariate truncated normal distribution and known as the Geweke–Hajivassiliou–Keane (GHK) recursive probability simulator. Although it fails to deliver unbiased multivariate truncated normal variates (as initially suggested by Ruud and detailed by Boersch-Supan and Hajivassiliou 1990), it does produce unbiased estimates of the choice probabilities. The approach is quick and generated draws and simulated probabilities depend continuously on the parameters β

and M (the covariance matrix). This latter dependence enables one to use conventional numerical methods, such as quadratic hillclimbing, to solve the first-order conditions for maximising the simulated likelihood function (equation (B6.23)). Hence the term simulated maximum likelihood (SML) (Stern 1997).

$$\bar{L}(\beta, M) = \prod_{r=1}^{R} \prod_{q=1}^{Q} \bar{P}_r(\{i_q\}). \qquad (B6.23)$$

Boersch-Supan and Hajivassiliou (1990) have shown that the choice probabilities are well approximated by the formula (B6.24), even for a small number of replications. Our experience suggests that 100 replications are sufficient for a typical problem involving five alternatives, 1000 observations and up to ten attributes. Such runs with appropriate software and a fast processor should take about 5–15 minutes to converge.

$$\bar{P}(\{i_q\}) = \frac{1}{R} \sum_{r=1}^{R} \bar{P}_r(\{i_{qn}\}). \qquad (B6.24)$$

The form of the RPL/ML model has important behavioural implications. The presence in ρ_{ki} of terms representing random tastes of an individual invariant across the choice set (i.e., unobserved heterogeneity) induces a correlation among the utility of different alternatives (Bhat 1997b, McFadden and Train 1996). This engenders a relatively free utility structure such that IIA is relaxed despite the presence of the IID assumption for the random components of the alternatives. That is, the RPL/ML model disentangles IIA from IID and enables the analyst to estimate models that account for cross-correlation among the alternatives. The example in table B6.5 compared to table 6.2 reinforces this result empirically. When the random utility parameters are all zero, the exact MNL model is produced. Applying the case study data, we find that all utility parameters with an RPL/ML form are not significantly different from zero, consequently the elasticities are identical to those of the MNL model (and are not reproduced in the table). Bhat (1997a) has superimposed random response heterogeneity over the systematic response heterogeneity by including parameterised covariates as shown in equations (B6.21) and (B6.22).

We have implicitly treated the RPL and ML models as if they are the same. The difference is entirely interpretation (Brownstone, Bunch and Train 1998). In the RPL specification the parameters of the attributes in the representative component of the utility expression (i.e., α_{ji} and β_{ji}) are random with a mean and deviations. When the deviations enter as components of the structure of the random component as illustrated in equations (B6.21) and (B6.22), they are an error-components model associated with the ML model. Any attributes associated with β_{ji} which do not enter the error components can be considered attributes whose parameters do not vary in the sampled population. Attributes of alternatives that are observed but are not included in the set of explicitly modelled attributes (i.e., with assigned β_{ji}s) but which consequently 'reside' in the error components, can be considered variables whose parameters vary in the sampled population but with zero means. Brownstone,

Page 202 — Stated Choice Methods

Table B6.5. *Random parameter logit model*

Variables	Coefficients	t-values
I. Random parameter logit model – replications for GHK simulators = 100		
Random parameters in utility functions		
AASC	7.2506	4.686
TASC	4.7941	4.450
BASC	3.9838	3.608
GC	−0.4245	−3.526
TTME	−0.9863	−5.507
Non-random parameters in utility functions		
HINCA	0.2557	1.976
Heterogeneity in mean, parameter : variable		
AASC:PSIZE	−1.1120	−1.568
TASC:PSIZE	−0.2533	−0.428
BASC:PSIZE	−0.2727	−0.420
GC:PSIZE	0.9919	1.548
TTME:PSIZE	−0.1169	−0.143
Diagonal values in Cholesky matrix L		
sAASC	0.2248	0.321
sTASC	0.1187	0.004
sBASC	0.1049	0.350
sGC	0.2385	0.489
sTTME	0.4567	0.146
*Below diagonal values in L matrix V = L * Lt*		
TASC:AASC	0.5552	0.100
BASC:AASC	0.5790	0.116
BASC:TASC	0.3233	−0.110
GC:AASC	0.1058	0.191
GC:TASC	0.2332	0.422
GC:BASC	−0.2344	−0.467
TTME:AASC	−0.4200	−0.457
TTME:TASC	0.9386	0.273
TTME:BASC	0.1911	0.511
TTME:GC	−0.1332	−0.378
Standard deviations of parameter distributions		
sdAASC	0.2248	0.321
sdTASC	0.5553	0.100
SdBASC	0.1241	0.360
SdGC	0.4212	0.807
sdTTME	0.4915	0.610
Log likelihood function	−182.6028	
Log likelihood at zero	−291.1218	
Pseudo-R^2	0.34576	

Table B6.5. (*cont.*)

Variables	Coefficients	*t*-values

I. Random parameter logit model – replications for GHK simulators = 100
Correlation matrix for random parameters

TTME	AASC	TASC	BASC	GC	TTME
AASC	0.1000	0.9999	0.4665	0.2513	0.8546
TASC	0.9999	0.1000	0.4608	0.2630	0.8503
BASC	0.4665	0.4608	0.1000	−0.4974	0.1197
GC	0.2512	0.2630	−0.4974	0.1000	0.4788
TTME	−0.8546	−0.8503	−0.1197	−0.4788	0.1000

II. Replications for simulated probabilities = 500

Variables	Coefficients	*t*-values

Random parameters in utility functions

AASC	7.3416	7.657
TASC	4.4425	8.830
BASC	3.6378	7.469
GC	−0.3610	−4.021
TTME	−0.1029	−11.791

Non-random parameters in utility functions

| HINCA | 0.2510 | 1.953 |

Heterogeneity in mean, parameter: variable

AASC:PSIZE	−1.098	−4.195
TASC:PSIZE	0.0000	
BASC:PSIZE	0.0000	
GC:PSIZE	0.6050	1.587
TTME:PSIZE	0.0000	

Diagonal values in Cholesky matrix L

sAASC	0.3166	0.048
sTASC	0.9685	0.040
sBASC	0.1378	0.045
sGC	0.6728	0.015
sTTME	0.1374	0.048

Below diagonal values in L matrix V = L ∗ Lt

TASC:AASC	0.2917	0.059
BASC:AASC	0.3585	0.008
BASC:TASC	0.2747	0.009
GC:AASC	−0.3367	−0.068
GC:TASC	0.1280	0.026
GC:BASC	0.1051	0.023
TTME:AASC	−0.4941	−0.058
TTME:TASC	−0.7440	−0.023
TTME:BASC	−0.2339	−0.075
TTME:GC	−0.7810	−0.025

Table B6.5. (*cont.*)

Variables	Coefficients	*t*-values
II. Replications for simulated probabilities = 500		
Standard deviations of parameter distributions		
sdAASC	0.3166	0.048
sdTASC	0.3073	0.065
sdBASC	0.1450	0.046
sdGC	0.3812	0.078
sdTTME	0.5739	0.077
Log likelihood	−184.2051	
Log likelihood at zero	−291.1218	
Pseudo-R^2	0.3433	

Correlation matrix for random parameters

	AASC	TASC	BASC	GC	TTME
AASC	0.1000	0.9490	0.2472	−0.8832	0.8610
TASC	0.9490	0.1000	0.2943	−0.7323	0.8580
BASC	0.2472	0.2943	0.1000	0.1074	0.6247
GC	−0.8832	−0.7323	0.1074	0.1000	0.5804
TTME	−0.8610	−0.8580	−0.6247	0.5804	0.1000

Notes: Method = BFGS; nodes for quadrature: Laguerre = 40; Hermite = 10; replications for simulated probabilities = 5.

Bunch and Train (1998) suggest that the RPL interpretation is '... useful when considering models of repeated choice by the same decision maker' (page 12). This is almost certainly the situation with stated choice data where choice sets in the range of 4 to 32 are common. The simplest model form is one in which the same draws of the random parameter vectors are used for all choice sets (essentially treating the choice sets as independent). Although a first-order autoregressive process for random parameters can be imposed, it is extremely complex. The error components approach, however, has the advantage of handling 'serial correlation' between the repeated choices in a less complex way (see below).

Developments in RPL and ML models are progressing at a substantial pace, with estimation methods and software now available. We can anticipate the greatest gains in understanding choice behaviour from continuing applications of the RPL/ML model. Table B6.5 illustrates the application of RPL. We present the MNL model as starting values for two models, respectively using 5 and 500 random draws in estimating the unconditional probabilities by simulated maximum likelihood. Revelt and Train (1998) suggest 100 draws are sufficient; in contrast, Bhat (1997a) suggests 1000. The importance of the number of draws is clearly demonstrated in table B6.5, where the source of individual heterogeneity, party size (PSIZE), when iterated with the alternative-specific constant for air travel, is statistically significant (*t*-value = −4.195) under 500 draws but not significant (*t*-value = −1.568) under 100 draws.

The number of draws also has an impact, albeit small, on the mean estimates of the random and non-random parameters in the utility expressions. The standard deviations of the random parameters for two attributes and three alternative-specific constants (given as the diagonal values in the Cholesky matrix) are not significant; hence these variables can all be treated as non-random (i.e., fixed) parameters. All of the *below diagonal* values in the Cholesky matrix are not significant, suggesting true independence. Finally, the standard deviations of parameter distributions, σ_k, which identify sources of heterogeneity that can vary across individuals and alternatives, are all statistically non-significant. Thus the only source of heterogeneity identified in this application is individual-specific (i.e., party size).

B6.4   Latent class heteroscedastic MNL model

This model introduces the additional complexity of taste heterogeneity along with the heteroscedasticity that is our central interest. In most econometric models that permit taste heterogeneity, a random parameters approach is usually adopted. That is, β_{iq} is assumed to be drawn from some joint density function (e.g., multivariate normal), and estimation recovers the parameters of the distribution. In marketing, latent class models often have been used instead of random parameter formulations (e.g., Dillon and Kumar 1994). Instead of a continuous joint distribution, latent class models assume that a discrete number of support points (say, S) are sufficient to describe the joint density function of the parameters.

Latent classes correspond to underlying market segments, each of which is characterised by unique tastes $\beta_s, s = 1, \dots, S$. However, Swait (1994) pointed out that these classes also can be characterised by variance differences. He postulated that members of class s have taste β_s and scale λ_s. If the indirect utility function for members of that class is

$$U_{iq|s} = \lambda_s \alpha_{i|s} + \lambda_s \beta_s X_{iq} + \varepsilon_{iq|s}, \tag{B6.25}$$

and the $\varepsilon_{iq|s}$ are conditionally IID extreme value type 1 within class, the choice probability for members of class s is

$$P_{iq|s} = \frac{\exp\left(\lambda_s \beta_s X_{iq}\right)}{\sum_{j \in C_q} \exp\left(\lambda_s \beta_s X_{jq}\right)}. \tag{B6.26}$$

The final specification of the choice model requires the development of a classification mechanism to predict an individual's membership in a class (see Swait (1994) for full details). If the probability of being in class s is given by W_{qs}, the unconditional probability of choosing alternative i is simply

$$P_{iq} = \sum_{s=1}^{S} P_{iq|s} W_{qs}. \tag{B6.27}$$

It is not possible to identify scale factors and utility parameters in this model simultaneously, but some possibilities for dealing with this are as follows:

1. let utility parameters vary across classes but constrain scale parameters to be equal (i.e., estimate $\beta_1, \ldots, \beta_S$ and set $\lambda_1 = \cdots = \lambda_S = 1$);
2. force taste parameter homogeneity but let scale parameters vary across classes (i.e., estimate $\beta_1 = \cdots = \beta_S = \beta$ and $\lambda_2, \ldots, \lambda_S$, normalising $\lambda_1 = 1$);
3. restrict combinations of utility and scale parameters such that either λ_s or β_s is estimated for any particular class s.

Each of these possibilities represents different behavioural assumptions concerning taste heterogeneity *vis-à-vis* error term variance within latent classes.

Gopinath and Ben-Akiva (1995) and Swait and Sweeney (1996) proposed similar models to that of Swait (1994). Differently from that earlier work, however, Gopinath and Ben-Akiva (1995) and Swait and Sweeney (1996) assume that the latent classes are ordered with respect to an additional underlying latent dimension (e.g., value of time, orientation towards value for money in a retail setting). Swait's (1994) model assumes that no particular relationship holds between latent classes and the multiple latent dimensions permitted in his segmentation framework.

B6.5   The multinomial probit model

The move to relaxing the IID assumption is now a practical reality since developments in estimation methods centred on simulated moments (McFadden 1989, Keane 1994, Geweke 1991, Boersch-Supan and Hajivassiliou 1990, Geweke, Keane and Runkle 1994), with special cases available in software such as LIMDEP. The gains in improved understanding and prediction of choice behaviour from covariance MNP remain central to ongoing research and are engendering a significant move from variants of GEV to MNP. We conclude this appendix with an overview of the MNP model, illustrating its empirical value in a cross-section and a repeated (stated) choice context.

Hausman and Wise (1978a) proposed the structured covariance matrix for the multinomial probit model to consider heterogeneity among individuals. They assumed parameter distributions of a utility function as normal, and derived the covariance matrix in which attributes of a utility function were incorporated. The covariance structure for error terms was described as equation (B6.28):

$$\text{cov}\left(\varepsilon_r, \varepsilon_q\right) = \sum_k \sigma_{\beta k}^2 Z_{rk} Z_{qk}. \tag{B6.28}$$

Here, r and q indicate alternatives, Z_{rk} is the kth attribute of alternative r and $\sigma_{\beta k}^2$ is an unknown variance of kth parameter β_k. Individual differences in the covariance matrix are expressed by equation (B6.28). Using this approach, let us consider an example in which the indirect utility function of a recreation destination choice model contains a trip distance variable that has heterogeneous parameters among individuals. The covariance between recreation destinations must be proportional to the product of two recreation destination distances from equation (B6.28). Assigning a larger co-variance for the combination of recreation destination further away seems to be reasonable as a covariance of errors, even though such a covariance structure may not represent the similarity among recreation destination alternatives.

Bolduc (1992) enriched this specification, proposing the following structure for the unobserved component of utility in the multinomial probit model:

$$\varepsilon_i = \rho \sum_{j \neq i} w_{ij}\varepsilon_j + \xi_i. \tag{B6.29}$$

In this equation, ε_i is a normally distributed error with a mean of zero and is corre-lated with the other errors ε_j ($j \neq i$). ξ is distributed normally and ρ is a parameter. w_{ij} indicates a weight between alternatives i and j. The model would be directly applicable to recreation destination choice models with a large choice set and/or may be applic-able to recreation destination choice behaviours by defining the distance-related func-tion to represent the relation among recreation destinations.

Another version of the multinomial probit model is a structured covariance matrix to represent any overlapped relation between recreation destination alternatives. The fundamental ideas of the model were presented in Yai, Iwakura and Ito (1993) and Yai and Iwakura (1994). The assumptions introduced in the model may be more realistic for recreation destination choice behaviours on a dense network of opportunities than the strict assumption of the IID property of the multinomial logit model. As the nested logit model assumes an identical dispersion parameter between two modelling levels for all sampled observations, the model has difficulty in expressing individual choice-tree structures. To improve the applicability of the MNP model to applications with non-independence among alternatives, a function can be introduced which represents the overlapping of pairs of alternatives, with a multinomial probit model form in the structured covariance matrix that uses the function to account for the individual choice-tree structures in the matrix and to improve the estimability of the new alter-native's covariances.

For MNP, a choice probability P_r with a choice set size R is calculated by multi-dimensional integration associated with ε, as below:

$$P_r = \int_{\varepsilon=-\infty}^{\varepsilon_r+V_r-V_1} \cdots \int_{\varepsilon_r=-\infty}^{\infty} \cdots \int_{\varepsilon_r=-\infty}^{\varepsilon_r+V_r-V_R} f(\varepsilon)\, d\varepsilon_R \ldots d\varepsilon_1, \tag{B6.30}$$

where the density function is described by

$$f(\varepsilon) = (2\pi)^{-(R/2)} \left| \sum \right|^{-(1/2)} \exp\left[-\frac{1}{2}\varepsilon \sum{}^{-1}\varepsilon^T\right] \tag{B6.31}$$

and the covariance matrix is

$$\sum = \begin{pmatrix} \sigma_1^2 & \sigma_{12} & \cdots & \sigma_{1R} \\ \sigma_{12} & \sigma_2^2 & & \vdots \\ \vdots & & \ddots & \\ \sigma_{1R} & \cdots & & \sigma_R^2 \end{pmatrix}. \tag{B6.32}$$

Table B6.6. *Multinomial probit results*

Variables	Utility parameters	t-values
Attributes in the utility functions		
A_TRAIN	−3.4758	−6.49
A_BUS	−2.6828	−6.69
BC	−0.02849	−4.93
BT	−0.06522	−5.76
A_AIR	−3.179	−5.32
s[AIR]	3.012	3.02
s[TRAIN]	1.000	
s[BUS]	1.000	
s[CAR]	1.000	
rAIR, TRA	0.000	
rAIR, BUS	0.000	
rTRA, BUS	*0.4117*	*1.97*
rAIR, CAR	*−0.1683*	*−1.88*
rTRA, CAR	0.000	
rBUS, CAR	0.000	
Log likelihood function	−203.81	
Log likelihood at zero	−291.12	
Pseudo-R^2	0.290	

We omit notation for an individual for simplicity, but can easily add the notation without any change in the model derivation. Elements of the symmetric covariance matrix Σ, usually defined as parameters, are estimated simultaneously with parameters of the utility function V_r. A set of the estimated elements in the matrix is constant for the population.

Estimation of this model requires the analyst to select the specific form of the error covariance matrix such as (B6.28) or (B6.29) and to select the off-diagonal correlations which should be non-zero. The non-zero covariances can be constrained as equal across specific pairs of alternatives; however, this requires parsimonious judgement to be exercised since the addition of a free covariance adds substantial complexity in estimation.[5] Each alternative also has a standard deviation for each of the diagonal elements, which requires setting at least one of them to equal 1.0 for identification. Experimentation with behaviourally reasonable differences should be undertaken with care; analysts should experiment with a number of optimisation algorithms such as BHHH and DFG, together with varying tolerances and steps in function evaluation.

The results of estimation of an MNP model with the data presented in chapter 6 are given in table B6.6. After extensive investigation of many combinations of

---

[5] The reader will have gathered by this time that specification of the MNP model can be complex, particularly in the case of the covariance matrix. We refer the reader to Bunch (1991) for detailed discussion of identification restrictions for the MNP model.

Table B6.7. *Probability weighted MNP, HEV and MNL GC elasticities*

	MNP	Random effects HEV	MNL
Alternative = Air			
Choice = Air	−1.677	−1.162	−1.069
Choice = Train	0.130	0.334	0.300
Choice = Bus	0.914	0.571	0.416
Choice = Car	2.082	0.583	0.519
Alternative = Train			
Choice = Air	0.674	0.432	0.392
Choice = Train	−0.291	−1.372	−1.197
Choice = Bus	0.650	0.818	0.542
Choice = Car	1.071	0.748	0.617
Alternative = Bus			
Choice = Air	0.372	0.278	0.223
Choice = Train	0.208	0.311	0.226
Choice = Bus	−1.659	−2.191	−1.495
Choice = Car	0.180	0.470	0.299
Alternative = Car			
Choice = Air	0.694	0.497	0.500
Choice = Train	0.090	0.439	0.416
Choice = Bus	0.773	0.767	0.507
Choice = Car	−0.390	−1.485	−1.193

non-zero covariances and non-unit standard deviations for the variances, we settled on a model in which the correlation between train and bus (0.411) and between car and plane (−0.168) were sufficiently interesting to report. The only identifiable and statistically significant standard deviation was for air travel (the most significant in table B6.1 for the HEV model). The GC elasticities reported in table B6.7 for MNP together with HEV and MNL show some relativity of similarity across the three models for each alternative, even though their absolute magnitudes are quite different. The particular specification of MNP is not necessarily as general as various versions of the HEV, CovHet and RPL/ML models; the degree of generality is heavily dependent on the number of free (off-diagonal) covariance terms and (diagonal) standard deviations. What we have established is that the air and car alternatives are slightly negatively correlated, whereas the correlation between train and bus is much more positively correlated, as might be expected. However, for the train and bus modes the standard deviations of the unobserved effects are not statistically significantly different from one. Indeed what we observe is the natural partitioning between FLY and GROUND alternatives as implemented in the NL model (table 6.7).

B6.6 Multi-period multinomial probit

The most general model, in terms of the specification of the variance-covariance matrix of random effect components, is the multiperiod-multinomial probit (MPMNP) model. Special cases of this model accommodate all variations of assumptions about the autoregressive structure, the correlation of unobserved effects between alternatives and time periods, explicit treatment of unobserved heterogeneity across individuals, and differential variances across alternatives. The models presented above are special applications of the more general model. The generalised utility expression can be written out as equation (B6.33):

$$u_{jqt} = X_{jqt}\alpha + y_{qt}\beta_j + \varepsilon_{jqt}, \tag{B6.33}$$

where

$u_{jqt} =$ latent *utility* of alternative j as perceived by individual q in time t, $i = 1, \ldots I, t = 1, \ldots T_i$ or in choice set t,

$X_{jqt} =$ alternative-specific *attributes* of alternative j as perceived by individual q in time t or in choice set t,

$y_{qt} =$ agent-specific *characteristics* of individual q in time t or in choice set t,

$\varepsilon_{jqt} =$ multinormal error with $\text{cov}(e_q) = \Omega(e_q = (e_{jqt})j = 1, \ldots I, t = 1, \ldots T^i)$,

$\Omega =$ is $I \times T_i$, permitting inter-alternative and inter-temporal correlation between e_{jqt} and e_{kqs} for the same individual q, and α, β_j, and Ω are unknown parameters to be estimated.

Specific covariance structures evolve from this general formulation. Contemporaneous correlations and heteroscedasticity of the form $e_{qt} = (e_{jqt})$, $j = 1 \ldots I$ can occur, resulting in general deviations from IIA, represented by MNP and RPL/ML. Intertemporal correlations between the random components $e_q = (e_{jqt})j = 1, \ldots, I, t = 1, \ldots T^i$ can occur, producing random effects, specific to alternatives, and first-order autoregressive errors (for investigating correlation amongst choice sets), specific to alternatives. Importantly, the random effects permissible from choice set variation are individual-specific (because we have multiple observations on an individual, enabling the analyst to account for the specific idiosyncrasies of an individual which do not change as individuals make choices). In a single cross section, the exposure of heterogeneity is dependent on variation across a sample of individuals.

To illustrate the behavioural implications of alternative assumptions, we estimated a series of models using a 1997 stated choice switching data set for high-speed rail in the auto-drive non-business market for the Sydney–Canberra corridor. Combinations of these error processes yield the models summarised in table B6.8. Full details of parameter estimates are available on request from the second author. (We use another data set because the data set used above is a single cross section, and thus not suitable for MPMNP.) All of the models can be described by a likelihood function which is a product of the choice probabilities across the sample of $q = 1, \ldots, Q$ individuals,

Table B6.8. *Alternative error processes in discrete-choice models: repeated stated choices*

Model	Error processes	RAN	AR1	MNP	VTTS*	log L
1	IID across SC replications, *IID across alternatives*	0	0	0	4.63	−1067.9
2	AR1 errors, *IID across alternatives*	0	1	0	4.98	−811.46
3	Random effects, *IID across alternatives*	1	0	0	5.22	−765.01
4	Random effects, AR1 errors, *IID across alternatives*	1	1	0	5.40	−775.68
5	IID across SC replications, correlated across alternatives	0	0	1	6.46	−1050.71
6	Random effects, correlated across alternatives	1	0	1	6.88	−759.57
7	Free variance, random effects, AR1 errors, correlated across alternatives	1	1	1	7.09	−759.04
8	Free variance and IID across SC replications	0	0	1	7.64	−1040.25
9	AR1 errors, correlated across alternatives	0	1	1	7.87	−770.38
10	Free variance, IID across SC replications, correlated across alternatives	0	0	1	8.06	−1044.3
11	Free variance, random effects, *IID across alternatives*	1	0	1	8.37	−759.71

Note: * Dollars per adult person hour.

$i = 1, \ldots, I$ alternatives and $t = 1, \ldots T$ choice sets (equation B6.34):

$$L(\beta, M) = \prod_{q=1}^{Q} P(\{i_{tq}\} | \{X_{itq}\}; \beta, M). \tag{B6.34}$$

Each sampled car traveller was asked to review four high-speed rail options defined by fare class (first, full economy, discount economy and off-peak), frequency (every 30 minutes, hourly and two hourly), and parking cost ($2–$20 per day), then asked to select one of them or stay with the car for the current trip. This was repeated for up to four choice sets; 355 individuals evaluated two choice sets and 81 evaluated four choice sets. To illustrate the behavioural implications of alternative assumptions, we have derived the mean behavioural values of non-business travel time savings (VTTS), also reported in table B6.8, together with the log likelihood at convergence. The variation in the VTTS is substantial, ranging from a low of $4.63/adult person hour for the most restrictive model, up to \$8.37/adult person hour for a less restrictive specification. This is nearly a doubling of the VTTS, having major implications for transport investments, given the important role played by time benefits in most transport project appraisals. Close inspection of table B6.8 suggests that the failure to account for non-constant variance and correlation between the alternatives are the major contributing influences to the downward biased MNL mean estimate of VTTS. Allowing for unobserved heterogeneity (through random effects – RAN) and serial correlation through a first-order autoregressive (AR1) structure, contributes far less to an increase in the mean VTTS (relative to the MNL estimate).

B6.7   Concluding thoughts

This appendix has provided an introduction to more advanced, yet operational, methods of modelling choice among a set of mutually exclusive discrete alternatives. The growing interest in combining preference data (see chapter 8), especially stated choice and revealed preference data, requires expertise in estimating models where the properties of the unobserved random component of indirect utility can be empirically determined and distinguished. Where appropriate, this applies between alternatives within a single discrete-choice data set, as well as between data sets with common and unique alternatives, contemporaneously and intertemporally. Adding complexity for its own sake is counterproductive; rather, we need to demonstrate empirical gains beyond the MNL model to justify the added modelling costs. Alternatively, ignoring these behaviourally richer opportunities might also be counterproductive; the price the analyst may pay is a denial of the ability to add behavioural depth and breadth to a discrete-choice problem. There are a growing number of empirical studies that suggest significant gains can be made from enriched behavioural realism. The examples in this chapter and appendix point to this; additional evidence will be accumulated in chapters 10–12, where we present case studies pertinent to marketing, transportation and environmental valuation.

7 Complex non-IID multiple choice designs

7.1 Introduction

This chapter focuses on design issues for multiple choice problems that involve violations of the IID error assumption of the simple MNL model. Much of the material in this chapter is new, and relies on recent work by Dellaert (1995) and Dellaert, Brazell and Louviere (1999), who first considered designs for choice problems involving non-constant error variances. Chapter 5 dealt with one form of non-constant error variance, in which the presence/absence of alternatives in choice sets can lead to violations of the IID error condition. We briefly revisit these availability designs in this chapter, and recast them in light of certain non-IID error variance model forms.

Let us begin by rewriting the basic random utility expression as equation (7.1) to recognise that the distribution of errors can differ by alternative, by individual or by combinations of alternatives and individuals.

$$U_{in} = V_{in} + \varepsilon_i + \varepsilon_n + \varepsilon_{in}. \tag{7.1}$$

Let us concentrate for the moment on the variance of the errors, and assume that the covariances are constant. Equation (7.1) allows alternatives to have different error variances, which could result from a variety of mechanisms, such as similarities in unobserved effects, duration of exposure in a market, types of advertising and promotional campaigns, etc. Similarly, error variances across individuals can differ owing to similarities in unobserved characteristics, differences in ability to discriminate among alternatives, knowledge or familiarity with alternatives, interest in the product category, etc. For completeness, equation (7.1) also allows error variances to differ jointly by alternatives and individuals, which can arise from interactions of the aforementioned influences and/or differences.

A more general form of equation (7.1) was considered by Dellaert, Brazell and Louviere (1999). They express the utility of the jth alternative for respondent r in measurement condition m as follows:

$$U_{jmr} = V_{jmr} + \varepsilon_j + \varepsilon_m + \varepsilon_r + \varepsilon_{jm} + \varepsilon_{jr} + \varepsilon_{mr} + \varepsilon_{jmr}, \tag{7.2}$$

where ε_j is the error component associated with choice alternative j, ε_m is the error associated with the use of measurement instrument and technique m, ε_r is the error between respondents, ε_{jm} is the unobserved effect of the measurement instrument and technique on the random component of alternative j, ε_{jr} and ε_{mr} are within-respondent unobserved effects jointly associated, respectively, with alternatives and measurement procedures, and ε_{jmr} are within-respondent unobserved effects associated jointly with alternatives and measurement procedures. Some of the sources of error variance are under the analyst's control, and can be held constant in properly designed experiments or surveys. For example, for a particular experiment or survey, the combined instrument and measurement procedure error (ε_m), between-respondent errors (ε_r) and within-respondent associated instrument and measurement procedure errors (ε_{mr}) should be constant. That is, an experiment typically involves the same instrument and measurement procedure, one respondent at a time makes a choice and that choice occurs within a constant instrument and procedure.

The remaining components may vary within choice sets because different options are offered which may have different error components, the measurement instrument and procedure may impact the variance of each option differently, and respondents' preferences for alternatives may be heterogeneous. Let us consider the case where alternatives differ in error variances (ε_j) but other terms are assumed constant. This can be modelled in several ways, including NL, HEV, CovHet, RPL/ML and MNP (see chapter 6). This topic is new, hence there is little discussion or empirical results for SP designs for these problems. Consequently, we restrict ourselves to nested logit and HEV models, which were discussed in chapter 6. These models are a logical first step in relaxing the constant variance assumption, insofar as they allow differing diagonal elements, but constant or zero off-diagonals.

7.2 Designs for alternatives with non-constant error variances

Because nested logit is a special case of the more general heterogeneous logit, we concentrate on the latter. Chapter 5 explained how one can use the more general model to diagnose and estimate the less general nested logit form. If we allow $J - 1$ different variances (or more correctly, 'variance ratios' relative to a reference alternative) for J total alternatives, an SP design must be able to estimate alternative-specific effects. Logically, better designs will permit more identification possibilities and yield efficient estimates. Little research is available on statistical efficiency, but it is reasonable to assume that more efficient designs will be those that minimise the number of cross-alternative attribute levels that are the same (i.e., zero-valued differences in attribute between alternatives); however, one also wants to estimate the means (Vs) and variances (σ_εs) for each alternative independently.

In the absence of mathematical or Monte Carlo results, the above conditions appear to be satisfied by two broad types of designs:

1. Designs for presence/absence in which attributes are arrayed according to an orthogonal fractional design when alternatives are 'present' (see chapter 5).

2. Designs in which all alternatives are 'present', and the attributes of all alternatives are arrayed according to an orthogonal fractional design (see chapter 5).

Designs in which some alternatives are present/absent while others are constantly 'present' are an intermediate case of these two design types. Both broad design types allow one to estimate all alternative-specific effects for each alternative independently of one another, as well as estimate the attribute effects within each alternative independently of one another. The key difference lies in the fact that presence/absence designs also allow the variances of each alternative to differ with presence/absence. It would be possible to parameterise the variance differences as a function of presence/absence, and hence, directly embed the effects in both means and variances. Cross-effects models implicitly embed presence/absence and/or more generally attribute cross-effects in the mean utilities, which obscures any variance differences and/or at best makes it difficult to interpret behavioural processes which impact means instead of, or in addition to, error variances.

7.3   Designs for portfolio, bundle or menu choices

This is a particularly interesting problem, not only because there are so many practical applications for such designs and the resulting models, but also because the process itself is behaviourally important. Consider the problem proposed by Dellaert (1995). Suppose a consumer is thinking about a short, weekend 'city break'. In reality a 'city break' is a composite good, consisting of destination/location, travel mode, accommodation, and food. Thus, the choice of a 'city break' option is at one and the same time the choice of a bundle of related components, which also are options.

For the sake of example and simplicity, assume that 'city breaks' can be described by these three choice dimensions: travel mode, type of city and accommodation. Travel modes might be private car, train, bus or plane depending on circumstances and distances involved; and each mode can have different times, costs and amenities/services. Examples of accommodation options might be hostel, pension, hotel or motel, which can vary in costs, levels of amenities/services and location *vis-à-vis* what a traveller wants to do and/or experience. Finally, cities can be described by potentially many attributes, such as size, expensiveness (apart from travel and accommodation), age/history, things to do and/or see, etc. A 'city break' is a combination of choices from each of these three general categories of goods.

It is highly likely that each of the component goods has a different error variance, such that the composite good will exhibit a complex error structure in which the component errors may be correlated. Thus we might have the following utility expression:

$$U_{in} = (V_{ijn} + \varepsilon_{ijn}) + (V_{ikn} + \varepsilon_{ikn}) + (V_{iln} + \varepsilon_{iln}), \tag{7.2a}$$

or

$$U_{in} = (V_{ijn} + V_{ikn} + V_{iln}) + (\varepsilon_{ijn} + \varepsilon_{ikn} + \varepsilon_{iln}), \tag{7.2b}$$

Table 7.1. *Fractional factorial designs for composite choices*

T	A	C
T	A	
T		C
	A	C

where j, k and l respectively index transport mode, accommodation and city type, i indexes composite alternatives and n indexes consumers. Equations (7.2a) and (7.2b) admittedly are simplistic, as the utilities of each component may interact or combine in non-additive ways. However, these expressions serve to illustrate the design problem, the primary purpose of this discussion. Let us now assume that the error components do not have constant variance, but rather differ for j, k and l, respectively. We ignore correlations in the error components to avoid complication.

Any of the designs previously discussed, with the possible exception of designs for presence/absence problems, force restrictions on this problem. For example, if we conceptualise the problem as a choice among a fixed set of M competing 'city breaks', each of which is described by the attributes of transport, accommodation and city type, we are led to designs discussed in chapter 5. That is, all component attributes can be treated as a collective factorial, from which the smallest, orthogonal, main effects fraction might be used to simultaneously create 'city break' options and choice sets. In this conceptual framework and resulting design implementation, each 'city break' may have a different variance, i.e., the random component can differ for each of the M options.

Importantly, if we conceptualise the problem in this way, and adopt this design approach, it is not clear if we can estimate separate variances for the component goods because they are not chosen *per se*. Additionally, even if all the attributes are orthogonal between the M 'city breaks', it does not necessarily follow that attributes within-components will be orthogonal. Thus, if we adopt this approach, we also must use designs that ensure orthogonality within and between components as well as within and between the M choice options. If one does not do this, one cannot guarantee that component variances can be estimated independently.

Thus, the analyst needs to develop designs that allow separate variance estimates for each component (relative to one as a referent). Dellaert (1995) proposes that this be achieved by creating one overall experiment, which is consistent with the conceptual approach just described, and combining it with sub-experiments in which components are systematically present/absent. For example, if we use capital letters T, A and C, respectively, to refer to transport, accommodation and city type components, we need the fractional factorial designs shown in table 7.1.

Dellaert's suggestion corresponds to designing all pairs and the one triple for this case. More generally, however, one wants to know if such a design approach not only can estimate different variance ratios for component goods, but also which

Table 7.2. *Suggested useful nested specifications*

1st	2nd	3rd
Order of choice in nest		
C	A	T
C	T	A
C & A	T	
C & T	A	
T	C	A
T & A	C	

types of choice models can be estimated. That is, we generally should prefer designs that can accommodate nested or more complex choice processes. For example, some consumers may first choose a city type, then choose accommodation and then transport. Other consumers may have frequent-flyer points, and hence choose transport, then city type and then accommodation. Yet others may choose airline and accommodation, then city type. Thus, designs need to be sufficiently flexible to accommodate these possibilities and allow tests of which is a better approximation to the true but unknown process.

Thus, Dellaert's (1995) suggestion that different variance components can be estimated by administering the above sub-experiments does not seem to apply in all cases, although it does in his application. Let us, therefore, consider the general case of nested processes for components, and design strategies that may be useful. In general, the *bundle choice* problem is one in which consumers evaluate a menu, from which they must assemble a package that suits them. Bernardino (1996) treats this problem as a fixed list of menu items from which consumers choose a solution, and uses McFadden's (1978) *sampling of alternatives approach* to develop choice sets and estimate models. Unfortunately, while easy to implement, this sampling approach relies on the constant variance IID assumption, and hence the MNL model, which is unlikely to be correct in such cases. The crux of the problem is that the number of alternatives which can be chosen increases exponentially with the number and complexity of the menu components; also, the error variances of at least some components are likely to differ, and at least some errors are likely to be correlated.

For example, for our simple case of T, A and C, there are eight possible options, including choice of 'no break'. Because each option consists of subsets of components, errors for each option may be (indeed, are likely to be) correlated, and their variances may not be (indeed, are unlikely to be) constant. Thus, designing for a nested process appears to be a sensible way to proceed. In the present case, some of the most likely nests (in our opinion) are shown in table 7.2.

As the number of components increase, the size of the choice set increases rapidly. The problem is more complicated if there are two or more vendors or competitors, each of which offer their own menu. Even more complicated (but highly realistic) are situations where consumers can mix and match components from different vendors. This brief discussion strongly suggests that one must impose constraints or structure on the problem to progress. A purely empiricist approach involving ever more general designs is not likely to prove fruitful in the absence of a clear behavioural theoretical view of the process a priori. Thus, *blind design* is not a substitute for conceptual thinking.

7.3.1 Simple bundle problems

Consider the single vendor case, such as a restaurant or mail-order company already chosen by consumers as a supplier. The consumer has to pick the bundle components. This problem can be approached in two ways:

1. Treat all menu items and their attributes as a collective factorial, and develop an appropriate fractional design to vary prices and other attributes, such that all attributes are orthogonal within and between menu items. Develop an appropriate behavioural model a priori to restrict the number of options and/or impose structure, such as modelling a sequence of choices in the restaurant case, categorising menu items in a meaningful way, such as kitchen appliances, bathroom accessories, etc., and modelling choice of category bundles.

    Alternatively, examine the choice combinations post hoc and develop a logical and sensible 'feasible set' from the empirical data. The latter is less satisfactory than the former because of capitalisation on chance and/or small sample sizes. In any case, the number of alternatives and the nature of the choice process must be determined to develop a model; such a model is unlikely to involve a constant variance, IID error structure.

2. The second alternative is less behaviourally realistic, but often may be feasible, and can be used in a Bayesian sense to learn about the process and improve the design on successive iterations. That is, one imposes structure and restricts the problem through the design process itself. In particular, one *designs* the bundles a priori, and uses the design as a basis for making inferences about the process. This allows one to control the dimensionality of the problem, and obtain behaviourally informative choice information.

We believe that the first alternative is behaviourally realistic, but fairly impractical and demanding of a priori knowledge. Having said that, if one has insight into the choice process (say, through supporting qualitative work, as described in chapter 9) and a very good reason for using the first design approach, it should be used in lieu of the second. In general, however, definitive insights often are not easy to obtain in many applied research contexts; instead, generally only vague hypotheses about process can be formulated. Moreover, few applied researchers have the necessary expertise to deal with complex non-IID choice processes involving large numbers of alternatives. For these reasons, we concentrate our discussion on the second design approach.

Let us reconsider Dellaert's (1995) *city break* problem. Assume that consumers can choose among four different cities (e.g., a resident of the Netherlands might choose

Table 7.3. *Choice sets constructed from 2^3 factorial + foldover*

Attributes	Set 1	Set 2	Set 3	Set 4	Set 5	Set 6	Set 7	Set 8
City A	Paris	Paris	Paris	Paris	Amster.	Amster.	Amster.	Amster.
Mode A	auto	auto	train	train	auto	auto	train	train
Hotel A	CBD	not CBD	CBD	not CBD	CBD	not CBD	CBD	not CBD
City B	Amster.	Amster.	Amster.	Amster.	Paris	Paris	Paris	Paris
Mode B	train	train	auto	auto	train	train	auto	auto
Hotel B	not CBD	CBD	not CBD	CBD	not CBD	CBD	not CBD	CBD
Not go								

between Amsterdam, Brussels, Paris and The Hague), four different transport modes (air, bus, train, private auto) and four types of accommodation (3/4 star hotel centrally located; 3/4 star hotel away from city-break destination (CBD); motel on city fringe; and pension/bed & breakfast away from CBD). This *small* problem produces sixty-four possible choice alternatives if consumers are presented with a menu from which to choose. The size of the problem can be reduced by designing the sets of options from which consumers choose instead of providing an unrestricted menu. (We later add complexity by introducing different prices, discounts and presence/absence.)

For example, consumers can be offered different *packages* consisting of a city, transport mode and accommodation type. Such an experiment can be designed as a simple choice among two (or more if appropriate) competing packages and/or the choice not to go. Such a design is constructed by treating Package A and Package B as separate alternatives, each of which is described by the three menu items, and each menu item has four levels. Viewed in this way, the overall design is a 4^6 factorial, from which an appropriate fraction can be selected, or if the problem is sufficiently small, the entire factorial can be used. The smallest *orthogonal* fraction produces thirty-two pairs, but a larger fraction that will produce sixty-four pairs allows all interactions between components to be estimated within alternatives. If this approach is adopted, the design should be inspected to ensure that the same package combinations are not paired with one another. If the latter occurs, it usually can be fixed by reordering or *swapping* levels within one or more columns in the design.

In the interests of space, let us reduce the problem to one involving two levels for each menu item to illustrate the design approach. We first make eight choice sets by constructing the 2^3 factorial for Package A and use its foldover to make Package B. For example, let the attribute levels be as follows: cities (Paris and The Hague); modes (auto and train); and accommodation (3/4 star hotel in CBD and 3/4 star hotel away from CBD). We generalise this design strategy immediately below to more than two levels per attribute, but at this point we use the simple approach to illustrate the idea of a design that forces trade-offs in each choice set. An example is shown in table 7.3.

The simple foldover approach cannot be used in cases in which attributes have more than two levels because foldovers contrast exact opposites; hence, non-linearities

Table 7.4. *Master sampling design to determine menu item levels in each foldover*

Foldover conditions	City	Mode	Accommodation
1	P & H	air, train	CBD, not CBD
2	P & H	air, auto	CBD, motel
3	P & H	train, auto	not CBD, motel
4	P & B	air, train	not CBD, motel
5	P & B	air, auto	CBD, not CBD
6	P & B	train, auto	CBD, motel
7	H & B	air, train	CBD, motel
8	H & B	air, auto	not CBD, motel
9	H & B	train, auto	CBD, not CBD

cannot be identified. The identification problem can be solved by creating separate foldover designs for each possible pair of levels. That is, continuing our C, T and A example, each four-level component has six pairs of levels (i.e., (4*3)/2); hence, there are 6^3 possible combinations of pairs, which can be reduced to a smaller number with an overall sampling design to select systematically from the total. For example, one can sample thirty-six sets of foldover designs using a Latin square to produce (36×8) 2^3 + foldover designs. This requires a total of 288 choice sets, which can be blocked to ensure that each consumer responds to, say, four sets of eight choice sets (or fewer if desired).

We can further simplify the design process, if required, by reducing the menu item levels to three each, which results in three pairs of levels for each menu item. For illustrative purposes we use a 3^{3-1} orthogonal fraction of the 3^3 to sample from the total set of foldovers. Each foldover is based on a 2^3, with the particular (two) levels in each foldover determined by the sampling design. In the interests of space, we do not present the entire design (i.e., all seventy-two choice sets); instead, we present (a) the 3^{3-1} orthogonal fraction of the 3^3 that generates the sample of foldovers, and (b) the first and last of the nine sets of foldovers required.

That is, there are nine sets of foldovers in the master sampling design, each of which requires eight choice sets (2^3 + its foldover), for a total of seventy-two choice sets overall. To illustrate the process, let the menu items levels be as follows: city (Paris, Hague, Brussels); mode (air, train, auto) and hotel (3/4 star CBD; 3/4 star outside CBD; motel on fringe). Tables 7.4 and 7.5 present, respectively, (a) the master sample design to determine which menu item levels apply to each of the nine foldovers, and (b) the resulting first and ninth foldover design conditions from the master sampling design. We deliberately restrict the illustration to only the first and ninth design conditions to conserve space, as there are lots of choice sets, and each is generated in exactly the same way according to the master design.

The 1st and 9th factorial + foldover designs from the master design plan above are shown in table 7.5. We omit the other seven designs in the interests of space, but what

Table 7.5. *1st and 9th foldover designs based on master sampling design*

Attributes	Set 1	Set 2	Set 3	Set 4	Set 5	Set 6	Set 7	Set 8
	1st set of choice sets constructed from 2^3 factorial + foldover							
City A	Brussels	Brussels	Brussels	Brussels	Hague	Hague	Hague	Hague
Mode A	auto	auto	train	train	auto	auto	train	train
Hotel A	CBD	not CBD	CBD	not CBD	CBD	not CBD	CBD	not CBD
City B	Hague	Hague	Hague	Hague	Brussels	Brussels	Brussels	Brussels
Mode B	train	train	auto	auto	train	train	auto	auto
Hotel B	not CBD	CBD	not CBD	CBD	not CBD	CBD	not CBD	CBD
Not go								
	9th set of choice sets constructed from 2^3 factorial + foldover							
City A	Paris	Paris	Paris	Paris	Hague	Hague	Hague	Hague
Mode A	air	air	train	train	air	air	train	train
Hotel A	CBD	not CBD	CBD	not CBD	CBD	not CBD	CBD	not CBD
City B	Hague	Hague	Hague	Hague	Paris	Paris	Paris	Paris
Mode B	train	train	air	air	train	train	air	air
Hotel B	not CBD	CBD	not CBD	CBD	not CBD	CBD	not CBD	CBD
Not go								

is shown below should be enough to construct the other designs and generate all the seventy-two choice sets included in the master design.

The above design strategy ensures that all pairs of attribute levels appear in the overall design in a balanced and orthogonal manner. In this way, non-linearities and interactions can be estimated, and each choice set forces consumers to make trade-offs. There are no dominant alternatives, no differences in attribute levels are equal and no alternatives are the same. To our knowledge this strategy only works for pairs of alternatives; hence, other strategies need to be used for more packages. One strategy discussed earlier involves (a) treating all attributes of all packages as a collective factorial, (b) selecting an appropriate orthogonal fraction and (c) ensuring that the same attribute combination(s) do not appear in the same sets.

The utility function that applies to such designs may be generic or alternative-specific. It would be generic if there were no reason to believe that the evaluation process differs for package A vs. B. Hence, for a generic specification, variance differences or covariances in error structures can be attributed to the menu items themselves and/or consumer heterogeneity. This is a vastly lower dimensional choice problem than that posed by the unrestricted menu approach. To the extent that options more closely match consumers' preferences, such packages will be chosen; otherwise, consumers should reject them. In reality, to take a city break, consumers implicitly must pick a package regardless of the task format. The advantage of this task is that it forces consumers to reveal their preferences in a simple way. As with other stated choice experiments in this book, random utility theory applies; hence, models estimated from these designs potentially can be rescaled to actual market choices.

Table 7.6. *Using separate prices to make choice sets from 2^{5-3} factorial + foldover*

Attributes	Set 1	Set 2	Set 3	Set 4	Set 5	Set 6	Set 7	Set 8
City A	Paris	Paris	Paris	Paris	Hague	Hague	Hague	Hague
Mode A	auto	auto	train	train	auto	auto	train	train
Cost	low	low	high	high	high	high	low	low
Hotel A	CBD	not CBD	CBD	not CBD	CBD	not CBD	CBD	not CBD
Cost	high	low	low	high	high	low	low	high
City B	Hague	Hague	Hague	Hague	Paris	Paris	Paris	Paris
Mode B	train	train	auto	auto	train	train	auto	auto
Cost	high	high	low	low	low	low	high	high
Hotel B	not CBD	CBD	not CBD	CBD	not CBD	CBD	not CBD	CBD
Cost	low	high	high	low	low	high	high	low
Not go								

7.3.2 Adding further complexity to a bundle choice

Let us now add some complexity by pricing individual menu items or the overall bundle and/or offering a discount for the bundle compared to buying the components separately. This can be accomplished in the following ways:

1. Add a separate price dimension to each menu item of each alternative as appropriate, or nest price levels within levels of each menu items.
2. Add an overall price to the package; i.e., add a single price dimension to the menu items to increase the total number of attributes by one.
3. Combine methods 1 and 2, but treat the overall price dimension levels as discounts off the total price of each component.

In the interests of continuity, we again use city breaks as an illustration. To further simplify, we restrict each menu item to two levels (as in a previous example) and also limit price to two levels. The menu items levels are city (Paris, Hague); mode (auto, train); accommodation (CBD, not CBD), and the price and/or discount levels are (low, high). We now illustrate each of the three approaches in tables 7.6 to 7.8.

The first approach requires us to either (i) add two price dimensions, one each for mode and accommodation, or (ii) nest price levels within each component. 'City' also could have a price dimension, which should be framed to include *other* costs such as food, ground transport, shopping, etc. To keep things simple, we omit city prices. The former option adds 'attributes' to the design, whereas the latter option adds levels to the menu items. Choice of one or the other depends on one's research purpose. We first illustrate design option (i) (table 7.6).

Next we illustrate design option (ii) by nesting two price levels within each mode and hotel level (table 7.7). To do this, we treat each mode by price combination as a level of a new dimension *mode and price*, and likewise for each hotel by price combination. As previously discussed, in order to ensure that all A and B options are different it may be necessary to reorder or *swap* levels or columns. If 'City' does not

Table 7.7. *Choice sets designed with an orthogonal fraction of $2^2 \times 4^4$ factorial*

Attributes	Set 1	Set 2	Set 3	Set 4	Set 5	Set 6	Set 7	Set 8	Set 9	Set 10	Set 11	Set 12	Set 13	Set 14	Set 15	Set 16
City A Mode A	1	0	1	0	1	0	1	0	0	1	0	1	0	1	0	1
Cost Hotel A	0	0	0	0	1	1	1	1	2	2	2	2	3	3	3	3
Cost	3	2	1	0	3	2	1	0	3	2	1	0	3	2	1	0
City B Mode B	0	1	1	0	1	0	0	1	0	1	1	0	1	0	0	1
Cost Hotel B	0	1	2	3	1	0	3	2	2	3	0	1	3	2	1	0
Cost	3	1	0	2	2	0	1	3	1	3	2	0	0	2	3	1
Not go																

Key to design codes in the table: City A (0 = Paris, 1 = Hague); Mode A: cost (0 = train, \$150; 1 = train, \$250; 2 = auto, petrol = \$4/L; 3 = auto, petrol = \$6/L); Hotel A: cost (0 = CBD, \$150/night; 1 = CBD, \$250/night; 2 = suburb, \$100/night; 3 = suburb, \$200/night); City B (0 = Hague, 1 = Paris); Mode A: cost (0 = train, \$250; 1 = train, \$150; 2 = auto, petrol = \$6/L; 3 = auto, petrol = \$4/L); Hotel A: cost (0 = suburb, \$200/night; 1 = suburb, \$100/night; 2 = CBD, \$250/night; 3 = CBD, \$150/night).

Table 7.8. *Choice sets designed with 2^{4-1} fraction + foldover (+ orthogonal two-way inter-actions of components and price)*

Attributes	Set 1	Set 2	Set 3	Set 4	Set 5	Set 6	Set 7	Set 8
City A	Paris	Paris	Hague	Hague	Paris	Paris	Hague	Hague
Mode A	auto	train	auto	train	auto	train	auto	train
Hotel A	CBD	not CBD	not CBD	CBD	CBD	not CBD	not CBD	CBD
Package \$	low	low	low	low	high	high	high	high
City B	Hague	Hague	Paris	Paris	Hague	Hague	Paris	Paris
Mode B	train	auto	train	auto	train	auto	train	auto
Hotel B	not CBD	CBD	CBD	not CBD	not CBD	CBD	CBD	not CBD
Package \$	high	high	high	high	low	low	low	low
Not go								

have its own price levels, the required design consists of a 2×4^2 for both A and B; hence, we use a fraction of the $2^2 \times 4^4$ factorial to make choice sets, as shown in table 7.7.

Finally, we illustrate a design in which we either price the entire package, or offer it at a discount from the total menu item prices (table 7.8). The former simply requires us to add a new dimension called overall package price (Package \$) with appropriate levels. The latter requires us to price each menu item using one of the above design strategies, and add an overall discount dimension expressed as a percentage of the total price of the separate menu items. For the present example, the former suggests the 2^4 factorial or an appropriate fraction if overall package price has two levels; otherwise, a fraction of the $2^3 \times P_l$, where P_l is the lth level of price, $l = 1, 2, \ldots, L$. In general, for $L > 2$ we must either treat all menu items and price for both A and B as a collective factorial, or use the sampling of foldovers strategy discussed earlier.

The example in table 7.8 represents a design for three menu items with two levels plus an overall price (two levels) for the entire package. We use a fraction plus its foldover to make the design for this example to save space, but as noted above, this problem is sufficiently small to use the entire 2^4 factorial plus its foldover. The design illustrated in table 7.8 allows one to estimate all main effects plus all two-way inter-actions with package price. In this way, one can estimate separate price effects for each menu item (assuming all other interactions are zero).

Additional complexity can be added by adopting a variant of Dellaert's (1995) approach. One can either have the attributes (levels) of each package component held constant or varied. Continuing the city break example, Anderson and Wiley (1992) and Lazari and Anderson (1994) proved that the necessary and sufficient con-ditions for independent estimation of presence/absence effects are satisfied by combin-ing the smallest orthogonal main effects presence/absence design with its foldover in one design. Constant/variable information designs are a special case of *availability* designs (see chapter 5). In our example there are three menu items, and we want to estimate the effects of constant vs. variable attribute (level) information, and if vari-able, we want to estimate the effects of attribute levels on choice. To simplify, we again limit the task to a pair of designed options plus an option not to choose, and limit each menu item to two levels. A master plan can be constructed to estimate these effects by combining the smallest orthogonal main effects design of the 2^6 factorial with its foldover. That is, we construct the 2^{6-3} and combine it with its foldover to make sixteen constant/variable conditions.

In each condition of this master plan a menu item is held constant at a certain level if the code is constant, or the menu item information varies if the code is variable. For example, condition 1 can be omitted or treated as a single choice set because all menu item information is constant. The 2^{3-1} fraction is used to make four sets in condition 2 because only three menu items vary, as shown in the master plan of table 7.9, which also lists the minimum number of choice sets required for each condition and the overall total number of sets.

Each menu item is balanced for constant vs. variable, and within each menu item level *variable* is contained an orthogonal fraction of the other menu items. For exam-ple, consider 'City' for option A. When City has the value *variable*, table 7.10 applies. For ease of examination we abbreviate *constant* (C) and *variable* (V), which makes it easy to verify by inspection that each of the remaining five columns are indeed ortho-gonal (see table 7.10). As previously illustrated in chapter 5, a simple verification method to determine this is to find whether each pair of columns contains exactly two of each of the following combinations: CC, CV, VC and VV. If each pair satisfies that condition, the columns will be orthogonal because all are pairwise probabilisti-

Table 7.9. *Constant/variable master plan: 2^{6-3} main effects design + foldover*

Condition	Package A			Package B			Min. sets
	City	Mode	Hotel	City	Mode	Hotel	
1	constant	constant	constant	constant	constant	constant	1
2	constant	constant	variable	constant	variable	variable	4
3	constant	variable	constant	variable	variable	variable	8
4	constant	variable	variable	variable	constant	constant	4
5	variable	constant	constant	variable	constant	variable	4
6	variable	constant	variable	variable	variable	constant	8
7	variable	variable	constant	constant	variable	constant	4
8	variable	variable	variable	constant	constant	variable	8
9	variable	variable	variable	variable	variable	variable	8
10	variable	variable	constant	variable	constant	constant	4
11	variable	constant	variable	constant	constant	constant	4
12	variable	constant	constant	constant	variable	variable	4
13	constant	variable	variable	constant	variable	constant	4
14	constant	variable	constant	constant	constant	variable	4
15	constant	constant	variable	variable	constant	variable	4
16	constant	constant	constant	variable	variable	constant	4
Total sets required in master design							77

Table 7.10. *Subdesign when City A is variable*

Condition	Package A			Package B		
	City	Mode	Hotel	City	Mode	Hotel
5	variable	C	C	V	C	V
6	variable	C	V	V	V	C
7	variable	V	C	C	V	C
8	variable	V	V	C	C	V
9	variable	V	V	V	V	V
10	variable	V	C	V	C	C
11	variable	C	V	C	C	C
12	variable	C	C	C	V	V

cally independent. A more rigorous method is to verify that all eigenvalues of the correlation matrix for the five columns equal one.

Each sub-matrix conditional on either V or C in the master design constitutes an orthogonal main effects design in the remaining columns. Thus, all constant/variable effects of each menu item can be estimated independently, including the effects of the attribute information when variable. The present example represents a very small problem, hence, problems of realistic and meaningful size may require many sets of choice sets even if the problem is restricted to a choice of pairs and a third no choice or other constant option.

7.4 Summary

This chapter has introduced variations in choice designs where additional degrees of freedom are required to identify the influence of relaxing the IID condition. In simple terms, as the analyst investigates more complex discrete-choice models, such as those presented in the appendix to chapter 6, the challenge in experimental design is to facilitate sufficient power in a design to evaluate statistically the role of each assumption in explaining choice behaviour. Chapter 7 has provided an introduction to this challenge.

8 Combining sources of preference data

8.1 Appreciating the opportunity

Figure 8.1 portrays the price history of two yogurt brands in a US city during the 1980s. There was little price differentiation between the brands during the 126-week period in the graph, and also clearly little price variation within each brand. In addition, product characteristics and marketing activities (e.g., advertising, promotions) varied little during this period. A choice model estimated from these scanner panel data for these brands[1] would indicate that the only significant explanatory attributes were the brand-specific constants and past behaviour (i.e., some form of behavioural inertia; see Guadagni and Little 1983).

A choice model cannot detect the effect of price and other marketing attributes in such data for the simple reason that the parameters of any statistical model are driven by the degree of variation in each attribute, not by the absolute levels of the attributes represented in the data. Hence, if there is little variation in an explanatory attribute, its parameter cannot be estimated.

The situation depicted in figure 8.1 is quite common, and is much more the rule than the exception in competitive markets. Indeed, think about how in your own experience the prices of many products/services move up or down at a market level: credit card interest rates, home mortgage rates, fuel, etc. This happens because competition tends to result in similar products with similar marketing activities. Even if some product differentiation exists, a similar tendency to homogenisation typically exists in each subclass of products and/or competitors tend to copy successful attributes/features. This state of affairs makes it difficult to estimate the impact of a firm's marketing activities on its own product and/or on its competitors' products because each competitor's independent attributes tend to track the others'.

The foregoing helps us to understand why the attributes in models estimated from choices in actual markets often cannot predict the impact of changing policy attributes

---

[1] The most common form of scanner panels is formed by (a large number of) households recruited by a control firm. The households receive a unique identifier that is linked to their purchases in local supermarkets. This results in a time series of choices across a large number of product classes.

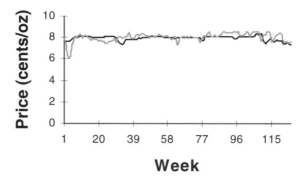

Figure 8.1 Price history for two yogurt brands

(e.g., prices). Unfortunately, however, this understanding does not help executives who must make decisions about what to do in response to competitor actions.

This chapter provides a very practical way to deal with the problem of insufficient variation in explanatory attributes within one choice (or, in general, preference) data source. The approach we will explain and discuss involves combining revealed preference (RP) data from real markets with stated preference (SP) or stated choice (SC) data from choice experiments or other sources of SP data using techniques developed in the last decade. We also show that this combination of data sources, which is sometimes called *data enrichment*, can be motivated by reasons other than the lack of variation in attributes, and we show that it also can be used to analyse and model multiple RP and SP sources. We also present a general characterisation of data generation processes that we believe can guide future research in this area.

8.2 Characteristics of RP and SP data

Besides the fact that RP data are generated by a choice process in the real world and SP/SC data are elicited in hypothetical markets, there are other differences in these data sources that may have implications for modelling choice behaviour.

8.2.1 RP data: the world as it is

Behaviour observed (i.e., data collected) in an actual market imparts information about a current market equilibrium process. Figure 8.2(a) shows a simple transport example of a market with five modes (Walk, Cycle, Bus, Train and Car) and certain cost and speed characteristics. The technology frontier reflected in choice data collected from this existing market will inevitably be characterised by the following:

- *Technological relationships* By definition, RP data describe only those alternatives that exist, which implies that existing absolute attribute levels and correlations between attributes will be in any model estimated from such data (plus limited ranges in attributes discussed above, as per figure 8.1).

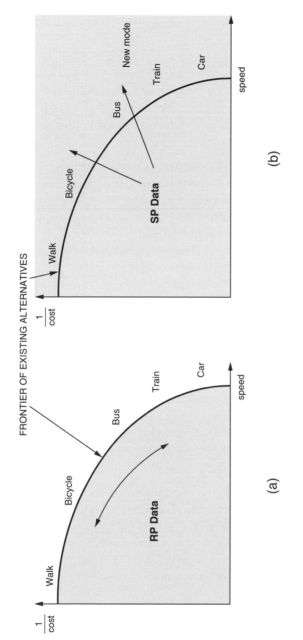

Figure 8.2 RP and SP data generation process

- *Brand sets* Brands are either in or not in a particular market, so it may be difficult to separate brand-related effects from attribute impacts. For example, the brand 'Bus' carries with it a series of images and associations that may not be separable from certain forms of access modes and associated levels of service, fare and travel time.
- *Market and personal constraints* Market and personal constraints (e.g., distribution or availability, work location, income, information availability) are reflected in such data. The embodiment of constraints in real market data are generally a good thing, but some marketing activities are directed towards such constraints, and RP data may not contain sufficient variability to permit identification of such effects.

In summary, RP data have high reliability and face validity (after all, these are real choices made by individuals who committed their actual, limited resources to make the choices possible). Hence, RP data are particularly well suited to short-term forecasting of small departures from the current state of affairs, which emphasises the tactical nature of the support RP-based models can give.

On the other hand, these same characteristics make RP data quite inflexible, and often inappropriate, if we wish to forecast to a market other than the historical one (whether in time, space or other dimension). Shifts in the technological frontier, as opposed to movements along the frontier, call for different data.

8.2.2 SP data: the world as it could be

Figure 8.2(b) shows how SP data come into their own. SP choice data can be used to model existing markets, but the data's strengths become far more apparent if we wish to consider markets fundamentally different from existing ones. Structural shifts in markets may occur because of technological advances (e.g., wireless communications), economic/financial reasons (e.g., a brand is removed from the market or a company goes bankrupt) or simply the passage of time. Some of the characteristics of SP data are as follows:

- *Technological relationships* Within reason, SP data can cover a much wider range of attributes and levels than RP data. Technological relationships can be whatever the experiment designer wishes (although attribute correlations often are built into SP experiments), so SP models tend to be more robust than RP models.
- *Brand sets* Like technology, brand presence/absence can be designed into SP data (e.g., Lazari and Anderson, 1994). It is also possible to explore issues such as line and/or brand extensions (e.g., Delta Airlines' vacation packages), co-branding (e.g., Fisher-Price and Disney toys) and/or affinity branding (e.g., a professional baseball club credit card, issued by a bank, that rewards usage through discounts to season events) without costly investments in actual market trials.
- *Market and personal constraints* Market constraints (e.g., distribution) often can be simulated and observed with SP data, either with attribute levels or presence/absence manipulations. In fact, even information-availability issues (e.g., real

market advertising and/or word-of-mouth) can be studied via SP methods, although these typically are more limited than would be the case in real markets. Unfortunately, as far as we are aware, it generally is difficult to simulate changes in personal constraints in SP tasks and obtain meaningful results.[2]

Thus, SP data can capture a wider and broader array of preference-driven behaviours than RP. SP data are particularly rich in attribute tradeoff information because wider attribute ranges can be built into experiments, which in turn, allows models estimated from SP data to be more robust than models estimated from RP data (see Swait, Louviere and Williams 1994). On the other hand, SP data are hypothetical and experience difficulty taking into account certain types of real market constraints; hence, SP-derived models may not predict well in an existing market without calibration of alternative-specific constants. As a consequence, SP-derived models may be more appropriate to predict structural changes that occur over longer time periods, although experience suggests that they also perform well in short-run prediction *if* calibrated to initial conditions.

8.2.3 Combining the strengths of RP and SP data

Previously we discussed strengths and weaknesses of RP and SP data sources, and noted that strengths could be exploited and weaknesses ameliorated. Now we discuss how to accomplish this by pooling both data sources. The process of pooling RP and SP data and estimating a model from the pooled data is called *data enrichment*. This process originally was proposed by Morikawa (1989), whose motivation was to use SP data to help identify parameters that RP data could not, and thereby improve the efficiency (i.e., obtain more precise and stable estimates) of his model parameters. This stream of research is illustrated by the work of Ben-Akiva and Morikawa (1990), Ben-Akiva, Morikawa and Shiroishi (1991), Bradley and Daly (1994), Hensher and Bradley (1993), Adamowicz, Louviere and Williams (1994), Adamowicz et al. (1997), Hensher (1998a) and others. A common theme of this paradigm is that RP data are viewed as the standard of comparison, and SP data are seen as useful only to the extent that they ameliorate certain undesirable characteristics of RP data.

The 'data enrichment paradigm' view is illustrated in figure 8.3, which suggests that the analyst's goal is to produce a model that can forecast to real market future scenarios. Bearing this objective in mind, RP data are collected that contain information about the equilibrium and attribute trade-offs in a particular current market. The RP information (especially the attribute trade-offs) may be deficient (i.e., identification may be problematic, or efficiency low), and hence SP data also are collected, although the RP and SP data may come from the same or different people. Significantly, the only SP information used involves the attribute trade-offs, which are pooled with the

---

[2] While this may be an over generalisation, it seems somewhat implausible to ask respondents in an SP choice task to consider changes to their personal contexts that they know are not under the control of the market forces being considered (e.g., home or work location in an SP mode choice task; change in the number of household members in an SP task about home mortgages).

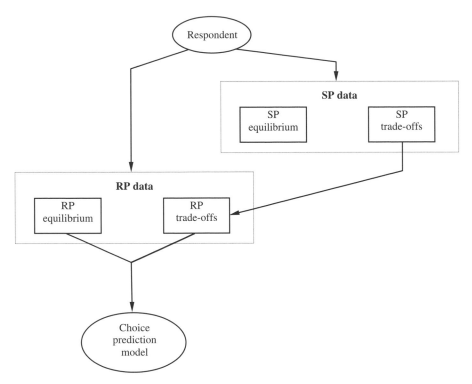

Figure 8.3 Enrichment paradigm 1

RP data to derive a final choice model (statistical details of the process are described in the next section).

A different view is represented by the work of Swait, Louviere and Williams (1994), and illustrated in figure 8.4. Their view is that each source of data should be used to capture those aspects of the choice process for which it is superior. For example, RP data is used to obtain current market equilibria, but the tradeoff information contained in RP data are ignored because of its deficiencies.[3] SP data typically cover multiple 'markets' or at least a wider range than a single RP market, hence the tradeoff information in SP is used, but equilibrium information is ignored. With regard to the latter, SP data provide information about equilibria over a large range of situations not necessarily directly relevant to the final objective, namely prediction to an actual RP market.

The statistical details necessary to implement both views are relatively straightforward, but this chapter focuses only on the approach consistent with the first, or *data enrichment paradigm*, which is the advanced state-of-the-practice in transportation and environmental economics. The reader is referred to Swait, Louviere and Williams (1994) for more detail on paradigm 2.

---

[3] We have had experiences with RP data in which not a single parameter was statistically significant. While this is not the rule, it drives home the point about data quality (or lack thereof).

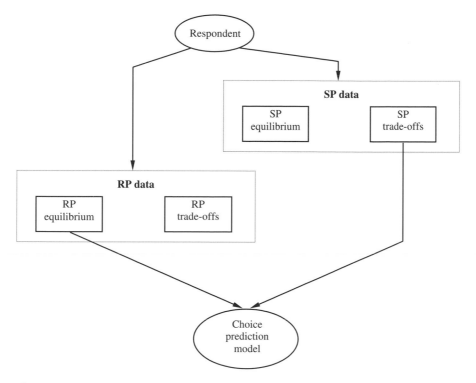

Figure 8.4 Enrichment paradigm 2

8.3 The mechanics of data enrichment

8.3.1 Some preliminaries

Suppose two preference data sources are available, one RP and another SP, and both deal with the same form of behaviour (say, choice of 8oz frozen orange juice concentrate). Each data source has a vector of attributes, and at least some of them are common to both data sets. For purposes of exposition, let the common attributes be X^{RP} and X^{SP} in the RP and SP data sets, respectively, and let there also be unique attributes Z and W, respectively, for each data set.

Invoking the now familiar random utility framework, we assume that the latent utility underlying the choice process in both data sets is given by equations (8.1) and (8.2).

$$U_i^{RP} = \alpha_i^{RP} + \beta^{RP} X_i^{RP} + \omega Z_i + \varepsilon_i^{RP}, \quad \forall i \in C^{RP}, \tag{8.1}$$

$$U_i^{SP} = \alpha_i^{SP} + \beta^{SP} X_i^{SP} + \delta W_i + \varepsilon_i^{SP}, \quad \forall i \in C^{SP}, \tag{8.2}$$

where i is an alternative in choice sets C^{RP} or C^{SP}, αs are data source-specific alternative-specific constants (ASCs), β^{RP} and β^{SP} are utility parameters for the common attributes and ω and δ are utility parameters or parameters for the unique attributes in each data set. It is important to note that the choice sets need not be the same in the two data sources, and in fact the alternatives need not be the same. Indeed, one attraction of SP data is their ability to manipulate and observe the effects on choice of introducing new products/brands and/or removing existing ones from consideration.

If we assume that the error terms in equations (8.1) and (8.2) are IID extreme value type 1 (EV1) within both data sources that are associated, respectively, with scale factors λ^{RP} and λ^{SP} (as introduced in chapters 3 and 6), the corresponding choice models can be expressed as follows:

$$P_i^{RP} = \frac{\exp\left[\lambda^{RP}(\alpha_{RP}i + \beta^{RP}X_i^{RP} + \omega Z_i)\right]}{\displaystyle\sum_{j \in C^{RP}} \exp\left[\lambda^{RP}(\alpha_{RP}j + \beta^{RP}X_j^{RP} + \omega Z_j)\right]}, \quad \forall i \in C^{RP}, \tag{8.3}$$

$$P_i^{SP} = \frac{\exp\left[\lambda^{SP}(\alpha_{SP}i + \beta^{SP}X_i^{SP} + \omega Z_i)\right]}{\displaystyle\sum_{j \in C^{SP}} \exp\left[\lambda^{SP}(\alpha_{SP}j + \beta^{SP}X_j^{SP} + \omega Z_j)\right]}, \quad \forall i \in C^{SP}. \tag{8.4}$$

8.3.2 A small digression: the scale factor

We now digress to discuss the EV1 scale factor and its role in the MNL model. As we later show, the scale factor plays a crucial role in the data enrichment process, so it is important to understand that role before proceeding further in our discussion of 'data enrichment'. Expressions (8.3) and (8.4) make it clear that any particular scale factor and parameters of its associated choice model are inseparable and multiplicative ($\lambda\kappa$), where κ is some parameter vector. *Thus, it is not possible to identify a scale factor within a particular data source.* None the less, the scale factor associated with any data source fundamentally affects the values of the estimated parameters, such that the larger (smaller) the scale, the bigger (smaller) the parameters.

Thus, there is a fundamental identification problem because scale (λ) and utility (β) parameters are confounded and cannot be separated in any one data source, which in turn, implies that *one cannot directly compare parameters from different choice models.* For example, one cannot compare price coefficients from two data sources directly to determine whether one is larger than the other. In particular, one cannot determine whether the observed difference is the result of differences in scale, true parameters or both. In fact, even if two data sources were generated by the same utility function (i.e., the same (parameters), but have different scale factors λ_1 and λ_2, the estimated parameters will differ (in one case they are $\lambda_1\beta$, and in the other $\lambda_2\beta$). If both parameters and scales can vary between data sets, it should be clear that parameter comparisons cannot rely on 'eyeballing' differences, but rather require a more sophisticated testing procedure.

Let us return to comparing two data sources that we believe reflect the same utilities, but (potentially) different scales. For example, in combining RP and SP data

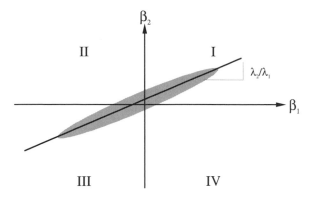

Figure 8.5 Visual test for parameter vector equality across two preference data sets

the key question is whether $(\lambda_1\beta_1) = (\lambda_2\beta_2)$. Let us rearrange the latter expression to obtain $\beta_1 = (\lambda_2/\lambda_1)\beta_2$, which shows that if the two taste vectors are equal, a graph of one parameter vector (e.g., RP) against the other (e.g., SP) should produce a cloud of points passing through the origin of the graph with (positive) slope equal to λ_2/λ_1 (i.e., the ratio of the error variance of set 2 to set 1). Figure 8.5 illustrates such a graphical plot, as suggested by chapter 13. To the extent that the cloud of points is too dispersed, or too many parameters have opposite signs in the data sources (implying points in quadrants II and IV), this provides evidence that parameter equality between data sets is less likely.

Plotting parameter vector pairs (or multiple vectors if more than two data sources are being compared – see chapter 13) is an easy way to investigate parameter equality in choice data, but there are problems with this simple method. For example, the parameter estimates contain errors not reflected in the graphical plots; hence, we generally require a more rigorous statistical test (described later) to determine if parameter equality holds between data sets, after accounting for scale differences. None the less, such plots are useful exploratory tools.[4]

More importantly, the influence of the scale factor of a data set is more meaningful than it might seem at first glance. Specifically, the scale factor in an MNL model is *inversely* related to the variance of the error term as follows for all alternatives and respondents:

$$\sigma^2 = \pi^2/6\lambda^2. \tag{8.5}$$

Thus, the higher the scale, the smaller the variance, which in turn implies that models that fit well will also display larger scales. Figure 8.6 demonstrates that

---

[4] Another useful exploratory tool suggested in chapter 13 is to perform principal components analysis on multiple parameter vectors. If a single dimension results, this is *supportive* of parameter equality up to a multiplicative constant.

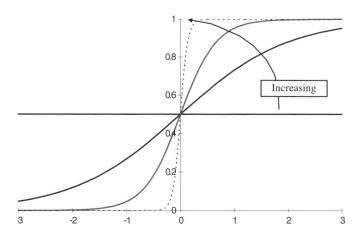

Figure 8.6 The effect of the scale parameter on choice probability

when scale is zero, choice probabilities are equal (for the binary case in figure 8.6, both probabilities equal 0.5), and as scale increases from that point, choice models predict outcomes that behave increasingly like a step function as the limit (∞) is approached. That is, as scale becomes infinitely large, the model perfectly discriminates between the two alternatives. This effect generalises to multiple alternatives.

The implication of these observations about the behaviour of the scale parameter is that it plays a role in choice models that is unique compared to more familiar statistical models such as OLS regression (with which many researchers are acquainted). That is, the model parameters and the characteristics of the error terms are intimately (even inextricably!) related. It may be wise to spend time thinking about and reviewing this notion because usual statistical and econometric education emphasises the role of the mean compared to other moments. In the case of choice models it is necessary to think of the variance (or, equivalently, *scale*) as an integral part of the model specification instead of being a nuisance parameter. The relationship between mean and variance exhibited by the MNL model is also a property shared by many other choice model forms, such as NL and MNP.

8.3.3   Data enrichment method

Recall again that our primary interest lies in testing the equality of the parameter vectors for SP and RP data. The process of combining the two data sources involves imposing the restriction that the common attributes have the same parameters in both data sources, i.e., $\beta^{RP} = \beta^{SP} = \beta$. However, because of the scale factor things aren't so simple! Remember that the estimated model parameters are confounded with the scale factors for each data set (see expressions (8.3 and (8.4)). Thus, even after imposing the restriction of common attribute parameter equality, we still must account for the scale factors, as shown in equations (8.6) and (8.7)

$$P_i^{RP} = \frac{\exp\left[\lambda^{RP}(\alpha_i^{RP} + \beta X_i^{RP} + \omega Z_i)\right]}{\sum\limits_{j \in C^{RP}} \exp\left[\lambda^{RP}(\alpha_i^{RP} + \beta_i^{RP} + \delta W_j)\right]}, \quad \forall i \in C^{RP}, \tag{8.6}$$

$$P_i^{SP} = \frac{\exp\left[\lambda^{SP}(\alpha_i^{SP} + \beta X_i^{SP} + \omega Z_i)\right]}{\sum\limits_{j \in C^{SP}} \exp\left[\lambda^{SP}(\alpha_i^{SP} + \beta_i^{SP} + \delta W_j)\right]}, \quad \forall i \in C^{SP}. \tag{8.7}$$

Equations (8.6) and (8.7) make it clear that if we wish to pool these two data sources to obtain a better estimate of β, we cannot avoid controlling for the scale factors.

So, data enrichment involves pooling the two choice data sources under the restriction that common parameters are equal, while controlling for the scale factors. Thus, the pooled data should enable us to estimate α^{RP}, β, ω, λ^{RP}, α^{SP}, δ and λ^{SP}. However, we cannot identify both scale factors, so one must be normalised. It is conventional to assume that the scale of the RP data set is one ($\lambda^{RP} \equiv 1$), and so the estimate of λ^{SP} represents a *relative scale* with respect to the RP data scale. Equivalently, we can view the problem as estimating the SP variance relative to the RP variance ($\sigma_{RP}^2 = \pi^2/6$).

The final parameter vector to be jointly estimated is $\psi = (\alpha^{RP}, \beta, \omega, \alpha^{SP}, \delta, \lambda^{SP})$. Assuming the two data sources come from independent samples, the log likelihood of the pooled data is simply the sum of the multinomial log likelihoods of the RP and SP data:

$$L(\psi) = \sum_{n \in R} \sum_{P_i \in C_n^{RP}} y_{in} \ln P_{in}^{RP}(X_{in}^{RP}, Z_{in} | \alpha^{RP}, \beta, \omega)$$

$$+ \sum_{n \in S} \sum_{P_i \in C_n^{SP}} y_{in} \ln P_{in}^{SP}(X_{in}^{SP}, W_{in} | \alpha^{SP}, \beta, \sigma, \lambda^{SP}) \tag{8.8}$$

where $y_{in} = 1$ if person n chooses alternative i, and $= 0$ otherwise. This function must be maximised with respect to ψ to determine the maximum likelihood parameter estimates, which can be accomplished in several ways, but we outline two of the easier methods below.

8.3.3.1 A manual method using existing MNL software

We first define a data matrix for the pooled data as a function of the scale factor for the SP data. Let this data matrix and its corresponding parameter vector (which omits the scale factor) be as follows:

$$Q(\lambda^{SP}) = \left[\begin{array}{c|c|c|c|c} \tilde{I}^{RP} & 0 & X^{RP} & Z & 0 \\ 0 & \lambda^{SP}\tilde{I}^{SP} & \lambda^{SP}X^{SP} & 0 & \lambda^{SP}W \end{array}\right], \tau' = (\alpha^{RP\prime}, \alpha^{SP\prime}, \beta', \omega', \delta'), \tag{8.9}$$

where $\tilde{I}^{RP}$ and $\tilde{I}^{SP}$ are identity matrices that multiply the ASCs in the RP and SP data sets, respectively; other quantities are as previously defined.

With this definition of the data matrix, the log likelihood of the joint sample, *conditional on the scale factor*, can be written as equation (8.10):

$$L(\tau|\lambda^{SP}) = \sum_{n \in RP \cup SP} \sum_{i \in C_n} y_{in} \ln P_{in}(Q(\lambda^{SP})|\tau). \tag{8.10}$$

For a given value of λ^{SP}, this log likelihood corresponds to estimating an MNL model from the pooled data. The catch is that we must multiply all rows in the SP data set by a value of λ^{SP}.

This suggests a simple procedure, originally proposed by Swait and Louviere (1993), to estimate the desired model parameters and the relative SP scale factor by manual search:

1. *Define a range of values of λ^{SP}* within which one expects the log likelihood function to be maximised. The lower bound cannot be less than zero, and the upper bound must be larger than the lower bound. Empirical experience suggests that scale factors tend to lie between 0 and 3, but in any particular pooled data set it is easy to define an upper bound by trial and error. Because the log likelihood in (8.10) is concave, there is a unique maximum.[5] Thus, one can try progressively larger values of λ^{SP} until one brackets the maximum.

2. *Implement a one-dimensional search* (e.g., fixed increment grid or golden-section searches) to obtain an estimate of the relative scale factor of the SP data. At each trial value of λ^{SP}, define data matrix $Q(\lambda^{SP})$ as in (8.9) and estimate the remaining parameters of the pooled MNL model using any standard MNL estimation package.

3. The estimates of λ^{SP} and τ are obtained from the model solution that maximises the value of the log likelihood function.

The above procedure yields consistent but inefficient estimates of λ^{SP} and τ. But it has the undeniable and worthy virtue of simplicity!

To illustrate the estimation method, consider an RP (with three alternatives) and an SP data set (with two alternatives). There are fifty-one common parameters, and only ASCs differ between data sets. Parameter estimates are first obtained by fitting MNL models to each data set separately; these are plotted against one another in figure 8.7. The graph in figure 8.7 strongly suggests that the parameters are the same in both data sources, although the scale factors may differ (figure 8.7 contains a 45° line plus another line that better fits the data). The graph also suggests that the constant of proportionality (the ratio of SP to RP) probably is larger than one (i.e., the slope is greater than 45°, indicating that the SP error variance is larger than the RP error variance (or conversely, the scale of the SP data is *smaller* than the RP scale). Table 8.1 contains the results of a fixed-step grid search for the relative scale. The search outcome

---

[5] The global concavity of the log likelihood function of the MNL choice model is a property unique to that model form. Other choice models (e.g., NMNL, MNP) have log likelihood functions that are *not* globally concave. However, this manual method can be used for those models also; we just have to be more careful during the search procedure to ensure that we have the global optimum of the scale factor and other parameters.

Table 8.1. *Fixed grid search results*

Relative scale trial value	Log likelihood	Relative scale trial value	Log likelihood
0.100	−1051.0	0.800	−711.5
0.150	−990.8	0.850	−713.4
0.200	−936.0	0.900	−716.5
0.250	−887.8	0.950	−720.6
0.300	−846.6	1.000	−725.6
0.350	−812.3	1.050	−731.3
0.400	−784.3	1.100	−737.5
0.450	−762.1	1.150	−744.1
0.500	−744.8	1.200	−751.1
0.550	−731.8	1.250	−758.3
0.600	−722.5	1.300	−765.6
0.650	−716.2	1.350	−773.1
0.675	−714.1	1.400	−780.7
0.700	−712.6	1.450	−788.3
0.725	−711.6	1.500	−795.9
0.750	−711.1		
0.775	−711.1		

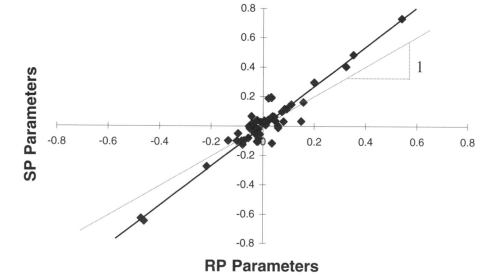

Figure 8.7 Parameter plot for example data combination exercise

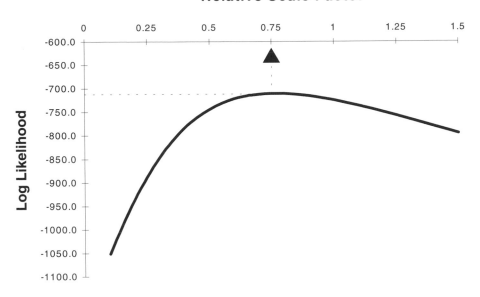

Figure 8.8 Plot of relative scale factor vs. log likelihood

log likelihood values are plotted in figure 8.8, which indicates the optimal value of the relative scale lies between 0.75 and 0.775, hence a midway point estimate would be 0.7625. Recall that the scale of the RP data set $= 1.0$, so what does our result tell us about the relative variances? To answer that question, consider the following ratio:

$$\frac{\sigma_{RP}^2}{\sigma_{SP}^2} = \frac{\pi^2/6\lambda_{RP}^2}{\pi^2/6\lambda_{SP}^2} = \frac{\lambda_{SP}^2}{\lambda_{RP}^2} = \left(\frac{\lambda_{SP}}{\lambda_{RP}}\right)^2 \approx \left(\frac{\hat{\lambda}_{SP}}{\hat{\lambda}_{RP}}\right)^2 = \left(\frac{0.7625}{1.0}\right)^2 \approx 0.58. \quad (8.11)$$

So, in fact, the variance of the RP data set is about 60 per cent of that of the SP data.

As noted above, the manual method yields consistent but not efficient parameter estimates. This is a problem because if the standard errors are not efficient they are likely to be *underestimated*, leading to inflated t-statistics. Thus, this first estimation method trades-off statistical efficiency for ease of implementation. The alternative is a method that simultaneously estimates model parameters and relative scale factors.

8.3.3.2 A FIML method: the NL trick

A full information maximum likelihood (FIML) method to estimate model parameters and relative scale factor(s) simultaneously must optimise (8.8) with respect to all parameters. One can develop estimation code to solve this specialised problem, but it is a time-honoured tradition in econometrics to try to find simpler ways to estimate the parameters (at a minimum, consistently, as in the manual method, and hopefully also

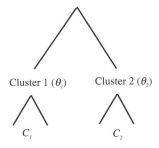

Cluster 1 (θ_1) Cluster 2 (θ_2)

C_1 C_2

Figure 8.9 A two-level, two-nest NMNL model

efficiently) instead of writing special code. Fortunately, such a solution is available for this problem, but it requires us to adopt a different conceptual view of the problem.

To pool the RP and SP data we have to assume that the data generation process for both data sources is IID EV1 with different scale factors, but with location (or mean) parameters that share some components but also have other unique components. Thus, MNL choice models must underlie the choices within each data source, as in equations (8.6) and (8.7). Now consider figure 8.9, which illustrates a Nested Logit (NL) model with two levels and two clusters of alternatives (which we call clusters 1 and 2 for presentation purposes). Cluster 1 contains alternatives in the set C_1, and Cluster 2 alternatives in C_2. Recall from chapter 6 that NL models are a hierarchy of MNL models, linked via a tree structure. MNL models underlie the data within each cluster, hence the constant variance (i.e., scale) assumption must hold within clusters. However, between clusters scale factors can differ. By explicitly accommodating different variances between clusters, NL provides a simple way to accomplish the estimation required to fuse the RP and SP data sources. In particular, the expressions for the conditional cluster choice models in figure 8.9 are as follows:[6]

$$P(i|C_1) = \frac{\exp[V_i/\theta_1]}{\displaystyle\sum_{j\in C_1}\exp[V_j/\theta_1]}, \tag{8.12}$$

$$P(k|C_2) = \frac{\exp[V_k/\theta_2]}{\displaystyle\sum_{j\in C_2}\exp[V_j/\theta_2]}. \tag{8.13}$$

In equations (8.12) and (8.13), V_i is the systematic portion of the utility of alternative i. The inclusive value parameters θ_1 and θ_2 play an interesting role in (8.12) and (8.13). That is, the systematic utility of all alternatives in the respective subnet of the tree is multiplied by the inverse of the inclusive value. The choice model in each subnet is MNL, which implies that *the scale of the utilities of the subnet is equal to the inverse of the subnet inclusive value*. The ratio of the variances for the two

---

[6] We do not develop the expressions for P(C_1) and P(C_2) since they are irrelevant to the point being made.

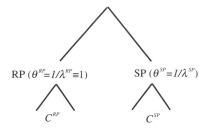

Figure 8.10 Combining RP and SP data using the NMNL model

clusters is given in (8.14)

$$\frac{\sigma_1^2}{\sigma_2^2} = \frac{\pi^2/6\lambda_1^2}{\pi^2/6\lambda_2^2} = \frac{1/\lambda_1^2}{1/\lambda_2^2} = \left(\frac{\theta_1}{\theta_2}\right)^2, \tag{8.14}$$

which can be compared to expression (8.11).

Let us now return to the problem of combining RP and SP data. Imagine that cluster 1 in figure 8.9 was renamed 'RP' and cluster 2 renamed 'SP', as in figure 8.10. Thus, if we estimate an NL model from the two data sources we obtain an estimate of the scale factor of one data set relative to that of the other, and our estimation objective is accomplished. This approach was proposed by Bradley and Daly (1992) and Hensher and Bradley (1993), who called the hierarchy in figure 8.10 an *artificial tree structure*.[7] That is, the tree has no obvious behavioural meaning, but is a useful modelling convenience. FIML estimation software for NL models is fairly widely available, and can be used to obtain FIML estimates of the inverse of relative scale factors. As with the manual search method presented earlier, one can identify only one of the relative scale factors, so figure 8.10 normalises the inclusive value of the RP data to unity.

As a further illustration, if we apply this technique to the data used to generate table 8.1 and figure 8.8, we obtain an estimate of the SP data inclusive value = 1.309, with a standard error of 0.067.[8] Equation (8.11) informs us that the variance of the RP data set is about $(1/1.309)^2 \approx 58\%$ that of the SP data set, which also was concluded from the manual search method. As previously noted, the manual search resulted in an estimate of the relative scale factor of 0.763, which compares closely with the FIML approach estimate of $(1.309)^{-1} \approx 0.764$. We also can conclude that our estimate of the true relative scale factor very likely does not equal one because 1.309 is 4.6 standard deviations from unity. Thus, it is unlikely that the two data sets have equal scales.

---

[7] Hensher and Bradley (1993) show a slightly different tree structure that is equivalent to the one we use here. Since the inclusive value of the RP cluster is one, they show the RP alternatives connected directly to the root. We believe the tree shown here will be more intuitive to those less acquainted with the intricacies of the NMNL model.

[8] The inclusive value in the artificial tree does not have to lie in the unit interval, the strictest condition for NMNL consistency with random utility maximisation (Hensher and Johnson 1981, Ben-Akiva and Lerman 1985), because individuals are not modelled as choosing from the full set of RP and SP alternatives.

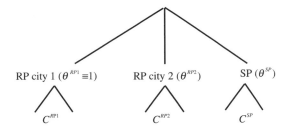

Figure 8.11 NMNL generalisation for multiple data source combination

The nested structure in figure 8.10 assumes that the inclusive value parameter(s) associated with all SP alternatives are equal and fixes the RP inclusive value parameter to unity. This assumption allows one to identify and estimate the variance and hence scale parameter of the SP data set relative to the RP normalisation, but forces within-data set homoscedasticity. Importantly, however, the NL estimation approach to the identification and estimation of relative scale ratios can be readily generalised. For example, another tree structure can be proposed that will allow scale parameters of each SP alternative to be estimated relative to that of all RP alternatives (as shown in Hensher 1998a). You may wish to try to imagine what such a tree would look like, and try drawing it yourself to better understand how NL can be generalised in this way. Further generalisation is possible if one treats the entire artificial tree as a set of degenerate alternatives (i.e., each cluster is a single alternative), resulting in a unique scale parameter for each alternative. However, identification conditions should be carefully evaluated before undertaking either exercise.

In addition, artificial trees can be extended to multiple data sources, instead of the two data sets considered thus far. For example, if we have RP data from city 1, RP data from city 2 and SP data from a nationwide sample, one can combine all these data sources with the single artificial tree structure shown in figure 8.11. If we normalise with respect to the scale of city 1, we can pool the three data sources to estimate joint model parameters and the relative scale factors of the RP data from city 2 and the nationwide SP data.

8.4 Is it always possible to combine preference data sources?

8.4.1 Testing if preference data sources can be combined

The concept of data enrichment originally arose in transportation (see, e.g., Morikawa 1989; Ben-Akiva and Morikawa 1990, Ben-Akiva, Morikawa and Shiroishi 1991, Hensher and Bradley 1993). As earlier noted, the motivation to combine RP and SP data was to exploit the improved data characteristics of SP to correct certain deficiencies in RP data (strong correlations between attributes, lack of identification of others, etc.). Hence, that paradigm implicitly assumes that (well-designed) SP data must necessarily improve corresponding RP data. More importantly, the implicit message in that literature is that the two data generation processes have the same model parameters for the common attributes (vector β in our notation).

If the common model parameters are not equal, this poses a problem for the data enrichment paradigm as currently conceived. That is, we noted with reference to figure 8.5 that common model parameters *may not be* equal. For example, the more spread out the 'cloud' of points representing pairs of model parameters, the less likely that this assumption holds. Swait and Louviere (1993) discussed this possibility, and proposed and illustrated a straightforward way to test the hypothesis that model parameters are equal, while controlling for scale differences between the data sets. That test procedure is as follows:

1. Estimate separate MNL models for each data set, namely, equations (8.3) and (8.4) in the case of RP and SP data. This yields ML estimates of $(\lambda^{RP}\alpha^{RP})$, $(\lambda^{RP}\beta^{RP})$, and $(\lambda^{RP}\omega)$, with a corresponding log likelihood of L^{RP} for the data; and $(\lambda^{SP}\alpha^{SP})$, $(\lambda^{SP}\beta^{SP})$, and $(\lambda^{SP}\delta)$ for the SP data, with a log likelihood of L^{SP}. (Note that scale parameters are not estimated, but nevertheless affect the estimated parameters, as earlier demonstrated.) Let the total number of parameters in model RP be K^{RP}, and K^{SP} in the SP model.
2. Estimate a pooled MNL model from the pooled data (expressions 8.6 and 8.7)) using one of the methods discussed above to obtain ML estimates of $(\alpha^{RP}, \beta, \omega, \alpha^{SP}, \delta, \lambda^{SP})$, and the L^{Joint}. The total number of parameters in the pooled data model is $[K^{RP} + K^{SP} - |\beta| + 1]$, where $|\cdot|$ is the number of elements in the vector, because the condition $\beta^{RP} = \beta^{SP} = \beta$ was imposed and an additional parameter estimated, namely the relative scale factor of the SP data.
3. Calculate the chi-squared statistic for the hypothesis that the common utility parameters are equal as follows:

$$-2[(L^{RP} + L^{SP}) - L^{Joint}]. \tag{8.15}$$

    This quantity is asymptotically chi-squared distributed with $|\beta| - 1$ degrees of freedom.

This test can be generalised to any number of data sources.

Let us return to the example in figure 8.7 and note that there seems to be rather close agreement in the common utility parameters between the two data sources. Hence, a priori we expect that the hypothesis of taste equality, with possible scale differences, to be retained. As previously noted, however, 'eyeball' tests of plots such as figure 8.7 can be misleading because the parameters in the graph are *estimates* that contain sampling errors. The formal test outlined above takes this into account, but requires that we have access to both data sets, hence we cannot conduct formal data enrichment hypothesis tests if we only have model parameters, which are often all that is available from journal articles. If the original data are unavailable, the graphical method (combined with the eigenvalue decomposition suggested in chapter 13) at least can provide tentative evidence regarding the appropriateness of data combination.

Table 8.2. *A comparison of stand-alone and joint models*

Data set	L	K
RP	−3501.4	52
SP	−4840.2	52
Joint	−8353.9	54

Following the above steps, estimation of the three models yields the results in table 8.2.

The associated chi-squared statistic is 24.6 (50 d.f.), and the critical value for the $\alpha = 0.05$ significance level is 36.4, which indicates that we should retain the hypothesis of parameter homogeneity between the two data sources. Therefore, we can proceed to predict behaviour in the market from which the RP data originated using the combined model. Chapter 13 uses a large number of empirical examples to argue that preference regularity (taste homogeneity across data sources and elicitation methods) may be more common than previously thought, based upon this type of testing. None the less, be warned that this is a testable hypothesis that must be verified on a case-by-case basis.

8.4.2 What if full data enrichment is rejected?

The hypothesis of data combination was retained in the above example. However, if it were rejected there are alternatives to using the RP model only, or collecting new SP data. For example, in the context of discussing how to model market segment differences in choice models, Swait and Bernardino (1997) argued that complete preference homogeneity may not hold for multiple segments (i.e., as multiple data sources), but partial preference homogeneity may. We can use the idea of partial preference homogeneity to help in data combination.

In particular, Swait, Louviere and Williams (1994) discuss RP/SP data enrichment for the case of package courier choice in three North American cities, and we use their city 1 data in what follows. Their RP data represent self-reports of the proportion of shipments sent via eight courier companies for a particular period of time, along with self-reported attribute levels for each courier company, and allow eleven model parameters and seven ASCs to be estimated. The SP data were derived from a binary choice experiment in which respondents could choose between two couriers, and the name of the courier company (brand) and the same attributes observed in the RP data were varied systematically and independently. Thus, both data sets have their own, unique ASCs and eleven attribute parameters in common, but apart from ASCs there are no data source-specific parameters. The estimation results for the data combination hypothesis test are given in table 8.3. The calculated test statistic is 72.0 (10 d.f.), whereas the critical value at $\alpha = 0.05$ confidence level is 18.3. Thus, we reject the

Table 8.3. *Comparison of stand-alone and joint models for courier service choice*

Data set	L	K
RP	−1412.6	18
SP	−940.2	18
Joint	−2388.69	26

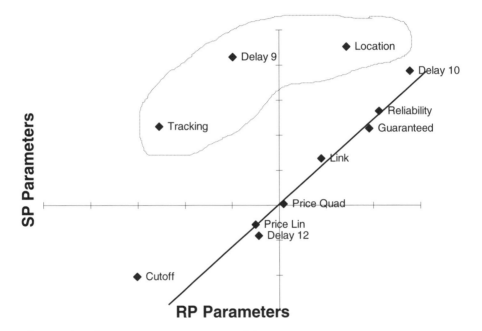

Figure 8.12 City 1 RP and SP MNL model common parameter comparison

hypothesis of preference homogeneity across the two data sources, while controlling for scale differences ($\theta^{SP} \approx 0.708$ with a standard error of about 0.038).

Figure 8.12 is a graph of the common parameters for the source-specific MNL models. It suggests that the rejection may be due to three specific parameters, shown within the dotted polygon. Aside from the three suspect parameters, the remaining parameters seem to lie along a positively sloped line passing through the origin. Two of the three suspect parameters (Tracking and Delay 9) exhibit sign reversals between data sets[9] and the third (Location) appears to have more effect in the SP compared to the RP data.

---

[9] In both cases, the SP sign is the correct one. RP data sets often exhibit counter-intuitive signs, so this result is not surprising.

Let us now consider a combined model in which we allow the 'suspect' parameters to be source-specific. Before proceeding, however, we need to clarify some details. For example, the model parameter for 'Delay 9' corresponds to one of three effects codes (Delay 9, 10, 12) that represent a four-level qualitative attribute. Although it is possible to allow different levels of an attribute to exhibit different effects in each data set, in this case we think that it makes more sense to treat the entire attribute as heterogeneous, rather than just one of its levels. Consequently, we allow five parameters to be data set-specific (Tracking, Location, Delay 9, Delay 10, Delay 12). The new combined model has a log likelihood value of -2355.6 with a total of thirty-one parameters, whereas the full preference homogeneity joint model has a log likelihood of -2388.6 and twenty-six parameters. If we again test whether preference homogeneity holds for a subset of parameters (i.e., partial enrichment), the test statistic is $-2[(-1412.6 - 940.0) - (-2355.6)] = 6.0$ (5 d.f.). The critical value at the $\alpha = 0.05$ confidence level is 11.1, so we retain the hypothesis of partial data enrichment. It is worth noting that $\theta^{SP} \approx 0.941$ (standard error ≈ 0.058), which is not significantly statistically different from one. (Readers may want to test their understanding thus far by considering what this result suggests about the relative variance of the SP data.)

So, the lesson from this example is that even if one rejects the hypothesis of full preference homogeneity, preference homogeneity may well hold for a subset of model parameters. However, partial parameter homogeneity presents the modeller with a potentially difficult decision: which set of parameters to use for prediction to the RP world? It is worth noting that this matter is not yet fully resolved in the literature, and is the subject of continuing discussion among academics and practitioners. Our view is that the prediction model should contain the RP ASCs and all parameters that were jointly estimated. The difficulty in the decision arises from two problems involving the non-jointly estimated parameters:

1. *Sign reversals* Only *very rarely* will SP tasks yield parameters with incorrect and statistically significant signs.[10] Hence, sign incompatibility almost always originates in the RP data. For this reason, if (non-joint) RP parameters have incorrect signs, we suggest that the corresponding SP parameters be used.
2. *Differential relative importance* If a particular (non-joint) RP parameter is smaller (or larger) than its SP counterpart, significant and has the correct sign, analysts must decide which one to use. To assist in this decision, if possible analysts should conduct tests with the two parameters (or a range of parameters) using a holdout data set or the RP data to determine how sensitive the results are to choice of parameter. If a certain model parameter is not significant, which may be associated with limited ranges of RP attribute variability, but we believe it should affect choices in the real market, it is not obvious that one should use the RP parameter. SP design matrices are almost always better conditioned than RP design matrices, hence SP parameter estimates may be more reliable than RP estimates.

---

[10] In our experience, reversed signs in SP data sets have been triggers for examining data processing errors.

Unfortunately, at the present time, this situation requires analysts to make decisions based on experience and expertise.

8.4.3 Reasons why data enrichment may not work

The hypothesis of preference equality across data sources could be rejected for a variety of reasons. In the case of RP and SP data enrichment, design, layout, framing, context, etc. of SP tasks are crucial to the success of the data combination exercise. If one's objective is to forecast the real market accurately, then tasks should reflect the choices made in that market as closely as possible, which includes (*inter alia*) the process of defining the task, attributes, levels, context, etc. The quality of the RP data also may affect the outcome of the statistical test, hence stringent quality control should be exercised to minimise errors and to ensure appropriate handling of missing data.

However, even after every care has been taken and all contingencies covered to the fullest extent possible, the hypothesis of preference equality between data sets may still be rejected in a particular empirical investigation. If this occurs, analysts must decide whether to disregard the statistical information and continue with a partially or fully pooled model. There probably are situations in which this is both warranted and will produce a good outcome, but at the present time there is too little empirical experience to permit generalisations. In any case, statistics and statistical tests are tools, and good scientists or scientific practitioners should be guided by theory, experience and expertise, as well as by study objectives. For example, incorrect parameter signs can result from many causes, including omitted attributes such as interaction effects, and parameter magnitudes can vary owing to linear approximations to non-linear effects, limited ranges of variation and other sources. Thus, all statistical models summarise information, and if the information is not biased, informed decisions are always preferable to ones made in the dark.

8.5 A general preference data generation process

We have mentioned several times in this chapter that the concept of data combination can be applied to many types of preference, or more generally, dominance data (RP choices, SP choices, SP rankings, SP ratings, etc.) and any number of data sources. We concentrated on illustrating how the techniques can be applied to a useful prototypical problem of combining RP and SP choice data sources. Our discussion demonstrated that an essential aspect of fusing preference or choice data sources (which indirectly reflects some latent structural framework, such as a utility function) is a consideration of the relative characteristics of the stochastic component of utility. Specifically, we demonstrated that if one assumes that data sources are generated by IID EV1 processes (i.e., MNL models underlie each data source), and the data sources share certain common preference parameters (but variances may differ), we must take into account *heteroscedasticity* between the data sources (chapter 6 discusses variants of the MNL models that do this).

In general, data combination requires an adequate model of the error structure of each data source, allowing for scale (or heteroscedasticity) and preference parameter differences. In other words, each data source has a data generation process (DGP), and that DGP must be accommodated in the joint model structure. This section presents a general DGP that can guide future work in combining data sources. In particular, the challenge in capturing real behavioural processes in statistical models is to adopt a framework that is sufficiently rich to accommodate the structure of all observed and unobserved influences on choices. Ideally, such a framework should be capable of allowing for both the real influences on choices as processed by the agents of choice (i.e., individuals, households, firms, groups) as well as variation in response opportunities associated with the means used by analysts to acquire information from agents. The latter include a wide array of data collection procedures (e.g., RP or SP methods), the complexity of tasks imposed on agents (e.g., the number of replications of SP tasks), observations of attributes of non-chosen alternatives in RP tasks, and methods of data collection (e.g., telephone, mail-out/mail-back and different interview methods).

Choice models provide opportunities to understand and capture real behavioural processes through deeper understanding of the behavioural implications of traditional statistical constructs such as mean, variance and covariance, scale and preference parameters. For example, understanding and modelling the effects of differences in error variances associated with the relative (indirect) utility of each alternative in a choice set is now a research focus because of opportunities to relax the IID error assumptions leading to MNL, and use variance properties to satisfy a common set of statistical assumptions when combining data from different sources (Morikawa 1989, Hensher and Bradley 1993, Bhat 1996, Swait and Louviere 1993). In addition, it is now recognised that the data collection process itself may be a source of variability in behavioural responses. Hence, if this source of variability is not isolated, it may confound the real behavioural role of the observed and unobserved influences on choice. Fortunately, it can be handled by appropriate functional specification of the structure of the variance of the unobserved effects. For example, the variance associated with an alternative can be a function of task complexity (Swait and Adamowicz 1996) or respondent characteristics that serve as proxies for ability to comprehend the survey task (Bhat 1996, Hensher 1998).

Developments in refining the specification of the indirect utility expression associated with a mutually exclusive alternative in a choice set can be summarised by equation (8.16) (see also equation (6.1) in chapter 6):

$$\tilde{U}_{int} = \alpha_{it} + \beta_{nt}X_{int} + \kappa_{nt}Y_{int-1} + \varphi_{nt}\tilde{U}_{int-1} + \tilde{\varepsilon}_{int}, \tag{8.16}$$

where

$\tilde{U}_{int}$ = indirect utility associated by person n with alternative i at time t

α_{it} = alternative-specific constant represents the mean of the distribution of unobserved effects in the random component associated with alternative i at time t

β_{nt} = utility parameters for person n, representing the relative level of or saliency associated with the attributes at time t

X_{int} = the attribute vector faced by individual n for alternative i, time period t

Y_{int-1} = choice indicator ($0 =$ not chosen, $1 =$ chosen) for person n, alternative i, time $t-1$

$\kappa_{nt}, \varphi_{nt}$ = utility weight associated with *state dependence* and *habit persistence* (see Heckman 1981), respectively, for person n, time period t

$\tilde{\varepsilon}_{int}$ = error term.

Assume that the scale of $\tilde{\varepsilon}_{int}$ (hence of $\tilde{U}_{int}$) is λ_{int}. Define $U_{int} = \lambda_{int}\tilde{U}_{int}$ and $\varepsilon_{int} = \lambda_{int}\tilde{\varepsilon}_{int}$.

Multiply both sides of (8.16) by λ_{int} to obtain equation (8.17):

$$U_{int} = \lambda_{int}\alpha_{it} + \lambda_{int}\beta_{nt}X_{int} + \lambda_{int}\kappa_{nt}Y_{int-1} + \lambda_{int}\varphi_{nt}\tilde{U}_{int-1} + \varepsilon_{int}. \tag{8.17}$$

This multiplication results in the error terms ε_{int} having unit scale. Note, however, that the habit persistence term in (8.17) involves the previous period's utility $\tilde{U}_{int-1}$, which associated scale λ_{int-1}. Thus, equation (8.17) can be rewritten to involve $U_{int-1} = \lambda_{int-1}\tilde{U}_{int-1}$ as equation (8.18):

$$U_{int} = \lambda_{int}\alpha_{it} + \lambda_{int}\beta_{nt}X_{int} + \lambda_{int}\kappa_{nt}Y_{int-1} + \left(\frac{\lambda_{int}}{\lambda_{int-1}}\right)\varphi_{nt}U_{int-1} + \varepsilon_{int}. \tag{8.18}$$

The term $\varphi_{nt}U_{int-1}$ is a person-specific, time-dependent unobserved heterogeneity effect which we subsume into a random attribute γ_{nt}. Thus, the final form of the utility function that we consider is given as equation (8.19):

$$U_{int} = \lambda_{int}\alpha_{it} + \left(\frac{\lambda_{int}}{\lambda_{int-1}}\right)\gamma_{nt} + \lambda_{int}\beta_{nt}X_{int} + \lambda_{int}\theta_{nt}Y_{int-1} + \varepsilon_{int}. \tag{8.19}$$

This form permits incorporation of (1) brand-specific temporal heterogeneity, (2) person-specific heterogeneity (which captures habit persistence, among other things), (3) state dependence, (4) temporal (for RP) or repeated measures (for SP) dependence in the error structure and (5) temporal, person-specific and product-specific heteroscedasticity.

Using equation (8.19) as an overarching structure, we note that the majority of discrete-choice models reported in the marketing, transport and environmental and resource economics literatures assume one or more of the following restrictions:

1. homoscedastic error terms, or scale parameters constant across people, products and time periods (but see Hensher et al. 1992, Bhat 1995, Swait and Adamowicz 1996, Swait and Stacey 1996);
2. temporal or repeated measures independence of errors (but see Morikawa 1994, Keane 1995, Swait and Naik 1996);
3. homogeneous utility parameters across the population (but see Keane 1997);
4. no unobserved heterogeneity (but see Morikawa 1994, Elrod and Keane 1995).

Overcoming these restrictions is a challenge if one has only a single source of choice or preference data. They are even greater challenges when combining multiple sources of data.

8.6 Summary

We began the chapter by trying to show why data combination (or enrichment) has become an important issue in several disciplines with interests in preferences or choices. Historically, research was motivated by recognition that the strengths of multiple data sources could compensate for each other's weaknesses, particularly apropos to RP and SP data sources.

However, research has evolved to try to deal with questions as to why data enrichment is possible in certain cases and not in others. In chapter 13 we show empirically that preference regularity (i.e., equivalent choice processes) seems to hold across a wide range of products, cultures and choice elicitation methods. Not only does this support the simple heteroscedasticity story underlying data enrichment techniques discussed in this chapter, but the results also suggest that independence of random components is a good first approximation in many empirical contexts. Also, simply accounting for variance scale ratios, or equivalently, variance differences between data sources, seems to account for much of the observed heterogeneity in utility parameters across (sometimes) vastly different choice contexts. This is supported by the importance of free variance in chapter 6 (appendix table B6.8).

It is indeed remarkable that such a simple process can explain so much variation between such widely differing choice processes. As a result of these empirical findings, we now believe that the role of the error variance (and other characteristics of the error structure) in choice processes represents one of the more interesting research opportunities in choice and consumer behaviour modelling. We will return to this topic again in chapter 13 when we review the general problem of comparing processes that underlie multiple sources of preference data, and review external and cross-validity evidence associated with models of these processes.

9 Implementing SP choice behaviour projects

9.1 Introduction

This chapter brings together many of the technical issues and details discussed in previous chapters, with the objective of illustrating how to implement SP choice projects. We use one specific project[1] as a vehicle to illustrate the stages and steps of most projects, and attempt to bring together all the details discussed in previous chapters. Over the course of several SP studies you may want to reread this chapter to help systematise the experience you gain.

The scope of this chapter is extensive because it covers (1) choice problem definition, (2) sample frame definition and sample size, (3) task and survey design, (4) data collection method, (5) data analysis and modelling and (6) model use. However, prior to turning our attention to these issues, we present a systematic overview of the choice process from the random utility perspective to focus the rest of the chapter.

9.2 Components of the choice process

One possible description of the choice process, within the random utility framework, is given by the specification below:

$$U_{in} = V_{in}(X_{in}, S_n|\beta_n) + \varepsilon_{in}(Z_{in}, S_n|\theta_n) \tag{9.1}$$

$$i^* = \tilde{R}_n \{U_{jn}\}. \tag{9.2}$$

$$\phantom{i^* = \tilde{R}}{}_{j \in C_n}$$

We assume that decision-makers form evaluations U_{in} of all goods $i \in C_n$, where C_n is the choice set (tautologically defined as that subset of the universal set of alternatives that are evaluated for choice). From an analyst's viewpoint, the evaluations can be decomposed into two components: the *deterministic utility* V_{in} and the *stochastic utility* ε_{in}. The first utility component, V_{in}, encapsulates analysts' knowledge of the preferences of decision maker n, which is affected by (a) attributes of the product X_{in},

---

[1] We would like to express our appreciation to Advanis Inc. for making these data available.

(b) characteristics of the decision maker S_n and (c) the marginal utilities β_n of these vectors (which in its most general form, can be assumed specific to each individual, hence subscript n). One way to think about this part of utility function (9.1) is that it is the mean of the utility distribution.

The second utility component, ε_{in}, represents an explicit statement of the degree of analysts' ignorance about the myriad idiosyncratic factors affecting individual n's choice, and also captures sampling error and model misspecification. An analyst traditionally assumes that the likelihood of observing a certain distribution of values of ε is known by the probability law that describes the shape of this distribution. For example, chapter 6 showed that if we assume that $(\varepsilon_{in}, \varepsilon_{jn}, \varepsilon_{kn}, \ldots)$ are jointly independent and identically distributed (IID) as type I extreme value (Gumbel) random variates, we can derive the multinomial logit (MNL) model. If they are distributed as generalised extreme value variates we derive the nested MNL; and if jointly multivariate normal, we derive the multinomial probit (MNP) model. These distributions are assumed to have deep parameters θ.

However, we note from (9.1) that we can make the stochastic utility component a function of alternative 'attributes' Z_{in} and decision-maker characteristics S_n. Although ε and its parameters traditionally have been considered a nuisance to be controlled to obtain better estimates (measures) of β_n, growing understanding of the role of the stochastic component in determining choice probabilities is causing many researchers to re-examine this view.

For example, the role of advertising (and in general, information) in the choice process traditionally was thought to influence mean utility, such that certain types of advertising provide specific information about such attributes as price, convenience, distribution channels, etc. Thus, such information helps decision makers to form product evaluations via the mean of the utility distribution. However, other types of advertising are geared towards creating images that appeal to segments of the population or reminds readers/viewers of particular brands; and yet other advertising is designed to increase/decrease risks of purchase and/or deliberately make it difficult to know the true attribute values. Although some effects of these types of advertising can be captured by the mean of the utility component, it also is reasonable to think that the distribution of the stochastic component can be affected by such marketing activity. For example, when consumers are reassured that their reference group status is enhanced by purchasing a certain product (e.g., a car), advertising may affect the variance of the utility distribution rather than its mean. That is, the product itself does not necessarily increase in utility; instead consumers become more certain of their evaluations. Some marketing actions such as advertising or distribution strategies may have more effect on consumers' certainty and confidence in their assessment of products, rather than the assessments themselves. Hence, we include Z_{in} and S_n in the stochastic utility term.

Manski showed that a very general two-stage process (screening followed by choice) can be formulated for any decision or choice:

$$P_i = \sum_{C \subseteq \Gamma} P(i|C)Q(C), \tag{9.3}$$

where P_i is the probability of choosing alternative i, $P(i|C)$ is the conditional probability of choice of i given the choice set is $C \subseteq \Gamma$, Γ is the set of possible choice sets, $Q(C)$ is the probability set and C is the choice set. Efforts were made to develop RP discrete-choice models on the basis of Manski's expression (Swait 1984; Swait and Ben-Akiva 1987a,b), but there has been little further progress because the size of Γ grows exponentially as a function of the number of alternatives (but see Roberts and Lattin 1991, Andrews and Srinivasan 1995 and Ben-Akiva and Boccara 1995).[2] In SP projects the universal set of alternatives typically is defined for consumers by the options in the choice scenarios. Consumers may or may not consider all the alternatives in the scenarios to make their final choices, so (9.3) could be used to model this decision. However, empirical difficulties discourage this approach (see Swait and Ben-Akiva 1987a,b), and it continues to be that SP choice models generally assume that consumers incorporate all alternatives in the choice scenario into their choice sets.

To reach a final decision, the consumer is assumed to apply a decision rule $\tilde{R}_n$ on the evaluations (see 9.2). The usual decision rule assumed in the random utility approach, and the only one to be considered here, is that of *utility maximisation*. That is to say, individuals are assumed to choose the good $i^* \in C_n$ with highest utility. As implemented in empirical choice modelling work, use of this decision rule requires that we assume decision makers have full information, use all information and are compensatory in their decisions (i.e., they are willing to trade-off any one attribute for others). The latter characteristic arises from the use of linear-in-the-parameters specifications of the systematic utility components. One reason for the almost exclusive use of the decision rule is that theoretical work in economics (where this rule is widely adopted) has guided much of the early developments in choice modelling. Secondly, this rule turns out to generate operational choice models, which has gained utility maximisation almost complete hegemony in empirical work. However, you should be aware that in many contexts this decision rule may not be appropriate. Work in psychology and the consumer behaviour area in marketing has shown that many other decision rules are not only possible, but may often be used by consumers (see a summary of these in Bettman, Johnson and Payne 1991). These are often termed *heuristics* because decision makers' motivation to use simpler rules than utility maximisation is often to reduce decision making costs (i.e., information gathering and processing).

What happens when we apply a compensatory, utility maximising model to a choice process that may not be so? Johnson and Meyer (1984) investigated this issue and found compensatory models (specifically, the MNL model) remarkably robust to violations of the compensatory, utility maximising assumptions. While their research was based on laboratory studies, it is supported by earlier research in the ability of non-linear model forms to capture non-compensatory behaviours (Einhorn 1970). Thus, on one hand, the reader should be reassured that there is supporting evidence that compensatory models of the type used in SP and RP choice studies are relatively

---

[2] If there are J objects from which choice sets can be formed, the number of sets in Γ is $|\Gamma| = 2^{J-1}$. For $J = 3$, $|\Gamma| = 7$, for $J = 10$, $|\Gamma| = 1024$, and for $J = 15$, $|\Gamma| = 32,768$. Clearly, it doesn't take many alternatives to make a full choice set generation model infeasible, practically speaking.

robust to a wide variety of decision-making patterns. On the other hand, it is necessary that further research be conducted in this area and appropriate model forms be investigated. In addition, knowing the decision rules used by consumers in a particular realm of decision making is an important piece of knowledge for any choice study. It can help the interpretation of modelling results and guide the design of marketing policy.

Our discussion thus far has highlighted several issues that we must be aware of when studying a particular choice process:

1. product attributes and decision-maker characteristics of relevance, that define the deterministic, or mean, utility (V_{in});
2. individual variations in preferences (β_n);
3. the characteristics of the stochastic utility term (ε_{in});
4. the choice set (C_n);
5. the decision rule ($\tilde{R}_n$).

9.3 The steps in an SP choice study

Every choice study goes through common stages, which we shall discuss in this chapter. These steps are:

1. define *study objectives*;
2. conduct supporting *qualitative study*;
3. develop and pilot the *data collection instrument*;
4. define *sample characteristics*;
5. perform *data collection*;
6. conduct *model estimation*;
7. conduct *policy analysis*.

Several of these steps are intertwined, which leads to an iterative evolution of an SP project. We shall attempt to transmit a sense of this dependence during the next few sections.

As we discuss these steps, we will use a particular study to highlight some of the issues and make the entire exercise more concrete.

9.3.1 Define study objectives

It is almost a truism that defining study objectives is often one of the most difficult stages in any project. A choice study is no exception. Difficulties generally arise from an inability to come to grips with the substantive questions to be answered through the study. Client and analyst are often working with different goals in mind: the former may have difficulty in coming to grips with the kernel of the problems that he or she must respond to, and is often labouring under organisational constraints that can adversely affect the usefulness of research; the latter is often less directed by the substantive issues and more affected by the limitations inherent to existing statistical methods. Thus, it behoves both analyst and client to work cooperatively to define the questions to be answered and establish the objectives of the particular study. A mutual understanding of these objectives will be key to the successful undertaking of any study, and will certainly affect the usefulness of results obtained from such an effort.

In for-profit companies, the type we shall consider here, the questions to be answered would seem straightforward: increase profit by increasing revenue or decreasing costs! However, this supposed 'clarity' of purpose is illusory. We must come to grips with far more specific issues here. An SP choice study can be geared towards

1. new product design,
2. market share, profitability or margin optimisation,
3. market strategy development (product and channel),
4. branding issues (brand equity, co-branding, affinity branding),
5. customer retention and profitability, or
6. combinations of the above, among others.

An SP study designed to optimise market share may or may not be useful for other purposes; and maximising share may not be an appropriate objective in some cases. Because of this wide variety of possible goals, research users often desire an *omnibus* study that can meet multiple needs (some not even known at the time of the study). The analyst, on the other hand, grapples with modelling issues and respondent burden (in data collection) that these multiple needs impose, with consequent effects on statistical technique and data quality. Every study involves reaching a working compromise between these opposing requirements.

Another issue that must be addressed is that of market segments (e.g., high vs. low product usage, East Coast vs. West Coast vs. Midwest, home-owners vs. renters, etc.). Often research buyers can specify subgroups of a population that should be studied, but just as frequently it is necessary for the analyst to help to define them more precisely. Indeed, market segments are important for several reasons: (1) segments often exhibit different preferences (β_n), so better descriptions of market behaviour can be obtained by taking them into account; (2) such differential preferences generally result in some groups being more profitable than others; (3) market segments help to define sampling frames, sample sizes and sampling methods.

Suppose one is retained by an auto rental company (say, brand A) operating in a particular North American city, that is interested in studying the demand for their services in that market. (Though we do not use the names of real brands in this study, the data used later are for actual brands from a real city.) The objective is to increase market share for the client firm. As part of this exercise, we want to study only rentals for personal purposes (e.g., vacations, substitute vehicles), not those for business purposes. In addition, the client wants to know how this demand varies by size of vehicle (compact, midsize, full size and luxury) among the major players (brands A, B, C and D, out of a field of eighteen car rental companies) in the particular market.

Thus, the response variable of interest is the choice of a pair (a, s), where a is an agency and s is the vehicle size. Finally, we wish to know how prior experience with car renting affects consumers' behaviour. Thus, we shall segment the sample a priori into those that were somewhat or extremely *satisfied* and those that were somewhat or extremely *dissatisfied* with their last rental experience.

9.3.2 Conduct qualitative study

Once study objectives are defined, and the client/analyst team believe their goals are sufficiently clear, it is time to consider consumers. This is an important stage because the study team should learn how consumers think about the decision process, how they gather information about products, when they make decisions, etc. We cannot overemphasise how important it is to conduct this kind of qualitative, exploratory work to guide subsequent phases of the SP study.

Focus groups are the usual means whereby qualitative information is gathered, although personal interviews are another source. Five to ten consumers from the target populations are recruited and brought to a central facility. A moderator leads the group through a prepared script that makes sure key topics are broached, but allows for other issues to be brought up during the session (which generally lasts between 30 and 90 minutes, though there are no hard and fast rules). There is considerable art to being an effective moderator: a good group moderator will keep the pace of discussion lively and on course, without letting any one person dominate the event. Focus group facilities generally provide for client and analyst observation of the session without their being seen or heard; sessions are also often recorded (both audio and video) for subsequent analysis. Both clients and analysts benefit from listening to some sessions, which can often lead study team members back to a redefinition of study objectives. Some consumers are unavailable to come to central facilities, so interviewers must go to them. The topics to be addressed are the same as in focus groups, but one is likely to lose interactions that often raise unexpected issues in focus groups. One-on-one interviews require experienced and flexible professionals who are cognisant of study objectives and know how to pursue important information as it comes up.

The key to the usefulness of the focus group is the quality of the script. Referring back to section 9.2, for an SP study this script should minimally broach the following subjects:

- *Product Attributes and Levels* Consumers and study team members generally do not think about products and services in the same way. The former are interested in satisfying certain needs, while the latter are generally interested in ascertaining which of several managerial actions should be taken in the market. *Study team members should keep in mind that consumers are always right about the way they think about products ... they buy the product, after all!* Hence, the study team should endeavour to understand the dimensions (e.g., price, convenience) along which the product is evaluated by consumers and how specific levels of these dimensions are expressed, and then translate the engineering variables into those terms. The primary objective is to be able to express the characteristics of the product to decision makers in the terms they employ.

- *Market segments* We previously noted that it is important to consider subgroups in the population for which preferences (β_n) may differ. However, other reasons that may lead groups to differ are different choice sets (C_n) or decision rules ($\tilde{R}_n$). A focus group is a good forum in which to explore these possibilities.
- *Choice Sets* Besides leading to possible market segment differences, focus groups should seek to clarify the number of alternatives consumers actually consider when making a choice, and how choice sets are defined (i.e., via habit, search, prior experience, word-of-mouth).

The useful outputs of this phase will be, using the notation developed earlier, (1) the attributes and levels of interest (X_i), (2) personal characteristics that affect choice (S_n), (3) sources of utility differences (β_n), (4) choice set characteristics, including size, and (5) whether different decision rules are used, and if so, why and when. Other possible issues that may be of interest are attitudes that affect demand, substitute and complementary products, etc.

Having emphasised the importance of the information that qualitative approaches can provide, it is just as important that over-reliance is not placed on the small samples involved. We seek insights and directions into consumer behaviour from this stage of the study, not precise measurements or strategic recommendations. In our applied work, we have observed cases in which clients have seized on statements made by one individual in one session, and used these to reach unwarranted generalisations. This can have a deleterious impact on any study; neither analyst nor client should succumb to such temptations.

Before proceeding to the next stage of the SP study, let us first consider the auto rental and vehicle size choice problem. Two focus groups were conducted in the target city, following a script based on the general guidelines above. We found that the seven classes of attributes in table 9.1 affect choice behaviour. The form in which we shall treat the brand attribute will be described later, but for now we note that brands A and B were the major rental companies in the market, while C and D, though national firms, had a smaller local presence.

Using market information and consumer experience from the focus groups, we defined the levels shown in the table. In addition to the attributes and levels, the focus group results indicated that respondents did not generally examine more than three car rental agencies on any given rental occasion. It also was unclear if respondents first considered agency, then vehicle size, or vice-versa.

9.3.3   Data collection instrument

The principal topic at this stage is the design of the choice task itself. However, it should not be forgotten that the SP choice task is generally one item among several in

Table 9.1. *Attributes and levels for example study*

Attribute	Type	Levels
Brand	Qualitative	A, B, C, D
Price/day	Continuous	Compact: $30, $34, $38, $42
		Mid-size: Compact + $2, Compact + $4
		Full-size: Compact + $4, Compact + $8
		Luxury: Compact + $20, Compact + $30
Price for kilometrage not included in daily rate	Continuous and qualitative	Unlimited kilometrage
		$0.10/km over 200 km
		$0.12/km over 200 km
		$0.15/km over 200 km
Type of vehicle	Qualitative	Compact: Geo Metro/Sunfire, Tercel/Cavalier
		Mid-size: Grand AM/Dodge Cirrus, Corsica/ Corolla
		Full-size: Grand Prix/Cutlass Supreme, Taurus/ Regal, Camry/Intrepid, Taurus/ Crown Victoria
		Luxury: BMW/Lexus, Lincoln Town Car/ Cadillac
Optional insurance ($/day)	Continuous	$12, $16
Airline reward	Continuous	None (0), 500
Fuel return policy and fuel price premium	Qualitative and continuous	Prepay full tank at discounted price
		Return at level rented
		Bring car back at lower level and pay $0.25 premium per litre
		Bring car back at lower level and pay $0.50 premium per litre

a survey. We recommend consultation of Dillman (2000) for further information on questionnaire design for mail and telephone surveys.

Traditionally, SP choice tasks are presented to respondents in paper and pencil surveys, in a tabular form. Attributes are arranged along the rows and alternatives along the columns, as in figure 9.1, which shows an example choice set generated for this study. However, there is nothing 'sacred' about this form; it should be adapted, changed as needed to reflect study objectives and decision-maker characteristics.

Our experience has shown that task layout should be carefully planned to enhance decision-maker understanding and use of the information provided. This is one of the main objectives of conducting pilot tests of the survey and choice task. Debriefing of respondents following administration of the choice task should lead to significant improvements on first and second drafts of choice tasks. *No significant survey should ever go to field without pilot testing!*

How does one determine how many choice sets like the one in figure 9.1 are needed? That is a function, of course, of the experimental design (see chapter 4). In our

Assume you are renting a car for *personal* use. Please indicate which car rental company and which size of car you would choose.

FEATURES	Brand A	Brand B	Brand C/D
Make of Car			
Sub-Compact/Compact	Tercel/Cavalier	Geo Metro/Sunfire	Geo Metro/Sunfire
Midsize	Corsica/Corolla	Corsica/Corolla	Corsica/Corolla
Full Size	Taurus/Crown Victoria	Taurus/Regal	Grand Prix/Cutlass Supreme
Luxury	Lincoln Town Car/Cadillac	BMW/Lexus	Lincoln Town Car/Cadillac
Price per Day			
Sub-Compact/Compact	$38	$42	$30
Midsize	$42	$46	$34
Full Size	$46	$50	$38
Luxury	$76	$80	$58
Kilometers Included (per day) and Extra Kilometer Price	Unlimited	Includes 200km/day; Extra km 15 cents/km	Includes 200km/day; Extra km 15 cents/km
Insurance Cost/Day	$12	$12	$16
Airline Points	No points	No points	No points
Gas Return Policy	Prepay full tank at discounted gas price	Bring car back at level you rented it at	Prepay full tank at discounted gas price
1) Which company would you rent from? (✓ only one)	☐₁	☐₂	☐₃

2) Which size of car would you rent? (✓ only one)

Sub-Compact/ Compact ☐₁
Midsize ☐₂
Full Size ☐₃
Luxury ☐₄

Figure 9.1 Example choice set

example, each of the three alternatives has twelve attributes, with differing numbers of levels. Brand was treated as fixed in the first two alternatives (alternative 1 was always brand A, and alternative 2 always brand B), but varied in the third alternative between brands C and D. We used a fractional factorial to create the $4^{12} \times 2^{25}$ orthogonal design (each of the three alternatives presented has four attributes with four levels each, and eight attributes with two levels each; and the brand factor in the third alternative represents a twenty-fifth two-level attribute) in sixty-four treatments to generate the choice sets for this example; this is only one of several possible design strategies that might be considered (see chapters 4 and 5 for other options).

Many researchers would suggest that it is inadvisable to make respondents evaluate all sixty-four choices because of data quality concerns. That is, as the burden on respondents grows, it is likely that the quality of the data they provide decreases. However, there is little rigorous empirical research to guide us in this matter, and existing results are somewhat contradictory. For example, Swait and Adamowicz (1996) show that task demands (namely, decision complexity and cumulative cognitive burden) can affect the variance of ε_{in}, which in turn can affect the efficiency of estimation of the parameter vector (ε_n). In fact, for over six different SP studies they find that there is a complexity level at which variance is minimised and that there is a cumulative cognitive load after which the variance of the stochastic utility term begins to grow. They find that variance is a convex function of decision complexity and cumulative cognitive load. On the other hand, Brazell and Louviere (1997) showed that survey response rates and model parameters are essentially equivalent when they compare groups of respondents given twelve, twenty-four, forty-eight and ninety-six choice sets in a particular decision task. Using the statistical test described in Swait and Louviere (1993), they found that after correcting for average variance differences between conditions, the parameter vectors were the same. Thus, more research is needed to guide such operational decisions.

But what should one do in the meantime? In most studies respondents evaluate between one and sixteen choice sets, with the average being somewhere around eight choice scenarios per respondent (Carson et al. 1994). Adaptations are made as a function of choice task complexity (number of attributes and alternatives), incentives, mode of elicitation (mail survey, personal interview, computerised interview), types of respondents and so forth. We recommend that one act conservatively for the present until better guidelines are available. (However, at least two of the co-authors have upon occasion and after due consideration given respondents tasks that exceed these average guidelines, with no apparent ill effects.)

A decision was made to implement the example choice study via a mail survey with no incentives. In addition to the choice task itself, the survey contained a number of other questions that might burden the respondent significantly. To increase response rates, it was decided to ask respondents to evaluate only four choice scenarios. The initial survey was pre-tested with twelve respondents, who were debriefed on various aspects of the instrument. This led to a number of improvements in the questionnaire and choice task.

9.3.4 Sampling frame and sample size

The *sampling frame* defines the universe of respondents from which a finite *sample* is drawn to administer the data collection instrument. Some examples of sampling frames are (1) residents of the state of New York, (2) all Australians eligible to have or already having current bank accounts, and (3) shipping managers for catalogue retailers in the Midwestern states of the USA.

Basically, the objectives of a study dictate *the sampling frame. While it may seem obvious, it is best that we clearly state that the sampling frame must be defined so as to enable the substantive questions to be answered with the model developed from the sample*. Careless definition of or miscommunication about sampling frames can invalidate the entire data collection effort, so it is a non-trivial matter.

Based on the sampling frame, which in many market applications can be considered infinite in size, one defines a sampling strategy and sample size. Two common sampling strategies for choice models are *simple random samples* (SRS) and exogenously stratified random samples (ESRS). See Ben-Akiva and Lerman (1985: chapter 8) for a description of and details about other sampling strategies for choice models. More general books on sampling theory are also available; see, for example, Levy and Lemeshow (1991). In the SRS, each decision maker in the sampling frame has an equal likelihood of being selected for the sample; for each selected individual, we observe personal characteristics S_n and Z_{in}, as well as the SP choices for a number of choice scenarios. With an ESRS, the sampling frame is divided into G mutually exclusive groups, each representing a proportion W_g of the population. The basis for creating the groups is any personal characteristic (e.g., income, residential location, age, gender,...) *except* the dependent variable being measured (i.e., the choice). Within each stratum, individuals have equal probability of selection (which means we take a random sample within stratum). The sample taken from each group need not result in the same sample proportions as in the population; instead, we might decide to have a proportion H_g of the sample from each group g.

For example, if we are interested in market segments, a properly executed SRS will capture market segments in the approximate proportion in which they exist in the sampling frame. Because some market segments of interest can occur relatively infrequently in an SRS, it is often necessary to use an ESRS. Suppose we wish to have an equal representation of rural and urban American residents in the sample, hence we stratify the sample into the two groups and set 50 per cent quotas for each group. Since only 25 per cent of the US population is classified as rural in the 1990 census, it is clear that the resulting sample will not be representative of the US population (i.e., the sampling frame). For exogenous stratification of sampling frames, it can be shown that consistent choice model parameter estimates can be obtained by weighting each respondent in group g by the ratio W_g/H_g. If the sample and the population proportions are equal, this is essentially equivalent to the case of simple random sampling.

Given a sampling strategy, we must define the sample size to be used. The study is being conducted to measure a choice probability (or proportion) with some desired level of accuracy. Elementary statistical theory proves the result that the asymptotic sampling distribution (i.e., the distribution as $n \to \infty$) of a proportion p_n, *obtained by an SRS of size n*, is normal with mean p (the true population proportion) and variance pq/n, where $q = 1 - p$. If we wish to estimate the true proportion within a per cent of the true value p with probability α or greater, then we must find the minimum sample size needed to satisfy the requirement that $\text{Prob}(|p_n - p| \leq ap) \geq \alpha$. Some algebraic manipulation will result in the expression below for the minimum sample size:

$$n \geq \frac{q}{pa^2}\, \Phi^{-1}\left(\frac{1+\alpha}{2}\right), \tag{9.4}$$

where $\Phi^{-1}(.)$ is the inverse cumulative normal distribution function.

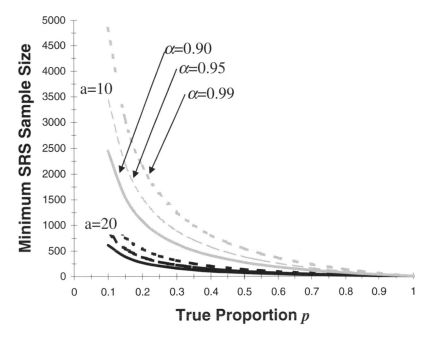

Figure 9.2 Minimum sample requirement for SRS

Figure 9.2 shows how this sample size requirement behaves as a function of the true proportion p, the relative accuracy a (10%, 20%) and the probability α (0.90, 0.95 and 0.99). According to (9.4), sample size requirements are quite modest for high proportions (say, above 0.5), but become *very high* for low (i.e., rare) proportions and high relative accuracy and confidence levels. Indeed it may be prohibitively expensive to obtain these sample sizes for very low proportions.[3]

In most SP studies, each respondent is given multiple choice scenarios in the choice task, so that each individual does r choice scenarios (i.e., replications). In practice, many projects try to obtain the required n choices from $\lceil n/r \rceil$ respondents, but we should remember that one of the assumptions behind the derivation of (9.4) is that the sampled choice observations are *independent*. While it is unlikely that the r choice replications from an individual are independent, practice has shown that a well-designed choice task that encourages respondents to view each choice scenario as unrelated to previous ones will yield parameter vectors that are proportional to those derived from models estimated on single choices from each respondent. As discussed in chapter 8, this is indicative that the only difference between the parameter vectors is in relative variance levels, which ultimately affects statistical efficiency but not unbiasedness. Hence, our recommendation is that (9.4) be viewed as the minimum

---

[3] Other sampling strategies, namely choice-based sampling, should be considered when dealing with rare alternatives. See Ben-Akiva and Lerman (1985), Cosslett (1978, 1981).

Table 9.2. *Choice probability estimation example*

p	Minimum number of choices required	Minimum number of respondents (for $r = 8$)
0.10	3457	432
0.20	1537	192
0.30	896	112
0.40	576	72
0.50	384	48
0.60	256	32
0.70	165	21
0.80	96	12

number of total choices to be collected, so that minimum SP random samples should be guided by the condition given below:

$$n \geq \frac{q}{rpa^2} \, \Phi^{-1}\left(\frac{1+\alpha}{2}\right). \tag{9.5}$$

To exemplify, if we wish to estimate a choice probability that will be approximately p in the real market situation with a relative accuracy of 10 per cent of p with probability of 0.95, and will require each respondent to evaluate eight replications, we obtain, using (9.5), the sample sizes shown in table 9.2. We stress that such numbers are only recommendations, and other factors (e.g., anticipated degree of taste variability, recruitment difficulties) will raise or lower the final sample size. Expression (9.5) can then be used to estimate the impact of the inevitable compromises that arise in every study.

Expression (9.5) applies to random samples, but if we use exogenous stratification, we can calculate total sample size in one of two ways: (1) apply (9.5) to obtain a total sample size, then apportion this among the strata in proportion to population representation or quotas decided upon; (2) apply (9.5) within each stratum (where an SRS is taken) and add up the component sample sizes. The second method will yield larger sample sizes because it requires that within-group proportions be estimated with a certain level of accuracy; the first method requires only that the overall proportion be estimated with a certain relative accuracy. If study objectives emphasise knowledge of segment-specific effects, it is advisable to use the second method above.

Sampling is a complex subject in its own right, and this section does not do it justice. The reader is directed to sources such as Ben-Akiva and Lerman (1985) and Cosslett (1981) for further direction on sampling for RP choice studies. In addition, general books on sampling theory are Cochran (1977) and Levy and Lemeshow (1991).

Before continuing to the next topic, we return to the car rental example. The client corporation currently has a market share of approximately 30 per cent in the target area. If we wish to predict market shares in this range with a relative accuracy of

10 per cent with a 95 per cent confidence level, with each respondent answering four choice scenarios, we need a sample of at least $896/4 = 224$ respondents. We used a simple random sample for this illustrative study, so a list of randomly selected residents of the city was purchased from a 'list house'. Note that quotas for the market segments we wish to investigate (satisfied vs. not satisfied with last rental experience) were not used, so they should be present in the sample in the proportion in which they occur in the population of car renters for personal purposes.

9.3.5 Data collection

Once the questionnaire is designed and tested, the sampling frame decided upon and the sample size calculated, the study can be put into the field. At this stage, the principal decisions that have to be made by the study team involve

1. respondent recruitment method,
2. how to bring respondent and instrument together, and
3. response collection mechanism.

The options for any particular study will be a function of the type of respondent, ease of identifying them, complexity and length of the questionnaire, the type of instrument (paper-and-pencil task, computerised interview), incentives, etc.

A singularly cost-effective form of data collection is the mail survey, which is most effective when respondents can be recruited a priori by telephone or other means. Following recruitment they are mailed surveys, supported by incentives and follow-up reminders that should increase response rates. At its simplest, respondents randomly selected from the sampling frame receive a questionnaire that includes a recruitment letter; incentives may or may not be used, and if used may or may not be contingent upon survey completion and return.[4] If there are stricter project time demands, express courier services can be used to send surveys to/from respondents, or in some cases, responses to the surveys can be collected by telephone.

However, other more complex (thus, more expensive) options are available and often used. Depending upon the type of respondent and the complexity of the decision or of the product being studied, it may be necessary to recruit respondents to come to central facilities where trained personnel provide appropriate information to respondents (personally, or through text or video presentations). In some cases it may be necessary to use personal interviewers; depending upon sample sizes this may be very expensive to execute, but accessing the sampling frame may require it none the less. These options usually require significant incentives for respondents.

Computerised interview methods are also available that come in several flavours: (1) a self-completion survey can be sent to respondents on floppy disk or CD-ROM, and which is mailed back to the researcher upon completion; (2) personal interviews are

---

[4] In certain countries there may be legal restrictions to the use of incentives that are linked to respondent performance.

conducted using a computer, with interviewers and/or respondents keying in responses to questions. The former method is often more useful in business-to-business applications (particularly in industries in which computers are relatively ubiquitous), whereas the latter is more often used for interviewing consumers. Computerised interviewing has the advantages of flexibility (i.e., questionnaire flow can be altered in real time) and improved data quality (i.e., error checking occurs at the time of response).

In the case of our example study, a simple mail survey was used, as indicated before. Respondents were not pre-recruited and did not receive an incentive. A survey packet, including a postage paid return envelope, was mailed to their home address. One follow-up reminder was sent a week after the survey itself. This approach produced a 34 per cent response rate, for a total of 264 usable surveys received by the closing date for the data collection phase.

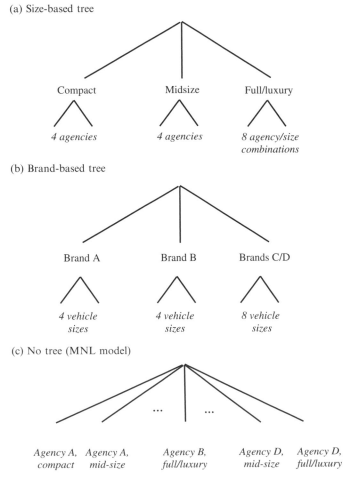

Figure 9.3 Tree specifications for rental agency and vehicle size NL choice model

Table 9.3a. *Dummy and contrast codings for compact vehicles*

Attributable level	Dummy coding	Effects coding
Geo Metro/Sunfire	1	+1
Tercel/Cavalier	0	−1

Table 9.3b. *Dummy and contrast codings for full-size vehicles*

Attribute level	Dummy coding			Contrast coding		
Grand Prix/Cutlass Supreme	1	0	0	1	0	0
Taurus/Regal	0	1	0	0	1	0
Camry/Intrepid	0	0	1	0	0	1
Taurus/Crown Victoria	0	0	0	−1	−1	−1

9.3.6 Model estimation

By this stage the formulation of the particular choice model specification to be estimated should have been determined. As discussed in chapters 4 and 7, this decision should have been used to guide the design of the experiment. We have decided to fit a nested logit (NL) model to the car rental data because we wanted to model the choice of car rental agency and car size. Hence, we were interested in whether there were IIA violations, and if so, whether we could capture them in the NL model through a hierarchical tree structure in a brand-related pattern or car-size pattern. This means that we needed to test which of the three trees in figure 9.3 was best able to describe the observed choices. Subsequently, we discuss the results of this test.

First, however, we discuss the variables included in the utility function. Historically, many SP models have treated qualitative variables using *effects-coded contrasts* instead of dummy codes (see chapter 4). For example, table 9.1 shows that compact vehicles were from two different brand groups: Geo Metro/Sunfire or Tercel/Cavalier. The dummy and contrast codings for this binary attribute are given in table 9.3a. For more than two levels, the contrast coding generalizes as shown in table 9.3b for the full size vehicle brand attribute (see also chapter 4). The decision of whether to use dummy or effects coding is largely up to the analyst. We use the latter in the example study.

RP and SP traditions also differ somewhat regarding coding of continuous variables. In RP models, variables have generally been expressed in the raw (e.g., time, money) of observation. In SP experiments, levels are often chosen in some regular

Table 9.4a. *Orthogonal polynomial coding formulae*

Order of polynomial term	2-level attribute	3-level attribute	4-level attribute	5-level attribute
Linear	$L = 2\left(\dfrac{x - \bar{x}}{d}\right)$	$L = \left(\dfrac{x - \bar{x}}{d}\right)$	$L = 2\left(\dfrac{x - \bar{x}}{d}\right)$	$L = \left(\dfrac{x - \bar{x}}{d}\right)$
Quadratic		$Q = 3L^2 - 2$	$Q = \left(\dfrac{L^2 - 5}{4}\right)$	$Q = L^2 - 2$

Notes: x = actual level of attribute; $\bar{x}$ = average value over all attribute levels; d = *equal* interval between levels.

Table 9.4b. *OP coding for compact car price obtained by applying formulae in table 9.4a*

Attribute level	Linear	Quadratic
$30	−3	+1
$34	−1	−1
$38	+1	−1
$42	+3	+1

pattern dictated by the range in the market and the objectives of the study (for example, price might be varied over four levels: $10, $12, $14 and $16). None of these prices might actually exist in the marketplace, although market values typically are within this range. In observations of actual behaviour from the marketplace, levels are not controlled by the observer, so such regularity might not obtain. Consequently, it may often happen that if one uses continuous variables with non-linear effects (such as a quadratic or higher-order terms) in RP models, high collinearity will be observed. This will also happen in SP models if one does not use exact (or at least approximate) *orthogonal polynomial* (OP) coding for continuous variables, which eliminates this collinearity between polynomials of the same attribute (see chapter 4).

Table 9.4 shows the equations needed to implement OP coding for linear and quadratic representations of 2-, 3-, 4- and 5-level attributes (orthogonal polynomial coding schemes for more than five levels can be found in Montgomery 1991.) As can be seen in table 9.1, the daily price of compact cars is a four-level attribute ($30, $34, $38, $42), and these levels are equidistant. Hence, if we use the appropriate formulae from table 9.4a (with $d = 4$ and $\bar{x} = 36$) we obtain the OP codes for this attribute (table 9.4b).

The formulae in table 9.4a generate integer values when levels are evenly spaced; when the levels are not equidistant one can use the formulae to generate codes that are not exactly orthogonal. We recommend that one *use OP coding whenever possible* because (1) OP coding makes it easy to compare coefficients from different attributes since the ranges of the transformed independent variables will be approximately the same; and (2) certain estimation algorithms (e.g., BHHH and secant methods such as the DFP and BFDP) are sensitive to variables ranges, and may be adversely affected by very different orders of magnitude (methods that use second-order information, e.g., Newton–Raphson, do not exhibit this type of sensitivity).

Of course, one can use any mathematically valid coding in SP choice models, including the raw units of measurement. Indeed, in some cases one may have good reasons to transform certain continuous variables using mathematical functions, such as the natural logarithm. In such cases, one may wish to recode the transformed variable to as orthogonal a form as possible using Robson's (1969) method.

Table 9.5 contains the attribute codes and estimated coefficients for the three models previously discussed. The models are based on the sample of 264 respondents, each of whom provided choice data from four replications. The MNL model has a log likelihood value at convergence of -2192.0, obtained from forty-four parameters. The brand-based NL model depicted in figure 9.3b has a log likelihood of -2185.9, with three additional inclusive value parameters. Thus we reject the hypothesis that the brand inclusive value parameters are simultaneously equal to one (implying that the MNL model holds): the chi-squared statistic for the hypothesis is 12.2 with three degrees of freedom, which is greater than the critical value of 7.8 at the 95 per cent confidence level. This result suggests that IIA violations occur, but since the inclusive value coefficients in the tree-based model are all greater than one, it indicates that this tree structure may be inconsistent with utility maximisation (see chapter 6).

The second NL model in table 9.5 has a vehicle size-based tree structure (see figure 9.3a), and all three inclusive value coefficients are significantly different from unity and less than one, which indicates that this structure is consistent with utility maximisation. If we test this tree against the MNL model (i.e., the hypothesis that all three inclusive value coefficients are unity), we obtain a chi-squared statistic of 132.8 (three degrees of freedom), and hence we reject the MNL model at the 95 per cent confidence level in favour of the vehicle size-based NL model.

Thus, we use the vehicle size-based NL as the preferred model. The model suggests that consumers (1) strongly prefer unlimited daily kilometrage, (2) react negatively to price increases in kilometrage charges, optional insurance and daily rates, (3) strongly prefer to return vehicles with fuel at the level when rented, are neutral with respect to prepaying a full tank at a *discounted* price, and dislike being charged price premiums to fill tanks back to original rental levels if returned at lower levels, (4) are somewhat attracted by airline points as rewards, and (5) do not significantly differentiate between vehicle brands except for mid-size vehicles. All significant coefficients were in the expected direction, and it is worth reiterating that it is *highly* unusual for SP data to exhibit significant *and* incorrect signs. When this rare eventuality occurs, one should consider the possibility of a problem in coding or data handling.

Half of the parameters in the choice model are interactions of the twenty-two independent variables with the socio-demographic variable S. S was coded $+1$ for

Table 9.5. *Estimation results for auto rental agency and vehicle size choice*

Variable descriptions	MNL model tree: flat parameter estimates (*t*-stats)	NL model tree: brand-based parameter estimates (*t*-stats)	NL model tree: size-based parameter estimates (*t*-stats)
Variable descriptions			
X_1: = 1 if Brand A, = −1 if brand D, = 0 o.w.	0.2102 (3.3)	−0.2574 (−0.6)	0.0919 (2.6)
X_2: = 1 if brand B, = −1 if brand D, = 0 o.w.	0.0476 (0.7)	0.2907 (0.9)	0.0225 (0.8)
X_3: = 1 if brand C, = −1 if brand D, = 0 o.w.	−0.2425 (−2.4)	−0.1415 (−0.6)	−0.1111 (−2.2)
X_4: = 1 if limited kilometrage, = −1 if unlimited	−0.6897 (−12.8)	−0.7069 (−13.0)	−0.3075 (−4.0)
X_5: price/km = $(x - 12.5)/2.5$, x in cents/km	−0.3115 (−4.3)	−0.3325 (−4.5)	−0.1404 (−3.1)
X_6: $(\text{price/km})^2 = 3(X_5)^2 - 2$	0.0328 (0.8)	0.0364 (0.9)	0.0135 (0.7)
X_7: price of optional insurance = $(x - 14)/2$, x in \$	−0.1704 (−2.6)	−0.1776 (−2.7)	−0.0862 (−2.4)
X_8: airline points = $(x - 250)/250$	0.2162 (4.1)	0.2185 (4.1)	0.0953 (2.9)
X_9: = 1 if prepay full gas tank, = −1 if bring back at lower level, = 0 o.w.	−0.0244 (−0.3)	−0.0177 (−0.2)	−0.0219 (−0.6)
X_{10}: = 1 if return @ level rented, = −1 if bring back at lower level, = 0 o.w.	0.2857 (3.9)	0.2954 (4.0)	0.1283 (2.8)
X_{11}: fuel price premium/litre for policy 'Bring back at lower level' = $(x - 37.5)/12.5$, = 0 for all other gas return policies	−0.1551 (−2.3)	−0.1578 (−2.3)	−0.0671 (−2.0)
X_{12}: compact vehicle type = 1 if Geo Metro/Sunfire, = −1 if Tercel/Cavalier	−0.0616 (−0.9)	−0.0408 (−0.4)	−0.0219 (−0.6)
X_{13}: compact price/day = $(x - 36)/2$, x in \$/day	−0.6096 (−9.0)	−0.6742 (−7.1)	−0.2802 (−3.3)
X_{14}: $(\text{compact price/day})^2 = [(X_{13})^2 - 5]/4$	0.0244 (0.3)	0.0609 (0.4)	0.2908 (2.9)
X_{15}: mid-size vehicle type = 1 if Grand AM/Dodge Cirrusm = −1 is Corsica/Corolla	0.2434 (4.2)	0.3389 (3.3)	0.1007 (2.1)
X_{16}: mid-size price/day = $(x - 39)$, x in \$/day	−0.2089 (−14.9)	−0.2603 (−9.0)	−0.0935 (−4.2)

	Col 1	Col 2	Col 3
X_{17}: full size vehicle type = 1 if Grand prix/Cutlass Supreme, = −1 if Taurus/Crown Victoria, = 0 o.w.	−0.1061 (−0.8)	−0.1777 (−0.9)	−0.0827 (−1.4)
X_{18}: full size vehicle type = 1 if Taurus/Regal, = −1 if Taurus/Crown Victoria, = 0 o.w.	0.0754 (0.6)	0.0901 (0.5)	0.0176 (0.3)
X_{19}: full size vehicle type = 1 if Camry/Intrepid, = −1 if Taurus/Crown Victoria, = 0 o.w.	0.0572 (0.5)	0.0690 (0.4)	0.0383 (0.7)
X_{20}: full size price/day = $(x - 42)/2$, x in \$/day	−0.3048 (−9.5)	−0.3475 (−7.4)	−0.1522 (−3.9)
X_{21}: luxury vehicle type = 1 = −1 if BMW/Lexus, = −1 if Lincoln Town Car/cadillac	0.1218 (0.8)	0.1499 (0.7)	0.0701 (1.2)
X_{22}: luxury price/day = $(x - 61)/5$, x in \$/day	−0.1778 (−1.6)	−0.0776 (−0.5)	−0.0864 (−1.8)
Segment interactions[1]			
$S \times X_1$	0.0157 (0.3)	0.0229 (0.4)	0.0032 (0.1)
$S \times X_2$	0.0049 (0.1)	0.0012 (0.0)	0.0085 (0.3)
$S \times X_3$	0.0226 (0.2)	0.0146 (0.1)	−0.0101 (−0.2)
$S \times X_4$	0.0762 (1.4)	0.0717 (1.3)	0.0347 (1.3)
$S \times X_5$	0.0020 (0.0)	−0.0001 (0.0)	−0.0006 (0.0)
$S \times X_6$	0.0282 (0.7)	0.01313 (0.8)	0.0067 (0.4)
$S \times X_7$	0.1106 (1.7)	0.1090 (1.7)	0.0477 (1.5)
$S \times X_8$	−0.0046 (−0.1)	−0.0034 (−0.1)	−0.0011 (−0.1)
$S \times X_9$	0.1075 (1.4)	0.1162 (1.5)	0.0643 (1.7)
$S \times X_{10}$	0.0065	0.0074 (0.1)	−0.0126 (−0.4)
$S \times X_{11}$	−0.0225 (−0.5)	−0.0314 (−0.5)	−0.0067 (−0.2)
$S \times X_{12}$	0.0298	0.0372 (0.4)	0.0244 (0.6)
$S \times X_{13}$	−0.0119 (−0.2)	0.0213 (0.2)	−0.0144 (−0.4)

Table 9.5. (cont.)

	MNL model tree: flat parameter estimates (t-stats)	NL model tree: brand-based parameter estimates (t-stats)	NL model tree: size-based parameter estimates (t-stats)
Segment interactions[1]			
$S \times X_{14}$	0.4500 (5.2)	0.7120)3.5)	0.4132 (5.2)
$S \times X_{15}$	0.0324 (0.6)	0.0439 (0.5)	0.0196 (0.5)
$S \times X_{16}$	−0.0234 (−1.7)	−0.0285 (−1.5)	−0.0154 (−1.6)
$S \times X_{17}$	0.1541 (1.1)	0.2490 (1.2)	0.1006 (1.7)
$S \times X_{18}$	−0.0299 (−0.2)	−0.0939 (−0.5)	0.0111 (0.2)
$S \times X_{19}$	−0.0277 (−0.2)	−0.0327 (−0.2)	−0.0317 (−0.6)
$S \times X_{20}$	−0.0384 (−1.2)	−0.0584 (−1.3)	−0.0047 (−0.3)
$S \times X_{21}$	−0.0686 (−0.5)	−0.0953 (−0.5)	−0.0549 (−0.9)
$S \times X_{22}$	0.0062 (0.1)	0.0013	0.0101 (0.2)
Inclusive values[2]			
Brand A	1.0	1.9613 (1.8)	
Brand B	1.0	1.4195 (1.2)	
Brand C or D	1.0	1.5170 (1.4)	
Compact			0.4372 (−4.3)
Mid-size			0.6288 (−2.5)
Full size/luxury			0.3478 (−7.6)
Log likelihood at zero	−2512.4	−2512.4	−2512.4
Log likelihood at convergence	−2192.0	−2185.9	−2125.6
Number of Parameters	44	47	47

Notes: [1] $S = 1$ is somewhat or extremely satisfied, $S = -1$ if somewhat or extremely dissatisfied; [2] asymptotic *t*-statistics of inclusive values are calculated with respect to one.

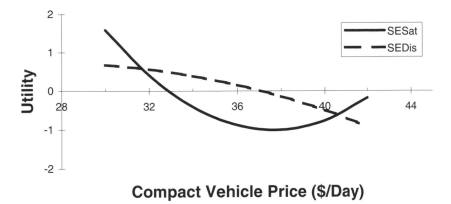

Figure 9.4 Compact vehicle utility as a function of price

individuals who were somewhat or extremely satisfied (group SESat) with their most recent auto rental experience, and -1 for those that were somewhat or extremely *dis*satisfied (group SEDis). Only one significant taste difference appears ($S \times X_{14}$, the quadratic daily price of compact vehicles), which is less than expected by chance. Hence, we will proceed on the basis of this evidence that both groups of previous experience renters have the same attribute preferences.

One small difficulty presented by the best model in table 9.4 concerns the compact vehicle daily rates. As shown in figure 9.4, the behaviour of the predicted utility function is counterintuitive in the higher range of the daily rates, for the SESat group: because of the quadratic segment interaction ($S \times X_{14}$), the model predicts an upturn of the utility function at a daily rate of about \$38 (see table 9.1 for the range of this attribute).

We therefore take the following steps to obtain our next model from the vehicle size-based NL model:

1. delete all segment effects, as explained above, and hopefully eliminate the counter-intuitive result for the compact car price (figure 9.4);
2. delete X_6, which is not significantly different from zero in table 9.5.

The ensuing model, while not presented here, has a log likelihood of -2151.9 with twenty-four parameters. This new model is nested within the NL model in the final column of table 9.4: a likelihood ratio test of the restrictions above has a calculated value of 52.6 with twenty-three degrees of freedom. However, note that the basic reason for this rejection is the deletion of the significant price interaction ($S \times X_{14}$), which has been eliminated for reasons other than statistical significance (i.e., essentially, the effect is believed to be spurious, not substantive). Hence, we shall proceed on the basis that the new model is our basis for comparison.

Unfortunately, the model resulting from the restrictions above continues to exhibit the counterintuitive increase of utility as compact car price increases. The solution we propose to circumvent this problem and obtain the final model is to redefine the price variables for the compact vehicle class; rather than use the linear and quadratic coding adopted thus far in the models, we shall define two piecewise linear terms, hinged at $36 (which is, conveniently, the midpoint of the data). We redefine X_{13} and X_{14} as follows:

$$X_{13} = \frac{\left(\left\{\begin{array}{ll} x & \text{if} \quad x \le 36 \\ 36 & \text{if} \quad x > 36 \end{array}\right\} - 36\right)}{4}, \tag{9.6}$$

$$X_{14} = \frac{\left(\left\{\begin{array}{ll} 0 & \text{if} \quad x \le 36 \\ x - 36 & \text{if} \quad x > 36 \end{array}\right\}\right)}{4}, \tag{9.7}$$

where x is the daily rate. Note that these new codes are *not* OP codes.

To obtain a final working model, we impose the restrictions mentioned before plus the following:

3. change the definitions of X_{13} and X_{14} from those in table 9.5 to expressions (9.6) and (9.7);
4. constrain the inclusive value of the mid-size group of alternatives to one, essentially connecting those alternatives to the root node of the tree (this constraint is not apparent from table 9.5, but arose as we refined the final specification with the new definitions for X_{13} and X_{14});
5. constrain the inclusive values for the two other branches of the tree to be equal (note how they are rather close in value in table 9.5).

These actions result in a vehicle size-based NL model with twenty-two parameters (see table 9.6) and a log likelihood value of -2155.9. Because of the redefinition of X_{13} and X_{14}, this latest model is not nested within the reduced form NL model discussed immediately above. Hence, we cannot use a likelihood ratio test to verify whether the twenty-four parameter NL model with a linear and quadratic compact car price is a better representation of the observed choices that the twenty-two parameter NL model with piecewise linear compact car prices. However, note that the log likelihood increased only about four points with the latest specification. While this intuitively seems like a good trade-off of model fit for parsimony, is this difference significant?

Ben-Akiva and Swait (1986) propose a test for non-nested choice models based on the Akaike Information Criterion. Suppose model 1 explains choices using K_1 variables, while model 2 explains the same choices using K_2 variables; assume that $K_1 \ge K_2$ (i.e., the second model is more parsimonious than the first) and that either (1) the two models have different functional forms or (2) the two sets of variables are different by at least one element. Define the fitness measure for model j, $j = 1, 2$:

$$\bar{\rho}_j^2 = 1 - \frac{L_j - K_j}{L(0)}, \tag{9.8}$$

where L_j is the log likelihood at convergence for model j and $L(0)$ is the log likelihood for the data assuming choice is random (i.e., all alternatives are equiprobable).

Ben-Akiva and Swait (1986) show that under the null hypothesis that model 2 (the more parsimonious specification) is the true model, the probability that the fitness measure (9.8) for model 1 will be greater than that of model 2 is asymptotically bounded by a function whose arguments are (1) the amount Z by which the fitness measures differ, (2) the difference in the number of parameters $(K_1 - K_2)$ and (3) the log likelihood for the equiprobable choice base model, $L(0)$ (since, assuming fixed choice set sizes, $L(0) = -N \ln J$, where N is the number of choice sets and J is the number of alternatives in the choice sets, this component captures the size of the sample and the degree to which either model is able to infer the choice process from the data). More precisely,

$$\text{prob}(|\bar{\rho}_2^2 - \bar{\rho}_1^2| \geq Z) \leq \Phi(-\sqrt{-2ZL(0) + (K_1 - K_2)}), \tag{9.9}$$

where $Z > 0$ and Φ is the standard normal CDF. Thus, if the more parsimonious model (model 2) has a higher fitness measure than model 1, then (9.9) sets an upper bound for the probability that one erroneously selects model 2 as the true model.

Using definition (9.8), models 1 and 2, respectively, have fitness measures of 0.1339 and 0.1331. Thus, the probability of observing a difference of 0.0008 in the fitness measures, given $L(0) = -2512.4$ and $(K_1 - K_2) = 2$, is less than or equal to $\Phi(-6.02) \approx 0$. So, we conclude that the model in table 9.6 is statistically superior to that of table 9.5.

Although there has not been much research on testing non-nested models for choice or other types of dependent variables, another test is provided by Pollak and Wales (1991) called the *likelihood dominance criterion*. Chapter 6 also presents a test for non-nested models involving choice-based samples.

We mentioned earlier that certain constraints were imposed on the inclusive value coefficients to arrive at the final model in table 9.6 (figure 9.6 shows the final tree). If we compare it to figure 9.3a, we might note that an assumption of this model is that the inclusive value coefficients for compact and full/luxury vehicles are the same. This indicates that the degree of within-nest correlation in the stochastic utilities is equal in these two classes of vehicles, but both differ from mid-size vehicles, which do not exhibit within nest correlation (i.e., the inclusive value is one). As a final comment on the model of table 9.6, we show in figure 9.5 the utility of all vehicle sizes as a function of price.

It is not easy to generalise about the decision to halt development and refinement of models. There always are more ideas that can be tested and things that could improve the model. For example, figure 9.5 shows the estimated utility vs. daily price relationships for all four vehicle classes and suggests that the price sensitivity of mid- and full-sized vehicles is very close over the range tested ($32–$46 vs. $34–$50). The normalised price variable coefficients are -0.1465 for mid-size and -0.2337 for full-size (see table 9.6); but because the normalisation rules differ by vehicle type (table 9.5), the price slopes for both classes are similar. Thus, one could test the model in table 9.6 to determine if these two slopes are statistically equivalent: this requires the two price variables to be normalised in the same way, the constraint that the slopes are equal to be imposed, and then a likelihood ratio statistic used to test for slope equality.

Table 9.6. *Final NL model for auto rental agency and vehicle size choice*

Variable descriptions[1]	NL Model tree: size-based parameter estimates (t-stats)
X_1	0.1249 (3.2)
X_2	0.0271 (0.7)
X_3	−0.142 (−2.3)
X_4	−0.4173 (−10.4)
X_5	−0.1978 (−4.5)
X_6	0 (−)
X_7	−0.0931 (−2.4)
X_8	0.1331 (4.2)
X_9	−0.0046 (−0.1)
X_{10}	0.1723 (3.8)
X_{11}	−0.0885 (−2.1)
X_{12}	−0.0109 (−0.3)
X_{13}: $= (\omega - 36)/4$ $\omega = x$ if $x \le 36$, $= 36$ if $x > 36$ $x =$ daily rate for compact vehicle	−0.4437 (−6.8)
X_{14}: $= \omega/4$ $\omega = 0$ if $x \le 36$, $= x - 36$ if $x > 36$ $x =$ daily rate for compact vehicle	−0.2436 (−3.0)
X_{15}	0.1664 (3.0)
X_{16}	−0.1465 (−10.7)
X_{17}	−0.0443 (−0.7)
X_{18}	0.0295 (0.5)
X_{19}	0.0315 (0.5)
X_{20}	−0.2337 (−10.8)
X_{21}	0.0667 (0.8)
X_{22}	−0.1232 (−1.9)
Inclusive values[2]	
Compact	0.5270 (−2.3)
Mid-size	1.0 (−)
Full-size/luxury	0.5270 (−)
Log likelihood at zero	−2512.4
Log likelihood at convergence	−2155.9
Number of parameters	22

Notes: [1] All variables are defined as in table 9.5 except for variables redefined in this table; [2] asymptotic t-statistics of inclusive values are calculated with respect to one; [3] Constrained to equal inclusive value of Compact vehicles.

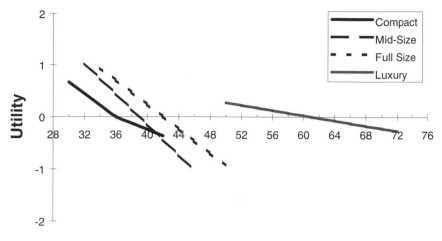

Figure 9.5 Compact vehicle piecewise linear utility as a function of price

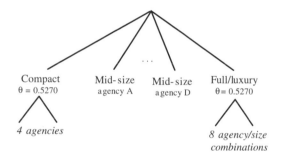

Figure 9.6 Final NL tree structure

9.3.7   Policy analysis

Once a satisfactory model has been developed, the study team can begin policy analysis, which usually involves three stages: (1) definition of a base case and calibration of the SP model; (2) calculation of certain figures of merit for individual attributes (holding other attributes constant) to summarise the behavioural information in the model (e.g., elasticities); and (3) analysis of aggregate market reaction to specific policies (i.e., multiple simultaneous changes of attributes). The latter policies usually involve the big issues that motivated the study.

The base case and SP model calibration   In almost every study some market situation constitutes the starting point of the analysis, or the 'base case.' Its specification involves brands (or, in general, alternatives) in the market and hence form the base case universal choice set (denoted C_B), together with prices and other attributes of

Table 9.7. *Actual and SP carrier market shares (%)*

Carrier	Actual	SP data	Actual	SP data	Actual	SP data
A	53.4	13.1	35.7	13.9	28.7	13.8
B	6.3	10.6	8.8	10.3	4.3	9.2
C	5.4	12.3	5.4	11.6	29.9	13.5
D	15.6	12.9	23.7	12.1	8.1	11.7
E	14.7	10.4	21.3	12.1	19.5	10.8
F	1.7	22.7	1.6	20.7	4.6	22.3
G	1.9	10.5	1.5	11.0	3.6	11.2
H	1.0	7.5	2.0	8.3	1.2	7.5

Source: Swait, Louviere and Williams (1994).

each product (denoted X_B). Importantly, shares of each alternative in the respective market must be known (MS_B) because the data collected in SP choice studies *do not* (and generally, *cannot*) reflect the aggregate shares of the existing market.

This point seems to elude choice modellers who have worked with RP data in the past. RP data automatically reflect the aggregate state of the market (even if the sample is not random it is possible to calculate aggregate market shares from RP data, given a known sampling plan). However, SP data do not reflect RP aggregate market shares because SP data reflect (by *designed intent*) as many markets as choice sets presented to respondents. Some of these hypothetical markets may be similar (or even identical) to the existing RP market, but the SP model parameters are estimated from all the hypothetical markets defined by the experimental design.

Ben-Akiva and Lerman (1985) show that for MNL choice models with a full set of alternative-specific constants (i.e., $J - 1$ constants if there are J alternatives), the *observed aggregate market share will be exactly equal to the predicted market share*. This is a mathematical property of MNL models, verifiable through the first-order conditions of the likelihood function being maximised to estimate the parameters. In other choice models (e.g., NL, MNP) this property holds approximately. Thus, SP choice model ASCs will exactly or closely predict the aggregate shares *in the estimation sample*; but that sample reflects a 'market' very different from the real market to which one wants to apply the final model.

Thus, one needs to *calibrate* SP models to reproduce base case market shares. Table 9.7 shows how aggregate SP shares can differ from the actual market, based on Swait, Louviere and Williams (1994), who reported SP and RP aggregate shares for freight shipper choice. One should note how similar aggregate SP distributions are across the three cities, but how different the aggregate SP and RP distributions are within each city.

One simple calibration process can be described as follows: adjust the ASCs in the SP model to predict aggregate shares in the marketplace at the base case choice set and attributes. Chapter 8 discusses how to combine SP and RP data to derive joint parameter estimates in such a way that the RP model has ASCs adjusted to the application market and other parameters affected by all the SP scenarios seen by respondents.

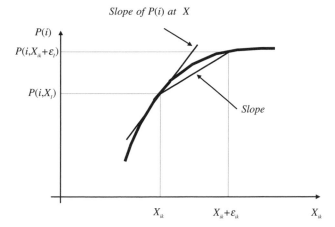

Slope of P(i) at X

Figure 9.7 The relationship between point and arc elasticities

That is, the data combination exercise yields a calibrated 'RP + SP' model. A related calibration process suggested by Swait, Louviere and Williams (1994) also will result in calibration of the SP model to allow policy analysis.

Analysis of individual attributes Before simulating complex policy scenarios that require simultaneous and multiple changes to different attributes, analysts should develop a 'feel' for how each attribute affects choice, holding all other attributes constant. Different figures of merit can be used to do this.

For example, one of the most commonly used evaluation measures is *elasticity* which expresses the percentage change in a response (e.g., market share) caused by a 1 per cent change in a certain variable. Suppose that the response of interest is the choice probability predicted by the model developed from the study data (i.e., $P(i)$, $\forall i \in C_B$) with respect to a continuous attribute X_{ik}. A *point elasticity* (so-called because it strictly is only valid at the point at which it is evaluated) is defined as follows:

$$E_{ik}^{P(i)} = \frac{\partial P(i)/P(i)}{\partial X_{ik}/X_{ik}} = \frac{\partial P(i)}{\partial X_{ik}} \cdot \frac{X_{ik}}{P(i)}, \tag{9.10}$$

which is then evaluated at $X = X_B$ (i.e., the base case). An *arc elasticity* represents the average elasticity over a certain range (it is essentially a point elasticity that uses finite differences rather than calculus), and is calculated thus:

$$\bar{E}_{ik}^{P(i)} = \frac{\Delta P(i)/P(i)}{\varepsilon_k/X_{ij}} = \frac{\Delta P(i)}{\varepsilon_k} \cdot \frac{X_{ik}}{P(i)}, \tag{9.11}$$

where $\Delta P(i) = P(i, X + \varepsilon_k) - P(i, X)$, $P(i, X)$ is $P(i)$ evaluated at X, and ε_k is a perturbation vector containing all zeros except for its kth element. To better interpret these expressions, consider figure 9.7, which makes it clear that the basis for a point elasticity is the instantaneous slope of the response function at the exact value X of the stimulus variable; on the other hand, the basis for the arc elasticity is the slope of the line chord connecting two values of the response function evaluated at X and $(X + \varepsilon)$. For relatively linear response functions these two elasticities are similar, but as functions become less linear the similarity diminishes. Thus, point elasticities are useful for evaluating the impact of small changes in stimulus variables, and arc elasticities are more robust measures valid over wider ranges of changes. Both have their roles in model evaluation and policy analysis (see, e.g., chapters 11 and 12).

What if the attribute of interest is not continuous (e.g., in the case study, whether or not the car rental has unlimited kilometrage or not, as opposed to the value of the kilometre limit)? In such cases, elasticities are not defined, but one can still calculate the change in the response variable generated by changing the qualitative variable from the base discrete level to another. For example, the market share gained or lost by changing the base rental market configuration for a brand from unlimited to limited kilometres per day will be helpful in gauging the relative importance of this attribute.

Another approach for establishing the relative importance of all attributes is to calculate the extent to which one attribute is valued in terms of a numeraire attribute, such as price. If X_{i1} is the price of the good, then $\partial P(i, X_i)/\partial X_{i1}$ is the price sensitivity of the choice probability. Likewise, for a continuous attribute X_{ik}, $\partial P(i, X_i)/\partial X_{ik}$ is the degree to which changes in the attribute affect the choice probability. The *marginal rate of substitution* between X_{ik} and price (X_{i1}) is, therefore,

$$\text{MRS}_{k1} = \frac{\partial X_{i1}}{\partial X_{ik}} = \frac{\partial P(i, X_i)/\partial X_{ik}}{\partial P(i, X_i)/\partial X_{i1}}. \tag{9.12}$$

The unit of the MRS_{k1} is the price equivalent of a unit of X_{ik}, or \$/(unit of X_{ik}). If an attribute is discrete, rather than continuous, then we can express the value of a change in that attribute as the price change (ΔX_{i1}) needed to exactly offset the change in market share created by the change in X_{ik} from the base case value to another level:

$$\text{VLC}_{k1} = \frac{\Delta X_{i1}}{P(i, X'_{Bk} - P(i, X_B)}, \tag{9.13}$$

where X'_{Bk} is the base case attribute vector except for the changed level of attribute k.

Expressions (9.12) and (9.13) are based on choice probability as the response function. Other possibilities for response functions are market shares MS_i and the latent indirect utility functions $U_i(X)$ themselves. If the utility functions are linear-in-the-parameters specifications, it is straightforward to see that (9.12) reduces to ratios of estimated parameters (or simple functions thereof) and (9.13) will generally simplify to the ratio of parameters.

We illustrate the use of the utilities as response functions to evaluate relative attribute importance in our case study. Figure 9.8 (which we term a 'tornado' graph) shows marginal rates of substitution and value of level changes for the attributes in the auto rental agency and car size choice model from table 9.6. The graph makes it apparent that unlimited kilometrage is an extremely positive characteristic to be offered, trans-

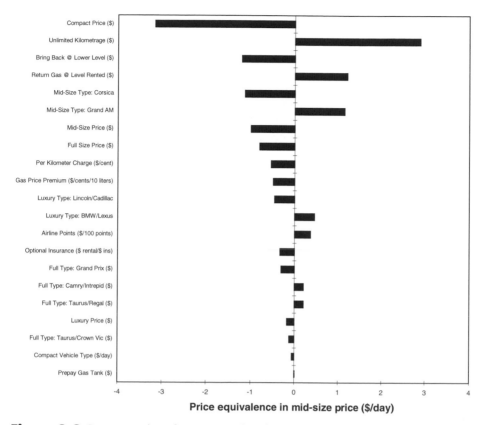

Figure 9.8 Price equivalents for auto rental and car size choice (based on utility functions)

lating into an equivalent $3/day in the mid-size rental rate. With respect to fuel return policies, another positive feature to offer is the ability to return the vehicle with the fuel at the level rented, which is valued at about $1.25/day. By comparison, bringing a vehicle back with fuel at a lower level and paying a premium ($0.10–$0.15/litre) to the rental agency to top up the tank is viewed quite negatively (also about $1.25/day); the third return policy, which is to prepay for a full tank at a discounted price, is valued somewhat neutrally (~$0/day). Renting a mid-size Grand Am vehicle is positively valued at $1.25, compared to −1.25 for renting a Corsica.

There are a number of other insights about the relative importance of different attributes that can be derived from the graph, which we invite the interested reader to undertake as a learning exercise.

Policy analysis   This is the most interesting and challenging stage of any project, in which the study team uses the model to answer the substantive questions of interest. To do this one must define a set of market scenarios to be compared with the base case. Each scenario usually involves multiple changes to the base case conditions and requires one to evaluate appropriate figures of merit (e.g., market share changes, profit) and formulate policy recommendations based on outcomes.

Very formal evaluation procedures are employed in some arenas. For example, in transportation planning and environmental economics, which both deal with public policy, *welfare analysis* provides a common framework for policy evaluation. Coverage of this topic is beyond the scope of this book, but can be obtained from standard microeconomics texts (e.g., Layard and Walters 1978). Instead, we merely note that the basis for use of choice models in welfare analysis is well-developed (e.g., Williams 1977, Small and Rosen 1981), and chapters 11 and 12 will discuss and illustrate the use of welfare analysis in transport and environmental applications.

9.4 Summary

The objective of this chapter was to equip the reader to conduct SP choice studies by integrating the myriad details from previous chapters into a coherent structure. We therefore covered a rather broad range of subjects:

- study objective definition;
- qualitative work needed to support choice studies;
- data collection instrument development and testing;
- sampling issues;
- data collection topics;
- model estimation; and
- model and policy analysis.

Coverage on these topics varied as a function of the scope of the text, but particular attention was given to the qualitative work, sampling issues and model estimation.

10 Marketing case studies

10.1 Introduction

The purpose of this chapter is to illustrate practical aspects of studying consumer choice behaviour in academic and commercial marketing settings using SP methods. The two case studies presented emphasise marketing applications, but nevertheless should be more broadly interesting to and useful for students of SP theory and methods.

SP preference elicitation methods have been used in academic and commercial marketing applications since the 1960s, and indeed, no other discipline has so widely and warmly embraced them. Rather than retrace well-known and well-worn topics and issues, this chapter tries to synthesise advances and insights from the past fifteen years with specific emphasis on advances in probabilistic discrete-choice models.

The case studies address the following topics:

- **Case study 1** deals with whether preference heterogeneity or variance heteroscedasticity is best able to describe consumer choices of brands of frozen orange juice concentrate. We investigate whether certain consumer characteristics (propensity towards planned shopping and deal proneness) are associated with differences in consumer attribute sensitivities, differences in choice variability or both. These types of behavioural differences matter in marketing applications because their policy implications are very different;
- **Case study 2** investigates choice set formation and its impacts on choice model outcomes. This case study deals with the difficult issue of properly specifying choice sets for consumers studied in choice modelling exercises. We show that misspecification of choice sets can have dramatic effects on choice model results and strategic marketing inferences derived therefrom.

10.2 Case study 1: preference heterogeneity vs. variance heteroscedasticity

The data in this case were collected in a major North American city for a study of consumer choice of frozen orange juice concentrate. The juice concentrate brands

EXAMPLE	Alternative A	Alternative B	Alternative C	Alternative D
Brand	McCain's	Old South	Generic	NONE
Grade	A	C	C	OF
Sweetness	Unsweetened	Sweetened	Sweetened	THESE
Sale Offer	Package of 4	Unit	Unit	PRODUCTS
Total Price/Package	$3.75	$1.75	$1.00	
I Would Purchase.... (✓Check Only One)	❑ ⇓	❑ ⇓	❑ ⇓	❑
How Many of the Selected Product?	_____ packages of 4	_____ cans	_____ cans	

Figure 10.1 Case study 1 SP task layout

studied are packaged in 8-ounce cans, which contain enough concentrate to make approximately eight cups of juice. The dependent variable of interest is the brand chosen by the consumers in the study, but it is worth noting that purchase quantity decisions conditional on brand choice also were elicited but not reported. This research problem was conceptualised and treated as a modified consumer packaged good (fast moving consumer good) discrete choice task, as shown in figure 10.1.

The primary research objective was to model the effect of including a non-purchase alternative in a choice task on the attractiveness of different package sizes and the perceived importance of certain product attributes (Olsen and Swait 1998). Consequently, the experiment manipulated whether a 'None' choice alternative was included in the task or not (hence, could/could not be chosen). This case study only uses choice data from subjects who offered 'None' as a choice option.

The larger sample consists of 405 grocery shoppers randomly chosen from a local telephone directory who agreed to participate (520 were recruited). Of the 405 who agreed to participate, 280 returned usable surveys (an effective response rate of 69 per cent).[1] This case uses 209 of those individuals.

Five attributes were used to describe possible packages of frozen orange juice concentrate (figure 10.1): (1) brand (levels: McCain's, Old South, Minute Maid and Generic), (2) grade (A vs. C, where grade C juices are made from lower quality oranges), (3) sweetness (sweetened vs. unsweetened), (4) package size (1 unit vs. package of 4) and (5) price per unit ($1.30 vs. $1.60/unit). These attributes and their levels were described in a separate glossary (table 10.1) to ensure that all participants had a set of common definitions for terms used in tasks. The attribute levels were taken from information found on labels of juice concentrate products in local supermarkets.

An orthogonal, one-half fraction of the 4×2^4 factorial design was used to create thirty-two orange juice profiles; this design has the property that all main-effects and two-way interactions are independent of one another. The remaining thirty-two

---

[1] While these higher response rates are not uncommon in marketing applications, particularly when higher incentives are employed, it is worthy of note that this study was conducted under the aegis of a university. Respondents were informed of this, which may have helped raise response rates.

Table 10.1. *Attribute glossary*

Term	Definition
Grade	Grade refers to the quality of the orange juice. <u>Grade A</u> orange juice is made only from the high quality oranges that pass a rigorous government screening programme. <u>Grade C</u> orange juices contain lower quality oranges (for example, those that were damaged by an unexpected frost).
Sweetness	This refers to whether sugar has been added to the natural orange juice. Some are <u>sweetened</u>, others are <u>unsweetened</u> (that is, no extra sugar has been added).
Sale offer	This refers to the number of cans that must be purchased together. You will see one of the following:
Unit	You may purchase one or more individual cans of this product at the stated price.
Package of 4	For this sale, multiples of 4 cans of orange juice will have to be purchased (that is, they are packaged together so that you can not just purchase a single can).
Total Price/Package	This represents the total amount of money that you would have to spend to purchase one package. The total price per package will be determined by both the discount being offered, and by the sale offer (the number of units required). For example, you might be offered a package of 4 for $5.60.

profiles from the 4×2^4 design were paired with the original thirty-two profiles by random assignment without replacement (chapter 5 and Louviere 1988a). A constant third option was added to each pair; it was described as generic, grade C, sweetened orange juice, sold by the unit at $1.00 per unit. The latter option was frequently promoted in local supermarkets. A fourth choice option (figure 10.1) was the 'None' option. In order to limit any one individual's task, each received a block of sixteen choice sets that comprised half the thirty-two pairs (choice sets), which were split into two blocks by random assignment.

Respondents were recruited by telephone, given a general description of the study (i.e., they would have to complete a survey about frozen orange juice concentrate), and asked how frequently they shopped for major grocery purchases. Those who went grocery shopping two or more times per month were asked to participate in the study, and offered a $2 incentive to participate, plus an additional $2 that would be donated to a charity of their choice. Those who agreed to participate were randomly assigned to one of the blocks described above.

In addition to the choice/quantity task, respondents also were asked about several personal and household characteristics, of which seven items (table 10.2) are germane to this case. The items were used to measure the two characteristics of 'deal proneness' and 'proneness to planned shopping trips'; scales were constructed by first analysing the seven-category agree/disagree item responses with principal component analysis

Table 10.2. *Item list*

1. Before going shopping I make out a detailed shopping list.
2. I only buy items on my shopping list.
3. I frequently use coupons when shopping.
4. I carefully look through the newspaper to see what specials are offered at different stores.
5. I frequently stock up on items when they are on sale.
6. I always try to get the best deal when shopping for groceries.
7. I frequently stock up on juice when it is on sale.

(PCA). The PCA results suggested that there were two latent dimensions: $PS \rightarrow propensity$ *towards planned shopping* (items 1–2) and $DP \rightarrow deal$ *proneness* (items 3–7). The PCA results are omitted in the interests of space, but the relevant items were summed to construct a score for each respondent on the two constructs as shown below:

$$PS = X_1 + X_2 \qquad\qquad (10.1a)$$

$$DP = X_3 + X_4 + X_5 + X_6 + X_7, \qquad\qquad (10.1b)$$

where X_j is the jth item score. The two constructs measured in this way are used as individual difference variables to test two competing hypotheses about the decision processes observed in the juice concentrate choice task:

Do the two constructs explain choice model parameter differences between individuals? That is, we specifically test whether the utility parameters are constant across individuals or vary for certain segments in a specific way. For example, a high score on the DP construct might indicate higher price sensitivity and a preference for package offers (4-can packs vs. units) than might otherwise be the case. Similarly, high scores on the PS construct might indicate less preference for 4-pack offers. Alternatively, these two constructs might explain the consistency (or variability) of individual consumers' choices. For example, high scores on the PS construct might be associated with more consistent choices of 'None', which can be modelled by parametrising both the utility function and the variance of the errors.

In order to compare these competing hypotheses we specified two variants of the basic MNL model:

1. A latent class model (see appendix B, section B6.4 in chapter 6).[2] This model assumes that there are S classes (or segments) in the population, each of which is associated with a different parameter vector β_s in the corresponding utility function (Swait 1994). The model simultaneously assigns individuals to segments with a polychotomous MNL model (with parameters γ_s to be estimated), and infers the utility parameters from a second MNL model. The explanatory

---

[2] Latent class models are only one way to model taste variation. See chapter 6 for more discussion.

variables in the classification comprise the vector Z_q containing DP and PS, where q is an individual. The juice attributes comprise vector X_i. The dependent variable is the chosen juice option because the number of segments and the segment membership of a particular consumer are not observed (hence, '*latent class model*').

2. A model that permits the random component variance to be parametrised as a function of DP and PS. We used the covariance heterogeneity (CovHet) HEV model of chapter 6 (appendix B, section B6.2) to model the variance as a function of these two covariates.

We fit and discuss both model specifications, and then test which specification is the best approximation to the observed choice behaviour.

10.2.1 The utility parameter heterogeneity hypothesis

To develop a discrete representation of the distribution of a vector of utility parameters in a population using a latent class model, one first must estimate the number of classes, S. This is a discrete, not a continuous, parameter, which creates problems for maximum likelihood theory because it requires continuity of the parameter space.

Thus, there is no one rigorous way to select the 'right' S, but rather a number of methods have been used based on the Akaike Information Criterion (AIC) and its variants. AIC-type measures encourage parsimonious model selection by penalising log likelihood improvements due to larger number of parameters; multiple measures tend to be used to guide selection of S. In a similar vein we used AIC and Consistent AIC (CAIC) to guide model selection. CAIC is a function of sample size as well as the dimensionality of the parameter space. For this model specification,

$$AIC = -2(LL(\hat{\theta}) - S \cdot K_\beta - (S-1)K_\gamma) \tag{10.2a}$$

$$CAIC = -2LL(\hat{\theta}) - (S \cdot K_\beta + (S-1)K_\gamma - 1)(\ln{(2N)} + 1), \tag{10.2b}$$

where $LL(\hat{\theta})$ is the log likelihood at the estimated parameters $\hat{\theta}$, $\theta = (\beta, \gamma)$, K_β is the number of elements in the utility function of the segment-specific choice models, K_γ is the total number of parameters in the classification model, and N is the number of observations in the sample. The value of S that minimises each of the measures suggests which model should be preferred.

The utility functions for the segment-specific choice models (see section B6.4 for details) contain brand-specific constants (four ASCs), the main effects of the four attributes (four utility parameters), and all two-order interactions of the four attributes (six utility parameters). The classification model involves three parameters for each segment to specify the effects of the two constructs and their interaction (DP, PS and $DP \times PS$). Thus, $K_\beta = 14S$ and $K_\gamma = 3(S-1)$. In order to be conservative, we used $N = 209$ (i.e., the number of respondents) rather than 209×16 (the number of choice observations) as the total number of observations in the analysis.

We estimated models for $S = 1, \ldots, 4$, and graphed AIC and CAIC (figure 10.2). For this range AIC decreases monotonically, while CAIC reaches a minimum at $S = 2$. We omit the three- and four-segment solutions in the interests of space, but

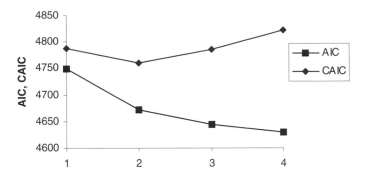

Figure 10.2 Selection of S

Table 10.3. *Latent 2-class parameter estimates*

Parameters	Parameter estimates (*t*-statistics in parentheses)	
	Segment 1	Segment 2
Utility function		
McCain's	1.476(1.6)	−0.727(−7.0)
MinMaid	2.631(3.0)	−0.608(−5.7)
OldSouth	2.478(2.8)	−1.043(−8.6)
Generic	0.405(0.0)	−1.659(−13.4)
None	0	0
Grade (+1 = A, −1 = C)	29.877(60.0)	0.756(11.0)
Sweetness (+1 = sweet, −1 = unsweet)	16.770(13.6)	−1.102(−15.8)
4 pack (+1 = 4 pack, −1 = unit)	−12.618(−10.7)	−0.124(−2.1)
Price = (x − 1.45)/0.15	−0.494(−1.7)	−0.491(−9.1)
Grade × sweetness	−16.035(0.0)	−0.003(0.0)
Grade × 4 pack	20.945(0.0	−0.007(−0.1)
Grade × price	−7.701(−25.4)	−0.028(−0.6)
Sweetness × 4 pack	−0.859(−0.7)	0.057(1.0)
Sweetness × price	−0.401(−1.1)	0.207(3.8)
4 pack × price	7.862(0.0)	−0.090(−1.7)
Predicted segment size (sample)	11.7%	88.3%
Latent segment membership scoring function		
PS	−1.556(−2.8)	
DP	−2.755(−6.8)	
DP × PS	1.397(1.5)	
Summary statistics		
Log likelihood (random choice)	−3083.12	
Log likelihood at convergence	−2304.54	
No. of parameters	31	

they yielded a large number of non-significant parameters, and in the four-segment solution produced a very small, counterintuitive segment. This led us to stop seeking further segments in this data. The results beyond two segments are likely to be unreliable because of the sample size we have available: latent class models are notoriously data-intensive. Selection of S is aided by these statistics, but analyst judgement should direct the decision.

We selected the two-segment solution as the best model to approximate utility parameter heterogeneity (see table 10.3). This model predicts that 12 per cent of the sample are in segment 1 and the other 88 per cent in segment 2. Membership in segment 1 *decreases* with increasing DP and PS, but the positive and statistically significant interaction term between these two characteristics indicates that the effect of increases in both factors is to ameliorate both main effects. The two constructs affect the membership probability for segment 2 exactly the opposite of segment 1 because segment 2's membership probability is simply one minus that of segment 1.

One can see differences in utility parameters for each segment more easily using the graphs in figure 10.3. These so-called 'radar' plots can be quite informative once one learns how to interpret them. That is, figure 10.3a displays the utility parameters of segment 1 that are statistically significant at the 90 per cent confidence level, each on a radial axis (not shown for clarity) with the name of the corresponding parameter at the outer extremity of its axis. The points are connected by straight lines to create an irregularly shaped polygon. The more the polygon resembles a circle, the more the parameters are equal in magnitude. If a polygon does not extend in a certain direction, the corresponding parameters are not statistically significant.

Thus, figure 10.3a suggests that segment 1 utilities are based partly on brand (particularly Minute Maid and Old South) and partly on attributes (grade, sweetness and package size). On average price is not statistically significant (main effect in table 10.3 for segment 1 reveals a t-statistic of -1.7, which is slightly below the 90 per cent confidence level), but the grade $\times$ price interaction is significant, implying more price sensitivity for grade A and less price sensitivity for grade C (the latter is somewhat counterintuitive). Finally, segment 1 exhibits a very low probability of choosing None (all brand-specific constants > 0, the implicit value of the ASC of the None option).

In contrast, segment 2 exhibits a high probability of choosing None (all brand-specific constants < 0), and a low probability of choosing generic orange juice (the most negative ASC). All brand and attribute main effects are significant at the 95 per cent confidence level (see table 10.3), and there is a significant sweetness $\times$ price interaction. This interaction implies less price sensitivity ($-0.284 = -0.491 + 0.207$) for sweetened compared with unsweetened juices ($-0.698 = -0.491 - 0.207$).

10.2.2 The variance heterogeneity hypothesis

The results of the CovHet HEV model that parameterises variance heterogeneity as a function of DP and PS are in table 10.4 (for the same data used to estimate the latent class model in table 10.3). In contrast to the latent class results, all ASCs and attribute

(a)

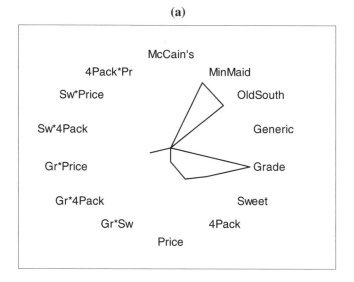

(b)

Figure 10.3 Radar plots of 2-class taste parameters (90 per cent confidence level)

main effects are significant, but no attribute interactions are significant. This suggests that the scale (variance) of the random component of utility increases (decreases) with increases (decreases) in PS and DP. That is, as both quantities increase, the impact on the scale (variance) decreases (increases), owing to the significant interaction term.

The log likelihood of the CovHet model is -2340.65 compared to the 2-class model, which has a log likelihood of -2304.54. The CovHet model does not explain choices as well as the latent class model, which should be expected because the latter has almost

Table 10.4. *CovHet HEV parameter estimates*

Parameters	Parameter estimates (*t*-statistics in parentheses)
Utility function	
McCain's	−0.156(−3.0)
MinMaid	−0.120(−2.8)
OldSouth	−0.203(−3.1)
Generic	−0.319(−3.1)
None	0
Grade (+1 = A, −1 = C)	0.149(3.1)
Sweetness (+1 = sweet, −1 = unsweet)	−0.202(−3.1)
4 pack (+1 = 4 pack, −1 = unit)	−0.031(−2.2)
Price = (x − 1.45)/0.15	−0.123(−3.1)
Grade × sweetness	−0.008(−0.8)
Grade × 4 pack	0.014(1.3)
Grade × price	0.003(0.3)
Sweetness × 4 pack	−0.007(-0.7)
Sweetness × price	0.016(1.7)
4 pack × price	−0.013(−1.3)
Covariates of scale function	
PS	1.750(3.4)
DP	2.271(4.9)
DP × PS	−2.573(−3.4)
Summary statistics	
Log likelihood (random choice)	−3083.12
Log likelihood at convergence	−2340.65
No. of parameters	17

twice the number of parameters. The empirical issue is whether the additional explanatory power from the model with more parameters is significant enough to reject the more parsimonious CovHet specification.

10.2.3 Testing the alternative behavioural hypotheses

Comparison of the two models is complicated by the fact that the specifications are non-nested. The non-nested test of Ben-Akiva and Swait (1986) based on the Akaike Information Criterion was discussed in chapter 9 (section 9.3.6), and we use this for the present test. The fit measures (equation (9.8)) for the models are respectively 0.2353 for the CovHet model (seventeen parameters) and 0.2425 for the two-class model (thirty-one parameters), or a difference of 0.0072. Hence, the probability that a model with fourteen more parameters is superior to the CovHet specification is less than or equal to 1.3×10^{-14} (equation (9.9)). Thus, it is highly likely that the CovHet model is a better description of the choices observed in this particular data set.

Some may find this result surprising because CovHet HEV is a relatively simple model that slightly extends MNL by allowing the error variances to be a function of individual characteristics and stochastically distributed over the population. Yet, this simple story reads better than a more complex utility heterogeneity story. Latent class models attempt to capture utility heterogeneity with a finite number of support points that can be generalised to a random parameters model (see appendix B, chapter 6).

We do not pursue the possibility here, but we acknowledge the fact such a flexible specification might perform better than the variance heterogeneity model, although Bunch (reported in Louviere, et al. 1999) recently showed that the number of observations required to satisfy asymptotic theory in such models was many times that for models such as MNL, and he only investigated 'small problems' (e.g., three choice alternatives and a few attributes).

We conclude this particular case study by noting that the results illustrate why it is important to consider random component heterogeneity when modelling choice data from any source. Chapter 13 presents more evidence of its pervasive role in preference data.

10.3 Case study 2: choice set generation analysis

This case study addresses a most challenging issue in choice modelling, namely making inferences about choice set structures. In chapter 9 (see discussions of expressions (9.1)–(9.3)) we noted that consumers make a certain choice from a given choice set C_n, and so we assumed that one knows C_n. In some situations it may be possible that one can know the 'true' choice set, but this is not the case in general. As pointed out by Swait (1984), Swait and Ben-Akiva (1985, 1987a,b), inferences about preference (and, by extension, variance) parameters will be biased if one misspecifies the choice set for the observation.

In the case of RP data, knowledge of C_n generally is not available, so many researchers assume that (1) all alternatives in existence are available to all observations, or (2) that some deterministic criteria can be used to eliminate alternatives from the universal set (e.g., autos are not choices for those who don't have cars or driving licences). The first option often is justified by arguing that the 'true set' is nested in the universal set, so it's better to include alternatives that shouldn't be in the set than omit alternatives that should be. Unfortunately, Swait and Ben-Akiva (1985) show that including irrelevant alternatives in choice sets *underestimates* the impact of attribute changes.

The issue of choice set generation probably is less likely to impact SP data because choice sets are controlled, but choice set generation issues cannot be ruled out. Specifically, SP tasks offer consumers arrays of options with certain characteristics, but they may consider only a subset of the options offered. That is, SP tasks control only the *universal set* of alternatives, not the individual's actual choice set.

Although choice set specification is critical, little effort has been devoted to it because modelling choice set generation is extremely complex owing to the potential

Now we're going to present you with the opportunity to do some shopping. Suppose you're shopping for jeans and find the following brands offered at the stated prices. In each scenario below, please indicate which one brand you would most prefer to buy, or if you like none of the offers, indicate you'd buy none of these. Consider each scenario independently of all others.

Scenario	Jeans					
X	CK $44.99	Gap $34.99	Lee $54.99	Levi's $24.99	Wranglers $34.99	I'd choose NONE
I would choose (√ only one):	⇩ □₁	⇩ □₂	⇩ □₃	⇩ □₄	⇩ □₅	⇩ □₆

Figure 10.4 Typical choice scenario for brand/price task

size of the problem. For example, expression (9.3) shows that for a universal set with J alternatives, $(2^J - 1)$ possible choice sets must be taken into account. If $J = 3$, there are only seven sets, but if $J = 10$, there are 1023 sets. If $J = 20$, there are 1,048,575 sets! Different approaches have been used to address this size issue (e.g., explicitly omitting certain choice sets, say by size of set), but it is safe to say that the modelling of choice set generation is still in its infancy and needs much more research attention.

This case study applies a particular model of choice set generation described below to SP choice data collected from a convenience sample of undergraduate students at a major North American university (see Erdem and Swait 1998 for more details). The SP task was based on a simple brand/price design for brands of jeans that included five brands (Calvin Klein, Gap, Lee, Levi's and Wrangler). All brands were present in every choice scenario, but their prices varied in each set (each brand had four price levels). As well, all choice sets offered a 'None of These' option so that respondents could choose none of the brands offered. Figure 10.4 shows a typical choice set; each of ninety-two respondents evaluated seventeen of these choice sets.

Respondents also rated each brand on a number of dimensions, and for our purposes we note that some of these ratings were used to construct a perceived quality (PQ) construct using LISREL (see Erdem and Swait 1998). We estimate a utility function for brand i that includes an ASC, the perceived quality measure and the natural logarithm of price. The choice set generation component is based on Swait's (1984) independent availability logit (IAL) model. That is, the probability of choosing brand i is

$$P_{in} = \sum_{C \subseteq \Gamma_n} P_{in|C} Q_{nC}, \tag{10.1}$$

where C is a choice set, Γ_n is the set of subsets of C_n, $P_{in|C}$ is the probability of choosing i given set C, and Q_{nC} is the probability set C is observation n's choice set. This model assumes that choice sets are latent, and the conditional choice model is MNL:

$$P_{in|C} = \frac{\exp(\beta X_{in})}{\sum_{j \in C} \exp(\beta X_{jn})}. \tag{10.2}$$

Table 10.5. *MNL and IAL parameter estimates*

Parameters	MNL parameter estimates (*t*-statistics in parentheses)	IAL parameter estimates (*t*-statistics in parentheses)
Utility function		
Calvin Klein	19.286(18.3)	27.656(11.7)
Gap	20.482(18.9)	26.942(11.8)
Lee	13.149(5.8)	18.069(5.0)
Levis	19.139(19.1)	25.396(12.4)
Wranglers	5.686(2.8)	15.359(3.0)
PQ(CK)	1.041(14.1)	1.493(10.3)
PQ(Gap)	1.000(13.2)	1.340(10.4)
PQ(Lee)	1.077(7.6)	1.548(7.0)
PQ(Levi's)	1.182(14.0)	1.580(10.8)
PQ(Wranglers)	1.350(9.8)	2.251(8.5)
ln(Price(CK))	−5.209(−17.6)	−7.549(−11.5)
ln(Price(Gap))	−5.547(−18.3)	−7.431(−11.5)
ln(Price(Lee))	−4.367(−6.5)	−5.953(−5.7)
ln(Price(Levi's))	−5.047(−18.3)	−6.837(−12.1)
ln(Price(Wranglers))	−2.467(−4.2)	−5.216(−3.5)
Availability functions		
Calvin Klein	0	1.636(6.6)
Gap	0	2.413(5.7)
Lee	0	0.618(0.8)
Levi's	0	2.493(6.0)
Wranglers	0	−0.814(−2.6)
None of these	0	0.920(2.3)
Summary statistics		
Log likelihood (random choice)	−2734.22	−2734.22
Log likelihood at convergence	−1398.57	−1382.46
No of parameters	15	21

The probability that the true choice set is $C \subseteq C_n$ is given by[3]

$$Q_{nC} = \frac{\prod_{j \in C} A_{jn} \prod_{j \in C_n - C} (1 - A_{jn})}{1 - \prod_{j \in C_n} (1 - A_{jn})},$$ (10.3)

where the probability A_{in} of alternative $i \in C_n$ being 'available' or in choice set C is specified by a parametrised logistic function, as follows:

$$A_{in} = \frac{1}{(1 + \exp(-\gamma Z_{in}))}.$$ (10.4)

[3] The normalisation factor in this expression is to account for the possibility that all alternatives are unavailable.

In this expression, γ is a parameter row vector and Z_{in} is a column vector of co-variates.

The IAL model assumes that alternatives (brands plus 'None') are in or out of the choice set independently. This clearly is a restrictive assumption because if Gap is in a choice set Calvin Klein also is likely to be there. However, the independence assumption does provide model tractability and permits an analysis of choice set structure without an a priori arbitrary imposition of some criteria to define choice set generation.

Table 10.5 presents MNL and IAL models estimated from 9156 choices. The IAL model only included ASCs in the availability functions (expression (10.4)). A test of the hypothesis that these availability ASCs are simultaneously zero produces a chi-squared statistic of 32.2 $(= -2[-1398.57 + 1382.46];$ 6 d.f.$)$. The critical value of χ^2 at the $\alpha = 0.05$ confidence level is 12.59, which strongly rejects the hypothesis that all individuals have a universal set of six alternatives as their choice set. (Note the caveat that the choice set generation model assumes alternatives are independently available.)

A comparison of utility parameters in both models reveals that slopes in the IAL model are greater in absolute value. This result is predicted by Swait and Ben-Akiva (1985) because inclusion of non-considered alternatives dampens the measured impact of attributes. In particular, the price sensitivity of Wranglers more than doubles in the IAL model. In the surveyed population, Wranglers is infrequently considered (it's the only brand with a negative coefficient in the availability function), so when we estimate price sensitivity without proper specification of choice set structure, the price sensitivity of Wranglers seems lower than it actually is among individuals who consider it.

The choice set generation portion of the model can be used to calculate the predicted distribution of choice set size (figure 10.5). The most likely sizes are four and five alternatives (including 'None'), and set sizes of one or two are unlikely (total probability of about 0.03). The marketing implications of this result are that no brands

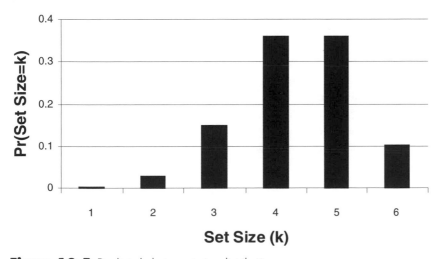

Figure 10.5 Predicted choice set size distribution

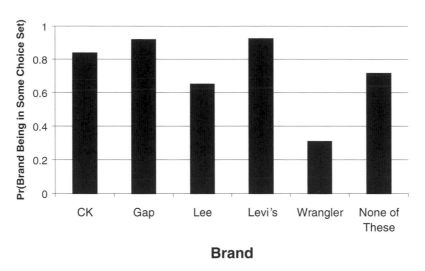

Figure 10.6 Predicted probability of inclusion in some choice set

in this sample have a 'captive' segment; instead, it is more likely that each brand competes with two or three others.

Figure 10.6 compares brands in terms of their likelihood of being in choice sets. For example, over the possible sixty-three sets of alternatives, Calvin Klein has a probability of approximately 0.83 of being in some choice set, Gap and Levi's are the brands most likely to be in all choice sets, Lee's inclusion probability is about 0.6 and Wranglers has a much lower inclusion probability of 0.3. 'None' has a high inclusion probability, indicating that consumers are ready to reject higher prices.

The most likely competitors for each brand can be estimated by calculating the probability of occurrence of each possible choice set to determine which specific sets are most likely. Nine choice sets jointly exhibit a total probability of 0.76 that the true choice set is among them (arrayed in decreasing order of likelihood in table 10.6). The most likely set is {CK, Gap, Levi's, None; probability = 0.23}, the next most likely set adds Lee and Wranglers to the most likely set (probability = 0.12).

This result supports the observation that all brands seem to compete with several other brands (if not all of them!). Thus, the probability of choice goes up for all brands because their consideration probabilities are higher, but the executives of CK, Gap and Levi's face the challenge that these brands need further differentiation to increase the likelihood of smaller choice sets! In fact, in this segment, it could be argued that Lee and Wranglers fare better because they are being considered outside their traditional market. We risk making more of this result than the small sample size and convenience sample justifies, hence we conclude by noting that the results illustrate the rich behavioural insights that choice set generation models can provide.

Additional information on the topic of choice set generation can be found in Swait and Ben-Akiva (1987a,b), Roberts and Lattin (1991), Ben-Akiva and Boccara (1995), Horowitz and Louviere (1995) and Andrews and Srinivasan (1995), among others.

Table 10.6. *Most likely choice sets*

Choice sets						Probability of occurrence
CK	Gap	Levi's	None of these			0.228
CK	Gap	Lee	Levi's	Wranglers	None of these	0.123
CK	Gap	Lee	Levi's			0.101
CK	Gap	Levi's	Wranglers	None of these		0.091
CK	Gap	Levi's				0.055
Gap	Lee	Levi's	None of these			0.049
CK	Gap	Lee	Levi's	Wranglers		0.044
Gap	Levi's	None of these				0.040
CK	Gap	Levi's	Wranglers			0.024

10.4 Summary

The purpose of this chapter was to illustrate how SP methods can be used to address marketing issues such as product design, pricing, distribution, etc. Case study 1 showed that variance differences may sometimes account for differences between segments better than preference heterogeneity. Case study 2 demonstrated the importance of correct specification of choice sets, and the important strategic and behavioural insights that can be obtained from models that incorporate better specifications of choice sets.

11 Transportation case studies

11.1 Introduction

Throughout this book we have used examples to help readers gain an appreciation of the way in which analysts study choice behaviour. This chapter presents a number of examples to illustrate how transport modellers might use stated choice and revealed preference data. The applications are sufficiently varied to give an appreciation of the ways to approach the study of traveller behaviour.

The first study is an extension of the application used in chapter 6 for intercity non-business travel between Sydney, Canberra and Melbourne. Revealed preference data is enhanced with stated preference data to evaluate the demand for a new mode of transport – high speed rail. The second case study continues the same theme of high-speed rail for the Sydney–Canberra corridor, but with a different choice experiment. Case study 1 is based on an experiment in which all existing modes plus a new alternative are included in the design of the stated choice experiment, but in case study 2 only the new alternative defines the attribute combinations in a fractional factorial design. The high speed rail alternative offered to the market is compared to each traveller's current mode and attribute levels in three choice scenarios in which the decision is framed as a switching task.

Case study 3 illustrates how stated choice models are used to derive attribute valuations. Behavioural values of travel time savings are obtained for car travel by trading between a proposed toll road offering travel time savings and an existing untolled route. Case study 3 uses a choice experiment in which alternatives are unlabelled, and analysed as ranked alternatives. We use this example to extend the idea of single value of travel time savings to a valuation function in which the value of travel time savings is a function of the level of toll and trip time.

The fourth case study brings together SP and RP data in the context of choice of ticket type and mode for commuting in Sydney. Case study 4 reinforces the warning that estimating and applying a stand-alone SP model when elasticities and predictions are required is not to be recommended. Case study 4 provides a comparison of the elasticities associated with an HEV and MNL model for combined SP–RP data and stand-alone SP data.

The emphasis in this chapter is on the way that stated choice data are used and not on the details of how the choice experiments are designed *per se*.

11.2 Case study 1: introducing a new alternative: high speed rail and the random effects HEV model in an SP—RP context

The data used to illustrate the application of the HEV model are drawn from a 1986 pre-feasibility market study associated with a Very Fast Train (VFT) project in Australia. We extracted 197 surveys of non-business travel between Sydney, Canberra and Melbourne for analysis. The revealed preference (RP) mode choice set comprised four modes (plane, car, coach and conventional train). The stated preference (SP) choice set included the four RP modes plus a new high speed rail alternative. For their most recent intercity trip, each sampled decision maker provided details of the travel time components (access, line-haul and egress), the cost, and transfers (if public transport was used) of their chosen means of transport and each of the modal alternatives. Hensher and Bradley (1993) used these same data to estimate a joint fixed effect RP/SP model with a constant scale factor ratio between the RP and SP sources.

The SP experiment involved three three-level attributes (access plus egress time, in-vehicle or line-haul time for the main mode and total cost) that were used to describe five mode choice options (drive, fly, bus, current train and very fast train). There are $(3^3)^5$ possible choice sets that could be described by combinations of the attribute levels, which are too many to be observed in any feasible sampling approach. We constructed a subset of this larger design by using an orthogonal design to make 108 choice sets from a 3^{15} factorial.

Each sampled respondent received four choice sets that included the four RP modes plus a new high speed rail alternative. The task was individualised as follows: for their most recent intercity trip, each respondent self-reported their travel time components (access, line-haul and egress), cost and a transfer (if public transport was used for the mode they actually chose) and provided the same information for each other mode alternative. Respondents ranked the five mode options in each choice set in order of preference. The first-preference rank was defined as the chosen mode in the current example application.

MNL models with constant variance were estimated from the RP and SP data, respectively (table 11.1). Examination and comparison of these models shows that the sensitivity to mode attributes (travel time and cost) are of the same order of magnitude in both data sources. However, as noted in previous chapters, direct comparisons of choice model utility parameters from different data sources are not possible without controlling for variance differences because the estimated parameters confound scale and utility.

Table 11.1. *Heteroscedastic extreme value model estimation*

Parameter	RP MNL model estimated parameters (*t*-stats in parentheses)	SP MNL model estimated parameters (*t*-stats in parentheses)	RP + SP HEV model estimated parameters[1] (*t*-stats in parentheses)
Utility function (taste) parameters			
Alternative-specific constants			
Plane–RP	−0.228(−0.5)		1.981(2.8)
Train–RP	0.725(+3.0)		1.983(3.1)
Coach–RP	−0.225(−0.9)		1.897(2.1)
Car–RP	0	0	
Plane–SP		0.502(+0.4)	1.714(0.7)
VFT–SP		2.014(+2.2)	2.019(2.6)
Train–SP		−0.546(−1.2)	1.705(1.1)
Coach–SP		−0.736(−2.2)	1.768(0.4)
Car–SP		0	0
Generic mode attributes			
Cost ($)	−0.0259(−3.9)	0.0317(−2.0)	−0.00184(−2.0)
Door-to-door time (min)	−0.0039(−5.3)	−0.0027(−1.8)	−0.00018(−2.1)
Scale parameters			
Plane–RP	1.00		0.167{8.37(1.1)}
Train–RP	1.00		0.179{7.77(1.4)}
Coach–RP	1.00		0.152{9.13(1.2)}
Car–RP	1.00		1.465{0.95(2.8)}
Plane–SP		1.00	0.182{7.65(1.7)}
VFT–SP		1.00	0.154{9.04(1.9)}
Train–SP		1.00	0.192{7.22(1.7)}
Coach–SP		1.00	0.150{9.26(1.7)}
Car–SP		1.00	1.392{1.00}
Goodness-of-fit			
Log likelihood at convergence	−244.9	−220.4	−536.6
Rho-squared	0.096	0.301	0.373

Note: [1]Parameters in {·} are estimated standard deviations of error terms, and corresponding *t*-values.

Table 11.1 also presents the HEV model on the pooled RP/SP data, which controls for scale differences between RP and SP, in this case at the mode-specific level (the scale parameter for Car in the SP data set is normalised to one). In contrast, most academic and commercial applications of data fusion have not controlled for scale differences at the alternative level (e.g., Adamowicz et al. 1997, Ben-Akiva and Morikawa 1991, Hensher and Bradley 1993, Swait and Louviere 1993); instead, error terms have typically been assumed IID within data source, leading to a single variance ratio to be estimated.

The HEV model in table 11.1 reveals some significant scale parameters in the data, suggesting interesting comparisons within and between data sources. For example, note the similarity between the car scale parameters in the RP and SP data. This observation seems to hold for all common mode pairs across the two data sources, such that the ratio of the RP to SP scale factors for each mode is about unity. This suggests that the SP experimental choice task was well designed in the sense that it captured error variability levels comparable to those in the RP data; intuitively, this should enhance our ability to pool these data.[1]

Another interesting insight provided by the mode-specific scale factors can be seen by noting that the ratio of the scale factors of all modes in either data set to that of car is quite small (on the order of one-eighth). Hence, these other modes have error variances with an order of magnitude *greater* than that of car, both in the real market place and in the SP choice task. This further suggests that consumers as a group behave much less consistently (i.e., reliably) when evaluating non-car modes than when evaluating the car mode. These rich behavioural insights are indicative of the benefits of modelling heteroscedasticity in choice models, and are the basis for formulating potentially rewarding avenues of research to explain the behavioural foundations of the heteroscedastic errors (see appendix B6).

11.3 Case study 2: high speed rail and random effects HEV in a switching context

In 1994 Speedrail Pty Ltd proposed a high speed rail system to link Sydney and Canberra with a through train service of 75 minutes. Typical door-to-door travel times of 120 minutes contrast with plane times of 140 minutes, car times of 200 minutes, coach times of 220 minutes and existing train times of 320 minutes. Drawing on an extensive feasibility study in all markets, we illustrate the use of a random effects HEV model by estimating switching mode choice models for the current business air market, the second largest market in the corridor.

Seven attributes of strategic or policy interest were varied in the choice experiment. They are travel time by HSR, frequency of service, a range of fares and discounts available for a family/group. Attribute levels are summarised in table 11.2. Because the primary interest centres on switching, the design problem involves the creation of HSR profiles that respondents will compare to their most recently chosen mode for a trip in the corridor, and decide if they would stay with their last chosen mode or switch to the new mode once it is available. There are seven attributes, and each is assigned three levels. The complete factorial of possible HSR profiles, therefore, is a 3^7 ($= 2187$ combinations). Because all attributes are numerical, and their preference directionality

---

[1] However, note that this is not a necessary or sufficient condition for two or more data sources to be poolable.

Table 11.2. *The attribute set and levels for HSR*

Attributes	Levels
Station to station travel time (minutes)	3: high, medium, low (3 hours, 2 hours, 1 hour)
Daily one-way service frequency/headway	3: high, medium, low (hourly, 2-hourly, 3-hourly)
First class fare (one-way)	3: high, medium, low ($115, $95, $75)
Full economy class fare (one-way)	3: high, medium, low ($70, $60, $50)
Discount economy fare (one-way)	3: high, medium, low ($45, $35, $25)
Off-peak discount fare (one-way)	3: high, medium, low ($40, $30, $20)
Additional discount for a family (2 adults, at least 1 child < 16 yrs old)	3: high, medium, low (50%, 30%, 10%)

is known a priori, there is the possibility of dominant or dominated profiles. In this case, such profiles were eliminated from the final fractional factorial design because they should provide no useful information (Hensher and Barnard 1990). However, it should be noted that there is controversy over the effects of dominant/dominated options because in many designs it is not clear whether they dominate or are dominated by options such as 'choose none'. Thus, one may wish to exercise caution in eliminating such options from designs because they can have significant impacts on the statistical properties of the resulting designs. In the present case, we used a 3^{7-4} orthogonal fraction to create twenty-seven profiles, which were further reduced to eighteen profiles after eliminating dominant/dominated profiles.

The eighteen profiles permitted us to estimate only the main effects of the attributes; hence, the utility function in this case is strictly additive in the attribute effects. We randomly assigned the eighteen profiles to blocks of three, each of which constitutes a 'version' of the choice experiment survey. The blocks are shown below for profiles numbered 1 to 18 (table 11.3 contains profiles corresponding to these numbers):

$$\{17, 2, 18\}\{4, 13, 3\}\{16, 12, 5\}\{1, 15, 6\}\{7, 11, 9\} \text{ and } \{8, 10, 14\}.$$

A surveyed respondent was asked to evaluate one choice set at a time and to choose between their current mode of travel and HSR; indicating which fare class they would select if choosing HSR. This choice process was undertaken three times.

The example herein is limited to air business travel, although all current modes (i.e., car, coach, conventional train and air) and trip purposes were investigated in the larger study. A self-administered questionnaire was handed out as air passengers boarded a flight in Canberra or Sydney, completed on board the aircraft and handed in at disembarkation. Flights were sampled over three days in 1994 and at various times of the day to capture both the peak business market and off-peak travellers. Of 1400 questionnaires distributed, 56 per cent were returned. The stated choice data were used to model the effects of the policy variables on switching between the mode used on the most recent business air trip in the corridor and HSR in one of four fare classes.

Table 11.3. *The final set of choice sets for Speedrail for full Sydney–Canberra trip*

Set	Time	Frequency	First class	Full economy	Discount economy	Off-peak	Family/Group Discount
A01	3 hours	2 hourly	115	70	25	40	10
A02	1 hour	2 hourly	95	70	35	30	30
A03	3 hours	3 hourly	75	60	35	20	30
B01	2 hours	hourly	95	60	35	40	10
B02	2 hours	hourly	75	70	45	40	30
B03	1 hour	3 hourly	115	60	45	40	50
C01	3 hours	hourly	95	50	45	30	50
C02	1 hour	3 hourly	95	70	45	20	10
C03	2 hours	2 hourly	115	50	45	20	30
D01	1 hour	hourly	75	50	25	20	10
D02	2 hours	3 hourly	115	50	35	20	50
D03	2 hours	3 hourly	75	70	25	30	50
E01	3 hours	hourly	115	70	35	20	50
E02	1 hour	2 hourly	75	50	35	40	50
E03	3 hours	3 hourly	95	50	25	40	30
F01	3 hours	2 hourly	75	60	45	30	10
F02	1 hour	hourly	115	60	25	30	30
F03	2 hours	2 hourly	95	60	25	20	50

Multinomial logit (MNL) and random effects HEV switching models (see appendix B, chapter 6) were estimated following extensive exploratory analysis of the data to ensure that the final models were both behaviourally plausible and parsimonious in application. The set of attributes influencing modal switching and fare class choice includes travel time, travel cost and a household's ability to pay. The business market currently served by air travel is defined by four classes of air travel (first class, business class, full economy and discount economy). Average air fares range from $212 for first class to $99 for discount economy. Three of the four HSR fare classes were analysed because the off-peak HSR ticket was only chosen by two people.

Table 11.4 contains the results for the MNL model with the constant variance (CV) assumption and the HEV model with free variance. The HEV scale parameters are the inverse of the standard deviation of the random component of the utility expressions associated with each alternative. If the CV assumption holds, one expects all variances to be statistically indistinguishable (i.e., = 1.0 on normalisation). Constraining variance to 1.0 (HSY-dy) enables one to test deviation from unit variance. We re-normalised the scale parameters to a base of 1.00 for HSY-dy to compare scale parameters instead of standard deviations. The scale parameters for Air-fc, Air-bc, and Air-dy are very similar; in contrast Air-fy is quite different, and substantially higher. This provides evidence of significantly different mean variance, which in turn requires analysts to explicitly take this into account through different

Table 11.4. *Empirical results for the current business air market*

Variable	Alternative	MNL Utility parameter	MNL t-statistic	HEV Utility parameter	HEV t-statistic
One-way adult cost ($)	All	−0.0231	−6.00	−0.0127	−2.10
One-way total time (mins)	Air-fc,bc HSR-fc	−0.0222	−10.63	−0.0138	−2.72
One-way total time (mins)	Air-fy HSR-fy	−0.0229	−12.11	−0.0157	−2.69
One-way total time (mins)	Air-dy HSR-dy	−0.0138	−5.78	−0.0097	−2.68
Personal income ($'000s)	Air-fc,bc, HSR-fc	0.0308	7.76	0.0194	2.50
Personal income ($'000s)	Air-fy HSR-fy	0.0071	1.89	0.0051	1.37
Party size	Air-dy HSR-dy	0.1974	3.45	0.1408	1.92
First and business class constant	Air-fc,bc	2.3861	2.95	1.8765	2.46
Full economy constant	Air-fy	4.7944	7.29	3.8715	4.37
Discount economy constant	Air-dy	1.6370	5.41	1.6529	3.41
First class constant	HSR-fc	1.8460	3.12	1.5386	3.03
Full economy constant	HSR-fy	3.1733	6.13	2.6220	5.74
Scale parameter air first class	Air-fc			1.5368	2.30
Scale parameter air business class	Air-bc			1.4387	2.32
Scale parameter air full economy	Air-fy			2.3930	2.04
Scale parameter air disc. economy	Air-dy			1.4025	2.26
Scale parameter first class	HSR-fc			1.2785	2.51
Scale parameter full economy	HSR-fy			1.1904	2.54
Scale parameter disc. economy	HSR-dy			1.00	—
Log likelihood at convergence		−1348.01		−1354.59	
Adjusted pseudo-r^2		0.207		0.203	
Sample size		876		876	
Door-to-door value of travel time Savings ($/hour per adult)					
First and busines class travel		58		65	
Full economy travel		59		74	
Discount economy travel		36		46	

scales associated with each observed attribute. As previously discussed, this is one of the attractive features of HEV.

The attributes that influenced choice between fare classes and modes for the current business air market were air and HSR fares, door-to-door travel times, personal incomes and party sizes. HSR will minimise time spent at airports due to scheduling and minimum check-in time, and is also considerably less expensive than air travel. Relative to the discount economy fare class for both air and HSR, there was a statistically significant positive personal income effect, almost four and a half times greater at the margin for first and business class compared to full economy travel. Party size had a statistically significant positive influence on the selection of a discount economy ticket, as might be expected. Even within the business market, there often are groups travelling on business who seek relatively low fares.

Table 11.5. *Direct and cross share fare elasticities for Air–HSR business market*

	Air-fc	Air-bc	Air-fy	Air-dy	HSR-fc	HSR-fy	HSR-dy
Air-fc	−4.884 (−4.750)	0.262	1.173	0.264	0.343	0.302	0.040
Air-bc	0.127	−3.093 (−3.804)	1.009	0.201	0.261	0.215	0.030
Air-fy	0.205	0.358	−2.454 (−2.339)	0.307	0.401	0.314	0.042
Air-dy	0.125	0.222	0.981	−1.590 (−2.008)	0.253	0.202	0.028
HSR-fc	0.114	0.204	0.892	0.182	−1.295 (−1.782)	0.184	0.026
HSR-fy	0.106	0.189	0.805	0.165	0.212	−0.704 (−1.026)	0.025
HSR-dy	0.086	0.156	0.617	0.136	0.175	0.146	−0.402 (−0.748)

Note: Interpret this table by column. For example, a 1 per cent increase in HSR first class fares will reduce the probability of choosing HSR-fc by 1.295 per cent. This 1 percent increase in first class fares on HSR will increase the probability of choosing a discount economy air fare by 0.253 per cent, *ceteris paribus*. (Direct share elasticities from MNL model are in parentheses.)

Behavioural values of travel time savings are reported in table 11.4. For the current business air market, the mean estimates are relatively high ($36 per adult/hour to $74 per adult/hour), and represent a weighted mix of the components of travel time (in-vehicle, walk, wait and transfer times). If we assume that access and egress time are approximately valued at 1.5 times the main mode in-vehicle time (a generally accepted ratio) then the approximate value of in-vehicle time savings for the business air market ranges from $14.50 per adult hour for discount economy travellers to $29.50 per adult hour for other fare classes. This result is similar to that of Bhat (1995, table 1); who found that travel time savings for in-vehicle time across all modes in the Toronto–Montreal corridor business market was $Aus18.80 per person hour (at an exchange rate of $Aus1.0 = $US0.78).

A full matrix of direct and cross market share elasticities for fares derived from the HEV model are summarised in table 11.5. The relatively high direct share elasticities in the business market for air travel in the presence of HSR for first class and full economy fares is to be expected because HSR fares are much lower than their air fare class counterpart, and HSR door-to-door travel times are also faster for most origin–destination pairs.

The MNL model cross-elasticities are not informative because the constant variance assumption restricts them to be invariant across all pairs of alternatives. The direct elasticities from the MNL model are in parentheses to illustrate the difference between MNL and HEV due to the constant variance assumption. For example, the MNL direct share elasticities differ significantly from HEV for five of the seven air market alternatives. Unlike MNL's constant cross share, HEV cross share elasticities reveal degrees of modal substitution. For example, the fares policy of an airline competing with HSR may lead to substitution within air classes/fares owing to changing relative air fares, but when HSR is introduced the greatest substitution potential in the first class market is full economy air and in HSR-full economy there is potential from both first class and full economy.

11.4 Case study 3: valuation of travel time savings and urban route choice with tolled options in an SP context

The most important user benefit of transport project appraisal is travel time savings. Social benefit–cost studies require dollar valuations of time savings (VTTS) as input into the determination of aggregate user benefits. Valuing travel time savings is complex and controversial, given the diverse set of circumstances in which travel time can be saved. In addition, the value of travel time savings may itself be a function of the size of the time savings and the total time committed to an activity.

Increasingly stated choice methods are being used to investigate empirical values of travel time savings, since, unlike in revealed preference methods, one can expose individuals to a richer array of variations in the amount of time saved, trip lengths and prices of travel. (Hensher et al. 1989, Fowkes and Wardman 1988, Bradley and Gunn 1990, Hensher et al. (1994, 1998a). The possibility that a *valuation function*, as distinct from a unique value of travel time savings within a market segment, would be more realistic than a point estimate has been raised in the past (see Hensher and Truong 1984, Bradley and Gunn 1990), although little consideration has been given to this idea. Stated-choice data provide a suitable empirical paradigm within which to estimate a valuation function as a function of levels of travel time, trip cost, income and any other characteristics thought to influence valuation variability. We present some empirical results based on a stated choice study undertaken in Sydney in 1994 (Hensher 1998a), in which a sample of car users were given a series of travel-time/toll-cost tradeoff experiments and asked to select an alternative route, given the levels of each attribute.

11.4.1 Establishing sources of variability in VTTS

To begin our analysis we need a general expression for the VTTS, which we now derive. Assume that the indirect utility expression associated with an alternative i is defined in terms of travel cost (C_i) and travel time (T_i) given by equation (11.1)

$$V_i = \alpha_i - \lambda C_i - \kappa_i T_i \tag{11.1}$$

and that κ_i is a function of C_i and T_i such that

$$K_i = \kappa(T_i, C_i). \tag{11.2}$$

A Taylor series expansion of (11.2) around the mean levels $\bar{T}$ and $\bar{C}$ for each alternative i (neglecting second-order terms) results in equation (11.3):

$$\kappa_i = \bar{\kappa} + (\partial\kappa/\partial T)_i(T_i - \bar{T}) + (\partial\kappa/\partial C)_i(C_i - \bar{C}). \qquad (11.3)$$

Substitution of (11.3) into (11.1) and some rearrangement of terms gives

$$V = \alpha_i - \lambda C_i - \bar{\kappa}T_i + (\beta T_i^2 + \gamma C_i T_i + \omega), \qquad (11.4)$$

where $\beta = (\partial\kappa/\partial T)_i$, $\gamma = (\partial\kappa/\partial C)_i$, and $\omega = -\beta\bar{T} - \gamma\bar{C}$.

We neglect second-order terms in (11.4), which implies that $\partial\kappa/T$ and $\partial\kappa/\partial C$ are constants, independent of alternative I, hence parameters ω, β and γ are unsubscripted. The VTTS can now be derived from (11.4) as follows (Hensher and Truong 1984):

$$\begin{aligned} \text{VTTS} &= \frac{\partial V/\partial T}{\partial V/\partial C_i}\bigg|V_i = \text{constant} \\ &= \frac{-\bar{\kappa} + \gamma C_i + 2\beta T_i}{-\lambda + \gamma T_i}. \end{aligned} \qquad (11.5)$$

Thus, VTTS depends on the levels of travel time and cost and (11.5) can be generalised to account for the disaggregation of travel time such as the distinction between free flow travel time and delay time. Furthermore, one can include interactions between each travel time component and between travel time and other attributes of alternatives and individuals.

Naturally, the latter ability to enrich the valuation function and test richer specifications is limited by the quality of data. In particular, RP data are somewhat limited in their ability to provide sufficient richness in variability and correlation structure to enable each potential influence to be included without confoundment. However, data from stated choice experiments provide more opportunity to account for the independent (i.e., additive) contribution of each source of variability in the valuation function. The latter reason (amongst others) has encouraged the use of SP methods as important features of a preferred empirical way to obtain behavioural values of travel time savings.

11.4.2 Developing an empirical valuation function for urban route choice

As part of the development of a system of privately financed toll roads and tunnels within the Sydney Metropolitan Area, in 1994 the New South Wales Roads and Traffic Authority (RTA) evaluated the costs and benefits of a tunnel under one of Sydney's busiest traffic intersections. The Taylor Square intersection is a bottleneck for north–south traffic which otherwise would enjoy more fully the benefits of a recent freeway system upgrade except for the few kilometres of road through Taylor Square. An SP experiment was designed to determine how travellers' route choice would be influenced by different toll/travel-time regimes, and identify the sensitivity of the relevant travelling population to alternative levels of tolls as a function of different potential savings in travel time.

Table 11.6. *Route choice alternatives*

Route choice set	Tolled route: toll	Tolled route: total time	Free route: total time	Free route: delay time
A	$0.50	1.5 mins	9 mins	3 mins
B	$0.50	3 mins	6 mins	4 mins
C	$0.50	4.5 mins	12 mins	2 mins
D	$1.00	1.5 mins	6 mins	2 mins
E	$1.00	3 mins	12 mins	3 mins
F	$1.00	4.5 mins	9 mins	4 mins
G	$1.50	1.5 mins	12 mins	4 mins
H	$1.50	3 mins	9 mins	2 mins
I	$1.50	4.5 mins	6 mins	3 mins

Table 11.7. *The set of choice sets*

	Route choice sets								
Grouped choices	A	B	C	D	E	F	G	H	I
1		▲		▲				▲	
2			▲		▲				▲
3	▲					▲	▲		

Note: ▲ to table: means present in the grouped choices

This case involves a route choice decision in which a sample of travellers made choices between toll and free routes. Toll and free route options were described by a total of four attributes, and each attribute was varied over three levels. The choice experiment involved asking each sampled traveller to choose a toll or free route from two routes offered. Toll routes were defined by toll and total travel time (total travel time = delay + free moving time) that were varied over three levels (toll levels = $0.50, $1, $1.50; travel time levels = 1.5 mins, 3 mins, 4.5 mins) and delay time was fixed at zero. Free routes were defined by zero toll, total travel time varied over three levels (levels = 6 mins, 9 mins and 12 mins) and delay travel time varied over three levels (2 mins, 3 mins and 4 mins). All possible choice sets that can be constructed from these attributes and choice options are given by a 3^4 factorial. We used a 3^{4-2} orthogonal fraction to make nine choice sets, which is the minimum number of choice sets with acceptable statistical properties (Louviere 1988a, Hensher 1994). The resulting nine choice sets are shown in table 11.6. Each respondent was randomly assigned three of the nine choice sets as shown in table 11.7.

Surveys were distributed to 3900 southbound motorists as they were stopped at the traffic lights at Taylor Square during the period 24–29 March 1994. The sampling plan took into account differences by days of week and time of day to represent the distribution of trip purposes of motorists travelling on that route. The survey asked questions about characteristics of the motorist's trip being undertaken when they received the questionnaire, three choice sets that offered toll and free routes, and some socioeconomic characteristics of motorists. Respondents returned their completed surveys by mail in a pre-addressed reply-paid envelope, with 958 questionnaires received within two weeks of the end of the distribution of the surveys (a response rate of 25 per cent). After editing the data, 848 responses were used to estimate the model in the case study (a useable response rate of 22 per cent). Six trip purposes were identified in the survey and aggregated into five trip purposes for model segmentation:

- private commuter (PC), defined as a trip to work by driving a privately registered household vehicle;
- business commuter (BC), defined as a trip to work driving a company-supplied vehicle;
- travel as part of work (PW), which includes trips such as driving a car to the airport to travel by air on a business trip, and travel in the Sydney Metropolitan Area associated with earning a living, such as travel by a salesperson;
- non-work related travel, which includes social and recreation trips (SR), shopping trips, travel to the airport for a personal trip; and
- other personal business (OB).

The route choice models were MNL models which provide estimates of the effects of tolls, travel time and other influences (e.g., personal income, other socioeconomic variables). These models were used to derive trip-purpose specific time values, and (if necessary) probabilistic switching curves for a range of time savings and levels of toll.

11.4.3 Developing a valuation function

To identify the underlying structure of the choice experiment and understand how the valuation function is derived from the information in this experiment, we begin by defining the information potential of each attribute. Recall that each attribute in the route choice experiment had three levels, hence each can be represented as coded values (-1, 0, 1) or as actual levels (e.g., $0.5, $1 and $1.5). Attribute non-linearity can be captured by specifying a polynomial of degree two (quadratics) because all the attributes have three levels. Linear and quadratic terms were represented by orthogonal polynomials (table 11.8), as described in section 9.3.6, table 9.4a.

Table 11.8. *The construction of a quadratic polynomial*

Linear attribute	Quadratic attribute	v (attribute)
-1	1	v_1
0	-2	v_2
1	1	v_3

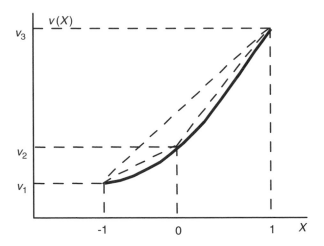

Figure 11.1 The role of the quadratic term

Let $v(X)$ denote the marginal utility arising from attribute X alone (e.g., travel time or cost). If $v(X)$ is non-linear in X, a second-order polynomial approximation for $v(X)$ can be written as equation (11.6):

$$v(X) = \alpha X + \beta X^2. \tag{11.6}$$

Information in table 11.8 allows one to derive relationships between $v(X)$ and X to illustrate the role of quadratic terms and why it is important to be able to test for non-linearity by separating out the independent contribution of X and X^2. The latter allows one to determine if both X and X^2 are required to capture the full effect of attribute X (which is limited to quadratic in this case because all attributes have three levels). That is, consider the two slopes in (11.6):

$$\alpha = (v_3 - v_2)/2, \tag{11.7}$$

$$\beta = [(v_3 - v_2) - (v_2 - v_1)]/6, \tag{11.8}$$

where α measures the mean slope between $X = 0$ and $X = 1$, and β measures the change in slope between $(X = -1, X = 0)$ and $(X = 0, X = 1)$ (see figure 11.1).

In addition to the non-linearity of each attribute's influence on the value of travel time savings, the possibility of two-way interactions between pairs of attributes needs to be considered. In fractional factorial designs the number of two-way interactions which are independent (i.e., orthogonal) of main effects (i.e., X and X^2) are determined by the fraction selected and the degrees of freedom of the design (see chapters 4 and 5). We are particularly interested in the interaction between toll and travel time, and hence will require a design that permits (at least) one independent two-way interaction. The quadratic term in the main effect of travel time and the interaction of toll and time allows us to evaluate the empirical form of the valuation function. As can be seen from

Table 11.9. *The orthogonal design for the route choice experiment*

Toll (C)	Total time toll route (T1)	Move time free route (T2)	Delay time free route (T3)	T_1^2	T_2^2	T_3^2	CT_1
−1	−1	0	0	1	−2	−2	1
−1	0	−1	1	−2	1	1	0
−1	1	1	−1	1	1	1	−1
0	−1	−1	−1	1	1	1	0
0	0	1	0	−2	1	−2	0
0	1	0	1	1	−2	1	0
1	−1	1	1	1	1	1	−1
1	0	0	−1	−2	−2	1	0
1	1	−1	0	1	1	−2	1

equation (11.4), a valuation function (as distinct from a single value) arises from a specification that includes quadratic and/or interaction terms. In addition to the relationships established amongst the attributes of the stated choice experiment, it is possible to interact other variables, such as socioeconomic characteristics, with the design attributes to enable further segmentation within the valuation function. The full design is in table 11.9 (for attributes shown in table 11.6).

The quadratic of an orthogonally coded attribute is not equivalent to the quadratic of the actual value of that attribute (i.e., (actual cost)^2 ≠ (orthogonal value)^2); hence a mapping from one metric to the other is required. The MNL model was estimated with the orthogonal codes, but we need to determine the value of travel time savings based on the actual levels of the attributes shown to the sampled population.

To do this, define the orthogonal level as N and the actual level as A. Then for a three-level attribute, we can define

$$N = \theta_0 + \theta_1 A, \tag{11.9}$$

$$N^2 = \delta_0 + \delta_1 A + \delta_2 A^2. \tag{11.10}$$

Denote the three levels for A as low (L), medium (M) and high (H) and L^2, M^2 and H^2 for A^2. Given the orthogonal codes for N (−1, 0, 1) and N^2 (1, −2, 1), substitution into equations (11.9) and (11.10) gives the following transformation functions:

$$-1 = \theta_0 + \theta_1 L, \tag{11.11}$$

$$0 = \theta_0 + \theta_1 M, \tag{11.12}$$

$$1 = \theta_0 + \theta_1 H, \tag{11.13}$$

where $\theta_1 = 1/\Delta_i$, $\theta_0 = -M/\Delta_i$, and $\Delta_i = M - L = H - M$ (assuming equal spacing for attribute i), and

$$1 = \delta_0 + \delta_1 L + \delta_2 L^2 \tag{11.14}$$

$$-2 = \delta_0 + \delta_1 M + \delta_2 M^2 \tag{11.15}$$

$$1 = \delta_0 + \delta_1 H + \delta_2 H^2 \tag{11.16}$$

and $\delta_2 = 3/\Delta_i^2$, $\delta_1 = -6M/\Delta_i^2$, and $\delta_0 = -2 + 3M^2/\Delta_i^2$.

The utility expressions associated with the tolled and free routes as estimated using orthogonal coded attribute levels can now be specified:

$$V_{\text{toll}} = \eta + \eta_1 C + \eta_2 T + \eta_3 T^2 + \eta_4 CT, \tag{11.17}$$

$$V_{\text{free}} = \eta_5 MT + \eta_6 MT^2 + \eta_7 DT + \eta_8 DT^2, \tag{11.18}$$

and translated from orthogonally coded to actual levels of attributes as follows:

$$V_{\text{toll}} = \omega + \omega_1 c + \omega_2 t + \omega_3 t^2 + \omega_4 ct, \tag{11.19}$$

$$V_{\text{free}} = \omega_5 mt + \omega_6 mt^2 + \omega_7 dt + \omega_8 dt^2. \tag{11.20}$$

Defining M_i as the actual mean level of attribute i and Δ_i as the step change in the level of attribute i, we derive the following conversion relationships:

$$\omega_1 = [\eta_1 \Delta_c - M_t \eta_4/(\Delta_c \Delta_t)]$$

$$\omega_2 = [\eta_2/\Delta_t - 6M_t \eta_3/\Delta_t^2 - M_c \eta_4/(\Delta_c \Delta_t)]$$

$$\omega_3 = [3\eta_3/\Delta_t^2]$$

$$\omega_4 = [\eta_4/\Delta_c \Delta_t]$$

$$\omega_5 = [\eta_5/\Delta_{mt} - 6M_{mt}\eta_6/\Delta_{mt}^2]$$

$$\omega_6 = [3\eta_6/\Delta_{mt}^2]$$

$$\omega_7 = [\eta_7/\Delta_{dt} - 6M_{dt}\eta_8/\Delta_{dt}^2]$$

$$\omega_8 = [3\eta_8/\Delta_{dt}^2],$$

where

M_c = medium level of toll (1)

Δ_c = \$0.50

Δ_t = 1.5 minutes

Δ_{dt} = 1 minutes

Δ_{mt} = 2 minutes

M_t = medium level of time on toll road (3 mins)

M_{mt} = medium level of move time (6 mins), and

M_{dt} = medium level of delay time (3 mins).

Table 11.10. *The partial correlation structure of actual attribute levels*

Free route	dt	dtsq	mt	mtsq	
delay time (*dt*)	1.0				
delay time squared (*dtsq*)	−0.995	1.0			
move time (*mt*)	−0.298	−0.295	1.0		
move time squared (*mtsq*)	−0.299	−0.295	0.982	1.0	

Toll route	tl	tlsq	tm	tmsq	tltm
toll (*tl*)	1.0				
toll squared (*tlsq*)	0.990	1.0			
time (*tm*)	−0.00068	−0.0099	1.0		
time squared (*tmsq*)	−0.00001	−0.0090	0.990	1.0	
toll by time (*tltm*)	0.664	0.650	0.692	0.686	1.0

Table 11.10 highlights the confoundment associated with utility parameter estimation if the attributes are not orthogonally coded. For the free route, the partial correlations vary from 0.995 for time and time-squared to −0.295 for all of the other combinations of attributes. For the tolled route the range is 0.991 to −0.00001.

Once we identify the values of η_i, $i = 1, \ldots, 8$, values of ω_i, $i = 1, \ldots, 8$, can be derived and the values of travel time savings calculated given actual values of travel times and toll. The behavioural values of travel time savings for each travel time (i.e., time of toll road, move time of free route and delay time of free route) can be obtained by substitution into equation (11.5). That expression assumes statistically significant parameter estimates for linear and quadratic time and the two-way interaction between toll and tollroad travel time. A distribution of values of travel time savings can be obtained by application of a range of tolls and travel times, and means, modes and medians can be estimated from the distribution. We now turn to the model estimation and derived results.

11.4.4 Empirical evidence

The final models for each of the five trip purpose segments are summarised in table 11.11. Each model has an interaction term between travel time and toll, but the quadratic term for time squared was not statistically significant in any model and so was eliminated. The behavioural values of travel time savings as a function of the level of toll and trip length (in minutes), expressed in dollars per person hour (see equation 11.5), are reported in table 11.12 for a reasonable range of tolls ($1 to $2) and trip lengths for the tolled section of the trip (5 to 10 minutes).

For each trip purpose segment VTTS increases for a given travel time as the toll level increases, and decreases for a given toll level as travel time increases; hence VTTS is inversely related to trip length. So, for a given toll individuals are willing to outlay

Table 11.11. *The route choice model results and time values*

	PC	BC	PW	SR	OB
Number of observations	1292	538	796	1034	1058
Toll-specific constant	−0.769	−0.279	0.599	0.050	0.410
	(−4.03)	(−0.95)	(2.48)	(2.26)	(1.58)
Toll	−1.0661	−0.984	−0.858	−0.997	−0.631
	(−8.34)	(−5.50)	(−5.89)	(−7.29)	(−3.47)
Travel time (toll route)	−0.311		−0.274	−0.303	−0.435
	(−2.98)		(−6.00)	(−2.21)	(−2.30)
Travel time (free route)	−0.532			−0.732	−0.304
	(−3.70)			(−4.53)	(−1.43)
Travel time (both routes)		−0.325			
		(−2.68)			
Toll × travel time	−0.274	−0.458	−0.418	−0.054	−0.310
(toll route)	(−1.60)	(−1.82)	(−1.78)	(−0.24)	(−1.06)
Personal income	−0.020	−0.018	−0.013	−0.017	−0.013
(free route) ($ pa)	(−4.59)	(−3.34)	(−2.69)	(−3.76)	(−2.22)
Likelihood ratio index	0.15	0.21	0.29	0.24	0.20

Note: *t*-statistics in brackets.

less money to save a unit of time for longer trips compared to shorter trips, a finding consistent with the results reported by Hensher (1976). As might be expected, the variation in VTTS is relatively flat in models where the two-way interaction between toll and travel time is not statistically significant (i.e., social-recreation travel).

To assess the empirical implications of deriving a valuation function and hence a distribution of VTTS from a model estimated on the *actual* attribute levels from revealed preference data, we re-estimate the private commuter model. The VTTS in brackets in table 11.12 derived from this model are consistently smaller and noticeably flat. The lack of variability and reduced values can be attributed to the amount of correlation in the model, which is revealed in table 11.10 (i.e., partial correlations between each main effect such as toll and travel time, and the two-way interaction is, respectively, 0.664 and 0.692). Lack of independence affects the mean parameter estimates for all three relevant attributes, and provides a strong cautionary about using actual levels of attributes to estimate *valuation functions*.

If we use the mean travel time and toll in the choice experiment for the toll route, we find that the VTTS is close to the figures in bold in table 11.12 for each trip purpose segment. It is worth noting that the travel time parameter in the free route alternative table 11.11, is more negative than the toll route parameters when statistically significant. The difference in travel time between the two routes is described by the component of travel time called 'delay time' in free routes. Consequently, the difference in the size of the parameters indicates the amount of congestion and possibly the degree of reliability associated with travel time on free routes compared to toll routes. Thus, the

Table 11.12. *Behavioural VTTS derived from a valuation function*

Toll	Time = 5 mins	Time = 7.5 mins	Time = 10 mins
Private commute			
Pinc = $19.81/hr			
$1	**4.35** (2.07)	3.29 (2.01)	2.65 (1.96)
$1.5	8.18 (2.44)	6.20 (2.33)	4.99 (2.30)
$2	12.01 (2.81)	9.10 (2.73)	7.33 (2.65)
Business commute			
Pinc = $26.17/hr			
$1	**7.07**	4.78	3.61
$1.5	12.81	8.66	6.54
$2	18.55	12.55	9.48
Travel as part of work			
Pinc = $23/hr			
$1	**4.59**	3.08	2.31
$1.5	10.50	7.04	5.29
$2	16.41	11.00	8.27
Social-recreation travel			
Pinc = $18.4/hr			
$1	**5.68**	5.23	4.85
$1.5	6.70	6.17	5.72
$2	7.73	7.12	6.60
Other personal business			
Pinc = $18.86/hr			
$1	**8.33**	5.57	4.19
$1.5	14.27	9.55	7.17
$2	20.21	13.52	10.16

Notes: Pinc = average hourly personal wage rate; Time refers to the trip length for the part of the trip where a toll would be incurred (and to the door-to-door trip time). Each VTTS (e.g., 4.35) is expressed in dollars per person hour. VTTS in brackets for private commute are derived from a model estimated on actual levels of attributes.

approach to the design of the stated choice experiment was useful for establishing the influence that trip reliability has on route choice.

11.5 Case study 4: establishing a fare elasticity regime for urban passenger transport: non-concession commuters with SP—RP and HEV

11.5.1 Background

Public transport operators increasingly use revenue optimising techniques in establishing mixtures of ticket types and fare levels. In predicting the response of the market to specific fare classes and levels (e.g., weekly tickets), a knowledge of how various market segments respond to both the choice of ticket type within a public transport mode and the choice between modes is crucial to the outcome. In some circumstances interest lies in evaluating the patronage and revenue implications of variations in offered prices for the existing regime of fare classes; in other circumstances interest lies in changes in fare class offerings via deletions and/or additions of classes.

A missing ingredient in many operational studies is a matrix of appropriate direct and cross fare elasticities that relate to specific fare classes within a choice set of *fare class* opportunities. Surprisingly, the research literature contains little empirical evidence detailed enough to distinguish sensitivities to particular fare class offerings within a predefined choice set of offerings. There is a plethora of empirical evidence on direct elasticities (Oum et al. 1992, Goodwin 1992), primarily treated as unweighted or weighted average fares within each public transport mode, but Mayworm, Lago and McEnroe (1980) and Oum et al. (1992) note that there is only limited evidence on cross-elasticities.

This case study does not rely on average fares, and distinguishes between fare classes for two public transport modes (train, bus) and the automobile for commuting in the Sydney Metropolitan area. Full matrices of direct and cross-share elasticities are derived for three train fare classes, three bus fare classes and car travel for commuters on non-concessionary tickets. We combined SP data with a knowledge of current modal attributes from RP data to assess travellers' ticket and mode choice decisions. This allowed us to evaluate sizeable variations in the levels of fares in each ticket class so that operators could extend policy intelligence beyond market experience.

11.5.2 Microeconomic specification of the indirect utility function for choice alternatives

The functional form of the conditional indirect utility expression defining the set of attributes that underlie the probability of mode choice is typically assumed in RP models to be linear and additive, although logarithmic or Box–Cox transformations sometimes are used to improve statistical 'fits' (e.g., Gaudry, Jara-Diaz and de Dios Ortuzar 1988), or quadratic terms are used in SP models with mean centred or orthogonal codes for each attribute (see previous case study, for example). Derivation of functional forms from microeconomic theory are exceptional in most transportation *modal choice* applications, although many more examples exist in other transport applications (especially automobile choice, see Hensher et al. 1992, Mannering and Winston 1985, Train 1986).

One exception in mode choice is Jara-Diaz and Videla (1989), who derived an appropriate functional form for the indirect utility expression for a discrete mode choice model from microeconomic principles, showing that the inclusion of the income effect is accommodated by the inclusion of a quadratic term in cost and segmentation of the sample by income. It has been known for some time (but often ignored) that the inclusion of income as a separate explanatory variable serves only as a proxy for unobserved attributes of alternatives such as comfort and convenience or other dimensions of preference, not captured by the utility parameters (e.g., Hensher 1984). One can interact cost and income by dividing modal cost by the wage rate (e.g., Train and McFadden 1978) and implicitly treat income as an endogenous variable that depends on the number of hours worked at a given wage rate, in contrast to its role as an exogenous variable in an individual's budget constraint.

In fact, if one estimates SP models with higher-order cost terms (e.g., quadratics), one consciously or unconsciously tests the presence/absence of the income effect. Unfortunately, all too often analysts also use income as an additive explanatory variable in $J - 1$ alternatives and interpret its utility parameter as a measure of the marginal utility of income. In fact, the marginal utility of income is a derivative of the cost variables, as shown by Jara-Diaz and Videla (1989); hence, an income effect must be included in the indirect utility expressions for *all* alternatives.

Formally, after Jara-Diaz and Videla (1989) and Hensher (1997b), for a sampled individual with a set of utility parameters and income I, define a vector of non-modal trip goods X and a vector of associated prices P. The attributes of available modes, including trip cost (c_j), are given by a vector A_j. These are the observed and unobserved sources of utility, introduced into an indirect utility function evaluated by a decision maker to arrive at a choice. Imposing the separability condition on the numeraire non-trip goods, and given modal alternatives defined by a set of utility-weighted modal attributes, individuals are assumed to behave as if they are maximising utility by comparing the set of modal alternatives, subject to the separability assumption for X and each of $A_j, j = 1, 2, \dots, M$ modes. That is,

$$\max\{\max[U_1(X) + U_2(A_j)] | PX' + c_j \leqslant I\}; \quad j \in \{1, \dots, M\}; \quad X \in x.$$
(11.21)

A conditional indirect utility function can be derived from (11.21) by the application of Roy's identity (a well-known relationship in economics between indirect utility, prices, income and demand for goods), to yield equation (11.22):

$$V(P, I - c_j, A_j) = V_1(P, I - c_j) + U_2(Q_j),$$
(11.22)

where the maximum conditional indirect utility is attributed to the chosen alternative from a mutually exclusive set of alternatives. Jara-Diaz and Videla (1989) demonstrate that if one takes a higher-order Taylor series expansion this implies solving equation (11.23), re-expressed as equation (11.24):

$$\max_j \left[V_1(P, I) + \sum_{i=1}^{n-1} \frac{1}{i!} V_1^i(P, I)(-c_j)^i + \frac{1}{n!} V_1^n(P, I)(-c_j)^n + U_2(A_j) \right]$$
(11.23)

$$\max_j \left[\sum_{i=1}^{n-1} \frac{1}{i!} V_1^i(P, I)(-c_j)^i + \frac{1}{n!} V_1^n(P, I)(-c_j)^n + U_2(A_j) \right].$$
(11.24)

Equation (11.24) provides an empirical opportunity to evaluate the dependency of mode choice on income. That is, if we include (at least) a quadratic term for cost (equation (11.25)), we establish the potential for income dependency:

$$V_i = \alpha_{0i} + \beta_{c1i}c_{1i} + \beta_{c2i}c_{2i}^2 + U_2(A_i).$$
(11.25)

In the words of Jara-Diaz and Videla (1989, 396):

> if a single model with utility in c_i, c_i^2, and A_i were run for the whole popula-
> tion, a null coefficient of c_i^2 would be consistent with a single coefficient for
> $c_i, \ldots$, but a significant coefficient of c_i^2 would be contradictory with the
> model, since V_I^i should be a function of I. Note that I is not explicitly
> included in V, but significant c_i^2 terms for each segment would suggest the
> existence of a more general $\ldots V(c_i, t_i, I)$ function.

Thus, if β_{c2i} is positive and statistically significant, an income effect exists and one
must segment by income so that income affects all alternatives in the choice set, or
include income in all indirect utility expressions. If one establishes that there is an
income effect, in the interest of maintaining a single discrete-choice model, one needs
to introduce income into all indirect utility expressions in a way that is consistent with
microeconomic theory. One appealing way is to adopt the approach promoted by
Train and McFadden (1978), Hensher et al. (1992), Jara-Diaz and de Dios Ortuzar
(1988), Jara-Diaz and Videla (1989) and Jara-Diaz (1998): a first-order expansion of
indirect utility yields a model in which money cost is divided by the expenditure rate,
the latter defined as the ratio of household income to leisure (or non-work) time. This
specification represents income as purchasing power. The marginal utility of income is
given by:

$$\frac{\partial V_i}{\partial I} = \beta_{c1i} + 2\beta_{c2i}c_{2i}. \tag{11.26}$$

When embedded in a discrete-choice model the cross-elasticities derived from equation (11.25) are choice elasticities. This case study concentrates on establishing a full
matrix of direct- and cross-choice (or share) fare elasticities using more behaviourally
appealing econometric methods and RP data combined with SP data. These estimates
become important inputs into a subsequent optimisation procedure proposed and
implemented by Taplin, Hensher and Smith (1999) to derive a matrix of ordinary
demand elasticities.

11.5.3 The empirical context

A sample of commuters and non-commuters was surveyed in the Sydney Metropolitan
Area in 1995 as part of a study of the mix and level of public transport fares. Within
each market segment patterns of modal and ticket use behaviour were captured to
identify both current behaviour and potentials to switch to alternative mode and ticket
uses under a range of alternative fare policies for the public bus, ferry and train
systems (Hensher and Raimond 1995). The choice of mode and ticket type is estimated
using a mixture of RP and SP data.

Respondents in the survey were asked to think about the last commuter trip they
made, where they went, how they travelled, how much it cost, etc. They were also
asked to describe another way that they could have made that trip if their current
mode had not been available. Their current behaviour constitutes the RP data.

Table 11.13. *Illustrative set of show cards for the SP experiment 1: bus or train for a short trip*

BUS FARES		TRAIN FARES	
Single	$0.60	Single	$0.80
Travel ten	$4.00	Off peak return	$0.90
(*10 single trips*)		(*purchase after 9am*)	
Travel pass	$8.60	Weekly	$6.80
(*7 days bus/ferry*)		(*7 days train only*)	
Travel pass	$10.00	Travel pass	$10.00
(*7 days bus/ferry/train*)		(*7 days bus/ferry/train*)	

Note: The experiment is based on answers to the following: 'You have told us that you could use either a Bus or Train as the main form of transport to travel to the destination that we have discussed. If public transport fares changed and were priced as shown, would you have used Bus or Train as the main form of transport for your trip? Which ticket type would you choose?'

This SP case involves a mode choice experiment in which public transport fares of current and alternative methods of travel were varied under a series of different pricing scenarios. The choice set was determined exogenously based on the physical availability of each alternative (including the availability of a car as a driver or passenger) for the journey to work. Fare (ticket) prices were varied over three levels (+50 per cent of current, current, −50 per cent of current). We developed separate fractional factorial designs for bus vs. train (eight ticket types), bus vs. car (four ticket types and car), and train vs. car (four ticket types and car). Respondents were asked to choose a mode of transport and, if they chose public transport, they also selected a fare. Automobile operating cost was fixed at the marginal perceived cost of 9 cents/km. Each respondent was randomly assigned four choice sets from the ultimate design. Table 11.13 contains an example of one choice set in the bus vs. train experiment.

A special challenge in this SP case is the need to present all individuals with realistic scenarios. People use different modes and travel over many different distances, hence one must develop a range of choice sets that contain different mode choice combinations and travel distances. The experiment is individualised in the sense that interviewers questioned respondents before the choice experiment was administered to determine which modes and levels of travel time/distance were appropriate for which respondents.

In order to accomplish the individualisation, the choice experiment was tailored to each individual's self-reported commuting trip attribute levels for their main mode (car, train, bus). Depending on their self-reporting of lengths of time spent in their main mode only (i.e., not access, egress or waiting times), they were assigned to experimental conditions for short trips (less than 15 minutes), medium trips (15–30

Table 11.14. *The stated choice experiment fare categories and levels*

	Low Fare	Current Fare	High Fare
Train: single (Off peak return)			
Short	$0.80 ($0.90)	$1.60 ($1.80)	$2.40 ($2.60)
Medium	$1.30 ($1.40)	$2.60 ($2.80)	$3.90 ($4.20)
Long	$1.80 ($2.00)	$3.60 ($4.00)	$5.40 ($6.00)
Train: Weekly			
Short	$6.80	$11.50	$18.30
Medium	$9.70	$19.40	$29.00
Long	$13.20	$26.00	$40.00
Train: Travel pass			
Short	$10.00	$20.00	$30.00
Medium	$14.00	$28.00	$42.00
Long	$20.00	$39.00	$59.00
Bus: Single			
Short	$0.60	$1.20	$1.80
Medium	$1.30	$2.50	$3.80
Long	$2.00	$3.90	$5.90
Bus: Travel ten			
Short	$4.00	$8.00	$12.00
Medium	$8.00	$16.00	$24.00
Long	$16.00	$32.00	$48.00
Bus:Travel pass (Bus/Ferry)			
Short	$8.60	$17.10	$26.00
Medium	$11.70	$23.00	$35.00
Long	$17.20	$34.00	$52.00
Bus: Travel pass (Bus/Ferry/Train)			
Short	$10.00	$20.00	$30.00
Medium	$14.00	$28.00	$42.00
Long	$19.50	$39.00	$59.00

minutes) or long trips (over 30 minutes).[2] An experimental design was developed based on one car choice option, four train ticket options (single, off-peak, weekly and travel pass) and four bus ticket options (single, travel ten, combined bus–ferry travel pass, and combined bus–ferry–train travel pass). Thus, as many as nine alternatives were possible for any respondent. The range of fares varied in the choice experiment is summarised in table 11.14.

11.5.4 Developing the stated choice experiment

The experimental designs were created as follows:

1. Car versus bus or ferry. Buses or ferries each had four ticket types, and the fares for each ticket type were varied over three levels (table 11.14). Thus the total

---

[2] Note that this application is ideal for computerized interviewing, as discussed in chapter 9.

number of possible ticket types for each choice experiment is a 3^4, from which we selected nine on the basis of an orthogonal 3^{4-2} fraction.

2. Bus versus train. As before, bus has four ticket types, and train has three. Each ticket type was assigned three fare levels (table 11.14), which means that there are 37 possible combinations of bus and train ticket options. We used an orthogonal main effects design based on the 6×3^6 factorial available in Hahn and Shapiro (1966) to make eighteen choice sets.

3. Car versus train. This design problem is the same as car versus bus or ferry, except that train has one less ticket type, so the number of combinations is 3^3. We used an orthogonal 3^{3-1} fraction to make nine choice sets.

4. Bus versus ferry. This design is identical to bus versus train, with the additional complication that both bus and ferry have four ticket types, and hence the number of possible choice sets is given by a 3^8 factorial. Thus, the design for this problem is larger than the design for bus versus train because the 6×3^6 is too small, so we used a 3^{8-5} fraction to generate twenty-seven choice sets for this experiment.

For each of the four modal choice contexts, a sampled individual was randomly assigned four choice sets. Face-to-face home interviews were conducted in households sampled by randomly choosing postcodes within each Local Statistical Area in Sydney, and within each postcode randomly by choosing a street to be cluster sampled. The sampling unit was the mode, to ensure enough sampled individuals currently choosing each alternative mode.

11.5.5 Empirical results

The RP choice set was choice-based, so correction of the RP subset of alternatives in the joint SP–RP model was undertaken by weighting that part of the likelihood function via the application of weights to the RP alternatives, defined by the ratio of the sample shares to the known population shares. This guarantees the reproduction of the base market shares at the ticket type level for the RP choice set. Additionally, all observations were exogenously weighted by the distribution of personal income for commuter demand as revealed in the 1991 Sydney Travel Survey. Although the survey included ferry and jet cat options, we excluded them from the analysis because most cities have only trains and buses available as public transport competing with the automobile. We also excluded taxis from the commuter sample.

The effective response rate was 37 per cent, which is about average for surveys of equivalent length (Richardson, Ampt and Meyburg 1995). While the full sample collected was 649 cases, not all cases had sufficient data to be suitable for modelling. The sample is a fairly broad representation of the Sydney population, though males and the elderly are slightly under-represented (see Hensher and Raimond 1995 for further details).

A final HEV model jointly estimated with seven SP and seven RP alternatives is given in table 11.16 (HEV) (summary statistics are in table 11.15). A joint SP–RP MNL model was estimated in which the scale parameter was fixed at 1.0 for the RP

Table 11.15. *Summary statistics of estimation sample*

Stated preference sub sample	Out of pocket cost ($)	Door to door time (mins)	Captive to PT (proportion)	Car available (proportion)	Sample size
Total sample					
Train single	2.89 (1.50)	69.4 (29.6)	0.081	–	540
Train weekly	2.11 (1.90)	69.4 (29.6)	0.081	–	540
Train travel pass	3.18 (1.61)	69.4 (29.6)	0.081	–	540
Bus single	2.34 (1.49)	53.6 (26.5)	0.119	–	472
Bus travel ten	1.67 (1.23)	53.6 (26.5)	0.119	–	472
Bus travel pass	1.54 (0.83)	53.6 (26.4)	0.119	–	472
Car	2.88 (2.63)	44.9 (33.3)	-	0.80	812
Sample who chose that alternative					
Train single	2.09 (1.18)	57.18 (31.3)	0.112	–	98
Train weekly	1.90 (0.92)	74.09 (28.3)	0.127	–	150
Train travel pass	2.31 (1.28)	71.58 (31.3)	0.083	–	60
Bus single	1.36 (0.63)	37.55 (21.4)	0.182	–	55
Bus travel ten	1.15 (0.74)	42.21 (21.3)	0.208	–	77
Bus travel pass	1.55 (1.16)	48.56 (21.2)	0.365	–	52
Car	2.14 (2.07)	34.17 (23.8)	–	1.0	420
Revealed preference sub sample					
Total sample					
Train single	1.64 (1.19)	64.29 (31.1)	0.044	–	272
Train weekly	2.46 (0.85)	72.58 (28.6)	0.317	–	248
Train travel pass	1.28 (1.32)	79.60 (27.8)	0.200	–	45
Bus single	2.37 (1.29)	51.26 (24.5)	0.074	–	324
Bus travel ten	1.17 (0.67)	60.60 (32.8)	0.160	–	100
Bus travel pass	1.94 (0.31)	46.25 (20.7)	0.333	–	48
Car	2.12 (2.04)	44.88 (33.3)	–	0.80	812
Sample who chose that alternative					
Train single	2.15 (1.21)	59.91 (30.7)	0.088		136
Train weekly	2.59 (0.79)	74.82 (27.8)	0.130		216
Train travel pass	2.40 (1.50)	82.50 (40.1)	0.500		32
Bus single	2.05 (1.19)	38.33 (19.0)	0.250		96
Bus travel ten	1.08 (0.54)	37.08 (21.7)	0.333		48
Bus travel pass	1.99 (0.30)	47.78 (20.9)	0.444		36
Car	1.39 (1.03)	33.23 (23.3)	–	1.00	372

Note: Standard deviations are in parentheses.

Table 11.16. *HEV model: joint estimation of SP and RP choices to evaluate the presence of an income effect*

Attribute	Units	Alternative	SP parameter estimates	*t*-value	RP parameter estimates	*t*-value
One-way trip cost (or fare)	Dollars	All	−0.3496	−4.15	−0.3496	−4.15
Trip cost squared	Dollars	All	0.0036	0.79	0.0036	0.79
Door-to-door time	Minutes	Train	−0.0186	−4.44	−0.0186	−4.44
Door-to-door time	Minutes	Bus	−0.0265	−4.95	−0.0265	−4.95
Door-to-door time	Minutes	Car	−0.0251	−5.86	−0.0251	−5.86
Train single constant		Train	7.8198	3.84	8.7959	3.98
Train weekly constant		Train	8.2091	3.93	10.319	4.17
Train travel pass constant		Train	8.0665	3.90	9.2150	3.31
Bus single constant		Bus	8.3482	4.00	9.4006	4.13
Bus travel ten constant		Bus	8.2200	3.95	9.6701	4.08
Bus travel pass constant		Bus	8.1234	3.94	9.7870	3.34
Car constant		Car	–	–	–	–
Captive to train dummy	1.0	Train	1.0657	2.42	1.0657	2.42
Captive to bus dummy	1.0	Bus	1.4792	3.44	1.4792	3.44
Car availability dummy	1.0	Car	9.2935	4.09	9.2935	4.09
Scale parameters						
Train single		Train	0.962 (1.3336)	3.58	1.515 (0.8467)	3.73
Train weekly		Train	0.527 (2.4358)	2.46	0.340 (3.7723)	1.33
Train travel pass		Train	0.559 (2.2941)	3.57	0.557 (2.3045)	1.11
Bus single		Bus	0.510 (2.5139)	3.14	0.307 (4.1828)	1.16
Bus travel ten		Bus	0.780 (1.6448)	3.51	0.353 (3.6309)	1.18
Bus travel pass		Bus	0.515 (2.4926)	3.01	0.615 (2.0844)	1.82
Car		Car	3.338 (0.3842)	4.25	1.283 (1.0000)	Fixed
Value of travel time savings						
Train	$/hour	3.36				
Bus	$/hour	4.75				
Car	$/hour	4.60				
Sample size		1824				
Log likelihood at convergence			−1547.64			
Pseudo R^2		0.730				

Notes: Value of travel time savings is calculated per one-way trip based on average number of one-way trips per ticket; the scale parameter is derived from the standard deviation estimate, the latter being set equal to 1.0 for the car alternative in the SP choice set. Given that , it follows that $\sigma_{iq}^2 = \pi^2/6\lambda^2$ will not be based on 1.0; standard deviations are in parentheses.

Table 11.17. *MNL model: joint estimation of SP and RP choices*

Attribute	Units	Alternative	SP parameter estimates	*t*-value	RP parameter estimates	*t*-value
One-way trip cost	Dollars	All	−0.4532	−9.74	−0.4532	−9.74
Door-to-door time	Minutes	Train	−0.0407	−10.49	−0.0407	−10.49
Door-to-door time	Minutes	Bus	−0.0469	−10.07	−0.0469	−10.07
Door-to-door time	Minutes	Car	−0.0363	−10.67	−0.0363	−10.67
Train single constatn		Train	1.8519	5.90	3.2493	8.36
Train weekly constant		Trai	2.1117	6.45	4.7789	12.03
Train travel pass cosntant		Train	1.5604	4.90	3.3961	5.16
Bus single constant		Bus	1.7664	5.65	3.1103	7.28
Bus travel ten constant		Bus	2.0134	6.36	3.6646	6.87
Bus travel pass constant		Bus	1.4553	4.50	4.2722	7.25
Car constant		Car	–	–	–	–
Captive to train dummy	1.0	Train	1.5632	4.21	1.5632	4.21
Captive to bus dummy	1.0	Bus	2.0861	4.73	2.0861	4.73
Car availability dummy	1.0	Car	2.9438	9.10	2.9438	9.10
Scale parameters						
Train single		Train	0.954	10.47	1.0	
Train weekly		Train	0.954	10.47	1.0	
Train travel pass		Train	0.954	10.47	1.0	
Bus single		Bus	0.954	10.47	1.0	
Bus travel ten		Bus	0.954	10.47	1.0	
Bus travel pass		Bus	0.954	10.47	1.0	
Car		Car	0.954	10.47	1.0	
Value of travel time savings						
Train	$/hour	5.41				
Bus	$/hour	6.22				
Car	$/hour	4.81				
Sample size		1824				
Loglikelihood at convergence		−2322.43				
Pseudo R^2		0.774				

choice set but estimated as a free (but fixed) parameter for all SP choice sets as summarised in table 11.17. The mean of cost for multi-trip tickets is derived from the ticket price divided by the number of one-way trips actually undertaken by each commuter, allowing for the use of the ticket for non-commuting travel (often overlooked in valuation). The off-peak train single trip option was deleted because few commuters chose it; and we had to combine the two bus travel passes (bus/ferry and bus/ferry/train) to ensure that enough commuters choose one of those ticket types. McFadden (1984: p. 1442) has stated that, 'As a rule of thumb, sample sizes which yield less than thirty responses per alternative produce estimators which cannot be analysed reliably by asymptotic methods.'

The distribution of SP costs encompasses the RP cost levels, although the composition of the sample in terms of captivity to public transport *given a ticket type* differs quite markedly. This is expected because all SP fare options within a mode were offered to each respondent, but the RP data defined only the chosen ticket (or mode) and the one (self-reported) viable alternative. One notable difference was multi-use tickets (e.g., train weekly, travel pass and bus travel ten), in which the higher incidence of RP captivity to public transport reflects reality much better than the SP profile. Including captivity and car availability in both SP and RP choice sets, however, is a valid application of contextual impacts on choices because one expects greater substitution between fare classes than between modes as a result of higher incidences of public transport captivity (all else equal). Importantly, this effect can be observed and modelled if ticket types are treated endogenously. Previous studies that used average fares or a single fare type per commuter to evaluate modal choice could not represent the amount of movement between ticket types as a contributing response to price changes. Thus mode choice models that ignore the reality of ticket-type switching may forecast some switching between modes that actually would be ticket switching within modes; hence there is a potential for overestimating the impact of fare policies on modal choice, unless within-mode cross elasticities approach zero.

Fare or cost was included initially as a non-linear effect estimated by linear and quadratic terms (equation (11.25)). The quadratic effect of cost was positive but not statistically significant (table 11.16) in the HEV model. Cost and cost-squared were mean centred to ensure that they were not highly correlated, which reduced their partial correlations from 0.95 to 0.33. Interestingly, the quadratic of cost was highly significant (*t*-value of 9.06) in the MNL model, suggesting confoundment of scale and utility parameters, which can be identified separately in HEV models. Previous studies that investigated income effects (e.g., Jara-Diaz and de Dios Ortuzar 1988, Jara-Diaz and Videla 1989 with a universal choice set of nine alternatives) may have incorrectly interpreted the presence/absence of income effects because they relied on simple MNL, which constrains the unobserved variance to be equal across alternatives. Consequently, based on HEV, we conclude that there is no income effect, which may be intuitively plausible in this case in which only a small amount of an individual's budget goes to commuting-use-related marginal costs.

The level-of-service attributes represented by mode-specific door-to-door travel time were statistically significant, producing behavioural values of travel time savings at the sample mean of fare or cost that were $3.36 per person hour for train, $4.60 per person hour for car, and $4.75 per person hour for bus. Public transport values were substantially lower than those derived from MNL ($5.41 for train and $6.22 for bus), but the value for car was only slightly lower (MNL value of $4.81). The HEV and MNL car values were comparable to the $4.35 per person hour value found in another recent Sydney route choice study (Hensher 1997b), and similar to findings of a recent commuter mode choice study for six capital cities in Australia (Hensher 1998a). Although somewhat premature, one might be tempted to suggest that relaxing the constant variance assumption redistributes the potential time benefits of modes in favour of the automobile, away from the relatively inflated behavioural values of travel time savings for public transport:

> in the basic logit model ... [is] ... the result of failure to account for some unobserved influences on relative utility which are suppressed through the constant variance assumption and consequently 'distributed' to the observed effects. (Hensher 1998b: 239).

If one identifies an income effect, personal income should be introduced into the utility expression for *every* alternative, in line with the theoretical requirement set out in section 11.5.2. We estimated a model in which cost was divided by the expenditure rate, but we do not discuss them because only one effect differed. None the less, it is worth noting that a likelihood ratio test yields a chi-square value of 52.06 with one degree of freedom which suggests that the two models differ significantly in goodness of fit, such that the zero income effect model has greater explanatory power than the income effect model.

When scale differences across all alternatives in both the SP and RP data are taken into account, parameter estimates for each attribute common to alternatives that appear in both SP and RP data sets should be generic (see chapter 8). There is no microeconomic theoretical reason (except for measurement differences) to treat them as data set specific, which traditionally has been the assumption in sequential and joint estimation of SP–RP models that link a single scale parameter to all alternatives in a specific data set (e.g., Morikawa 1989, Hensher and Bradley 1993).

11.5.6 Fare type and car cost direct and cross share elasticities

The final set of direct and cross-elasticities are reported in table 11.18. The reported results are probability weighted average estimates, derived from estimates for each individual in the sample. Each column provides one direct share elasticity and six cross share elasticities. These direct or cross elasticities represent the relationship between a percentage change in fare level and a percentage change in the proportion of daily one-way trips by the particular mode and ticket type.

For example, the column headed TS tells us that a 1 per cent increase in the train single trip fare leads to a 0.218 per cent reduction in the proportion of daily one-way trips by train on a single fare. In addition, this 1 per cent single fare increase leads to a 0.001 per cent higher proportion of one-way trips on a train travel pass and 0.001 per cent increase in one-way trips on a train weekly ticket.

The set of fare elasticities associated with a joint SP–RP model are based on the SP parameter estimates of fare and cost, rescaled to the RP model to provide the choice probabilities and fare (or car cost) attribute levels. The HEV model is not a closed form expression, hence its elasticity formula is complex (see appendix B to chapter 6). For completeness and comparison, table 11.18 contains direct and cross elasticities from the SP partition of the joint SP–RP HEV model, the joint SP–RP MNL model and the stand-alone SP-MNL and RP-MNL model. The cross elasticities for a joint and stand-alone MNL model are uninformative.

Table 11.18. *Direct and cross share elasticities*

	TS	TW	TP	BS	BT	BP	Car
Train weekly (TS)	**-0.218** (-0.702) [-0.161, -0.517] {-0.057, -0.317}	0.001 (0.289) [0.146, 0.110] {0.134, 0.073}	0.001 (0.1490) [0.031, 0.067] {0.004, 0.039}	0.057 (0.012) [0.052, 0.035] {0.048, 0.023}	0.005 (0.015) [0.025, 0.041] {0.012, 0.029}	0.005 (0.009) [0.021, 0.024] {0.018, 0.018}	0.196 (0.194) [0.427, 0.601] {0.134, 0.199}
Train weekly (TW)	0.001 (0.213) [0.062, 0.087] {0.054, 0.053}	**-0.093** (-0.635) [-0.057, -0.313] {**-0.018**, -0.197}	0.001 (0.358) [0.031, 0.067] {0.004, 0.039}	0.001 (0.025) [0.052, 0.035] {0.048, 0.023}	0.001 (0.024) [0.025, 0.041] {0.012, 0.029}	0.006 (0.019) [0.021, 0.024] {0.018, 0.018}	0.092 (0.229) [0.427, 0.601] {0.134, 0.199}
Train travel pass (TP)	0.001 (0.210) [0.062, 0.087] {0.054, 0.053}	0.001 (0.653) [0.146, 0.110] {0.134, 0.073}	**-0.196** (-1.23) [-0.111, -0.597] {**-0.002**, -0.368}	0.001 (0.023) [0.052, 0.035] {0.048, 0.023}	0.012 (0.022) [0.025, 0.041] {0.012, 0.029}	0.001 (0.017) [0.021, 0.024] {0.018, 0.018}	0.335 (0.218) [0.427, 0.601] {0.134, 0.199}
Bus single (BS)	0.067 (0.023) [0.062, 0.087] {0.054, 0.053}	0.001 (0.053) [0.146, 0.110] {0.134, 0.073}	0.001 (0.031) [0.031, 0.067] {0.004, 0.039}	**-0.357** (-0.914) [-0.217, -0.418] {**-0.141**, -0.239}	0.001 (0.248) [0.025, 0.041] {0.012, 0.029}	0.001 (0.286) [0.021, 0.024] {0.018, 0.018}	0.116 (0.096) [0.427, 0.601] {0.134, 0.199}
Bus travel ten (BT)	0.020 (0.020) [0.062, 0.087] {0.054, 0.053}	0.004 (0.037) [0.146, 0.110] {0.134, 0.073}	0.002 (0.023) [0.031, 0.067] {0.004, 0.039}	0.001 (0.206) [0.052, 0.035] {0.048, 0.023}	**-0.160** (-0.462) [-0.083, -0.268] {**-0.017**, -0.159}	0.001 (0.163) [0.021, 0.024] {0.018, 0.018}	0.121 (0.090) [0.427, 0.601] {0.134, 0.199}
Bus travel pass (BP)	0.007 (0.025) [0.062, 0.087] {0.054, 0.053}	0.036 (0.063) [0.146, 0.110] {0.134, 0.073}	0.001 (0.034) [0.031, 0.067] {0.004, 0.039}	0.001 (0.395) [0.052, 0.035] {0.048, 0.023}	0.001 (0.290) [0.025, 0.041] {0.012, 0.029}	**-0.098** (-0.700) [-0.072, -0.293] {**-0.005**, -0.154}	0.020 (0.103) [0.427, 0.601] {0.134, 0.199}
Car (C1)	0.053 (0.014) [0.062, 0.087] {0.054, 0.053}	0.042 (0.023) [0.146, 0.110] {0.134, 0.073}	0.003 (0.013) [0.031, 0.067] {0.004, 0.039}	0.066 (0.009) [0.052, 0.035] {0.048, 0.023}	0.016 (0.011) [0.025, 0.041] {0.012, 0.029}	0.003 (0.066) [0.021, 0.024] {0.018, 0.018}	**-0.197** (-0.138) [-0.130, -0.200] {**-0.265**, -0.361}

Note: Elasticities relate to the price per one-way trip. The RP elasticity precedes the SP elasticity in any pair. SP direct and cross elasticities from the HEV model (table 11.16) are in parentheses ( ). The direct elasticities from the stand-alone RP- and SP-MNL models are in square brackets [ ]. Cross elasticities for the stand-alone SP-MNL model and the stand-alone RP-MNL model are given in [ ]. The MNL RP and SP direct and cross elasticities are in braces { } from the joint SP–RP MNL model in table 11.17. The interpretation for a specific fare class is obtained under each column heading.

A comparison of the HEV and MNL RP elasticities shows a systematically lower set of direct elasticity estimates for all public transport alternatives in the MNL model (and vice versa for car). We might conclude that an SP model tends to produce lower elasticities than its RP counterpart when the SP choice probabilities are higher than the RP probabilities (which is the situation here). The MNL direct elasticity estimates for public transport alternatives tend to be lower than their HEV counterparts in both RP and SP models (and vice versa for car). The implication, *if generalisable* (given the observation that the less-chosen modes in an RP setting are chosen more often in an SP setting), is that previous studies that used an MNL and/or a stand-alone SP model specification may have sizeable errors in estimation of direct share elasticities.

11.5.7 Conclusions

The results for case study 4 are based on estimation of MNL and HEV models using a mixture of SP and RP data. The utility parameters associated with trip fares in the SP model were rescaled by the ratio of the variances associated with fare for a particular alternative across the two data sources, so that the richness of the fare data in the SP experiment could enrich the RP model. The resulting matrix of direct and cross elasticities reflects the market environment in which commuters make actual choices, while benefiting by an enhanced understanding of how travellers respond to fare profiles not always observed in real markets, but including fare profiles which are of interest as potential alternatives to the current market offerings.

A better understanding of market sensitivity to classes of tickets is promoted as part of the improvement in management practices designed to improve fare yields. In this final case study we have examined a number of approaches to estimating a matrix of direct and cross price share elasticities, and provide for the first time a complete asymmetric matrix.

11.6 Conclusions to chapter

The case studies presented in this chapter present a broad perspective on how transportation analysts have used and can use SP methods to predict demand and market share as well as derive marginal rates of substitution between attributes that influence choices. The number of applied studies is expanding rapidly as the benefits of combining revealed preference and stated choices are realised. The reader should have enough background from earlier chapters to be able to use the methods discussed in a wide range of transport applications in both passenger and freight sectors.

12 Environmental valuation case studies

12.1 Introduction

During the past thirty years the valuation of environmental goods and services has become one of the most heavily researched areas within environmental economics. Several techniques for valuing goods and services that do not ordinarily enter the market system have been devised. One of the emerging areas in valuation is the use of SP theory and methods in the valuation of environmental goods and services. SP techniques offer many advantages in this area, and their consistency with random utility theory allows them to be used to generate economic measures of benefits (or costs) associated with changes in environmental service flows.

This chapter reviews the general topic of environmental valuation, and more specifically, the use of SP techniques in valuation. This is followed by an examination of two case studies. The first case study illustrates the use of SP in measuring the value of recreation, in which SP is used as a stand-alone tool for valuation and combined with RP data for the same activity. The second case study examines the use of SP in the valuation of an endangered-species conservation programme, in which SP is used to elicit consumer preferences over environmental goods and services where there is no behavioural trail (i.e., no market in which to compare SP and RP data). Finally, advanced issues in the use of SP for environmental valuation are discussed, including the relationship between SP and the most common direct environmental valuation technique: contingent valuation.

12.2 Environmental valuation: theory and practice

Many aspects of the natural environment are 'valuable' to people but their value may not be reflected in the market system. People value such activities as hiking and camping, but prices paid for these activities tend to be set administratively, and are

This chapter © 1998 Wiktor Adamowicz, and has been prepared for inclusion in this volume.

often quite low (or even zero). The public values clean air, but cannot easily buy it in a market-like setting. The economic value of these activities, if priced and offered in market-like settings, would result from the interaction of supply and demand.[1] However, for a variety of reasons, environmental goods and services have not been incorporated into the market system, and hence their economic values are largely unknown and often under-represented in economic analysis.[2] In the past thirty years economists (and others) have devised methods to determine the value of environmental goods and services and express them in monetary terms. Thus, the process of environmental valuation represents an attempt to place environmental goods on a par with market goods so that they can be evaluated using the same money metric.

Environmental values include values for recreation, scenery, aesthetics and health. Linkages between the environment and water quality, air quality and other aspects of environmental quality also can be viewed as environmental values. Some environmental goods may have administrative fees that reflect a portion of their value (e.g., licence fees for hunting), but others have no apparent market or price (e.g., scenery). As with the assessment of any other economic value, environmental values are measured as the amount an individual would be willing to pay for an increase in the quality or quantity of a good or service, or the amount they would be willing to accept in compensation for a decrease in the quality or quantity.

There are two types of environmental values, namely *use values* and *passive use values*. Use values are values related to some use, activity or traceable economic behavioural trail. Outdoor recreation consumption (of any form) typically requires expenditures on travel and other goods, and despite the fact that recreation may not be priced in a market, expenditures on recreation-related items provide a behavioural trail that can be used to develop a value of the environmental good. Effects of changes in scenery or aesthetic attributes of forest environments on real estate values also can be viewed as use values. Passive use values, on the other hand, have no clear behavioural trail. These values include existence values, bequest values and other values not typically expressed directly or indirectly through any market.

In the past, use values have been measured by a number of techniques, depending on the issue at hand and the data available. Techniques for measuring use values can be characterised either as direct (i.e., they use conversational or hypothetical question approaches) or indirect (i.e., they use existing use data to develop models of behaviour in the face of environmental change). Direct methods include contingent valuation[3]

---

[1] Economic value is often defined as the amount one is willing to pay or willing to accept for a good or service. However, there are significant technical complexities in the actual determination of such values, even for market goods (see Freeman 1993).

[2] Environmental goods and services are often not incorporated into the economic system because they possess 'public goods' characteristics. That is, one person's consumption of clean air does not come at the expense of another person's consumption, and one person cannot generally exclude another person from consuming 'their' clean air. These characteristics make it difficult to construct market-like systems for environmental goods.

[3] Contingent valuation is a direct questioning technique that asks individuals what they would be willing to pay for a change, contingent on there being a market for the good. This technique will be discussed and compared to SP methods later in the chapter.

(Mitchell and Carson 1989; Freeman 1993) and SP methods, while indirect techniques include travel cost models commonly used in recreation demand (Freeman 1993, Bockstael et al. 1991), hedonic price models used in property value analysis (Freeman 1993) and a host of production function methods that examine the impact of environmental change on outputs or expenditures (Freeman 1993; Braden and Kolstad 1991).

Passive use value is defined as an individual's willingness to pay for an environmental good, even though he or she may never intend to make (or may be barred from making) any active use of it. That is, the individual derives satisfaction from the mere existence of the good. There is no behavioural trail, hence only direct methods such as contingent valuation can be used to elicit passive use values. It is worth noting that there is still some controversy about the existence of passive use values (not just their measurement), and whether they are an economic phenomenon (Diamond and Hausman 1994). Passive use values (assuming they exist and are relevant) are associated with public goods or quasi-public goods. Wilderness areas, wildlife habitat, protected areas and other such environmental goods may have passive use values associated with them.

Because they elicit preferences or trade-offs for attributes of goods or services that may or may not currently exist, SP techniques can be used to measure use or passive use values. It also is easy to combine SP techniques with RP methods to develop improved choice models. We now turn to an analysis of the use of SP in the context of measuring the value of outdoor recreation, one of the most heavily researched non-market activities.

12.3 Case study 1: use values – recreational hunting site choices

The demand for recreation has been heavily researched in the environmental economics literature. This is partly because recreation forms a natural link between market activities (travel, expenditures on campsites, etc.) and the environment (scenery, wildlife, etc.). Environmental changes often affect recreationists, and through these changes in demand, economic activities in regions located near recreation sites are affected. During the early 1960s advances in benefit–cost analysis and efforts to improve the use of non-market benefits in benefit–cost analysis focused on incorporating recreation values (and changes therein) in benefit–cost calculations.

In the case study that follows we examine the links between recreation and industrial forestry in western Canada. Industrial forestry activities change landscapes and affect wildlife populations, and change access to forest areas because roads are constructed as part of forestry activities. Thus, forestry impacts on recreation are not necessarily positive or negative. For example, certain wildlife populations may improve after forestry activity and access may also be enhanced. Yet, if forest harvesting activity takes place in certain ways, wildlife populations may decline partly from changes in habitat and also from too many additional recreationists.

This case study examines recreational hunting site choice in the north-western region of Alberta, Canada.[4] Recreational hunting is an important regional activity that generates a significant amount of economic impacts. Forestry activity also is sizeable, and has a major influence on the landscape. The research question is 'What are the likely effects of forest harvesting (and associated access changes) on recreational hunting site choices and values?' Thus, our objective is to understand the impact of changes in environmental attributes (access, landscape, wildlife populations, etc.) on the recreational hunting population and to translate these changes into economic values. The measures of economic values ultimately are used to help design forest harvesting activities that maximise the sum of forestry and recreation values by choosing appropriate levels and areas for forest harvesting.

12.3.1 Study objectives

The objectives of the study were to develop a decision support tool that could be used to predict recreational hunting site choice[5] in the face of changes to the landscape brought about by forestry activities and other forces. This decision support tool was intended to provide industry with a way to evaluate the non-market value of recreation along with the market values of forest harvesting as input to decisions about where and when to harvest. Thus, the SP study objective was to design a task (SP survey) for recreationists that would reveal how their site choice behaviour would be likely to change in response to changing environmental characteristics. Secondary objectives were to collect RP data on actual choice so that these data could be combined with SP data (or used on their own) and obtain information on perceptions of environmental quality attributes at the hunting sites.

It is worth noting that RP data alone could be used to answer some of the questions described above. However, as described in chapter 8, RP data often suffer from the fact that attributes are very collinear and/or their range of values is limited and may not include levels important to policy analysts. In this study there was little variation in some RP attributes, such as level of access to recreation sites and degree of congestion at sites. Thus SP data were required to accurately assess changes in these types of attributes. Furthermore, one easily can imagine situations in which congestion levels could rise to levels not previously experienced. Responses to this type of change require SP data because RP data contain no such information. Such examples often arise in environmental economic analysis. For instance, in a recent case in the north-western United States, changes to river and reservoir levels were proposed in an attempt to restore salmon populations to viable levels (see Cameron et al. 1996 for details). Recreationists (boaters, water skiers, swimmers, etc.) had not previously experienced these water level change magnitudes; hence, it is unlikely that RP data

---

[4] This case study is based on research reported in McLeod et al. 1993, Adamowicz et al. 1997 and Boxall et al. 1996. Further details can be found in these papers.

[5] The choice set in this case is the set of Wildlife Management Units (WMUs) in the west central region of Alberta, Canada. This set of WMUs overlaps with the forest management area of interest.

could predict responses to changes. Moreover, water quality and recreation facility attributes tend to be quite correlated because areas with good water quality and high scenic quality also tend to have developed beach facilities. Thus, SP analysis is required to separate the effects of water quality from the effects of development and facilities.

12.3.2 Qualitative study

Focus groups with hunters were used to provide qualitative input to the study (see chapter 9 for a discussion of the use of focus groups in SP choice studies). Sessions were held in a central facility and tape recorded so the discussions could be more fully analysed subsequently. The main purpose of the focus groups was to identify and refine the site attributes that were important to the group. Also, focus groups are useful for understanding the words and phrases (or more generally 'language') that individuals use to describe and discuss the attributes. For example, moose hunters are interested in harvesting animals. Thus one assumes that moose populations in a region would be an important attribute in site choice. Yet, listing the 'number of moose per square kilometre' meant little to the focus group participants. Instead, they were more comfortable with such descriptions like as 'seeing or hearing moose' or 'seeing signs of 1 or 2 moose per day'. Similarly, for such attributes as degree of site congestion, the absolute number of people encountered was not relevant; instead, hunters wanted to know if they would encounter people on foot or people in vehicles.

The focus groups allowed us to identify the attributes in table 12.1, which are actually quite small in number. The focus groups also provided information relevant to describe the attributes in the SP task. We experimented with written site descriptions and artists' renderings of site characteristics, but the focus groups demonstrated the superiority of written descriptions.

12.3.3 Data collection, instrument design and sampling frame

Surveys were administered to samples of hunters selected from Alberta Fish and Wildlife Services licence records. The hunters were sampled from five locations, four located within the study area plus Edmonton, a large metropolitan centre located about 200 km outside the area. Each hunter was sent a letter notifying them that a study was being conducted and that they would be phoned to ask them to participate. Next, hunters were phoned and asked to attend a group in their town or city. Hunters were provided with incentives to attend the groups (commemorative pins containing the likeness of a moose were given to each participant at the meetings, a cash prize was drawn at each meeting and one large cash prize was awarded after all meetings were completed). A total of 422 hunters were phoned, 312 of which confirmed that they would attend the groups, and of these, 271 (87 per cent of recruitments) actually attended. There were eight central facility group sessions held in various locations in the study area, with group sizes ranging from twenty to fifty-five hunters. Sessions were tape recorded (there was discussion during the completion of survey tasks), and a

Table 12.1. *Attributes used in the moose hunting stated preference experiment*

Attribute	Level
Moose populations	Evidence of <1 moose per day
	Evidence of 1–2 moose per day
	Evidence of 3–4 moose per day
	Evidence of more than 4 moose per day
Hunter congestion	Encounters with no other hunters
	Encounters with other hunters on foot
	Encounters with other hunters in ATV
	Encounters with other hunters in trucks
Hunter access	No trails, cutlines, or seismic lines
	Old trails passable with ATV
	Newer trails, passable with 4WD vehicle
	Newer trails, passable with 2WD vehicle
Forestry activity	Evidence of recent forest activity
	No evidence of forestry activity
Road quality	Mostly paved, some gravel or dirt
	Mostly gravel or dirt, some paved sections
Distance to site	50 km
	150 km
	250 km
	350 km

Note: ATV = All terrain vehicle; 2(4)WD = 2(4) wheel drive.

representative of the Provincial Fish and Wildlife Agency was at each meeting to answer general questions about hunting issues.

Each hunter completed five survey components: (1) demographics, (2) SP task, (3) a record of moose hunting trips (RP information), (4) a contingent valuation question[6] and (5) site-by-site estimates of perceptions of hunting site quality. The order of the last four components was randomised to test for section-order bias. Further details of the survey design and data collection process can be found in McLeod et al. (1993).

The SP task consisted of a series of SP choice sets (hunting site scenarios) with two hunting site options and a third option of not going hunting. The situation was presented as '. . . If these were the only sites available on your next trip – which alternative would you choose?' Hunters are familiar with situations in which sites (Wildlife Management Units or WMUs) are closed for all or part of the season, hence, it was credible for them to consider choosing between only two alternatives or not going at all. The set of attributes and levels presented in table 12.1 were used to create choice sets using a $(4^4 \times 2^2) \times (4^4 \times 2^2)$ orthogonal main effects design, which produced thirty-two choice sets that were blocked into two versions of sixteen choice sets

---

[6] A discrete-choice contingent valuation question was included to compare the results of this approach with the SP task. These results are reported in Boxall et al. 1996.

Table 12.2. *Example choice set from the moose hunting site task*

Features of hunting area	Site A	Site B
Distance from home to hunting area	50 kilometres	50 kilometres
Quality of road from home to hunting area	Mostly gravel or dirt, some paved	Mostly paved, some gravel or dirt
Access within hunting area	Newer trails, cutlines or seismic lines, passable with a 2WD vehicle	Newer trails, cutlines or seismic lines passable with a 4WD truck
Encounters with other hunters	No hunters, other than those in my hunting party, are encountered	Other hunters, on ATVs, are encountered
Forestry activity	Some evidence of recent logging found in the area	No evidence of logging
Moose population	Evidence of less than 1 moose per day	Evidence of less than 1 moose per day
Tick ONE box only:	☐ A	☐ B ☐ Neither

each. Each respondent was randomly assigned to one version. Each therefore evaluated sixteen pairs of descriptions of moose hunting sites plus the option of choosing neither site (hence, not going moose hunting). An example of one of the choice sets is presented in table 12.2.

12.3.4 Model estimation

A variety of models can be estimated using the data collected in this study.[7] The SP data alone can be used to estimate models, the RP data about choices plus data on the 'objective measures'[8] attributes of the actual sites could be used, and/or RP data plus data on the perceptions of attributes of the actual sites can be used. Of course all three

---

[7] The estimation results reported here are based on Adamowicz et al. 1997 in which more detail on the estimators can be found.

[8] Even within 'objective measures' of attributes like moose population level and levels of hunter congestion there is a certain amount of variation or error since these measures are not perfectly collected. These 'objective measures' typically provided by government agencies can be considered a form of agency perception of the attributes of the sites.

types of data could be combined in joint estimation (data fusion, as it is sometimes called – see chapter 8). A further issue is the degree to which preferences for hunting sites differ between segments in the hunter population. A key finding from previous research in this area is that preferences differ between hunters who reside in urban areas and those who reside in rural areas. Below we investigate issues of data fusion and heterogeneity using a variety of model forms, but for simplicity as well as comparison purposes we begin by presenting MNL estimates of the SP model parameters.

Estimates of the MNL choice model parameters are in the first column of table 12.3. Two alternative-specific constants represent the two hunting alternatives in the choice set (the 'don't go hunting alternative' has a constant equal to zero for identification purposes). These constants are positive and statistically significant at the 95 per cent level, indicating that, everything else held constant, the respondents receive more utility from hunting than not hunting. Travel cost (measured as the distance to the alternative times a factor that converts distance into travel costs) is negative and significant. All remaining variables are effects coded (see chapter 9) and are either two- or four-level variables. (For example, road quality is a two-level attribute, and the tabled negative parameter represents poor road quality (unpaved roads). Thus, the parameter for the better road quality (paved roads) is positive (1 – the parameter for unpaved roads). Nevertheless, this parameter is not significant, suggesting that hunting site choice is unaffected by the site's road quality.) Levels of access significantly affect choice, and the first level of access (no trail) and the fourth level of access (2WD access) are both negative. The estimate of the parameter corresponding to the reference (in this case, fourth) level of an effects coded attribute is the negative of the sum of parameters of the other attributes (again, see chapter 9). Thus, as congestion increases from no hunters to hunters in vehicles, utility declines. Similarly, as moose populations increase, utility increases.

The second model in table 12.3 includes interactions of rural or urban residence (individual characteristics) with the attributes in the SP model. These interactions involve effects codes (urban hunters = 1, rural hunters = −1); hence, interaction coefficients are added to main effects for urban hunters and subtracted for rural hunters. Urban hunters have smaller absolute travel cost parameters, which may be because they tend to take fewer but longer trips, hence are less sensitive to distance and cost. Urban hunters also seem significantly more sensitive to lack of trails (no-trails), but their preferences for other attributes (including moose populations) appear similar to rural hunters.

Table 12.3 also presents results of an RP model based on hunters' actual trips, and a combined model for both RP and SP data (see chapter 8 for a description of the estimation methods for combined RP–SP models). Note that several parameters in the RP model could not be estimated because there was insufficient variation in the 'real world' data to identify the preferences for some attributes. All parameters can be estimated in the pooled model, including alternative specific constants for every real wildlife management unit. Our results indicate that both models (RP and SP) capture the same underlying preferences once error variance differences are taken into account (see Adamowicz et al. 1997). That is, error variance differences reflected in the θ_1 term in table 12.3 account for differences in preference parameters between the two data sets.

12.3.5 Policy analysis: economic welfare measurement

The objective of the SP task and associated model estimates was to understand the economic impact of changing attributes of moose hunting sites. In economic terms this is known as *welfare measurement*, which refers to the amount that individuals are willing to pay for quality or quantity changes. In this study, welfare measures refer to the amounts that individuals are willing to pay in additional travel costs for quality improvements. This provides a way to 'monetise' the benefits of environmental improvements to measure them on the same scale as and compare them to other land uses already measured in monetary terms (e.g., forest harvesting benefits).

The SP model results can be used to forecast changes in hunting site choice if attributes of a site are changed. For example, if companies engage in forest harvesting practices that enhance moose populations, individuals are attracted to sites; and conversely, if forest harvesting results in lower moose populations, hunters will go elsewhere. In the present case SP results are used to help predict what will happen to the visitation rates for fourteen actual wildlife management units (WMUs).

To determine the economic welfare impact of a change we go one step beyond predicting changes, as explained in the following example. Suppose there is only one WMU and hunters always choose to go hunting (an abstraction, of course, but it helps to understand welfare measurement). To examine the monetary impact of a quality change, one could compare situations before and after the change. In particular, let V^0 be the 'utility' before the change, defined by the utility expression estimated from the MNL model (e.g., column 2 of table 12.3). If we simplify V^0 to include only price (travel cost) and a generic quality factor Q, utility can be expressed as

$$V^0 = \beta_1 \text{(Price)} + \beta_2(Q). \tag{12.1}$$

Suppose we wish to examine a change from level of quality Q to Q'. Assume for the time being that $Q' > Q$ and $\beta_1 < 0$, $\beta_2 > 0$. The economic welfare impact of the change from Q to Q' is the price increase in the new situation (CV, or compensating variation in equation 12.2) that makes a person as well off in the original situation as they will be under the quality improvement. That is, we wish to find the CV quantity (amount) that solves the following expression:

$$V_0 = \beta_1 \text{(Price)} + \beta_2(Q) = \beta_1 \text{(Price} + CV) + \beta_2(Q') = V^1. \tag{12.2}$$

Thus, CV is the amount of money that equates the original utility level (V^0) with the subsequent utility level (V^1).[9]

---

[9] Much of the fundamental theory behind welfare measurement in discrete-choice models has been developed by Small and Rosen (1981) and Hanemann (1982). For a discussion of economic welfare theory including applications to discrete-choice models see Freeman (1993) or Braden and Kolstad (1991).

Table 12.3. *Estimation results for moose hunting site choice task*

	SP – no interactions	SP (urban/rural interactions)	RP (urban/rural interactions)	RP–SP
Site A (SP ASC)	2.1133	1.8437	—	1.8501
	(30.08))	(22.2)		(22.4)
Site B (SP ASC)	2.0741	1.7744	—	1.7790
	(29.78)	(21.4)		(21.7)
Travel cost	−0.0056	−0.0047	−0.0098	−0.0127
	(−22.6)	(−17.8)	(−5.4)	(−6.4)
Road quality	−0.0185	−0.0494	0.1303	−0.0627
(unpaved)	(−0.071)	(−1.5)	(0.60)	(−0.8)
Access	−0.3210	−0.1082	—	−0.2913
No trail	(−6.88)	(−1.8)		(−1.7)
Old trail	0.4006	0.3301	1.4911	0.7078
	(8.02)	(5.3)	(1.5)	(3.7)
4WD Trail	0.1702	0.0624	—	0.2055
	(3.99)	(1.1)	(1.5)	
Congestion				
No hunters	0.6030	0.5967	−2.8610	1.6297
	(13.64)	(10.6)	(−2.5)	(5.2)
On foot	0.0687*	0.0044	—	−0.0048
	(1.42)	(0.1)		(−0.0)
In ATV	−0.2784	−0.2677	—	−0.7550
	(−6.00)	(−4.5)		(−4.1)
Logging	−0.0452*	0.0370	0.0726	0.0316
	(1.75)	(1.1)	(0.1)	(0.4)
Moose Population				
Moose 1	−1.238	−1.2218	0.0023	−3.2069
	(−24.35)	(−18.5)	(0.0)	(−5.6)
Moose 2	−0.0622*	0.0040	−0.0900	−0.2534
	(−1.40)	(0.1)	(−0.2)	(−1.9)
Moose 3	0.4440	0.4447	−1.3721	1.2469
	(10.08)	(7.8)	(−1.5)	(5.1)
Interactions				
Urban*Site a		0.0413	—	−0.0288
		(0.3)		(−0.1)
Urban*site b		0.1427		−0.2497
		(1.1)	—	(−0.7)
Urban*travel cost		0.0014	0.0048	0.0044
		(3.2)	(3.4)	(5.0)
Urban*unpaved		0.1147	—	0.1911
		(2.2)		(1.6)
Urban*no trail		−0.4006	—	−1.0630
		(−4.4)	—	(−3.4)
Urban*old trail		0.0753	0.4071	0.6396
		(0.8)	(2.6)	(3.3)
Urban*4WD trail		0.2145	—	0.3732
		(2.5)		(2.1)

Table 12.3. (*cont.*)

	SP – no interactions	SP (urban/rural interactions)	RP (urban/rural interactions)	RP–SP
Interactions				
Urban*no hunters		0.0576	0.1845	0.0680
		(0.6)	(0.6)	(0.3)
Urban*on foot		0.1065	—	0.3191
		(1.1)		(1.2)
Urban*in ATV		−0.0067	—	−0.0295
		(−0.1)		(−0.1)
Urban*logging		−0.0020	−0.1348	0.0900
		(−0.0)	(−0.8)	(0.8)
Urban*moose 1		−0.0145	−0.1173	−0.2643
		(−0.4)	(−0.5)	(−1.4)
Urban*moose 2		−0.1103	0.5351	0.3871
		(−1.2)	(3.3)	(2.7)
Urban*moose 3		0.0187	−0.0693	−0.0949
		(0.2)	(−0.4)	(−0.6)
RP ASCs				
WMU337		—	−0.7385	0.5863
		—	(−0.8)	(0.9)
WMU338		—	0.7149	−0.8366
			(0.7)	(−1.1)
WMU340		—	0.1614	1.6713
			(0.1)	(2.7)
WMU342		—	0.1614	3.5135
			(=WMU340)	(3.6)
WMU344		—	−1.7154	4.1400
			(−1.4)	(5.0)
WMU346		—	—	0.0170
				(0.0)
WMU348		—	0.7149	−1.7593
			(=WMU338)	(−2.0)
WMU350		—	−0.9133	1.6122
			(−0.7)	(2.7)
WMU352		—	—	3.7260
				(3.9)
WMU354		—	1.4147	1.6235
			(2.3)	(2.2)
WMU356		—	—	2.2300
				(2.4)
WMU437		—	—	−1.7588
				(−1.5)
$\theta_1 = \ln(scale)$				−0.9840
				(−5.8)
ρ^2	0.2514	0.2581	0.2437	0.2566

Note: Asymptotic *t*-statistics are in parentheses; SP = stated preference, RP = revealed preference.
Source: Adamowicz et al. (1997).

While this provides a measure of economic welfare (or willingness to pay) for a quality change in the case of one alternative, it does not address situations involving many alternatives. Put another way, equation (12.2) is the economic welfare measure that would obtain if there were no uncertainty about the alternative that an individual would choose. If we know the individual definitely will choose alternative i, then any changes to alternative i can be assessed using the formula above.[10] However, with discrete-choice models we only know that an individual has a *certain probability of choosing a particular alternative*, and we need a way to extend the welfare measurement expression to cases in which individuals have probabilities of choosing alternatives. The solution is to 'weight' each alternative by the probability that it will be selected. This is somewhat analogous to the concept of *expected utility*, in which the utility of being in several states of the world is weighted by the probability that each occurs, and the weighted utility sum equals the expected utility.

The MNL model requires a slight modification to examine the expected value of the maximum utility of the alternatives because the alternative with the highest utility should be the chosen one. Fortunately, given the MNL model assumptions (EV1 error terms, see chapters 3 and 6), the expected value of the maximum is easily computed. Given a set of alternatives $i = 1, \ldots n$, with utilities V_i, the expected value of the maximum is

$$\ln \sum_{i=1}^{n} e^{V_i}. \tag{12.3}$$

This expression appeared earlier as the 'inclusive value' or 'log-sum' (chapter 6), which summarises information about alternatives and converts it into expected values. Now the welfare expression can be modified to incorporate the expected value concept. A change from initial conditions V_I^0 to new conditions V_I^1 can be expressed as

$$CV = \frac{-1}{\mu} \left[\ln \sum_{i=1}^{n} e^{V_i^0} - \ln \sum_{i=1}^{n} e^{V_i^1} \right], \tag{12.4}$$

where μ is the 'marginal utility of money' or the change in utility that arises from a 1-unit change in money or price. The marginal utility of money term can be derived from a MNL model. For example, the price coefficient in a linear model reflects the change in utility for a change in the price of a good, which captures the marginal utility of money. However, the price coefficient is negative, reflecting the fact that higher prices result in lower utilities. In order to change this into the marginal utility of money, one simply multiplies the price coefficient by -1 (to change this term into the marginal utility of income, rather than the marginal disutility of price).

Having discussed the mechanics of welfare measurement, we now turn to some examples from the case study. For example, recall that we want to estimate impacts

---

[10] Note that a simple linear form is assumed in the example. However, any functional form may be employed. In general the welfare expression is $V(Y, Q) = V(Y - CV, Q')$ where Y is money or income, Q is the original environmental quality level and Q' is the new or 'improved' environmental quality level. See Freeman (1993) for a discussion on the technical aspects of welfare measurement.

of changing moose population levels (for example) on recreational hunting. There are fourteen actual alternatives, hence, the expression for calculating the welfare measure is:

$$CV = \frac{-1}{\mu} \left[\ln \sum_{i=1}^{14} e^{V_i^0} - \ln \sum_{i=1}^{14} e^{V_i^1} \right].$$

(12.5)

Suppose that V_0 indicates the original environmental situation and V^1 is a situation in which moose populations at one site move to a higher level. Thus, we examine a site improvement that moves from the lowest to the second level of moose population. The parameter estimates in column 2 of table 12.3, applied to the best available information on the attributes at each of the fourteen sites, permit us to calculate the first summation in equation (12.5). Travel cost is a function of distance, hence we compute it for a representative person in the sample. Next, we change moose population at WMU344 from level 1 to level 2 and recalculate the summation, which becomes the second summation in expression (12.5). Finally, the marginal utility of money is derived from the travel cost parameter and the CV is calculated. That is, we calculate the amount of money an individual would be willing to pay per trip for a change in moose population at WMU344. In the present case this is \$8.93,[11] which is the amount that the representative hunter would be willing to pay. Persons who live further from WMU344 (hence, have higher travel costs to 344, or equivalently have lower probability of visiting site 344, all else equal), should have less WTP (willingness to pay).

One can programme an expression such as equation (12.5) into a spreadsheet or decision support system (DSS). With such a DSS, the attributes of alternatives can be varied and the impact of changing any one (or a combination) of attributes can be examined. This provides decision makers (e.g., forest managers) with the information that they need to compare the impacts of various alternatives.

This completes case study 1, but we note in closing the discussion that the analysis can be extended in many directions. However, we will forego these extensions to return to more general issues in modelling recreation or use values and examine some advanced topics in environmental valuation associated with measuring use values.

12.3.6 Frequency and choice

This case study provides some measures of how choices of alternative sites may be affected by changing environmental quality. Economic welfare measures were described by per-trip measures, but what if the changes affect not only where a person chooses to go but also how often she or he goes? In market goods contexts, this refers to a 'frequency' or demand effect as opposed to a choice effect. The economic impact of frequency versus choice matters because reductions in environmental quality may have very large effects if they result in reduced participation (frequency) as well as changes in site choice.

---

[11] See Adamowicz et al. (1997) for additional details and further information on welfare calculations in such models.

A simple way to model participation is to include an alternative in the choice set such as 'do not participate'. In the case study presented above such an option was included in each three alternative choice set, but it may not completely reflect the true situation. That is, individuals may assume that choice sets will change so that 'better' options will appear in later choice sets, which will allow them to continue to make the number of trips they wish. Another possibility is that one can ask individuals which alternative they would choose, and how many trips (in a season) they would make to the sites assuming they represented their only available choices, but even this is somewhat problematic. Such an approach was used by Adamowicz, Louviere and Williams (1994), but their respondents found it somewhat difficult to state how many trips they would make to hypothetical sites. Furthermore, modelling the data generated by such responses is challenging.

A formal approach to modelling frequency and choice in the context of recreation trips was proposed and implemented by Hausman, Leonard and McFadden (1995). They jointly estimated a model in which the number of trips each person takes per season is conditional on the choices each makes. That is, one only observes trip frequency for choices made. The inclusive value (or log-sum) from the choice model is linked through to the frequency equation as a measure of the relative attractiveness of the full set of alternatives, which is assumed to determine the total number of trips. Although theoretically consistent and appealing, their approach requires joint data on trip frequency and choice, and assumes that trip frequencies can be accurately explained with information on individual characteristics and site level variables.[12]

12.3.7 Dynamics

The models discussed to this point describe choice behaviour in static environments. Recreation sites are chosen based on their attribute levels and current levels of individual income, experience, etc. However, individuals may be subject to habits and continue to choose particular sites on the basis of habit-forming preference structures. Alternately, individuals may be variety-seekers and wish to choose different sites on each trip, or they may remember recent bad experiences at certain sites and avoid them until these memories decay. These possible dynamic aspects of choice are seldom taken into account in SP approaches, but may be significant elements of choice behaviour, especially if temporal planning horizons are quite long (e.g., vacation trips).

There has been relatively little research into choice dynamics in recreation or environmental valuation. A simple-minded approach would use RP data and include a variable to indicate if an alternative was chosen on the last occasion or not (see, e.g., Guadagni and Little (1983) for a marketing example). However, such an approach is conceptually unappealing because it confounds the dynamic element (previous choice) with the other attributes, and begs the question of what explains the previous choice(s). A person may continue to visit a site because it has the best

---

[12] Similar approaches to the frequency–choice problem can be found in Yen and Adamowicz (1994) and Feather, Hellerstein and Tomasi (1995).

attributes, or the same person may simply exhibit habit-forming behaviour. More sophisticated approaches included Adamowicz's (1994) formal model of intertemporal choice behaviour for recreation site choice, or Provencher and Bishop's (1997) approach which simultaneously estimates the parameters of an MNL choice model while solving a dynamic programming site selection problem. The latter approach, in particular, requires complex data and specialised estimation software. The issue is relevant because in reality choices probably are dynamic, hence may be strongly influenced by habit, learning and other dynamic elements. Stated choice models typically do not examine such issues, but SP data could be used to enhance the RP data used to estimate such models. This would allow RP data to play a major role in identifying dynamic processes, and the SP data to play a major role in determining attribute trade-offs.

12.3.8 Summary

In this section was described the application of stated choice models to environmental valuation of recreational hunting. The process of defining the study objectives, performing qualitative analysis, implementing data collection, analysing data and performing policy analysis is very similar for any stated choice case study. The largest difference in this case is probably that the policy analysis goes beyond calculating market shares or predicted choice probabilities. The analysis of economic welfare measures is an extension of probability calculations that allows one to 'value' changes in environmental quality not reflected in market prices. Thus, stated choice methods provide mechanisms for the valuation of environmental goods and services, either as stand alone methods or in combination with revealed preference information. The next section deals with a different but related issue in environmental valuation, namely valuing goods and services that do not have any linkage with expenditures, purchases or other observable market behaviours.

12.4 Case study 2: passive use values

Some of the most contentious issues in the environmental area involve what can be viewed as passive use values. For example, in the Pacific northwest region of the United States, the well-known battle over the use of old-growth forest habitat where spotted owls live is basically a conflict between individuals who wish to see old-growth forests remain as is and those who can benefit from logging them. In this case the policy question is, 'How much are people willing to pay to ensure that spotted owls exist?' Or, alternatively, 'How much decrease in timber output and associated employment will society trade-off for maintenance of old-growth forest habitat?' This particular conflict remains unresolved and tensions continue between the various parties involved in the dispute. The *Exxon-Valdez* oil spill in Prince William Sound, Alaska, impacted use values (fishing, recreation, etc.), but the legal action brought against Exxon also sought recovery of passive use values lost because of the impact on the ecosystem (Carson et al. 1994 detail this case).

Passive use values are difficult to measure because there is no behavioural trail and hence no 'actual' value to use as a benchmark or basis for calibration. Yet, measurement of passive use values has become very important, partly due to their policy implications, but also because damage assessment legislation in the United States has legislated their consideration and use in court cases. In this section we examine a case study which uses SP to measure passive use values.

12.4.1 Passive use values: contingent valuation and stated preference

Contingent valuation methods (CVM) have been used by economists for approximately thirty years to value changes in natural resources and environments. In the CVM approach respondents receive detailed information about the current state of the environment (including economic and biological information) and the proposed change (an improvement or reduction in environmental quality). Once respondents 'digest' the information, they are asked if they would vote to accept the changes and pay a certain amount of money or vote against the initiative.[13] Responses to such questions are analysed to determine the average willingness to pay for the sample of individuals.

The CVM approach is somewhat similar to methods used in marketing to evaluate new concepts for goods or products. For example, concept tests typically provide detailed descriptions of products for which demand forecasts are to be made (e.g., Urban and Hauser 1993). Descriptions may consist of models, mockups, prototypes, multimedia presentations, etc., but in any case, the description is used to estimate the demand or value. In contrast, the SP approach views a product as one of many possible products that differ in the values or positions they occupy on key attribute characteristics. In the SP approach, characteristics are used to develop descriptions to which consumers react.

A concern with CVM is that it relies very heavily on the accuracy of descriptions, but any errors in a description discovered after the fact cannot be changed. Hence, the provision of detailed information is crucial to the analysis. Also, CVM typically cannot value the separate components of the situation. In contrast, SP methods rely less on the accuracy and completeness of any particular alternative, but more on the accuracy and completeness of the product characteristics and attributes used to describe alternatives. Thus, instead of asking about a single event in detail, consumers are asked about a sample of events drawn from the universe of possible events of that

---

[13] The form of contingent valuation described here is referendum contingent valuation. There are other forms including discrete choice (which involves asking respondents if they would pay a certain amount but does not describe the situation as a referendum) and open-ended approaches (asking an individual how much they would be willing to pay for the environmental improvement). Note that these questions are described as willingness-to-pay questions but that the same questions could be carried out in a willingness-to-accept framework. For details on contingent valuation see Mitchell and Carson (1989), Freeman (1993) or Carson (1991).

type. SP tasks may provide some advantages relative to contingent valuation, and we review these issues in the later part of this chapter. However, relatively little research has examined the use of SP tasks in passive use value settings,[14] hence this issue requires further examination.

We now turn our attention to a case study involving the measurement and modelling of passive use values using SP methods.

12.4.2 Study objectives

A common example of passive use value is the value that people place on endangered or threatened animal species. This case study examines one such species, the woodland caribou in Alberta, Canada. Mountain dwelling, woodland caribou rely on old-growth forests in west central Alberta, an area also involved in considerable industrial (forestry, oil and gas) and recreational activity. Lands allocated under forest management agreements (FMAs) in Alberta contain superior woodland caribou habitat. To establish protected areas and conditions considered optimal for caribou preservation by biologists, holders of FMAs may have to be compensated and recreational uses of the land may be restricted. It should be noted that these are public lands; hence, preferences of the general public are relevant to land-use decision making. These issues form the basis for our valuation exercise.

12.4.3 Qualitative study

Focus groups were used to help understand how individuals viewed protection of caribou habitat and the aspects of this situation that mattered. A typical CVM exercise would involve the development of a detailed description of the proposed changes to management under a 'caribou protection plan' and an elicitation of the amount that individuals would be willing to pay (or willing to vote for in a referendum format) to implement the plan. In the SP approach the characteristics of the situation are identified, i.e., the attributes associated with protection of woodland caribou. Such attributes include the landbase that supports caribou, forestry activity and employment, recreational opportunities, habitat for other species (which may be negatively correlated with caribou) and other items. Understanding of the aspects of land use that matter to people is critical in developing scenario descriptions. Also, the issue of a payment vehicle or a linkage between the actions people prefer and how each person will be affected must be examined (e.g., individuals may pay to protect caribou with tax funds). The SP task was constructed from the attributes found to matter most to focus group participants (caribou populations, wilderness area, employment, taxes paid per household, etc., see table 12.4).

---

[14] For a discussion on the potential advantages and disadvantages of stated choice methods see Adamowicz, Swait and Louviere (1993) or Adamowicz, Boxall, Louviere et al. (1998).

Table 12.4. *Attributes and levels used in the caribou passive use value experiments*

Attribute	Levels
Mountain caribou population (number of caribou)	50 400 (current situation) 600 1600 (historical maximum)
Wilderness Area (hectares)	100,000 150,000 (current situation) 220,000 300,000
Recreation restrictions (categories)	Level 1 No restrictions Level 2 Activities in designated areas (current situation) Level 3 No hunting, fishing, off-road vehicles, helicopters; horses and overnight camping in designated areas Level 4 No hunting, fishing, off-road vehicles, helicopters, horses; hiking on designated trails, limited access overnight camping.
Forest industry employment (direct employment)	450 900 1200 (current situation) 1250
Changes to provincial income tax (annual change)	$50 decrease No change (current situation) $50 increase $150 increase
Additional Attributes (*confounded with attributes above, listed to make descriptions complete*)	
Moose populations (negatively correlated with caribou populations: moose and caribou populations are inversely related)	14,000 8,000 6,000 2,000
Forest management agreement area (hectares) (this area decreases as the size of wilderness area increases)	1,061,000 1,012,000 942,000 862.000

Table 12.5. *Choice task for woodland caribou–passive use value case study*

Attributes	Current situation	Alternative situation 1 (future situation)	Alternative situation 2 (future situation)
Mountain caribou	400 caribou	1600 caribou	600 caribou
Moose population	8000 moose	2000 moose	6000 moose
Wilderness area	150,000 hectares	150,000 hectares	220,000 hectares
FMA area	1,012,000 hectares	1,012,000 hectares	1,012,000 hectares
Recreation restrictions	Level 2	Level 2	Level 1
Forest industry employment	1200 jobs	1200 jobs	1200 jobs
Provincial income tax change	No change in taxes/year	$50 increase in taxes/year	$50 decrease in taxes/year

12.4.4 Data collection, instrument design and sampling frame

The attributes determined in the qualitative study were assigned levels to represent the ranges that occur in the study area, and were combined to construct choice scenarios by using a $4^5 \times 4^5 \times 2$ orthogonal, main effects design. The two 4^5 components relate to two 'alternative futures' options presented in the choice task, and the last component is a two-level blocking factor used to create two versions of scenarios and reduce the number of choice sets each individual faced. Where possible, such orthogonal blocking factors like this should be used to create versions because they ensure balance in the attribute levels within and between versions. Each choice set included the status quo (described by the attributes at current levels) and two 'alternative futures' (see table 12.5). Individuals were asked to choose the alternative they preferred as if they were voting on the options. Each respondent received eight choice set scenarios and was asked to choose one situation from the three offered for each scenario.

Survey respondents were a random sample of residents of Edmonton, Canada. Initial telephone contact was used to recruit individuals to complete a follow-up mail survey. Random digit dialling procedures were used to contact 900 Edmonton residents who agreed to complete the survey. Surveys were sent to them, and reminder cards were then sent after two weeks. Non-respondents were sent new survey packages after four weeks. The overall response rate by the cutoff date was 65 per cent, which was considered good in view of the complexity of the survey.

12.4.5 Model estimation

A basic MNL model was estimated from the choice data. Caribou populations, wilderness area, changes in tax payments, and changes in forest industry employment were modelled as quantitative (continuous) variables, whereas recreation restrictions

Table 12.6. *Coefficients of linear and quadratic caribou choice experiment MNL models*

Variable	Linear model	Quadratic model
ASC (for non-status quo choices)	−0.6740	−0.4715
	(−9.19)	(−5.76)
Caribou	0.0501	0.5453
	(9.25)	(17.71)
Caribou squared		−0.0269
		(−16.85)
Wilderness area	0.0391	0.0756
	(9.33)	(2.30)
Wilderness area squared		−0.0008
		(−1.16)
Recreation level 1[a]	0.3334	0.2786
	(6.55)	(5.22)
Recreation level 2[a]	0.1669	0.1747
	(3.23)	(3.15)
Recreation level 3[a]	−0.2168	−0.1503
	(−3.87)	(−2.65)
Employment	0.0080	0.1329
	(0.81)	(1.56)
Employment squared		−0.0086
		(−1.73)
Tax[b]	−0.0033	−0.0055
	(−7.54)	(−5.86)
Tax squared[b]		−0.0002
		(−2.77)
ρ^2	0.09	0.14
Log likelihood	−2840.68	−2669.23

Notes: [a]Effects coded variable; [b]Linear tax variable represents (Income − Tax) but is estimated using tax only (since income is constant across alternatives). Quadratic tax variable is (Income − Tax)^2/(10000)).
Source: Adamowicz, Boxall, Williams and Louviere, (1998).

were modelled as qualitative variables (four levels represented by three effects-coded variables). The estimation results are reported in table 12.6 and reveal that almost all attributes are statistically significant. Caribou populations and wilderness area had significant and positive marginal utilities. Tax payments were negative and significant as expected. The effect of recreation restrictions decreases in size as restrictions become more severe. As expected, adding restrictions to an individual's recreation opportunities decreases utility. Finally, forest industry employment was not statistically significant, indicating that, in this case, people do not consider increasing employment in the forest industry to be personally welfare enhancing. A quadratic form of the model also was estimated, which fit better than the linear model and suggests, for example, that preferences for caribou populations rise rapidly to a population size of about 600, and then flatten.

An interesting issue arises in the interpretation of the alternative-specific constant. Here the ASC represents the utility of choosing something other than the status quo, all else equal. That is, this ASC represents either alternative future a or alternative future b. The ASC parameter is significant and negative, indicating a preference for the status quo, all else equal, which is consistent with results in other literatures. That is, a so-called status quo 'bias' seems to arise when people are asked to consider moving away from their present situation (Samuelson and Zeckhauser (1988) offer a more general discussion).

12.4.6 Policy analysis

The model describes and predicts preferences over 'states of the world'; hence one can examine the amount an individual would be willing to pay to move from the status quo to a situation in which a caribou conservation programme was instituted. Suppose that a certain programme involved an increase in the caribou population from 400 to 600, an increase in area in wilderness reserves and a ban on recreational activities in the area (no hunting, fishing or off-road vehicles). Economic welfare measures can be constructed using the methods described above by comparing individuals' utility at the status quo with their utility in the alternative future. Using the notation presented above (equation (12.2)), let Q reflect the status quo levels of environmental attributes (caribou population level, wilderness area, recreation restrictions) and Q' represent the proposed caribou conservation plan (increased caribou population, increased wilderness area, restricted recreation access). The amount of money that an individual would be willing to pay for the caribou conservation plan is estimated by computing the value of CV in equation (12.6)

$$V^0 = \beta_1\,(\text{Price}) + \beta_2(Q) = \beta_1\,(\text{Price} + CV) + \beta_2(Q') = V^1. \tag{12.6}$$

Of course, one could compute the value of any programme defined by changes in the attributes of the choice task. Thus, willingness to pay for a programme that increases caribou populations but also restricts recreation opportunities and reduces forest industry employment also can be calculated. This project's modelling results suggest that the average sample household was willing to pay about \$75 per year in additional taxes for a project that increased caribou population and extended wilderness area (at the expense of FMAs), but decreased recreation access by one level relative to the status quo. A very wide range of policy analyses can be based on the estimated model parameters. For example, average sample willingness to pay to increase caribou populations one level more than the status quo was relatively low. That is, increasing caribou populations from 600 to 800 was worth about \$26 per household per year (all else equal). This result suggests that once caribou levels are well beyond significant threats to their population, individual preferences (as revealed by the quadratic model) for further population increases and increased taxes are quite small.

12.4.7 Summary

This section presented a case study involving the use of SP methods to estimate passive use values. The basic approach is the same for any SP application, but the issue is complicated by the following factors:

1.   Individuals have relatively little familiarity with 'choosing' goods such as environmental quality or endangered species management plans.
2.   Individuals may feel that they do not have enough background or knowledge to actually make such choices, although they frequently make important and complex social choices in elections and referenda. Thus, these issues are not outside of the purview of social choice situations.
3.   In any situation with passive use values, there is no easy way to 'ground truth' the results as there is no behavioural trail. Thus, issues of strategic behaviour, or individuals misrepresenting their preferences in order to achieve individual gain, is always a concern.

It has been suggested that describing the situation as a referendum may alleviate the problems associated with strategic behaviour, but even this frame may not eliminate such problems.

Eliciting the public's preferences for environmental services is a very important yet challenging area of research. Many of the environmental issues we face today, such as endangered species, global climate change, industrial pollution, etc., have elements of use and/or passive use value. In order to make informed decisions regarding policy actions, accurate models of human choice and preferences are required. However, accuracy in an arena filled with scientific uncertainty, political agendas and interest groups is difficult. In the conclusion to this section we turn to a discussion of one of the most difficult issues in applying SP to environmental issues.

12.5 The passive use value controversy: can SP help?

In 1989 the *Exxon Valdez* ran aground and the ensuing oil spill generated a variety of damage assessment cases and calls for compensation. One element of compensation demanded by the State of Alaska was lost passive use value. A vigorous debate began in the economics profession contesting the existence of passive use values and the merit of the CVM method. After several years of panels, debates and papers, the National Oceanic and Atmospheric Administration (NOAA, the agency responsible for the guidelines for damage assessment under the Oil Pollution Act), an agency in the Department of Commerce of the United States Federal government, approved CVM methods for determining passive use values and initiating discussion on compensation (Arrow et al. 1993). The NOAA panel report also issued guidelines for the conduct of CVM studies.

Passive use values will continue to be important elements of resource management. CVM probably will continue to be used as a tool. However, researchers are beginning to explore the use of SP or choice experiment approaches in which the attributes of the situation become important. In that regard, there may be several advantages to the SP approach relative to CVM:

1. SP tasks allow researchers to 'value' attributes as well as situational changes. Thus, response surfaces or valuation functions can be developed to permit a range of values to be examined (e.g., a range of estimated ecological impacts).
2. In the case of damage to a particular attribute, compensating amounts of other goods (rather than compensating variation based on money) can be calculated. For example, in our earlier recreational hunting example, a reduction in moose population could be 'compensated' by changing access conditions at different sites. Such a use of compensating 'goods' is now employed in resource damage assessment cases (Jones and Pease 1995, NOAA 1997). For further detail see Adamowicz, Louviere and Swait (1998).

Calculation of compensation in non-monetary terms appeals to some researchers and policy makers because it avoids having to ask people how much money they would be willing to pay for environmental improvements. Similarly, in the more common case of damage assessment, it avoids asking how much money they would be willing to accept for reductions in environmental quality. Individuals tend to feel uncomfortable trading off money for environmental attributes, particularly in the case of the latter question. A non-monetary compensation approach provides for environmental damages to be compensated with improvements to other environments, perhaps even in different locations.

However, this approach also has limitations because one needs to design SP tasks to elicit preferences for environmental quality, and even if one has a 'true' representation of preferences, determination of resource compensation may be complex. For example, some people may want habitat near their home improved to compensate for damages, but others may want distant national parks improved. As well, environmental improvement projects may last for several years, requiring that some way be found to compare the benefits of a multi-year environmental improvement to a single year's damage. These are only two complications that may arise when moving to resource compensation. Nevertheless, there is so much controversy over the use of money as a metric for measuring damages, and the CVM method itself, that this SP approach is being given serious consideration.

Another potential advantage associated with SP is that it may decrease concerns about certain phenomena observed in past empirical research, such as strategic behaviour and 'yea-saying'.[15] That is, respondents are asked to choose from various

---

[15] Yea-saying is a phenomenon that occurs in contingent valuation and in other hypothetical voting tasks. Individuals vote 'yes' for the environmentally friendly alternative because they would like to be in favour of environmental protection and they find the environmentally unfriendly alternative unpalatable. There are no significant consequences in this case associated with this form of strategic behaviour.

scenarios, which may make it more difficult for them to behave strategically. Modern CVM methods use referendum formats or present choices in public referenda contexts. This format may minimise individuals' strategic behaviour because referenda appear to be 'incentive compatible' mechanisms that induce individuals to reveal their true values (see Mitchell and Carson 1989). SP tasks such as those illustrated above can also be framed as referenda. Finally, issues of embedding (Kahneman and Knetsch 1992), scoping and/or sequencing (Carson and Mitchell 1995) have dominated the recent CVM debate. That is, individuals may value goods presented as subsets of composite goods (e.g., a muffin as part of a breakfast) differently than they value the good when presented on its own (only a muffin). SP is based on attributes and incorporates different subsets of goods within the design; hence, embedding is part of SP experiments, and the empirical results reveal if individuals are sensitive to attribute levels (termed 'scope' in the CVM literature). Finally, the repeated response approach of SP allows for within-sample verification or consistency tests, which are uncommon in the CVM literature.

Despite these potential advantages of SP tasks, SP designs may create some problems. SP experiments are often based on orthogonal main effects fractions of complete factorial designs. Such designs limit the way in which attribute effects can enter utility functions. More complex designs can be used, but they can lead to more complex surveys. Also, issues of information provision, survey design, and survey administration apply as much to SP surveys as they do to any survey-based method.

A recent test of SP methods for measuring passive use values was performed by Adamowicz, Boxall, Williams and Louviere (1988). This experiment also examined combining SP and CVM tasks to use the information generated by both. The results suggested that SP performs at least as well as CVM and the advantage of attribute-based valuation is significant.

It is likely that the use of SP methods in the environmental area will increase in the future. In environmental economics research has focused on detailed examination of CVM as a preference elicitation tool. However, the controversy generated by the *Exxon Valedez* incident and the resulting NOAA panel have begun to broaden economic researchers' quest for tools that can describe preferences and elicit trade-offs. It is not clear that any methods yet proposed can solve the puzzle of passive use values because obtaining 'truth' in this context is difficult. Nevertheless, there appears to be a concerted effort to employ methods such as SP in the search for information on environmental preferences.

12.6 Conclusions

Forms of SP methods have been in use for some time in environmental economics. The CVM method has been in existence for over thirty years. Recently economists have begun to expand their stated choice repertoire to include the methods examined in detail in this volume. These methods have been used in two distinct cases. First, they are used to reflect, or help reflect, human behaviour related to environmental quality. The choices that humans make in the areas of recreation, housing choice and even food choice can be related (at least in part) to some aspect of environmental quality. Models of behaviour or demand can then be used to understand the implications of changing environmental quality and also the economic value of these changes.

The second use of stated preference methods in environmental economics is to measure passive use values, or preferences for public goods or social choices. These choices do not necessarily involve any explicit behavioural changes, and hence SP tasks take on more of a role of public opinion elicitation or referendum modelling. This form of choice is difficult to model for several reasons, not the least of which is the fact that individuals are not used to such tasks and there are rarely actual choice data available to calibrate stated choices.

We presented two case studies in this chapter, one use value case and one passive use value case. Throughout the chapter we noted that the objective of these studies either was to develop planning tools (the recreational hunting case) or was to value environmental quality changes so that damage assessments and compensation requirements can be computed. However, there are other uses of SP tasks and non-market valuation. These tools can be used to help determine full cost prices, or prices in which damages to environmental quality is built in. For example, in the case of electrical utilities, SP methods are used to determine the environmental cost of generating electricity and then factoring this cost back into the price. SP methods can also be used to develop natural resource accounts. Natural resource accounts have been proposed as a parallel to traditional national accounts (GNP or GDP), except that the value of the natural capital (forests, water, soil, etc.) is measured and accounted for in the measure of wealth. If water quality declines, its value in the natural resource account declines. In order to be measured in consistent terms these accounts are often formulated in monetary terms, thus requiring a non-market valuation method to transfer the physical account into dollar terms.

SP methods are likely to continue to grow in use and popularity in the environmental economics profession. They are consistent with economic theory and they provide a way to alleviate some of the difficulties associated with relying on market data. In environmental economics individuals are somewhat used to operating in areas outside of traditional markets; hence SP methods fit very well within their tool kits.

13 Cross validity and external validity of SP models

13.1 Introduction

At the heart of psychological and economic theories of consumer choice behaviour lie implicit or explicit assumptions about regularities (i.e., consistencies) in evaluation processes and decision rules across individuals, product classes, time periods, cultures, etc. Demonstrating the existence of such regularities is a crucial step in establishing the external and cross validity of SP theory and methods, but there are also two broader reasons to seek regularities in consumer choices:

1. To provide support for psychological and economic theories of choice in a variety of contexts of interest to academic disciplines interested in and practitioners of choice modelling; and
2. To support the development and generalisability of theory dealing with specific, substantive empirical issues.

The purpose of this chapter is to describe and provide a theoretical rationale for seemingly fairly widespread empirical regularities in published and unpublished research on the analysis and modelling of preferences and choices. In particular, we provide evidence that theory discussed in previous chapters (especially chapter 8) predicts that a simple behavioural mechanism can explain a wide range of empirical comparisons of preference and choice models estimated from different conditions, contexts, times, geographical location and/or product classes. In this chapter our objective is to explain this mechanism, demonstrate how it arises naturally as a consequence of random utility theory and illustrate its generality in a wide range of empirical contexts.

In marketing, transport, resource economics and other social sciences, choice data (more generally, *preference*, or even more generally, *dominance* data) come in many flavours:

*   cross-sectional observations of past, present or future preferences or choices, including most recent or last choice,
*   observations of preferences or choices in controlled experiments,

- longitudinal observations of choices from scanner or other panels,
- judgements (more generally, 'evaluations') of alternatives on latent dimensions like 'attractiveness,' 'purchase intent', etc., measured magnitude estimation/production, rating or ranking scales, and/or discrete choices of one or perhaps no alternatives,
- observations of decisions made by single persons or groups of people; and so forth.

Without seeking to be exhaustive, this short list yields many possible combinations of preference data types and decision contexts. Indeed, with such disparity in preference data sources, a search for regularities in decision and choice processes would seem daunting, and, it is fair to say, has thus far yielded little in the way of reductionism.

We believe that the lack of substantial progress to date in identifying regularities in preference and choice processes can be traced in part to the fact that any such search faces formidable difficulties without a guiding theoretical framework. Thus, building on material in earlier chapters, we attempt to show that random utility theory (hereafter, RUT) can provide such a framework (see Manski 1977, McFadden 1981, Ben-Akiva and Lerman 1985). We also attempt to show that a relatively simple phenomenon predicted by RUT seems to account for many seemingly unrelated empirical results previously reported in marketing, transport and other areas. In particular, as discussed in chapter 3, RUT posits that the utility of a product or service can be decomposed into systematic and random components. This decomposition is well known, but until recently it was less well known that the behaviour of the random component in preference data sources impacts inferences from estimates of utilities (i.e., utility parameters) within data sources and comparisons of estimates between data sources (Morikawa 1989; Swait and Louviere 1993).

Variability in the random utility component plays a key role in the derivation and estimation of random utility theory based choice models (see Ben-Akiva and Lerman 1985; Swait and Louviere 1993). Thus, it is important not only to understand this role, but also to test its implications in empirical research; fortunately, recent methodological advances permit tests of hypothesised preference and choice process regularities. For example, Ben-Akiva and Morikawa (1990) and Swait and Louviere (1993) explained why and how error variability differences must and can be taken into account when comparing different sources of choice data, and how to test the hypothesis that two or more sets of choice data differ only in levels of error variability. More recently, Louviere (1994) proposed that many conjoint type experiments could be conceptualised in a random utility framework, and modelled by means of some form of nested submodel within the family of generalised logistic regression models. One key implication of Louviere's new conceptualisation of classical conjoint analysis is to create a level playing field for model comparisons. That is, the RUT framework allows one to test if parameter estimates differ after accounting for differences in levels of error variability. For example, Ben-Akiva, et al. (1994) discuss and Louviere, Fox and Moore (1993) demonstrate that one can apply Louviere's (1994) argument to many forms of preference data, whether (a) conjoint or other stated preference (generically termed SP) sources or (b) revealed preference (RP) sources. That is, one now can compare and test preference (utility) parameters across different (a) sources of preference data, (b) types of decision tasks, (c) types of task manipulations such as attribute or profile orderings, (d) groups of people, (e) time periods, geographical locations, etc.

Thus, the purpose of this chapter is threefold:

1. to propose an operational definition of preference process regularity,
2. to outline a general way to compare and test models and sources of dominance data based on the previously cited recent advances, and
3. demonstrate that accounting for differences in the random utility component among sources of preference data frequently may account for a significant portion of the reliable differences in model parameter estimates.

To achieve our objectives, the remainder of the chapter is organised as follows:

- We first review past literature to show that comparisons of model parameters between diverse conditions/situations/manipulations have been and still are of interest to the research community.
- We then formalise the concept of preference regularity, and relate it to the random utility component, specifically through the concept of measurement reliability.
- Next, we briefly describe and present the results of model comparison tests for a variety of empirical data sets, the results of which strongly support the notion that much of the observed differences in preference measurements can be attributed simply to differences in the magnitudes of error variability among the data sets compared.
- We end by discussing the significance of the findings and implications for further research directions that flow logically from them.

13.2 A brief review of preference model comparisons

Comparison of utility parameters from different sets of preference data has a long history in marketing, transport and other fields. For example, Meyer (1977) investigated the impact of profile ordering on attribute weight, while Meyer and Eagle (1982) investigated the effect of varying attribute ranges on utility parameters. Johnson (1989) reported on attribute order effects on utility parameters. Olsen et al. (1995) found differences in utility parameters as a function of type of task (rating vs. choice), presentation format (sequential vs. simultaneous), whether subjects had prior practice, etc. Oliphant et al. (1992) compared utility parameters from ratings and choice tasks, and profile or choice set order within type of task. Elrod, Louviere and Davey (1993) compared rating and choice tasks under conditions in which choice sets were Pareto optimal. Chrzan (1994) reported differences in choice task utility parameters due to three kinds of order effects. Ben-Akiva, Morikawa and Shirioshi (1991) and Bradley and Daly (1994) compared logit model parameters estimated from different depths of preference ranking data, and found differences by depth. These references make it evident that there has been, and continues to be, considerable interest in the effects of task manipulations, order effects and response mode differences on utility parameters in conjoint and other types of decision and choice tasks.

More recently, comparisons of revealed (RP) and stated preference (SP) data have been of research interest. For example, Ben-Akiva and Morikawa (1990) compared RP and SP data for transport mode choice in the Netherlands, and were unable to reject the hypothesis that both data sets produced comparable utility parameters. Hensher and Bradley (1993) reported a similar result in a study of a new fast train proposed for the Melbourne–Sydney corridor. Other related research includes the following: (a) Louviere, Fox and Moore (1993) compared different RP and SP measures for vacation trips; (b) Swait, Louviere and Williams (1994) compared RP and SP measures for freight shipper choices; and (c) Adamowicz, Louviere and Williams (1994) and Adamowicz (1997) compared RP and SP measures for water-based recreation and moose-hunting destination choices. Hence, not only is interest in comparing models from different sources of preference data growing, but interest in combining multiple sources of RP and SP data to test whether common parameters can be estimated from the combined sources also is growing (Swait and Louviere 1993, Ben-Akiva et al. 1994, Carson et al. 1994; see chapter 8 of this book).

Finally, there are numerous examples of preference model parameter comparisons among different 'a priori' segments and/or groups of consumers. For example, Currim (1981) compared choice models for different consumer segments identified from conjoint tasks, while Gensch (1985) proposed an approach to test for parameter differences among segments. Arnold, Oum and Tigert (1983) compared differences in preference model parameters in supermarket choice models by city, time period and country. More recently, research interest in so-called latent segmentation methods applied to preference modelling has been increasing (see Dillon and Kumar (1994) for a review). These methods explicitly impose model parameter differences (i.e., implied parameter comparisons) across segments uncovered in the analysis. This brief and non-comprehensive review demonstrates broad interest in preference model comparisons in many different areas in several academic disciplines.

13.3 Preference regularities

13.3.1 Conceptual structure

As a first step we develop a conceptual framework based upon RUT to study and compare differences in choice or preference (more generally, *dominance*) data sources. In the discussion below we define 'preference regularity' precisely, despite having used the term somewhat loosely above. Although previous research addressed this concept (e.g., Swait and Louviere 1993, Ben-Akiva et al. 1994), the conceptual framework we discuss below formalises much previous work, which may be useful for future research.

To motivate what follows, suppose a sample of consumers respond to a survey in which they make choices from experimentally designed pairs of alternatives that describe some product. Call this choice elicitation procedure 1 (CEP1), and its associated design matrix X_1. Suppose a second source of preference or choice data for this same product also is available, such as the responses of a second (independent) sample of individuals to questions that elicit (a) which product or service they last purchased and (b) their associated perceived (attribute) design matrix X_2. Call this choice elicitation procedure 2 (CEP2). Further, let X_1 and X_2 have some attributes in common (represented respectively by matrices X_{c1} and X_{c2}), but other attributes are elicitation procedure-specific (call these matrices Z_1 and Z_2, respectively). Thus, $X_1 = (X_{c1}, Z_1)'$ and $X_2 = (X_{c2}, Z_2)'$.

For simplicity, let us assume that the total preference evaluation U_k of a product profile in CEP_k, $k = 1, 2$, is the sum of the individual partworth utility parameters of the common attributes. That is, for now we assume that the utility function is strictly additive in each common attribute, and we denote these common utility parameters $V_{ck}(X_{ck}, \beta_k)$ for each CEP. Let the partworth utility parameters for the procedure-specific components be denoted $W_k(Z_k, \gamma_k)$, $k = 1, 2$. Finally, we must associate certain stochastic terms with each common and procedure-specific utility component to account for usual statistical (econometric) concerns of measurement error, omitted variables, incorrect functional forms, etc. These error components are denoted as ζ_1, ζ_2, ζ_{c1}, ζ_{c2}, ε_1, and ε_2, and associated with the different data sources and partworth components as follows:

$$U_1 = \theta_1 + [V_{c1}(X_{c1}, \beta_1) + \zeta_{c1}] + [W_1(Z_1, \gamma_1) + \zeta_1] + \varepsilon_1,$$

$$U_2 = \theta_2 + [V_{c2}(X_{c2}, \beta_2) + \zeta_{c2}] + [W_2(Z_2, \gamma_2) + \zeta_2] + \varepsilon_2,$$

where θ_1, θ_2 are intercepts to capture average preference levels in each data source. These expressions can be straightforwardly rearranged to be

$$U_1 = \theta_1 + V_{c1}(X_{c1}, \beta_1) + W_1(Z_1, \gamma_1) + (\zeta_{c1} + \zeta_1 + \varepsilon_1), \tag{13.1}$$

$$U_2 = \theta_2 + V_{c2}(X_{c2}, \beta_2) + W_2(Z_2, \gamma_2) + (\zeta_{c2} + \zeta_2 + \varepsilon_2). \tag{13.2}$$

In each equation the dimensionality of the corresponding preference measure is defined by its own elicitation procedure. For example, in the present case U_1 has two rows (it's a paired alternative task), but U_2 can exhibit variable numbers of rows per respondent, depending upon the number of products that comprised the respondents' choice set when they made their last real purchase. Figure 13.1 provides additional insight into equations (13.1) and (13.2) by depicting the entire set of relationships previously described as a path-like diagram familiar to structural equation modellers (Bollen 1989). Although figure 13.1 shows only a two-source case, it is easy to extend it to any number of preference data sources.

A key issue suggested by the literature previously reviewed is whether different elicitation procedures, situational contexts, etc., measure the same underlying preference process. Intuitively, this issue deals with a comparison of common utilities

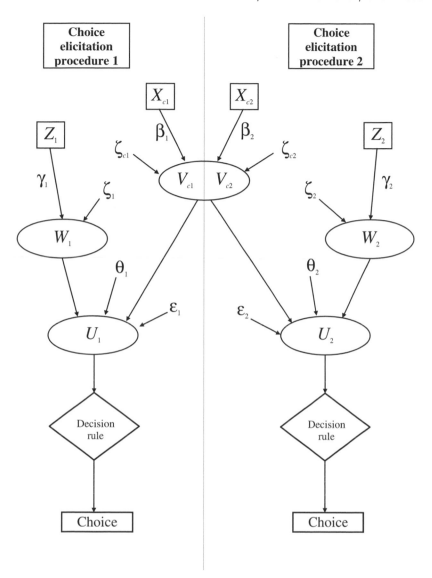

Figure 13.1 Conceptual framework for preference data comparison

$V_{ck}(X_{ck}, \beta_k)$ derived from each elicitation procedure, context, etc. This motivates us to propose a formal definition of the concept of *preference regularity*:

Definition PR: $K \geq 2$ preference elicitation procedures exhibit *preference regularity* if the marginal common utilities $MU_{k|X_{ck}=X_{c0}} = [\partial V_{ck}(X_{ck}, \beta_k)/\partial X_{ck}]_{X_{ck}=X_{c0}}$ are equal up to positive constants of proportionality, i.e. $MU_{k|X_{ck}=X_{c0}} = \lambda_{k,k'} MU_{k'|X_{c'k}=X_{c0}}$ for any pair of data sources (k, k'), where the scalar $\lambda_{k,k'} > 0$, and X_{c0} is a vector of common attribute levels.

A key to understanding the basis for this definition is the recognition that it is not the absolute magnitudes of common utilities *per se* that matter in comparing multiple measures, but rather the comparability of the implied sensitivity of the measures to changes in attribute levels. Definition PR also requires that the *algebraic signs* of the multiple measures agree (hence, the constants of proportionality be positive).

Note that if common partworth utilities are linear-in-the-parameters, the following definition for preference regularity will hold:

Definition PR′: When $V_{ck}(X_{ck}, \beta_k) = \beta_k X_{ck}$, $k = 1, \ldots, K$, the preference elicitation procedures are said to exhibit *preference regularity* if the parameter vectors β_k are equal up to positive constants of proportionality, i.e., $\beta_k = \lambda_{k,k'} \beta_{k'}$ for data sources (k, k').

Definition PR′ is more restrictive than PR, but in practice it should be more widely applicable because many, if not most, estimated choice models are linear-in-the-parameters specifications.

Our definition of preference regularity for multiple preference data sources requires that the marginal common utility partworths measured in each source be equal up to a multiplier for all common attributes. Figure 13.2 graphically illustrates the proportionality condition that underlies definition PR′ in the two data source case. That is, if preference regularity holds between the two data sources, the marginal common utilities should be linearly related with a positive slope. More intuitively, if definition PR′ holds, a graph of the estimated parameters β_1 vs. β_2 should plot as a straight line intersecting the origin. Hence, the 'cloud' of points should occupy quadrants I and III, but not II and IV of the graph. If this graphical pattern is not satisfied in a particular empirical situation, it is unlikely that the two data sources capture the same underlying preferences.

Graphs such as figure 13.2 can help diagnose possible regularities, but a more rigorous test is needed because the data are *estimates* of $\partial V_{ck}(X_{ck}, \beta_k)/\partial X_{ck}$. Thus, a statistical test that takes the errors in the estimates into account is needed to make

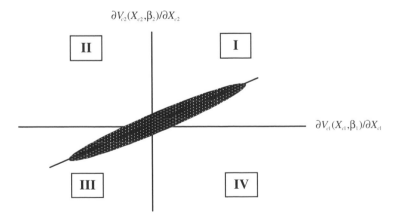

Figure 13.2 Preference regularity hypothesis generated by definition PR

inferences about preference regularities. Such a test can be developed as a straight-forward generalisation of the likelihood ratio test proposed by Swait and Louviere (1993) for the two-source case, which allows definition PR$'$ to be operationalised.

As figure 13.2 indicates, definition PR$'$ is a very strong requirement for preference regularity, and its stringency increases with the number of attributes involved. Thus, the quality and strength of evidence for/against preference regularity in empirical applications will be associated with care taken to design the attribute space for each data source, the degree of attribute overlap, the relative importance of source-specific attributes, bias induction and measurement reliability of each elicitation procedure, etc. In turn, this implies that such conditions should be specified and documented when reporting the results of such comparisons.

Other factors also may explain rejection of this (relatively stringent) preference regularity hypothesis. For example, RUT requires three items to be specified in pre-ference models: (1) a preference rule (utility function) that can be decomposed into systematic and random components, (2) a choice set of alternatives and (3) a decision (choice) rule that selects an alternative from a choice set. Differences in any of these three items between data sources may lead to violations of preference regularity. For example, suppose that two data sources represent identical designed choice experi-ments that differ only in that the first source was a forced choice between two designed alternatives, and the second contained an additional (third) 'no-choice' alternative. Thus, the first data source represents choices from sets C_r, $r = 1, \ldots, R$, but the second represents choices from sets $D_r = C_r \cup \{\text{'No choice'}\}$, $r = 1, \ldots, R$. Previous beha-vioural research would suggest that behaviour in the forced choice condition will differ significantly from the condition containing the option to not choose (e.g., Tversky and Shafir 1992, Olsen et al. 1995). In fact, if there is a difference it implies utility model parameter inequality, not preference regularity.

Unfortunately, definition PR does not inform us as to what represents a 'reason-able' attribute dimensionality from which to make inferences about preference regu-larities between multiple data sources. Nevertheless, it seems reasonable that comparisons involving fewer attributes generally should represent weaker support for preference regularity across data sources than comparisons involving more. In addition, the strength of evidence should increase as the number of attributes in the comparison increases.

It is also important to understand why tests of preference regularity should not involve alternative-specific constants (ASCs). In part this is due to the fact that our definition of preference regularity involves the sensitivity of multiple latent utility functions to attribute changes. However, more specifically, ASCs are simply the loca-tion parameters of the random utility component and not associated with any one attribute; they also capture the average effect of omitted variables, which varies between contexts. For example, in the case of the MNL model it is well known that if one includes all (identifiable) ASCs, the aggregate predicted marginal choice dis-tribution *will necessarily equal* the observed aggregate marginal choice distribution (see Ben-Akiva and Lerman 1985). ASCs have no other substantive interpretation (but with certain coding conventions, they can be forced to equal the expected utility if all attributes exactly equal zero). Although some non-IID error models do not share this property with MNL, ASCs none the less are specific to each data source; hence, including them in the common utility cannot enhance preference regularity tests. Furthermore, as we later show, the proportionality constants in our preference regularity definitions are related to assumptions about the random utility components $(\zeta_{ck} + \zeta_k + \varepsilon_k)$; hence, it is necessary to allow differences in measurement reliability to test preference regularity between data sources.

13.3.2 Stochastic variability and preference regularity

It is well known that the latent utility scale associated with a particular choice model cannot be determined absolutely, but rather has an arbitrary origin (zero point). However, what seems to be less well appreciated is that the *scale* of the latent utility construct also cannot be uniquely identified. This identification restriction is the same as that encountered by structural equation modellers in identifying the variances of latent constructs.

For example, consider a binary probit choice model with latent utilities $U_i = V_i + \varepsilon_i$, where $i = 1, 2$ is the alternative index, V_i is the deterministic utility and $(\varepsilon_1, \varepsilon_2)'$ is a bivariate normal random component with variances $\text{var}(\varepsilon_i)$ and $\text{cov}(\varepsilon_1, \varepsilon_2)$. The observed dependent variable is $Y = (y_1, y_2)$, where y_1 equals 1 if $U_1 > U_2$, 0 otherwise, and $y_2 = 1 - y_1$. The choice probability of alternative 1 is given by

$$\text{prob}(1) = \Phi[(V_1 - V_2)/\sigma] = \Phi[\alpha(V_1 - V_2)], \tag{13.3}$$

where Φ is the $N(0, 1)$ CDF, $\sigma^2 = \text{var}(\varepsilon_1) + \text{var}(\varepsilon_2) - \text{cov}(\varepsilon_1, \varepsilon_2)$ and $\alpha = 1/\sigma$. Equation (13.3) reveals two properties about the scale (α) of the underlying utility construct: (1) it is determined by one's assumptions about the random stochastic utility component, and (2) it is confounded with the partworth utility estimates. This situation is not unique to binary probit, which can be seen if we consider the same latent utility model but assume that the εs are IID Gumbel with scale factor $\lambda^2 (= \pi^2/6\sigma^2$, where $\sigma^2 = \text{var}(\varepsilon_1) = \text{var}(\varepsilon_2))$. Then the choice probability for alternative 1 is

$$\text{prob}(1) = \{1 + \exp[-\lambda(V_1 - V_2)]\}^{-1}. \tag{13.4}$$

We note without formal proof that confounding of scale and partworth estimates is common to *all* preference models that link latent constructs to observable categorical or discrete ordered outcomes. Thus, binary and multinomial versions of linear, MNL, HEV, GEV and probit models, as well as ordered logit and probit models, inherently confound scale and partworths (see chapter 6 of this book; also McFadden 1981, Ben-Akiva and Lerman 1985, Maddala 1983, Bunch 1991).

As noted in Ben-Akiva and Lerman (1985) and Swait and Louviere (1993), estimation of these models requires one to assume an appropriate normalising condition, such as $\alpha \equiv 1$ in (13.3) or $\lambda \equiv 1$ in (13.4). However, figure 8.6 demonstrates that one's choice of scaling constant makes a difference. That is, as scale increases, even for a fixed difference in systematic utilities, the probability model becomes more like a step-function. In fact, as $\lambda \to \infty$, choice becomes deterministic because alternative 1 will be chosen whenever $(V_1 - V_2) \geq 0$ (Ben-Akiva and Lerman 1985). Conversely, as $\lambda \to 0$, choice probabilities converge to $1/J$, for J alternatives (i.e., a uniform distribution).

Unfortunately, the need to normalise the scale constant in empirical applications of choice models tends to obscure the fact that the estimated model parameters are actually estimates of (scale × partworth). This confound is irrelevant for prediction, but is crucial for comparison of partworths across market segments, elicitation procedures, experimental conditions, time periods, geographical locations, etc. That is, it must be taken into account because not to do so can result in real preference similarities being obscured.

To illustrate why this can be so we will examine two typical preference function comparison situations in the next section. We will also demonstrate how to formally test for preference regularity.

13.4 Procedures for testing preference regularity

13.4.1 Case 1: multiple experimental conditions/response variable = choice

Suppose we design L (≥ 2) experimental conditions to test some behavioural hypothesis. We randomly assign respondents to each of the L conditions, and expose them to condition-specific information prior to completing an identical choice task. For the sake of discussion, assume that the utility function in condition l is (using the notation of the previous section)

$$U_l = \theta_l + \beta_l X_l + \nu_l, l = 1, \ldots, L, \tag{13.5}$$

where $\nu_i = (\zeta_{cl} + \varepsilon_l)$. That is, there are no context-specific utility components (i.e., $W_l(Z_l, \gamma_l) = 0$ and $\zeta_l = 0$, $\forall l$), but ASCs and utility parameters may differ between conditions. We also assume that the ν_l are IID Gumbel (EV1) with scale factor λ_l in each condition, which has two consequences: (1) choice processes in both conditions conform to a MNL model, and (2) levels of error variance in each condition may differ because $\lambda_l \propto 1/\sigma_l$. Other assumptions would lead to multinomial probit or other random utility models in each condition, but do not alter our logic. Thus, the choice probabilities in condition l are generated by MNL models that may seem superficially similar, but actually involve different values of λ_l:

$$P_{il} = \exp\left[\lambda_l(\theta_{il} + \beta_l X_{il})\right] \Big/ \sum_l \exp\left[\lambda_l(\theta_{il} + \beta_l X_{jl})\right]. \tag{13.6}$$

The null hypothesis of interest is that the experimental manipulations do not affect utility parameters $B_l, l = 1, \ldots, L$, or essentially, that $H_0: \beta_1 = \beta_2 = \cdots = \beta_L = \beta$. For a linear-in-the-parameters preference function specification, this hypothesis is equivalent to stating that preference regularity exists across the L conditions. If we estimate

MNL models from data in each of the L conditions, we estimate $(\lambda_l \beta_l)$, $l = 1, \ldots, L$, not the β_ls of real interest. If we compare model coefficients across conditions and find differences, we cannot know if these differences are due to (a) differences in utility parameters, (b) differences in scale factors, (c) sampling error or (d) combinations of all three.

One might begin an initial investigation into preference regularity by means of simple graphs. Specifically, by definition PR$'$, if H_0 holds and one graphs pairs of estimated utilities from each data source (i.e., $(\lambda_1 \beta_1)$ vs. $(\lambda_2 \beta_2)$, $(\lambda_1 \beta_1)$ vs. $(\lambda_3 \beta_3)$, etc.), the result should be a 'cloud' of points consistent with a straight-line passing through the origin of the graph (as in figure 8.6, p. 236). Alternatively, one can calculate the eigenvalues of the correlation matrix of the L estimated parameter vectors to investigate the number of linearly independent dimensions needed to describe the L points in K-space (K is the number of elements in β, denoted $K = |\beta|$). In the latter case, if H_0 holds, all the estimated utility vectors must be perfectly linearly related except for estimation and sampling errors; hence, only one dimension can underlie the data. Of course, one can do both things: (a) locate the parameter vector components in a space of reduced dimensions, and (b) graph all vectors against the first dimension. Again, if H_0 holds, one should obtain a family of proportional straight lines, and if slopes differ, the differences are due to scale factor differences.

Unfortunately, graphs and simple matrix reduction techniques do not take into account the sampling and estimation errors (i.e., the estimated parameter vectors are random variables). Swait and Louviere (1993) discuss the two-condition extension to the informal procedure above that accounts for these errors. A straightforward adaptation of the Swait and Louviere test permits one to correctly test H_0, as follows:

1. Estimate L separate choice models, obtaining the log likelihood value at convergence, LL_l, for each.
2. Pool all L data sources to estimate a joint model that imposes H_0, but allows different λ_l, $l = 1, \ldots, L$; call the log likelihood at convergence LL_J.
3. Form the statistic $-2(LL_J - \sum LL_l)$, which is asymptotically chi-squared distributed with $K(L - 1)$ degrees of freedom, where $K = |\beta|$. If the calculated chi-squared value is greater than the critical chi-squared value at the desired significance level, reject H_0.

The key points involved in this procedure are that step (1) estimates $(\lambda_l \beta_l)$, $l = 1, \ldots, L$, which permits both scale and partworths to vary from condition to condition; step (2) estimates a single β across conditions and λ_l, $l = 1, \ldots, L$, which permits scale to vary while imposing a single partworth vector across all conditions. It is important to note that one cannot identify all L Gumbel scale factors in estimating the joint model in step (2) above. Instead, one of them, say λ_1, must be normalised (conveniently, to one), with the remaining $(L - 1)$ scale factor ratios (λ_l / λ_1) identified by the procedure.

The advantage of this formal statistical test is that it accounts for all three sources of differences in parameters. A disadvantage is that one needs original data, which may preclude rigorous post-hoc investigation of some previously published results that contain only parameter estimates. Graphs and eigenvalue analyses can be applied to published results, but as mentioned earlier they lack the statistical properties and power of a full information maximum likelihood (FIML) test. Thus, several fields, most notably marketing and transport research, could benefit from having all researchers who publish model results make their original data available to others who request them (a practice common in several other fields, e.g., environmental and resource economics).

The immediately preceding case is of general interest, despite its deceptively simple nature. For example, several researchers recently reported hypotheses consistent with the general structure described above: Swait and Louviere (1993) for $L = 2$; Adamowicz, Louviere and Williams (1994), Adamowicz et al. (1997) for $L = 2$ and $L = 3$; and Louviere, Fox and Moore (1993) for $L = 7$. The foregoing were comparisons of alternative preference elicitation procedures, but could have been comparisons of segments (a priori or latent) or product classes. Indeed, to illustrate the generality of application, we now consider a comparison across product classes.

For example, Deighton, Henderson and Neslin (1994) examined the effects of advertising on switching and repeat purchase behaviour in three mature product classes (ketchup, and liquid and powdered detergent) using scanner panel data from Eau Claire, Wisconsin. They estimated separate MNL models from these data, which resulted in eleven common parameters associated with variables related to advertising exposure, price, promotional status, loyalty and recent purchase behaviour (coefficients and associated standard errors are in Deighton et al. 1994, table 3). The eigenvalues of the correlation matrix for these three parameter vectors were, respectively 2.88, 0.09 and 0.02. Thus, the first eigenvalue explains 96 per cent of the variance, which suggests that the common utility partworths for the three product classes can be arrayed along a single underlying dimension. This expectation is confirmed by figure 13.3, which graphs the components of the three vectors against the first latent dimension. As expected, the elements of the three vectors cluster closely together and their slopes appear to be quite similar, suggesting equality of scale factors. We lack access to their data, but it appears likely that a formal test of the hypothesis of preference regularity would not be rejected for these three data sets. Thus, a simple mechanism (i.e., differences in the error variances of the three products) is able to account for nearly all of the differences in the parameter vectors for three distinct product classes (especially ketchup versus the other two).

The latter result is significant because if the hypothesis of preference regularity holds across the three product classes, Deighton et al. (1994) could have pooled the three data sources to estimate a common vector of utility partworths, while controlling for possible scale differences. At a minimum, this would increase their sample size, and thereby the efficiency of their parameter estimates; but more significantly, it would imply process invariance across data sets and product categories. Indeed, data pooling might have led them to report more robust findings with respect to their substantive hypotheses concerning the impact of advertising on switching and repeat purchase behaviour.

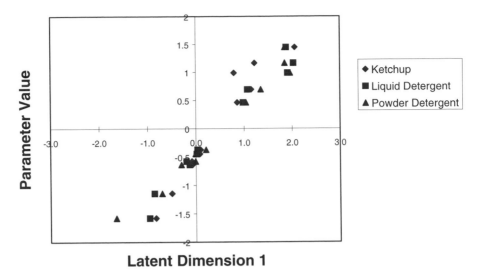

Latent Dimension 1

Figure 13.3 Parameter plot. *Source:* Deighton et al. (1994, table 3)

13.4.2 Case 2: categorical versus ordinal response variables

As before, let us randomly assign respondents to one of two preference elicitation procedures:

1. One sample reports (a) the brands in a particular category that they considered and purchased on their last visit to a supermarket, and (b) the perceived attributes of the chosen and other considered products. We will call this the revealed preference, or RP, choice data (we also could observe the purchases of a random sample while in a store and ask them questions in part (b)).
2. A second sample indicates their likelihood of purchasing (on a seven-point ordinal scale) a single hypothetical product profile from the same category described by a vector of attribute levels. We will call this stated preference, or SP, ordinal data.

As before, interest centres on whether the two elicitation methods evoke the same preferences.

Let the utility function in the RP data set be given by

$$U_{RP} = \theta_{RP} + \beta_{RP} X_{c,RP} + \gamma_{RP} Z_{RP} + (\zeta_{c,RP} + \zeta_{RP} + \varepsilon_{RP}), \tag{13.7}$$

where we allow for choice-task-specific effects through Z_{RP}. Assume that the $(\zeta_{c,RP} + \zeta_{RP} + \varepsilon_{RP})$ are IID Gumbel with scale λ_{RP}. The probability of choice of brand i is, therefore,

$$P_i = \frac{\exp\left[\lambda_{RP}(\theta_{i,RP} + \beta_{RP} X_{ic,RP} + \gamma_{RP} Z_{i,RP})\right]}{\sum_j \exp\left[\lambda_{RP}(\theta_{j,RP} + \beta_{RP} X_{jc,RP} + \gamma_{RP} Z_{j,RP})\right]}. \tag{13.8}$$

Let us now turn our attention to the SP group, who provided the 'intent-to-purchase' ordinal response to a single product profile (we assume that 'brand' is not a profile attribute, hence task attributes are 'generic'). Assume that the observed ordinal response Y_n (a value from 1 to 7) is based on an underlying latent scale U_{SP}, as below:

$$U_{SP} = \beta_{SP}X_{c,SP} + (\zeta_{c,SP} + \varepsilon_{SP}), \tag{13.9}$$

and that $\nu_{SP} = (\zeta_{c,SP} + \varepsilon_{SP})$ is logistic distributed with location parameter 0 and standard deviation σ_{SP}. Hence, the cumulative density function for U_{SP} is

$$G_{SP}(u) = \{1 + \exp[\lambda_{SP}(\beta_{SP}X_{c,SP} - u)]\}^{-1}, \quad -\infty < u < \infty, \tag{13.10}$$

where $\lambda_{SP} = \pi 3^{-1/2}/\sigma_{SP}$ (see Johnson, Kotz and Balakrishnan, 1995). To fully specify the SP model, we must relate the underlying latent scale to the observed responses Y_n. Suppose that when the U_{SP} is less than or equal to some value τ_1, the respondent answers $Y_n = 1$. Using the CDF above, this event has probability $G_{SP}(\beta_{SP}X_{c,SP} + \tau_1)$. If U_{SP} lies between τ_1 and τ_2, which occurs with probability $[G_{SP}(\beta_{SP}X_{c,SP} + \tau_2) - G_{SP}(\beta_{SP}X_{c,SP} + \tau_1)]$, the respondent answers $Y_n = 2$. The full probability distribution for Y_n is given below:

$$\text{prob}\,(T_n = y)$$

$$= \begin{cases} G_{SP}(\beta_{SP}X_{c,SP} + \tau_1) & \text{if } y = 1 (\beta_{SP}X_{c,SP} \leq \tau_1) \\ G_{SP}(\beta_{SP}X_{c,SP} + \tau_2) - G_{SP}(\beta_{SP}X_{c,SP} + \tau_1) & \text{if } y = 2 (\tau_1 \leq \beta_{SP}X_{c,SP} \leq \tau_2) \\ 1 - G_{SP}(\beta_{SP}X_{c,SP} + \tau_6) & \text{if } y = 7 (\tau_6 \leq \beta_{SP}X_{c,SP}) \end{cases}$$

$$\tag{13.11}$$

The parameters $\tau = (\tau_1, \dots, \tau_6)'$ are called threshold parameters, and it is required that $\tau_1 \leq \tau_2 \leq \cdots \leq \tau_6$ (only five can be identified, so we can set $\tau_1 \equiv 0$). Similar to the choice model case, the latent variable U_{SP} has an unidentifiable variance (or scale factor) that is confounded with the parameter vectors β_{SP} and τ (see equation (13.10)).

As in case 1, we are interested in whether preference regularity holds between the two elicitation methods. That is, does H_0: $\beta_{RP} = \beta_{SP} = \beta$ hold? The hypothesis test procedure is virtually identical to that for case 1:

1. Estimate two separate models, obtaining LL_{RP} and LL_{SP}, the log likelihood values at convergence.
2. Estimate a joint model that imposes H_0, but allows λ_{RP} and λ_{SP} to differ (both cannot be estimated, so normalise one (=1), and estimate the other); call the log likelihood at convergence LL_J.
3. Form the statistic $-2[LL_J - (LL_{RP} + LL_{SP})]$, which is asymptotically chi-squared distributed with K degrees of freedom, where as before $K = |\beta|$. If the calculated chi-squared value is greater than the critical chi-squared value at the desired significance level, reject H_0.

To illustrate this case, Morikawa (1994) combined RP choice data and SP preference rating data using a model system similar to the one above. The RP choice data were choices between rail and car for intercity travel in the Netherlands, while the SP data were ordered responses to a designed paired comparison experiment. Morikawa was interested in combining RP and SP data to improve the statistical properties of his estimates, but his paper contains the results needed to perform the descriptive tests discussed in this and prior sections. We subjected the common six parameters to a principal components analysis (RP generated by a binary logit model, and SP by an ordered probit model), and obtained eigenvalues of 1.442 and 0.558. Thus, the first eigenvalue accounts for approximately 72 per cent of the variation in the average utility parameters in both data sources. Not surprisingly, therefore, Morikawa's formal test retained the null that the parameters of the two models were equal up to scale at an $\alpha = 0.05$ level (calculated chi-squared = 11.5, with seven degrees of freedom; critical value = 14.1). The estimated scale ratio ($\lambda_{SP}/\lambda_{RP}$) was 0.27, which suggests that SP data error variances were approximately four times larger than RP variances.

This second case demonstrates that testing the existence of preference regularity across multiple data sources involves controlling for variance (or reliability) differences, even if one or more of the dependent measures are *not* indicators of choice, *per se*. This reinforces our earlier comments that the conceptual framework proposed and discussed in this chapter can be used to compare any forms of dominance data.

13.4.3 Summary

The foregoing discussion demonstrated that the scale factor (which is inversely related to the error variance) is a measure of the statistical information contained in preference (or more generally, dominance) data. Consequently, if two preference data sets contain the same underlying preference structure, but differ significantly in magnitudes of random error, the two sets of estimated parameters will appear to differ significantly in absolute magnitudes. This has far-reaching implications for interpreting and testing the results of empirical model comparisons. For example, Swait and Louviere (1993) noted that few previous researchers in marketing took error variance differences into account in statistical tests of parameter differences in preference model comparisons, and showed how this can lead to misinterpretation of hypothesis tests. Similarly, it was recognised only recently that many preference measures such as ratings and rankings can be treated as implied choices (although see Chapman and Staelin 1982). More specifically, Louviere (1994) discussed ways to treat discrete (multiple) choices, binary responses (yes/no, like/dislike, consider/not consider, etc.), rankings, ratings and resource allocations in a random utility framework, and estimate probabilistic discrete-choice models from each data source.

Louviere's (1994) observation also applies to designed preference experiments such as conjoint, paired or multiple comparisons, as well as similar measures observed for real choice alternatives in surveys or other sources of observational data, including but not limited to revealed preference data such as scanner panel data in marketing and labour participation panels in applied economics work. In turn, this establishes a common basis for comparison of dominance data sources. Now that we can compare these data sources on a level playing field, and we know that each source may exhibit different magnitudes of random component variation, some previously published results of parameter comparisons may need to be reconsidered. Thus, future research opportunities now can be pursued that can enrich our understanding of similarities as well as differences in preference measures, methods and models.

Equally significantly, now that we understand the role played by the scale parameter more fully, it begs the question as to how and why differences in error variability arise in different sets of preference data. We ignore this issue in this chapter, but note in passing that answers to this question should be keenly pursued in future research. Instead, to fulfil our objectives of (1) reviewing cross- and external validity results, (2) motivating future research and (3) illustrating the generality of the empirical conclusions that arise from the conceptual framework, the next section presents empirical preference regularity results spanning a wide range of contexts.

13.5 Empirical case studies and results

This section presents sixteen comparisons of preference data model parameters spanning a wide range of product/service categories, types of preference data, data collection procedures, types of consumers, geographical locations, time periods, etc. The examples we present are organised into three major groups:

1. *Revealed preference (RP) data* These include examples of survey and scanner panel data sources that permit tests of preference regularities between market segments, time periods and product categories. These comparisons are included to illustrate that even though RP data have long been the preferred source from which to estimate preference models, cross-validity comparisons still have much to reveal about underlying processes.
2. *Stated Preference (SP) data* Examples of survey-based choice experiments (Louviere and Woodworth 1983) and best/worst conjoint (Louviere and Swait 1996a) are examined with respect to market segments and comparisons across multiple SP elicitation methods. These comparisons specifically address cross-validity issues, that is, whether different measures of the same underlying preference structure result in the same inferences about the preference process.
3. *RP and SP data* A number of examples examine preference regularities between actual choices (RP) and stated choices (SP), making possible comparisons across space and elicitation methods for different product classes. These comparisons specifically address the case of external validity, that is, whether SP models capture the underlying preference process revealed in RP data.

We want to point out that these sixteen data sets were not chosen to make SP look good. Instead, they are a subset of a much larger set of empirical results that we have compiled over the past eight years in our research programme, and are representative of this larger body of research. All examples in this section involve categorical response variables and MNL functional forms (hence, case 1 applies). Although we focus on MNL models in this section, it is important to reiterate that *all* choice models (in fact, all preference ranking models) are subject to the preference regularity concepts introduced earlier in this chapter.

The 'main hypothesis' that underlies our examination of these cases is that preference regularity (as in definition PR) exists between the conditions examined. All model specifications presented are linear-in-the parameters, and the null is that there are no reliable differences between model parameters estimated from the different sources of preference data, once differences in error variability are taken into account. To test this hypothesis we adopt the view that each type of preference data and its associated preference model constitutes a measurement system, and the parameters estimated from each system constitute the measurements of interest. Thus, the main hypothesis can be restated as: 'All sources of preference data and the model parameters estimated from these data are equally valid measures of the underlying, latent preferences, but the sources of preference data can differ in their measurement reliability.'

Viewed from the latter perspective, the problem can be conceptualised as a multi-trait, multi-method issue. In this view, we expect the vectors of estimated preference parameters to form a single measurement system, comprising a single, common factor. Ideally, this latter hypothesis can be tested using confirmatory factor analysis; however, in most of our cases, either the number of estimated parameters is too small for a reliable analysis or the number of different parameter vectors is too small. Hence, we use non-confirmatory principal components analysis, which provides strong circumstantial evidence for the main hypothesis. As shown earlier, a FIML extension of the Swait and Louviere (1993) likelihood ratio test can be used to test preference regularity. In our discussion below, we present the results of this formal test whenever available.

For the sake of brevity, results are summarised in table 13.1, and we now discuss them in some detail. Some examples strongly support the existence of preference regularity in particular situations, while others suggest that it may not hold in certain situations. Reasons why the data in any one example do/do not support preference regularity is not the issue. Instead, the more important issue is that regularity seems to hold in such a surprisingly large number of cases. These results should stimulate subsequent research into rigorous explanations for the existence of preference regularities and the conditions under which they can or cannot be expected, etc.

13.5.1 Revealed preference (RP) data sources

Examples 1–5 deal with choices made in real markets. The first two cases involve work trip mode choices by residents of Washington, DC and Bogotá, Colombia, respectively. The first example is from Ben-Akiva and Lerman (1985), and involves three MNL models estimated for different income groups defined a priori. Excluding the ASCs for reasons explained earlier, each model vector contains nine parameters. When we subject these three nine-parameter vectors to a principal components analysis, we find that the first eigenvalue accounts for 81 per cent of the variance, hence the vast majority of the reliable variance can be summarised by a single common factor. Example 2 is from Kozel (1986), who compared work trip mode choice models in

Bogotá, Colombia, in 1972 and 1978. Similar to the Ben-Akiva and Lerman result above, the first eigenvalue derived from a principal components analysis accounts for 78 per cent of the variance in the vectors of estimated parameters.

In both cases the original data are unavailable to conduct a formal test of the main hypothesis, but it none the less is noteworthy that the parameter vectors in both cases appear to be highly comparable across market segments (example 1) and time periods (example 2). This finding is somewhat ironic in light of the fact that nearly a decade ago there was great interest in spatial and temporal choice model transferability in the transportation planning literature (e.g., Kozel 1986). If preference regularity holds in this area, savings in data collection costs could amount to many millions of dollars worldwide, which was then and again should be a key motivation for interest in transferability of choice models.

Examples 3–5 are published examples involving scanner panel data, and all are analysed using principal components analysis to extract the eigenvalues associated with successive linear combinations of the data columns representing each vector of model parameters. Example 1 (Deighton et al. 1994), which was previously discussed, shows that the first eigenvalue explains 96 per cent of the variability between the MNL parameter vectors for three different product classes (ketchup, liquid and powdered detergent). Examples 4 and 5 are included because (a) they involve other product classes and (b) they try to model consumer heterogeneity with latent class procedures. Example 4 involves a five-latent-class MNL model for an unspecified product (Kamakura and Russell 1989). The eigenvalues of the correlation matrix of the five four-parameter vectors are, respectively, 3.60, 1.01, 0.39, 0 and 0; hence, the first dimension captures 72 per cent of the variability. This suggests that the number of latent classes may be overspecified, and only two classes may be warranted once one allows for scale factor differences between classes. That is, an alternative model would involve hierarchically structured heterogeneity classes, in which two meta-classes exist at an upper level because their utility parameters truly differ; and within each meta-class, at a lower level, the five classes differ because of scale factors (or variability) differences, but not taste differences. Such a result obtains because current latent class choice modelling procedures cannot distinguish between model parameter differences due to error variability differences and real parameter differences; instead, absolute parameter magnitudes are used to distinguish latent classes. Example 5 involves the identification and estimation of three latent classes in households who purchase ground coffee (Bucklin et al., 1995). The first eigenvalue accounts for 67 per cent of the variability in the correlation matrix representing the estimated latent class parameter vectors (the eigenvalues are, respectively, 2.01, 0.73 and 0.26). This result suggests that the number of latent classes may be overspecified by one, or perhaps more, classes.

Latent class choice models have become popular in survey and scanner panel applications in marketing. Latent classes are one way to operationalise the concept of market segments, and are often a relatively straightforward way to account for consumer heterogeneity (e.g., compared to random parameter specifications). Nevertheless, the results in the foregoing examples suggest that attributing differences

Table 13.1. *Empirical case studies*

Example	Example description	Comments	No. of parameter vectors	No. of parameters	% variance dimension 1	Hypothesis test results
1	Work trip mode choice; Multiple income segments	• Washington, DC 1968 RP data, 3 income segments • 1136 observations • Source; Ben-Akiva and Lerman (1985: 196–7)	3	9	81	NA
2	Work trip mode choice; Two time periods	• Bogotá, Colombia, RP data for • 1972: 732 observations • 1978: 1244 observations • Source: Kozel (1986: 263–4)	2	17	78	NA
3	Scanner panel data; Multiple product classes	• Eau Claire, WI RP panel data • Product classes: *Ketchup*: 481 households, 3897 purchases *Liquid detergents*: 167 households, 1519 purchases *Powder detergents*: 313 households, 3527 purchases • Source: Deighton et al. (1994: table 3)	3	11	96	NA
4	Scanner panel data with latent segments (I)	• Product: unknown food item, • 585 households, 78-week observation period • 5 latent segments • Source: Kamakura and Russell (1989: table 2)	5	4	72	NA

5	Scanner panel data with latent segments (II)	• Product: ground caffeinated coffee, 4 brands • 376 households, 4985 purchases • 3 latent segments • Source: Bucklin et al. (1995: table 1)	3	7	67	NA
6	Best/worst conjoint, two attitudinal segments	• Best/worst conjoint for retail outlets attributes • Segments: 2 groups created based on response to an ordinal scale about attitude towards shopping • Source: convenience sample of 64 University of Florida undergraduate students	2	12	97	Scalable, at the 95% significance level
7	Elicitation method comparison: SP choice and SP consideration	• Product: bicycle trail choice • Sample of Chicago residents • *SP1*: trinomial bike trail choice, 16 profiles • *SP2*: Yes/No bike trail consideration, 16 profiles • Source: Swait and Louviere (1993: 311)	2	53	94	Scalable, at the 95% significance level (not including ASCs)
8	Multiple SP elicitation methods: vacation destination preference (I)	• Sample: convenience group of 168 residents of Edmonton, Canada • *SP1*: next choice • *SP2*: choice experiment • *SP3*: yes/no consideration • *SP4*: consideration (exploded) • *SP5*: ideal ratings (exploded) • *SP6*: ideal ratings (logistic regression) • Source: Louviere et al. (1993: table 1)	6	34	63	NA

Table 13.1. (cont.)

Example	Example description	Comments	No. of parameter vectors	No. of parameters	% variance dimension 1	Hypothesis test results
9	Multiple SP elicitation methods: vacation destination preference (II)	• Sample convenience group of 168 residents of Edmonton, Canada • SP1: next choice SP2: choice experiment SP3: yes/no consideration SP6: ideal ratings (logistic regression) • Source: Louviere et al. (1993: table 1)	4	34	83	NA
10	Geographic and elicitation method comparison	• Product: freight shipper choice of carrier • Sample: 600 businesses in each of 3 North American cities • For each city, RP data: proportion of shipments by carriers SP data: trinomial choice experiment, 16 profiles per respondent • Source: Swait et al. (1994)	6 (2 methods × 3 cities)	18	83	– Hypothesis of RP/SP scalability rejected at 95% significance level in all 3 cities – Hypothesis of geographic transferability not tested
11	Elicitation method comparison: RP and SP choice	• Product: housing mortgage provider • RP: choices made by recent home buyers • SP: choice experiment with 4 alternatives, 8 profiles per respondent • Source: confidential	2	77	55	Not rejected at 95% significance level

12	Elicitation method comparison: RP, SP choice and best/worst conjoint	• Product: ski area destination • *RP*: most recent ski area choice, 152 respondents *CB*: trinomial, generic ski area choice, 10 sets per respondent, 282 respondents *BW*: 16 profiles per respondent, 195 respondents • Source: Louviere and Swait (1996a)	3	28	59	– RP and BW scalability: not rejected at 95% significance level – RP and CB scalability: not rejected at 95% significance level
13	Elicitation method comparison: RP marginal distribution and SP next choice	• Product: shopping mall destination • Sample: Orlando 1992 • Source: Jordan Louviere	3	17	93	NA
14	Elicitation method comparison: RP last choice, RP marginal distribution	• Product: shopping mall destination • Sample: Edmonton 1993 • Source: Jordan Louviere	2	31	70	NA
15	Elicitation method comparison: RP last choice, RP marginal distribution, 2 SP consideration measures	• Product: shopping mall destination • Sample: Oslo, 1992 • Source: Jordan Louviere	4	21	93	NA
16	Elicitation method comparison across 2 cities: RP last choice, RP marginal distribution, 2 SP consideration measures	• Product: shopping mall destination • Sample: Oslo 1992 and Edmonton 1993 • Source: Jordan Louviere	8	7	89	NA

among consumers to utility parameter variation which actually are due to differences in reliability may possibly mislead formulation and execution of policy. Swait (1994: 80) noted the following:

> Clearly, different marketing actions are implied if segments have the same underlying response patterns with respect to product attributes but some are more variable in their behaviour than others, compared to the situation in which the underlying response patterns are truly different. Thus, it is felt that this distinction between behavioural response to stimuli and variability in behaviour is important to producing meaningful segments for managerial decision-making.

13.5.2 Stated preference (SP) data sources

This group of data sources generally involves comparisons of consumer preferences inferred from different SP elicitation procedures and constitutes examples 6–10.

Example 6 is based on the best/worst conjoint elicitation method (Finn and Louviere 1993; Louviere and Diener 1997), in which consumers are asked to choose one most and one least attractive conjoint profile feature. In this study retail stores were described by six attributes and evaluated by a convenience sample of undergraduate students at the University of Florida in the USA. Each student indicated his/her attitude towards retail shopping, and was subsequently classified into one of two groups ('hate to shop' and 'love to shop'). Segment-specific MNL models were estimated on the attribute level counts. Naive pooling of the data from the two segments (i.e., not controlling for scale differences) rejects the hypothesis of utility parameter equality ($\chi^2 = 31.6$, 13 d.f., 95 per cent confidence level critical value $= 22.36$). This is somewhat surprising given the homogeneity of the sample, but might be justified on the basis of segment utility parameter differences.

A principal components analysis of both segment-specific twelve-parameter vectors results in a first eigenvalue that accounts for 97 per cent of the variance, which strongly suggests that preference regularity should hold between the two consumer types after accounting for scale differences. Thus, not surprisingly, a formal test of the main hypothesis retains the null at $\alpha = 0.05$ significance level ($\chi^2 = 11.8$, 12 d.f.), and illustrates how apparently significant model segment differences may be explained by reliability (or segment error variance) differences. That is, respondents in both 'love to shop' and 'hate to shop' segments seem to have the same utility parameters, but the level of random error variance in the 'love to shop' segment is less than that in the 'hate to shop' segment, and the latter difference led to initial rejection of parameter equality.

Example 7 involves bicycle trail discrete choice and consideration SP responses elicited from a sample of 367 Chicago residents. The same choice experiment was used to elicit both choice and consideration responses. The main hypothesis could not be rejected at the $\alpha = 0.05$ significance level for these two data sources (Swait and Louviere 1993). Table 13.1 also reveals that the first eigenvalue from a principal components analysis of the two estimated parameter vectors accounts for 94 per cent of the variance. Hence, these results suggest that the choice and consideration elicitation procedures (1) capture the same attribute trade-offs, but different overall utility levels, and (2) have different levels of response reliability (i.e., error variance).

Example 8 involves six different SP preference elicitation methods (Louviere, Fox and Moore 1993). Preference data were obtained from a convenience sample of 158 Edmonton residents, who evaluated sixteen different vacation destinations in different ways. We analysed the six parameter vectors using principal components analysis, and the first eigenvalue accounted for 63 per cent of the variance in the correlation matrix of the parameter estimates. Two elicitation methods (denoted SP4 and SP5, in table 13.1) used rank-order data explosion to create implied choices (Chapman and Staelin, 1982; Louviere, Fox and Moore 1993), and graphs of the estimated parameter suggest that SP4 and SP5 coefficients are similar to each other, but not to other SP estimates. Pairwise comparisons using the Swait and Louviere (1993) sequential test of the main hypothesis were reported in the paper, and demonstrated high levels of support for the main hypothesis, except for the data representing rating of 'ideal' alternatives.

Example 9 is a further analysis of example 8 in which SP4 and SP5 coefficients are deleted from the principal components analysis. This yields a first eigenvalue that accounts for 83 per cent of the variance among elicitation procedures SP1, SP2, SP3 and SP6, and suggests that methods SP4 and SP5 measure something other than the other four elicitation procedures. The remaining four procedures exhibit a much higher degree of preference regularity, hence, we would conclude that their cross-validity is high. This outcome is consistent with recent research on preference orderings (e.g., Ben-Akiva, Morikawa and Shiroishi 1991), which suggests that models estimated from ranking and discrete-choice data do not yield comparable utility estimates.

13.5.3 Combinations of RP and SP data sources

In this section we consider combining multiple sources of preference data, especially RP and SP data. This topic has been of considerable recent interest in transportation research and environmental/resource economics (e.g., see chapters 11 and 12 of this book; see also Ben-Akiva and Morikawa 1990; Hensher and Bradley 1993; Swait, Louviere and Williams 1994; Ben-Akiva et al. 1994; Adamowicz, Louviere and Williams 1994; Adamowicz et al. 1997; Swait and Adamowicz 1996), and should interest researchers in marketing and other fields. The pioneering work of Ben-Akiva and associates was motivated by a desire to improve the statistical properties of RP parameter estimates with supplemental SP data. In contrast, Swait and Louviere (1993) were motivated by a need for a test to determine *if* one is justified in pooling multiple preference data sources. The latter is a more general concern because pooling preference data sources requires the satisfaction of preference regularity defined earlier in this chapter.

Example 10 compares six sources of RP and SP choice data from each of three North American cities (Swait, Louviere and Williams 1994). Two hundred respondents in each of three North American cities supplied data about their previous

Table 13.2. *Principal components results for example 10*

Condition	No. of parameter vectors	% variance dimension 1
All cities, RP and SP	6	83
3 cities, RP only	3	90
3 cities, SP only	3	88
City 1, RP and SP	2	84
City 2, RP and SP	2	88
City 3, RP and SP	2	94

choices of freight shippers during a stipulated prior time period. SP data were obtained from the same respondents using a designed choice experiment. Each individual supplied choice data for sixteen scenarios, from which MNL models (eighteen parameters each) were estimated. The correlation matrix of the resulting six RP and SP parameter vectors was analysed by principal components (eigenvalues were, respectively, 4.95, 0.45, 0.35, 0.14, 0.07 and 0.03). The first eigenvalue explains 83 per cent of the variance in the between-conditions models correlation matrix, but Swait, Louviere and Williams (1994) rejected the RP vs. SP preference regularity hypothesis across the three cities at the $\alpha = 0.05$ significance level (see table 13.1). Shipper alternatives varied from city to city although some were common to all, and different shipping companies dominated each market. Thus, it is not surprising that the overall set of six vectors does not satisfy preference regularity.

Nevertheless, the principal components results in table 13.2 help to interpret the results of the hypothesis test. In particular, parameter vectors for the RP and SP data sources seem to be internally consistent across cities; but a comparison of elicitation methods within cities suggests that the rejection may be due to city 1's RP and SP data sets being less similar to one another. This, in turn, suggests that the overall failure to satisfy preference regularity is primarily due to differences in RP and SP data from city 1, which affected the comparison tests on the remaining parameter vectors. These data are proprietary, but we can say that city 1 is a very different North American city, and differences in behaviour in that city and other cities are often reported.

Choice of housing mortgage provider is example 11. Details of this study are confidential, but the study involved collection of RP data from a sample of approximately 350 recent home buyers and SP experimental choice data from a sample of approximately 800 respondents close to purchase. The first eigenvalue of the correlation matrix of two estimated MNL parameter vectors (each with 77 parameters) explains only 55 per cent of the variance, suggesting a much weaker relationship between the RP and SP data sources than previously encountered (see also example 8 above). However, a FIML test retains preference regularity at the $\alpha = 0.05$ significance level because many RP parameters were not statistically significant and had signs opposite to the SP parameters (see also example 8). Similar results motivated research into data fusion in transport and environmental economics; that is, RP data are often characterised by ill-conditioned design matrices with limited ranges in the design variables. For example, the explanatory variable 'loan interest rate' in example 11 exhibited little range in the real market (e.g., differences of 1/4 to 1/8 of a percentage point). SP data often can overcome such limitations (Adamowicz, Louviere and Williams 1994).

Example 12 compares preference elicitation based on best/worst (BW) conjoint (Louviere and Swait 1996a; Louviere and Diener 1997) with choice-based conjoint (CB) and RP choices in the context of ski area destination choice. Aggregate MNL models (28 parameters per vector) were calibrated for each elicitation procedure. Louviere and Swait (1996a) report FIML tests of preference regularity between BW and RP, and CB and RP, which retained the null hypothesis that the parameter vectors were equal after taking error variability differences into account. In contrast, the first eigenvalue in a principal components analysis explained only 59 per cent of the variance in the correlation matrix of the RP, BW and CB parameter vectors, which reinforces the need for a rigorous (FIML) test of preference regularity. Additional analyses of parameter vector pairs (RP,BW), (RP,CB) and (BW,CB) resulted in first eigenvalues that explained 75, 71 and 61 per cent of the variance, respectively. This latter result suggests that differences between BW and CB methods most likely account for the differences in the earlier analysis.

Examples 13–16 are a single case with sub-examples involving shopping mall destination choices. Similar surveys were administered to randomly sampled households in Orlando (USA), Edmonton (Canada) and Oslo (Norway) in 1992 and 1993 (Finn and Louviere 1996). In each survey, multiple RP (last mall visited, distribution of previous month's mall visits) and SP (next visit, two different mall consideration) measures were elicited. In each case, the first eigenvalue from a principal components analysis explained at least 70 per cent, and generally over 90 per cent, of the variability in the correlation matrix of the estimated parameter vectors. Especially notable is example 16, in which all RP and SP measures for Edmonton and Oslo were jointly analysed, yielding a first principal component that explained 89 per cent of the variability in the correlation matrix of the common utility partworths. The latter results suggest that preference regularity may hold for shopping mall destination choice across cultures, countries, urban forms and so forth.

13.6 Summary and conclusions

Several disciplines, primarily economics and psychology, have developed theoretical models to describe consumer behaviour in the marketplace, from which operational preference measurement models can be derived and applied. One of the most fruitful streams of research in that tradition has been random utility theory based choice models, which assume that some level of uncertainty is associated with analysts' inferences of consumer preferences. This chapter brought together three independent streams of research in consumer behaviour and preference measurement, with random utility theory serving as the underlying conceptual framework:

1. *Model transferability (over space and time)*   In the 1970s transportation research-ers tried to establish a basis for transferring travel demand models across space and time (see Kozel 1986) because of the potential for significant economies of cost and effort.
2. *Elicitation method comparisons*   Since the late 1970s interest in comparing and contrasting alternative preference elicitation methods in marketing and other fields has increased (e.g., Meyer 1977; Elrod, Louviere and Davey 1993; Olsen et al. 1995; Adamowicz, Louviere and Williams 1994);
3. *Data fusion*   Since the late 1980s, interest has steadily risen in combining prefer-ence data sources in which the strengths of one complement the other's weak-nesses and improve the statistical properties of design matrices. The ultimate goal of this research in transportation planning and resource economics is to obtain better utility parameter estimates (e.g., Ben-Akiva and Morikawa 1990; Adamowicz, Louviere and Williams et al. 1994).

This chapter has attempted to unify these three streams of research by proposing a relatively simple mechanism to explain *preference regularities* across multiple pre-ference data conditions (e.g., elicitation methods, cultures, time periods, and/or experimental conditions). Thus, we proposed that the existence of preference regula-rities should be evaluated on the basis of the marginal utility of attributes common to conditions, and tested on the basis of whether the marginal utilities are equal up to positive constants of proportionality. We demonstrated that a simple mechanism gives rise to these constants of proportionality that is inversely related to the variance (or scale) of the stochastic utility component in random utility models.

We developed a formal definition of preference regularity and illustrated how it could be applied to two cases often found in practice: (1) categorical responses com-pared across multiple conditions (e.g., conditions in an experiment); (2) one data source with a categorical response and another with an ordinal response. In both cases, we demonstrated that the positive constants of proportionality are directly related to the variances of the random utility component. We also discussed how failure to recognise their role will lead to improper comparisons of marginal utilities, and proposed a basic test for the existence of preference regularities, which generalises the likelihood ratio test proposed by Swait and Louviere (1993). In addition, we also presented two simple techniques to complement formal tests: (1) simple graphs of marginal utilities (or parameter values, if utility functions are linear-in-the-para-meters); and (2) matrix decomposition techniques such as principal components ana-lysis applied to the estimated parameter vectors to test for a single, common underlying factor. The latter two techniques do not account for the random nature of the estimated parameter vectors, but constitute useful exploratory analysis tools.

We presented a relatively large number of examples involving tests of prefer-ence regularities across multiple elicitation methods (RP: survey, scanner panel; SP:

best/worst, choice experiment, yes/no consideration, ratings conjoint), market segments (a priori and latent), space (between cities and countries), time periods, etc. The overwhelming majority of these examples supported our main hypothesis that the variance of the stochastic utility component generally accounts for a large proportion of the observed differences in preference parameters from different conditions, elicitation procedures, etc.

There are many implications of the existence of preference regularities for research into choice behaviour, of which the following are supported by the examples presented in this chapter:

1. If various SP elicitation methods can be shown to be equivalent (i.e., to capture preference regularities), albeit with different levels of reliability, this suggests new research to determine factors that underlie degrees of preference regularity, comparability and reliability of methods, conditions under which generalisations hold, etc.
2. To specify a priori or latent segments in choice and other preference-based data, it is important to test whether the data support (a) utility parameter variation or (b) utility parameter homogeneity with variance differences (i.e., preference regularity). The two outcomes do not imply the same policy actions (Swait 1994), and failure to recognise the existence of preference regularities in sub-classes in latent class models may lead to over-specification of the number of classes and incorrect strategic inferences.
3. If preference regularities can be shown to hold across combinations of product classes (e.g., as in Deighton et al. 1994), cultures and time periods (e.g., Finn and Louviere 1996), this would support generalisability of empirical observations, which should lead to more general theory.
4. Support for fusion of RP and SP data would be greatly increased if it could be shown that certain SP preference elicitation methods (and/or conditions of application) lead to more frequent satisfaction of preference regularity with RP sources. This would increase the usefulness of certain RP choice data sources (e.g., scanner panel data) by making it possible to add more flexible survey-based SP preference data from independent samples for which a wider variety of complementary information with improved statistical properties can be derived.

The above constitute only a partial list of insights that preference regularity research may bring to academic and applied research. The results in this chapter supporting the main hypothesis suggest that it is fair to conclude that further research along these lines is not only warranted, but seems likely to greatly enhance our understanding of preference formation and choice processes in real and simulated market environments.

References

Adamowicz, W. (1994): 'Habit formation and variety seeking in a discrete choice model of recreation demand', *Journal of Agricultural and Resource Economics*, 19: 19–31

Adamowicz, W., Boxall, P., Louviere, J., Swait, J. and Williams, M. (1998): 'Stated preference methods for valuing environmental amenities', in Bateman, I. and Willis, K. (eds.), *Valuing environmental preferences: theory and practice of the contingent valuation method in the US, EC and developing countries*, London: Oxford University Press, pp. 460–79

Adamowicz, W., Boxall, P., Williams, M. and Louviere, J. (1998): 'Stated preference approaches for measuring passive use values: choice experiments and contingent valuation', *American Journal of Agricultural Economics* 80(1), 64–75

Adamowicz, W., Louviere, J. and Swait, J. (1998): *An introduction to stated choice methods for resource based compensation*, prepared by Advanis Inc. for the National Oceanic and Atmospheric Administration, US Department of Commerce

Adamowicz, W., Louviere, J. and Williams, M. (1994): 'Combining stated and revealed preference methods for valuing environmental amenities', *Journal of Environmental Economics and Management* 26: 271–92

Adamowicz, W., Swait, J., Boxall, P., Louviere, J. and Williams, M. (1997): 'Perceptions versus objective measures of environmental quality in combined revealed and stated preference models of environmental valuation', *Journal of Environmental Economics and Management* 32: 65–84

Algers, S., Daly, A., Kjellman, P. and Widlert, S. (1996): 'Stockholm model system (SIMS): application', in Hensher, D.A., King, J. and Oum, T. (eds.), *World transport research: modelling transport systems*, Oxford: Pergamon, pp. 345–62

Algers, S., Daly, A. and Widlert, S. (1997): 'Modelling travel behaviour to support policy making in Stockholm', in Stopher P.R. and Lee-Gosselin M. (eds.), *Understanding travel behaviour in an era of change*, Oxford: Pergamon, 547–70

Allenby, G. and Ginter, J. (1995): 'The effects of in-store displays and feature advertising on consideration sets', *International Journal of Research in Marketing* 12: 67–80

Amemiya, T. (1978): 'On a two-step estimation of multinomial logit models', *Journal of Econometrics* 8(1): 13–21

(1981): 'Qualitative response models: a survey', *Journal of Economic Literature* 19: 1483–536

(1985): *Advanced econometrics*, Oxford: Basil Blackwell

Anderson, D.A. and Wiley, J.B. (1992): 'Efficient choice set designs for estimating availability cross-effects models', *Marketing Letters* 3(3): 357–70

Anderson, N.H. (1981): *Foundations of information integration theory*, New York: Academic Press

(1982): *Methods of information integration theory*, New York: Academic Press

(1996): *A functional theory of cognition*, Majwah, N.J.: Lawrence Erlbaum

Anderson, N.H., and Shanteau, J. (1977): 'Weak inference with linear models', *Psychological Bulletin* 85: 1155–70

Anderson, S., de Palma, A. and Thisse, J. (1992): *Discrete choice theory of product differentiation*, Cambridge, Mass.: MIT Press

Andrews, R. and Srinivasan, T.C. (1995): 'Studying consideration effects in empirical choice models using scanner panel data', *Journal of Marketing Research* 32: 30–41

Arnold, S.J., Oum, T.H, and Tigert, D.J. (1983): 'Determinant attributes in retail patronage: seasonal, temporal, regional and international comparisons', *Journal of Marketing Research* 20: 149–57

Arrow, K., Solow, R., Portnoy, P., Leamer, E., Radner, R. and Schuman, H. (1993): 'Report of the NOAA panel on contingent valuation', *Federal Register,* pp. 4601–14

Bates, J. (1995): *Alternative-specific constants in logit models,* Oxford: John Bates and Associates (mimeo)

(1999): 'More thoughts on nested logit', mimeo, John Bates Services, Oxford, January

Batsell, R.R. and Louviere, J. (1991): 'Experimental analysis of choice', *Marketing Letters* 2: 199–214

Ben-Akiva, M.E. (1977): 'Passenger travel demand forecasting: applications of disaggregate models and directions for research', paper presented at World Conference on Transport Research, Rotterdam, April

Ben-Akiva, M.E. and Boccara, B. (1995): 'Discrete choice models with latent choice sets', *International Journal of Research in Marketing* 12(1): 9–24

Ben-Akiva, M.E. and Bolduc, D. (1996): 'Multinomial probit with a logit kernel and a general parametric specification of the covariance structure', unpublished working paper, Department of Civil Engineering, MIT

Ben-Akiva, M.E., Bolduc, D. and Bradley, M. (1993): 'Estimation of travel choice models with randomly distributed values of time', *Transportation Research Record* 1413: 88–97

Ben-Akiva, M.E., Bradley, M., Morikawa, T., Benjamin, J., Novak, T., Oppewal, H. and Rao, V. (1994): 'Combining revealed and stated preferences data', *Marketing Letters* 5(4) (Special Issue on the Duke Invitational Conference on Consumer Decision-Making and Choice Behaviour: 335–51

Ben-Akiva, M.E. and Lerman, S. (1985): *Discrete choice analysis: theory and application to travel demand*, Cambridge, Mass: MIT Press

Ben-Akiva, M.E. and Morikawa, T. (1990): 'Estimation of switching models from revealed preferences and stated intentions', *Transportation Research* A 24A(6): 485–95

(1991): 'Estimation of travel demand models from multiple data sources', in Koshi, M. (ed.) *Transportation and traffic theory,* Proceedings of the 11th ISTTT, Amsterdam: Elsevier, pp. 461–76

Ben-Akiva, M. E., Morikawa, T. and Shiroishi, F. (1991): 'Analysis of the reliability of preference ranking data', *Journal of Business Research* 23: 253–68

Ben-Akiva, M.E. and Swait, J. (1986): 'The akaike likelihood ratio index', *Transportation Science* 20(2): 133–36

Berkovec, J., Hausman, J. and Rust, J. (1984): 'Heating system and appliance choice', MIT (mimeo)

Berkovec, J. and Rust, J. (1985): 'A nested logit model of automobile holdings for one vehicle households', *Transportation Research* 19B(4): 275–86

Berkson, J. (1953): 'A statistically precise and relatively simple method of estimating the bio-assay with quantal response based on the logistic function', *Journal of the American Statistical Association* 48: 565–99

Bernadino, A. (1996): *Telecommuting: modeling the employer's and the employee's decision-making,* New York: Garland

Bettman, J., Johnson, E. and Payne, J. (1991): 'Consumer decision making', in Robertson, T. and Kassarjian, H. (eds.), *Handbook of consumer behaviour,* New York: Prentice-Hall, pp. 50–84

Bhat, C. (1995): 'A heteroscedastic extreme value model of intercity travel mode choice', *Transportation Research* 29B(6): 471–83

    (1996): 'Accommodating variations in responsiveness to level-of-service measures in travel mode choice modelling', Department of Civil Engineering, University of Massachusetts at Amherst, May

    (1997a): 'An endogenous segmentation mode choice model with an application to inter-city travel', *Transportation Science* 31(1), 34–48

    (1997b): 'Recent methodological advances relevant to activity and travel behavior analysis', Conference Pre-prints, IATBR'97, 8th Meeting of the International Association of Travel Behavior Research, Austin, Tex. September

    (1998): Accommodating flexible substitution patterns in multi-dimensional choice modelling: formulation and application to travel mode and departure time choice, *Transportation Research* 32A: 495–507

Bishop, Y., Fienberg, S. and Holland, P. (1975): *Discrete multivariate analysis,* Cambridge, Mass: MIT Press

Bockstael, N.E., McConnell, K.E. and Strand, I.E. (1991): 'Recreation', in Braden, J.B. and Kolstad, C.K. (eds.), *Measuring the demand for environmental quality,* Amsterdam: North-Holland, pp. 227–70

Boersch-Supan, A. (1984): 'The Demand for housing in the United States and West Germany: a discrete choice analysis', Unpublished PhD thesis, Department of Economics, MIT, June 1984

    (1985): 'Hierarchical choice models and efficient sampling with applications on the demand for housing', *Methods of Operations Research* 50: 175–86

    (1990): 'On the compatibility of nested logit models with utility maximisation', *Journal of Econometrics* 43: 373–88

Boersch-Supan, A. and Hajvassiliou, V. (1990): 'Smooth unbiased multivariate probability simulators for maximum likelihood estimation of limited dependent variable models', *Journal of Econometrics* 58(3): 347–68

Bolduc, D. (1992): 'Generalised autoregressive errors in the multinomial probit model', *Transportation Research* 26B(2): 155–70

Bollen, K. (1989): *Structural equations with latent variables,* New York: Wiley

Boxall, P., Adamowicz, W., Williams, M., Swait, J. and Louviere, J. (1996): 'A comparison of stated preference approaches to the measurement of environmental values, *Ecological Economics* 18: 243–53

Braden, J.B. and Kolstad, C.D. (1991): *Measuring the demand for environmental quality,* New York: North Holland

Bradley, M.A. and Daly, A.J. (1992): 'Uses of the logit scaling approach in stated preference analysis', paper presented at the 6th World Conference on Transport Research, Lyon, July

Bradley, M.A. and Daly, A.J. (1994): 'Use of the logit scaling approach to test rank-order and fatigue effects in stated preference data', *Transportation* 21(2): 167–84

Bradley, M.A. and Daly, A.J. (1997): 'Estimation of logit choice models using mixed stated preference and revealed preference information', in Stopher, P.R. and Lee-Gosselin, M. (eds.) *Understanding travel behaviour in an era of change,* Oxford: Pergamon, pp. 209–32

Bradley, M.A. and Gunn, H. (1990): 'Stated preference analysis of values of travel time in the Netherlands', *Transportation Research Record* 1285: 78–89

Bradley, M., Rohr, C. and Heywood, C. (1996): 'The value of time in passenger transport: a cross-country comparison', paper presented at the 7th World Conference of Transport Research, Sydney, July

Brazell, J. and Louviere, J. (1997): 'Respondents' help, learning and fatigue', paper presented at INFORMS Marketing Science Conference, University of California at Berkeley, March

Brewer, A. and Hensher, D.A. (1999): 'Distributed work and travel behaviour: the dynamics of interactive agency choices between employers and employees', paper presented at the International Conference on Travel Behavior Research, Austin, Tex., September)

Brownstone, D., Bunch, D. and Train, K. (1998): 'Joint mixed logit models of stated and revealed preferences for alternative-fuelled vehicles', Conference Pre-prints, IATBR'97, 8th Meeting of the International Association of Travel Behaviour Research, Austin, Tex., September

Brownstone, D. and Small, K.A. (1985): 'Efficient estimation of nested logit models', School of Social Sciences, University of California at Irvine, June

Brownstone, D. and Train, K. (1999): 'Forecasting new product penetration with flexible substitution patterns', *Journal of Econometrics* 89(1-2): 109–30

Bucklin, R., Gupta, S. and Han, S. (1995): 'A brand's eye view of response segmentation in consumer brand choice behaviour', *Journal of Marketing Research* 32: 66–74

Bunch, D. (1991): 'Estimability in the multinomial probit model', *Transportation Research* 25B(1): 1–12

Bunch, D.S. and Batsell, R.R. (1989): 'A Monte Carlo comparison of estimators for the multinomial logit model', *Journal of Marketing Research* 26: 56–68

Bunch, D.S., Louviere, J. and Anderson, D.A. (1996): 'A comparison of experimental design strategies for choice-based conjoint analysis with generic-attribute multinomial logit models', unpublished working paper, UC Davis Graduate School of Management, May

Butler, J. and Moffitt, R. (1982): 'A computationally efficient quadrature procedure for the one factor multinomial probit model', *Econometrics* 50: 761–64

Cailliez, F. and Pagés, J.P. (1976): *Introduction à l'analyse des données,* Paris: SMASH

Cameron, T.A. (1982): 'Qualitative choice modelling of energy conservation decisions: a microeconomic analysis of the determinants of residential space-heating', unpublished PhD thesis, Department of Economics, Princeton University

Cameron, T.A. (1985): 'Nested logit model of energy conservation activity by owners of existing single family dwellings', *Review of Economics and Statistics* 68(2): 205–11

Cameron, T.A., Shaw, W.D., Ragland, S.E., Callaway, J.M. and Keefe, S. (1996): 'Using actual and contingent behaviour with differing levels of time aggregation to model recreation demand', *Journal of Agricultural and Resource Economics* 21: 130–49

Carson, R., Louviere, J., Anderson, D., Arabie, P., Bunch, D., Hensher, D., Johnson, R., Kuhfeld, W., Steinberg, D., Swait, J., Timmermans, H. and Wiley, J. (1994): 'Experimental analysis of choice', *Marketing Letters* 5(4): 351–68

Carson, R.T. (1991): 'Constructed markets', in Braden, J.B. and Kolstad, C.D. (eds.), *Measuring the demand for environmental quality,* Amsterdam: North-Holland: pp. 121–62

Carson, R.T. and Mitchell, R.C. (1995): 'Sequencing and nesting in contingent valuation surveys', *Journal of Environmental Economics and Management* 28: 155–74

Carson, R.T., Mitchell, R.C., Haneman, W.M., Kopp, R.J., Presser, S. and Ruud, P.A. (1994): 'Contingent valuation and lost passive use: damages from the *Exxon Valdez*', Resources for the future discussion paper, Washington, DC

Chapman, R. and Staelin, R. (1982): 'Exploiting rank ordered choice set data within the stochastic utility model', *Journal of Marketing Research* 19: 288–301

Chrzan, K. (1994): 'Three kinds of order effects in choice-based conjoint analysis', *Marketing Letters* 5(2): 165–72

Cochran, W.G. (1977): Sampling techniques, 3rd edition, New York: Wiley

Cosslett, S. (1978): 'Efficient estimation of discrete choice models from choice-based samples', unpublished PhD thesis, Department of Economics, University of California at Berkeley

    (1981): 'Efficient estimation of discrete choice models', in Manske, C.F. and McFadden, D.L. (eds.), *Structural analysis of discrete data with econometric application,* Cambridge, Mass: MIT Press, pp. 51–113

Cox, D.R. (1972): 'Regression models and life table', *Journal of the Royal Statistical Society* B34: 187–220

Currim, I. (1981): 'Using segmentation approaches for better prediction and understanding from consumer mode choice models', *Journal of Marketing Research* 18: 301–9

Daganzo, C. (1980): *Multinomial probit,* New York: Academic Press

Daly, A.J., (1985): 'Estimating "tree" logit models', *Transportation Research* 21B(4): 251–68

Daly, A. and Zachary, S. (1978): 'Improved multiple choice models', in Hensher, D.A. and Dalvi, M.Q. (eds.), *Determinants of travel choice,* Westmead: Saxon House, pp. 321–62

    (1997): ALOGIT, Hague Consulting Group, The Hague

Dandy, G. and Neil, R. (1981): 'Alternative mathematical structures for modelling mode choice', Report No. R30, Department of Civil Engineering, University of Adelaide

Daniels, R. (1997): 'Combining stated choice methods and discrete choice models in the development of valuation functions for environmental attributes influencing choice behaviour', PhD thesis, Institute of Transport Studies, University of Sydney, August

Daniels, R. and Hensher, D.A. (1998): 'Understanding differences in private and citizen preferences: do environmental attributes really matter and how can we capture them in preference measurement?', Institute of Transport Studies, University of Sydney, November

Dawes, R. and Corrigan, B. (1974): 'Linear models in decision making', *Psychological Bulletin* 81: 95–106

de Palma, A., Myers, G.M. and Papageorgiou, Y.Y. (1994): 'Rational choice under an imperfect ability to choose', *American Economic Review* 84: 419–40

Deighton, J., Henderson, C. and Neslin, S. (1994): 'The effects of advertising on brand switching and repeat purchasing', *Journal of Marketing Research* 31: 28–43

Dellaert, B.G.C. (1995): 'Conjoint choice models for urban tourism, planning and marketing', PhD thesis, Bouwstenen 35, Faculty of Architecture, Building and Planning, Eindhoven University of Technology

Dellaert, B.G.C., Brazell, J.D. and Louviere, J.J. (1999): 'The effect of attribute variation on consumer choice consistency', *Marketing Letters* 10: 139–47

DeSerpa A.C. (1971): 'A theory of the economics of time', *Economic Journal* 828–45

Diamond, P. and Hausman, J. (1994): 'Contingent valuation: is some number better than no number?', *Journal of Economics Perspectives* 8: 45–64

Dillman, D.A. (2000): *Mail and Internet Surveys: The Tailored Design Method* (2nd edn), New York: Wiley

Dillon, W. and Kumar, A. (1994): 'Latent structure and other mixture models in marketing: an integrative survey and overview', in Bagozzi, R. (ed.), *Advanced methods of marketing research*, London: Blackwell, pp. 295–351

Domencich, T. and McFadden, D. (1975): *Urban travel demand: a behavioural approach,* Amsterdam: North-Holland

DuWors, R. and Haines, G.H. (1990): 'Event history analysis measures of brand loyalty', *Journal of Marketing Research* 28: 485–93

Econometric Software (1999): LIMDEP 7.0 for Windows, Econometric Software Inc., New York and Sydney

Efron, B. (1977): 'Efficiency of Cox's likelihood function for censored data', *Journal of the American Statistical Association* 72: 557–65

Einhorn, H. (1970): 'The use of nonlinear, noncompensatory models in decision-making', *Psychological Bulletin* 73: 221–30

Elrod, T. and Keane, M. (1995): 'A factor analytic probit model for representing the market structure in panel data', *Journal of Marketing Research* 32: 1–16

Elrod, T., Louviere, J. and Davey, K. (1993): 'A comparison of ratings-based and choice-based conjoint models', *Journal of Marketing Research* 24(3): 368–77

Englin, J. and Cameron, T.A. (1996): 'Augmenting travel cost models with contingent behavior data', *Environmental and Resource Economics* 7: 133–47

Erdem, T. and Keane, M.P. (1996): 'Decision-making under uncertainty: Capturing dynamic brand choice processes in turbulent consumer goods markets', *Marketing Science* 15(1): 1–20

Erdem, T. and Swait, J. (1998): 'Brand equity as a signaling phenomenon,' *Journal of Consumer Psychology* 7(2): 131–57

Feather, P., Hellerstein D. and Tomasi, T. (1995): 'A discrete choice count model of recreational demand', *Journal of Environmental Economics and Management* 29: 228–37

Finn, A. and Louviere, J. (1993): 'Determining the appropriate response to evidence of public concern: the case of food safety', *Journal of Public Policy and Marketing* 11(1): 12–25

    (1996): 'Comparisons of revealed and stated preference model parameters over time and types of retail activities', unpublished working paper, Faculty of Business, University of Alberta, Edmonton, Canada

Fleming, T. and Harrington, D. (1990): *Counting processes and survival analysis*, New York: Wiley

Fowkes, T. and Wardman, M. (1988): 'The design of stated preference travel choice experiments', *Journal of Transport Economics and Policy* 13(1): 27–44

Freeman, A.M. (1993): *The measurement of environmental and resource values,* Baltimore: Resources for the Future Press

Frisch, R. (1951): 'Some personal reminiscences of a great man', in Harris, S.E. (ed.), *Schumpeter, Social Scientist*, Cambridge, Mass: MIT Press, pp. 1–10

Gaudry, M., Jara-Diaz, S. R. and de Dios Ortuzar, J. (1988): 'Value of time sensitivity to model specification', *Transportation Research* 23B: 151–8

Gensch, D. (1985): 'Empirically testing a disaggregate choice model for segments', *Journal of Marketing Research* 22: 462–7

Geweke, J. (1991): 'Efficient simulation from the multivariate normal and student-t distributions subject to linear constraints', in *Computer Science and Statistics: proceedings of the Twenty-Third Symposium on the Interface,* Alexandria, Va.: American Statistical Association, pp. 571–8

Geweke, J., Keane, M. and Runkle, D. (1994): 'Alternative computational approaches to inference in the multinomial probit model', *Review of Economics and Statistics* 76(4): 609–32

Gifi, A. (1990): *Nonlinear multivariate analysis,* Chichester: Wiley

Gilbert, C.C.M. (1992): 'A duration model of automobile ownership', *Transportation Research B,* 26B(2): 97–114

Gillen, D.W. (1977); 'Estimation and specification of the effects of parking costs on urban transport mode choice', *Journal of Urban Economics* 4(2): 186–99

Gittins, R. (1985): *Canonical analysis: a review with applications in ecology,* Berlin: Springer-Verlag

Goldfeld, S.M. and Quandt, P.E. (1972): *Nonlinear methods in econometrics,* Amsterdam: North-Holland

Goodman, L.A. (1970): 'The multivariate analysis of qualitative data; interactions among multiple classification', *Journal of the American Statistical Association* 65: 225–56

  (1972): 'A modified multiple regression approach to the analysis of dichotomous variables', *American Sociological Review* 37: 28–46

Goodwin, P.B. (1992): 'A review of new demand elasticities with special reference to short and long run effects of price changes', *Journal of Transport Economics and Policy* 26: 155–69

Gopinath, D. and Ben-Akiva M.E. (1995): 'Estimation of randomly distributed value of time', working paper, Department of Civil Engineering, MIT

Green, P. and Srinivasan, V. (1978): 'Conjoint analysis in consumer research: issues and outlook', *Journal of Consumer Research,* 1: 61–8

  (1990): 'Conjoint analysis in marketing research: new developments and directions', *Journal of Marketing* 54(4): 3–19

Green, P. and Wind, Y. (1971): *Multiattribute decisions in marketing: a measurement approach,* Hinsdale: Dryden Press

Greene, W. (1996): 'Heteroskedastic extreme value model for discrete choice', working paper, New York University

Greene, W.G. (1997): 'The HEV model: A note', Department of Economics, Stern School of Business, New York University (mimeo)

Guadagni, P.M. and Little, J.D. (1983): 'A logit model of brand choice calibrated on scanner data', *Marketing Science* 2(3): 203–38

Hahn, G.J. and Shapiro, S.S. (1966): 'A catalog and computer program for the design and analysis of orthogonal symmetric and asymmetric fractional factorial experiments', technical report 66-C 165, General Electric Research and Development Center, Schenectady, N.Y.

Han, A. and Hausman, J. (1990): 'Flexible parametric estimation of duration and competing risk models', *Journal of Applied Econometrics* 5: 1–28

Hanemann, W.M. and Kanninen B. (1999): 'The statistical analysis of discrete-response CV data', in Bateman, I.J. and Willis, K.G. (eds.), *Valuing environmental preferences: theory and practice of the contingent valuation method in the US, EC and developing countries,* Oxford: Oxford University Press, pp. 302–441

Hanemann, W. M. (1984): 'Welfare evaluations in contingent valuation experiments with discrete responses', *American Journal of Agricultural Economics* 66: 332–41

Hanemann, W.M. (1982): 'Applied welfare analysis with qualitative response models', working paper no. 241, University of California at Berkeley

Hatanaka, T. (1974): 'An efficient two-step estimator for the dynamic adjustment model with autocorrelated errors', *Journal of Econometrics* 10: 199–220

Hausman, J.A., Leonard G.K. and McFadden D. (1995): 'A utility-consistent combined discrete choice and count data model assessing recreational use losses due to natural resource damage', *Journal of Public Economics* 56: 1–30

Hausman, J.A. and McFadden, D. (1984): 'Specification tests for the multinomial logit model', *Econometrica* 52: 1219–40

Hausmann, J. and Wise, D.A. (1978a): 'A conditional probit model for qualitative choice: discrete decisions recognising interdependence and heterogeneous preferences', *Econometrica* 46: 403–26

(1978b): 'AFDC participation: measured variables or unobserved characteristics, permanent or transitory, working paper, Department of Economics, MIT

Heckman, J. (1981): 'Statistical models for discrete panel data', in Manski, C.F. and McFadden, D. (eds.), *Structural analysis of discrete data with econometric applications,* Cambridge, Mass.: MIT Press, 114–78

Heckman, J. and Singer, B. (1984): 'A method for minimising the impact of distributional assumptions in econometric models for duration data', *Econometrica* 52: 271–320

Hensher, D.A. (1976): 'The value of commuter travel time savings: empirical estimation using an alternative valuation model', *Journal of Transport Economics and Policy* 10(2): 167–76

(1983): 'A sequential attribute dominance model of probabilistic choice', *Transportation Research* 17A(3): 215–18

(1984): 'Achieving representativeness of the observable component of the indirect utility function in logit choice models: an empirical revelation', *Journal of Business* 57: 265–80

(1985): 'An econometric model of vehicle use in the household sector', *Transportation Research* 19B(4): 303–13

(1986): 'Sequential and full information maximum likelihood estimation of a nested logit model', *Review of Economics and Statistics,* 68(4): 657–67

(1989): 'Behavioural and resource values of travel time savings: a bicentennial update' *Australian Road Research* 19(3): 223–9

(1991): 'Efficient estimation of hierarchical logit mode choice models', *Journal of the Japanese Society of Civil Engineers* 425/IV-14: 117–28

(1994): 'Stated preference analysis of travel choices: the state of the practice', *Transportation* 21: 107–33

(1997a): 'A practical approach to identifying the market for high speed rail: a case study in the Sydney–Canberra corridor', *Transportation Research* 31A(6): 431–46

(1997b): 'Value of travel time savings in personal and commercial automobile travel', in Greene, D. Jones, D. and Delucchi, M. (eds.), *Measuring the full costs and benefits of transportation,* Berlin: Springer-Verlag, pp. 245–80

(1998a): 'Extending valuation to controlled value functions and non-uniform scaling with generalised unobserved variances', in Garling, T., Laitila, T. and Westin, K. (eds.), *Theoretical foundations of travel choice modelling,* Oxford: Pergamon, pp. 75–102

(1998b): 'Establishing a fare elasticity regime for urban passenger transport: non-concession commuters', *Journal of Transport Economics and Policy* 32(2): 221–46

Hensher, D.A. and Barnard, P.O. (1990): 'The orthogonality issue in stated choice designs', in Fischer, M., Nijkamp, P. and Papageorgiou, Y. (eds.), *Spatial choices and processes*, Amsterdam: North-Holland, 265–78

Hensher, D.A., Barnard, P., Milthorpe, F. and Smith, N. (1989): 'Urban tollways and the valuation of travel time savings', *Economic Record* 66(193): 146–56

Hensher, D.A. and Bradley, M. (1993): 'Using stated response choice data to enrich revealed preference discrete choice models', *Marketing Letters* 4(2): 139–51

Hensher, D.A. and Greene, W.G. (1999): 'Nested logit model estimation: clarifying the rules for model specification', Institute of Transport Studies, University of Sydney, May

Hensher, D.A. and Johnson, L. (1981): *Applied discrete choice modelling,* London: Croom Helm

Hensher, D.A. and Louviere, J. (1983): 'Identifying individual preferences for alternative international air fares: an application of functional measurement theory', *Journal of Transport Economics and Policy* 17(2): 225–45

(1998): 'A comparison of elasticities derived from multinomial logit, nested logit and heteroscedastic extreme value SP-RP discrete choice models', paper presented at the 8th World Conference on Transport Research, Antwerp, July

Hensher, D.A., Louviere, J. and Swait, J. (1999): 'Combining sources of preference data', *Journal of Econometrics* 89(1–2): 197–222

Hensher, D.A. and Raimond, T. (1995): *Evaluation of fare elasticities for the Sydney region,* report prepared by the Institute of Transport Studies for the NSW Government Pricing Tribunal, Sydney

Hensher, D.A., Smith, N.C., Milthorpe, F.M. and Barnard, P.O. (1992): *Dimensions of automobile demand: a longitudinal study of automobile ownership and use,* Amsterdam: North-Holland

Hensher, D.A. and Truong, T.P. (1984): 'Valuation of travel time savings from a direct experimental approach', *Journal of Transport Economics and Policy* 19(3): 237–261

Herriges, J.A. and Kling, C.L. (1996): 'Testing the consistency of nested logit models with utility maximisation', *Economic Letters* 50: 33–9

Hicks, J.R. (1946): *Value and capital,* 2nd edn, Oxford: Oxford University Press

Horowitz, J. (1983): 'Statistical comparison of non-nested probabilistic discrete choice models', *Transportation Science* 17, 319–50

(1998): *Semi-parametric estimation methods,* Berlin: Springer-Verlag

Horowitz, J., Hensher, D.A. and Zhu, W. (1993): 'A bounded-size likelihood test for non-nested probabilistic discrete choice models estimated from choice-based samples', working paper ITS-WP-93-15, Institute of Transport Studies, University of Sydney

Horowitz, J. and Louviere, J. (1993): 'Testing predicted probabilities against observed discrete choices in probabilistic discrete choice models', *Marketing Science* 12(3): 270–9

(1995): 'What is the role of consideration sets in choice modeling?', *International Journal of Research in Marketing* 12(1): 39–54

(1990): The external validity of choice models based on laboratory experiments', in Fischer, M., Nijkamp, P. and Papageorgiou, Y. (eds.), *Spatial choices and processes,* Amsterdam: North-Holland, pp. 247–63

Huber, J. and Zwerina, K. (1996): 'The importance of utility balance in efficient choice set designs', *Journal of Marketing Research* 33: 307–17

Hunt, G.L. (1998): 'Nested logit models with partial degeneracy', Department of Economics, University of Maine, November (mimeo)

Hutchinson, J.W., Kamakura, W.A. amd Lynch, J.G. (1997): 'Unobserved heterogeneity as an alternative explanation for "reversal" effects in behavioral research', unpublished working paper, Department of Marketing, Wharton School of Business, University of Pennsylvania

Jara-Diaz, S. (1998): 'Time and income in discrete choice models', in Garling, T., Laitila, T. and Westin, K. (eds.), *Theoretical foundations of travel choice modelling,* Oxford, Pergamon: pp. 51–74

Jara-Diaz, S. and de Dios Ortuzar, J. (1988): 'Introducing the expenditure rate in mode choice models', *Journal of Transport Economics and Policy* 23(3): 293–308

Jara-Diaz, S. and Videla, J. (1989): 'Detection of income effect in mode choice: theory and application', *Transportation Research* 23B: 393–400

Johnson, E.J. and Meyer R.J. (1984): 'Compensatory choice models of noncompensatory processes: the effect of varying context', *Journal of Consumer Research* 11(1): 528–41

Johnson, N., Kotz, S. and Balakrishnan, N. (1995): *Continuous univariate distributions, II*, 2nd edn, New York:Wiley

Johnson, R. (1989): 'Making decisions with incomplete information: the first complete test of the inference model', *Advances in Consumer Research* 16: 522–8

Johnson, R.M. and Orme, B.K. (1996): 'How many questions should you ask in choice-based conjoint studies?', paper presented to the American Marketing Association's Advanced Research Techniques Forum, Beaver Creek, Colo. (June)

Jones, C.A. and Pease, K.A. (1995): 'Resource based measures of compensation in liability statutes for natural resource damages', paper presented at the AERE workshop on Government Regulation and Compensation, Annapolis, Md., June

Kahneman, D. and Knetsch, J.L. (1992): 'Valuing public goods: the purchase of moral satisfaction', *Journal of Environmental Economics and Management*, 22: 57–70

Kahneman, D. and Tversky, A. (1979): 'Prospect theory: an analysis of decisions under risk', *Econometrica* 47, 263–91

(1984): 'Choices, values and frames', *American Psychologist* 39: 341–50

Kamakura, W. and Russell, G. (1989): 'A probabilistic choice model for market segmentation and elasticity structure', *Journal of Marketing Research* 26: 379–90

Kamakura, W., Wedel, M. and Agrawal, J. (1994): 'Concomitant variable latent class models for conjoint analysis', *International Journal of Research in Marketing* 11(5): 451–64

Keane, M. (1994): 'Modelling heterogeneity and state dependence in consumer choice behavior', working paper, Department of Economics, University of Minnesota

(1997): 'Current issues in discrete choice modelling', *Marketing Letters* 8(3): 307–22

Keane, M.P. and Wolpin, K.I. (1994): 'The solution and estimation of discrete choice dynamic programming models by simulation and interpolation: Monte Carlo evidence', *Review of Economics and Statistics*, 76(4): 648–72

Keeney, R.L. and Raiffa, H. (1976): *Decisions with multiple objectives: preference and value tradeoffs*, New York: Wiley

Keller, K.L. (1993): 'Conceptualizing, measuring and managing customer-based brand equity', *Journal of Marketing* 57(1): 1–22

Kessler, R.C. and Greenberg, D.F. (1981): *Linear panel analysis*, New York: Academic Press

Koppelman, F.S. and Wen, C.H. (1997): 'The paired combinatorial logit model: properties, estimation and application', Department of Civil Engineering, Northwestern University, Evanston, Illinois

'Alternative nested logit models: structure, properties and estimation', *Transportation Research* 32B(5): 289–98

Kozel, V. (1986): 'Temporal stability of transport demand models in a colombian city', in *Annals of the 1985 International Conference on Travel Behaviour*, April 16–19, Noordwijk, Holland, pp. 245–67

Krantz, D.H. and Tversky, A. (1971): 'Conjoint-measurement analysis of composition rules in psychology', *Psychological Review* 78: 151–69

Krantz, D.H., Luce, R.D., Suppes, P. and Tversky, A. (1971): *Foundations of measurement*, New York: Academic Press

Kuhfeld, W.F., Tobias, R.D. and Garratt, M. (1994): 'Efficient experimental design with marketing research applications', *Journal of Marketing Research* 31: 545–57

Lancaster, K. (1966): 'A new approach to consumer theory', *Journal of Political Economy* 74: 132–57

(1971): *Consumer demand: a new approach,* New York: Columbia University Press

Langdon, M.G. (1984): 'Methods of determining choice probability in utility maximising multiple alternative models', *Transportation Research* 18B(3): 209–34

Layard, P.R.G. and Walters, A.A. (1978): *Microeconomic theory,* New York:McGraw-Hill

Lazari, Andreas and Anderson, D. (1994): 'Designs of discrete choice set experiments for estimating both attribute and availability cross effects', *Journal of Marketing Research* 31: 375–83

Lerman, S.R. and Louviere, J. (1978): 'On the use of functional measurement to identify the functional form of the utility expression in travel demand models', *Transportation Research Record,* 673: 78–86

Levy, P. and Lemeshow, S. (1991): *Sampling of populations: methods and applications,* New York: Wiley

Louviere, J. (1974): 'Predicting the evaluation of real stimulus objects from an abstract evaluation of their attributes: the case of trout streams', *Journal of Applied Psychology* 59(5): 572–77

(1988a): *Analyzing decision making: metric conjoint analysis,* Newbury Park, Calif.: Sage

(1988b): 'Conjoint analysis modelling of stated preferences: a review of theory, methods, recent developments and external validity', *Journal of Transport Economics and Policy* 20: 93–119

(1994): 'Conjoint analysis', in Bagozzi R. (ed.), *Advanced methods of marketing research,* Cambridge, Mass.: Blackwell, pp. 223–59

(1995): 'Relating stated preference measures and models to choices in real markets: cali-bration of CV responses', in Bjornstad, D.J. and Kahn, J.R. (eds.), *The contingent valuation of environmental resources,* Brookfield: Edward Elgar, pp. 167–88

Louviere, J., Fox, M. and Moore, W. (1993): 'Cross-task validity comparisons of stated preference choice models', *Marketing Letters* 4(3): 205–13

Louviere, J. and Hensher D.A. (1983): 'Using discrete choice models with experimental design data to forecast consumer demand for a unique cultural event', *Journal of Consumer Research* 10(3): 348–61

(1996) *Stated preference analysis: applications in land use, transportation planning and envir-onmental economics,* short course delivered in USA (Portland), Sweden (Stockholm) and Australia (Sydney, Melbourne)

Louviere, J., Hensher, D.A., Anderson, D.A., Raimond, T. and Battellino, H. (1994): *Greenhouse gas emissions and the demand for urban passenger transport: design of the stated preference experiments,* Report 3, Institute of Transport Studies, University of Sydney

Louviere, J. and Swait, J. (1996a): 'Best/worst conjoint working paper', Department of Marketing, Faculty of Economics, University of Sydney, Australia

(1996b): 'Searching for regularities in choice processes, or the little constant that could', working paper, Department of Marketing, Faculty of Economics, University of Sydney, Australia

Louviere J. and Timmermans, H. (1990a): 'A review of recent advances in decompositional preference and choice models', *Journal of Economic and Social Geography* 81(3): 214–24

(1990b): 'Stated preferences and choice models applied to recreation research: a review', *Leisure Sciences* 12: 9–32

Louviere, J. and Woodworth, G. (1983): 'Design and analysis of simulated consumer choice or allocation experiments: an approach based on aggregate data', *Journal of Marketing Research* 20: 350–67

Louviere, J., Meyer, R., Bunch, D., Carson, R., Dellaert, B., Hanemann, W. M., Hensher, D. and Irwin, J. (1999); 'Combining sources of preference data for modeling complex decision processes', *Marketing Letters* 10(3): 187–217

Lu, X. (1996): 'Bayesian methods in choice model estimation: a summary of multinomial probit estimation methods', paper presented at the 76th Annual Meeting of the Transportation Research Board, Washington, DC, January

Luce, R.D. (1959): *Individual choice behavior: a theoretical analysis,* New York: Wiley

Luce, R.D. and Suppes P. (1965): 'Preference, utility and subjective probability', in Luce, R.D., Bush, R.R. and Galanter, E. (eds.), *Handbook of mathematical psychology,* III, New York: Wiley, pp. 249–410

Lynch, J. (1985): 'Uniqueness issues in the decompositional modeling of multiattribute overall evaluations', *Journal of Marketing Research* 22: 1–19

Machina, M.J. (1987): 'Choice under uncertainty: problems solved and unsolved', *Economic Perspectives* 1(1): 121–54

Maddala, G. (1983): *Limited-dependent and qualitative variables in economics,* Cambridge: Cambridge University Press

Mannering, F. and Winston, C. (1985): 'Dynamic empirical analysis of household vehicle ownership and utilisation', *Rand Journal of Economics* 16: 215–36

Manski, C.F. (1977): 'The structure of random utility models', *Theory and Decision* 8: 229–54

Manski, C.F. and Lerman, S.R. (1977): 'The estimation of choice probabilities from choice-based samples', *Econometrica* 45(8): 1977

Matzoros, A. (1982): 'The estimation of nested logit choice models', unpublished MSc thesis, Institute of Transport Studies, University of Leeds

Mayworm, P., Lago, A.M. and McEnroe, J.M. (1980): *Patronage impacts of changes in transit fares and services,* Bethesda, Md, Ecosometrics Inc.

Mazzotta, M., Opaluch, J. and Grigalunas, T.A. (1994): 'Natural resource damage assessment: the role of resource restoration', *Natural Resources Journal* 34: 153–78

McClelland, G.H. and Judd, C.M. (1993): 'Statistical difficulties of detecting interactions and moderator effects', *Psychological Bulletin,* 114(2): 376–90

McFadden, D. (1974): 'Conditional logit analysis of qualitative choice behaviour', in Zarembka, P. (ed.), *Frontiers in econometrics,* New York: Academic Press, pp. 105–42

(1976): 'The revealed preferences of a governmental bureaucracy', *Bell Journal of Economics* 7: 55–72

(1978): 'Modeling the choice of residential locations', in Karlqvist, K., Lundquist, E., Snickars, F. and Weibull, J.L. (eds.), *Spatial interaction theory and planning methods,* Amsterdam: North-Holland, pp. 75–96

(1979): 'Quantitative methods for analysing travel behaviour of individuals: some recent developments', in Hensher, D.A. and Stopher, P.R. (eds.), *Behavioural travel modelling,* London: Croom Helm, pp. 279–318

(1981): 'Econometric models of probabilistic choice', in Manski, C. and McFadden, D. (eds.), *Structural analysis of discrete data with econometric applications,* Cambridge, Mass.: MIT Press, pp. 198–272

(1984): 'Econometric analysis of qualitative response models', in Griliches, Z. and Intriligator, M.D. (eds.), *Handbook of Econometrics,* II, Amsterdam: Elsevier Science, pp. 1395–457

(1986): 'The choice theory approach to marketing research', *Marketing Science* 5(4): 275–97

(1987): 'Regression-based specification tests for the multinomial model', *Journal of Econometrics* 34(1/2): 63–82

(1989): 'A method of simulated moments for estimation of discrete response models without numerical integration', *Econometrica* 57(5): 995–1026

McFadden, D. and Ruud, P.A. (1994): 'Estimation by simulation', *Review of Economics and Statistics*, 76(4): 591–608

McFadden, D. and Train, K. (1996): 'Mixed MNL models for discrete response', Department of Economics, University of California at Berkeley

McFadden, D., Tye, W. and Train, K. (1977): 'An application of diagnostic tests for independence from irrelevant alternatives property of the multinomial logit model', *Transportation Research Record*, 637: 39–46

McLeod, K., Boxall, P., Adamowicz, W., Williams, M. and Louviere, J. (1993): *The incorporation of nontimber goods and services in integrated resource management, I, An introduction to the Alberta moose hunting study*, Department of Rural Economy Project Report 9312, University of Alberta

Meyer, R. (1977): 'An experimental analysis of student apartment selection decisions under uncertainty', *Great Plains-Rocky Mountains Geographical Journal* 6 (special issue on human judgment and spatial behaviour): 30–8

Meyer, R. and Eagle, T. (1982): 'Context induced parameter instability in a disaggregate-stochastic model of store choice', *Journal of Marketing Research* 19: 62–71

Meyer, R. and Johnson, E. (1995): 'Empirical generalizations in the modeling of consumer choice', *Marketing Science* 14(3) (special issue on empirical generalizations): G180–G189

Meyer, R., Levin, I. and Louviere, J. (1984): 'Functional analysis of mode choice', *Transportation Research Record* 673: 1–7

Mitchell, R.C. and Carson, R.T. (1989): *Using surveys to value public goods: the contingent valuation method*, Baltimore: Johns Hopkins University Press for Resources for the Future

Montgomery, D. (1991): *Design and analysis of experiments*, 3rd edn, New York: Wiley

Morikawa, T. (1989): 'Incorporating stated preference data in travel demand analysis', PhD dissertation, Department of Civil Engineering, MIT

(1994): 'Correcting state dependence and serial correlation in RP/SP combined estimation method', *Transportation* 21(2): 153–66

Muth, R. F. (1966): 'Household production and consumer demand functions', *Econometrica*, 34(3): 699–708

Nash, J.F. (1950): 'Equilibrium points in *n*-person games', *Proceedings of the National Academy of Sciences* 36: 48–9

NOAA (1997): 'Scaling compensatory restoration actions: damage assessment and restoration program', Silver Spring, Md: NOAA

Norman, K.L. and Louviere, J. (1974): 'Integration of attributes in public bus transportation: two modelling approaches', *Journal of Applied Psychology* 59(6): 753–58

Oak, D. (1977): 'The asymptotic information in censored survival data', *Biometrika*, 64: 441–48

Oliphant, K., Eagle, T., Louviere, J. and Anderson, D. (1992): 'Cross-task comparison of ratings-based and choice-based conjoint', paper presented at the 1992 Advanced Research Techniques Forum of the American Marketing Association, June, Beaver Creek, Colo.

Olsen, G.D. and Swait, J. (1998): 'Nothing is important', working paper, Faculty of Management, University of Calgary, Alberta, Canada

Olsen, G.D., Swait, J., Johnson, R. and Louviere, J. (1995): 'Response mode influences on attribute weight and predictive ability when linear models are not certain to be robust', working paper, Faculty of Business, University of Calgary, Alberta, Canada

Ortuzar, J. de Dios (1983): 'Nested logit models for mixed-mode travel in urban corridors', *Transportation Research* 17A(4): 282–99

Oum, T.H., Waters II, W.G. and Yong, J-S. (1992): 'Concepts of price elasticities of transport demand and recent empirical estimates', *Journal of Transport Economics and Policy* 26: 139–54

Payne, C. (1977): 'The log-linear model for contingency tables', in O'Muircheartaigh, C.A. and Payne, C. (eds.), *The analysis of survey data, II, Model Fitting,* London: Wiley, pp. 105–44

Payne, J. W., Bettman, J. R. and Johnson, E. J. (1992): 'Behavioral decision research: a constructive processing perspective', *Annual Review of Psychology,* 43: 87–131

 (1993): *The adaptive decision maker,* New York: Cambridge University Press

Pollak, R. and Wales, T. (1991): 'The likelihood dominance criterion – a new approach to model selection', *Journal of Econometrics* 47: 227–42

Prentice, R.L. and Gloeckler, L.A. (1978): 'Regression analysis of grouped survival data with applications to breast cancer data', *Biometrics* 34: 57–67

Press, W.H., Flannery, B.P., Teukolsky, S.A. and Vetterling, W.T. (1986): *Numerical recipes,* Cambridge: Cambridge University Press

Provencher, B. and Bishop, R.C. (1997): 'An estimable dynamic model of recreation behavior with an application to Great Lakes angling', *Journal of Environmental Economics and Management* 33: 107–27

Quigley, J. (1985): 'Consumer choice of dwelling, neighborhood, and public services', *Regional Science and Urban Economics* 15: 41–63

Raghavarao, D. and Wiley, J.B. (1994): 'Experimental designs for availability effects and cross effects with one attribute', *Communications in Statistics* 23(6): 1835–46

Rao, C.R. (1973): *Linear statistical inference and its applications,* New York: Wiley

Rao, P. and Miller, R.L. (1971): *Applied econometrics,* Belmont: Wadsworth

Restle, F. (1961): *Psychology of judgment and choice,* New York: Wiley

Revelt, D. and Train, K. (1998): 'Incentives for appliance efficiency in a competitive energy environment: random parameters logit models of households' choices', *Review of Economics and Statistics* 80(4): 647–57

Richardson, A.J., Ampt, E. and Meyburg, A.H. (1995): *Survey methods for transport planning,* Melbourne: Eucalyptus Press

Roberts, J. and Lattin, J. (1991): 'Development and testing of a model of consideration set composition', *Journal of Marketing Research,* 28: 429–40

Rosen, S. (1974): 'Hedonic prices and implicit markets: product differentiation in pure competition', *Journal of Political Economy,* 82(1): 34–55

Rushton, G. (1969): 'Analysis of spatial behaviour by revealed space preference', *Annals of the Association of American Geographers* 59: 391–400

Samuelson, P.A. (1948): *Foundations of economic analysis,* Cambridge, Mass.: McGraw-Hill

Samuelson, W. and Zeckhauser, R. (1988): 'Status quo bias in decision making', *Journal of Risk and Uncertainty* 1: 7–59

Senna, L. (1994): 'Users' response to travel time variability', unpublished PhD thesis, Department of Civil Engineering, University of Leeds

Silk, A.J. and Urban, G. (1978): 'Pre-test-market evaluation of new packaged goods: a model and measurement methodology', *Journal of Marketing Research* 15(2): 171–91

Small, K. (1987): 'A discrete choice model for ordered alternatives', *Econometrica* 55(2): 409–24

(1994): 'Approximate generalized extreme value models of discrete choice', *Journal of Econometrics* 62: 351–82

Small, K.A. and Rosen, H.S. (1981): 'Applied welfare economics with discrete choice models', *Econometrica* 49(1): 105–30

Small, K.A. and Brownstone, D. (1982): 'Efficient estimation of nested logit models: an application to trip timing', Research Memorandum No. 296, Econometric Research Program, Princeton University

Small, K.A. and Hsiao, C. (1985): 'Multinomial logit specification tests', *International Economic Review* 26: 619–27

Sobel, K.L. (1981): 'Travel demand forecasting by using the nested multinomial logit model', *Transportation Research Record* 775: 48–55

Stern, S. (1997): 'Simulation-based estimation', *Journal of Economic Literature* 35: 2006–39

Street, A.P. and Street D.J. (1987): *Combinatorics of experimental design*, New York: Oxford University Press

Struyk, R.J. (1976): *Urban homeownership – the economic determinants*, Lexington, Lexington Books

Suzuki, S., Harata, N. and Ohta, K. (1995): 'A study on the measurement methods of the value of time', paper presented at the 7th World Conference of Transport Research, Sydney, July

Swait, J. (1984): 'Probabilistic choice set formation in transportation demand models', unpublished PhD thesis, Department of Civil Engineering, MIT

(1994): 'A structural equation model of latent segmentation and product choice for cross-sectional revealed preference choice data', *Journal of Retailing and Consumer Services* 1(2): 77–89

Swait, J. and Adamowicz, W. (1996): 'The effect of choice environment and task demands on consumer behaviour: discriminating between contribution and confusion', Department of Rural Economy, Staff paper 96-09, University of Alberta, Alberta, Canada

Swait, J. and Ben-Akiva, M. (1985): 'An analysis of the effects of captivity on travel time and cost elasticities', in *Annals of the 1985 International Conference on Travel Behavior*, April 16–19, Noordwijk, Holland, pp. 113–28

(1987a): 'Incorporating random constraints in discrete choice models of choice set generation', *Transportation Research* 21B: 91–102

Swait, J. and Ben-Akiva, M. (1987b): 'Empirical test of a constrainted choice discrete model: mode choice in Sao Paulo, Brazil', *Transportation Research* 21B: 103–15

Swait, J. and Bernadino, A. (1997): 'Seeking taste homogeneity in choice processes: distinguishing taste variation from error structure in discrete choice data', working paper, Intelligent Marketing Systems, Edmonton, Canada

Swait, J., Erdem, T., Louviere, J. and Dubelaar, C. (1993): 'The equalization price: a measure of consumer-perceived brand equity', *International Journal of Research in Marketing* 10: 23–45

Swait, J. and Louviere, J. (1993): 'The role of the scale parameter in the estimation and use of multinomial logit models', *Journal of Marketing Research* 30: 305–14

Swait, J., Louviere, J. and Williams, M. (1994): 'A sequential approach to exploiting the combined strengths of SP and RP data: application to freight shipper choice', *Transportation* 21: 135–52

Swait, J. and Naik, P. (1996): 'Consumer preference evolution and sequential choice behavior', working paper, Department of Marketing, College of Business Administration, University of Florida

Swait, J. and Stacey, E.C. (1996): 'Consumer brand assessment and assessment confidence in models of longitudinal choice behavior', presented at the 1996 INFORMS Marketing Science Conference, March 7–10, 1996, Gainesville, Fla.

Swait, J. and Sweeney, J. (1996): 'Perceived value and its impact on choice behavior in a retail setting', working paper, Department of Marketing, College of Business Administration, University of Florida

Taplin, J.H.E., Hensher, D.A. and Smith, B. (1999): 'Imposing symmetry on a complete matrix of commuter travel elasticities', *Transportation Research* 33B(3): 215–32

Ter Braak, C.J.F. (1990): 'Interpreting canonical correlation analysis through biplots of structure correlations and weights', *Psychometrika* 55: 519–31

Theil, H. (1970): 'On the estimation of relationships involving qualitative variables', *American Journal of Sociology* 76(1); 103–54

(1971): *Principles of Econometrics*, New York: Wiley

Thurstone, L. (1927): 'A law of comparative judgment', *Psychological Review* 34: 273–86

Train, K. (1986): *Qualitative choice analysis: theory, econometrics and an application to automobile demand*, Cambridge, Mass.: MIT Press

(1995): 'Simulation methods for probit and related models based on convenient error partitioning', working paper 95-237, Department of Economics, University of California at Berkeley

(1997): 'Mixed logit models for recreation demand', in Kling, C. and Herriges, J. (eds.), *Valuing the environment using recreation demand models,* New York: Elgar, pp. 140–63

(1998): 'Recreation demand models with taste differences over people', *Land Economics* 74(2): 230–9

Train, K. and McFadden, D. (1978): 'The goods/leisure trade-off and disaggregate work trip mode choice models', *Transportation Research* 12: 349–53

Truong, T.P. and Hensher, D.A. (1985): 'Measurement of travel times values and opportunity cost from a discrete-choice model', *Economic Journal* 95(378): 438–51

Tversky, A. and Shafir, E. (1992): 'Choice under conflict: the dynamics of deferred decision', *Psychological Science* 3(6): 358–61

Tye, W., Sherman, L., Kinnucan, M., Nelson, D. and Tardiff, T. (1982): *Application of disaggregate travel demand models*, National Cooperative Highway Research Program Report 253, Transportation Research Board, Washington, DC

Urban, G. and Hauser, J. (1993): *Design and marketing of new products,* 2nd Edn, Englewood Cliffs, Prentice-Hall

Urban, G., Hauser, L., Qualls, J.R., Weinberg, W.J., Bruce, D., et al. (1997): 'Information acceleration: validation and lessons from the field', *Journal of Marketing Research* 34(1): 143–53

Urban, G., Hauser, L., Roberts, J. R. and John, H. (1990): 'Prelaunch forecasting of new automobiles', *Management Science* 36(4): 401–21

Verboven, F. (1996): 'The nested logit model and representative consumer theory', *Economic Letters* 50: 57–63

Vovsha, P. (1997): 'The cross-nested logit model: application to mode choice in the Tel-Aviv metropolitan area', paper presented at the 76th Annual Meeting of the Transportation Research Board, Washington, DC, January

Wardman, M. (1988): 'A comparison of revealed and stated preference models of travel behaviour', *Journal of Transport Economics and Policy* 22(1): 71–92

Warner, S. (1963): 'Multivariate regression of dummy variates under normality assumptions', *Journal of the American Statistical Association* 58: 1054–63

(1967): 'Asymptotic variances for dummy variate regression under normality assumptions', *Journal of the American Statistical Association* 62: 1305–14

Westin, R.B. (1974): 'Predictions for binary choice models', *Journal of Econometrics* 2(1): 1–16

Wilks, S.S. (1962): *Mathematical statistics,* New York: Wiley

Williams, H.C.W.L. (1977): 'On the formation of travel demand models and economic evaluation measures of user benefit', *Environment and Planning* A 9(3): 285–344

(1981): 'Random theory and probabilistic choice models', in Wilson, A.G., Coelho, J.D., Macgill, S.M. and Williams, H.C.W.L. (eds.), *Optimization in locational and transport analysis*, Chichester: Wiley, pp. 46–84

Winer, B.J. (1971): *Statistical principles in experimental design,* New York: McGraw-Hill

Yai, T. and Iwakura, S. (1994): 'Route choice modelling and investment effects upon a metropolitan rail network', pre-prints of the 7th International Conference on Travel Behaviour, Santiago, Chile, pp. 363–74

Yai, T., Iwakura, S. and Ito, M. (1993): 'Alternative approaches in the estimation of user demand and surplus of rail network' (in Japanese), *Infrastructure Planning Review* 11: 81–8

Yai, T., Iwakura, S. and Morichi, S. (1997): 'Multinomial probit with structured covariance for route choice behaviour', *Transportation Research* 31B(3), 195–207

Yen, S.T. and Adamowicz, W. (1994): 'Participation, trip frequency and site choice: a multinomial poisson hurdle model of recreation demand', *Canadian Journal of Agricultural Economics* 42: 65–76

Index

399